arihant
SUCCESS AND NOTHING LESS

AF819878

Be a TOP SCORER
in ISC Exams 2025

i Succeed

15 Sample Question Papers

with Quick Study Notes

Chemistry 12th

AUTHORS
Shikha Soni,
Saleha Pervez

List of *i Succeed* Sample Papers for ISC 12

- Physics
- Chemistry
- Maths
- Biology
- Accounts
- Economics
- Commerce
- English Language
- Literature in English

Arihant Prakashan
(School Division Series)

Administrative & Production Offices

Regd. Office

'Ramchhaya' 4577/15, Agarwal Road, Darya Ganj, New Delhi -110002
Tele: 011- 47630600, 43518550

Head Office

Kalindi, TP Nagar, Meerut (UP) - 250002
Tel: 0121-7156203, 7156204

Sales & Support Offices

Agra, Ahmedabad, Bengaluru, Bareilly, Chennai, Delhi, Guwahati, Hyderabad, Jaipur, Jhansi, Kolkata, Lucknow, Nagpur & Pune.

PRICE ₹275.00

PO No : TXT-XX-XXXXXXX-X-XX

Published by Arihant Publications (India) Ltd.

For further information about the books published by Arihant, log on to www.arihantbooks.com or e-mail at info@arihantbooks.com

Follow us on

i Succeed

SAMPLE QUESTION PAPERS

THE **BEST CHOICE** OF TEACHERS & STUDENTS, Why?

01 Exact Exam Pattern

All Sample Papers have been designed on the actual exam format of ISC

02 Complete Syllabus

Complete coverage of syllabus through different types of questions across all the sample papers

03 Latest Specimen & Examination Question Paper

Latest Specimen & ISC examination Question Paper with detailed solutions.

04 Detailed Solutions

Step-by-step solutions to help you understand concepts and improve problem-solving skills.

05 All Type of Questions

Coverage of all type of exam pattern questions, analysis, understanding, recall, application & evaluation.

Free Doubt Solving APP

To help you sort out your doubts at any time any place.

i Succeed

Chemistry Class 12

Course Structure
2024-25

Time: 3 Hrs		Max. Marks : 70
S. No.	UNIT	TOTAL WEIGHTAGE
1.	Solutions	Physical Chemistry 25 Marks
2.	Electrochemistry	
3.	Chemical Kinetics	
4.	*d* and *f*-Block Elements	Inorganic Chemistry 14 Marks
5.	Coordination Compounds	
6.	Haloalkanes and Haloarenes	Organic Chemistry 31 Marks
7.	Alcohols, Phenols and Ethers	
8.	Aldehydes, Ketones and Carboxylic Acids	
9.	Organic Compounds containing Nitrogen	
10.	Biomolecules	
	TOTAL	**70 Marks**

SOLUTIONS

Study of concentration of solutions of solids in liquids, liquid in liquid, solubility of gases in liquids, solid solutions, Colligative properties - Raoult's law of relative lowering of vapour pressure (1st & 2nd), elevation of boiling point, depression of freezing point, osmotic pressure. Use of colligative properties in determining molecular masses of solutes, abnormal molecular mass association and dissociation, van't Hoff factor.

Normality, molality, molarity, mole fraction, ppm, as measures of concentration. Definition of the above with examples. Simple problems based on the above.

(i) Solubility of gases in liquids – Henry's Law, simple numericals based on the above.

(ii) Raoult's Law for volatile solutes and non volatile solutes, ideal solution, non-ideal solution. Azeotropic mixtures – definition, types, graphical representation, fractional distillation with examples.

(iii) Colligative properties – definition and examples, and its use in determination of molecular mass.

(a) Relative lowering of vapour pressure: Definition and mathematical expression of Raoult's Law. Determination of relative molecular mass by measurement of lowering of vapour pressure.

(b) Depression in freezing point: molal depression constant (cryoscopic constant) – definition and mathematical expression (derivation included).

(c) Elevation in boiling point method: molal elevation constant (ebullioscopic constant) definition and mathematical expression (derivation included).

(d) Osmotic pressure: definition and explanation. Natural and chemical semipermeable membranes, reverse osmosis, isotonic, hypotonic and hypertonic solutions. Comparison between diffusion and osmosis.

Application of osmotic pressure in the determination of relative molecular mass. van't Hoff- Boyle's Law, van't Hoff – Charles' Law, van't Hoff - Avogadro's law.

(e) Abnormal molecular mass: Dissociation and Association with suitable examples.

(f) van't Hoff factor for the electrolytes which dissociate and the molecules which associate in solution. Modification of the formula of colligative 178 properties based on van't Hoff factor. Simple problems. Calculation of degree of dissociation and association. Experimental details not required.

Numerical problems based on all the above methods. Experimental details not required.

ELECTROCHEMISTRY

Electrolytic and electrochemical cells. Redox reactions in electrochemical cells. Electromotive Force (emf) of a cell, standard electrode potential, Nernst equation and its application to chemical cells. Relation between Gibb's energy change and emf of a cell.

Conductance in electrolytic solutions, specific, equivalent and molar conductivity, variations of conductivity with concentration, graphs; Kohlrausch's Law of electrolysis and Faraday's Laws of electrolysis. Dry cell and lead accumulator, fuel cells, corrosion.

(i) Electrochemical cells: introduction, redox reactions (principle of oxidation and reduction in a cell).

(ii) Galvanic cells - introduction; representation, principle – oxidation reduction. Mechanism of production of electric current in a galvanic cell.

(iii) Measurement of potential. Single electrode potentials. Standard hydrogen electrode (E^{o}) - definition, preparation, application and limitations.

Standard electrode potential - Measurement of standard electrode potential of Zn^{2+} / Zn , Cu^{2+} / Cu, half-cell (using standard hydrogen electrode).

Cell notation – representation. Factors affecting electrode potential with explanation - main emphasis on the temperature, concentration and nature of the electrode.

(iv) Electrochemical series. Its explanation on the basis of standard reduction potential. Prediction of the feasibility of a reaction.

(v) Nernst equation and correlation with the free energy of the reaction with suitable examples.

Prediction of spontaneity of a reaction based on the cell emf.

Numericals on standard electrode potential of half-cells, cell emf, relationship between free energy and equilibrium constant, standard electrode potential and free energy.

(vi) Comparison of metallic conductance and electrolytic conductance. Relationship between conductance and resistance. Specific resistance and specific conductance. **Cell Constant** Calculation of cell constant. Meaning of equivalent conductance. Meaning of molar conductance. General relationship between specific conductance, molar conductance and equivalent conductance (units and graphs). Units, numericals. Molar conductance of a weak electrolyte at a given concentration and at infinite dilution. Kohlrausch's Law– definition, applications and numericals.

(vii) **Faraday's Laws of Electrolysis:** Faraday's First Law of electrolysis. Statement, mathematical form. Simple problems. Faraday's Second Law of electrolysis:

Statement, mathematical form. Simple problems. Relation between Faraday, Avogadro's number and charge on an electron. $F = N_A e$ should be given (no details of Millikan's experiment are required).

(viii) **Batteries:** Primary and Secondary Cells: Leclanche cell, mercury cell, Lead storage battery and fuel cell - structure, reactions and uses.

(ix) **Corrosion:** Concept, mechanism of electrochemical reaction, factors affecting it and its prevention.

CHEMICAL KINETICS

Meaning of Chemical Kinetics - slow and fast reactions. Rate of a reaction - average and instantaneous rate (graphical representation). Factors affecting rate of reaction: surface area, nature of reactants, concentration, temperature, catalyst and radiation. Order and molecularity of a reaction, rate law and specific rate constant. Integrated rate equations and half-life (only for zero and first order reactions), concept of collision theory (elementary idea, no mathematical treatment). Concept of threshold and activation energy, Arrhenius equation.

(i) Meaning of chemical kinetics, Scope and importance of Kinetics of the reaction, slow and fast reactions - explanation in terms of bonds.

(ii) **Rate of Reaction:** definition, representation of rate of reaction in terms of reactants and products, determination of rate of reactions graphically, instantaneous and average rate of reaction. Factors affecting rate of reaction.

(iii) Law of mass Action: statement and meaning of active mass. Explanation with an example - general reactions.

(iv) Effect of concentration of reactants on the rate of a reaction: Qualitative treatment, based on the law of mass action, statement of rate law, General rate equation - Rate = k(concentration of the reactant)$_n$, where, *k* is rate constant and n is the order of the reaction, relationship between the rate of the reaction with rate constant with respect to various reactants.

(v) Order of a reaction: meaning, relation between order and stoichiometric coefficients in balanced equations, order as an experimental quantity, rate equation for zero order reaction and its unit, mathematical derivation of rate equation for first order reaction, characteristics of first order reaction - rate constant is independent of the initial concentration, units to be derived, definition of half-life period, derivation of expression of half-life period from first order rate equation.

Problems based on first order rate equation and half-life period.

(vi) Molecularity of the reaction: Meaning - physical picture, relation between order, molecularity and the rate of a reaction, Differences between order and molecularity of a reaction.

(vii) The concept of energy: Exothermic and endothermic reactions, concept of energy barrier, threshold and activation energy, formation of activated complex, effect of catalyst on activation energy and reaction rate.

(viii) **Collision Theory** Condition for a chemical change - close contact, particles should collide. Collisions to be effective - optimum energy and proper orientation during collision. Energy barrier built-up when the collision is about to take place, Activated complex formation, difference in energy of the reactant and the product - exothermic and endothermic reactions with proper graphs and labelling.

(ix) Mechanism of the reaction: meaning of elementary reaction, meaning of complex and overall reaction, explanation of the mechanism of the reaction, slowest step of the reaction. Relationship between the rate expression, order of reactants and products at the rate-determining step, units of rate constant – explanation with suitable examples.

(x) Effect of temperature on the rate constant of a reaction: Arrhenius equation $-K=Ae^{-Ea/RT}$, meaning of the symbols of Arrhenius equation, related graph, evaluation of E_a and A from the graph, meaning of slope of the graph, conversion from exponential to log form of the equation, relationship between the increase in temperature and the number of collisions. Numerical based on Arrhenius equation.

d and *f*-BLOCK ELEMENTS

Position in the periodic table, occurrence, electronic configuration and characteristics of transition metals, general trends in properties of the *3d*-series of transition metals - metallic character, ionisation enthalpy, oxidation states, ionic radii, colour of ions, catalytic property, magnetic properties, interstitial compounds, alloy formation, preparation and properties of $K_2Cr_2O_7$ and $KMnO_4$.

Lanthanoids and actinoids

(i) *d*-Block: 3*d*, 4*d* and 5*d* series : Study in terms of metallic character, atomic and ionic radii, ionisation enthalpy, oxidisation states, variable valency, formation of coloured compounds, formation of complexes, alloy formation.

(ii) *f*-Block: 4*f* and 5*f* series: Electronic configuration, atomic and ionic radii, oxidisation states, formation of coloured compounds, formation of complexes, alloy formation. Lanthanoid contraction and its consequences. Chemical reactivity – with oxygen, hydrogen, halogen, sulphur, nitrogen, carbon and water. Actinoids - oxidation states and comparison with lanthanoids.

(iii) Potassium permanganate: structure, shape, equation of extraction from pyrolusite ore, its oxidising nature in acidic, basic and neutral medium, use in redox titration. Oxidising nature in acidic [$FeSO_4$, $(COOH)_2 \cdot 2H_2O$, KI], basic (KI) and neutral (H_2S) mediums to be done.

(iv) Potassium dichromate: structure, shape, equation of extraction from chromite ore and its use in titration. Oxidising nature in acidic, basic and neutral medium, use in redox titration. Interconversion of chromate and dichromate ion (effect of pH).

COORDINATION COMPOUNDS

Concept of complexes, definition of ligands, coordination number, oxidation number. IUPAC nomenclature of mononuclear coordination compounds. Isomerism (structural and stereo). Bonding, Werner's theory, VBT and CFT. Colour, magnetic properties and shapes. Importance of coordination compounds (in qualitative analysis, extraction of metals and biological system).

(i) Definition of coordination compounds / complex compounds, differences with a double salt, study of ligands – mono-, bi-, tri-, tetra-, penta-, hexa- and polydentate, chelating ligands, definition of coordination number,
its calculation for a complex coordination sphere, study of oxidation state of an element in a complex, its calculation, IUPAC rules of nomenclature of coordination compounds.

(ii) Isomerism – structural, stereo types and examples.

(iii) Valence bond theory of coordination compounds – examples of formation of inner orbital and outer orbital complexes (high and low spin, octahedral, tetrahedral and square planar), prediction of magnetic character.

(iv) Crystal field theory – crystal field splitting in tetra and octahedral systems. Explanation of colour and magnetic character.

(v) Stability of coordination compounds (explain stability on the basis of magnitude of K) as mentioned above.

(vi) Importance and uses.

HALOALKANES AND HALOARENES

Haloalkanes: General formula, nomenclature and classification. Nature of C—*X* bond, physical and chemical properties, mechanism of substitution reactions, optical rotation.

Haloarenes; Basic idea, nature of C—*X* bond, substitution reactions (directive influence of halogen in monosubstituted compounds only).

Uses and environmental effects of - dichloromethane, trichloromethane, tetrachloromethane, iodoform, freons and DDT.

Nature of C—*X* bond

Naming the halogen derivatives of alkanes by using common system and IUPAC system for mono, di and tri-halo derivatives.

Preparation of haloalkanes from:

Alkane and halogen, Alkene and hydrogen halide, Alcohols with PX_3, PCl_5 and $SOCl_2$, Halide exchange method (Finkelstein and Swarts), Silver salt of fatty acids (Hunsdiecker).

Physical properties: state, melting point, boiling point and solubility.

Chemical properties : nucleophilic substitution reactions (S_N1, S_N2) mechanism in terms of primary, secondary and tertiary halides). Reaction with : sodium hydroxide, water sodium iodide, ammonia, primary amine, secondary amine, pottasium cyanide, silver cyanide, potassium nitride, silver nitride, silver salt of fatty acid and lithium-aluminium hydride.

Elimination reaction (Saytzeff's rule)/b-elimination. Reaction with metals : sodium and magnesium (Wurtz's reaaction, Grignard's reagent preparation). Chloroform and iodoform : preparation and properties : Structure of freons. Preparations of haloarenes by Sandmeyer's and Gattermann's reaction, by electrophillic substitution.

Physical Properties :

State, melting point, boiling point and solubility.

Chemical properties:

Electrophilic substitution (chlorination nitration and sulphonation) with mechanism, Nucleophilic substitution (replacement of chlorine with —OH, —NH_2) with mechanism, Reduction to benzene, Wurtz-Fittig reaction, Fittig reaction, Addition reaction with magnesium (formation of Grignard reagent), Structure of DDT.

ALCOHOLS, PHENOLS AND ETHERS

Alcohols Classification, general formula, structure and nomenclature. Methods of preparation, physical and chemical properties (of primary alcohols only), identification of primary, secondary and tertiary alcohols, mechanism of dehydration, uses with special reference to methanol and ethanol.

(i) Classification into monohydric, dihydric and polyhydric alcohols, general formulae, structure and nomenclature of alcohols. Difference between primary, secondary and tertiary alcohols in terms of structure, physical properties and chemical properties.

(ii) **Methods of preparation:**

Hydration of Alkenes – direct hydration, indirect hydration, hydroboration oxidation, From Grignard's reagent, Hydrolysis of alkyl halides, Reduction of carbonyl compounds, From primary amines.

Manufacture of methanol by Bosch process and ethanol by fermentation of carbohydrates, chemical equations required (only outline of the method of manufacture, detail not required).

Properties:

Acidic nature of alcohols:, Reaction with sodium, Esterification with mechanism,

Reaction with hydrogen halides.
Reaction with PCl_3, PCl_5, and $SOCl_2$, Reaction with acid chlorides and acid anhydrides, Oxidation, Dehydration with mechanism.

Uses of alcohols.

(iii) Conversion of one alcohol into another.

(iv) Distinction between primary, secondary and tertiary alcohols by Lucas' test.

Phenols Classification and nomenclature. Methods of preparation, physical and chemical properties, acidic nature of phenol, electrophilic substitution reactions, uses of phenols.

Preparation of phenol from diazonium salt, chlorobenzene (Dow's process) and from benzene sulphonic acid. Manufacture from Cumene.

Physical properties state and solubility

Chemical properties:

Acidic character of phenol, Reaction with sodium hydroxide, Reaction with sodium, Reaction with zinc, Reaction with acetyl chloride and acetic anhydride, Reaction with phosphorus penta chloride, Bromination, nitration and sulphonation (Electrophilic substitution reactions), Kolbe's reaction (formation of salicylic acid), Reimer – Tiemann reaction, Test for phenol – $FeCl_3$ test, azo dye test.

Aliphatic Ethers General formula, structure and nomenclature. Methods of preparation, physical and chemical properties, uses.

Ethers: structure of ethereal group. Preparation from alcohol (Williamson's synthesis).

Physical properties state, miscibility.

Chemical properties:

Reaction with chlorine, Oxidation (peroxide formation), Reaction with HI, Reaction with PCl_5.

Aryl Ethers

Physical properties – state and solubility.

Chemical properties – preparation of anisole (Williamson's synthesis), electrophilic substitution (halogenation, nitration and Friedel-Crafts reaction.) Uses of ether.

ALDEHYDES, KETONES AND CARBOXYLIC ACIDS

Aldehydes and Ketones : Nomenclature, structure of methods of preparation of aldehydes and ketones, physical and chemical properties, mechanism of nucleophilic addition, reactivity of alpha hydrogen in aldehydes and uses.

Preparation: From alcohol, From alkenes (ozonolysis), From alkynes (hydration), From acid chlorides (Rosenmund's reduction, reaction with dialkyl cadmium), From calcium salt of carboxylic acids, From nitriles (Stephen reaction, Grignard's reagent), From esters.

Physical properties – state and boiling point.

Chemical properties: Nucleophilic addition reactions with mechanism (ammonia and its derivatives, HCN, $NaHSO_3$ and Grignard's reagent), Oxidation reactions, iodoform reaction, Reduction: reduction to alcohol and alkanes (Clemmensen's reduction, Wolff-Kishner reduction, red phosphorus and HI), Base catalysed reactions (with mechanism): Aldol condensation, cross aldol condensation, Cannizzaro's reaction.

Tests: difference between formaldehyde and acetaldehyde; aldehydes and ketones.

Uses of aldehydes and ketones.

Aromatic aldehyde (Benzaldehyde)

Lab preparation from toluene by oxidation with chromyl chloride.

Physical properties: state and stability.

Chemical properties: Oxidation and reduction, Nucleophilic addition reaction (hydrogen cyanide and sodium bisulphite), Reactions with ammonia and its derivatives (hydroxyl amine, hydrazine and phenyl hydrazine), Reaction with phosphorus pentachloride, Cannizzaro reaction, Benzoin condensation, Perkin's reaction, Electrophilic substitution - halogenation, nitration and sulphonation.

Test: distinction between aromatic and aliphatic aldehydes.

Uses of benzaldehyde.

Carboxylic Acids: Classification, general formula and structure of carboxylic group. Nomenclature, acidic nature, methods of preparation, physical and chemical properties and uses.

Classification of mono and dicarboxylic acids with examples.

Preparation of aliphatic and aromatic carboxylic acid:

From alcohols, aldehydes, From nitriles, From Grignard's reagent.

Physical properties: state, boiling point and solubility.

Chemical properties:

Acidic character: (aliphatic, aromatic carboxylic acids with the effect of substituents on the acidic character – to be dealt with in detail), Reaction with active metals, alkalies, carbonates and bicarbonates, Formation of acid derivatives.

Decarboxylation (chemical and Kolbe's electrolytic reaction), HVZ reactions, Substitution of benzene ring (meta directive effect of carboxylic acid group) nitration and sulphonation.

Tests for acids: Formic acid, acetic acid and benzoic acid.

Uses of formic acid, acetic acid and benzoic acid.

ORGANIC COMPOUNDS CONTAINING NITROGEN

Aliphatic amines: General formula and, classification of amines. Structure of the amino group, nomenclature. Methods of preparation, physical and chemical properties, uses, identification of primary, secondary and tertiary amines.

Amines

Nomenclature, classification with examples, structure, general formula.

Methods of preparation:

From alcohol, From alkyl halide, From cyanide, From amide (Hofmann's degradation), From nitro compounds, Gabriel phthalimide synthesis.

Physical properties:

comparison between primary, secondary and tertiary amines in terms of – state, solubility, boiling point (hydrogen bonding), comparison with alcohols.

Chemical properties:

Basic character of amines – comparison between primary, secondary and tertiary alkyl amines/ ammonia/ aniline. Effect of substituents on the basic strength of aniline, Alkylation and acylation with mechanism, Reaction with nitrous acid, Carbylamine reaction.

Distinction between primary, secondary and tertiary amines (Hinsberg's Test).

Aniline

Preparation reduction of nitrobenzene.

Physical properties – state, solubility and boiling point.

Chemical properties:

Reaction with HCl and H_2SO_4, Acetylation, alkylation, Benzoylation, Carbylamine reaction, Diazotisation, Electrophilic substitution (bromination, nitration and sulphonation)

Tests for aniline.

Uses of aniline.

Cyanides and Isocyanides

Methods of preparation:

Cyanides:

From alkyl halide, From amide, Isocyanides, From alkyl halide, From primary amines

Diazonium salts: Preparation, chemical reactions and importance in synthetic organic chemistry.

Preparation from aniline;

Properties: Sandmeyer's reaction, Gattermann reaction and Balz – Scheimann reaction, replacement of diazo group by —H, —OH, $—NO_2$, coupling reaction with phenol and aniline.

BIOMOLECULES

Carbohydrates – Definition, classification (aldoses and ketoses), monosacahrides (glucose and fructose), D-L configuration oligosaccharides (sucrose, lactose, maltose), polysaccharides (starch, cellulose, glycogen); Importance of carbohydrates.

Carbohydrates: definition, classification - mono (aldose, ketose), oligo (di, tri, tetra saccharides) and polysaccharides with examples: reducing sugars and non-reducing sugars – examples and uses.

Establishment of structures for glucose and fructose (open and cyclic).heating with HI, reaction with hydroxylamine, bromine water, acetic anhydride, nitric acid and phenyl hydrazine.

Test for glucose and fructose (bromine water test with equation).

Disaccharides – structures of sucrose, maltose and lactose (glycosidic linkage).

Polysaccharides – starch, cellulose, glycogen.

Proteins – structural units of proteins. Basic idea of - amino acids, peptide bond, polypeptides, proteins, structure of proteins - primary, secondary, tertiary structure and quaternary structures (qualitative idea only), denaturation of proteins. Enzymes, hormones - elementary idea only.

Proteins: Amino acids – general structure, classification and zwitter ion formation. Isoelectric point. Classification of proteins on the basis of molecular shape; primary, secondary, tertiary and quaternary, structures of proteins, denaturation of proteins. (Definitions only. Details and diagrams are not required).

Vitamins - Classification and functions.

Vitamins A, B, C, D, E and K: classification (fat soluble and water soluble), deficiency diseases. (Chemical names and structures are not required).

Nucleic Acids - DNA and RNA.

Nucleic acids: basic unit – purine and pyrimidine, DNA – structure (double helical), RNA (No chemical structure required). Differences between DNA and RNA.

Preparation Assessment Zone

Welcome to the Preparation Assessment Zone !

In this section, you'll find **ISC Specimen Paper** and **Board Examination Paper 2024** to help you assess your readiness. Attempt these papers to familiarise yourself with the exam format and identify areas that need improvement.

Progress Tracker **Tick the papers as you complete them.**

☐ ISC Specimen Paper

☐ Board Examination Paper 2024

ISC Specimen Paper

Session 2024-25

Chemistry (Code 862)

Class 12

General Instructions

1. This paper is divided into four sections-A, B, C and D. Answer all questions.
2. **Section A** consists of **one** question **having sub-parts** of **one** mark each. **Section B** consists of **ten** questions of **two** marks each. **Section C** consists of **seven** questions of **three** marks each and **Section D** consists of **three** questions of **five** marks each.
3. Internal choices have been provided in one question each in Section B, Section C and Section D.
4. All working, including rough work, should be done on the same sheet as, and adjacent to the rest of the answer.
5. The intended marks for questions or parts of questions are given in brackets [].
6. Balanced questions must be given, wherever possible and diagrams where they are helpful. When solving numerical problems, all essential working must be shown.
7. In working out problems, use the following data:
   Gas constant (R) = 1.987 cal deg^{-1} mol^{-1} = 8.314 JK^{-1} mol^{-1} = 0.0821 dm^3 atm K^{-1} mol^{-1}
   1L atm = 1 dm^3 atm =101.3 J, 1 Faraday =96500 Coulombs.
   Avogadro's number (N_A) = 6.023 × 10^{23}.

- No. of Questions : 21
- No. of Sections : 4
- Time Alloted : 3 Hrs.
- Max. Marks : 70

Section A

[14 Marks]

1. (A) Fill in the blanks by choosing the appropriate word(s) from those given in the brackets: [4×1]

[four, three, remains same, propane, ns^{1-2}, increases, six, propan-2-ol, $(n-1)\, d^{1-10}$, two, decreases, Clemmensen's, Wolff-Kishner]

(i) The molar conductance of a solution .... on dilution but the specific conductance of a solution .... on dilution. • *Understanding*

(ii) In the complex ion $[CoCl(en)_2\,ONO]^+$, the coordination number and the oxidation number of the central metal ion are .... and .... • *Understanding*

(iii) Propanone on reaction with zinc amalgam in the presence of concentrated HCl gives .... and the reaction is called ...... reduction. • *Recall*

(iv) The variation and magnitude of oxidation state in coordination complexes is due to the participation of inner .... electrons in addition to outer .... electrons. • *Understanding*

(B) Select and write the correct alternative from the choices given below. [7×1]

(i) The correct order of the increasing basic nature of ammonia, methylamine and aniline is • *Analysis*

(a) Methylamine < Aniline < Ammonia
(b) Aniline < Methylamine < Ammonia
(c) Ammonia < Aniline < Methylamine
(d) Aniline < Ammonia < Methylamine

(ii) Colligative properties of a solution are • *Understanding*

(P) Independent of the nature of solute
(Q) Proportional to molecular mass of solute

(R) Proportional to concentration of solute
(S) Independent of the amount of solvent
(a) Only P and Q are correct
(b) Only P and R are correct
(c) Only P and S are correct
(d) Only Q and S are correct

(iii) According to Markownikoff's rule, "The negative part of the halogen acid attaches itself with that C-atom of an unsymmetrical alkene which has least number of H-atom."

Anti-Markownikoff's addition of HBr is not observed in • *Analysis*
(a) propene
(b) but-2-ene
(c) but-1-ene
(d) pent-2-ene

(iv) Most of the naturally occurring α-amino acids are optically active and have *L*-configuration. Which of the following amino acids is not asymmetric? • *Recall*
(a) Valine (b) Alanine
(c) Glycine (d) Leucine

(v) Which one of the following complex ions has geometrical isomers? • *Understanding*
(a) $[Ni(NH_3)_5Br]^+$
(b) $[Cr(NH_3)_4en]^{3+}$
(c) $[Co(NH_3)_2(en)_2]^{3+}$
(d) $[Co(NH_3)_6]^{3+}$

(vi) Given below are two statements marked Assertion and Reason. Read the two statements carefully and select the correct option.

Assertion (A) Tertiary butyl bromide undergoes Wurtz reaction to give 2,2,3,3 tetramethyl butane.

Reason (R) In Wurtz reaction, when same alkyl halides react with sodium in dry ether to give hydrocarbon; the hydrocarbon formed contains double the number of carbon atoms present in the alkyl halide. • *Analysis*
(a) Both Assertion and Reason are true and Reason is the correct explanation of Assertion.
(b) Both Assertion and Reason are true but Reason is not the correct explanation for Assertion.
(c) Assertion is true but Reason is false.
(d) Both Assertion and Reason are false.

(vii) Given below are two statements marked Assertion and Reason. Read the two statements carefully and select the correct option.

Assertion (A) There is a continuous increase in size among lanthanoids with an increase in atomic number.

Reason (R) Lanthanoids do not show lanthanoid contraction. • *Analysis*
(a) Both Assertion and Reason are true and Reason is the correct explanation of Assertion.
(b) Both Assertion and Reason are true but Reason is not the correct explanation for assertion.
(c) Assertion is true but Reason is false.
(d) Both Assertion and Reason are false.

(C) Read the passage carefully and answer the questions that follow. [3×1]

A plant or any other living being maintains a reasonable balance of C-14 (radioactive carbon) in its tissue during its lifetime. C-14 is used to determine the age of fossils. In the upper atmosphere, neutrons present in the cosmic rays are captured to produce the following nuclear reaction.

$${}_7N^{14} + {}_0n^1 \longrightarrow {}_6C^{14} + {}_1H^1$$

C-14 isotope is circulated in the atmosphere and gets absorbed by living organism during photosynthesis. The ratio of C-14 to C-12 in living being is $1:10^{12}$.

Once the living being dies, the level of C-14 in the dead being decreases due to the following reaction.

$${}_6C^{14} \longrightarrow {}_7N^{14} + {}_{-1}e^0 + \gamma \text{ rays}$$

The death of the plant brings an end to its tendency to take up C-14. The half-life period of C-14 is 5770 years. By knowing the concentration of C-14 in the living plant and the piece of dead material at a particular time, the age of the material (fossil) can be determined.

(i) Write the relation between the decay constant and half-life period. • *Recall*

(ii) In a piece of dead wood, the activity or concentration of C-14 is found to be one third of its initial activity. Calculate the age of the old wood. • *Application*

(iii) The half-life period ($t_{1/2}$) for a first order reaction is 30 minutes. Calculate the time taken to complete 87.5% of the reaction. • *Application*

Section B

[20 Marks]

2. The solution of two electrolytes A and B are diluted. Λ_m of B increases 1.5 times while that of A increases 25 times. Which of the two is a strong electrolyte? Give a reason. • *Understanding* [2]

3. An organic compound [A] which has characteristic odour, reacts with conc. NaOH to give two compounds [B] and [C]. Compound [B] has molecular formula C_7H_8O which upon oxidation gives back compound [A]. Compound [C] is the sodium salt of the acid and upon treatment with sodalime yields an aromatic hydrocarbon [D]. Identify the compounds [A], [B], [C] and [D]. [2] • *Understanding*

4. Devise a scheme for the synthesis of *n*-butane using CH_3I as the only source of carbon. Is it possible to obtain propane in pure state by applying this scheme? Give a reason for your answer. • *Evaluate* [2]

5. It is generally observed that the rate of a chemical reaction becomes double with every 10°C rise in temperature. If the generalisation holds true for a reaction in the temperature range of 298 K to 308 K, what would be the value of activation energy (E_a) for the reaction? • *Application* [2]

6. An organic compound [X] of molecular formula C_3H_5N, in one reaction produced a primary amine with $LiAlH_4$. In another case, the organic compound [Y] of same molecular formula C_3H_5N produced a secondary amine with $LiAlH_4$. Identify both the compounds [X] and [Y]. Why do these compounds form two different products? • *Understanding* [2]

7. During chemistry class, a teacher wrote $[Ni(CN)_4]^{2-}$ as a coordination complex ion on the board. The students were asked to find out the magnetic behaviour and shape of the complex. Pari, a student, wrote the answer paramagnetic and tetrahedral whereas another student Suhail wrote diamagnetic and square planer. • *Evaluate* [2]
Evaluate Pari's and Suhail's responses.

8. An organic compound 'X' with molecular formula $C_4H_{10}O$ is found to be soluble in conc. H_2SO_4 and does not react with sodium metal or $KMnO_4$. Compound 'X' when heated with excess of HI gives a single alkyl halide. Deduce the structure of the compound 'X'. Explain all the reactions involved. [2] • *Understanding*

9. (i) Identify the compounds [A] and [B] in the following reactions. [2] • *Understanding*

(a) $C_6H_5CHO \xrightarrow[\text{(2) SOCl}_2]{\text{(1) K}_2\text{Cr}_2\text{O}_7/\text{H}_2\text{SO}_4} [A] \xrightarrow{\text{C}_6\text{H}_6\text{ (anhy. AlCl}_3)} [B]$

(b) $CH_3—C\equiv CH \xrightarrow[\text{(2) Vigorous oxidation, conc. HNO}_3]{\text{(1) H}_2\text{SO}_4/\text{HgSO}_4} [A] \xrightarrow[\text{[Conc. H}_2\text{SO}_4]]{\text{C}_2\text{H}_5\text{OH}} [B]$

Or (ii) Three organic compounds A, B and C are non cyclic functional isomers of carbonyl compounds with molecular formula C_4H_8O. Isomers A and C give positive Tollen's test while compound B does not give positive Tollen's test but gives positive iodoform test. Compounds A and B on reduction with Zn amalgam and conc. HCl give the same product.

(a) Write the structures of the compounds A, B and C. • *Understanding*

(b) Out of the compounds A, B and C, which one will be the least reactive towards addition of HCN. • *Understanding*

10. Calculate the value of E°_{cell}, E_{cell} and ΔG that can be obtained from the following cell at 298 K.

$Al/Al^{3+}_{(0.01\ M)} // Sn^{2+}_{(0.015\ M)}/Sn$ • *Application* [2]

Given, $E^\circ_{Al^{3+}/Al} = -1.66$ V, $E^\circ_{Sn^{2+}/Sn} = -0.14$ V

11. Write the chemical test to distinguish between the following pairs of compounds. [2]

(i) Propan-1-ol and propan-2-ol

(ii) Phenol and ethanol • *Understanding*

Or

(a) Calculate the boiling point of urea solution when 8.0 g of urea is dissolved in 250 g of water. Boiling point of pure water is 373 K. (k_b of water = $0.52\ K\ kg\ mol^{-1}$, molecular mass of urea = $60\ g\ mol^{-1}$) • *Application*

(b) Ethylene glycol is used as an antifreeze agent. Calculate the amount of ethylene glycol to be added to four kilogram of water to prevent it from freezing at –6°C.

(K_f of water = $1.86\ K\ kg\ mol^{-1}$) Assume that ethylene glycol ($CH_2OH \cdot CH_2OH$) does not dissociate or associate in aqueous solution. • *Application*

(c) What will be the effect on the value of molality and molarity of a solution with change in temperature? • *Understanding*

Solutions *in Topper's Style*

My Commitment *I affirm that I am reviewing these solutions only after I have solved the Specimen Paper on my own. My purpose of looking the solutions is solely to verify whether my answers/solutions were correct or not and to identify my mistakes in case my solutions were wrong or I could not solve that.*

1. (A) (i) increases, decreases

(ii) six, three

(iii) propane, Clemmensen's

(iv) $(n-1)\ d^{1-10},\ ns^{1-2}$

(B) (i) (d) Methylamine is a stronger base than ammonia due to + *I*-effect (electron-donating power) of alkyl group. On the other hand, aniline is a weaker base than ammonia due to electron withdrawing nature of aryl group. Thus, the correct order of the increasing basic nature is

Aniline < Ammonia < Methylamine

(ii) (b) Colligative properties of a solution depends only on the number of solute particles irrespective of their nature to the total number of particles present in the solution. Further, it is proportional to concentration of solute.

Thus, only statements (P) and (R) are correct.

(iii) (b) Anti-Markownikoff's addition of HBr is not observed in case of but-2-ene. This is because it a symmetrical alkene.

(iv) (c) The general formula of amino acid is

$$R-\underset{\displaystyle NH_2}{\underset{|}{CH}}-COOH$$

where, *R* represents side chain. The characteristic feature of *R* of given amino acids are follows :

Glycine-H

Alanine- $-CH_3$

Valine- $-HC(CH_3)_2$

Leucine - $-(H_3C)_2CH-CH_2-$

Thus, glycine is not an asymmetric amino acid.

(v) (c) Geometrical isomerism is shown by $[Co(NH_3)(en_2)]^{3+}$ due to different possible geometric arrangements of the ligands. The structures of isomers are as follows :

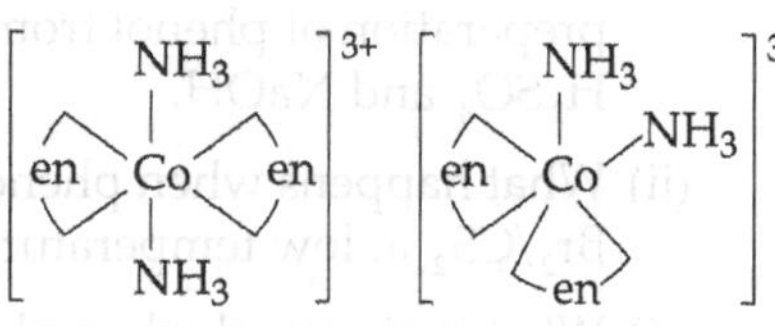

trans-isomer *cis*-isomer

(vi) (a) Tertiary butyl bromide undergoes Wurtz reaction to give 2, 2, 3, 3-tetramethyl butane. The reaction is as follows

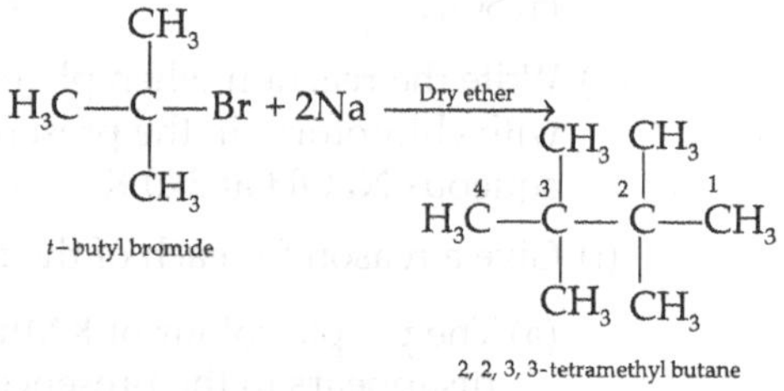

Here, the hydrocarbon formed contain double the number of carbon atoms present in the alkyl halide. Thus, both Assertion and Reason are true and Reason is the correct explanation of Assertion.

(vii) (d) There is a gradual decrease in size among lanthanoids with an increase in

(C) (i) The radioactive decay of C-14 takes place by first order kinetics. Therefore, the relation between the decay constant (k) and half-life period is given as

$$t_{\frac{1}{2}} = \frac{0.693}{k}$$

or $$k = \frac{0.693}{t_{\frac{1}{2}}}$$

(ii) Given, $t_{1/2} = 5770$ years

$$(a - x) = \frac{a}{3}$$

As we know that, for first order reaction

$$t = \frac{2.303}{k} \log \frac{a}{(a-x)}$$

and, $$k = \frac{0.693}{t_{\frac{1}{2}}}$$

$$\therefore \quad t = \frac{2.303 \times 5770}{0.693} \log \frac{a}{a/3}$$

$$\Rightarrow \quad t = \frac{2.303 \times 5770 \times \log 3}{0.693}$$

$$t = \frac{2.303 \times 5770 \times 0.4771}{0.693}$$

$$[\because \log 3 = 0.4771]$$

$$\therefore \quad t = 9148.4 \text{ years}$$

(iii) Given, $t_{1/2} = 30$ minutes

If $a = 100$, $(a - x) = (100 - 87.5) = 12.5$

As we know that, for first order reaction,

$$t = \frac{2.303}{k} \log \frac{a}{a-x} \quad \left[\because k = \frac{0.693}{t_{1/2}}\right]$$

$$\therefore \quad t = \frac{2.303 \times 30}{0.693} \times \log \frac{100}{12.5}$$

$$\Rightarrow \quad t = \frac{2.303 \times 30}{0.693} (\log 100 - \log 12.5)$$

$$\text{or } t = \frac{2.303 \times 30}{0.693} (2 - 1.097) \quad \left[\begin{array}{l}\because \log 100 = 2 \\ \log 12.5 = 1.097\end{array}\right]$$

$$\therefore \quad t = 99.70 \times 0.903 \text{ mins}$$

$$= 90.03 \text{ mins}$$

2. B is a strong electrolyte as on dilution, Λ_m increases to a little extent. This is because in case of strong electrolyte, on dilution, number of ions remains almost the same and only inter ionic attraction decreases.

3. Compound $[A]$ has characteristic odour which means it can be benzaldehyde. It undergoes Cannizzaro reaction with NaOH to give alcohol and sodium salt of acid.

Compound $[B]$ can be benzyl alcohol as it contains only one oxygen atom, which on oxidation gives back compound $[A]$.

The reaction involved is

$$\underset{(B)}{C_6H_5CH_2OH} \xrightarrow{CrO_3} \underset{(A)}{C_6H_5CHO}$$

Compound 'C' can be sodium salt of benzoic acid which on heating with sodalime yields an aromatic compound 'D' which may be benzene.

Thus, $[A] = C_6H_5CHO$ (Benzaldehyde),

$[B] = C_6H_5CH_2OH$ (Benzyl alcohol)

$[C] = C_6H_5COONa$ (Sodium salt of benzoic acid)

$[D] = C_6H_6$ (Benzene)

4. The scheme/sequence of reactions for the synthesis of n-butane using CH_3I as the only source of carbon is as follows :

$$\underset{\text{Methyl iodide}}{2CH_3I} \xrightarrow[\text{Wurtz reaction}]{\text{Na, dry ether}} \underset{\text{Ethane}}{CH_3-CH_3} \xrightarrow{Cl_2/h\nu} \underset{\text{Ethyl chloride}}{CH_3CH_2Cl}$$

$$2CH_3CH_2Cl \xrightarrow[\text{Wurtz reaction}]{\text{Na, dry ether}} \underset{n\text{-butane}}{CH_3CH_2CH_2CH_3}$$

Propane cannot be obtained in pure state by the above scheme. This is because, Wurtz reaction between CH_3I and C_2H_5I will give three products, i.e., ethane, propane and butane.

5. Given, $T_1 = 298$ K and $T_2 = 308$ K

$$\frac{k_2}{k_1} = 2, \ R = 8.314 \text{ J K}^{-1} \text{ mol}^{-1}$$

According to Arrhenius equation,

$$\log \frac{k_2}{k_1} = \frac{Ea}{2.303\,R}\left[\frac{1}{T_1} - \frac{1}{T_2}\right]$$

$$\log 2 = \frac{E_a}{2.303 \times 8.314 \text{ J/K/mol}}\left[\frac{-1}{298} - \frac{1}{308}\right]$$

$$0.3010 = \frac{E_a}{2.303 \times 8.314} \times \frac{10}{298 \times 308}$$

$$E_a = \frac{0.3010 \times 2.303 \times 8.314 \times 298 \times 308}{10} (\text{J mol}^{-1})$$

$$E_a = 52897.78 \text{ J/mol or } 52.898 \text{ kJ/mol}$$

6. Since, compound $[X]$ having molecular formula C_3H_5N produces primary amine on reaction with $LiAlH_4$. Therefore, it must be propanenitrile or ethyl cyanide (C_2H_5CN).

However, compound $[Y]$ of same formula (C_3H_5N) produces secondary amine on reaction with $LiAlH_4$. Therefore, it must be ethyl isocyanide (C_2H_5NC). The reactions are as follows :

$$\underset{\substack{\text{Ethyl cyanide} \\ [A]}}{CH_3CH_2C{\equiv}N} + LiAlH_4 \longrightarrow \underset{\substack{\text{Propanamine} \\ \text{(Primary amines)}}}{CH_3CH_2CH_2NH_2}$$

$$CH_3CH_2—\overset{\oplus}{N}\equiv\overset{\ominus}{C} \xrightarrow{LiAlH_4} CH_3CH_2NHCH_3$$

Ethyl isocyanide [B] → N-methyl ethanamine (Secondary amines)

7. In the complex $[Ni(CN)_4]^{2-}$, the oxidation state of Ni is +2.

Ni (atom (Z = 28)

$= [Ar]3d^8 4s^2 =$ 3d: [⇅][⇅][⇅][↑][↑] 4s: [⇅] 4p: [ ][ ][ ]

$Ni^{2+} = [Ar]3d^8 =$ 3d: [⇅][⇅][⇅][↑][↑] 4s: [ ] 4p: [ ][ ][ ]

Since, CN^- is a strong field ligand, so pairing of electrons will take place.

$[Ni(CN)_4]^{2-} =$ 3d: [⇅][⇅][⇅][⇅][ ] [××][××][××][××]

dsp^2-hybridised

Thus, $[Ni(CN)_4]^{2-}$ is diamagnetic and the shape of the complex is square planar.

Therefore, out of Pari and Suhail's responses, Suhail's response was correct.

8. (i) As compound 'X' does not react with sodium metal or potassium permanganate, it cannot be an alcohol.

(ii) As compound 'X' dissolves in conc. H_2SO_4, it may be an ether.

(iii) As compound 'X' on heating with excess of HI, gives a single alkyl halide, therefore compound 'X' must be a symmetrical ether.

(iv) The only symmetrical ether having molecular formula $C_4H_{10}O$ is diethyl ether.

Thus, compound 'X' is diethyl ether,
$CH_3—CH_2—O—CH_2—CH_3$.

$$CH_3CH_2—O—CH_2CH_3 \xrightarrow{Conc.\ H_2SO_4} \left[CH_3—CH_2—\overset{+}{\underset{H}{O}}—CH_2—CH_3\right]HSO_4^-$$

Soluble oxonium salt

$$CH_3CH_2OCH_2CH_3 \xrightarrow[\Delta]{HI} 2\ CH_3CH_2—I$$

(X) Diethyl ether → Ethyl iodide

9. (i) (a) $C_6H_5CHO \xrightarrow[(2)\ SOCl_2]{(1) K_2Cr_2O_7/H_2SO_4} C_6H_5COCl$

Benzladehyde → Benzoyl chloride (A)

$\xrightarrow{C_6H_6\ (Anhy.\ AlCl_3)} C_6H_5COC_6H_5$

Benzophenone (B)

(b) $CH_3—C\equiv CH \xrightarrow[(2)\ Vigorous\ oxidation,\ conc.HNO_3]{(1) H_2SO_4/HgSO_4}$

Propyne

$CH_3COOH \xrightarrow[conc.H_2SO_4]{C_2H_5OH} CH_3COOC_2H_5$

Acetic acid (A) → Ethyl ethanoate (B)

Or

(ii) (a) The possible functional isomers of carbonyl compound with molecular formula, C_4H_8O are

$$CH_3—\underset{}{\overset{CH_3}{\overset{|}{C}H}}—CHO,\ CH_3CH_2CH_2CHO,$$

$$CH_3CH_2—\overset{O}{\overset{||}{C}}—CH_3$$

- Isomers (A) and (C) give positive Tollen's test, thus they must be aldehydes.

$$RCHO + 2[Ag(NH_3)_2]^+ + 3OH^- \xrightarrow{\Delta}$$

Aldehyde, Tollen's reagent

$$RCOO^- + 2Ag\downarrow + 2H_2O + 4NH_3\uparrow$$

Silver mirror

$$CH_3—\underset{CH_3}{\underset{|}{CH}}—CHO \text{ and } CH_3CH_2CH_2CHO$$

- Isomer (B) does not give Tollen's test, but gives positive Iodoform test, thus it must be a ketone with $CH_3—\overset{O}{\overset{||}{C}}—$ group.

$$RCOCH_3 \xrightarrow{NaOX} RCOONa + CHX_3\ [X = Cl, Br, I]$$

Isomers (A) and (B) on reduction with Zn(Hg) / conc. HCl give same product.

$$CH_3—\overset{CH_3}{\overset{|}{C}H}—CHO + 4[H] \xrightarrow{Zn-Hg/conc.\ HCl} CH_3\overset{CH_3}{\overset{|}{C}H}—CH_3 + H_2O$$

$$CH_3—CH_2—CH_2—CHO + 4[H] \xrightarrow{Zn-Hg/conc.\ HCl} CH_3—CH_2—CH_2—CH_3 + H_2O$$

$$CH_3CH_2COCH_3 + 4[H] \xrightarrow{Zn-Hg/conc.\ HCl} CH_3CH_2CH_2CH_3 + H_2O$$

So, the structures of (A), (B) and (C) are

$CH_3CH_2CH_2CHO$ (A), $CH_3CH_2COCH_3$ (B), $CH_3\overset{CH_3}{\overset{|}{C}H}—CHO$ (C)

(b) The isomer (B) is least reactive towards addition of HCN.

Since, aldehydes are more reactive towards nucleophilic addition reactions than ketones due to inductive and steric effects.

10. Given, $E^{\circ}_{Al^{3+}/Al} = -1.66$ V

$E^{\circ}_{Sn^{2+}/Sn} = -0.14$ V

For the given cell,

Al/Al^{3+} (0.01 M) || Sn^{2+} (0.015 M)/Sn

$$E^{\circ}_{cell} = E^{\circ}_{cathode} - E^{\circ}_{anode}$$
$$= -0.14\text{ V} - (-1.66)\text{ V}$$
$$= 1.52\text{ V}$$

The half-cell reactions are as follows

At anode

$$Al(s) \longrightarrow Al^{3+}(aq) + 3e^-] \times 2$$

At cathode

$$Sn^{2+}(aq) + 2e^- \longrightarrow Sn(s)] \times 3$$

Overall reaction

$$2Al(s) + 3Sn^{2+}(aq) \longrightarrow 2Al^{3+}(aq) + 3Sn(s)$$

$$E_{cell} = E^{\circ}_{cell} - \frac{0.0591}{n}\log\frac{[Al^{3+}]^2}{[Sn^{2+}]^3}$$

Here, n = number of electrons transferred, i.e., 6

$$\therefore\ E_{cell} = 1.52 - \frac{0.0591}{6}\log\frac{[0.01]^2}{[0.015]^3}$$

$$E_{cell} = 1.52 - \frac{0.0591}{6}(\log(10)^5 - \log(15)^3)$$

$$\Rightarrow\quad E_{cell} = 1.52 - \frac{0.0591}{6}\times(5 - 3.528)$$

$$\therefore\quad E_{cell} = 1.5056\text{ V}$$

Now, $\Delta G = -nFE^{\circ}_{cell}$

$$\therefore\quad \Delta G = (-6\text{ mol})\times(96500\text{ C mol}^{-1})\times(1.5056\text{ V})$$
$$= -871742\text{ J}$$

11. (i) **Propan-1-ol and propan-2-ol**

Propan-1-ol and propan-2-ol can be distinguished by Lucas test.

$$\underset{\substack{\text{Propan-1-ol}\\\text{(Primary alcohol)}}}{CH_3CH_2CH_2OH} + HCl \xrightarrow[ZnCl_2]{\text{Anhydrous}} \underset{\substack{n\text{-propyl chloride}\\\text{(Do not produce turbidity}\\\text{at room temperature)}}}{CH_3CH_2CH_2Cl} + H_2O$$

$$\underset{\substack{\text{Propan-2-ol}\\\text{(Secondary alcohol)}}}{CH_3-\underset{OH}{\underset{|}{C}H}-CH_3} + HCl \xrightarrow{\text{Anhydrous } ZnCl_2} \underset{\substack{\text{2-chloropropane}\\\text{(Produces turbidity after 5}\\\text{mins at room temperature)}}}{CH_3-\underset{Cl}{\underset{|}{C}H}-CH_3} + H_2O$$

(ii) **Ethanol and phenol**

Phenol gives violet colouration complex with $FeCl_3$ solution but ethanol does not

$$\underset{\text{Phenol}}{6C_6H_5OH} + FeCl_3 \longrightarrow \underset{\text{Violet colour complex}}{[Fe(COC_6H_5)_6]^{3-}} + 3H^+ + 3HCl$$

12. (i) $\underset{\text{Nitrobenzene}}{C_6H_5NO_2} \xrightarrow[Sn/HCl]{6[H]} \underset{\substack{\text{Aniline}\\(A)}}{C_6H_5NH_2} \xrightarrow[273-278K]{HNO_2 + HCl}$

$$\underset{\substack{\text{Benzene diazonium}\\\text{chloride}\\(B)}}{C_6H_5N_2^+Cl^-} \xrightarrow[\text{(Coupling reaction)}]{C_6H_5NH_2} \underset{\substack{p\text{-aminoazobenzene}\\(C)}}{C_6H_5N{=}NC_6H_4NH_2}$$

(ii) $\underset{\text{Ethanamine}}{CH_3CH_2NH_2} \xrightarrow[(2)\text{Red }P/Cl_2]{(1)HNO_2} \underset{\substack{\text{Ethyl chloride}\\(A)}}{CH_3CH_2Cl} \xrightarrow[(2)H_2O/H^+]{(1)KCN}$

$$\underset{\substack{\text{Propanoic acid}\\(B)}}{CH_3CH_2COOH} \xrightarrow[(2)Br_2/KOH]{(1)NH_3/\text{heat}} \underset{\substack{\text{Ehanamine}\\(C)}}{CH_3CH_2NH_2}$$

13. (i) For case A,

Given, $W_2 = 5.85$ g

$W_1 = 100$ g

$T_f = -3.348°C = 269.652$ K

$K_f = 1.86$ K Kg mol^{-1}

Molecular mass = 58.5 g/mol

As we know that,

$$\Delta T_f = T_f^{\circ} - T_f$$

$$\therefore\ \Delta T_f = 273 - 269.652 = 3.348\text{ K}$$

$\because$ Observed molecular mass

$$M_2 = \frac{K_f \times W_2 \times 1000}{\Delta T_f \times W_1}$$

$$\therefore\quad M_2 = \frac{1.86 \times 5.85 \times 1000}{3.348 \times 100} = 32.5\text{ g/mol}$$

Now, For case B,

Given, $W_2 = 0.2$ g

$W_1 = 20$ g

$\Delta T_f = 0.45°C = 0.45$ K

$K_f = 5.12$ Kg mol^{-1}

Molecular mass = 60 g/mol

$\because$ Observed Molecular mass

$$M_2 = \frac{K_f \times W_2 \times 1000}{\Delta T_f \times W_1}$$

$$\therefore\quad M_2 = \frac{5.12 \times 0.2 \times 1000}{0.45 \times 20} = 113.78\text{ g/mol}$$

(ii) As we know that,

$$\text{Van't Hoff factor} = \frac{\text{Normal molecular mass}}{\text{Observed molecular mass}}$$

Therefore, $[A]$ will undergo dissociation as its van't Hoff factor (i) value is 18. Whereas, $[B]$ will undergo association as its van't Hoff factor (i) value is 0.53.

(iii) The given order of depression in freezing point is correct. This is because ΔT_f depends on the number of moles of solute molecules.

14. (i) **Rosenmund's Reaction**

Acyl chloride or acid chloride is hydrogenated in the presence of palladium catalyst supported over and partially poisoned by the addition of sulphur or barium sulphate.

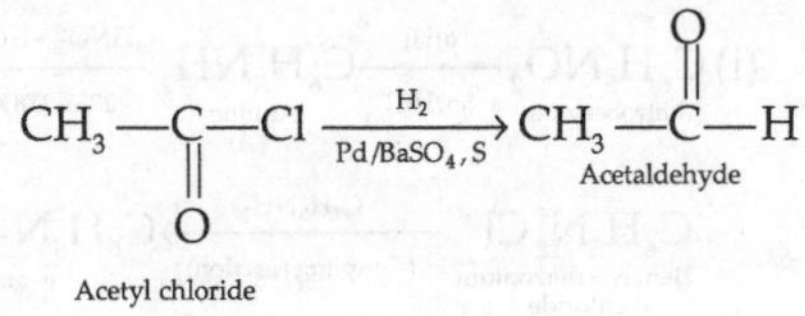

(ii) **Benzoin Condensation**

The addition reaction between two kinds of aromatic aldehydes especially benzaldehyde in presence of cyanide ions as a catalyst to form, α-hydroxy ketone.

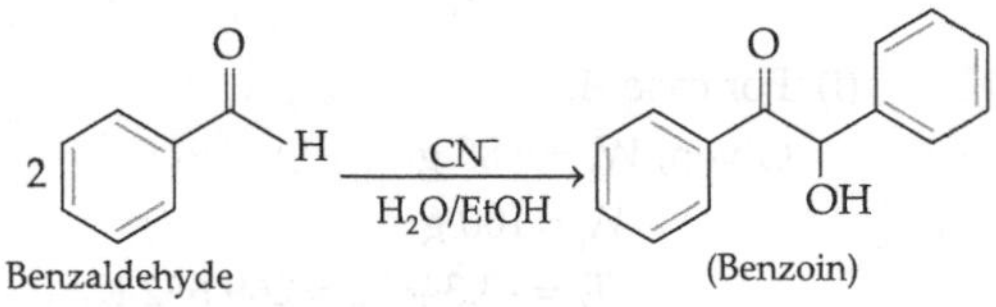

(iii) **Perkin's Reaction**

This reaction gives an α, β-unsaturated aromatic acid *via* Aldol condensation of aromatic aldehyde and an acid anhydride. It occurs in the presence of alkali, which acts as a base catalyst in the reaction.

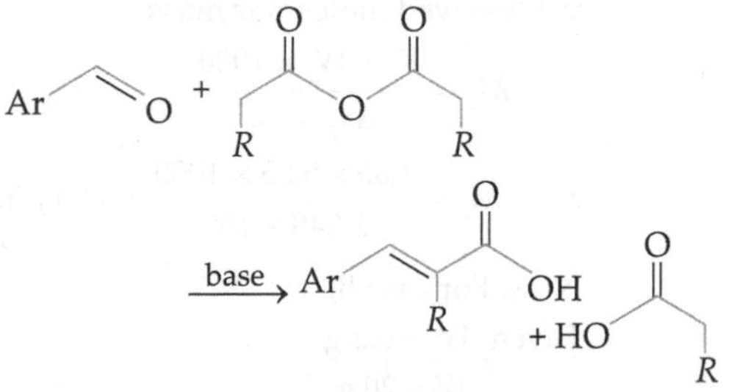

15. (i) The formula and IUPAC name of two coordination complex ions (C.N = 6) with cyanide ligand and iron as central metal atom is as follows

- $[Fe(CN)_6]^{4-}$

  IUPAC name — Hexacyanidoferrate (II) ion

- $[Fe(CN)_6]^{3-}$

  IUPAC name — Hexacyanidoferrate (III) ion

(ii) (a) If $\Delta_o > P$, then ligand will be a strong ligand. Therefore, it will become more energetically favourable for the fourth electron to occupy t_{2g} orbital with configuration $t_{2g}^4 e_g^0$.

If $\Delta_o < P$, then ligand will be a weak field ligand. Therefore, the fourth electron will enter one of the e_g orbitals giving the configuration $t_{2g}^3 e_g^1$.

16. (i) (a) • Dry cell consists of a zinc container which acts as the anode.

• The cathode is a carbon (graphite) rod surrounded by a mixture of powdered manganese dioxide and carbon.

(b) The space between anode and cathode is filled with moist paste of ammonium chloride and zinc chloride.

(c) Dry cell do not have a long life because the acidic NH_4Cl corrodes the zinc container.

Or

(ii) (a) If salt bridge is removed from the two half-cells, then cell will not function. This is because, electricity flow will stop after sometime as positive charge will accumulate at oxidation half-cell and negative at reduction half-cell which balance the redox free energy and thus, will stop the redox reaction.

(b) Copper sulphate solution cannot be stored in a zinc pot because zinc being more reactive than copper, displaces copper from its salt solution.

(c) The density of H_2SO_4 in a lead storage battery decreases as it is discharged. This is because sulphate is consumed from the electrolyte due to the formation of lead sulphate.

17. (i) The peptide bond linkage in glycylalanine is shown below.

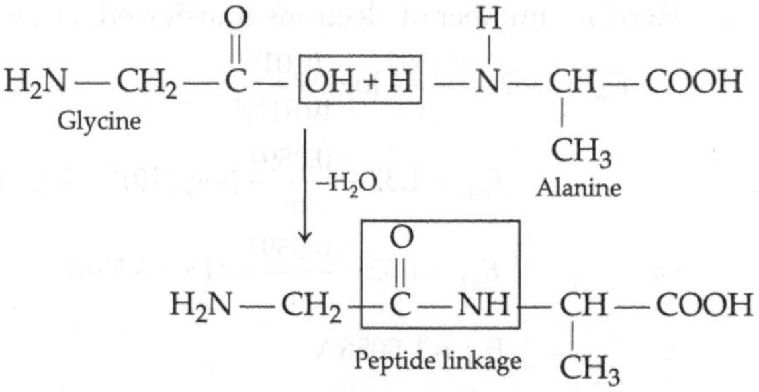

(ii) When a nucleotide from DNA containing thymine is hydrolysed, then β-D-2-deoxyribose (pentose sugar), phosphoric acid and thymine (nitrogenous base) are obtained as products.

(iii) Reducing sugars are the carbohydrates in which ketonic or aldehydic groups are free and are capable of reducing Fehling's solution or Tollen's reagent.

e.g. Glucose, fructose, ribose etc.

18. (i) Rate law for the given reaction

$A + B \rightarrow$ Product may be expressed as

$$\text{Rate} = k[A]^x[B]^y$$

$$(\text{Rate})_1 = 4.0 \times 10^{-4} = k(0.1)^x(0.1)^y \quad \ldots\text{(i)}$$

$$(\text{Rate})_2 = 1.6 \times 10^{-3} = k(0.2)^x(0.2)^y \quad \ldots\text{(ii)}$$

$$(\text{Rate})_3 = 1.0 \times 10^{-2} = k(0.5)^x(0.1)^y \quad \ldots\text{(iii)}$$

$$(\text{Rate})_4 = 1.0 \times 10^{-2} = k(0.5)^x(0.5)^y \quad \ldots\text{(iv)}$$

On dividing Eq^n (iii) by Eq^n (ii), we get

$$\frac{(\text{Rate})_3}{(\text{Rate})_1} = \frac{1.0 \times 10^{-2}}{4.0 \times 10^{-4}} = \frac{k(0.5)^x(0.1)^y}{k(0.1)^x(0.1)^y}$$

$$\Rightarrow (5)^2 = (5)^x$$

$$\therefore \quad x = 2$$

On dividing Eq^n (iv) by Eq^n (iii), we get

$$\frac{(\text{Rate})_4}{(\text{Rate})_3} = \frac{1.0 \times 10^{-2}}{1.0 \times 10^{-2}}$$

$$= \frac{k\,(0.5)^x(0.5)^y}{k\,(0.5)^x(0.1)^y}$$

$$(1)^0 = (5)^y$$

$$\therefore \quad y = 0$$

Thus, order with respect A is 2 and with respect to B is 0.

(ii) Now, Rate $= k\,[A]^2[B]^0$

Putting values in Eq. (i), we get

$$4.0 \times 10^{-4} = k\,[0.1]^2$$

$$\therefore \quad k = \frac{4.0 \times 10^{-4}}{0.1 \times 0.1}$$

$$= 4 \times 10^{-2}\ \text{mol}^{-1}\ \text{L sec}^{-1}$$

(iii) If $[A] = 0.2$ mol L^{-1}sec^{-1} and $[B] = 0.35$ mol L^{-1}sec^{-1}

Then, reaction rate can be calculated as

$$\text{Rate} = k\,[A]^2[B]^0$$

$$\therefore \quad \text{Rate} = 4 \times 10^{-2}\,[0.2]^2\,[0.35]^0$$

$$\Rightarrow \text{Rate} = 4 \times 10^{-2} \times 4 \times 10^{-2}$$

$$= 1.6 \times 10^{-3}\ \text{mol L}^{-1}\text{sec}^{-1}$$

19. (i)

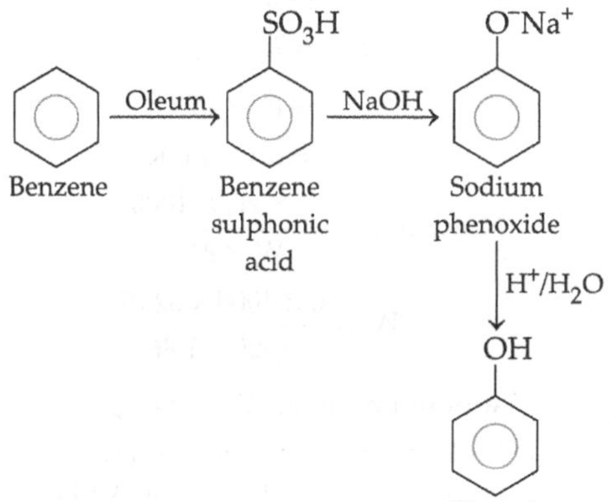

Phenol

(ii) When phenol reacts with Br_2 / CS_2 at low temperature, then monobromophenols are formed. The reaction is as follows

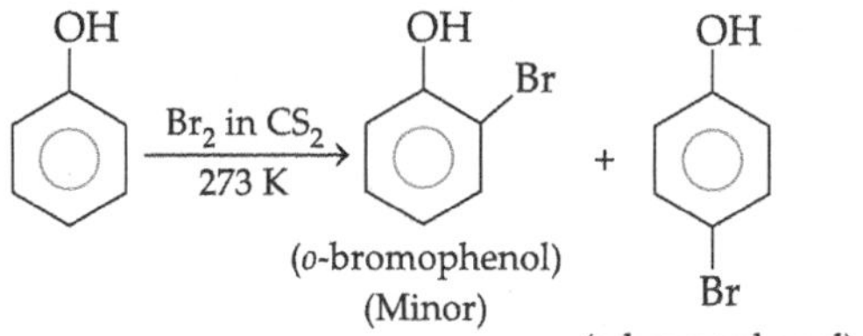

(o-bromophenol) (Minor)

(p-bromophenol) (Major)

(iii) When phenol reacts with neutral $FeCl_3$ solution, then ferric phenoxide complex is formed.

Following reaction takes place

$$6C_6H_5OH + FeCl_3 \longrightarrow \underset{\text{Violet colour complex}}{[Fe(OC_6H_5)_6]^{3-}} + 3H^+ + 3HCl$$

(iv) Picric acid is prepared by first treating phenol with conc. H_2SO_4 at 373 K and then with HNO_3.

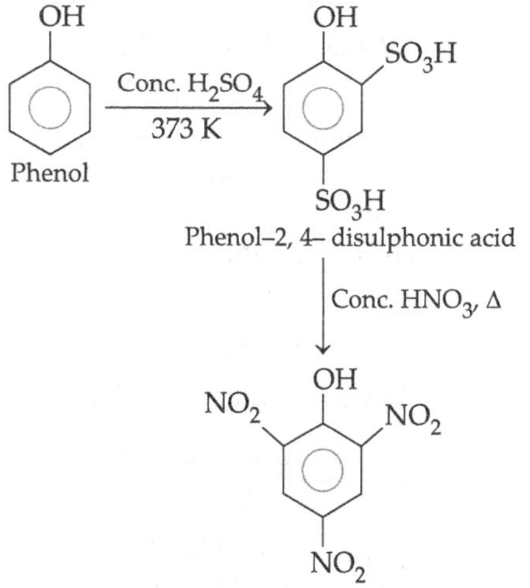

Picric acid

(v) On treating phenol with chloroform in the presence of sodium hydroxide, —CHO group is introduced at *ortho*-position of benzene ring.

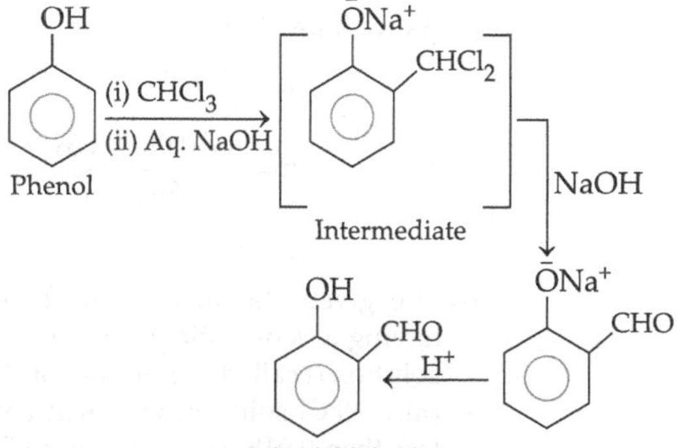

Salicylaldehyde

20. (i) (a) When oxalic acid is added to acidic solution of $KMnO_4$, its colour disappear due to the reduction of MnO_4^- ion to Mn^{2+}. Following chemical reaction takes place.

$$5C_2O_4^{2-} + 2MnO_4^- + 16H^+ \longrightarrow \underset{\text{(Colourless)}}{2Mn^{2+}} + 8H_2O + 10CO_2$$

(b) Some transition metals and their compounds are attracted towards magnetic field due to presence of unpaired electrons in d-orbitals.

(c) Mn^{2+} compounds (E.C, [Ar]$3d^5$) are more stable towards (+3) oxidation state due to half-filled d-orbitals.

On the other hand, Fe^{2+} compounds (E.C, [Ar]$3d^6$) are comparatively less stable as they have six electrons in their orbitals.

So, they tend to lose one electron from Fe^{3+} and get stable $3d^5$ configuration.

(ii) (a) $2KMnO_4 + 8H_2SO_4 + 10FeSO_4 \longrightarrow K_2SO_4 + 2MnSO_4 + 5Fe_2(SO_4)_3 + 8H_2O$

(b) $K_2Cr_2O_7 + 7H_2SO_4 + 6KI \longrightarrow 4K_2SO_4 + Cr_2(SO_4)_3 + 3I_2 + 7H_2O$

21. (a) Two solutions having same osmotic pressure at a given temperature are called isotonic solutions.

(b) Given, $\pi = 8.21$ atm

$T = 273 + 27 = 300\,K$

$V = 100\,mL = 0.1\,L$

As we know that, $\pi = \frac{n}{V} RT$

$$\therefore 8.21 = \frac{W_2 \times 0.0821 \times 300}{180 \times 0.1}$$

$$\Rightarrow W_2 = \frac{8.21 \times 180 \times 0.1}{0.0821 \times 300} = 6\,g$$

(c) Given, $\pi = 8.21$ atm

$T = 273 + 37 = 310\,K$

$V = 0.1\,L$

As we know that,

$$\pi = \frac{n}{V} RT$$

$$\therefore \quad \pi = \frac{6 \times 0.0821 \times 310}{180 \times 0.1}$$

$$\pi = 8.48 \text{ atm}$$

(d) The given statement is false. As solution having less osmotic pressure than the other solution is called hypotonic solution. Thus, a pure NaCl solution with salt concentration less than 0.91% (mass/volume) is hypotonic with human blood.

(e) Edema is caused by taking a lot of salt or salty food. This happens because people experience water retention in tissue, cells and intercellular spaces because of osmosis.

Or

(a) Mass of urea, $W_2 = 8.0$ g

Mass of water, $W_1 = 250$ g

$T_b^\circ = 373\,K$

$K_b = 0.52\,K\,kg\,mol^{-1}$

Molecular mass of urea, $M_2 = 60$ g/mol

As we know that,

$$\Delta T_b = \frac{K_b \times W_2 \times 1000}{M_2 \times W_1}$$

$$\therefore \quad \Delta T_b = \frac{0.52 \times 8 \times 1000}{250 \times 60}$$

$$\Delta T_b = 0.277\,K$$

Now, $\Delta T_b = T_b - T_b^\circ$

$\because$ Freezing point of urea solution,

$$T_b = (0.277 + 373)\,K = 373.277\,K$$

(b) Mass of water, $W_1 = 4$ kg or 4000 g

$T_f = -6°C$

$K_f = 1.86\,K\,kg\,mol^{-1}$

As we know that,

$$\Delta T_f = T_f^\circ - T_f = 0 - (-6°C) = 6°C \text{ or } 6\,K$$

Now, $$\Delta T_f = \frac{K_f \times W_2 \times 1000}{W_1 \times M_2}$$

$$W_2 = \frac{6 \times 4000 \times 62.07}{1000 \times 1.86}$$

Amount of urea, $W_2 = 800.9$ g

(c) Molality does not change with change in temperature. While, molarity of a solution decrease with rise in temperature due to increase in volume.

Write your Roll No.

Examination Paper 2024

Chemistry 12th (Code 862)

No. of Ques : 21 **No. of Sections :** 4 **Time :** 3 Hrs. **Max. Marks :** 70

General Instructions

1. This paper is divided into four Sections A, B , C and D. Answer all questions.
2. **Section A** consists of one question having sub-parts of one mark each.
3. **Section B** consists of ten questions of two marks each.
4. **Section C** consists of seven questions of three marks each, and
5. **Section D** consists of three questions of five marks each.
6. Internal choices have been provided in one question each in Section B, Section C, Section D.
7. All working, including rough work, should be done on the same sheet as, and adjacent to the rest of the answer.
8. The intended marks for questions or parts of questions are given in brackets [].
9. Balanced equations must be given wherever possible and diagrams where they are helpful.
10. When solving numerical problems, all essential working must be shown.
11. In working out problems, use the following data :
    Gas constant $R = 1.987$ cal deg^{-1} mol^{-1} = 8.314 J K^{-1} mol^{-1} = 0.0821 dm^3 atm K^{-1} mol^{-1}
    11 atm = 1 dm^3 atm = 101.3 J. 1 Faraday = 96500 coulombs. **Avogadro's number** = 6.023×10^{23}.

Section A **[14 Marks]**

1. (A) Fill in the blanks by choosing the appropriate word(s) from those given below in the brackets. [4×1]

[lead poisoning, zero, phosgene, dependent, cancer, independent, diethyl ether, first, ethyl carbonate, ethene]

(i) For a particular reaction, the value of rate constant is 0.05 s^{-1}. The reaction is of .... order and will be .... of the initial concentration.

(ii) EDTA is used in the treatment of .... while *cis*-platin is used in the treatment of ....

(iii) The addition of small quantity of ethanol to chloroform prevents the formation of .... and converts it into the harmless compound ....

(iv) The dehydration of ethyl alcohol with conc. H_2SO_4 at 140°C mainly yields .... while at 170°C the main product formed is ....

(B) Select and write the correct alternative from the choices given below. [7×1]

(i) Which one of the following statement is correct regarding the dry cell?

(P) Zinc container acts as an anode in dry cell.

(Q) Zinc container touches the paste of MnO_2 and carbon.

(R) Dry cell can be charged easily.

(S) Graphite rod acts as a cathode in dry cell.

(a) Only (P) and (R) (b) Only (Q) and (R)
(c) Only (P) and (S) (d) Only (Q) and (S)

(ii) The metal complex ion that is paramagnetic is
(Atomic number of Fe = 26, Cu = 29, Co = 27 and Ni = 28)

(a) $[Fe(CN)_4]^{2-}$ (b) $[Co(NH_3)_6]^{3+}$
(c) $[Ni(CN)_4]^{2-}$ (d) $[Cu(NH_3)_4]^{2+}$

(iii) When $KMnO_4$ is heated with acidified oxalic acid, gas bubbles are evolved. These gas bubbles are evolved due to the formation of

(a) SO_2 (b) CO_2 (c) SO_3 (d) O_2

(iv) The reaction of ethanamide with alcoholic sodium hydroxide and bromine gives

(a) ethylamine (b) methylamine
(c) propylamine (d) aniline

(v) An equimolar solution of non-volatile solutes *A* and *B*, shows a depression in freezing point in the ratio of 2:1. If *A* remains in its normal state in the solution, the state of *B* in the solution will be

(a) normal (b) hydrolysed
(c) associated (d) dissociated

(vi) **Assertion** (A) Specific conductivity of all electrolytes decreases on dilution.

Reason (R) On dilution, the number of ions per unit volume decreases.

(a) Both Assertion and Reason are true and Reason is the correct explanation of Assertion.

(b) Both Assertion and Reason are true but Reason is not the correct explanation of Assertion.

(c) Assertion is true but Reason is false.

(d) Assertion is false but Reason is true.

(vii) **Assertion** (A) Ammonolysis of alkyl halides involves the reaction between alkyl halides and alcoholic ammonia.

Reason (R) Ammonolysis of alkyl halides produces secondary amines only.

(a) Both Assertion and Reason are true and Reason is the correct explanation for Assertion.

(b) Both Assertion and Reason are true but Reason is not the correct explanation for Assertion.

(c) Assertion is true but Reason is false.

(d) Assertion is false but Reason is true.

(C) Read the passage given below and answer the questions that follow. **[3 × 1]**

When two solutions are separated by a semipermeable membrane, the solvent molecules move from a solution of lower molar concentration to a solution of higher molar concentration through osmosis.

(i) Samar removed the outer hard shell of two different eggs while cooking at home. He then placed one egg in pure water and the other egg in saturated solution of sucrose. What change is he likely to observe in the eggs after few hours?

(ii) Which solution, hypertonic or hypotonic, has a higher amount of solute in same quantity of solution?

(iii) A 5% aqueous solution of glucose (molar mass = 180 g mol^{-1}) is isotonic with 1.66% aqueous solution of urea. Calculate the molar mass of urea.

Section B **[20 Marks]**

2. (i) Write a chemical test to distinguish between ethanol and phenol.

(ii) Give a chemical reaction to convert acetaldehyde into secondary propyl alcohol. **[2]**

3. Give reason for each of the following.

(i) Zinc, cadmium and mercury are considered as *d*-block elements but not regarded as transition elements.

(ii) Transition metals possess a great tendency to form complex compounds. [2]

4. Convert the following by giving chemical equations for each. [2]
   (i) Ethyl bromide to diethyl ether
   (ii) Phenol to salicylaldehyde

5. Account for each of the following. [2]
   (i) Zirconium (Zr) and Hafnium (Hf) are difficult to separate.
   (ii) Salts of cupric (Cu^{2+}) ion are coloured whereas salts of cuprous (Cu^{+}) ion are colourless.

6. How will you bring the following conversions? [2]
   (i) Benzene to biphenyl
   (ii) Iodoform to acetylene

7. Calculate the maximum possible electrical work that can be obtained from a galvanic cell under standard conditions at 298 K. [2]

$$Zn \mid Zn^{2+}_{(aq)} \mid\mid Ag^{+}_{(aq)} \mid Ag$$

Given $E^\circ_{(Zn^{2+}/Zn)} = -0.76$ V; $E^\circ_{Ag^+/Ag} = +0.80$ V

8. (i) Give reason for each of the following.
   (a) Ethoxyethane does not react with sodium, but ethanol does. [2]
   (b) Ethoxyethane with conc. HI at 373 K gives C_2H_5OH and CH_3I but not CH_3OH and C_2H_5I.

Or

(ii) An organic compound [*A*] having molecular formula $C_4H_{10}O$ forms a compound [*B*] with molecular formula C_4H_8O on oxidation. Compound [*B*] gives a positive iodoform test. The reaction of compound [*B*] with CH_3MgBr followed by hydrolysis gives compound [*C*] with molecular formula $C_5H_{12}O$.

Identify the compounds [*A*], [*B*] and [*C*]. Write the reaction for the conversion of compound [*A*] and compound [*B*].

9. If 200 cm^3 of an aqueous solution of protein contains 1.26 g of protein, the osmotic pressure of the solution at 300 K is found to be 2.57×10^{-3} atm. [2]

Calculate the molar mass of protein.

($R = 0.0821$ L atm K^{-1} mol^{-1})

10. (i) Benzaldehyde is less reactive than propionaldehyde. Why? [2]
   (ii) In the preparation of ethanal by the oxidation of ethanol, ethanal should be removed immediately as it is formed. Why?

11. (i) Why is Mn^{+2} ion more stable than Fe^{+2} ion?
   (Atomic number of Mn = 25 and Fe = 26) **[2]**
   (ii) Trivalent lanthanoid ions such as La^{3+} (Z = 57) and Lu^{+3} (Z = 71) do not show any colour in their solution. Give reason.

Section C **[21 Marks]**

12. For the reaction $A + B \rightleftharpoons$ Product, following data was obtained. [3]

Experiment number	Initial concentration of [*A*] (mol L^{-1})	Initial concentration of [*B*] (mol L^{-1})	Initial rate (mol L^{-1} min^{-1})
1	0.15	0.15	9.6×10^{-2}
2	0.30	0.15	3.84×10^{-1}
3	0.15	0.30	1.92×10^{-1}
4	0.30	0.30	7.68×10^{-1}

Calculate the following.
   (i) The overall order of the reaction.
   (ii) The rate law equation.
   (iii) The value of rate constant.

13. (i) Illustrate the following reactions by giving one suitable example in each case. [3]
   (a) Coupling reaction
   (b) Acetylation of ethylamine
   (ii) Aniline does not give Friedel - Crafts reaction. Give reason.

14. (i) Aradhana visits a physician as she is suffering from rickets and joint pain. Which fat-soluble vitamin should the physician prescribe to her? [3]
   (ii) Somesh put few drops of vinegar in milk. What change do you think he observed in

the milk after some time? What is this phenomenon known as?

(iii) Name the product of hydrolysis of sucrose. Is it a reducing sugar or a non-reducing sugar?

15. An aqueous solution containing 12.50 g of barium chloride in 1000 g of water boils at 373.0834 K. Calculate the degree of dissociation of barium chloride. **[3]**
[Given K_b for $H_2O = 0.52$ K kg mol^{-1}; molecular mass of $BaCl_2 = 208.34$ g mol^{-1}]

16. An organic compound C_2H_4O gives red precipitate when heated with Fehling solution. It also undergoes aldol condensation in the presence of dilute NaOH. **[3]**

(i) Identify the organic compound and write its IUPAC name.

(ii) Which compound will be formed when this organic compound reacts with hydroxylamine?

(iii) What is observed when the compound, referred to in subpart (i), is heated with ammoniacal silver nitrate?

17. (i) Identify the compounds [*A*], [*B*] and [*C*] in each of the following reactions. **[3]**

(a) $C_2H_5OH \xrightarrow{PCl_5} [A] \xrightarrow{KCN} [B] \xrightarrow{H_3O^+} C_2H_5COOH \xrightarrow[\Delta]{NH_3} [C]$

(b) $C_6H_5OH \xrightarrow{Zn/Dust} [A] \xrightarrow[\text{Anhy. } AlCl_3]{CH_3Cl} [B] \xrightarrow[K_2Cr_2O_7 + H_2SO_4]{[O]} [C]$

Or (ii) Give a chemical test to distinguish between the following pairs of compounds.

(a) Ethanol and methanol

(b) Ethanol and ethanal

(c) Propan-2-ol and 2-methyl propan-2-ol

18. (i) The rate constant of a reaction at 500 K and 700 K are 0.02 s^{-1} and 0.07 s^{-1} respectively. Calculate the value of E_a (activation energy). **[3]**

(ii) A radioactive substance which emits alpha particle follows first order reaction. The half-life period of this radioactive substance is 30 hours. Calculate the fraction in percent (%) of the radioactive substance which remains after 90 hours.

Section D **[15 Marks]**

19. (i) An organic compound [*A*], having a specific smell forms two compounds [*B*] and [*C*] by reacting with conc. sodium hydroxide. The molecular formula of compound [*B*] is C_7H_8O, which forms compound [*A*] again on oxidation. Compound [*C*] forms benzene on heating with soda lime.

Write the structures of compounds [*A*], [*B*] and [*C*]. Also, write the reactions involved.

(ii) Identify the compounds [*A*] and [*B*] in the reactions given below.

(a) $C_6H_6 \xrightarrow[AlCl_3 \text{ (anhy.)}]{CH_3Cl} [A] \xrightarrow[K_2Cr_2O_7 + H_2SO_4]{[O]} [B]$

(b) $CH_3—CHOH—CH_3 \xrightarrow[K_2Cr_2O_7 + H_2SO]{[O]} [A] \xrightarrow{NH_2OH} [B]$

20. (i) A coordination compound has a formula $CoCl_3 \cdot 4NH_3$. It precipitates silver ions as AgCl and its molar conductance corresponds to a total of two ions.

Based on this information, answer the following questions.

(a) Deduce structural formula of the complex compound.

(b) Write the IUPAC name of the complex compound.

(c) Draw the geometrical isomers of the complex compound.

(ii) Give a chemical test to show that $[Co(NH_3)_5Cl]SO_4$ and $[Co(NH_3)_5SO_4]Cl$ are ionisation isomers.

21. (i) (a) Study the diagram given below that represents Cu-Ag electrochemical cell and answer the questions that follow.

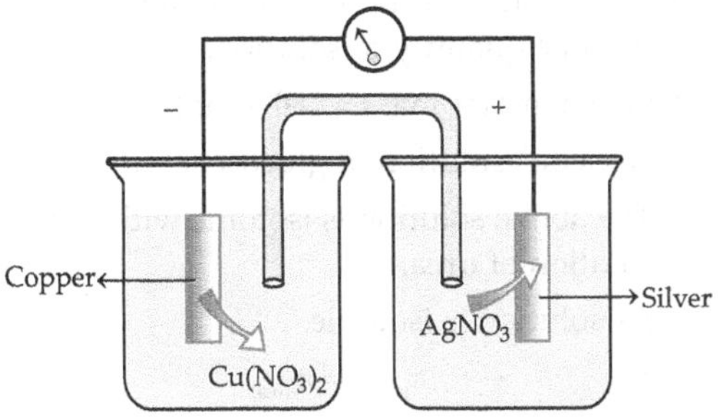

Given, $E^\circ_{(Cu^{2+}/Cu)} = 0.337$ V; $E^\circ_{(Ag^+/Ag)} = 0.799$ V

(1) Write the cell reaction for the above cell.

(2) Calculate the standard emf of the cell.

(3) If the concentration of $[Cu^{2+}]$ is 0.1 M and E_{cell} is 0.422 V, at 25°C, calculate the concentration of $[Ag^+]$

(4) Calculate ΔG for the cell.

(b) Calculate Λ°_m for $BaCl_2$ and $Al_2(SO_4)_3$ from the following data.

For $\Lambda^\circ_m\ Ba^{2+} = 127.2$ S cm^2 mol^{-1},
$\Lambda^\circ_m Al^{3+} = 189$ S cm^2 mol^{-1}
$\Lambda^\circ_m Cl^- = 76.3$ S cm^2 mol^{-1},
$\Lambda^\circ_m SO_4^{2-} = 160$ S cm^2 mol^{-1}

Or (ii) (a) A 0.05 M NH_4OH solution offers the resistance of 30.8 ohms to a conductivity cell at 298 K. If the cell constant is 0.343 cm^{-1} and molar conductance of NH_4OH at infinite dilution is 471.4 S cm^2 mol^{-1}, calculate the following.

(1) Specific conductance

(2) Molar conductance

(3) Degree of dissociation

(b) In the diagram of the electrolytic cell given below, *A*, *B* and *C* are connected in series having electrolytes of $ZnSO_4$, $AgNO_3$ and $CuSO_4$ respectively. A steady current of 1.5 A was passed until 1.45 g of Ag was deposited at the cathode of cell *B*.

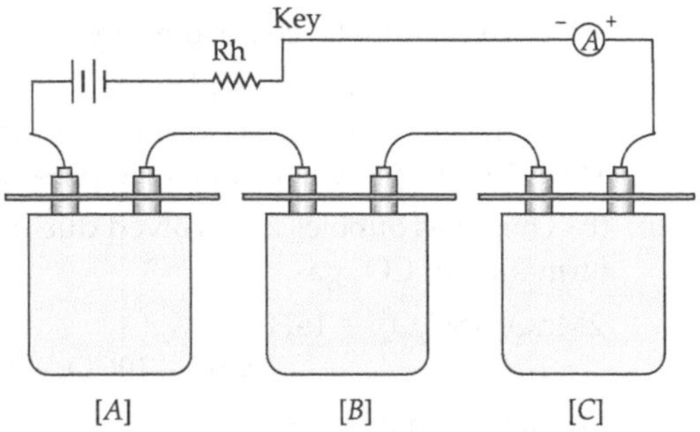

(Atomic mass of Ag = 108, Cu = 63.5, Zn = 65.3)

Answer the following questions.

(i) How long did the current flow?

(ii) What weight of Cu and Zn was deposited at cathode?

Solutions *in Topper's Style*

1. A. (i) first; independent

(ii) lead poisoning; cancer

(iii) phosgene; diethyl carbonate

(iv) diethyl ether; ethene

B. (i) (c) Among the given statements (P) and (S) are correct while (Q) and (R) are incorrect.

- Zinc container cannot touches the paste of MnO_2 and carbon as the space between the electrode is filled with moist paste of ammonium chloride and zinc chloride.
- Dry cell cannot be charged easily.

(ii) (d) The $[Cu(NH_3)_4]^{2+}$ complex is paramagnetic as Cu^{2+} has d^4 configuration. Thus, four unpaired electrons are present.

(iii) (b) These gas bubbles are evolved due to the formation of CO_2 gas.

$$2MnO_4^- + 5C_2O_4^{2-} + 16H^+ \longrightarrow 2Mn^{2+} + 10CO_2 + 8H_2O$$

(iv) (b) Methylamine is formed.

$$\underset{\text{Ethanamide}}{CH_3-\overset{\overset{\displaystyle O}{||}}{C}-NH_2} + Br_2 + \underset{\text{(Alcoholic)}}{4\,NaOH} \longrightarrow \underset{\text{Methylamine}}{CH_3-NH_2} + 2NaBr + Na_2CO_3 + 2H_2O$$

(v) (d) The state of *B* in the solution will be dissociated.

(vi) (a) Both Assertion and Reason are true and Reason is the correct explanation for Assertion.

(vii) (c) Assertion is true but Reason is false.

The correct Reason is : Ammonolysis of alkyl halides produces primary amines only.

C. (i) The egg placed in water will get swollen. It is due to the osmosis of pure water into the egg.

While, when the egg is placed in the saturated solution of sucrose, it will shrink because osmosis always occurs from higher concentration of solvent to lower concentration of solvent.

(ii) Hypertonic solution has a higher amount of solute in same quantity of solution.

(iii) Given, molar mass = 180 g mol^{-1}

Aqueous solution of glucose = 5%

The above solution is isotonic with 1.66% aqueous solution of urea.

As solution is isotonic.

$$\therefore \quad \pi_{sugar} = \pi_{urea}$$

$$C_1RT = C_2RT$$

$$\text{or} \quad C_1 = C_2$$

$$\frac{5}{180} = \frac{1.66}{M}$$

$$M = \frac{1.66}{5} \times 180$$

$$= 59.76 \text{ g}$$

2. (i) Iodoform test can be used to distinguish between ethanol and phenol.

- $\underset{\text{Ethanol}}{CH_3CH_2OH} + 4NaOI \longrightarrow \underset{\substack{\text{Iodoform} \\ \text{(Yellow ppt.)}}}{CHI_3} + HCOONa + NaI + H_2O + 2NaOH$
- $\underset{\text{Phenol}}{C_6H_5OH} + NaOH \longrightarrow$ No yellow ppt.

(ii) Conversion of acetaldehyde into secondary propyl alcohol.

$$\underset{\text{Acetaldehyde}}{CH_3-\overset{\overset{\displaystyle H}{|}}{C}=O} + CH_3MgBr \longrightarrow CH_3-\overset{\overset{\displaystyle H}{|}}{\underset{\underset{\displaystyle CH_3}{|}}{C}}-OMgBr$$

$$\xrightarrow[\text{Hydrolysis}]{H_2O/H^+} \underset{\text{Secondary propyl alcohol}}{CH_3-\overset{\overset{\displaystyle H}{|}}{\underset{\underset{\displaystyle CH_3}{|}}{C}}-OH} + Mg\begin{matrix} OH \\ Br \end{matrix}$$

3. (i) As zinc, cadmium and mercury of group 12 have completely filled *d*-orbitals in their common oxidation states, thus they are not regarded as transition metals, but they are studied along with the chemistry of the transition metals.

(ii) The transition metals form a large number of complex compound due to the comparatively smaller size of the metal ions, their high charge density and vacant *d*-orbitals for bond formation.

4. (i) **Ethyl bromide to diethyl ether**

$$\underset{\text{Ethyl bromide}}{CH_3CH_2Br} + \underset{\text{Sodium ethoxide}}{NaO-C_2H_5} \longrightarrow \underset{\text{Diethyl ether}}{CH_3CH_2-O-CH_2CH_3}$$

(ii) **Phenol to salicylaldehyde**

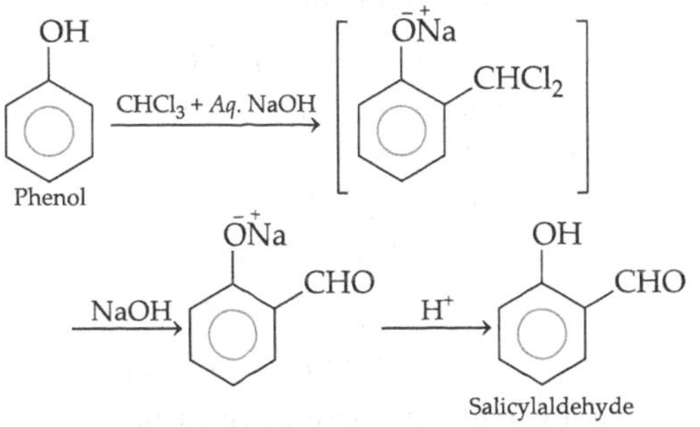

5. (i) Due to lanthanoid contraction, there is a small difference in the size of Zr and Hf. So, there is difference in some properties of lanthanoids like solubility, degree of hydration and complex formation. These differences enable the separation of lanthanoids by ion exchange method.

(ii) Cu^{2+} ion has an electronic configuration $3d^9$ whereas Cu^+ ion has $3d^{10}$. Hence, an unpaired electron is present in Cu^{2+} due to which $d-d$ electronic transition takes place. The energy of excitation corresponds to the frequency of light absorbed.

The colour observed corresponds to the complementary colour of the light absorbed. In contrast, due to lack of unpaired electrons Cu^+ is colourless.

6. (i) **Benzene to biphenyl**

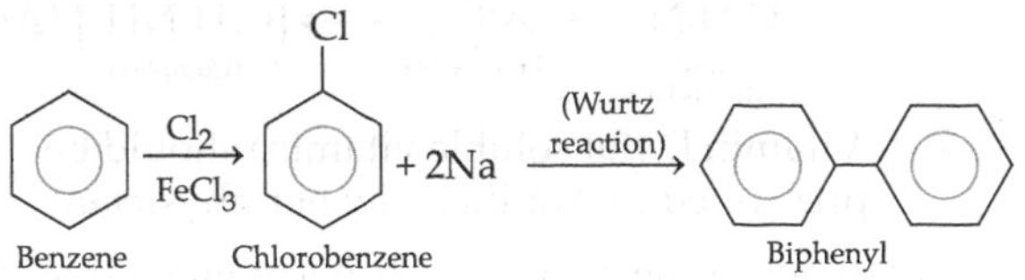

(ii) **Iodoform to acetylene**

$$\underset{\text{Iodoform}}{2CHI_3} + 6Ag \longrightarrow \underset{\text{Acetylene}}{CH\equiv CH} + \underset{\text{ppt.}}{6AgI\downarrow}$$

7. Given, $E^\circ_{(Zn^{2+}/Zn)} = -0.76\text{ V}$

$E^\circ_{(Ag^+/Ag)} = 0.80\text{ V}$

$E^\circ_{cell} = 0.8-(-0.76)$

$= 1.56\text{ V}$

$W_{electrical} = -nFE^\circ_{cell}$

$= -2\times 96500 \times [1.56]$

$= -301,080\text{ J}$

$= -301.1\text{ kJ}$

8. (i)(a) Alcohols react with active metals like Na to produce corresponding alkoxides with the evolution of hydrogen gas. This shows that alcohols are acidic in nature (and can donate a proton to a stronger base).

Whereas diethyl ether does not contain any ionic functional group nor can deprotonate readily. Thus, in the absence of available hydrogen atoms or other ionic species, the sodium ions will not react with sodium.

(b) In case of unsymmetrical ethers having two different alkyl groups, the alcohol and the alkyl halide formed depends on the nature of the alkyl group.

In ethoxy ethane, alkyl groups are present, thus, lower alkyl group forms alkyl iodide (CH_3I) and higher alkyl group forms alcohol, i.e. C_2H_5OH. This is an example of S_N2 reaction.

Or

(ii) According to the given question compound *B*, i.e. C_4H_8O gives positive iodoform test. Thus, it is a ketone containing $CH_3-\overset{O}{\overset{\|}{C}}-$ group. As only one aldehyde, i.e. acetaldehyde gives positive iodoform test, hence, the formula of *B* may be

$$CH_3-\underset{O}{\underset{\|}{C}}-CH_2CH_3$$

- As *B* is formed by the oxidation of *A*, thus *A* must be an alcohol. Thus, the formula of alcohol forming *B* is $CH_3-\overset{OH}{\overset{|}{\underset{H}{\underset{|}{C}}}}-CH_2CH_3$, i.e. butanol.

The reaction involve is

- $$\underset{\substack{\text{Butanol}\\(A)}}{CH_3-\overset{OH}{\overset{|}{C}H}-CH_2CH_3} \xrightarrow[\text{agent}]{\text{Mild oxidising}} \underset{\substack{\text{Butan-2-one}\\(B)}}{CH_3-\overset{O}{\overset{\|}{C}}-CH_2CH_3}$$

The reaction of (*B*) with CH_3MgBr followed by hydrolysis gives (*C*). The reaction is given as

$$\underset{\substack{\text{Butan-2-one}\\(B)}}{CH_3-\overset{O}{\overset{\|}{C}}-CH_2CH_3} + CH_3MgBr \xrightarrow[H^+,\,H_2O]{\text{Hydrolysis}}$$

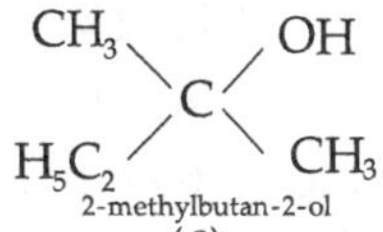

+ Mg(OH)Br

2-methylbutan-2-ol
(*C*)

Thus, compounds *A*, *B* and *C* are butanol, butan-2-one and 2-methylbutan-2-ol respectively.

9. Given, Volume of aqueous solution of a protein $= 200\ cm^3$

Amount of protein = 1.26 g

Osmotic pressure, $\pi = 2.57 \times 10^{-3}$ atm

$R = 0.0821$ L atm $K^{-1} mol^{-1}$ or $T = 300$ K

as $\pi = CRT$

$$\therefore 2.57 \times 10^{-3} = \frac{1.26 \times 1000 \times 0.0821 \times 300}{M \times 200}$$

$$M = \frac{1.26 \times 1000 \times 0.0821 \times 300}{2.57 \times 10^{3} \times 200}$$

$$= 0.06 \times 10^{6}\ g/mol^{-1}$$

10. (i) The carbon atom of carbonyl group of benzaldehyde is less electrophilic than carbon atom of the carbonyl group present in propionaldehyde. As the polarity of >C=O group is reduced in benzaldehyde due to resonance hence it is less reactive.

(ii) In oxidation of ethanol to ethanal, ethanal is readily oxidised to carboxylic acid if allowed to remain in the reaction mixture. Therefore, ethanal should be removed immediately as it is formed.

11. (i) Mn^{2+} ion has half-filled configuration, i.e. $3d^5$, while Fe^{2+} ion does not (i.e. $3d^6$). Therefore, Mn^{2+} ion is more stable than Fe^{2+} ion.

(ii) Ion which does not have unpaired electrons does not impart colour to the solution. La^{3+} has $5d^0 6s^0$ and Lu^{3+} has $4f^{14} 5d^0 6s^0$ configuration. Thus, both do not have unpaired electron. Thus, they do not shown any colour in their solution.

12. Let, the order w.r.t A and B be α and β, respectively. Rate law expression may be written as

Rate $= k[A]^{\alpha} [B]^{\beta}$

$\therefore \quad 9.6 \times 10^{-2} = k[0.15]^{\alpha} [0.15]^{\beta}$ ...(i)

or $\quad 3.84 \times 10^{-1} = k[0.3]^{\alpha} [0.15]^{\beta}$ ...(ii)

or $\quad 1.92 \times 10^{-1} = k[0.15]^{\alpha} [0.3]^{\beta}$ ...(iii)

orf $\quad 7.68 \times 10^{-1} = k[0.3]^{\alpha} [0.3]^{\beta}$ ...(iv)

Dividing Eqs. (i) by (ii), we get

$$\frac{9.6 \times 10^{-2}}{3.84 \times 10^{-1}} = \frac{k[0.15]^{\alpha} \cancel{[0.15]^{\beta}}}{k[0.3]^{\alpha} \cancel{[0.15]^{\beta}}}$$

$$\left[\frac{1}{4}\right] = \left[\frac{1}{2}\right]^{\alpha} \Rightarrow \left[\frac{1}{2}\right]^{2} = \left[\frac{1}{2}\right]^{\alpha}$$

$\therefore \quad \alpha = 2$

Dividing Eqs. (i) by (iii), we get

$$\frac{9.6 \times 10^{-2}}{1.92 \times 10^{-1}} = \frac{k\cancel{[0.15]^{\alpha}}[0.15]^{\beta}}{k\cancel{[0.15]^{\alpha}} [0.3]^{\beta}}$$

$$\Rightarrow \left[\frac{1}{2}\right]^{1} = \left[\frac{1}{2}\right]^{\beta} \Rightarrow \beta = 1$$

(i) The overall order of the reaction is 3.

(ii) Rate law expression.

Rate $= k[A]^2 [B]^1$

(iii) From expression (i) rate constant can be calculated as

$$9.6 \times 10^{-2} = k[0.15]^2 [0.15]^1$$

$$k = \frac{9.6 \times 10^{-2}\ mol\ L^{-1} min^{-1}}{[0.15]^3\ (mol\ L^{-1})^3}$$

$$= 28.44\ mol^{-2} L^2 min^{-1}$$

13. (i) (a) **Example of Coupling reaction**

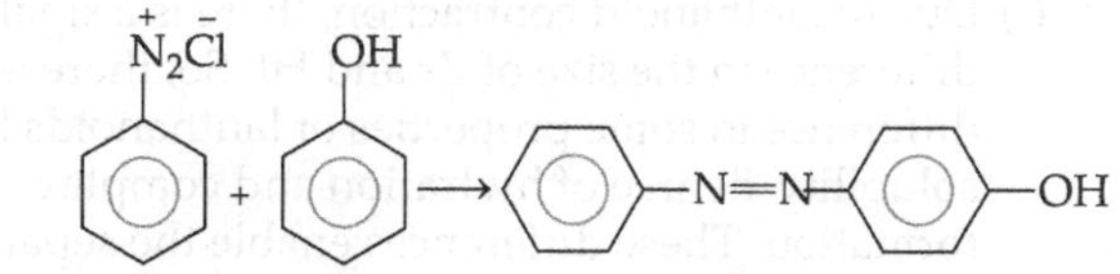

Benzene diazonium chloride Phenol *p*-hydroxyazobenzene

(b) **Example of acetylation of ethylamine**

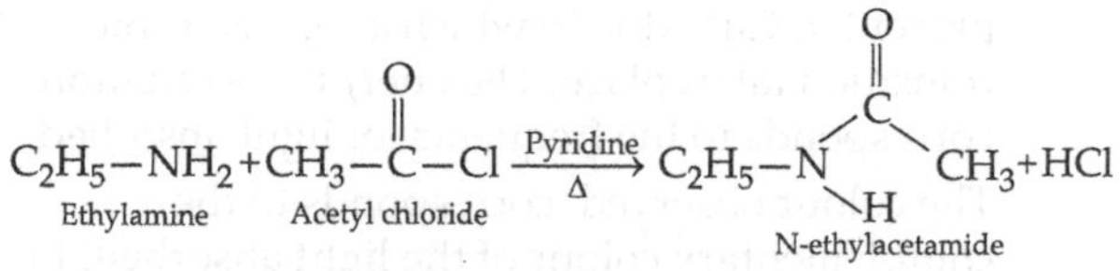

(ii) Aniline does not undergo Friedel-Craft's reaction it is due to salt formation with aluminium chloride which is used as Lewis acid catalyst.

$$\underset{\substack{\text{Aniline} \\ \text{(Lewis base)}}}{C_6H_5NH_2} + \underset{\text{(Lewis acid)}}{AlCl_3} \longrightarrow \underset{\text{(Complex)}}{[C_6H_5NH_2]^+[AlCl_3]^-}$$

14. (i) Vitamin D (fat soluble vitamin) should be prescribed to Aradhana by her physician.

(ii) When Somesh put few drops of vinegar in milk, small white chunks or curds become visible in the mixture.

This phenomenon is known as denaturation of protein.

(iii) • On hydrolysis with acids or enzyme, sucrose gives equimolar mixture of D-(+)-glucose and D-(−)-fructose.

• Sucrose is a non reducing sugar.

15. Given, boiling point of water $(T_b) = 373.0834$ K

Actual boiling point of water $(T_b^{\circ}) = 373$ K

As, $\Delta T_b = T_b - T_b^{\circ}$

$\therefore \quad \Delta T_b = 373.0834 - 373 = 0.0834$ K

Amount of $BaCl_2$ = 12.5 g

Amount of water = 1000 g

K_b for $H_2O = 0.52$ K kg mol^{-1}

Molecular mass of $BaCl_2 = 208.34$ g mol^{-1}.

$$\text{Moles of } BaCl_2 = \frac{12.5}{208.34} = 0.0599 \approx 0.06$$

$$\text{Molality } (m) = \frac{0.06 \times 1000}{1000} = 0.06 \text{ mol/kg}$$

Now, $\Delta T_b = K_b \cdot m \cdot i$

$$0.0834 = 0.52 \times 0.06 \times i$$

$$i = \frac{0.0834}{0.52 \times 0.06} = 2.67 \simeq 2.7.$$

$$\text{As, } \underset{1-x}{BaCl_2} \rightleftharpoons \underset{x}{Ba^{2+}} + \underset{2x}{2Cl^-}$$

$$i = 1 - x + x + 2x$$

$$2.7 = 1 + 2x \Rightarrow x = \frac{1.7}{2} = 0.85$$

Therefore, degree of dissociation is 85%.

16. (i) According to the given information that C_2H_4O gives red ppt. with Fehling solution and undergoes aldol condensation in presence of dil. NaOH. This means C_2H_4O is an aldehyde having an α-H atom. Thus, it can be CH_3—CHO. Its IUPAC name is ethanal.

$$\underset{\text{Ethanal}}{CH_3CHO} + \underset{\text{Fehling solution}}{2Cu^{2+}} + 4\bar{O}H \xrightarrow{\Delta} \underset{\text{Acetic acid}}{CH_3-\overset{\overset{\large O}{||}}{C}-OH} + \underset{\text{Red ppt.}}{Cu_2O\downarrow} + 2H_2O$$

$$\underset{\text{Ethanal}}{2CH_3-\overset{\overset{\large O}{||}}{C}-H} \xrightarrow[H_2O]{\text{Dil. NaOH}} \underset{\text{3-hydroxybutanal}}{CH_3-\overset{\overset{\large OH}{|}}{CH}-CH_2-\overset{\overset{\large O}{||}}{C}-H}$$

(ii) Reaction of ethanal with hydroxylamine.

$$\underset{\text{Ethanal}}{CH_3-\overset{\overset{\large O}{||}}{C}-H} + \underset{\text{Hydroxylamine}}{H_2N-OH} \xrightarrow{H^+} \underset{\text{Acetaldoxime}}{CH_3-\underset{\underset{\large H}{|}}{C}=N-OH} + H_2O$$

(iii) Reaction of ethanal with ammoniacal silver nitrate.

$$\underset{\text{Ethanal}}{CH_3-\overset{\overset{\large O}{||}}{C}-H} + \underset{\text{(Tollen's reagent)}}{2[Ag(NH_3)_2]^+} + 2\bar{O}H \xrightarrow{\Delta} \underset{\text{Acetic acid}}{CH_3-\overset{\overset{\large O}{||}}{C}-OH} + 2Ag\downarrow + 4NH_3 + H_2O$$

17. (a)

$$C_2H_5OH \xrightarrow{PCl_5} \underset{(A)}{C_2H_5Cl} \xrightarrow{KCN} \underset{(B)}{C_2H_5-CN} \xrightarrow{H_3O^+} C_2H_5COOH \xrightarrow[\Delta]{NH_3} \underset{(C)}{CH_3-CH_2-\overset{\overset{\large O}{||}}{C}-NH_2}$$

(b)

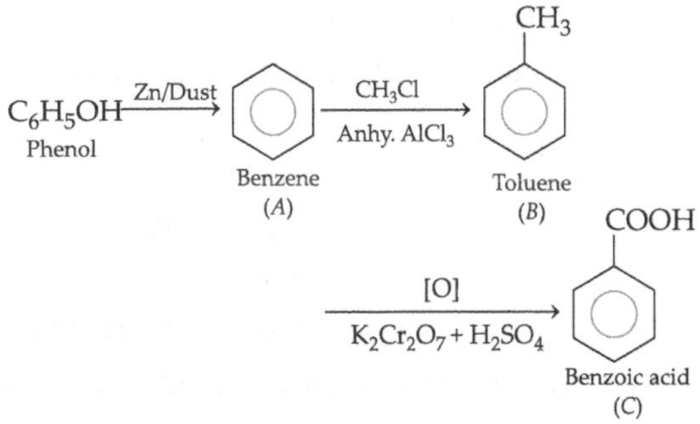

Or (ii) (a) **Ethanol and methanol** Ethanol gives positive iodoform test when warmed with iodine in presence of NaOH while methanol does not.

$$\underset{\text{Ethanol}}{CH_3CH_2OH} \xrightarrow{3I_2 + 4\,NaOH} CHI_3 + HCOO^-Na^+ + 5NaI + 5H_2O$$

$$\underset{\text{Methanol}}{CH_3-OH} \xrightarrow{NaOH, I_2} \text{No reaction}$$

(b) **Ethanol and ethanal** Ethanal gives positive Tollen's test while ethanol does not.

$$\underset{\text{Ethanol}}{CH_3-\overset{\overset{\large O}{||}}{C}-H} + 2[Ag(NH_3)_2]^+ + 3\bar{O}H \longrightarrow \underset{\text{Acetic acid}}{CH_3-\overset{\overset{\large O}{||}}{C}-OH} + 2Ag\downarrow + 4NH_3 + 2H_2O$$

$$CH_3CH_2-OH + 2[Ag(NH_3)_2]^+ + 3\bar{O}H \longrightarrow \text{No reaction}$$

(c) **Propan-2-ol and 2-methylpropan-2-ol**

Propan-2-ol when passed over heated copper at 573 K, a ketone is formed.

$$\underset{\text{2° alcohol (Propan-2-ol)}}{(CH_3)_2\overset{\overset{\large H}{|}}{C}-OH} \xrightarrow[573\,K]{Cu,} \underset{\text{Acetone}}{(H_3C)_2C=O} + H_2\uparrow$$

whereas, when 2-methylpropan-2-ol passed over heated copper at 573 K, it gives an alkene.

$$\underset{\substack{\text{(3° alcohol)}\\\text{(2 methylpropan-2-ol)}}}{CH_3-\overset{\overset{\large CH_3}{|}}{\underset{\underset{\large OH}{|}}{C}}-CH_3} \xrightarrow[573\,K]{Cu} \underset{\text{2-methylpropene}}{CH_3-\overset{\overset{\large CH_3}{|}}{C}=CH_2} + H_2O$$

18. (i) Given, $T_1 = 500\text{ K}, T_2 = 700\text{ K}$

$k_1 = 0.02\text{ s}^{-1}, k_2 = 0.07\text{ s}^{-1}$

We know that,

$$\log\frac{k_2}{k_1} = \frac{E_a}{2.303R}\left(\frac{1}{T_1} - \frac{1}{T_2}\right)$$

$$\log\left(\frac{0.07}{0.02}\right) = \frac{E_a}{2.303 \times 8.314}\left(\frac{1}{500} - \frac{1}{700}\right)$$

$$\log(3.5) = \frac{E_a}{19.15}\left[\frac{200}{350000}\right]$$

$$E_a = \frac{0.54 \times 19.15 \times 350000}{200}$$

$$= 18096.75\text{ J mol}^{-1} = 18.096\text{ kJ mol}^{-1}$$

(ii) Given, Half-life of radioactive substance $= 30$ hr

$= 1800$ min

We know that, $t_{1/2} = \frac{0.693}{k}$

$$\Rightarrow \quad k = \frac{0.693}{t_{1/2}} = \frac{0.693}{1800} = 0.000385\text{ min}^{-1}$$

Also for first order reaction,

$$t = \frac{2.303}{k}\log\frac{[N_0]}{[N]}$$

$$90 \times 60 = \frac{2.303}{0.000385}\log\frac{[N_0]}{[N]}$$

$$\log\left[\frac{N_0}{N}\right] = \frac{90 \times 60 \times 0.000385}{2.303} = 0.9027$$

$$\frac{N_0}{N} = \text{Antilog }[0.9027] = 7.9928$$

19. (i) It is given that the molecular formula of B is C_7H_8O. The possible compound having this molecular formula may be benzyl alcohol ($C_6H_5CH_2OH$), anisole ($C_6H_5OCH_3$), *ortho, meta* or *para*-cresol ($CH_3—C_6H_4OH$).

- *o*-, *m*-, *p*-cresol on oxidation give complex products and anisole cannot be easily oxidised. Thus, the compound (B) must be benzyl alcohol.
- It is given that compound (B) forms compound (A) on oxidation, which has characteristic smell, that means compound (D) may be benzaldehyde.
- Benzaldehyde (A) on treatment with NaOH undergoes Cannizzaro reaction to give compounds (B) and (C). We know that compound (B) is benzyl alcohol, therefore compound (C) may be sodium benzoate ($C_6H_5CO\bar{O}\overset{+}{Na}$).

Also, it is given that compound (C) forms benzene on heating with soda lime.

Thus, it confirms that compounds (C) must be sodium benzoate ($C_6H_5CO\bar{O}\overset{+}{Na}$).

The chemical equation of all the reactions involved are as follows

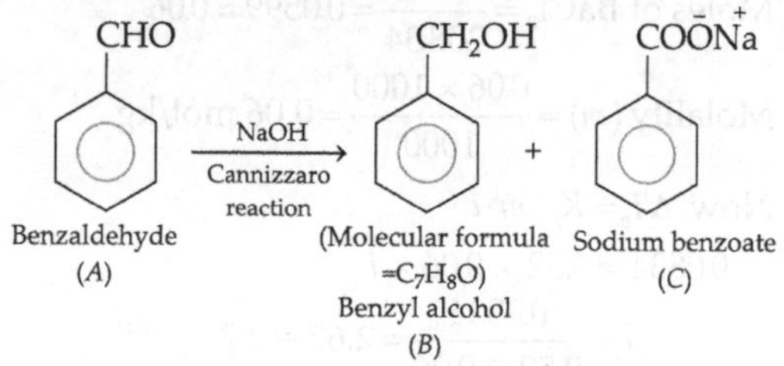

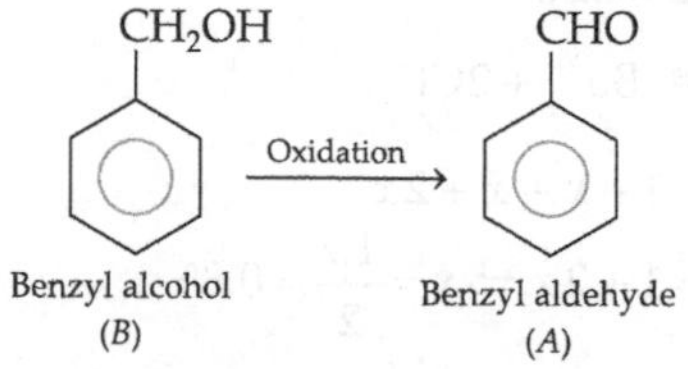

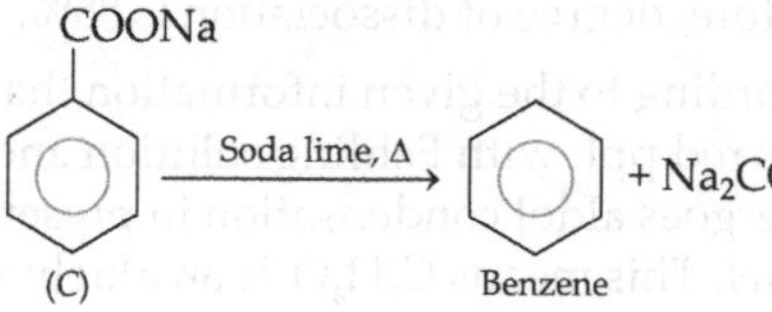

Thus, $A = C_6H_5CHO$, (Benzaldehyde)

$B = C_6H_5CH_2OH$, (Benzyl alcohol)

$C = C_6H_5COONa$, (Sodium benzoate))

(ii) (a)

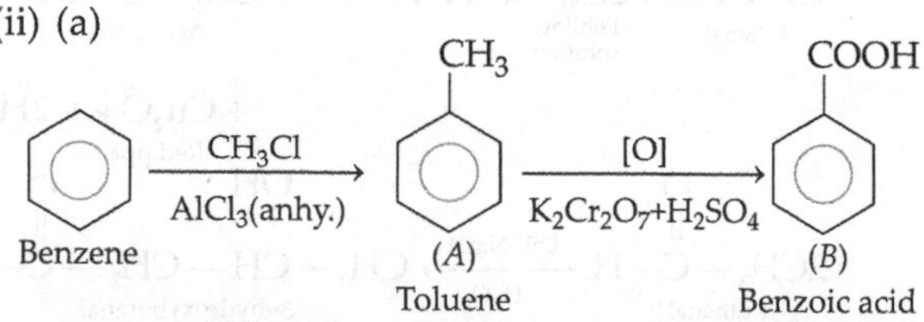

(b)

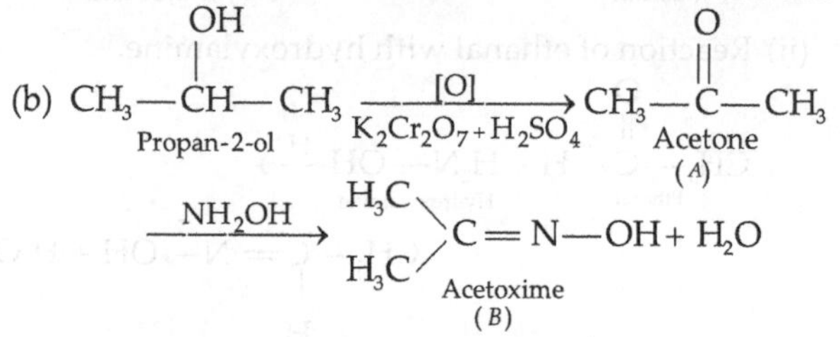

20. (i) It is given that $CoCl_3 \cdot 4NH_3$ precipitates silver ions as AgCl and its molar conductance corresponds to a total of two ions. Thus, the formula of the compound will be $[CoCl_2(NH_3)_4]Cl$ as it satisfies both the conditions.

(a) The structural formula of the complex compound is $[CoCl_2(NH_3)_4]Cl$.

(b) IUPAC name =

Tetraamminedichloridocobalt(III) chloride

(c) Geometrical isomers of $[CoCl_2(NH_3)_4]Cl$ are as follows

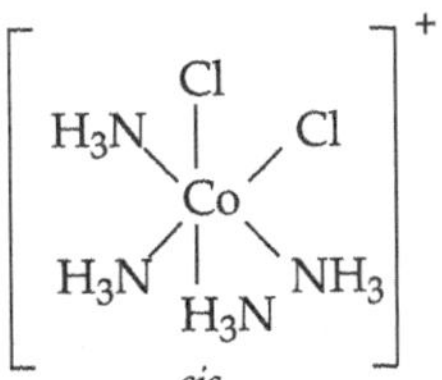

cis

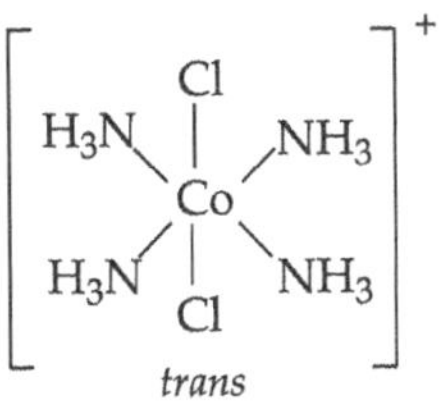

trans

(ii) The $[Co(NH_3)_5SO_4]Cl$ complex gives white precipitate with silver nitrate solution while $[Co(NH_3)_5Cl]SO_4$ does not gives such precipitate. This shows that $[Co(NH_3)_5SO_4]Cl$ and $[Co(NH_3)_5Cl]SO_4$ are ionisation isomers.

21. (i)(a) (1) The cell reaction for the given cell

$2Ag^+(aq) + 2e^- \longrightarrow 2Ag(s)$ [Reduction half-cell]

$Cu(s) \longrightarrow Cu^{2+}(aq) + 2e^-$ [Oxidation half-cell]

Overall reaction is given as

$2Ag^+(aq) + Cu(c) \longrightarrow 2Ag(s) + Cu^{2+}(aq)$

(2) Standard emf of the cell, i.e. E°_{Cell}

$= E_{Cathode} - E_{Anode} = E^\circ_{Ag^+/Ag} - E_{Cu^{2+}/Cu}$

$= (0.799 - 0.337)$ V

$E^\circ_{cell} = 0.462$ V

(3) Given, concentration of Cu^{2+}, i.e. $[Cu^{2+}] = 0.1M$

$E_{cell} = 0.422$ V and $T = 25°C$

Concentration of Ag^+, i.e. $[Ag^+] = ?$

As, we know that,

$$E_{cell} = E^\circ_{cell} - \frac{0.059}{2}\log\frac{[Cu^{2+}]}{[Ag^+]^2}$$

$$0.422 = 0.462 - \frac{0.059}{2}\log\frac{[0.1]}{[Ag^+]^2}$$

$0.422 = 0.462 - 0.0295\,[\log[0.1] - \log[Ag^+]^2]$

$0.422 = 0.462 - 0.0295\log[0.1] + 0.0295 \times 2\log[Ag^+]$

$0.422 = 0.462 + 0.0295 + 0.059\log[Ag^+]$

$0.422 = 0.4915 + 0.0591\log[Ag^+]$

$-0.0695 = 0.059\log[Ag^+]$

$-1.178 = \log[Ag^+]$

$[Ag^+] = 0.066$ M

(4) $\Delta G^\circ = -nFE^\circ_{cell} = -2 \times 96500 \times 0.462$

$= -89166\ J\ mol^{-1}$

$= -89.166\ kJ\ mol^{-1}$

(b) Given, $\Lambda^\circ_{m\,(Ba^{2+})} = 127.2\ S\ cm^2\ mol^{-1}$

$\Lambda^\circ_{m\,(Al^{3+})} = 189\ S\ cm^2\ mol^{-1}$

$\Lambda^\circ_{m\,(Cl^-)} = 76.3\ S\ cm^2\ mol^{-1}$

$\Lambda^\circ_{m\,(SO_4^{2-})} = 160\ S\ cm^2\ mol^{-1}$

$\Lambda^\circ_{m\,(BaCl_2)} = \Lambda^\circ_{m\,(Ba^{2+})} + 2\Lambda^\circ_{m\,(Cl^-)}$

$= 127.2 + 2 \times 76.3 = 127.2 + 152.6$

$= 279.8\ S\ cm^2\ mol^{-1}$

$\Lambda^\circ_{m\,[Al_2(SO_4)_3]} = 2\Lambda^\circ_{m\,(Al^{3+})} + 3\Lambda^\circ_{m\,(SO_4^{2-})}$

$= 2 \times 189 + 3 \times 160 = 858\ S\ cm^2\ mol^{-1}$

Or

(ii)(a) Given, concentration of NH_4OH solution = 0.05 M

Resistance = 30.8 ohm

Temperature = 298 K

Cell constant $(G^*) = \frac{l}{A} = 0.343\ cm^{-1}$

Molar conductance (Λ^∞_m) of NH_4OH at infinite dilution = $471.4\ S\ cm^2\ mol^{-1}$

(1) **Specific conductance** $= \frac{1}{\rho} = \frac{1}{R} \times \frac{l}{A}$

$$= \frac{1}{30.8\ (ohm)} \times 0.343\ cm^{-1}$$

$= 0.01113\ ohm^{-1}\ cm^{-1}$

(2) **Molar conductance,** $\Lambda^c_m = \frac{\kappa \times 1000}{Molarity}$

$$= \frac{0.01113 \times 1000}{0.05} \approx 222\ S\ cm^2\ mol^{-1}$$

(3) **Degree of dissociation** $\alpha = \frac{\Lambda^c_m}{\Lambda^\infty_m} = \frac{222}{471.4} = 0.472$

(b) (i) Given, Current = 1.5 A, Amount of Ag = 1.45 g

For Cell *B* Atomic mass of Ag = 108, Cu = 63.5, Zn = 65.3

As, $Ag^+ + e^- \rightleftharpoons Ag$ (at cathode)

1 mole of Ag is deposited by 96500 C

1.45 g of Ag will be deposited by

$$= \frac{96500 \times 1.45}{108} = 1295.6\ C$$

Now, $Q = It$

$1295.6 = 1.5 \times t \Rightarrow t = 864$ s

(ii) **For Cell *A*,** $Zn^{2+} + 2e^- \longrightarrow Zn$

$\therefore$ 2 moles of electrons (2 × 96500 C of current) produces 1 mole (65.3 g) of zinc.

$\therefore$ 1295.6 of electricity will deposit

$$= \frac{65.3}{2 \times 96500} \times 1295.6 = 0.438\ g\ of\ zinc$$

For Cell C, $Cu^{2+} + 2e^- \longrightarrow Cu$

2 moles of electrons (2 × 96500 C of current) produces 1 mole (63.5 g) of Cu

1295.6 C of electricity will deposit

$$= \frac{63.5 \times 1295.6}{2 \times 96500} = 0.426\ g\ of\ Cu$$

Proficiency Building Zone

Welcome to the Proficiency Building Zone !

This section contains **15 Sample Question Papers** designed to enhance your problem-solving skills and proficiency. Use these papers to practice regularly and track your progress. Remember, consistent practice is key to Chemistry.

Progress Tracker **Tick the papers as you complete them.**

- ☐ Sample Paper 1 ______ (Fill your score)
- ☐ Sample Paper 2 ______ (Fill your score)
- ☐ Sample Paper 3 ______ (Fill your score)
- ☐ Sample Paper 4 ______ (Fill your score)
- ☐ Sample Paper 5 ______ (Fill your score)
- ☐ Sample Paper 6 ______ (Fill your score)
- ☐ Sample Paper 7 ______ (Fill your score)
- ☐ Sample Paper 8 ______ (Fill your score)
- ☐ Sample Paper 9 ______ (Fill your score)
- ☐ Sample Paper 10 ______ (Fill your score)
- ☐ Sample Paper 11 ______ (Fill your score)
- ☐ Sample Paper 12 ______ (Fill your score)
- ☐ Sample Paper 13 ______ (Fill your score)
- ☐ Sample Paper 14 ______ (Fill your score)
- ☐ Sample Paper 15 ______ (Fill your score)

SPQ Code : **PB-01/15** Series ***i*-Succeed 01-25/15** Roll No.

Sample Question Paper 01

Chemistry 12th (Code 862)

General Instructions

1. This paper is divided into four sections-A, B, C and D. Answer all questions.
2. **Section A** consists of **one** question **having sub-parts** of **one** mark each. **Section B** consists of **ten** questions of **two** marks each. **Section C** consists of **seven** questions of **three** marks each and **Section D** consists of **three** questions of **five** marks each.
3. Internal choices have been provided in one question each in Section B, Section C and Section D.
4. All working, including rough work, should be done on the same sheet as, and adjacent to the rest of the answer.
5. The intended marks for questions or parts of questions are given in brackets [].
6. Balanced questions must be given, wherever possible and diagrams where they are helpful. When solving numerical problems, all essential working must be shown.
7. In working out problems, use the following data:
Gas constant (R) = 1.987 cal deg^{-1} mol^{-1} = 8.314 JK^{-1} mol^{-1} = 0.0821 dm^3 atm K^{-1} mol^{-1}
1L atm = 1 dm^3 atm =101.3 J, 1 Faraday =96500 Coulombs.
Avogadro's number (N_A) = 6.023 × 10^{23}.

Time : 3 Hrs.

Max. Marks : 70

Section A **[14 Marks]**

1. (A) Fill in the blanks by choosing the appropriate word(s) from those given in the brackets. [4×1]
[oxidation, *para*, blue, black, reduction, red, *p*-benzoquinone, endothermic, green, dia, tetrahedral, *o*-benzoquinone, high, octahedral, exothermic, low]

(i) Formic acid gives .... ppt. with Tollen's reagent and ...... ppt. with Fehling solution. • *Recall*

(ii) Dissolution of sugar in water is an .... process and therefore .... temperature will favour the dissolution of sugar in water. • *Understanding*

(iii) The complex $[Co(NH_3)_6]^{3+}$ has .... geometry and is .... magnetic in nature. • *Understanding*

(iv) Phenol on .... with chromic acid gives .... • *Recall*

(B) Select and write the correct alternative from the choices given below. [7×1]

(i) Which of the following statements is correct regarding acidic character of phenols? • *Understanding*

I. Phenol are weaker acids than alcohols.
II. *o*-nitrophenol is more acidic than *m*-nitrophenol.
III. pK_a value of *p*-cresol is more as compared to pK_a value of *m*-cresol.
IV. Cresols are more acidic than phenols.

(a) Only I and II (b) Only II and III
(c) Only I and IV (d) Only III and IV

(ii) *d-d* transition means a shifting of electrons between the lower energy *d*-orbitals to a higher energy *d*-orbital by absorption of energy and *vice-versa*. Due to *d-d* transition, elements are coloured. The transition element which is not coloured in aqueous medium is • *Analysis*

(a) Sc^{3+} (b) Ti^{2+}
(c) Cu^{3+} (d) Mn^{2+}

(iii) Conductors are the materials or substances which allow electricity to flow through them. Which of the following substance is not conductor ? • *Recall*

(a) Graphite
(b) Glass
(c) Silver
(d) Alloys of metal

(iv) The IUPAC name of the given compound is

$$CH_3-CH_2-\underset{\displaystyle CHO}{\underset{|}{CH}}-\underset{\displaystyle CH_3}{\underset{|}{CH}}-CH_2-CH_3$$

(a) 4-methyl-2-ethyl pentanal
(b) 4-ethyl-3-methyl pentanal
(c) 2-ethyl-3-methyl pentanal
(d) 4-methyl hexanal • *Understanding*

(v) 75% of a first order reaction was completed in 32 mins. When was 50% of the reaction completed?

(a) 24 mins • *Application*
(b) 16 mins
(c) 8 mins
(d) 4 mins

SP-01

(vi) **Assertion** (A) D-(+)-glucose is dextrorotatory in nature.

Reason (R) 'D' represents its dextrorotatory nature. • *Understanding*

(a) Both Assertion and Reason are true and Reason is the correct explanation of Assertion.
(b) Both Assertion and Reason are true but Reason is not the correct explanation of Assertion.
(c) Assertion is true but Reason is false.
(d) Both Assertion and Reason are false.

(vii) **Assertion** (A) Specific conductance keep on increasing with dilution.

Reason (R) On increasing dilution, degree of ionisation of weak electrolyte decreases and volume of solution also decreases. • *Analysis*

(a) Both Assertion and Reason are true and Reason is the correct explanation of Assertion.
(b) Both Assertion and Reason are true but Reason is not the correct explanation of Assertion.
(c) Assertion is true but Reason is false.
(d) Both Assertion and Reason are false.

(C) Read the passage given below and answer the questions that follows [3×1]

Phenols are the compounds that possess a hydroxyl group directly attached to an aromatic carbocylic nucleus. Phenol is the trivial name for monohydroxy- benzene. The *o*, *m* and *p*-cresols are monohydroxytoluenes and are distinct in their properties and reactions from the isomeric side chain hydroxy compound, benzyl alcohol, which is a typical aromatic alcohol.

Simple monohydric phenols are either corrosive liquids or low melting solids. The dihydric and trihydric phenols are solids.

The mono-hydroxy compounds are only slightly soluble in water but are miscible with organic solvents.

Water solubility increases and solubility in organic solvent decreases with the introduction of additional hydroxyl groups. They are all characterised and distinguished from the aliphatic or aromatic alcohols by their different solubility in aqueous alkali.

(i) What are the products obtained on reaction of phenol with dil. HNO_3? • *Understanding*

(ii) Write the structure of picric acid. • *Recall*

(iii) Among *o*-nitrophenol and *p*-nitrophenol, which will prefer to undergo intramolecular H-bonding? • *Understanding*

Section B [20 Marks]

2. Give reason for the following. • *Understanding* [2]
   (i) *d*-block elements exhibit a large number of oxidation states than *f*-block elements.
   (ii) Sc^{3+} ion does not show paramagnetism.

3. Sita was making noodles in boiling water and added common salt to it. • *Application*[2]
   Calculate the boiling point of a solution prepared by adding 15.0 g of NaCl to 250.0 g of water (K_b for water = 0.512 K kg mol^{-1} and molar mass of NaCl = 58.44 g mol^{-1}).

4. (i) For the cell reaction at 25°C.
   $$Zn(s)\,|\underset{(0.1M)}{Zn^{2+}(aq)}\,||\,\underset{(0.01M)}{Cd^{2+}(aq)}\,|Cd(s)$$
   Given, $E^{\circ}_{cathode} = -0.403V$, $E^{\circ}_{anode} = -0.763V$
   (a) Write the reaction at anode. • *Analysis*
   (b) Write the reaction at cathode. [2]
   (ii) Find E_{cell} of the given cell. • *Application*

5. Explain • *Understanding* [2]
   (i) Why the dipole moment of chlorobenzene is lower than that of cyclohexyl chloride?
   (ii) Why Grignard reagents should be prepared under anhydrous conditions?

6. Which compound in each of the following pairs will react faster in S_N2 reaction with OH^- and why? • *Understanding* [2]
   (i) CH_3Br or CH_3I (ii) $(CH_3)_3CCl$ or CH_3Cl

7. (i) Which of the following species cannot act as a ligand ? Give reason. • *Understanding* [2]
   $$OH^-, NH_4^+, CH_3NH_2, H_2O$$
   (ii) The complex $[Co(NH_3)_5(NO_2)]Cl_2$ is red in colour. Give IUPAC name of its linkage isomer. • *Understanding*

8. How will the following be obtained? (Give chemical equations) [2]
   (i) Toluene from phenol
   (ii) Propan-2-ol from ethanal • *Understanding*

Or Devise a scheme for the synthesis of 2-methylbutanal which is racemised in acid or base using 2-methylbutanol (optically active is nature). Is the product is also optically active. Give reason for your answer. • *Evaluate*

9. (i) Arrange the following compounds of same molarity in the increasing order of freezing point. (Assume 10% ionisation in electrolytes) • *Understanding*
   Urea, $Al_2(SO_4)_3$, NaCl, $CaCl_2$. [2]
   (ii) It is advised to add ethylene glycol to water in car radiator while driving in hill station. Why? • *Understanding*

10. How will you convert the following? [2]
   (i) Ethanal to 2-hydroxy propanoic acid
   (ii) Toluene to benzoic acid • *Understanding*

11. (i) Draw the diagram showing splitting of *d*-orbital in tetrahedral complex. • *Recall* [2]
   (ii) How will you distinguish between the following isomeric pair?
   $[CoBr(NH_3)_5]SO_4$ and $[Co(SO_4)_5(NH_3)_5]Br$ • *Understanding*

Section C

[21 Marks]

12. (i) Rohan specifically used lemon juice while marinating meat. What can be the possible reason of doing that? Name the phenomena associated with it. • *Recall* [3]

(ii) Name the base that is found in nucleotide of RNA only. • *Recall*

(iii) Glucose on reaction with acetic acid gives glucose pentaacetate. What does it suggest about the structure of glucose? • *Understanding*

13. An alcohol $A(C_4H_{10}O)$ on oxidation with acidified potassium dichromate gives acid $B(C_4H_8O_2)$. Compound A when dehydrated with conc. H_2SO_4 at 443 K gives compound C. Treatment of C with aqueous H_2SO_4 gives compound D $(C_4H_{10}O)$ which is an isomer of A.

Compound D is resistant to oxidation but compound A can be easily oxidised.

Identify A, B, C and D. Name the type of isomerism exhibited by A and D.

• *Understanding* [3]

14. (i) The half-life time for the decomposition of a substance dissolved in CCl_4 is 2.5 h at 30°C. [3]

How much of the substance will be left after 10 h, if the initial weight of the substance is 160 g? • *Application*

(ii) First order decomposition reaction takes 40 min for 30% decomposition. Calculate its $t_{1/2}$ value. • *Application*

15. In order to account for the extent of association and dissociation, van't Hoff introduced a factor, i called as van't Hoff factor. In case of association, value of 'i' is less than one while in case of dissociation, value of 'i' is greater than one.

Consider the case given below and answer the questions that follow.

When 2g of benzoic acid dissolves in 25 g of benzene (C_6H_6), it shows a depression in freezing point equal to 1.62 K. Molal depression constant of benzene is $4.9\ K\ mol^{-1}\ kg$. [3]

(i) Inferring the value of van't hoff factor, find out whether the solute undergoes association or dissociation?

• *Analysis and Understanding*

(ii) What is the percentage ionisation of acid, if it forms dimer in solution?

• *Application*

16. How will the following be converted? (Give chemical equations) • *Understanding* [3]

(i) Nitrobenzene into aniline

(ii) Ethanoic acid into methanamine

(iii) Nitrobenzene to 2, 4, 6-tribromoaniline

Or Write the reactions involved in the following. • *Recall*

(i) Hofmann bromamide degradation reaction

(ii) Diazotisation

(iii) Gabriel phthalimide synthesis

17. Consider the following reaction,

$$2NO(g) + Cl_2(g) \longrightarrow 2NOCl(g) \quad [3]$$

The following data were collected at 263 K.

Exp. No.	Initial [NO] (M)	Initial $[Cl_2]$ (M)	Initial rate of disappearance of Cl_2 (M/min)
1.	0.15	0.15	0.60
2.	0.15	0.30	1.20
3.	0.30	0.15	2.40
4.	0.25	0.25	?

Answer the following questions.

(i) What is the order of reaction with respect to NO and Cl_2. • *Application*

(ii) Determine the rate constant of reaction. • *Application*

(iii) Determine the initial rate of disappearance of Cl_2 in exp. 4. • *Evaluate*

18. Identify the compounds A, B and C in the following reactions. • *Understanding* [3]

(i) $CH_3CH_2I \xrightarrow{NaCN} [A] \xrightarrow[\text{Partial hydrolysis}]{OH^-} [B] \xrightarrow{NaOH + Br_2} [C]$

(ii) $CH_3CN \xrightarrow{H_2O/H^+} [A] \xrightarrow[\Delta]{NH_3} [B] \xrightarrow{Br_2+KOH} [C]$

Section D

[15 Marks]

19. (i) Calculate E°_{cell} for the following reaction at 298 K: [5]

$$2\,Al(s) + 3Cu^{2+}(0.01M) \longrightarrow 2\,Al^{3+}(0.01M) + 3Cu(s)$$

Given, $E_{cell} = 1.98$ V • *Application*

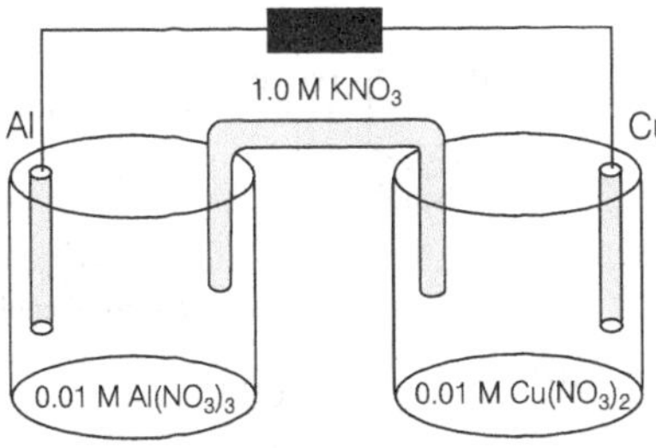

(ii) Calculate the potential of hydrogen electrode in contact with a solution whose pH is 10. • *Application*

Or (i) A steady current of 2 amperes was passed through two electrolytic cells *X* and *Y* connected in series containing electrolytes $FeSO_4$ and $ZnSO_4$ until 2.8 g of Fe deposited at the cathode of cell *X*.

How long did the current flow? Calculate the mass of Zn deposited at the cathode of cell *Y*. • *Application*

(Molar mass : Fe = 56 g mol^{-1}, Zn = 653 g mol^{-1}, 1F = 96500 C mol^{-1})

(ii) A solution of $Ni(NO_3)_2$ is electrolysed between platinum electrodes using a current of 5.0 A for 20 min. What mass of nickel will be deposited at the cathode? • *Application*

20. (i) The elements of 3*d* transition series are given as [5]

Sc Ti V Cr Mn Fe Co Ni Cu Zn

Answer the following.

(a) Write the element which shows maximum number of oxidation states. Give reason. • *Understanding*

(b) Which element has the highest melting point? • *Understanding*

(c) Which element is a strong oxidising agent in +3 oxidation state and why? • *Understanding*

(ii) What is lanthanoid contraction? What is its effect on the chemistry of the elements which follow the lanthanoids? • *Recall*

21. Account the following. • *Understanding* [5]

(i) (a) Electrophilic substitution in benzoic acid takes place at *meta*-position.

(b) Carboxylic acids do not give characteristic reactions of carbonyl group.

(ii) How can you distinguish between acetophenone and benzaldehyde, as well as benzoic acid and ethylbenzoate?

Solutions *in Topper's Style*

My Commitment *I affirm that I am reviewing these solutions only after I have solved the Sample Question Paper on my own. My purpose of looking the solutions is solely to verify whether my answers/solutions were correct or not and to identify my mistakes in case my solutions were wrong or I could not solve that.*

1. (A) (i) black, red

(ii) endothermic, high

(iii) octahedral, dia

(iv) oxidation, *p*-benzoquinone

(B) (i) (b) Statements II and III are correct while statements I and IV are incorrect. Their correct form are as follows

- Phenols are more acidic than alcohols because phenoxide ion left after the release of a proton is stabilised by resonance.
- Cresols are less acidic than phenols due to presence of electron releasing group (alkyl group).

(ii) (a) Sc^{3+} has no unpaired electron in its *d*-subshell due to which *d*-*d* transition is not possible. So, it is colourless.

(iii) (b) Glass is an insulator.

(iv) (c) The IUPAC name of the following compound is

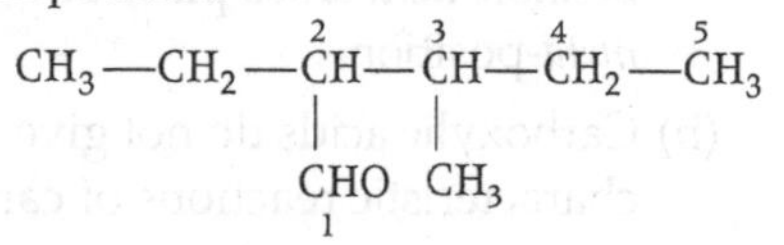

2-ethyl-3-methylpentanal

(v) (b) For a first-order reaction,

we have : $t_{75\%} = 2t_{50\%}$

Given : $t_{75\%} = 32$ mins

$32 \text{ min} = 2\,t_{50\%}$

$t_{50\%} = 16$ mins

Hence, 50% of the reaction would have been completed in 16 mins.

(vi) (c) Assertion is true but Reason is false. D-(+)-glucose is dextrorotatory because it rotates the plane polarised light to right.

Here, D represents relative configuration of glucose with respect to glyceraldehyde.

(vii) (d) Thus, both Assertion and Reason are false.

On dilution, the number of ions and the volume of the solution increases, but the increase in volume is higher than increase in number of ions.

Hence, number of ions per unit volume decreases and specific conductance (κ) also decreases.

(C) (i)

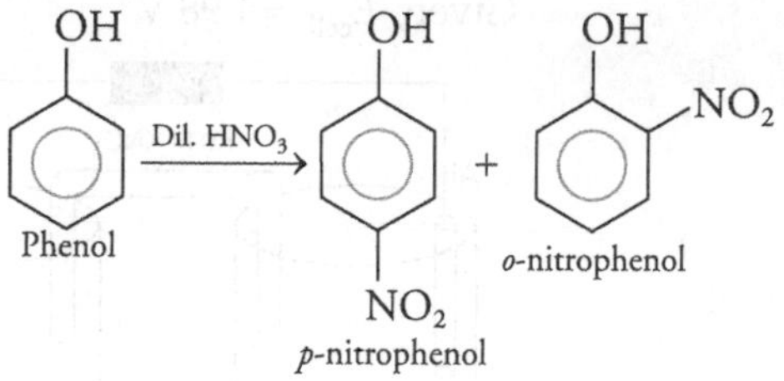

(ii)

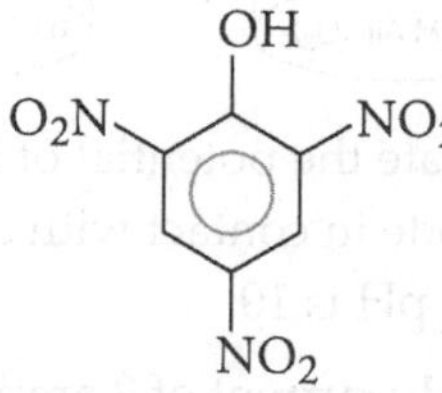

2,4,6-trinitrophenol (Picric acid)

(iii) *o*-nitrophenol shows intramolecular H-bonding.

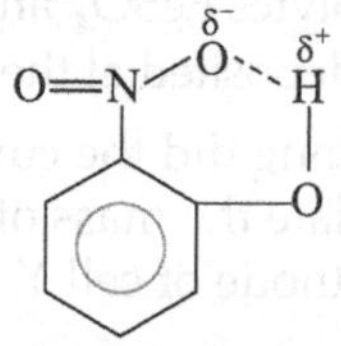

2. (i) In case of *d*-block elements, the difference of energy between $(n-1)\,d$ and *ns*-orbitals is very small. Hence, electrons from both the energy levels can be removed to exhibit variable oxidation states.

However, in case of *f*-block elements, there is a large gap in energy of 4*f* and 5*d*-subshells, thus the number of oxidation states of *f*-block is limited.

(ii) Sc^{3+} ion does not show paramagnetism because it has noble gas configuration of Ar (argon). Therefore, its *d*-orbital is empty and hence, no unpaired electron is present.

3. Given, amount of NaCl, $w_1 = 15.0$ g, amount of water, $W_2 = 250.0$ g, molar mass of NaCl, $M = 58.44 \text{ g mol}^{-1}$, $K_b = 0.512 \text{ K kg mol}^{-1}$

∵ 1 mole of NaCl gives 2 ionic particles, i.e. Na^+ and Cl^-.

∴ $i = 2$

We know that, $\Delta T_b = iK_b m$,

$$\Delta T_b = \frac{i \times K_b \times w_1 \times 1000}{M \times W_2}$$

$$\Rightarrow \quad \Delta T_b = \frac{2 \times 0.512 \times 15 \times 1000}{58.44 \times 250} = 1.051 \text{ K}$$

Also, $\Delta T_b = T_b - T_b^{\circ}$

or, $T_b = \Delta T_b + T_b^{\circ}$

Thus, boiling point of a solution $(T_b) = 373\text{ K} + 1.051$
$= 374.051\text{ K}.$

4. (i) The cell reaction is

(a) At anode, $Zn(s) \longrightarrow Zn^{2+}(aq) + 2e^-$

(b) At cathode, $Cd^{2+}(aq) + 2e^- \longrightarrow Cd(s)$

(ii) $E°$ of the cell is given by,

$E^{\circ}_{cell} = E^{\circ}_{cathode} - E^{\circ}_{anode} = -0.403 - (-0.763) = 0.36\text{ V}$

Applying Nernst equation to the cell reaction,

$$E_{cell} = E^{\circ}_{cell} - \frac{0.059}{n}\log\frac{[Zn^{2+}(aq)]}{[Cd^{2+}(aq)]}$$

$$E_{cell} = 0.36 - \frac{0.059}{2}\log\frac{0.1}{0.01} \qquad [\because n = 2]$$

$$E_{cell} = 0.36 - 0.0295\log 10$$
$$= 0.36 - 0.0295 \times 1 = 0.3305\text{ V}$$

5. (i)

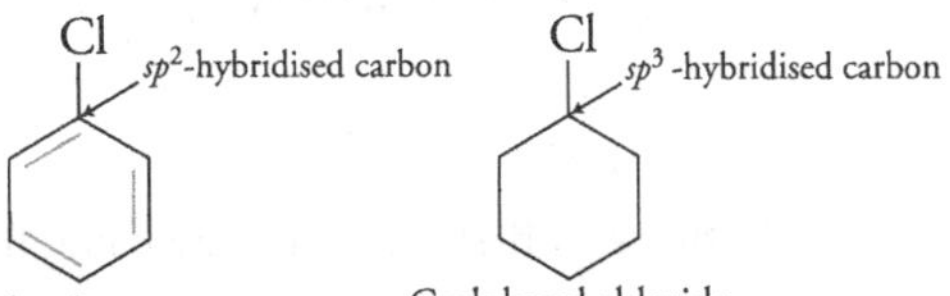

Chlorobenzene   Cyclohexyl chloride

Due to sp^2-hybridisation of C-atom in chlorobenzene, C-atom is more electronegative (greater *s*-character), whereas in cyclohexyl chloride, C-atom is sp^3-hybridised, i.e. less electronegative (lesser *s*-character). So, polarity of C—Cl bond in chlorobenzene is less than the C—Cl bond in cyclohexyl chloride.

Further, due to delocalisation of lone pair of electrons of Cl-atom over the benzene ring, C—Cl bond in chlorobenzene acquires some double bond character, while C—Cl bond in cyclohexyl chloride is a pure single bond.

Thus, C—Cl bond in chlorobenzene is shorter than in cyclohexyl chloride. As dipole moment is a product of charge and distance, therefore, the dipole moment of chlorobenzene is lower than that of cyclohexyl chloride.

(ii) Grignard reagents $(R\text{—Mg—}X)$ are readily decomposed by water to produce alkanes. That is why, they should be prepared under anhydrous conditions. Instead, ether is used as a solvent during the preparation of Grignard reagent.

$$R\text{—Mg—}X + H_2O \xrightarrow{\text{Ether}} \underset{\text{Alkane}}{R\text{—H}} + Mg\begin{smallmatrix} X \\ OH \end{smallmatrix}$$

6. (i) CH_3Br and CH_3I both are primary halogen compounds. The reactivity will depend upon the size of the halogen atom. Iodine is a better leaving group because of larger size, therefore, CH_3I will react faster than CH_3Br.

(ii) Out of $(CH_3)_3CCl$ and CH_3Cl, the molecule being a primary halide, i.e. CH_3Cl, will react faster with OH^-. This is because in S_N2 reaction, 1° halide reacts faster than 3° halide.

7. (i) NH_4^+ ion does not have a lone pair of electrons which it can donate to central metal ion. Hence, it cannot behave as a ligand.

(ii) $[Co(NH_3)_5(ONO)]Cl_2 \rightarrow$ Pentaaminenitrito-O- cobalt (III) chloride.

8. (i) **Toluene from phenol**

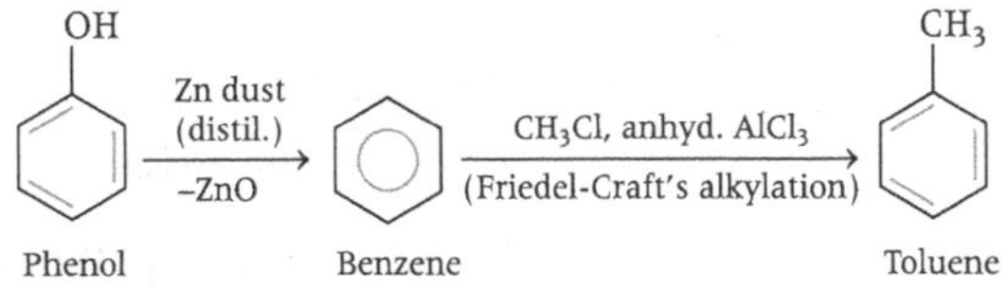

(ii) **Propan-2-ol from ethanal**

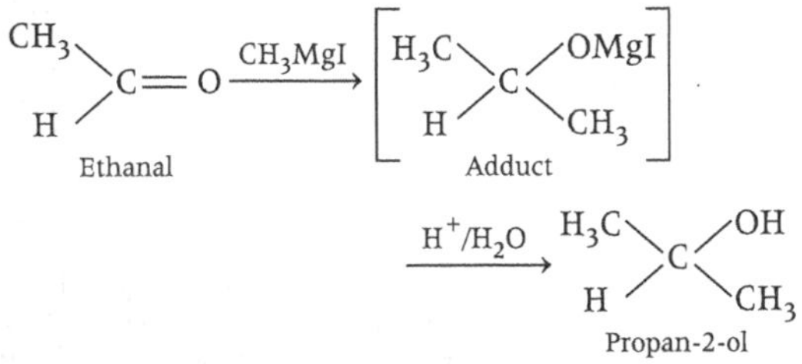

Or

The compound, 2-methylbutanol on oxidation with PCC, forms 2-methylbutanal.

The reactions are as follows

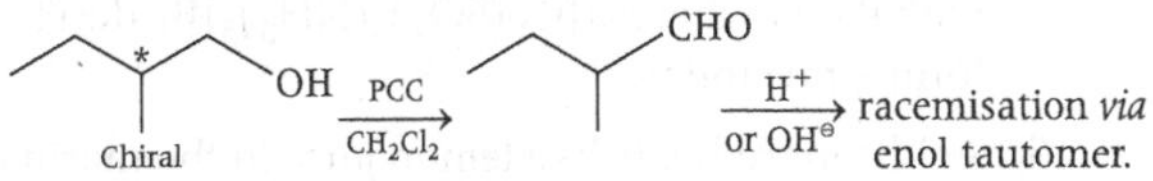

2-methylbutanal is an optically active compound due to presence of chiral centre.

9. (i) We know, $\Delta T_f = ik_f m = T_f^{\circ} - T_f$

The more the value of '*i*', the more is the ΔT_f value and hence, less is the T_f value.

$\Rightarrow$ For, i = number of particles.

	i
Urea (NH_2CONH_2)	1 (does not ionise)
NaCl	2
$CaCl_2$	3
$Al_2(SO_4)_3$	5

$\therefore$ Increasing order of T_f is,

$Al_2(SO_4)_3 < CaCl_2 < NaCl < NH_2CONH_2$(Urea).

(ii) Ethylene glycol lowers the freezing point of water, therefore, water does not freeze in hill station.

10. (i) **Ethanal to 2-hydroxy propanoic acid**

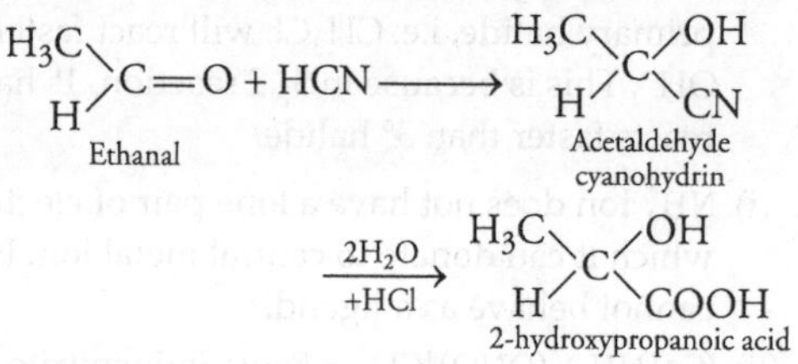

(ii) **Toluene to benzoic acid**

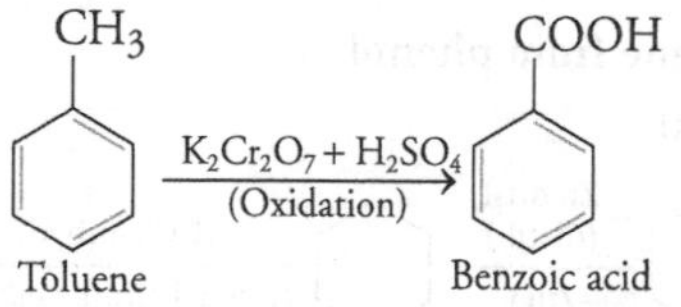

11. (i) Following is the diagram showing splitting of *d*-orbital in tetrahedral complex.

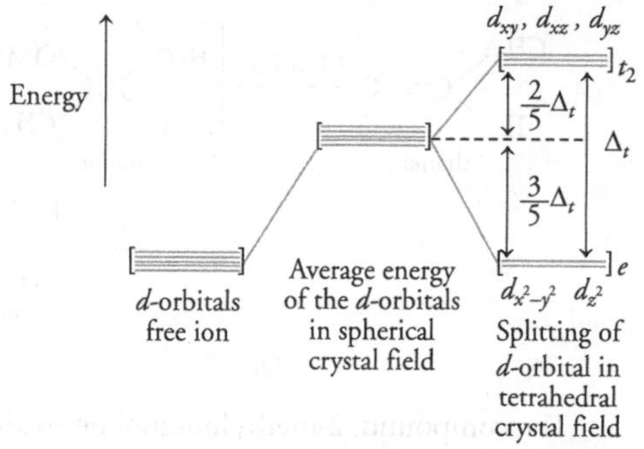

d-orbital splitting in a tetrahedral crystal field

(ii) $[CoBr(NH_3)_5]SO_4$ gives white precipitate of $BaSO_4$ with $BaCl_2$ whereas $[Co(SO_4)_5(NH_3)_5]Br$ don't form a precipitate.

12. (i) Acidic ingredients like lemon juice in the marinate will tenderise the meat by unwinding the long protein present in the meat. This phenomena is known as denaturation of protein.

(ii) DNA and RNA both contain three common bases, adenine (A), guanine (G) and cytosine (C). Thymine (T) is present in DNA but in place of thymine, RNA contains uracil (U).

(iii) Acetylation of glucose with acetic acid gives glucose pentaacetate which confirms the presence of five —OH groups.

13. An alcohol '*A*' ($C_4H_{10}O$) on oxidation with acidified $K_2Cr_2O_7$ gives acid '*B*' ($C_4H_8O_2$).

Thus, '*A*' is 1° alcohol and *B* is a carboxylic acid. Compound *A* when dehydrated with conc. H_2SO_4 at 443 K gives compound '*C*'.

Thus, '*C*' is an alkene. Treatment of *C* with aqueous H_2SO_4 gives *D* ($C_4H_{10}O$) which is an isomer of *A* and resistant to oxidation. Thus, '*D*' is a hindered alcohol.

The reactions are as follows

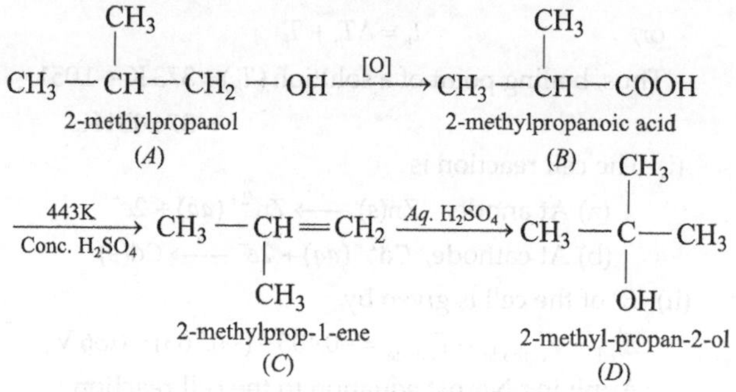

Thus, '*A*' and '*D*' are position isomers of each other.

14. (i) Number of half-life periods

$$= \frac{\text{Total time}}{\text{Time of one half-life period}} = \frac{10}{2.5} = 4$$

Amount of substance left after *n* half-life periods

$$= \left(\frac{1}{2}\right)^n \times \text{initial quantity} = \left(\frac{1}{2}\right)^4 \times 160\text{ g}$$

$$= \frac{160}{2 \times 2 \times 2 \times 2}\text{ g} = 10\text{ g}$$

(ii) To find $t_{1/2}$, first calculate *k* by using the formula,

$$k = \frac{2.303}{t}\log\frac{[R]_0}{[R]}$$

Given, $t = 40$ mins for 30% decomposition means $[R]_0 = 100$ M and $[R] = 70$ M

$$\therefore \quad k = \frac{2.303}{40}\log\frac{[R]_0}{[R]} = \frac{2.303}{40}\log\frac{100}{70}$$

$$= \frac{2.303}{40}\log 1.4286 = \frac{2.303 \times 0.1549}{40} = 0.0089\text{ min}^{-1}$$

Calculate $t_{1/2}$ by using the formula,

$$t_{1/2} = \frac{0.693}{k} = \frac{0.693}{0.0089} = 77.865\text{ mins}$$

15. Depression in freezing point is given by the formula,

$$\Delta T_f = K_f \times m = \frac{1000 \times K_f \times w_{\text{solute}}}{M \times W_{\text{solvent}}}$$

$$\left[\because m = \frac{1000 \times w_{\text{solute}}}{M \times W_{\text{solvent}}}\right] \quad \ldots\text{(i)}$$

Where, w_{solute} = mass of solute
W_{solvent} = mass of solvent
M = molar mass

Firstly, molar mass of benzoic acid is calculated, then van't Hoff factor and degree of association is calculated.

Given that, mass of benzoic acid, $w = 2$ g; mass of benzene, $W = 25$ g

$K_f = 4.9\text{ K mol}^{-1}\text{kg}$; depression in freezing point, $\Delta T_f = 1.62$ K

Molar mass of benzoic acid,

$$M = \frac{1000 \times 4.9 \times 2}{1.62 \times 25} = 242 \text{ g mol}^{-1}$$

The normal mass of benzoic acid $= 122 \text{ g mol}^{-1}$

(i) van't Hoff factor, $i = \dfrac{\text{Normal molar mass}}{\text{Observed molar mass}}$

$$\Rightarrow \quad i = \frac{122 \text{ g/mol}}{242 \text{ g/mol}} = 0.504$$

Thus, benzoic acid will undergo association in solution.

(ii) Degree of association $(\alpha) = \dfrac{i-1}{\frac{1}{n}-1}$

$$\alpha = \frac{0.504 - 1}{\frac{1}{2} - 1} = 0.496 \times 2 = 0.992$$

[Here, $n = 2$ as it forms dimer]

$\therefore$ Percentage ionisation of acid

$= 100 \times \alpha$

$= 100 \times 0.992 = 99.2\%.$

Common Mistake Generally, we can make mistake being confused in w and W in the formula of depression in freezing point. It should be noted that w is always used as mass of solute in the numerator while W is used as mass of solvent in the denominator.

16. (i) **Nitrobenzene into aniline**

$$\underset{\text{Nitrobenzene}}{C_6H_5NO_2} + 3H_2 \xrightarrow[\text{or Fe + HCl}]{\text{Sn + HCl}} \underset{\text{Aniline}}{C_6H_5NH_2} + 2H_2O$$

(ii) **Ethanoic acid into methanamine**

$$\underset{\text{Ethanoic acid}}{CH_3COOH} \xrightarrow{SOCl_2} \underset{\text{Ethanoyl chloride}}{CH_3COCl} \xrightarrow{NH_3(\text{excess})}$$

$$\underset{\text{Ethanamide}}{CH_3CONH_2} \xrightarrow[\text{(Hofmann bromamide reaction)}]{Br_2/KOH} \underset{\text{Methanamine}}{CH_3NH_2}$$

(iii) **Nitrobenzene to 2, 4, 6-tribromoaniline**

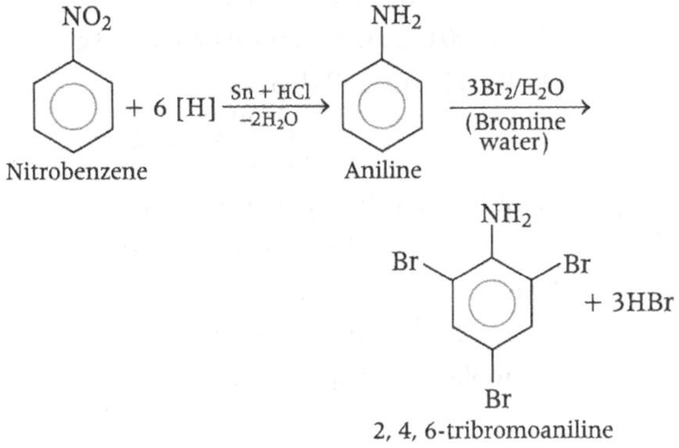

Or

(i) **Hofmann bromamide degradation reaction** This reaction is used for preparing amine containing one carbon less than the starting amide. This method was developed for the preparation of primary amines by reacting an amide with Br_2/Cl_2 in NaOH/KOH.

In this reaction, migration of an alkyl or aryl group takes place from carbonyl carbon of the amide to the N-atom.

$$R{-}\overset{O}{\overset{\|}{C}}{-}NH_2 + Br_2 + 4NaOH \longrightarrow R{-}NH_2 + Na_2CO_3 + 2NaBr + 2H_2O$$

e.g. $\underset{\text{Propanamide}}{CH_3CH_2CONH_2} + Br_2 + 4NaOH \longrightarrow$

$$3\underset{\text{Ethanamine}}{CH_3CH_2NH_2} + Na_2CO_3 + 2NaBr + 2H_2O$$

(ii) **Diazotisation** The conversion of primary aromatic amines into their diazonium salts is called diazotisation.

Benzene diazonium chloride is prepared by the reaction of aniline with nitrous acid (which is produced by the reaction of $NaNO_2$ and HCl) at 273-278 K or 0-5°C as shown below.

$$\underset{\text{Aniline}}{C_6H_5NH_2} + NaNO_2 + 2HCl \xrightarrow{273\text{-}278\text{ K}} \underset{\text{Benzene diazonium chloride}}{C_6H_5\overset{+}{N_2}\overset{-}{Cl}} + NaCl + 2H_2O$$

Due to its unstability, the diazonium salt is not generally stored and is used immediately after its preparation.

(iii) **Gabriel phthalimide synthesis** When a phthalimide is treated with ethanolic KOH, it forms potassium salt of phthalimide which on heating with alkyl halide followed by alkaline hydrolysis forms corresponding primary amines as shown below.

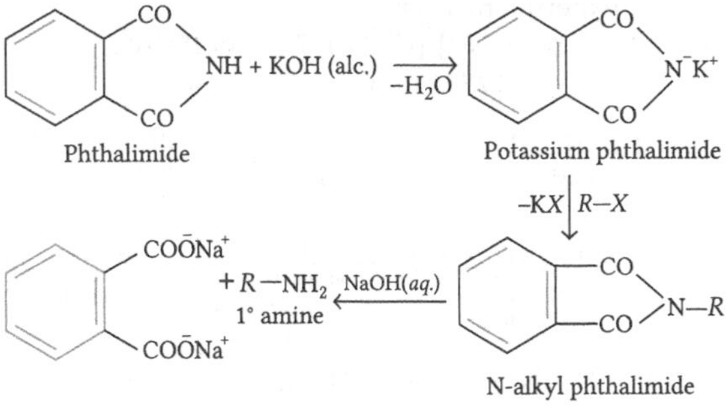

Primary amines are produced through this method without the traces of secondary or tertiary amines.

So, this method is preferred for the synthesis of primary amines.

17. (i) Rate law may be expressed as :

$$\text{Rate} = k[NO]^x[Cl_2]^y$$

$$(\text{Rate})_1 = 0.60 = k(0.15)^x(0.15)^y \quad \ldots(i)$$

$$(\text{Rate})_2 = 1.20 = k(0.15)^x(0.30)^y \quad \ldots(ii)$$

$$(\text{Rate})_3 = 2.40 = k(0.39)^x(0.15)^y \quad \ldots(iii)$$

On dividing Eq. (i) by Eq. (iii), we get,

$$\frac{(\text{Rate})_1}{(\text{Rate})_3} = \frac{0.60}{2.40} = \frac{k(0.15)^x(0.15)^y}{k(0.30)^x(0.15)^y}$$

or $$\frac{1}{4} = \frac{(0.15)^x}{(0.30)^x} = \left(\frac{15}{30}\right)^x$$

$$\left(\frac{1}{2}\right)^2 = \left(\frac{1}{2}\right)^x$$

$\therefore$ $x = 2$

Similarly, on dividing Eq. (i) by Eq. (ii), we get,

$$\frac{(\text{Rate})_1}{(\text{Rate})_2} = \frac{0.60}{1.20} = \frac{k(0.15)^x(0.15)^y}{k(0.15)^x(0.30)^y}$$

or $$\frac{1}{2} = \frac{(0.15)^y}{(0.30)^y} = \left(\frac{15}{30}\right)^y$$

$$\left(\frac{1}{2}\right)^1 = \left(\frac{1}{2}\right)^y$$

$\therefore$ $y = 1$

Hence, rate law is $k[NO]^2[Cl_2]^1$.

The order of reaction with respect to NO and Cl_2 are 2 and 1 respectively.

(ii) Rate constant can be calculated by substituting the value of rate, [NO] and $[Cl_2]$ from any of the experiments.

$$k = \frac{\text{Rate}}{[NO]^2[Cl_2]}$$

$$= \frac{0.60}{(0.15)^2(0.15)} = \frac{0.60}{0.00338}$$

$$= 177.51 \text{ mol}^{-2}\text{L}^2\text{min}^{-1}$$

(iii) Let initial rate of disappearance of Cl_2 in experiment 4 is r_4.

$\therefore$ $r_4 = k[NO]^2[Cl_2] = 177.51 \times (0.25)^2(0.25)$

$= 2.77$ M/min

18. (i) $\underset{\text{Ethyl iodide}}{CH_3CH_2I} \xrightarrow{NaCN} \underset{\substack{\text{Ethyl cyanide} \\ (A)}}{CH_3CH_2CN} \xrightarrow[\text{Partial hydrolysis}]{OH^-}$

$\underset{\substack{\text{Propanamide} \\ (B)}}{CH_3CH_2CONH_2} \xrightarrow[\substack{\text{Hofmann bromamide} \\ \text{degradation}}]{NaOH + Br_2} \underset{\substack{\text{Ethylamine} \\ (C)}}{CH_3CH_2NH_2}$

(ii) $\underset{\text{Acetonitrile}}{CH_3CN} \xrightarrow{H_2O/H^+} \underset{\substack{\text{Acetic acid} \\ (A)}}{CH_3COOH} \xrightarrow[\Delta]{NH_3}$

$\underset{\substack{\text{Acetamide} \\ (B)}}{CH_3CONH_2} \xrightarrow[\substack{\text{Hofmann bromamide} \\ \text{degradation}}]{Br_2 + 4KOH} \underset{\substack{\text{Methylamine} \\ (C)}}{CH_3NH_2}$

19. (i) $2Al(s) + 3Cu^{2+}(0.01\text{ M}) \longrightarrow$

$2Al^{3+}(0.01\text{ M}) + 3Cu(s);\ E_{cell} = 1.98$ V

Applying Nernst equation for the given cell reaction,

$$E_{cell} = E^\circ_{cell} - \frac{0.0591}{n}\log\frac{[Al^{3+}]^2}{[Cu^{2+}]^3}$$

$$E^\circ_{cell} = E_{cell} + \frac{0.0591}{n}\log\frac{[Al^{3+}]^2}{[Cu^{2+}]^3}$$

Here, $n = 6$ (n = number of electrons transferred)

$$= 1.98 + \frac{0.0591}{6}\log\frac{(0.01)^2}{(0.01)^3}$$

$$= 1.98 + \frac{0.0591}{6}\log 100 = 1.98 + \frac{0.0591}{6} \times 2$$

$[\because \log 100 = \log 10^2 = 2\log 10 = 2 \text{ as } \log 10 = 1]$

$= 1.9997 \text{ V} \approx 2.0 \text{ V}$

(ii) For hydrogen electrode, $H^+ + e^- \longrightarrow \frac{1}{2}H_2$

Applying Nernst equation,

$$E_{(H^+/1/2H_2)} = E^\circ_{(H^+/1/2H_2)} - \frac{0.0591}{n}\log\frac{1}{[H^+]}$$

$$= 0 - \frac{0.0591}{1}\log\frac{1}{(10^{-10})}$$

$(\because \text{pH} = 10, [H^+] = 10^{-10}\text{ M})$

$$= 0 - \frac{0.0591}{1} \times (10\log 10) = -0.591 \text{ V}$$

Thus, $E_{(H^+/1/2H_2)} = -0.591$ V

Or

(i) $Fe^{2+} + \underset{2F}{2e^-} \longrightarrow \underset{56g}{Fe}$

$\because$ 56 g of Fe is deposited by 2F or 2×96500 C charge.

$\therefore$ 2.8 g of Fe will be deposited by

$$\frac{96500 \times 2 \times 2.8}{56} \text{ C charge} = 9650 \text{ C}$$

Now, $Q = It$

$\therefore$ Time, $t = \frac{9650}{2} = 4825$ s $[\because I = 2\text{A (given)}]$

$Zn^{2+} + 2e^- \longrightarrow Zn$

$\because 2 \times 96500$ C charge deposits Zn = 65.3 g

$\therefore$ 9650 C charge will deposit

$$Zn = \frac{65.3 \times 9650}{96500 \times 2} = 3.27 \text{ g}$$

(ii) Quantity of electricity passed $= i \times t$

$= 5 \times (20 \times 60) = 6000$ C

The electrode reaction is

$Ni^{2+} + 2e^- \longrightarrow Ni$

i.e. 1 mole of Ni requires electricity = 2F

2×96500 C deposits Ni $= 58.7$ g

$\therefore$ 6000 C will deposits Ni $= \dfrac{58.7}{2 \times 96500} \times 6000$

$= 1.825$ g

20. (i) (a) Mn shows the maximum number of oxidation states. This is because Mn with electronic configuration $[Ar]3d^5 4s^2$ has maximum no. of unpaired electrons in *d*-orbitals and all the electrons in *s*-orbital as well as in *d*-orbital can take part in bond formation.

(b) Chromium has highest melting point among all the given elements.

(c) In the $+3$ oxidation state, Mn is a strong oxidising agent because in Mn^{3+} ion, Mn exists in $3d^4$ configuration which is less stable and it can reduce to Mn^{2+} giving a more stable $3d^5$ configuration. Hence, it acts as a strong oxidising agent.

(ii) **Lanthanoid contraction** The overall decrease in atomic and ionic radii from lanthanum to lutetium, due to the imperfect shielding of one electron by another in the same subshell is known as lanthanoid contraction.

The cumulative effect of the contraction of the lanthanoid series causes the radii of the members of third transition series to be similar to those of corresponding members of second series.

Zr (160 pm) and Hf (159 pm) have identical radii. Due to their similar radii, they have same physical and chemical properties.

21. (i) (a) Electrophilic substitution in benzoic acid takes places at *meta*-position because carboxylic group is a deactivating group.

The presence of electron withdrawing carboxylic group results in a decreased electron density at *o*- and *p*-position.

(b) Due to resonance, electrophilicity of carbonyl carbon is reduced.

Therefore, carboxylic acids do not give characteristic reactions of carbonyl carbon.

(ii) **Acetophenone and benzaldehyde** Add NaOH and I_2 to acetophenone and benzaldehyde and heat them.

Acetophenone forms yellow precipitate of iodoform while benzaldehyde does not.

Benzoic acid and ethyl benzoate Add $NaHCO_3$ solution to both the compounds. Benzoic acid will given effervescence and liberate CO_2, while ethyl benzoate does not.

SPQ Code : **PB-02/15** Series ***i*-Succeed 02-25/15** Roll No.

Sample Question Paper 02

Chemistry 12th (Code 862)

General Instructions

1. This paper is divided into four sections-A, B, C and D. Answer all questions.
2. **Section A** consists of **one** question **having sub-parts** of **one** mark each. **Section B** consists of **ten** questions of **two** marks each. **Section C** consists of **seven** questions of **three** marks each and **Section D** consists of **three** questions of **five** marks each.
3. Internal choices have been provided in one question each in Section B, Section C and Section D.
4. All working, including rough work, should be done on the same sheet as, and adjacent to the rest of the answer.
5. The intended marks for questions or parts of questions are given in brackets [].
6. Balanced questions must be given, wherever possible and diagrams where they are helpful. When solving numerical problems, all essential working must be shown.
7. In working out problems, use the following data:
Gas constant (R) = 1.987 cal deg^{-1} mol^{-1} = 8.314 JK^{-1} mol^{-1} = 0.0821 dm^3 atm K^{-1} mol^{-1}
1L atm = 1 dm^3 atm =101.3 J, 1 Faraday =96500 Coulombs.
Avogadro's number (N_A) = 6.023×10^{23}.

Time : 3 Hrs.

Max. Marks : 70

Section A

[14 Marks]

1. (A) Fill in the blanks by choosing the appropriate word(s) from those given in the brackets. [4×1]

[acetaldehyde cyanohydrin, lactic acid, butyric acid, thymine, chemical, physical, electrical, independent, fast, mechanical, adenine, uracil, guanine]

(i) Acetaldehyde reacts with HCN to give ....which on hydrolysis gives .... • *Understanding*

(ii) The purine bases present in nucleic acid are ...... and .... • *Recall*

(iii) A galvanic cell converts .... energy into .... energy. • *Recall*

(iv) The rate of zero order reaction is .... of the concentration of reactants and the reaction is extremely .... • *Understanding*

(B) Select and write the correct alternative from the choices given below. [7×1]

(i) Which of the following compounds will react with sodium hydroxide in water? • *Analysis*

(a) C_6H_5OH (b) $C_6H_5CH_2OH$
(c) $(CH_3)_3COH$ (d) C_2H_5OH

(ii) Half-life period of a first order reaction is 9 min. What percentage of the reaction will be completed in 90 min? • *Application*

(a) 99.9% (b) 75%
(c) 25% (d) 50%

(iii) Which of the following factors does not affect the electrode potential of an electrode? • *Recall*

(a) Nature of the electrode (metal)
(b) Temperature of the solution
(c) Molarity of the solution
(d) Size of the electrode

(iv) The correct order of the decreasing basic nature of methylamine, ethylamine and aniline is • *Analysis*

(a) methylamine > ethylamine > aniline
(b) ethylamine > methylamine > aniline
(c) aniline > methylamine > ethylamine
(d) aniline > ethylamine > methylamine

(v) Which of the following statements is incorrect regarding nucleophilic substitution reactions? • *Understanding*

I. Nucleophilic substitution reactions in aryl halides occur only under drastic conditions.
II. Primary alkyl halide will prefer S_N1 reaction.
III. S_N2 reaction of optically active alkyl halides are always accompanied by the retention of configuration.

(a) Only I and III (b) Only II and III
(c) Only III and IV (d) Only I and II

(vi) **Assertion** (A) High blood pressure patients are advised to take the minimum quantity of salt.
Reason (R) From salt, Na^+ and Cl^- ion concentration increases in the body fluid which may rupture the blood cells. • *Analysis*

(a) Both Assertion and Reason are true and Reason is the correct explanation of Assertion.
(b) Both Assertion and Reason are true but Reason is not the correct explanation for Assertion.
(c) Assertion is true but Reason is false.
(d) Both Assertion and Reason are false.

(vii) **Assertion** (A) A carboxylate ion ($RCOO^-$) is stabilised by resonance to a greater extent as compared to the acid ($RCOOH$).
Reason (R) The contributing structures of $RCOO^-$ are equivalent, while those of $RCOOH$ are not. • *Analysis*

(a) Both Assertion and Reason are true and Reason is the correct explanation of Assertion.
(b) Both Assertion and Reason are true but Reason is not the correct explanation for Assertion.
(c) Assertion is true but Reason is false.
(d) Both Assertion and Reason are false.

(C) Read the passage given below carefully and answer the questions that follow [3×1]

The *d*-block, which lies between *s* and *p*-blocks contains, elements of groups 3-12, in which *d*-orbitals are progressively filled in each of four long periods of periodic table. These elements are also called **transition elements** or **metals**. In general, the electronic configuration of outer orbitals of these elements is $(n-1)d^{1-10}ns^{1-2}$. The electronic configuration of outer orbitals of Zn, Cd and Hg are represented by the general formula $(n-1)d^{10}ns^2$.

The elements constituting the *f*-block are those in which $4f$ and $5f$-orbitals are progressively filled. The series of $4f$-orbitals is called lanthanoids while series of $5f$-orbitals is called actinoids. They are place in a separate panel at the bottom of the periodic table. The elements of *f*-block are also called **inner-transition elements**.

(i) Transition metals are very good catalyst. Why? • *Understanding*

(ii) Transition metals form a large number of interstitial compounds. Give reason. • *Understanding*

(iii) What are the different oxidation states exhibited by lanthanoids? • *Recall*

SP-02

Section B

[20 Marks]

2. (i) At 298 K, [2]
$Al | Al^{3+} (0.01\ M) || Sn^{2+} (0.015\ M) | Sn$
Given : $E^\circ_{Al^{3+}/Al} = -1.66\ V$ and
$E^\circ_{Sn^{2+}/Sn} = -0.14\ V$
(a) Write the anode reaction. • *Analysis*
(b) Write the cathode reaction.
(ii) Calculate the value of E°_{cell} for the given cell. • *Application*

3. When 9.0 g of non-volatile solute, *B* is dissolved in 100 g of water, a lowering of freezing point by 0.93 K is observed.
Calculate the molar mass of B (K_f of water $= 1.86\ K\ molal^{-1}$). [2]
• *Application*

4. During chemistry class, a teacher wrote $[Fe(CN)_6]^{4-}$ as a coordination complex ion on blackboard. The students were asked to find out the number of unpaired electrons and magnetic behaviour of complex. Anil, a student, wrote the answer 2 and paramagnetic whereas another student Rita, wrote 0 and diamagnetic. Evaluate Anil's and Rita's responses. • *Evaluate* [2]

5. Give reasons for the following. • *Understanding* [2]
   (i) Mn^{3+} is a good oxidising agent.
   (ii) $E^\circ_{M^{2+}/M}$ values are not regular for first row of transition metals (3*d*-series).

6. Give reason for the following. • *Understanding* [2]
   (i) Transition metals show variable oxidation states.
   (ii) The basicity of lanthanoids decreases from $La(OH)_3$ to $Lu(OH)_3$.

7. Write the main product in the following reaction. • *Understanding* [2]
   (i) $2CH_3COCl + (CH_3)_2Cd \longrightarrow$
   (ii) $CH_3CH_2CHO \xrightarrow{Zn(Hg)/Conc.HCl}$

8. Give one chemical test for each to distinguish between the following pair of compounds. • *Understanding* [2]
   (i) Acetone and diethyl ketone.
   (ii) Formic acid and acetic acid.

9. (i) What is the relationship between osmotic pressure at 273 K, when 10 g of glucose (p_1), 10 g of urea (p_2) and 10 g of sucrose (p_3) are dissolved in 250 mL of water? • *Application* [2]
   (ii) A solution containing 4 g of polyvinyl chloride in 1L of dioxane was found to have an osmotic pressure of 6×10^{-4} atm at 300 K.
   Then, what will be the molar mass of polymer polyvinyl chloride? • *Understanding/Application*

10. Write the product(s) formed when • *Understanding* [2]
   (i) 2-bromopropane undergoes dehydrohalogenation reaction.
   (ii) chlorobenzene undergoes nitration reaction.

   Or

   An alkyl halide (*A*) of molecular formula $C_6H_{13}Cl$ on treatment with alcoholic KOH gives two isomeric alkenes (*B*) and (*C*) of molecular formula C_6H_{12}. Both alkenes on hydrogenation give 2, 3-dimethylbutane. Write the structures of (*A*), (*B*) and (*C*). • *Understanding*

11. (i) Which one of the following would feel attraction when placed in magnetic field Co^{2+}, Ag^{+}, Ti^{4+} and Zn^{2+}? [2] • *Understanding*
   (ii) It has been observed that first ionisation energy of 5*d*-series of transition elements are higher than that of 3*d* and 4*d* series, explain why? • *Understanding*

SP-02

Section C **[21 Marks]**

12. In the Arrhenius equation for a certain reaction, the value of *A* (frequency factor) and E_a (activation energy) are $4\times10^{13}\ s^{-1}$ and 98.6 kJ mol^{-1}, respectively. If the reaction is of first order, then find that at what temperature will its half-life period be 10 min? • *Application* [3]

13. How are the following conversions carried out? [3]
   (i) Ethyl cyanide to ethanoic acid
   (ii) Butan-1-ol to butanoic acid
   (iii) Benzoic acid to *m*-bromobenzoic acid • *Understanding*

   Or

   An organic compound *A* (molecular formula $C_8H_{16}O_2$) was hydrolysed with dilute sulphuric acid to give a carboxylic acid *B* and an alcohol *C*.
   Oxidation of *C* with chromic acid also produced *B*. On dehydration *C* gives but-1-ene. Write the equations for the reactions involved. • *Understanding*

14. (i) Suresh visits a doctor as he was suffering from night blindness. What can be the possible deficiency of vitamin doctor told him? Name some sources of this vitamin. • *Recall* [3]

(ii) What is the structural difference between a nucleoside and a nucleotide? • *Recall*

(iii) The two strands of DNA are not identical but are complementary. Explain. • *Understanding*

15. The following data were obtained during the first order thermal decomposition of SO_2Cl_2 at a constant volume,

$$SO_2Cl_2(g) \longrightarrow SO_2(g) + Cl_2(g) \quad [3]$$

Exp. No.	Time/s^{-1}	Pressure/atm
1.	0	0.5
2.	100	0.6

Show how this data can be used to deduce the rate constant for the given reaction and find the rate of reaction when total pressure is 0.65 atm. • *Evaluate and Application*

16. Arrange the following compounds in the increasing order of their acidic strength. • *Analysis* [3]

(i) *p*- cresol, *p*-nitrophenol, phenol

(ii) catechol, resorcinol, quinol, phenol

17. Identify the compounds *A*, *B* and *C* in the following reactions. • *Understanding* [3]

(i) $C_6H_5\overset{+}{N}_2Cl^- \xrightarrow{CuCN} [A] \xrightarrow{H_2O/\ H^+} [B] \xrightarrow[\Delta]{NH_3} [C]$

(ii) $C_6H_5NO_2 \xrightarrow{Sn + HCl} [A] \xrightarrow[273\ K]{NaNO_2\ + HCl} [B] \xrightarrow[\Delta]{H_2O/H^+} [C]$

18. A solution containing 0.011 kg of barium nitrate in 0.1 kg of water boils at 100.46°C. For water, K_b is 0.52 K kg mol^{-1} and the molar mass of barium nitrate is 0.2613 kg mol^{-1}. [3]

(i) Find ΔT_b. • *Application*

(ii) Calculate degree of ionisation of the salt. • *Application*

Section D **[15 Marks]**

19. (i) Identify the product formed when propan-1-ol is treated with conc. H_2SO_4 at 413 K. Write the mechanism involved for the above reaction. [5] • *Understanding*

(ii) Given the structures and IUPAC name of the products expected from the following reactions. • *Understanding*

(a) Reaction of methanal with

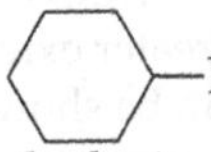

—MgBr following by hydrolysis.

(b) Reaction of phenol with $Br_2(aq)$.

20. (i) (a) What type of isomerism is shown by the complex $[Co(NH_3)_5(SCN)]^{2+}$? • *Recall* [5]

(b) Why $[NiCl_4]^{2-}$ is paramagnetic, while $[Ni(CN)_4]^{2-}$ is diamagnetic? (Atomic number of Ni = 28) • *Understanding*

(c) Why are low spin tetrahedral complexes rarely observed? • *Understanding*

(ii) When a coordination compound $CrCl_3 \cdot 6H_2O$ is mixed with $AgNO_3$, 2 moles of AgCl are precipitated per mole of the compound. Write • *Understanding*

(a) structural formula of the complex.

(b) IUPAC name of the complex.

SP-02

21. Galvanic cells are electrochemical cells in which the electrical energy is produced from suitable redox reactions. In a galvanic cell, the two electrodes must be joined externally to complete the electrical circuit with an external load to avoid short circuit.

Consider the galvanic cell, [5]

$Pt|VO^{2+}(0.35M), V^{2+}(0.15\ M), V^{3+}(0.15\ M), H^+(0.70M)||Tl^{3+}(0.50\ M), Tl^+(0.10\ M)|Pt$ and the following data:

$$Tl^{3+} + 2e^- \rightleftharpoons Tl^+;\ E^- = +1.25\ V\ vs\ SHE$$

$$VO^{2+} + 2H^+ + e^- \rightleftharpoons V^{3+} + H_2O;$$

$$E^\circ = +0.36\ V\ vs\ SHE$$

Answer the following questions.

(i) Write the two half-reactions and the overall (conventional) cell reaction that occurs spontaneously, when the cell is short-circuited. • *Understanding*

(ii) Calculate the actual voltage (E_{cell}) of the cell and the equilibrium constant (K_{eq}) for the overall (conventional) cell reaction. • *Application*

Or (i) The specific conductivity of a solution containing 5g of anhydrous $BaCl_2$ (molecular weight = 208 g mol^{-1}) in 1000 cm^3 of a solution is found to be 0.0058 ohm^{-1} cm^{-1}. Calculate the molar and equivalent conductivity of the solution. • *Application*

(ii) What is an electrochemical series? How is it useful in predicting whether a metal can liberate hydrogen from an acid or not? • *Recall*

Solutions *in Topper's Style*

My Commitment *I affirm that I am reviewing these solutions only after I have solved the Sample Question Paper on my own. My purpose of looking the solutions is solely to verify whether my answers/solutions were correct or not and to identify my mistakes in case my solutions were wrong or I could not solve that.*

1. (A) (i) acetaldehyde cyanohydrin, lactic acid
(ii) adenine, guanine
(iii) chemical, electrical
(iv) independent, fast

(B) (i) (a) Phenol, (C_6H_5OH) reacts with sodium hydroxide in water to give sodium phenoxide and water.

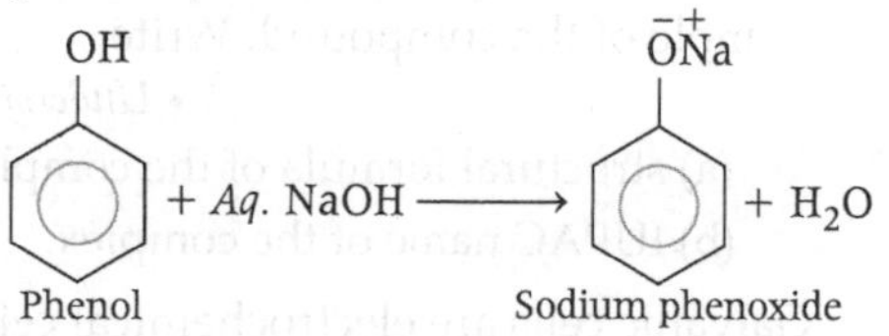

Phenol Sodium phenoxide

(ii) (a) Given, $t_{1/2} = 9$ mins, $t = 90$ mins

As we know that, $t_{1/2} = \frac{0.693}{k}$

$$k = \frac{2.303}{t}\log\frac{a}{a-x}$$

$$\Rightarrow \frac{0.693}{9} = \frac{2.303}{90}\log\frac{100}{100-x}$$

$$\Rightarrow 3.00912 = \log\frac{100}{100-x}$$

$$x = 99.9\%$$

(iii) (d) Electrode potential depends on the nature of the electrode, temperature of the solution and the concentration of metal ions in the solution.

(iv) (b) $C_2H_5NH_2 > CH_3NH_2 > C_6H_5NH_2$

(v) (b) Statements I and IV are correct whereas statements II and III are incorrect. Their correct form are as follows

- Primary alkyl halide will prefer S_N2 reaction.
- S_N2 reaction of optically active alkyl halides are always accompanied by the inversion of configuration.

(vi) (a) High blood pressure patients are advised not to take salt because Na^+ ion enter into body fluid by raising the concentration of solute which may rupture the blood cells.

Thus, both (A) and (R) are true and (R) is the correct explanation of (A).

(vii) (a) Both (A) and (R) are true and (R) is the correct explanation of (A).

A carboxylate ion ($RCOO^-$) is stabilised by resonance to a greater extent as compared to *R*COOH. This can be shown by the following resonating structures.

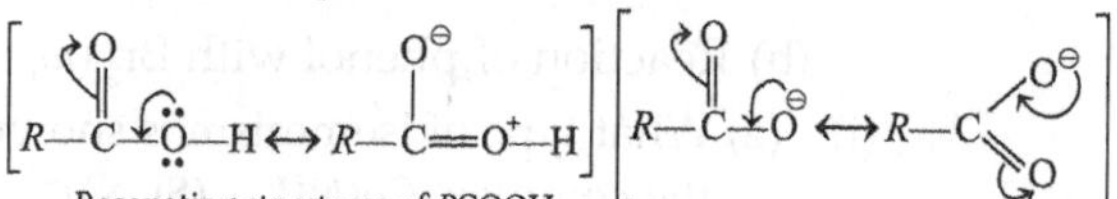

Resonating structures of *R*COOH (non-equivalent)

Resonating structures of $RCOO^-$ (equivalent)

(C) (i) Transition metals are very good catalyst due to their ability to adopt multiple oxidation state and form complexes.

(ii) Transition metals form a large number of interstitial compounds because there are vacant spaces in the lattice of transition metals which can be filled by small atoms like H, C, N etc.

(iii) Different oxidation state exhibited by lanthanoids are +2, + 3 and + 4.

2. (i) (a) At anode, $Al(s) \longrightarrow Al^{3+}(aq) + 3e^-$

(b) At cathode, $Sn^{2+}(aq) + 2e^- \longrightarrow Sn(s)$

(ii) Given, $E^\circ_{Al^{3+}/Al} = -1.66\ V$

and $E^\circ_{Sn^{2+}/Sn} = -0.14\ V$

$$E^\circ_{cell} = E^\circ_{cathode} - E^\circ_{anode}$$
$$= -0.14\,V - (-1.66\,V)$$
$$= -0.14\,V + 1.66\,V = 1.52\ V$$

3. Depression in freezing point is given by the formulae;

$$\Delta T_f = K_f \times m$$

or, $$M_B = \frac{K_f}{\Delta T_f} \times \frac{w_B}{W_A}$$

w_B = mass of solute = 9.0 g

W_A = mass of solvent = 100 g

$K_f = 1.86\ K\ molal^{-1}$

∴ $$M_B = \frac{1.86\ K\ kg\ mol^{-1}}{0.93\,K} \times \frac{9.0\,g}{100\,g}$$
$$= 0.180\ kg\ mol^{-1}$$
$$= 180\ g\ mol^{-1}$$

4. Electronic configuration of

$Fe_{26} = [Ar]3d^6 4s^2$

$Fe^{2+} = [Ar]3d^6 4s^0$

$[Fe(CN)_6]^{4-}$ = [Ar] 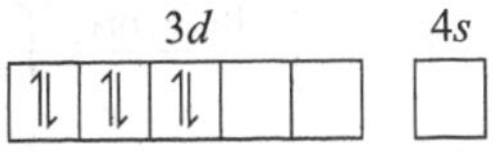

No unpaired electron

$[Fe(CN)_6]^{4-}$ is diamagnetic in nature as it has no unpaired electron. Therefore, Rita's response was correct.

5. (i) Mn^{3+}/Mn^{2+} has large positive E° value. Hence, Mn^{3+} can be easily reduced to Mn^{2+}. It is because Mn^{2+} has half-filled electronic configuration, so it is stable and Mn^{3+} is least stable. Therefore, Mn^{3+} is a good oxidising agent.

(ii) There is decrease in negative electrode potentials of M^{2+}/M in the first transition series due to increase in the sum of IE_1 and IE_2. It shows that in general, the stability of +2 oxidation state decreases from left to right.

Exceptions are Mn and Zn in which the greater stability of +2 state for Mn is due to half-filled *d*-subshell (d^5) in Mn^{2+} and that of Zn is due to completely filled *d*-subshell (d^{10}) in Zn^{2+}.

6. (i) Transition metals show variable oxidation states in its compounds (except the first and last element) because of the fact that difference in the energy of $(n-1)d$ electrons and ns- electrons is very less and hence both the energy levels can take part in bonding.

(ii) Due to lanthanoid contraction, the basic character of hydroxides decreases from $La(OH)_3$ to $Lu(OH)_3$ as the covalent nature of Ln—OH bond increases.

7. (i) $$\underset{\text{Acetyl chloride}}{2CH_3COCl} + (CH_3)_2Cd \xrightarrow{\text{Dry ether}} \underset{\text{Propanone}}{2CH_3COCH_3} + CdCl_2$$

(ii) $$\underset{\text{Propanal}}{CH_3CH_2CHO} \xrightarrow{Zn(Hg)/\text{conc. }HCl} \underset{\text{Propane}}{CH_3CH_2CH_3}$$

8. (i) **Test to distinguish between acetone and diethyl ketone**

Acetone gives yellow precipitate of iodoform when treated with NaOI (I_2/ NaOH) but diethyl ketone does not give this test.

$$\underset{\text{Acetone}}{CH_3COCH_3} + 3NaOI \longrightarrow \underset{\text{Sodium acetate}}{CH_3CO\overset{-}{O}\overset{+}{Na}} + 2NaOH + \underset{\text{(Yellow ppt.)}}{\underset{\text{Iodoform}}{CHI_3\downarrow}}$$

$$\underset{\text{Diethyl ketone}}{(CH_3CH_2)_2C{=}O} \xrightarrow{NaOI} \text{No yellow ppt. of } CHI_3$$

(ii) **Test to distinguish between formic acid and acetic acid** Formic acid gives silver mirror test with Tollen's reagent while acetic acid does not give this test.

$$\underset{\text{Formic acid}}{HCOOH} + \underset{\text{Tollen's reagent}}{2\,[Ag(NH_3)_2]^+} + 2OH^- \longrightarrow CO_2 + 2H_2O + 4NH_3 + \underset{\text{Silver mirror}}{2Ag\downarrow}$$

$$\underset{\text{Acetic acid}}{CH_3COOH} + \underset{\text{Tollen's reagent}}{2\,[Ag(NH_3)_2]^+} + 2OH^- \longrightarrow \text{No reaction}$$

9. (i) Greater is the molar concentration of solution, more is the osmotic pressure. Also, lesser the molecular weight, more is the osmotic pressure.

$$\pi \propto C;\ \pi \propto \frac{n}{V};\ \pi \propto \frac{1}{M}$$

∴ p_2 (urea) > p_1 (glucose) > p_3 (sucrose)

(ii) Given, $w_B = 4\,g$ and $\pi = 6 \times 10^{-4}$ atm

We know, $$\pi V = \frac{w_B}{M_B} RT$$

$$6 \times 10^{-4}\ atm \times 1\,L = \frac{4g}{M_B} \times 0.082\ L\,atm\,K^{-1}mol^{-1} \times 300\,K$$

∴ $$M_B = 1.64 \times 10^5\ g/mol$$

10. (i) $$\underset{\text{2-bromopropane}}{CH_3{-}\overset{\overset{\displaystyle Br}{|}}{CH}{-}CH_3} \xrightarrow{\text{Alc. KOH}} \underset{\text{Prop-1-ene}}{CH_3{-}CH{=}CH_2}$$

(ii) 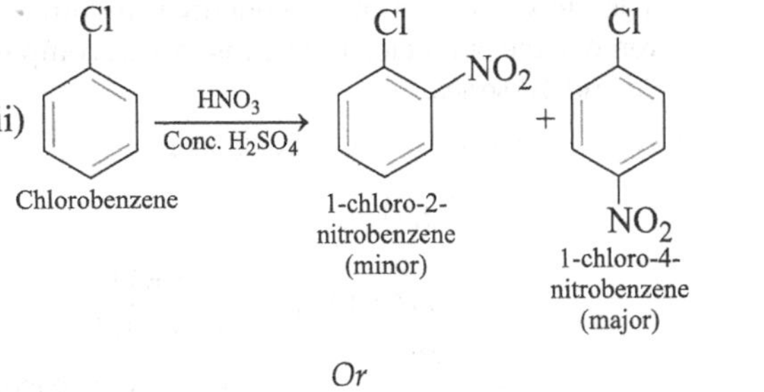

Or

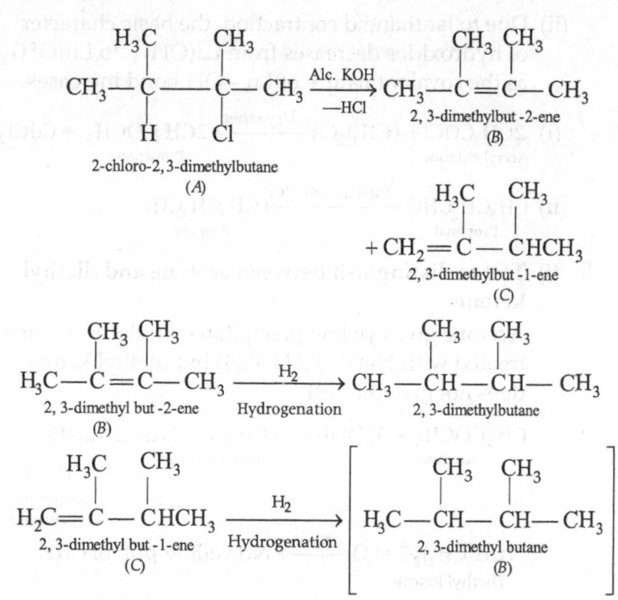

11. (i) Electronic configuration of Co^{2+} : $[Ar]3d^7$

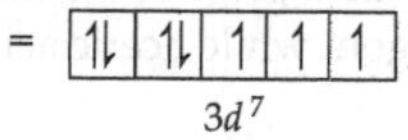

It has **three unpaired electrons.**

Electronic configuration of Ag^+ : $[Kr]4d^{10}5s^0$

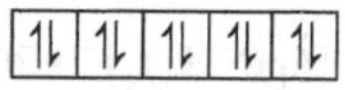

It does **not have any unpaired electron.**

Electronic configuration of Ti^{4+} : [Ar]

No unpaired electron.

Electronic configuration of Zn^{2+} : $[Ar]3d^{10}$

No unpaired electron.

Since, unpaired electrons is present only in Co^{2+}. Thus, it is paramagnetic in nature and hence, Co^{2+} ion would be attracted to magnetic field.

(ii) First ionisation energy of $5d$-series of transition elements are higher than that of $3d$ and $4d$-series because $5d$-series have intervening $4f$-orbitals.

There is greater effective nuclear charge acting on outer valence electrons due to the weak shielding by $4f$-electrons.

Therefore, large amount of energy is required to remove the outer electron in this case as compared to $3d$ and $4d$-series.

12. Given, $A = 4 \times 10^{13}\,s^{-1}$, $E_a = 98.6\,kJ\,mol^{-1}$

$$\because \quad \log k = \log A - \frac{E_a}{2.303RT}$$

$$\therefore \quad \log k = \log(4 \times 10^{13}) - \frac{98600}{2.303 \times 8.314 \times T} \quad \ldots(i)$$

Now, $\quad t_{1/2} = \frac{0.693}{k} \quad$ [For first order reaction]

$$k = \frac{0.693}{600s} = 1.155 \times 10^{-3}\,s^{-1} \quad \ldots(ii)$$

On putting value of k in Eq. (i), we get,

$$\therefore \log(1.155 \times 10^{-3}) = \log(4 \times 10^{13}) - \frac{98600}{2.303 \times 8.314 \times T}$$

$$\log(1.155 \times 10^{-3}) - \log(4 \times 10^{13}) = \frac{-98600}{2.303 \times 8.314 \times T}$$

$$-16.539 = \frac{-98600}{2.303 \times 8.314 \times T}$$

$$\Rightarrow \quad T = 311.36\,K$$

13. (i) **Ethyl cyanide to ethanoic acid**

$$\underset{\text{Ethyl cyanide}}{C_2H_5CN} \xrightarrow{H_2O/H^+} \underset{\text{Propanoic acid}}{C_2H_5COOH} \xrightarrow{NH_3/\Delta}$$

$$\xrightarrow{HNO_2} \underset{\text{Ethylamine}}{C_2H_5NH_2} \xleftarrow{Br_2/KOH} \underset{\text{Propionamide}}{C_2H_5CONH_2}$$

$$\underset{\text{Ethanol}}{C_2H_5OH} \xrightarrow{\text{Alkaline } KMnO_4} \underset{\text{Ethanoic acid}}{CH_3COOH}$$

(ii) **Butan-1-ol to butanoic acid**

$$\underset{\text{Butanol}}{CH_3CH_2CH_2CH_2OH} \xrightarrow[\text{(b) Dil. } H_2SO_4]{\text{(a) } K_2Cr_2O_7} \underset{\text{Butanoic acid}}{CH_3CH_2CH_2COOH}$$

(iii) **Benzoic acid to *m*-bromobenzoic acid**

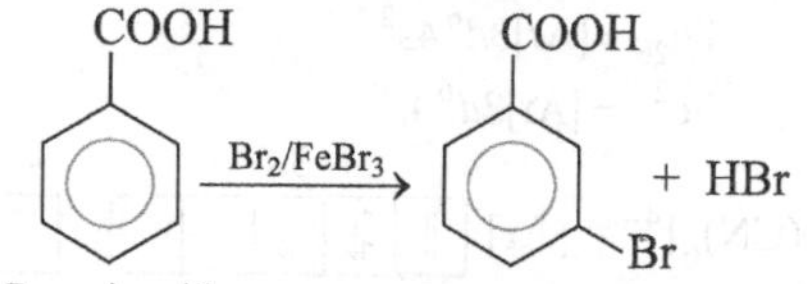

Benzoic acid *m*-bromobenzoic acid

Or

Compound *C* on dehydration gives but-1-ene ($CH_3CH_2CH{=}CH_2$), so it must be butan-1-ol. When subjected to oxidation *C* gives butanoic acid *B*.

Thus, compound *A* is

$CH_3CH_2CH_2COOCH_2CH_2CH_2CH_3$.

The reactions involved are as follows

$$\underset{(A)}{CH_3CH_2CH_2COOCH_2CH_2CH_2CH_3} \xrightarrow{H_2O/H^+}$$

$$\underset{(B)}{CH_3CH_2CH_2COOH} + \underset{(C)}{CH_3CH_2CH_2CH_2OH}$$

$$\underset{(C)}{CH_3CH_2CH_2CH_2OH} \xrightarrow[\text{(Oxidation)}]{CrO_3} \underset{(B)}{CH_3CH_2CH_2COOH}$$

$$\underset{(C)}{CH_3CH_2CH_2CH_2OH} \xrightarrow[\substack{H_2SO_4 \\ \text{(Dehydration)}}]{\text{Conc.}} \underset{\text{But-1-ene}}{CH_3CH_2CH = CH_2}$$

14. (i) Deficiency of vitamin A causes night blindness. Sources of vitamin A are fish liver oil, carrots, butter and milk.

(ii) **Structural difference between a nucleoside and nucleotide**

Nucleoside A unit formed by the attachment of a base to 1' position of sugar is known as nucleoside.

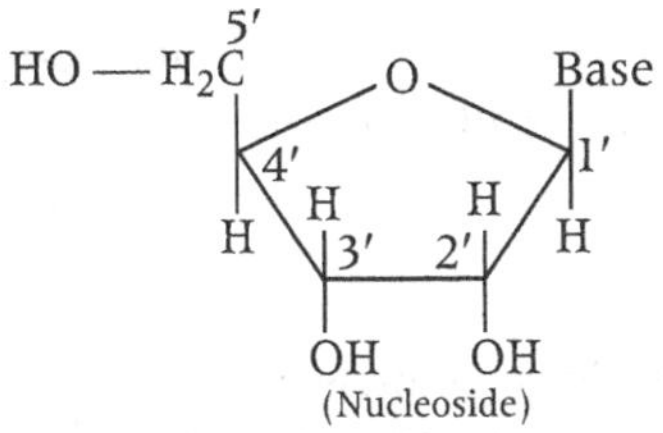

(Nucleoside)

Nucleotide When nucleoside is linked to phosphoric acid at 5′ position of sugar moeity, a nucleotide is obtained.

Thus, a nucleotide contains three basic components of nuclei acids, i.e. a phosphoric acid, a nitrogenous base and a pentose sugar.

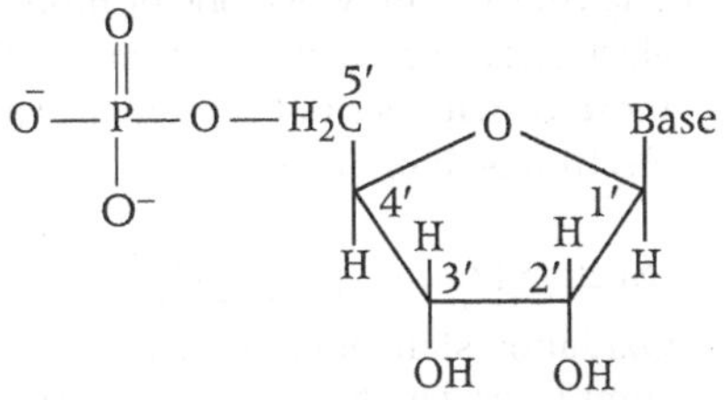

(Nucleotide)

(iii) The two strands of DNA are not identical because their sequence of bases has to be complementary to each other. e.g. If one sequence is ATCG, then the other has to be TAGC.

15. $SO_2Cl_2(g) \longrightarrow SO_2(g) + Cl_2(g)$

	$SO_2Cl_2(g)$	$SO_2(g)$	$Cl_2(g)$
Initially at $t=0$	p_i	0	0
After time t	$p_i - p$	p	p

Total pressure after time t, i.e.

$$p_t = p_i - p + p + p = p_i + p$$

$\therefore$ $p = p_t - p_i$

So, $p_{SO_2Cl_2} = p_i - p = p_i - (p_t - p_i)$

$$= p_i - p_t + p_i = 2p_i - p_t$$

$\because$ $k = \frac{2.303}{t}\log\left(\frac{p_i}{p_i - p}\right)$

$\therefore$ $k = \frac{2.303}{t}\log\frac{p_i}{(2p_i - p_t)}$

Calculation of rate constant, k

Given, $p_i = 0.5$ atm; $p_t = 0.6$ atm

$$k = \frac{2.303}{t}\log\frac{p_i}{(2p_i - p_t)}$$

$$= \frac{2.303}{(100\,s)}\log\frac{0.5\text{ atm}}{0.4\text{ atm}}$$

$$= \frac{2.303}{(100\,s)}\log 1.25$$

$$= \frac{2.303}{(100\,s)} \times 0.0969$$

$$= 2.23 \times 10^{-3}\,s^{-1}$$

Calculation of reaction rate when total pressure is 0.65 atm

$$p_{SO_2Cl_2} = 0.5 - (0.65 - 0.50)$$

$$= (0.5 - 0.15)$$

$$= 0.35\text{ atm}$$

and $k = 2.23 \times 10^{-3}\,s^{-1}$

$$\text{Rate} = k \times p_{SO_2Cl_2}$$

$$= (2.23 \times 10^{-3}\,s^{-1}) \times (0.35\text{ atm})$$

$$\text{Rate} = 7.8 \times 10^{-4}\text{ atm s}^{-1}$$

16. (i) Electron withdrawing group such as $-NO_2$, increases the acidic character of phenols while electron donating group such as $-CH_3$, decreases the acidic character of phenols.

Thus, increasing order of acidic strength is

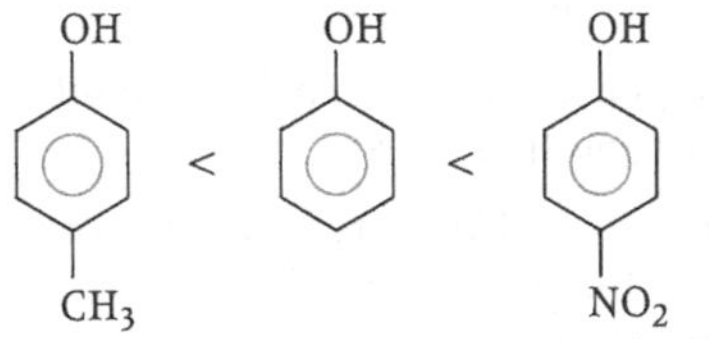

(p-cresol) (Phenol) (p-nitrophenol)

(ii) $+I$ and $+R$ effect decreases the acidity while $-I$ and $-R$ effect increases the acidity of phenols.

Thus, increasing order of acidic strength is

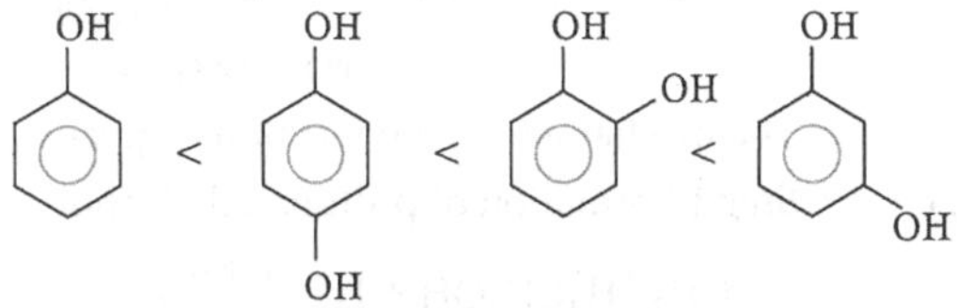

(Phenol) (Quinol) $+R, -I$ (Catechol) $+R, -I$ (more) (Resorcinol) $-I$

17. (i) $C_6H_5N_2^+Cl^- \xrightarrow{CuCN} C_6H_5CN \xrightarrow{H_2O/H^+}$

Benzene diazonium chloride; Benzonitrile (A)

$C_6H_5COOH \xrightarrow[\Delta]{NH_3} C_6H_5CONH_2$

Benzoic acid (B); Benzamide (C)

(ii) $C_6H_5NO_2 \xrightarrow{Sn+HCl} C_6H_5NH_2 \xrightarrow[273\,K]{NaNO_2 + HCl}$

Nitrobenzene; Aniline (A)

$C_6H_5N_2^+Cl^- \xrightarrow[\Delta]{H_2O/H^+}$ 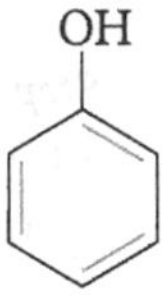

Benzene diazonium chloride (B); Phenol (C)

18. (i) Given, w_B = mass of solute = 0.011 kg

W_A = mass of solvent = 0.1 kg

Molar mass of solute, $M_B = 0.2613\text{ kg mol}^{-1}$,

$K_b = 0.52\text{ K kg mol}^{-1}$

$\because$ $\Delta T_b = T_b - T_b^\circ$

$\therefore$ $\Delta T_b = 100.46°C - 100°C$

$= 0.46°C = 0.46\text{ K}$

(ii) Now, $\Delta T_b = i\,K_b \times m$

$$= i\,K_b \times \frac{w_B}{M_B \times W_A}$$

$$i = \frac{\Delta T_b}{K_b \times m}$$

$$= \frac{\Delta T_b \times M_B \times W_A}{K_b \times w_B}$$

$$= \frac{0.46\,\text{K} \times 0.2613\,\text{kg mol}^{-1} \times 0.1\,\text{kg}}{0.52\,\text{K kg mol}^{-1} \times 0.011\,\text{kg}}$$

$i = 2.10$

For $Ba(NO_3)_2 \rightleftharpoons Ba^{2+} + 2NO_3^-$

Total number of particles $(n) = 1 + 2 = 3$

As we know that,

$$\alpha = \frac{i-1}{n-1} = \frac{2.10-1}{3-1} = \frac{1.10}{2} = 0.55$$

The degree of ionisation of barium nitrate in aqueous solution = 0.55.

19. (i) When propan -1-ol is treated with conc. H_2SO_4 at 413 K, the product obtained is 1-propoxypropane.

The reaction is given as,

$$\underset{\text{propan-1-ol}}{2CH_3CH_2CH_2OH} + \text{Conc.} H_2SO_4 \xrightarrow{413\,K} \underset{\text{1-propoxypropane}}{CH_3CH_2CH_2-O-CH_2CH_2CH_3} + H^+$$

The mechanism of the reaction is given as

***Step* I** Formation of protonated alcohol.

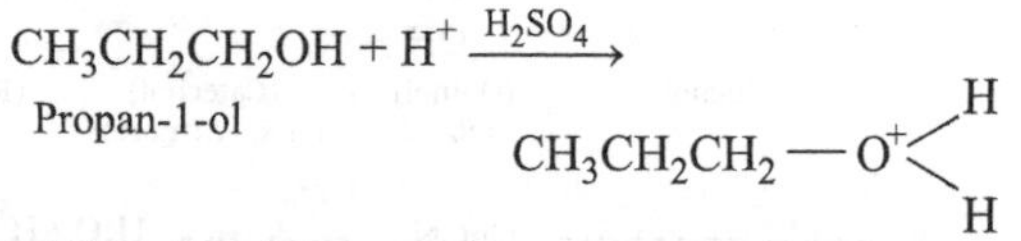

***Step* II** Nucleophilic attack by non-protonated alcohol molecule on protonated alcohol molecule.

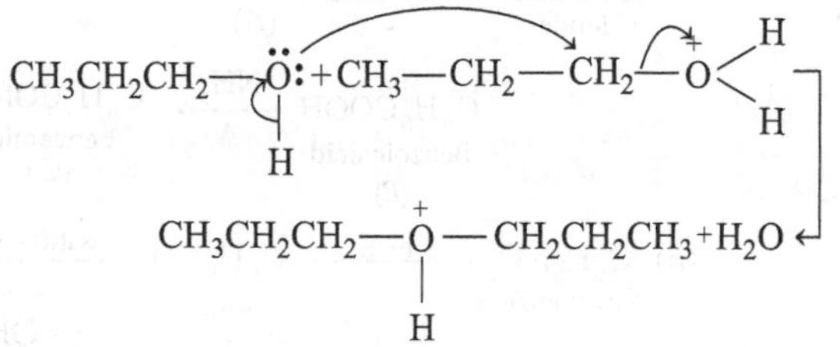

***Step* III** Loss of proton to form 1-propoxypropane.

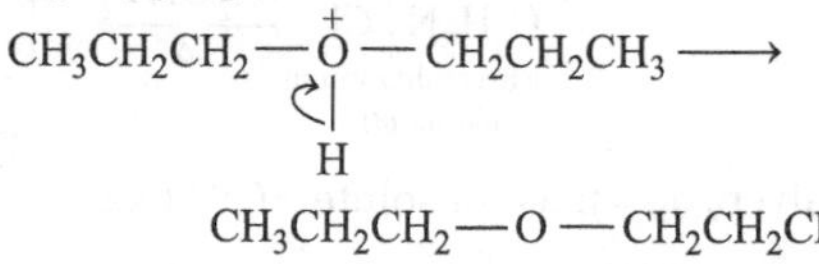

(ii) (a)

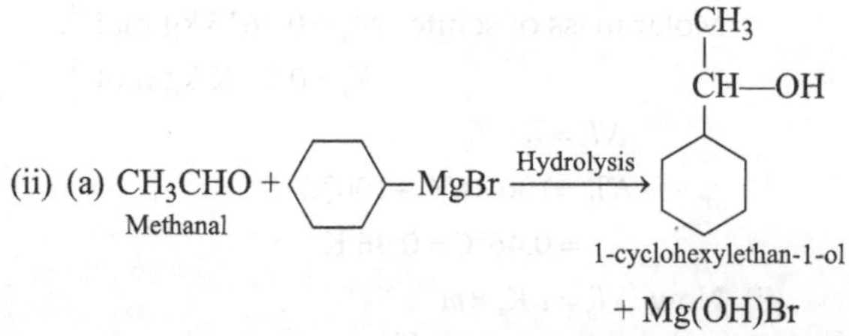

(b)

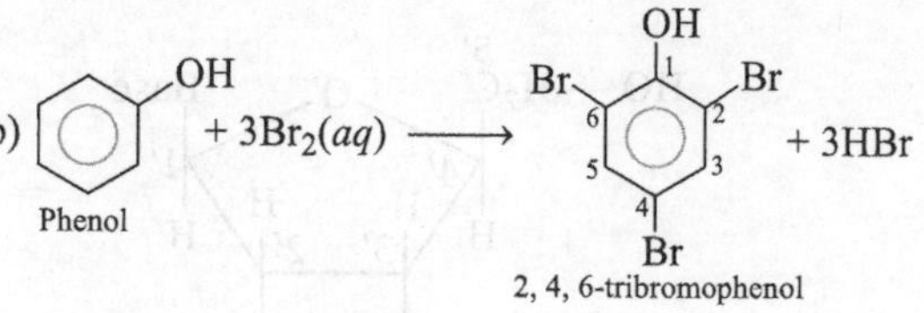

20. (i) (a) Linkage isomerism arises in a coordination compound containing ambidentate ligand. Hence, $[Co(NH_3)_5(SCN)]^{2+}$ exhibit linkage isomerism due to presence of SCN, which is an ambidentate ligand and can linked with metal either through N or S.

$[Co(NH_3)_5SCN]^{2+}$ and $[Co(NH_3)_5NCS]^{2+}$

(b) The complex in which one or more unpaired electrons are present is paramagnetic while, those which does not contain any unpaired electron is diamagnetic.

Ni atom $(Z = 28)$

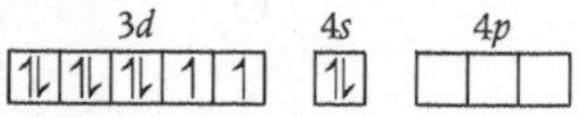

Oxidation state of Ni is + 2 in both the complexes, i.e. $[NiCl_4]^{2-}$ and $[Ni(CN)_4]^{2-}$.

$Ni^{2+} =$

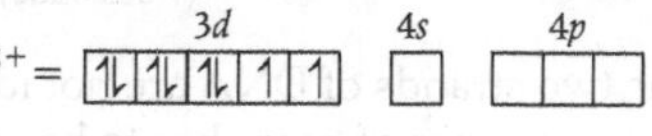

In case of $[NiCl_4]^{2-}$, Cl^- is a weak field ligand so pairing of electrons in 3*d*-orbital does not occur, hence compound is paramagnetic with two unpaired electrons. In $[Ni(CN)_4]^{2-}$, CN^- is a strong field ligand, hence pairing occurs and $[Ni(CN)_4]^{2-}$ is diamagnetic.

(c) For tetrahedral complexes, the crystal field stabilisation energy is lower than pairing energy, so they are rarely formed in low spin state.

(ii) (a) When one mole of $CrCl_3 \cdot 6H_2O$ is mixed with $AgNO_3$, two moles of AgCl are precipitated which indicates that two ionisable chloride ions in the complex are present.

Hence, its structural formula is $[Cr(H_2O)_5Cl]Cl_2 \cdot H_2O$.

(b) IUPAC name of the complex $[Cr(H_2O)_5Cl]Cl_2 \cdot H_2O$ is pentaaquachloridochromium (III) chloride.

21. (i) At anode, $[V^{3+} + H_2O \rightleftharpoons VO^{2+} + 2H^+ + e^-] \times 2$

At cathode, $Tl^{3+} + 2e^- \rightleftharpoons Tl^+$

Overall cell reaction $2V^{3+} + Tl^{3+} + 2H_2O \rightleftharpoons 2VO^{2+} + 4H^+ + Tl^+$

(ii) Nernst equation is given by,

$$E_{cell} = E^\circ_{cell} - \frac{0.0592}{n} \log\left[\frac{\text{Products}}{\text{Reactants}}\right]$$

$$E^\circ_{cell} = E^\circ_{cathode} - E^\circ_{anode}$$

$$= 1.25 - 0.36 = 0.89\,\text{V}$$

$$\therefore \ E_{cell} = E^\circ_{cell} - \frac{0.0592}{2}\log\frac{[VO^{2+}]^2\,[H^+]^4\,[Tl^+]}{[V^{3+}]^2[Tl^{3+}]}$$

$$= +0.89 - \frac{0.0592}{2}\log\frac{(0.35)^2(0.70)^4(0.1)}{(0.15)^2\,(0.50)}$$

$$= +0.89 + 0.017$$

$\therefore$ Actual voltage,

$$E_{cell} = +0.91\,V$$

$$\because \quad E^\circ_{cell} = \frac{0.0592}{n}\log K_{eq}$$

$$\therefore \quad \log K_{eq} = \frac{nE^\circ_{cell}}{0.0592} = \frac{(2)(+0.89)}{(0.0592)} = 30.07$$

$$\Rightarrow \quad K_{eq} = 1.17\times10^{30}$$

Or

(i) Conductivity $(\kappa) = 0.0058\ \text{ohm}^{-1}\ \text{cm}^{-1}$
Molar mass of $BaCl_2 = 208\ \text{g mol}^{-1}$
As 5 g of $BaCl_2$ is present in 1000 cm^3 of the solution.

$\therefore$ Molar concentration (C)

$$= \frac{1}{208}\times\frac{5}{1000}\times1000 = 0.0240\ \text{mol L}^{-1}$$

$\because$ Molar conductivity, $\Lambda_m = \dfrac{\kappa\times1000}{M}$

$$\therefore \quad \Lambda_m = \frac{0.0058\,\text{ohm}^{-1}\text{cm}^{-1}\times1000\,\text{cm}^3\text{L}^{-1}}{0.0240\ \text{mol L}^{-1}}$$

$$= 241.67\ \text{ohm}^{-1}\ \text{cm}^2\text{mol}^{-1}$$

In $BaCl_2$, equivalent weight

$$= \frac{\text{molecular weight}}{2} = \frac{208}{2} = 104$$

$$\lambda_{eq} = \Lambda_m \times \frac{\text{Eq. wt. of } BaCl_2}{\text{Mol. wt. of } BaCl_2}$$

$$= \Lambda_m \times \frac{\frac{208}{2}}{208} = \frac{241.67}{2}$$

$$= 120.835\ \Omega^{-1}\ \text{cm}^2\ \text{eq.}^{-1}.$$

(ii) The arrangement of various standard half-cells in the order of their decreasing values of standard reduction potentials is called **electrochemical series.**

In the electrochemical series, metals that are placed above hydrogen are reactive metals and reacts with acids like HCl (dil.), H_2SO_4 (dil.) to produce salt and hydrogen gas and metals that have placed below hydrogen are unreactive with acids.

$$\text{Metal} + \text{Dil. acid} \longrightarrow \text{Salt} + \text{Hydrogen}$$

e.g. $\underset{\text{Zinc}}{Zn(s)} + \underset{\text{(Dil.)}}{2HCl(aq)} \longrightarrow \underset{\text{Zinc chloride}}{ZnCl_2(aq)} + \underset{\text{Hydrogen gas}}{H_2(g)\uparrow}$

Value Points To get maximum marks one must write one example along with the explanation of question.

SPQ Code : **PB-03/15** Series ***i*-Succeed 03-25/15** Roll No. | | | | | | | | |

Sample Question Paper 03

Chemistry 12th (Code 862)

General Instructions

1. This paper is divided into four sections-A, B, C and D. Answer all questions.
2. **Section A** consists of **one** question **having sub-parts** of **one** mark each. **Section B** consists of **ten** questions of **two** marks each. **Section C** consists of **seven** questions of **three** marks each and **Section D** consists of **three** questions of **five** marks each.
3. Internal choices have been provided in one question each in Section B, Section C and Section D.
4. All working, including rough work, should be done on the same sheet as, and adjacent to the rest of the answer.
5. The intended marks for questions or parts of questions are given in brackets [].
6. Balanced questions must be given, wherever possible and diagrams where they are helpful. When solving numerical problems, all essential working must be shown.
7. In working out problems, use the following data:
Gas constant (R) = 1.987 cal deg^{-1} mol^{-1} = 8.314 JK^{-1} mol^{-1} = 0.0821 dm^3 atm K^{-1} mol^{-1}
1L atm = 1 dm^3 atm =101.3 J, 1 Faraday =96500 Coulombs.
Avogadro's number (N_A) = 6.023×10^{23}.

Time : 3 Hrs.

Max. Marks : 70

Section A

[14 Marks]

1. (A) Fill in the blanks by choosing the appropriate word(s) from those given in the brackets.

[Freons, $T = 0°$ C, $T = 10°$ C, dsp^2, propellants, foams, tripled, doubled, hexacyanoferrate(III); d^2sp^3, sp^3d^2, phenol, phenoxide ion] [4×1]

(i) Chlorofluorocarbon compounds of methane and ethane are collectively known as .... They are used as ...... for aerosols. • *Recall*

(ii) ...... is less reactive than......towards electrophilic aromatic substitution. • *Understanding*

(iii) The IUPAC name and hybridisation of the complex $[Fe(CN)_6]^{3-}$ are .... and ...., respectively. • *Understanding*

(iv) It has been found that for a chemical reaction with rise in temperature by ......, the rate constant is nearly .... • *Recall*

(B) Select and write the correct alternative from the given choices below. [7×1]

(i) Vapours of an alcohol when passed over hot reduced copper, produced an alkene, the alcohol is • *Analysis*

(a) primary alcohol (b) secondary alcohol
(c) tertiary alcohol (d) dihydric alcohol

(ii) Which of the following statement is incorrect regarding positive deviation from ideal behaviour?

I. The intermolecular interactions between $A—B$ are weaker than those between $A—A$ or $B—B$.

II. The value $\Delta_{mix} V$ is negative.
III. Heating increases solubility.
IV. Water + nitric acid is an example of this type of solution. • *Recall*

(a) Only I and II (b) Only II and IV
(c) Only I and III (d) Only III and IV

(iii) Which of the following solutions of KCl will have the highest value of molar conductivity? • *Application*

(a) 0.01 M (b) 1 M (c) 0.5 M (d) 0.1 M

(iv) In the reaction,

$$\text{Phenol} \xrightarrow[\text{(b) } CO_2/400K]{\text{(a) NaOH}} [A] \xrightarrow{H^+/H_2O} [B] \xrightarrow[\text{(ii) } FeCl_3]{\text{(i) } Ac_2O} [C]$$

The end product *C* is • *Understanding*

(a) phenyl acetate (b) salicylic acid
(c) salicylaldehyde (d) aspirin

(v) Lanthanoid contraction is observed in second and third rows of transition elements. • *Recall*

The group which does not have similar radii is

(a) Sc, Y, La (b) Ti, Zr, Hf
(c) V, Nb, Ta (d) All of these

(vi) **Assertion** (A) Chlorine is an *ortho-para* directing group in electrophilic aromatic substitution reaction.

Reason (R) Chlorine is an electron withdrawing group. • *Analysis*

(a) Both Assertion and Reason are true and Reason is the correct explanation of Assertion.
(b) Both Assertion and Reason are true but Reason is not the correct explanation of Assertion.
(c) Assertion is true but Reason is false.
(d) Both Assertion and Reason are false.

(vii) **Assertion** (A) Kohlrausch law helps to find the molar conductivity of weak electrolyte at infinite dilution.

Reason (R) Molar conductivity of a weak electrolyte at infinite dilution cannot be determined experimentally. • *Analysis*

(a) Both Assertion and Reason are true and Reason is the correct explanation of Assertion.
(b) Both Assertion and Reason are true but Reason is not the correct explanation of Assertion.
(c) Assertion is true but Reason is false.
(d) Both Assertion and Reason are false.

(C) Read the passage given below carefully and answer the questions that follow [3×1]

Carboxylic acid having an α-hydrogen when treated with chlorine or bromine in presence of small amount of red phosphorus gives α-halocarboxylic acid. This reaction is known as Hell-Volhard-Zelinsky reaction.

$$R{-}CH_2{-}COOH + X_2 \xrightarrow{\text{Red, } P} R{-}\underset{\underset{X}{|}}{CH}{-}COOH$$

The mechanism of the reaction can be explained as the phosphorus reacts with bromine to give phosphorus tribromide and in the first step this converts the carboxylic acid into an acyl bromide.

$$\frac{3}{2}Br_2 + P \longrightarrow PBr_3$$

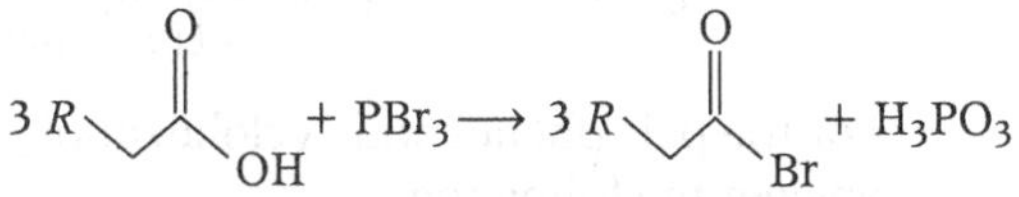

An acyl bromide can readily exist in the enol form and this tautomer is rapidly brominated at the α-carbon. The monobrominated compound is much less nucleophilic, so the reaction stops at this stage. This acyl intermediate compound can undergo bromide exchange with unreacted carboxylic acid *via* the anhydride which allows the catalytic cycle to contribute until the conversion is complete.

(i) Will $(CH_3)_3CCOOH$ give HVZ reaction? If not, why? • *Understanding*

(ii) Among the α-halocarboxylic acids and $R{-}CH_2{-}COOH$, which is more acidic and why? • *Understanding*

(iii) Give the reaction and the product of acetic acid reacting with Cl_2 in presence of red phosphorus. • *Analysis*

Section B

[20 Marks]

2. Devise a scheme for the synthesis of anthracene using benzene as the only source of organic compound. Is it possible to obtain naphthalene in pure state by applying this scheme. Give reason for your answer. • *Evaluate* [2]

3. Give a reason for each of the following. [2]
   (i) Transition elements usually form coloured ions.
   (ii) Zn^{2+} salts are white while Ni^{2+} salts are blue in colour. • *Understanding*

4. Complete and balance the following chemical equations. [2]
   (i) $K_2Cr_2O_7 + H_2SO_4 + H_2S \longrightarrow$
   (ii) $Fe^{2+} + MnO_4^- + H^+ \longrightarrow$ • *Recall*

5. Account for the following.
   (i) The colour of $KMnO_4$ disappears when oxalic acid is added to its solution in acidic medium?
   (ii) Third ionisation enthalpy of manganese is exceptionally high. [2] • *Understanding*

6. For the pair phenol and cyclohexanol, answer the following.
   (i) Why is phenol more acidic than cyclohexanol ?
   (ii) Give one chemical test to distinguish between the two. • *Understanding* [2]

SP-03

7. (i) Write the chemical reaction for the following. • *Recall*
   (a) Sulphonation reaction of phenol.
   (b) Nitration reaction of phenol.
   (ii) In Reimer-Tiemann reaction, write the mechanism for the generation of electrophile and name it. • *Recall*

8. How will the following be obtained? (Give chemical equations) [2]
   (i) Benzamide from benzoic acid
   (ii) 3-hydroxybutanal from ethanol • *Understanding*

Or *A*, *B* and *C* are three non-cyclic functional isomers of a carbonyl compound with molecular formula C_4H_8O. Isomers *A* and *C* give positive Tollen's test whereas isomer *B* does not give Tollen's test, but gives positive iodoform test.
Isomers *A* and *B* on reduction with Zn(Hg)/conc. HCl give the same product *D*. Write the structures of *A*, *B*, *C* and *D*. • *Understanding*

9. The vapour pressure of water is 12.3 kPa at 300 K. Calculate the vapour pressure of a one molal solution of a non-volatile, non-ionic solute in water. • *Application* [2]

10. (i) The conductivity of 0.2 M KCl solution is 3×10^{-2} $ohm^{-1}\,cm^{-1}$. Calculate its molar conductance. • *Application*
   (ii) Calculate the cell constant if two Pt electrode fitted in a conductance cell are 1.5 cm apart and the cross-sectional area of each electrode is $0.75\,cm^2$. [2] • *Application*

11. (i) What is the molality of KCl that should be added to 1 kg of water to lower its freezing point to $-8.0°C$? (K_f for water $=1.86°C\,kg\,mol^{-1}$) • *Application*
   (ii) What is the ratio of value of van't Hoff factor for $K_4[Fe(CN)_6]$ to that of $Fe_4[Fe(CN)_6]_3$ solution? • *Application* [2]

Section C

[21 Marks]

12. The following data were obtained during the first order thermal decomposition of SO_2Cl_2 at a constant volume, [3]

$$SO_2Cl_2(g) \longrightarrow SO_2(g) + Cl_2(g)$$

Experiment	Time	Total pressure/atm
1.	0	0.4
2.	100	0.7

Determine the value of rate constant.

(Given, $\log 4 = 0.6021, \log 2 = 0.3010$)

• *Evaluate*

13. Arrange the following compounds. [3]

Pentan-1-ol, 2-methyl butan-2-ol, 3-methyl butan-2-ol.

(i) In the increasing order of their boiling point. • *Analysis*

(ii) In the increasing order of their reactivity towards Lucas reagent. • *Analysis*

14. (i) Rakesh put few drops of lemon in milk. What change does he observed after sometime? What is this phenomenon known as? • *Recall* [3]

(ii) Rubina while her visit to a doctor, found out, she is having deficiency of vitamin B_{12}. What are the sources of vitamin advised by the doctor to her to cure this deficiency? • *Analysis*

(iii) Give an example of reducing and non-reducing sugar. • *Recall*

15. Using colligative properties, calculated molar mass is sometimes differ from experimentally determined molar mass. This is known as abnormal molecular mass. The difference is due to the solute particles that undergo association or dissociation.

Consider the two cases given below and answer the following questions that follow.

(A) 19.5 g of CH_2FCOOH is dissolved in 500 g of water. The depression in the freezing point of water observed is 1.0°C. [3]

(B) The freezing point of a solution decreases by 0.45 K when 0.4 g of acetic acid dissolved in 40 g of benzene.

Answer the following questions.

(i) Calculate the abnormal molecular mass of solute in both the cases. • *Application*

(ii) Inferring the value of van't Hoff factor in both the cases, find out which solution undergoes association and which solution undergoes dissociation. • *Analysis*

(iii) Given below is the increasing order of freezing points of equimolar solutions.

$$AlCl_3 < KNO_3 < \text{Glucose}$$

Provide a reason to explain if the above ordered arrangement is correct or not. • *Understanding*

16. Identify the structures of *A*, *B* and *C* in the following reactions. [3]

(i) $C_6H_5\overset{+}{N_2}Cl^- \xrightarrow{CuCN} [A] \xrightarrow[\Delta]{H_2O/H^+} [B] \xrightarrow[\Delta]{NH_3} [C]$

(ii) $C_6H_5NO_2 \xrightarrow{Sn + HCl} [A] \xrightarrow[273\text{ K}]{NaNO_2 + HCl} [B] \xrightarrow[\Delta]{H_2O/H^+} [C]$

• *Understanding*

17. Write chemical equation for the following conversions. [3]

(i) Nitrobenzene to benzoic acid

(ii) Benzyl chloride to 2-phenylethanamine

(iii) Aniline to benzyl alcohol • *Understanding*

Or

Arrange the following in increasing order of property specified.

(i) Aniline, ethanamine, 3-ethyl ethanamine (solubility in water).

(ii) Ethanoic acid, ethanamine, ethanol (boiling point).

(iii) Methanamine, N, N- dimethyl methanamine and N-methylmethanamine (basic strength in aqueous phase). • *Analysis*

18. (i) Calculate the activation energy for first order reaction when 50% of reaction is completed in 40 min and 20 min at 300 K and 320 K respectively.

• *Application*

(ii) For the reaction,

$$2N_2O_5(g) \longrightarrow 4NO_2(g) + O_2(g),$$

the rate of formation of $NO_2(g)$ is $2.8 \times 10^{-3} \text{ Ms}^{-1}$.

Calculate the rate of disappearance of $N_2O_5(g)$. • *Application* [3]

Section D **[15 Marks]**

19. (i) A coordination compound having a formula $CoCl_3 \cdot 4NH_3$ precipitates silver ions as AgCl. Its solution conductivity corresponds to 1 : 1 electrolyte. [5]

Coordination compounds are formulated and named according to the IUPAC system. Few rules for naming coordination compounds are

(1) In ionic complex, the cation is named first and then the anion.

(2) In the coordination entity, the ligands are named first and then the central metal ion.

(3) When more than one type of ligands are present, they are named in alphabetical order of preference without any consideration of charge.

Based on this information, answer the following questions.

(a) Write the structural formula of the complex compound. • *Understanding*

(b) Give the IUPAC name of the complex compound. • *Understanding*

(c) Name the type of isomerism involved. • *Recall*

(ii) Using IUPAC norms, write the formulae for the following.

(a) Sodium dicyanoaurate (I)

(b) Tetraammine chlorido nitrito-N-platinum (IV) sulphate. • *Understanding*

20. (i) Starting with acetone, how will 2-methylpropan-2-ol and propane be synthesised? • *Understanding* [5]

(ii) Explain why benzoic acid is stronger than acetic acid. • *Understanding*

(iii) Name the reagent (*A*) used in the following reaction. • *Understanding*

$$CH_3—CO—CH_3 \xrightarrow{(A)} CH_3—\underset{\displaystyle OH}{\underset{|}{CH}}—CH_3$$

21. (i) Given below the depiction of a fuel cell. [5]

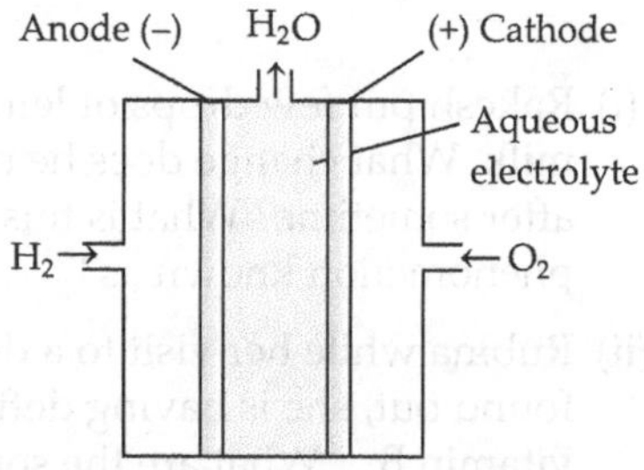

Fuel cell using H_2 and O_2 produces electricity

(a) Write the working of fuel cell by giving the reaction at anode and cathode. Also, write the overall reaction. • *Recall*

(b) What is the formula for efficiency of fuel cell? • *Recall*

(c) Write any one use of fuel cell and one of its disadvantage. • *Recall*

(ii) How many Coulombs are required to produce 40 g of aluminium from molten Al_2O_3? • *Application*

Or (i) 0.05N solution of a salt occupying a volume between two platinum electrodes separated by a distance of 1.72 cm and having an area of 4.5 cm^2 has a resistance of 250 ohm.

Calculate the equivalent conductance and *K*. • *Application*

(ii) Write the applications of Kohlrausch's law. • *Application*

Solutions in Topper's Style

My Commitment *I affirm that I am reviewing these solutions only after I have solved the Sample Question Paper on my own. My purpose of looking the solutions is solely to verify whether my answers/solutions were correct or not and to identify my mistakes in case my solutions were wrong or I could not solve that.*

1. (A) (i) Freons, propellants

(ii) Phenol, phenoxide ion

(iii) hexacyanoferrate (III), d^2sp^3

(iv) 10° C, doubled

(B) (i) (c) Tertiary alcohols undergoes dehydration to form alkene when passed over heated copper at 573 K.

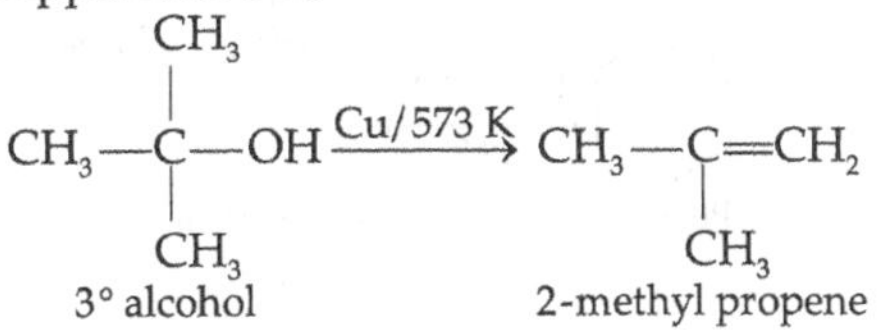

(ii) (b) Only statements (II) and (IV) are incorrect. Their correct form are as follows

- The value of $\Delta_{mix}V$ is positive.
- Water + nitric acid is an example of solutions showing negative deviation from Raoult's law.

(iii) (a) $\Lambda_m = \dfrac{\kappa \times 1000}{M}$

$\Lambda_m \propto \dfrac{1}{M}$ at constant κ

Therefore, Λ_m will be highest if molarity of solution will be lowest.

Hence, option (a) is correct.

(iv) (d)

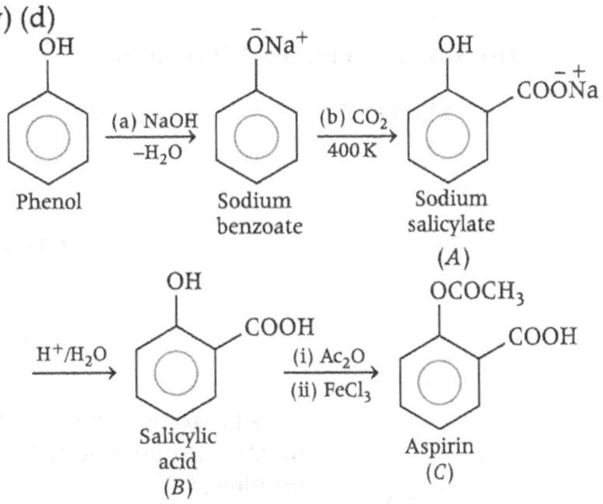

(v) (a) Due to lanthanoid contraction, the atomic radii of the second and third rows of transition elements is almost same.

So, they resemble each other much more as compared to first row elements and show similar characteristics.

(vi) (b) Chlorine is an electron withdrawing group yet it acts as *ortho, para*-directing group in electrophilic aromatic substitution reaction due to its +*R* effect. Thus, both Assertion and Reason are true but Reason is not the correct explanation of Assertion.

(vii) (a) Both Assertion and Reason are true and Reason is the correct explanation of Assertion.

(C) (i) $(CH_3)_3CCOOH$ will not give HVZ reaction as it does not have an α-hydrogen.

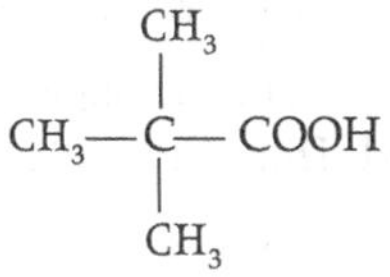

(ii) In α-halocarboxylic acids, there is an electronegative halogen atom at α-position to carboxyl group. It helps in stabilisation of ion formed after lose of proton from —COOH group. Hence, it is more acidic than unsubstituted carboxylic acids.

(iii) Acetic acid will react with Cl_2 in presence of red phosphorus to give α-chloroacetic acid.

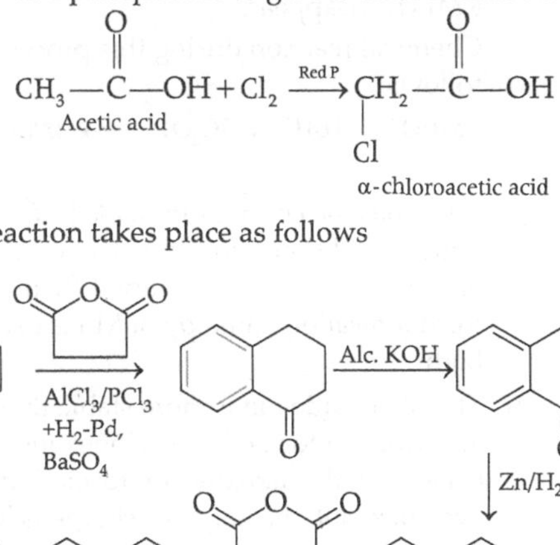

2. The reaction takes place as follows

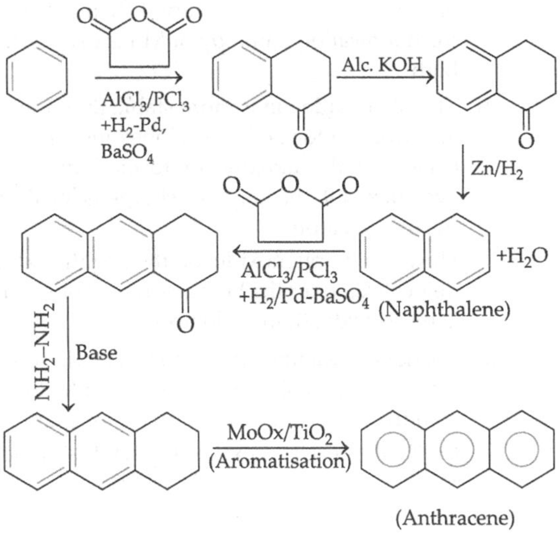

Yes, naphthalene can be obtain in pure state by applying this scheme by carrying out the reaction only upto naphthalene.

3. (i) Most of the complexes of transition elements are coloured. This is because of the absorption of radiation from visible light region to promote an unpaired electron from one of the *d*-orbitals to another.
When ligand has free electrons, the transfer of electron takes place from anion to cation. In this case, energy absorbed during the process is responsible for colour.

(ii) Electronic configuration of $Zn^{2+} = [Ar]3d^{10}4s^0$

↿⇂	↿⇂	↿⇂	↿⇂	↿⇂

Electronic configuration of $Ni^{2+} = [Ar]3d^8 4s^0$

↿⇂	↿⇂	↿⇂	↿	↿

Compounds that contain unpaired electrons are coloured. Thus, Ni^{2+} salts are blue in colour.

4. (i)
$$\underset{\text{Potassium dichromate}}{K_2Cr_2O_7} + \underset{\text{Sulphuric acid}}{4H_2SO_4} + \underset{\text{Hydrogen sulphide}}{3H_2S} \longrightarrow \underset{\text{Potassium sulphate}}{K_2SO_4} + \underset{\text{Chromium sulphate}}{Cr_2(SO_4)_3} + \underset{\text{Water}}{7H_2O} + \underset{\text{Sulphur}}{3S}$$

(ii) $5Fe^{2+} + MnO_4^- + 8H^+ \longrightarrow Mn^{2+} + 5Fe^{3+} + 4H_2O$

5. (i) MnO_4^- ion gets reduced to Mn^{2+} ion and oxalic acid oxidises to CO_2 due to which the colour of $KMnO_4$ disappears.
Chemical reaction during this process is as follows
$$2MnO_4^- + 16H^+ + 5C_2O_4^{2-} \longrightarrow 2Mn^{2+} + 8H_2O + 10CO_2\uparrow$$

(ii) Mn^{2+} has the configuration [Ar] $3d^5$ which is a highly stable configuration. Hence, the removal of third electron will be very difficult. Therefore, third ionisation enthalpy of Mn is exceptionally high.

6. (i) The phenoxide ion is more stable than the alkoxide ion formed by cyclohexanol. This is because in the alkoxide ion formed by cyclohexanol, the negative charge is localised on the oxygen atom.
However, in phenoxide ion the negative charge is delocalised over the benzene ring. Thus, phenol is more acidic than cyclohexanol.

(ii) Phenol on reacting with ferric chloride solution gives a violet colour compound while it remains colourless when reacted with cyclohexanol.
$$6C_6H_5OH + FeCl_3 \longrightarrow \underset{\text{Violet colour}}{[Fe(OC_6H_5)_6]^{3-}} + 3H^+ + 3HCl$$

7. (i) Sulphonation and nitration are electrophilic substitution reaction of phenol.

(a) **Sulphonation**

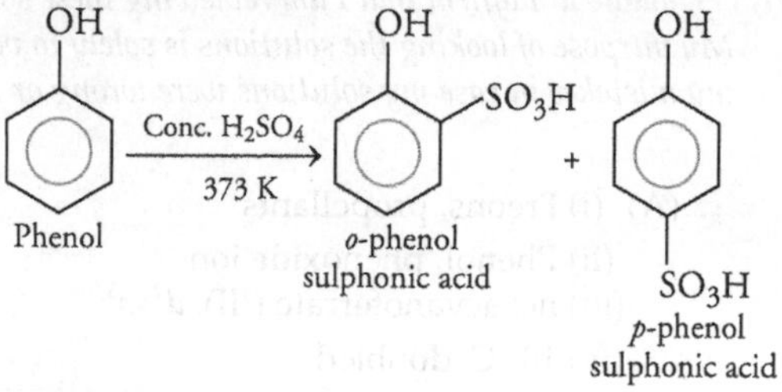

(b) **Nitration**

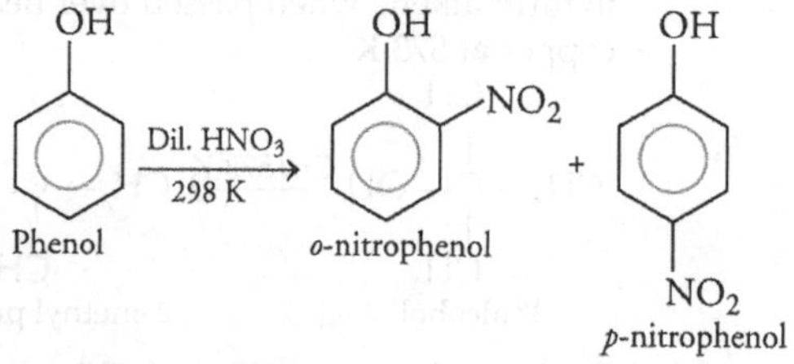

(ii) In Reimer-Tiemann reaction, the generation of electrophile takes place as follows
$$\underset{\text{(Chloroform)}}{CHCl_3} + OH^- \rightleftharpoons HOH + :\bar{C}Cl_3 \longrightarrow Cl^- + \underset{\text{Dichloro carbene}}{:CCl_2}$$

8. (i) **Benzamide from benzoic acid**

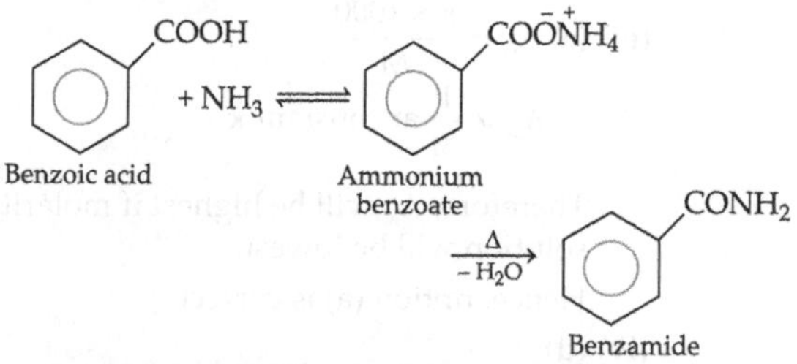

(ii) **3-hydroxybutanal from ethanol**
$$\underset{\text{(Ethanol)}}{CH_3CH_2OH} \xrightarrow[CrO_3]{\text{Oxidation}} \underset{\text{(Ethanal)}}{CH_3CHO} \xrightarrow{\text{Aldol condensation}} \underset{\text{3-hydroxybutanal}}{CH_3CH(OH)-CH_2-CHO}$$

> **Value Points** To get maximum marks following points must be included in conversion problem.
> - Write the reagents involved in each step.
> - Also, write the IUPAC name of each reactant and product.

Or

The possible functional isomers of carbonyl compound with molecular formula, C_4H_8O are

$CH_3-CH(CH_3)-CHO$, $CH_3CH_2CH_2CHO$, $CH_3CH_2-\overset{O}{\overset{\|}{C}}-CH_3$

- Isomers (A) and (C) gives positive Tollen's test, thus they must be aldehydes.
- Isomer (B) does not give Tollen's test, but gives positive iodoform test, thus it must be a ketone with $CH_3-\overset{O}{\overset{\|}{C}}-$ group.
- Isomers (A) and (B) on reduction with Zn(Hg) / conc. HCl give same product (D).

$$\underset{(C)}{CH_3-CH(CH_3)-CHO} + 4[H] \xrightarrow{\text{Zn-Hg/Conc. HCl}} CH_3CH(CH_3)-CH_3 + H_2O$$

$$\underset{(A)}{CH_3-CH_2-CH_2-CHO} + 4[H] \xrightarrow{\text{Zn-Hg/conc. HCl}} \underset{(D)}{CH_3-CH_2-CH_2-CH_3} + H_2O$$

$$\underset{(B)}{CH_3CH_2COCH_3} + 4[H] \xrightarrow{\text{Zn-Hg/conc. HCl}} \underset{(D)}{CH_3CH_2CH_2CH_3} + H_2O$$

So, the structures of (A), (B), (C) and (D) are

$\underset{(A)}{CH_3CH_2CH_2CHO}$, $\underset{(B)}{CH_3CH_2COCH_3}$, $\underset{(C)}{CH_3CH(CH_3)-CHO}$, $\underset{(D)}{CH_3CH_2CH_2CH_3}$

9. As solution is 1 molal, it means that 1 mole of solute is dissolved in 1000 g of solvent (water).

Moles of solute = 1 mole

Moles of water $= \frac{1000}{18} = 55.55$ moles

$\therefore$ Total number of moles = 56.55 moles

Mole fraction of solute $(\chi_B) = \frac{1}{1+55.55} = 0.018$

$$\left[\therefore \text{Mole fraction of solute } (\chi) = \frac{\text{Moles of solute}}{\text{Total moles}}\right]$$

As we know that, lowering in vapour pressure of solvent is

$$\frac{p_1^\circ - p_1}{p_1^\circ} = \chi_B$$

$$\therefore \quad \frac{12.3 - p_1}{12.3} = 0.018$$

$$\Rightarrow \quad p_1 = 12.08 \text{ kPa}$$

10. (i) We know that molar conductance and conductivity of a solution are related as

$$\Lambda_m = \frac{1000}{C} \times \kappa \qquad \ldots(i)$$

where, Λ_m is molar conductance, C = concentration and κ is specific conductance or conductivity of a solution.

Given, $C = 0.2$ M, $\kappa = 3 \times 10^{-2}\ \Omega^{-1}\ \text{cm}^{-1}$

Putting values in Eq. (i), we get

$$\Lambda_m = \frac{1000}{0.2} \times 3 \times 10^{-2} = \frac{30}{0.2}$$

$$= 1.5 \times 10^2\ \Omega^{-1}\ \text{cm}^2 \text{mol}^{-1}$$

(ii) Given, $l = 1.5$ cm, $a = 0.75 \text{cm}^2$

We know,

$$\text{Cell constant} = \frac{l}{a} = \frac{1.5}{0.75} = 2.0 \text{cm}^{-1}$$

11. (i) KCl dissociates as, $KCl \longrightarrow K^+ + Cl^-$

$\because$ 1 mole of KCl gives 2 moles of particles

$\therefore \quad i = 2$

We know that, depression in freezing point,

$$\Delta T_f = iK_f m \qquad (\text{where, } m = \text{molality})$$

Here, $\Delta T_f = 0 - (-8.0) = 8°C$

$$\therefore \text{ Molality, } m = \frac{8°C}{2 \times 1.86°C \text{ kg mol}^{-1}} = 2.15 \text{ mol/kg}$$

(ii) van't Hoff factor of $K_4[Fe(CN)_6] = 5$

and van't Hoff factor of $Fe_4[Fe(CN)_6]_3 = 7$

$\therefore$ Ratio of van't Hoff factor value $= \frac{5}{7} = 0.71$

12.

	$SO_2Cl_2(g) \longrightarrow$	$SO_2(g)$ +	$Cl_2(g)$
Initial pressure	p_i	0	0
After time, t	$p_i - p$	p	p

Total pressure after time t,

i.e. $\quad p_t = p_i - p + p + p = p_i + p$

$\Rightarrow \quad p = p_t - p_i$

Thus, $a = p_i$ and $a - x = p_i - p = p_i - (p_t - p_i)$

$$= p_i - p_t + p_i = 2p_i - p_t$$

Substituting the values of a and $(a - x)$ in equation,

$$k = \frac{2.303}{t} \log \frac{a}{a-x}$$

$$k = \frac{2.303}{t} \log \frac{p_i}{(2p_i - p_t)}$$

Calculating rate constant (k), when $t = 100$s

Given, $p_i = 0.4$ atm and $p_t = 0.7$ atm

$$\text{Then, } k = \frac{2.303}{100} \log \frac{p_i}{(2p_i - p_t)}$$

$$= \frac{2.303}{100} \log \frac{0.4}{(2 \times 0.4 - 0.7)}$$

$$= \frac{2.303}{100}\log\frac{0.4}{0.1} = \frac{2.303}{100}\log 4$$

$$= \frac{2.303}{100} \times 0.6021 = 0.01387$$

$$= 1.387 \times 10^{-2} s^{-1}$$

13. (i) With the increase in branching, the shape of the molecule becomes more compact and hence, less surface contact is available for van der Waals' forces and thus, boiling point decreases.

Therefore, increasing order of the boiling point is,

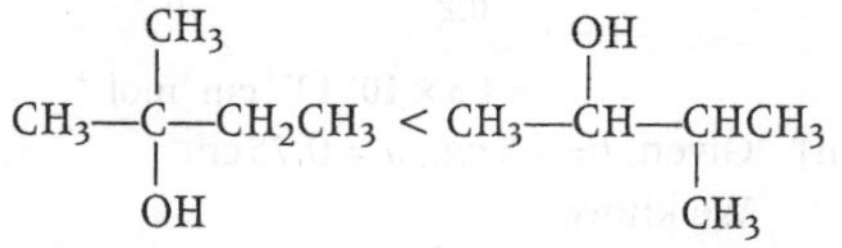

2-methylbutan-2-ol < 3-methylbutan-2-ol

$< n\text{-}C_4H_9CH_2OH$
Pentan-1-ol

(ii) For the reactivity towards Lucas reagent, the order of appearance of turbidity is 3°> 2°> 1° (alcohols).

Thus, increasing order of the given alcohols towards Lucas reagent is,

Pentan-1-ol < 3-methylbutan-2-ol < 2-methylbutan-2-ol

14. (i) After sometime, curdling of milk has occured due to the formation of lactic acid by the bacteria present in the milk. This phenomenon is known as denaturation of protein.

(ii) The sources of vitamin B_{12} are meat, fish, egg and curd.

(iii) Glucose and fructose are reducing sugars whereas sucrose and raffinose are non-reducing sugars.

15. (i) (A) Here, $w_2 = 19.5$ g, $W_1 = 500$ g,

$K_f = 1.86 \text{ K kg mol}^{-1}$, $(\Delta T_f)_{obs} = 1.0°C$

$$\therefore M_2(\text{observed}) = \frac{1000 K_f w_2}{W_1 \Delta T_f}$$

$$= \frac{(1000)(1.86 \text{ K kg mol}^{-1})(19.5 \text{ g})}{(500 \text{ g})(1.0 \text{ K})}$$

$$= 72.54 \text{ g mol}^{-1}$$

M_2 (calculated) for CH_2FCOOH

$$= 14 + 19 + 45 = 78 \text{ g mol}^{-1}$$

(B) Here, $w_2 = 0.4 \times 10^{-3}$ kg,

$W_1 = 0.04$ kg

$K_f = 5.12 \text{ K kg mol}^{-1}$,

$(\Delta T_f)_{obs} = 0.45$ K

$$\therefore M_2 \text{ (observed)} = \frac{K_f w_2}{w_1 \Delta T_f}$$

$$= \frac{(5.12 \text{ K kg mol}^{-1})(0.4 \times 10^{-3} \text{ kg})}{(0.04 \text{ kg})(0.45 \text{ K})}$$

$$= 113.78 \times 10^{-3} \text{ kg mol}^{-1}$$

$$= 113.78 \text{ g mol}^{-1}$$

M_2 (calculated) for $CH_3COOH = 60 \text{ g mol}^{-1}$

(ii) (A) van't Hoff factor $(i) = \frac{(M_2)_{cal}}{(M_2)_{obs}}$

$$= \frac{78 \text{ g mol}^{-1}}{72.54 \text{ g mol}^{-1}} = 1.0753$$

$\because i > 1$, thus dissociation occurs.

(B) van't Hoff factor $(i) = \frac{(M_2)_{cal}}{(M_2)_{obs}}$

$$= \frac{60 \text{ g mol}^{-1}}{113.78 \text{ g mol}^{-1}} = 0.527$$

$\because i < 1$, thus association occurs.

(iii) The given order of freezing point is correct as the value of i for glucose, KNO_3 and $AlCl_3$ are 1, 2 and 4, respectively.

16. (i) $C_6H_5N_2^+Cl^- \xrightarrow{CuCN} C_6H_5CN \xrightarrow{H_2O/H^+}$

Benzene diazonium chloride; Benzonitrile (A)

$C_6H_5COOH \xrightarrow[\Delta]{NH_3} C_6H_5CONH_2$

Benzoic acid (B); Benzamide (C)

(ii) $C_6H_5NO_2 \xrightarrow{Sn + HCl} C_6H_5NH_2 \xrightarrow[273 K]{NaNO_2 + HCl}$

Nitrobenzene; Aniline (A)

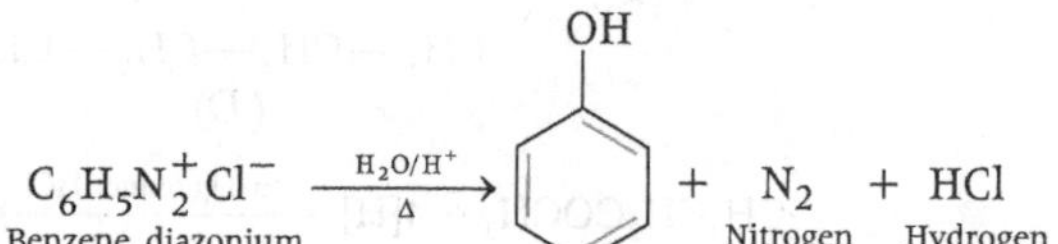

Benzene diazonium chloride (B); Phenol (C); Nitrogen; Hydrogen chloride

17. (i) **Nitrobenzene to benzoic acid**

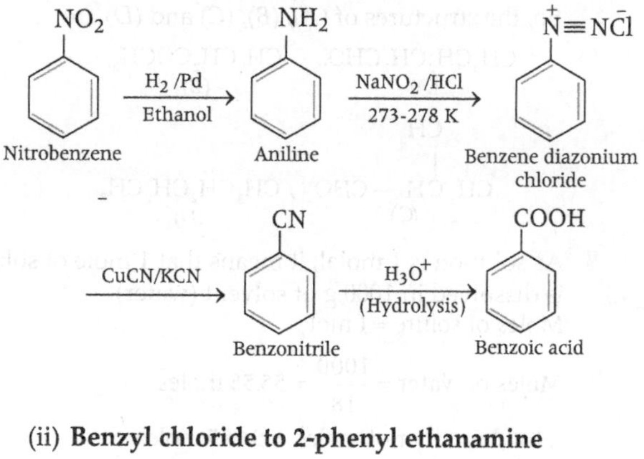

(ii) **Benzyl chloride to 2-phenyl ethanamine**

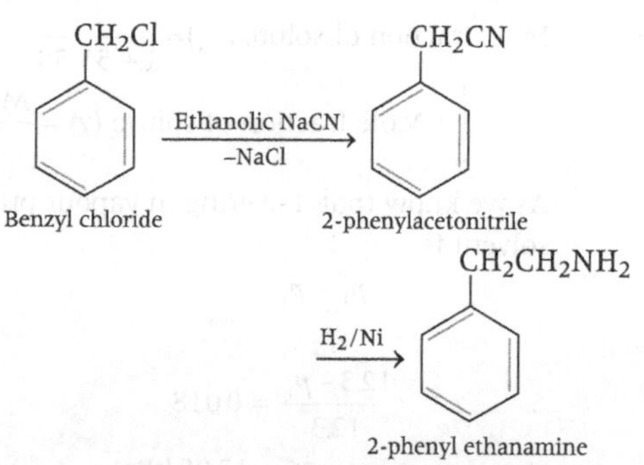

(iii) **Aniline to benzyl alcohol**

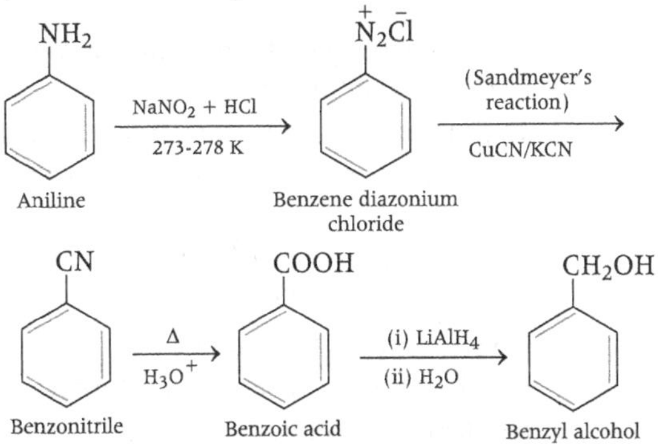

Or

(i) The correct increasing order of solubility in water is
aniline < 3 - ethylethanamine < ethanamine.
Solubility of amines decreases with increase in molar mass due to increase in the hydrophobic part which retard the formation of H - bonds.

(ii) The correct increasing order of boiling point is ethanamine < ethanol < ethanoic acid.
Carboxylic acids have higher boiling points because they have high extent of hydrogen bonding with water, due to which they exists as associated molecules.

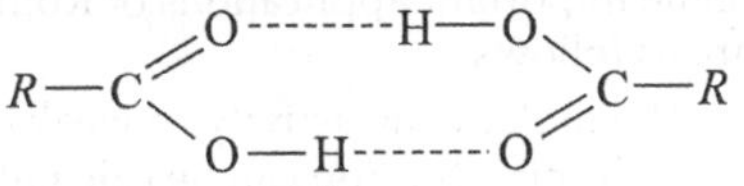

Dimer

(iii) The correct increasing order of basic strength in aqueous phase is
N, N - dimethyl methanamine (3°) < methanamine (1°) < N - methyl methanamine (2°)
Basic strength in aqueous phase depends upon the stabilisation of their conjugate acids by a number of factors such as H-bonding, steric hindrance of alkyl groups and + *I*-efffect of alkyl groups. The first two factors are favourable for 2° amines.

18. (i) $t_{1/2}$ for first order reaction is given by $t_{1/2} = \frac{0.693}{k}$

For 300 K, $k_1 = \frac{0.693}{t_{1/2}} = \frac{0.693}{40}$

At 320 K, $k_2 = \frac{0.693}{20}$

Arrhenius equation is,

$$\log\frac{k_2}{k_1} = \frac{E_a}{2.303R}\left(\frac{1}{T_1} - \frac{1}{T_2}\right)$$

$$\log\frac{40}{20} = \frac{E_a}{2.303 \times 8.314}\left[\frac{1}{300} - \frac{1}{320}\right]$$

$$\log 2 = \frac{E_a}{19.15}\left[\frac{20}{300 \times 320}\right]$$

$$0.301 = \frac{E_a}{19.15\,\text{J mol}^{-1}\text{K}^{-1}} \times 20.8 \times 10^{-5}\text{K}$$

$$E_a = 0.27712 \times 10^5\ \text{J mol}^{-1}$$

$$E_a = 27712\ \text{J mol}^{-1}$$

$$E_a = 27.712\,\text{kJ/mol}$$

(ii) For the reaction,

$$2N_2O_5(g) \longrightarrow 4NO_2(g) + O_2(g)$$

Overall rate of reaction is

$$-\frac{1}{2}\frac{d[N_2O_5]}{dt} = +\frac{1}{4}\frac{d[NO_2]}{dt} = +\frac{d[O_2]}{dt}$$

Given, $\frac{d[NO_2]}{dt} = 2.8 \times 10^{-3}\ \text{Ms}^{-1}$, $\frac{d[N_2O_5]}{dt} = ?$

$$\therefore\quad -\frac{1}{2}\frac{d[N_2O_5]}{dt} = \frac{1}{4}\frac{d[NO_2]}{dt}$$

Putting the given values in the above equation, we get

$$\frac{-d[N_2O_5]}{dt} = \frac{1}{4} \times 2 \times 2.8 \times 10^{-3}\ \text{Ms}^{-1}$$

$$= 1.4 \times 10^{-3}\ \text{Ms}^{-1}$$

19. (i) (a) $CoCl_3 \cdot 4NH_3$ precipitates silver ions as AgCl and its solution conductivity corresponds to 1 : 1 electrolyte. Thus, the formula of the compound will be $[CoCl_2(NH_3)_4]Cl$.

(b) IUPAC name—Tetraamminedichlorido cobalt(III) chloride.

(c) This complex compounds shows geometrical isomerism as $[CoCl_2(NH_3)_4]^+$ and $[CoCl_2(NH_3)_4]^+$ have same molecular and structural formula but different arrangement in space.

(ii) (a) $Na[Au(CN)_2]$

(b) $[Pt(NH_3)_4Cl(NO_2)]SO_4$

20. (i)

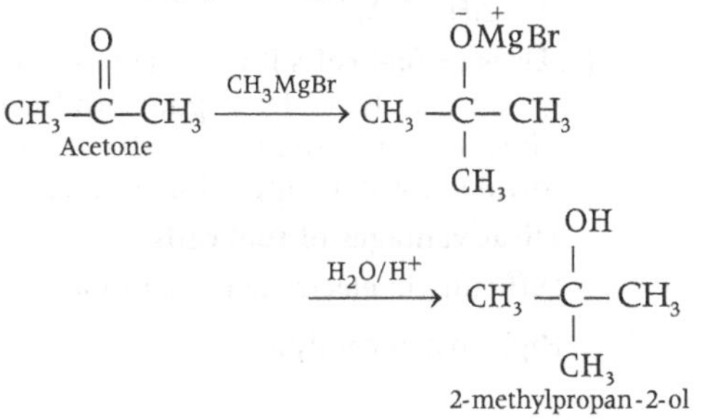

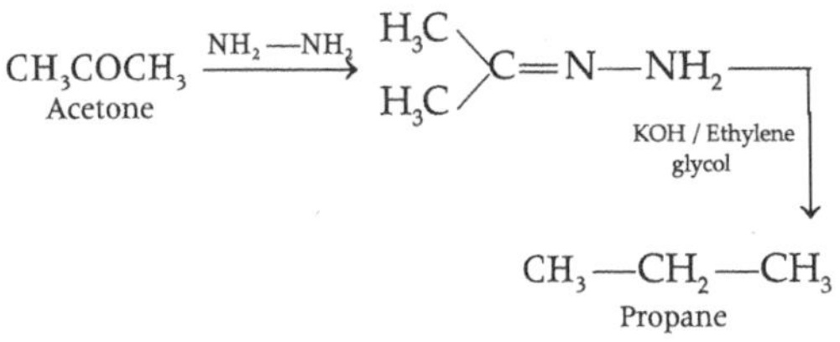

(ii) Benzoic acid is a stronger acid than acetic acid because the carboxyl group of benzoic acid is attached to a sp^2-hybridised carbon, which is more electronegative and electron withdrawing than the sp^3-hybridised carbon attached to acetic acid.

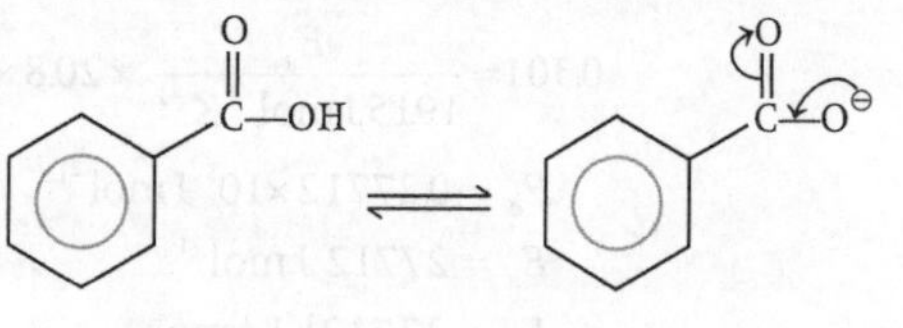

More electronegativity stabilise the anion and hence, increases the acidity. Whereas, methyl group in acetic acid induces $+I$ effect and destabilise the anion.

$$CH_3-COOH \rightleftharpoons CH_3 \rightarrow COO^{\ominus}$$

($+I$ effect destabilise the anion)

(iii) $$\underset{\text{Propanone}}{CH_3-\overset{\overset{O}{\|}}{C}-CH_3} \xrightarrow{NaBH_4\ (A)} \underset{\text{Propan-2-ol}}{CH_3-\overset{\overset{OH}{|}}{CH}-CH_3}$$ (2)

21. (i) (a) Galvanic cells that are designed to convert the energy of combustion of fuels such as hydrogen, methane and methanol directly into electrical energy are called fuel cells.

In this type of galvanic cells, reactants are continuously feed to the electrodes which react to produce electricity and product thus formed are continuously removed.

The electrode reactions for the cell are

At anode, $2H_2(g) + 4OH^-(aq) \longrightarrow 4H_2O(l) + 4e^-$

At cathode, $O_2(g) + 2H_2O + 4e^- \longrightarrow 4OH^-(aq)$

Overall reaction, $2H_2(g) + O_2(g) \longrightarrow 2H_2O(l)$

(b) **Efficiency of fuel cell (n)**:

$$n = \frac{\text{Electrical work done during redox change}}{\Delta H \text{ formed during reaction}}$$

$$n = \frac{\Delta G}{\Delta H} = \frac{-nFE}{\Delta H}$$

(c) **Uses of fuel cells** It was used in Apollo space program. The water vapour produced during the reaction were condensed and added to the drinking water supply for astronauts.

Disadvantages of fuel cells

- Difficulty in electrode preparation.
- High cost of catalyst.

(ii) $$Al_2O_3(l) + \underset{(6F)}{6e^-} \longrightarrow \underset{\substack{2\times 27\\ = 54\,g}}{2Al} + 3O^{2-}$$

To produce 54 g of Al from molten Al_2O_3, electricity required = 6F.

To produce 40 g of Al from molten Al_2O_3,

$$\text{electricity required} = \frac{6\text{ F}}{54\text{ g}} \times 40\text{ g} = 4.44\text{ F}$$

$$= 428460\text{ C} \quad [\because 1F = 96500\text{ C}]$$

Or

(i) Given, normality (N) = 0.05N

length (l) = 1.72 cm, area (A) = 4.5 cm^2 and resistance (R) = 250 Ω

$\because$ Specific conductance = Conductance × Cell constant

$$\because \quad \kappa = C \times \frac{l}{A} = \frac{1}{R} \times \frac{l}{A}$$

$$= \frac{1}{250} \times \frac{1.72}{4.5} \quad \left[\because C = \frac{1}{R}\right]$$

$$= 1.5289 \times 10^{-3}\ \text{ohm}^{-1}\text{cm}^{-1}$$

We know that, $\Lambda_{eq} = \kappa \times \frac{1000}{N}$

$$\therefore \quad \Lambda_{eq} = \frac{1.5289 \times 10^{-3}\ \text{ohm}^{-1}\text{cm}^{-1} \times 1000\ \text{cm}^{-3}\text{L}^{-1}}{0.05\text{g eq L}^{-1}}$$

$$= 30.578\ \text{ohm}^{-1}\text{cm}^2\text{eq}^{-1}$$

(ii) Some important applications of Kohlrausch's law are as follows

(a) The molar conductivity of weak electrolytes at infinite dilution can be calculated by using Kohlrausch's law.

(b) Degree of dissociation of weak electrolyte (like acetic acid) at a given concentration can be calculated.

(c) Knowing the degree of dissociation (α), the dissociation constant (K) of the weak electrolyte at a given concentration of the solution, can be calculated.

(d) Solubility of sparingly soluble salts can be calculated as solubility,

$$= \frac{\kappa \times 1000}{\Lambda_m^{\circ}} \text{ (mol / L)}$$

SPQ Code : **PB-04/15**   Series *i*-**Succeed 04-25/15**   Roll No. | | | | | | | | |

Sample Question Paper 04

Chemistry 12th (Code 862)

General Instructions

1. This paper is divided into four sections-A, B, C and D. Answer all questions.
2. **Section A** consists of **one** question **having sub-parts** of **one** mark each. **Section B** consists of **ten** questions of **two** marks each. **Section C** consists of **seven** questions of **three** marks each and **Section D** consists of **three** questions of **five** marks each.
3. Internal choices have been provided in one question each in Section B, Section C and Section D.
4. All working, including rough work, should be done on the same sheet as, and adjacent to the rest of the answer.
5. The intended marks for questions or parts of questions are given in brackets [].
6. Balanced questions must be given, wherever possible and diagrams where they are helpful. When solving numerical problems, all essential working must be shown.
7. In working out problems, use the following data:
Gas constant (R) = 1.987 cal deg^{-1} mol^{-1} = 8.314 JK^{-1} mol^{-1} = 0.0821 dm^3 atm K^{-1} mol^{-1}
1L atm = 1 dm^3 atm =101.3 J, 1 Faraday =96500 Coulombs.
Avogadro's number (N_A) = 6.023 × 10^{23}.

Time : 3 Hrs.
Max. Marks : 70

Section A **[14 Marks]**

1. (A) Fill in the blanks by choosing the appropriate word(s) from those given in the bracket. [4×1]

[HCl, $\frac{2}{3}$, tetrahedral, anhydrous $ZnCl_2$, H_2SO_4, pentanedioic acid, $\frac{7}{3}$, octahedral, 1, $ZnCl_2$, square planar, butanedioic acid, 2]

(i) The geometry of $[Fe(CN)_6]^{4-}$ and $[Cu(CN)_4]^{2-}$ are ...... and ...... respectively. • *Understanding*

(ii) Lucas reagent is a mixture of conc. .... and .... • *Recall*

(iii) The IUPAC name of succinic acid is .... It has ...... number of carboxylic groups attached to it. • *Recall*

(iv) The order of reaction with respect to A and B is .... and .... respectively, whose rate law is $k[A]^{\frac{7}{3}}[B]^{\frac{2}{3}}$. • *Understanding*

(B) Select and write the correct alternative from the choices given below. [7 × 1]

(i) The element belonging to 3rd series of d-block elements is • *Recall*

(a) La (b) Zn
(c) Zr (d) Rh

(ii) For a non-spontaneous reaction, ΔG° and E°_{cell} will be respectively. • *Recall*

(a) – ve and + ve (b) + ve and – ve
(c) + ve and + ve (d) – ve and – ve

(iii) Hinsberg reagent is used to distinguish between 1°, 2° and 3° amine. Which of the following amines does not react with Hinsberg reagent? • *Analysis*

(a) $CH_3CH_2NH_2$ (b) $(CH_3)_3N$
(c) $(CH_3)_2NH$ (d) $H_3C—CH(NH_2)—CH_3$

(iv) Which of the following compound give a white precipitate with $BaCl_2$ solution? • *Analysis*

(a) $[Cr(H_2O)_5Br]\ SO_4$
(b) $[Cr(H_2O)_5SCN]$
(c) $[Co(NH_3)_5SO_4]Br$
(d) $[Pt(NH_3)_2Cl_4]$

(v) Which of the following statements is incorrect regarding structure of methanol? • *Understanding*

I. C—OH bond angle is more than tetrahedral angle.
II. There are two lone pair of electrons.
III. Bond angle between H_3C–O–H bond is 108°9′.
IV. Total number of σ bond are four.

(a) Only I and IV (b) Only II and III
(c) Only III and IV (d) Only I and II

(vi) **Assertion** (A) The $t_{1/2}$ of zero order reaction depends on concentration of reactants.

Reason (R) $t_{1/2}$ and rate constant of zero order reaction are related to each other as

$$t_{1/2} = \frac{[R]_0}{2k}$$ • *Analysis*

(a) Both Assertion and Reason are true and Reason is the correct explanation of the Assertion.
(b) Both Assertion and Reason are true but Reason is not the correct explanation of Assertion.
(c) Assertion is true but Reason is false.
(d) Both Assertion and Reason are false.

(vii) **Assertion** (A) KCN reacts with methyl chloride to give methyl isocyanide.

Reason (R) CN^- is an ambident electrophile. • *Analysis*

(a) Both Assertion and Reason are true and Reason is the correct explanation of the Assertion.
(b) Both Assertion and Reason are true but Reason is not the correct explanation of Assertion.
(c) Assertion is true but Reason is false.
(d) Both Assertion and Reason are false.

(C) Read the passage given below carefully and answer the questions that follow [3 × 1]

Boiling point or freezing point of liquid solution would be affected by the dissolved solids in the liquid phase. A soluble solid in solution has the effect of raising its boiling point and depressing its freezing point.

The addition of non-volatile substances to a solvent decreases the vapour pressure and the added solute particles affect the formation of pure solvent crystals.

According to many researches the decrease in freezing point directly correlated to the concentration of solutes dissolved in the solvent. This phenomenon is expressed as freezing point depression and it is useful for several applications such as to freeze concentration of liquid food and to find the molar mass of an unknown solute in the solution. The phenomenon of freezing point depression has also many practical uses.

The radiator fluid in an automobile is a mixture of water and ethylene glycol. The freezing point depression prevents radiator from freezing in winter.

(i) Why the addition of non-volatile substances to a solvent decreases the vapour pressure of solvent? • *Understanding*

(ii) Out of 1% sucrose and 1% NaCl which has least freezing points? • *Analysis*

(iii) The freezing point of a solution having 50 cm^3 of ethylene glycol in 50 g water is found to be –34°C. Calculate the density of ethylene glycol, assuming ideal behaviour. [K_f = 1.86°C kg/mol] • *Application*

Section B

[20 Marks]

2. (i) The conductivity of 0.20 M solution of KCl, at 298 K is 0.0248 S cm^{-1}. Calculate its molar conductivity. [2]
• *Application*

(ii) If a reaction has an equilibrium constant $K < 1$, then $E°$ is positive or negative? What is the value of K when $E° = 0$ V?
• *Application*

3. During chemistry class, a teacher wrote acetone and chloroform as azeotropic mixture on the board. The students were asked to find out the type of azeotropic mixture and type of deviation shown by them. Anjali, a student wrote the answer minimum boiling azeotropes and positive deviation from Raoult's law whereas another student Saif wrote maximum boiling azeotropes and negative deviation from Raoult's law.

Evaluate Anjali's and Saif's responses.
• *Evaluate* [2]

4. Identify the reaction and write the IUPAC name of the product formed. [2]
• *Recall*

(i) $CH_3CH_2—COOH \xrightarrow{Br_2/\text{Red } P_4}$

(ii) 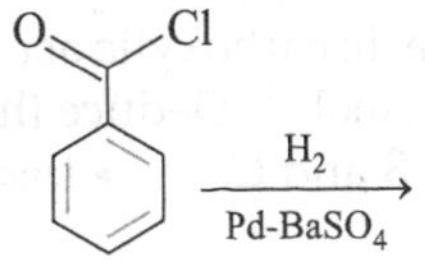

5. State reasons for the following. [2]

(i) *n*-butyl bromide has higher boiling point than *t*-butyl bromide.

(ii) Racemic mixture is optically inactive.
• *Understanding*

6. Compare the chemistry of actinoids with that of the lanthanoids with reference to

(i) electronic configuration

(ii) oxidation state [2]
• *Recall*

7. Give one chemical test for each to distinguish between the following pair of compounds. [2]

(i) Acetaldehyde and benzaldehyde

(ii) Acetaldehyde and acetone
• *Understanding*

8. Give balanced chemical equation to convert the following. [2]

(i) Salicylaldehyde from phenol

(ii) Propan-1-ol from propene
• *Understanding*

Or

When ethene reacts with HBr, a compound (X) is formed. When compound (X) reacts with sodium ethoxide, compounds Y and Z are formed. Y on reaction with excess of hydrogen halides under drastic conditions forms an alcohol (A). Identify the compound X, Y, Z and A. [2]
• *Understanding*

9. The rate of a particular reaction doubles, when temperature changes from 27°C to 37°C. [2]

Calculate the energy of activation of such a reaction.
• *Application*

10. Write the chemical equations for the following reactions:

(i) Oxidation of nitrite ion by MnO_4^- in acidic medium.

(ii) Acidification of potassium chromate solution. [2]
• *Analysis*

11. (i) Give a reason to explain why transition metal ions possess a great tendency to form complexes? [2]
• *Understanding*

(ii) The paramagnetic character in 3*d*-transition series elements increases upto Mn and then decreases. Why?
• *Understanding*

Section C **[21 Marks]**

12. In a reaction between A and B, the initial rate of reaction (r_0) was measured for different initial concentrations of A and B as given below.

A/ mol L^{-1}	0.20	0.20	0.40
B/mol L^{-1}	0.30	0.10	0.05
r_0/ mol L^{-1} s^{-1}	5.07×10^{-5}	5.07×10^{-5}	1.43×10^{-4}

(i) What is the order of the reaction with respect to A and B? • *Application* [3]

(ii) Calculate the rate constant • *Application*

(iii) Determine the reaction rate when the concentration of A and B are 0.30 mol/L and 0.45 mol/L • *Evaluate*

13. At 25°C, the vapour pressures of benzene (C_6H_6) and toluene (C_7H_8) are 93.4 torr and 26.9 torr, respectively. A solution is made by mixing 35.0 g of benzene and 65.0 g of toluene. [3]

(i) Calculate mole fraction of benzene and toluene. • *Application*

(ii) At what applied pressure in torr, will this solution boil at 25°C? • *Application*

14. Write chemical equations to illustrate the following name reactions: [3]

(i) Clemmensen reduction
(ii) Cannizzaro reaction
(iii) Stephen reaction • *Recall*

SP-04

15. (i) A child is suffering from bleeding gums. Doctor advised him to intake amla, lemon, oranges and green leafy vegetables. By deficiency of which vitamin does the child is suffering? [3] • *Analysis*

(ii) How are carbohydrates stored in animal's body? Mention any one organ where they are present. • *Recall*

(iii) What is the basic structural difference between starch and cellulose? • *Recall*

16. Explain the following behaviours. [3]

(i) Alcohols are more soluble in water than the hydrocarbons of comparable molecular masses.

(ii) *Ortho*-nitrophenol is more acidic than *ortho*-methoxyphenol.

(iii) Cumene is a better starting material for the preparation of phenol.

• *Understanding*

17. Write structures of compounds A, B and C in each of the following reactions: [3]

(i) $C_6H_5Br \xrightarrow{\text{Mg/dry ether}} [A] \xrightarrow[(b)\ H_3O^+]{(a)\ CO_2(g)} [B] \xrightarrow{PCl_5} [C]$

(ii) $CH_3CN \xrightarrow[(b)\ H_3O^+]{(a)\ SnCl_2/HCl} [A] \xrightarrow{\text{Dil.NaOH}} [B] \xrightarrow{\Delta} [C]$

• *Undserstanding*

Or A compound $A(C_2H_6O)$ on oxidation by PCC gave B, which on treatment with aqueous alkali and subsequent heating furnished C. B on oxidation by $KMnO_4$, forms a monobasic carboxylic acid with molar mass 60 g mol^{-1}. Deduce the structures of A, B and C. • *Understanding*

18. Complete the following reactions. [3]

(i) $CH_3CH_2—Br$ - - - Ag + $CH_3CH_2—Br$ - - - Ag $>O \longrightarrow A$

(ii) $CH_3—O—CH_2Cl + CH_3MgI \xrightarrow{\text{Dry ether}} B$

(iii) 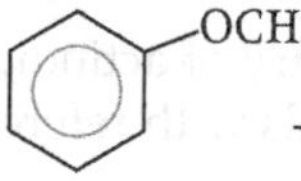 $\xrightarrow{CH_3COCl/\text{Anhyd. }AlCl_3}$

• *Understanding*

Section D **[15 Marks]**

19. (i) An organic aromatic compound 'A' with the molecular formula C_6H_7N is sparingly soluble in water. 'A' on treatment with dil. HCl gives a water soluble compound 'B'. 'A' also reacts with chloroform in presence of alcoholic KOH to form an obnoxious smelling compound 'C'. 'A' reacts with $NaNO_2$ and benzene sulphonyl chloride to form an alkali soluble compound 'D'. 'A' reacts with $NaNO_2$ and HCl to form a compound 'E'

which on reaction with phenol forms an orange red dye 'F'. Elucidate the structures of the organic compounds from 'A' to 'F'. • *Understanding* [5]

(ii) How will you bring about the following conversions?

(a) Methylamine into iodomethane.

(b) Chlorobenzene into *p*-chloroaniline. • *Understanding*

20. (i) The following figure, represents variation of (Λ_m) *vs* $\sqrt{C}$ for an electrolyte. Here, Λ_m is the molar conductivity and *C* is the concentration of the electrolyte. [5]

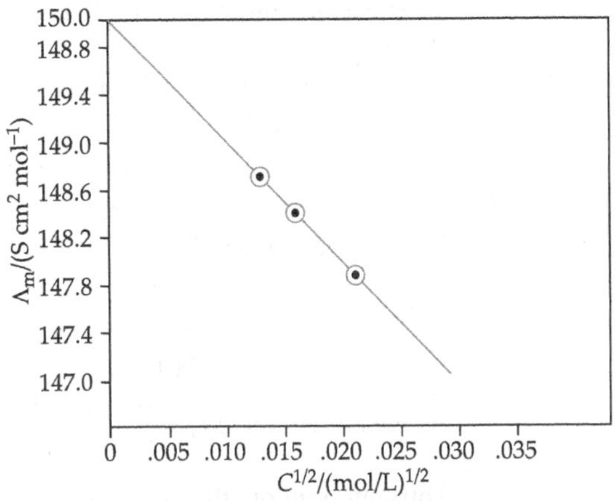

(a) Identify the nature of electrolyte on the basis of the above plot. Justify your answer. • *Recall*

(b) Determine the value of Λ_m° for the electrolyte. • *Application*

(c) Show how to calculate the value of *A* for the electrolyte using the above graph. • *Understanding*

(ii) What is the amount of charge required to carry out the conversion of 1 mole of Al^{3+} ions to Al according to the following reaction ?

$Al^{3+} + 3e^- \longrightarrow Al$ • *Application*

Or

(i) At 25°C, the specific conductance of a saturated solution of AgCl is $3.41 \times 10^{-6} \Omega^{-1} cm^{-1}$ and that of water is $1.61 \times 10^{-6} \Omega^{-1} cm^{-1}$.

The molar conductance at infinite dilution for Ag^+ and Cl^- ions are $61.92 \Omega^{-1} cm^2 mol^{-1}$ and $76.34 \Omega^{-1} cm^2 mol^{-1}$ respectively.

Calculate the solubility of AgCl in gram litre at the given temperature. [5]

$AgCl \rightleftharpoons Ag^+ + Cl^-$ • *Application*

(ii) How is metallic conduction differ from electrolytic conduction? • *Recall*

21. For understanding the structure and bonding in transition metal complexes, the magnetic properties are very helpful. Larger the number of unpaired electrons, stronger will be the paramagnetism. However, magnetic behaviour of a complex can be confirmed from magnetic moment measurement. A metal complex having composition $Cr(NH_3)_4Cl_2Br$ has been isolated in two forms *A* and *B*. The form *A* reacts with $AgNO_3$ to give a white precipitate readily soluble in dilute aqueous ammonia whereas *B* gives a pale yellow precipitate soluble in concentrated ammonia. [5]

(i) Write the formulae of isomers *A* and *B*. • *Understanding*

(ii) State the hybridisation of chromium in each of them. • *Understanding*

(iii) State the magnetic behaviour of each isomers *A* and *B*. • *Understanding*

(iv) Calculate the magnetic moment (spin only value) of the isomer *A*. • *Application*

(v) How coordination compounds are helpful to determine hardness of water. • *Application*

Solutions *in Topper's Style*

My Commitment *I affirm that I am reviewing these solutions only after I have solved the Sample Question Paper on my own. My purpose of looking the solutions is solely to verify whether my answers/solutions were correct or not and to identify my mistakes in case my solutions were wrong or I could not solve that.*

1. (A) (i) octahedral, square planar

(ii) HCl, anhydrous $ZnCl_2$

(iii) Butanedioic acid, 2

(iv) $\frac{7}{3}, \frac{2}{3}$

(B) (i) (a) Among the given elements, only La belongs to 3rd series, Zn belongs to 1st series, Rh and Zr belongs to 2nd series of transition metals.

(ii) (b) For a non-spontaneous reaction, the standard change in Gibbs free energy, ΔG° and the standard cell potential, E°_{cell} will be positive and negative respectively.

(iii) (b) Hinsberg reagent forms an alkali soluble product with 1° amine, alkali insoluble product with 2° amine and do not react with 3° amine.

Hence, $(CH_3)_3N$ is a correct choice.

(iv) (a) $[Cr(H_2O)_5Br]SO_4$ gives a white ppt. of $BaSO_4$ when reacted with $BaCl_2$ solution as it gives SO_4^{2-} ions in the solution.

(v) (a) Only statements (I) and (IV) are incorrect. Their correct forms are as follows:

- C—OH bond angle in methanol is less than tetrahedral angle due to the repulsion between the unshared electron pairs of oxygen.
- Total number of σ bond in methanol are five. The structure is as follows

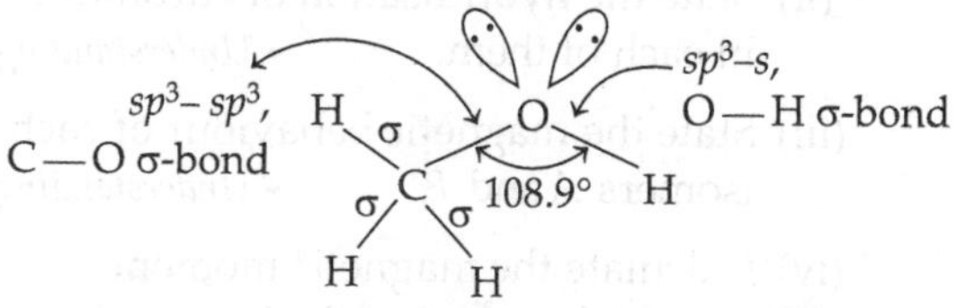

(vi) (a) $t_{1/2}$ of zero order reacion is $t_{1/2} = \frac{[R]_0}{2k}$ and therefore, $t_{1/2}$ of zero order reaction depends on concentration of reactant.

Thus, both Assertion and Reason are true and Reason is the correct explanation of Assertion.

(vii) (d) KCN reacts with methyl chloride to give methyl cyanide as KCN is ionic in nature. Moreover, CN^- is an ambident nucleophile. Thus, both (A) and (R) are false.

$$\underset{\text{Methyl chloride}}{CH_3—Cl} + KCN \longrightarrow \underset{\text{Methyl cyanide}}{CH_3CN} + KCl$$

(C) (i) When a non-volatile solute is dissolved in a solvent, the number of solvent molecules near the surface decreases. As some of the surface is now occupied by solute particles hence, the vapour pressure of the solvent decreases.

(ii) Depression in freezing point is a colligative property (depends only upon the number of solute particles). Thus, the compound which produce maximum ions has the least freezing point.

$$\text{Sucrose} \longrightarrow \text{No ions}$$
$$NaCl \longrightarrow Na^+ + Cl^-$$

Hence, NaCl has least freezing point.

(iii) Given, Volume of ethylene glycol = 50 cm^3

Mass of water $(w_1) = 50$ g

$$T_f = -34\,°C$$
$$\therefore \quad \Delta T_f = 0°C - (-34°C) = 34°C$$

As we know that, $\Delta T_f = \frac{K_f \times w_2 \times 1000}{W_1 \times M_2}$

Thus, amount of ethylene glycol (w_2)

$$= \frac{M_2 \times \Delta T_f \times W_1}{K_f \times 1000} = \frac{62 \times 34 \times 50}{186 \times 1000} = 56.67\text{ g}$$

(as, molar mass ethylene glycol is 62 g mol^{-1})

$$\because \text{Density, } d = \frac{\text{Mass of solute}}{\text{Volume}} = \frac{56.67}{50} = 1.13\text{ g/cm}^3$$

2. (i) Given, Molarity $(M) = 0.20$ M

Conductivity $(\kappa) = 0.0248$ S cm^{-1}

Molar conductivity (M)

$$\lambda_m = \frac{\kappa \times 1000}{\text{Molarity}} = \frac{0.0248 \times 1000}{0.20\text{ mol cm}^{-3}} = 124\text{ S cm}^2/\text{mol}$$

(ii) $E^\circ = \frac{0.0591}{n} \log K$

If $K < 1$ (say 0.01), then

$$E^\circ = \frac{0.0591}{n} \log 0.01 = \frac{-2 \times 0.0591}{n}$$

Thus, E° is negative. If $E^\circ = 0$ V, then $k = 1$

3. The mixture of acetone and chloroform is an example of maximum boiling azeotropes.

The mixture shows negative deviation from Raoult's law because of increase in intermolecular forces of attraction between acetone and chloroform.

Thus, Saif's responses were correct.

4. (i) $CH_3—CH_2—COOH \xrightarrow{\text{(a) } Br_2 / \text{Red } P_4} \underset{\alpha\text{-bromopropanoic acid}}{CH_3—\underset{\underset{Br}{|}}{C}H—COOH}$

This reaction is known as **Hell-Volhard-Zelinsky reaction**.

(ii) 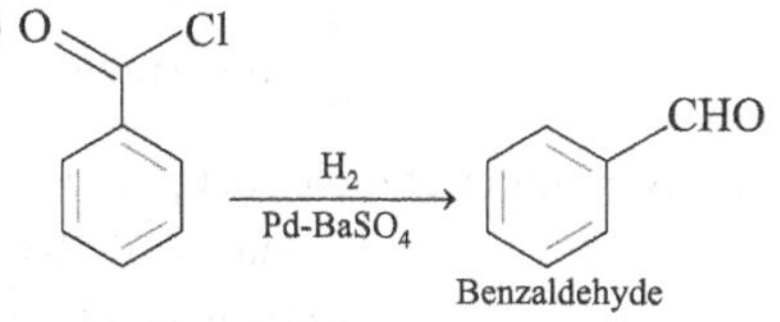

This reaction is known as **Rosenmund reduction reaction.**

5. (i) For isomeric alkyl halides, the boiling points decreases as the branching increases. This is because with increase in branching, the surface area of the alkyl halide decreases and hence, the magnitude of van der Waals' forces of attraction decreases.

Therefore, *n*-butyl bromide ($CH_3CH_2CH_2CH_2Br$) has higher boiling point than *tert*-butyl bromide ($(CH_3)_3CBr$).

(ii) Racemic mixture contains two enantiomers, i.e. *d* and *l*- forms in equal proportions and possesses zero optical rotation as the rotation of plane polarised light due to one isomer will be cancelled by the rotation due to the other isomer. Thus, the mixture will be optically inactive.

6. (i) **Electronic configuration** The general electronic configuration of actinoids is $5f^{1-14}, 6d^{0-1}, 7s^2$ whereas the general electronic configuration of lanthanoids is

$$4f^{1-14}, 5d^{0-1}, 6s^2$$

(ii) **Oxidation states** Lanthanoids mainly show + 3 oxidation state and + 2 and + 4 oxidation states also exist. On the other hand, in addition to + 3 oxidation state, actinoids also show higher oxidation states like. + 4, + 5, + 6 and + 7.

7. (i) **Acetaldehyde and benzaldehyde** Acetaldehyde acts as reducing agent which reduces Fehling's solution. It gets oxidised to carboxylate ion and reduce Cu^{2+} to cuprous oxide.

$$\underset{\text{Acetaldehyde}}{CH_3—\overset{}{\underset{\underset{O}{||}}{C}}—H} + 2Cu^{2+} + 5OH^- \xrightarrow{\Delta} \left[\underset{\text{Carboxylate ion}}{CH_3—\overset{\overset{O}{||}}{C}—O^-}\right] + Cu_2O\downarrow + 3H_2O$$

Benzaldehyde is not oxidised by Fehling's solution.

(ii) **Acetaldehyde and acetone** Acetaldehyde gives a silver mirror test when heated with Tollen's reagent.

$$\underset{\text{Acetaldehyde}}{CH_3CHO} + \underset{\text{Tollen's reagent}}{2[Ag(NH_3)_2]^+} + 3OH^- \longrightarrow CH_3COOH + \underset{\text{Silver mirror}}{2Ag\downarrow} + 4NH_3 + 2H_2O$$

Acetone does not give this test because it lacks reducible hydrogen (directly bonded to carbonyl group).

8. (i) 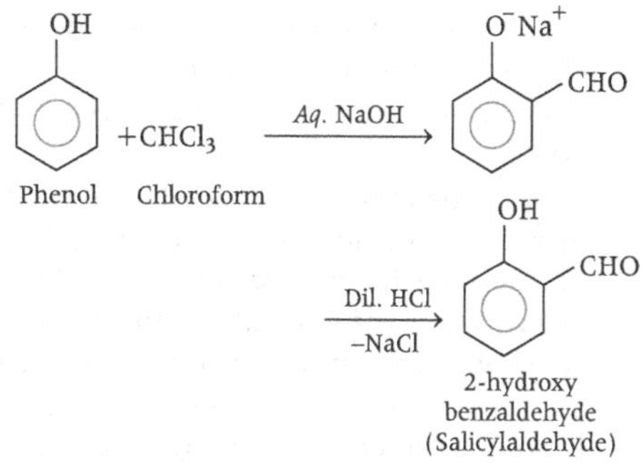

(ii) $3\underset{\text{Propene}}{CH_3—CH{=}CH_2} + \underset{\text{Diborane}}{3(H—BH_2)_2} \xrightarrow[3H_2O_2,\ OH^-]{H_2O} \underset{\text{Propan-1-ol}}{3CH_3—CH_2—CH_2OH} + B(OH)_3$

Or When ethene reacts with hydrogen bromide (HBr) it forms bromoethane (X) which on reaction with sodium ethoxide forms ethoxyethane (Y) and sodium bromide (Z).

Ethoxyethane (Y) on reaction with HX under drastic condition forms an alcohol, i.e. ethyl alcohol (A).

The reactions involved are as follows:

$$CH_2{=}CH_2 + HBr \longrightarrow \underset{(X)}{CH_3—CH_2—Br} \xrightarrow{C_2H_5O^-Na^+} \underset{(Y)}{C_2H_5OC_2H_5} + \underset{(Z)}{NaBr}$$

$$\underset{(Y)}{C_2H_5OC_2H_5} + HX \xrightarrow{373\text{ K}} \underset{(A)}{C_2H_5OH} + C_2H_5X$$

9. Given, $T_1 = 27°C = (27 + 273) K = 300 K$,

If $k_1 = k$, then at $T_2 = 37°C$
$= (37 + 273) K = 310 K$, $k_2 = 2k$

According to Arrhenius equation,

$$\log \frac{k_2}{k_1} = \frac{E_a}{2.303R}\left(\frac{T_2 - T_1}{T_1 T_2}\right) \quad \ldots(i)$$

On putting values in Eq. (i), we get,

$$\log \frac{2k}{k} = \frac{E_a}{2.303 \times 8.314 \text{ JK}^{-1}\text{ mol}^{-1}} \times \frac{(310 - 300) \text{ K}}{(300 \times 310) \text{ K}}$$

$$\log 2 = \frac{E_a}{2.303 \times 8.314} \times \frac{10}{300 \times 310} (\text{J mol}^{-1})$$

$\therefore \quad E_a = 53598.59 \text{ J mol}^{-1} = 53.6 \text{ kJ mol}^{-1}$

10. (i) **Oxidation of nitrite ion by MnO_4^- in acidic medium**

$$2MnO_4^- + 5NO_2^- + 6H^+ \longrightarrow 2Mn^{2+} + 5NO_3^- + 3H_2O$$

(ii) **Acidification of potassium chromate solution**

$$2K_2CrO_4 + 2H^+ \longrightarrow K_2Cr_2O_7 + 2K^+ + H_2O$$

or $2CrO_4^{2-} + 2H^+ \longrightarrow Cr_2O_7^{2-} + H_2O$

11. (i) Due to small size and high effective nuclear charge of transition metal atoms or their cations, they have a high positive charge density on them. This high positive charge density makes the atoms or cation to attract the lone pair of electrons from the ligand, in their vacant *d*-orbital and thus can form $L \rightarrow M$ coordinate bonds.

(ii) Paramagnetic character increases with the increase in the number of unpaired electrons. The larger is the number of unpaired electrons of central atom or ion greater is the paramagnetic character. Since, number of unpaired electrons increases from Sc to Mn and then decreases from Fe to Zn. Therefore, paramagnetic character also increases from Sc to Mn and then decreases from Fe to Zn.

12. Rate law states that rate $= k[A]^x[B]^y$

$$(\text{Rate})_1 = k[0.20]^x[0.30]^y = 5.07 \times 10^{-5} \quad \ldots(\text{i})$$

$$(\text{Rate})_2 = k[0.20]^x[0.10]^y = 5.07 \times 10^{-5} \quad \ldots(\text{ii})$$

$$(\text{Rate})_3 = k[0.40]^x[0.05]^y = 1.43 \times 10^{-4} \quad \ldots(\text{iii})$$

On dividing Eq. (i) by Eq. (ii), we get

$$\frac{(\text{Rate})_1}{(\text{Rate})_2} = \frac{k[0.20]^x[0.30]^y}{k[0.20]^x[0.10]^y} = \frac{5.07 \times 10^{-5}}{5.07 \times 10^{-5}}$$

$$[3]^y = 1$$

or, $[3]^y = [3]^0$

$\therefore \quad y = 0$

Now, on dividing Eq. (iii) by Eq. (ii), we get

$$\frac{(\text{Rate})_3}{(\text{Rate})_2} = \frac{k(0.40)^x(0.05)^0}{k(0.20)^x(0.10)^0} = \frac{1.43 \times 10^{-4}}{5.07 \times 10^{-5}}$$

$$2.8205 = 2^x\left(\frac{1}{2}\right)^0 = 2^x$$

On taking log on both sides, we get

$$\log 2.8205 = x \log 2$$

$$x = \frac{0.4503}{0.3010} = 1.496 \approx 1.5$$

(i) Thus, order of the reaction with respect to *A* and *B* are 1.5 and 0, respectively.

(ii) Rate law equation is $R = k[A]^{1.5}[B]^0$

Thus, $k = \dfrac{5.07 \times 10^{-5}}{(0.20)^{1.5}}$ mol/L/s

$$= 5.7 \times 10^{-4}\ \text{mol}^{-1/2}\text{L}^{1/2}\text{s}^{-1}$$

(iii) Since, $R = k[A]^{1.5}$

$\therefore \quad R = [5.7 \times 10^{-4}(0.30)^{1.5}]$ mol/L/s

$$= 0.937 \times 10^{-4}\ \text{mol/L/s}$$

13. (i) Partial vapour pressure of C_6H_6, $p^\circ_{C_6H_6} = 93.4$ torr

Partial vapour pressure of $C_6H_5CH_3$, $p^\circ_{C_6H_5CH_3} = 26.9$ torr

Given, mass of $C_6H_6 = 35$ g and mass of $C_6H_5CH_3 = 65$ g

Therefore, number of moles of C_6H_6

$$= \frac{\text{Mass of } C_6H_6}{\text{Molar mass of } C_6H_6}$$

Molar mass of $C_6H_6 = 12 \times 6 + 1 \times 6$

$$= 72 + 6 = 78\ \text{g mol}^{-1}$$

Thus, the number of moles of C_6H_6

$$= \frac{35}{78} = 0.449 \text{ moles}$$

Similarly, number of moles of $C_6H_5CH_3$

$$= \frac{\text{Mass of } C_6H_5CH_3}{\text{Molar mass of } C_6H_5CH_3}$$

Molar mass of $C_6H_5CH_3$

$$= 12 \times 6 + 1 \times 5 + 12 + 1 \times 3$$

$$= 92\ \text{g mol}^{-1}$$

Therefore, the number of moles of $C_6H_5CH_3$ is

$$n_{C_6H_5CH_3} = \frac{65}{92} = 0.707$$

Now, the mole fractions of C_6H_6 and $C_6H_5CH_3$ are

$$\chi_{C_6H_6} = \frac{n_{C_6H_6}}{n_{C_6H_6} + n_{C_6H_5CH_3}} = \frac{0.449}{0.449 + 0.707}$$

$$= \frac{0.449}{1.156} = 0.388$$

$$\chi_{C_6H_5CH_3} = \frac{n_{C_6H_5CH_3}}{n_{C_6H_5CH_3} + n_{C_6H_6}}$$

$$= \frac{0.707}{0.707 + 0.449}$$

$$= \frac{0.707}{1.156} = 0.612$$

(ii) $p_{C_6H_6} = p^\circ_{C_6H_6} \times \chi_{C_6H_6}$

$$= 93.4 \times 0.388 = 36.24 \text{ torr}$$

$$p_{C_6H_5CH_3} = p^\circ_{C_6H_5CH_3} \times \chi_{C_6H_5CH_3}$$

$$= 26.9 \times 0.612 = 16.46 \text{ torr}$$

Total vapour pressure of the solution is

$$p_{\text{total}} = p_{C_6H_6} + p_{C_6H_5CH_3}$$

$$= 36.24 + 16.46 = 52.7 \text{ torr}$$

14. (i) **Clemmensen reduction**

$$(CH_3)_2C{=}O + 4[H] \xrightarrow{\text{Zn—Hg/Conc. HCl}} CH_3CH_2CH_3 + H_2O$$

Acetone → Propane

It involves the reduction of carbonyl group ($>$C=O) to $>CH_2$ group and it is carried out in the presence of Zn amalgam and conc. HCl.

(ii) **Cannizzaro reaction**

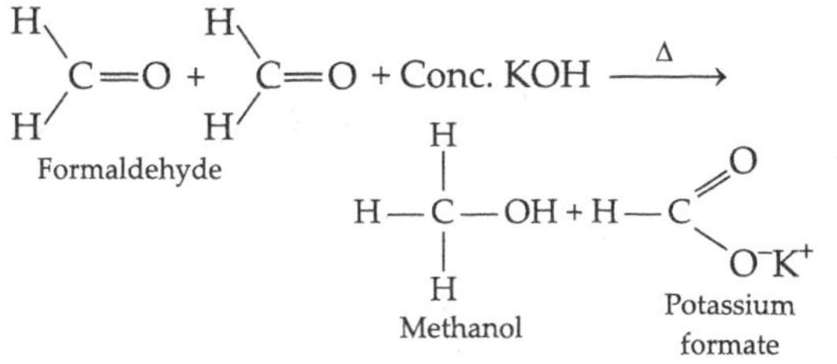

Aldehydes which do not have α—H atom undergo self oxidation and reduction reaction on heating with conc. alkali.

(iii) **Stephen reaction** Nitriles are reduced to corresponding imine with stannous chloride in the presence of hydrochloric acid, which on hydrolysis give corresponding aldehyde.

$$RCN + SnCl_2 + HCl \longrightarrow RCH{=}NH \xrightarrow{H_3O^+} RCHO$$

15. (i) The child is suffering from deficiency of vitamin C (ascorbic acid).

(ii) Carbohydrates are stored in animal's body in the form of glycogen. It is stored in liver.

(iii) The main structural difference between starch and cellulose is that the glucose units in the starch are connected by α-linkage and the glucose units in cellulose are connected by β-linkages.

16. (i) Alcohols can form H-bonds with water. Therefore, they are water soluble.

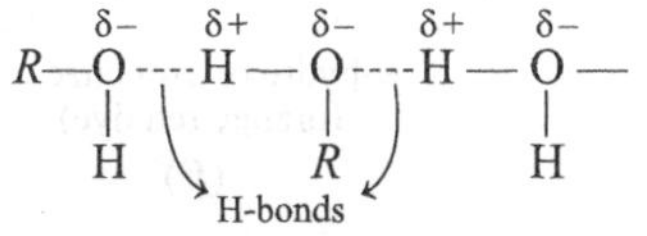

On contrary, hydrocarbons cannot form H-bonds with water and thus are insoluble in water.

(ii) Due to strong $-R$ and $-I$-effect of the $—NO_2$ group, electron density at the O—H bond decreases and hence, the loss of a proton becomes easy.

Now, after the loss of a proton, the *o*-nitrophenoxide ion left behind is stabilised by resonance and thus making *o*-nitrophenol a stronger acid.

In contrast, due to + *R*-effect, — OCH_3 group increases the electron density between the O—H bond. Thereby, making the loss of proton difficult.

Resonating structures of *o*-nitrophenoxide ion and *o*-methoxyphenol is as follows

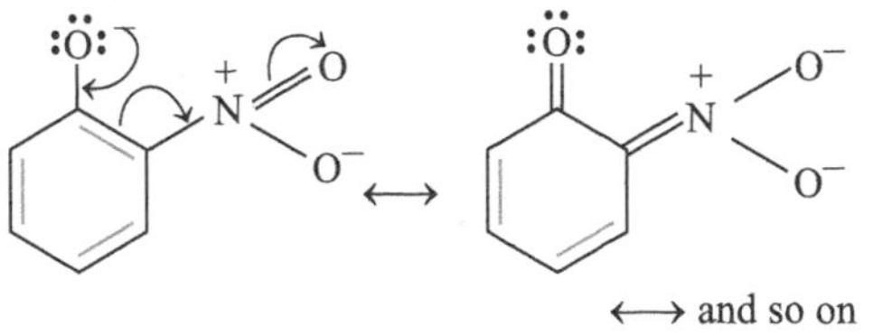

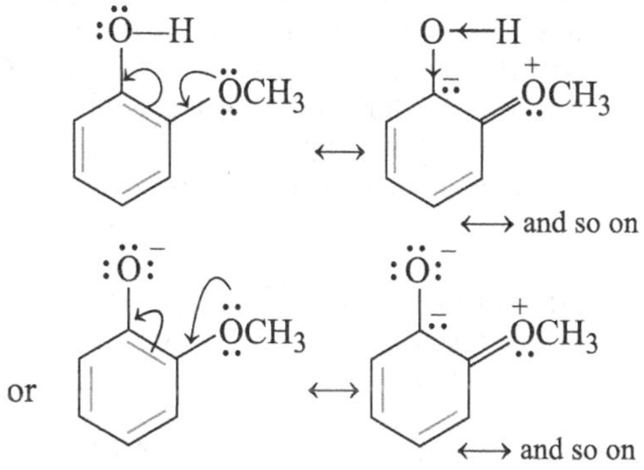

Therefore, *o*-nitrophenol is more acidic than *o*-methoxyphenol.

(iii) Cumene (*iso*-propylbenzene) upon aerial oxidation, form cumene hydroperoxide which upon subsequent hydrolysis with dilute acid gives phenol and propanone (acetone).

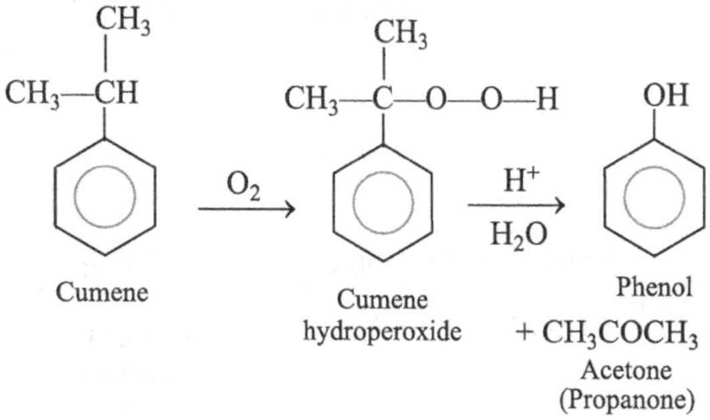

Since, the side product formed in the above reaction is acetone which is another important organic compound, hence cumene is better starting material for the preparation of phenol.

17. (i)

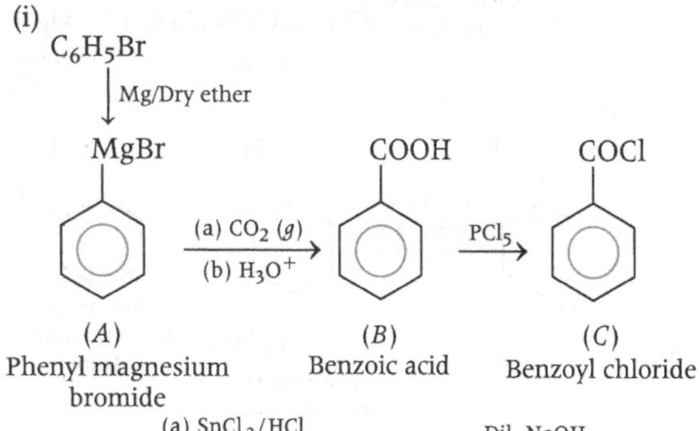

(ii) $CH_3CN \xrightarrow[(b)\ H_3O^+]{(a)\ SnCl_2/HCl} CH_3CHO$ (*A*) Acetaldehyde $\xrightarrow{\text{Dil. NaOH}}$

$CH_3—CH(OH)—CH_2—CHO$ 3-hydroxy butanal (*B*) $\xrightarrow{\Delta}$ $CH_3—CH{=}CH—CHO$ But-2-enal (*C*)

Or

Monobasic carboxylic acid = *R*COOH. Given that, molar mass of *R*COOH = 60 g mol^{-1}

i.e. $x + 12 + 16 + 16 + 1 = 60$; $x = 15$

Thus, $R = — CH_3$ (molar mass 15) and the acid is CH_3COOH.

Since, the acid is obtained by the oxidation of aldehyde, so *B* is an aldehyde, i.e. CH_3CHO and *A* is CH_3CH_2OH as it gives *B* on oxidation by PCC. *C* is an alkene as it is formed by subsequent heating of aldehyde (*B*) with aqueous alkali.

Thus, the involved reactions are as follows

$$\underset{\text{(Ethanol) } (A)}{CH_3-CH_2-OH} \xrightarrow{PCC} \underset{\text{(Ethanal) } (B)}{CH_3-\overset{O}{\overset{\|}{C}}-H} \xrightarrow{KMnO_4} \underset{\text{(Ethanoic acid) (Molecular weight } = 60\text{ g mol}^{-1})}{CH_3-\overset{O}{\overset{\|}{C}}-OH}$$

$$\underset{(B)}{2CH_3-\overset{O}{\overset{\|}{C}}-H} \xrightarrow[\text{Aldol condensation}]{OH^-} \underset{\text{3-hydroxybutanal}}{CH_3-\overset{OH}{\overset{|}{CH}}-CH_2-\overset{O}{\overset{\|}{C}}-H} \xrightarrow[-H_2O]{\text{Heat}} \underset{\text{But-2-enal } (C)}{CH_3-CH=CH-\overset{O}{\overset{\|}{C}}-H}$$

18. (i)

$$\begin{matrix} CH_3CH_2-Br\cdots Ag \\ + \\ CH_3CH_2-Br\cdots Ag \end{matrix} \rangle O \longrightarrow \underset{\text{Diethyl ether } (A)}{\begin{matrix} CH_3CH_2 \\ CH_3CH_2 \end{matrix} \rangle O} + \underset{\text{Silver bromide}}{2AgBr}$$

(ii) $\underset{\text{Chloromethoxy methane}}{CH_3-O-CH_2Cl} + CH_3MgI \xrightarrow{\text{Dry ether}} \underset{\text{Ethyl methyl ether}}{CH_3-OCH_2CH_3} + \underset{\text{Chloromagnesium iodide}}{Mg(Cl)I}$

(iii)

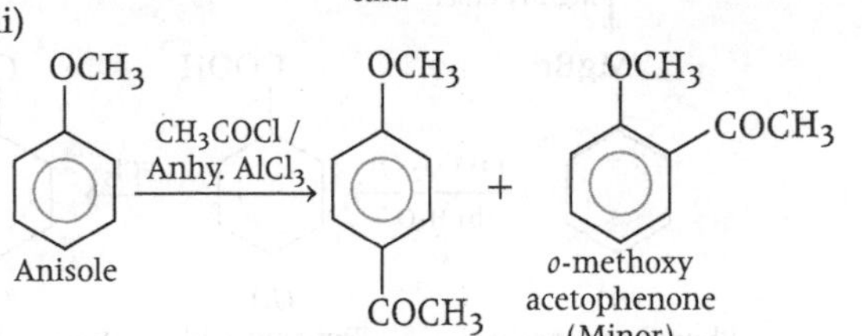

Anisole; *p*-methoxy acetophenone (Major); *o*-methoxy acetophenone (Minor)

19. (i)

(a)

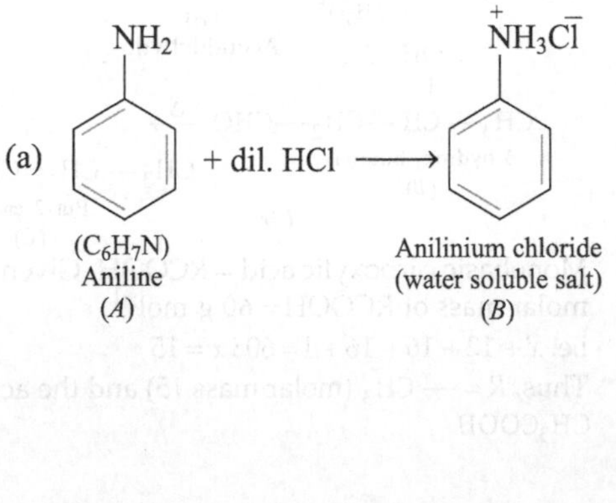

(C_6H_7N) Aniline (*A*); Anilinium chloride (water soluble salt) (*B*)

(b)

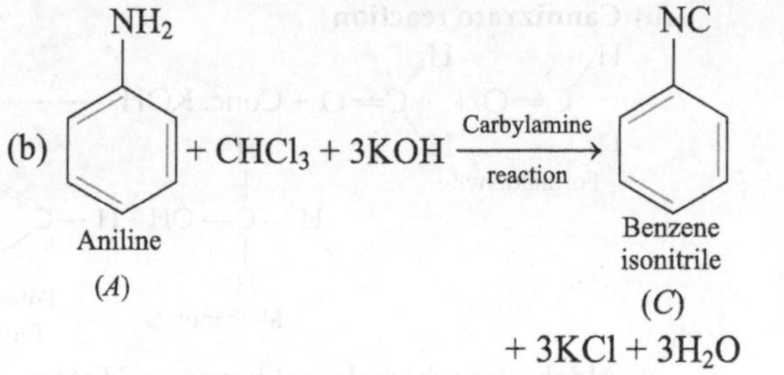

Aniline (*A*); Benzene isonitrile (*C*)

(c)

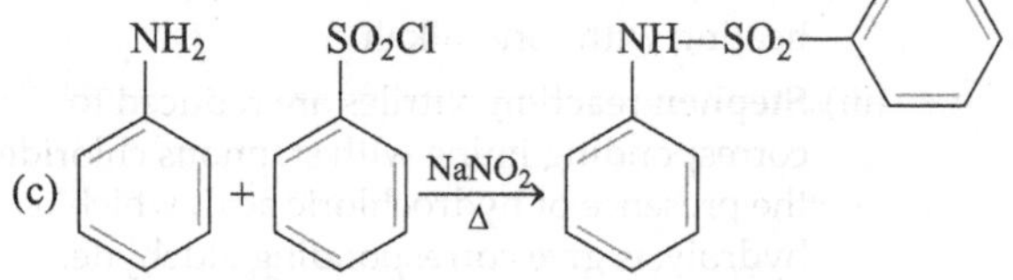

Aniline (*A*); Benzene sulphonyl chloride; N-phenylbenzene sulphonamide (soluble in alkali) (*D*)

(d)

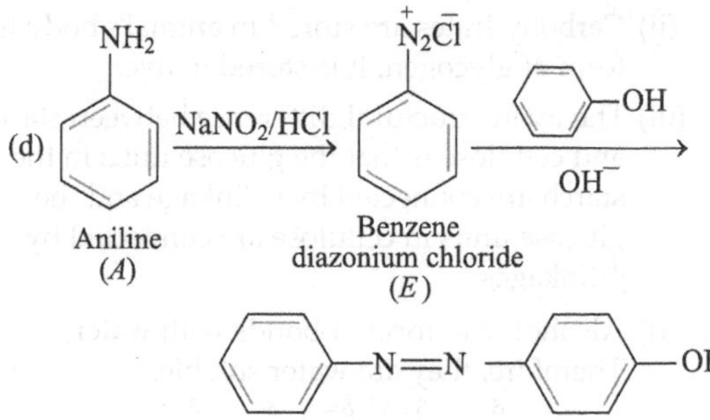

Aniline (*A*); Benzene diazonium chloride (*E*); *p*-hydroxy azobenzene (orange red dye) (*F*)

(ii) (a) **Methylamine into iodomethane**

$$\underset{\text{Methylamine}}{CH_3NH_2} + HNO_2 \xrightarrow{H_2O/H^+} CH_3OH \xrightarrow{P/I_2} \underset{\text{Iodomethane}}{CH_3I}$$

(b) **Chlorobenzene into *p*-chloroaniline**

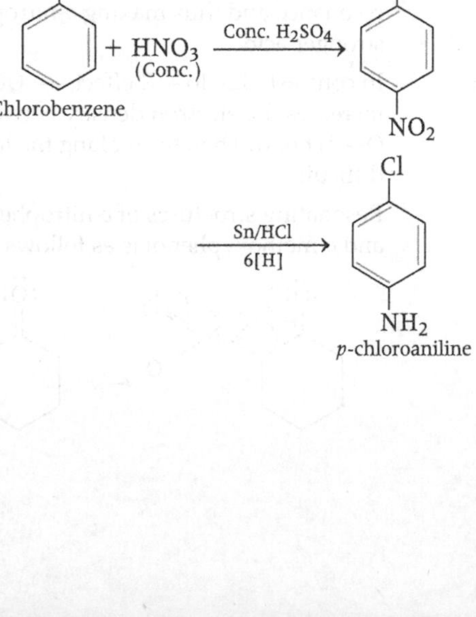

Chlorobenzene; *p*-chloroaniline

20. (i) (a) The nature the electrolyte on the basis of plot is strong electrolyte. For strong electrolyte, Λ°_m increases slowly with dilution.

(b) Using Debye-Huckel Onsager equation,

$$\Lambda_m = \Lambda^\circ_m - A\sqrt{C}$$

Λ°_m value from graph is 150 $S\,cm^2 mol^{-1}$.

(c)

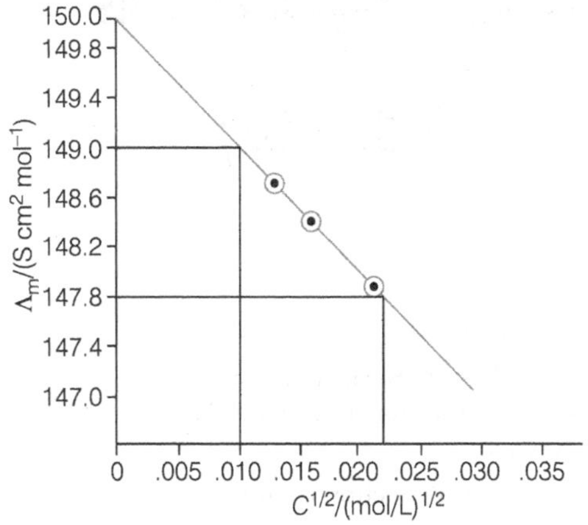

$$A = -\text{slope} = \left(\frac{y_2 - y_1}{x_2 - x_1}\right) = -\frac{(149 - 147.8)}{(0.010 - 0.022)}$$

$$= 100\ S\,cm^2 mol^{-1} / (mol / L^{-1})^{1/2}$$

(ii) The number of electrons involved in the reaction is three. Therefore, the amount of electricity required for one mole of Al^{3+} ions = 3F or $3 \times 96500\ C = 289500\ C$

Or

(i) Given, $\Lambda^\infty_{Ag^+} = 61.92\Omega^{-1}cm^2mol^{-1}$;

$\Lambda^\infty_{Cl^-} = 76.34\Omega^{-1}cm^2\ mol^{-1}$

Since, AgCl is a sparingly soluble salt, its saturated solution may be regarded as an infinitely dilute solution. Thus,

$$\Lambda^{salt}_m = \Lambda^\infty_{Ag^+} + \Lambda^\infty_{Cl^-}$$

$$\Lambda^{salt}_m = 61.92 + 76.34 = 138.26\Omega^{-1}cm^2\ mol^{-1}$$

Moreover, $\kappa_{salt} = \kappa_{solution} - \kappa_{water}$

$$= (3.41 \times 10^{-6} - 1.61 \times 10^{-6})\Omega^{-1}cm^{-1}$$

$$= 1.80 \times 10^{-6}\ \Omega^{-1}cm^{-1}$$

The molar conductivity is related to specific conductivity as

$$\Lambda^{salt}_m = \frac{\kappa_{salt} \times 1000}{M} \Rightarrow M = \frac{\kappa_{salt} \times 1000}{\Lambda^{salt}_m}$$

$$= \frac{1.8 \times 10^{-6} \times 1000}{138.26} = 1.3 \times 10^{-5}\ mol\ L^{-1}$$

$\therefore$ Solubility of AgCl $= 1.3 \times 10^{-5}\ mol\,L^{-1}$

$= (1.3 \times 10^{-5}) \times 143.5$

[Molar mass of AgCl = 143.5 g/mol]

$= 1.87 \times 10^{-3}\ gL^{-1}$

(ii) **Comparison of Metallic and Electrolytic Conduction**

S.N.	Metallic Conduction	Electrolytic Conduction
1.	Electric current flows due to the movement of electrons.	Electric current flows due to the movement of ions.
2.	No chemical change occurs.	Ions are oxidised or reduced at the electrodes.
3.	It does not involve the transfer of any matter.	It involves transfer of matter in the form of ions.
4.	Resistance increases with increase in temperature.	Resistance decreases with increase in temperature.
5.	Faraday's law is not followed.	Faraday law is followed.

21. 'A' gives white precipitate with $AgNO_3$ which is readily soluble in dilute aqueous ammonia, so in it Cl is present outside the coordination sphere.
'B' gives a pale yellow precipitate soluble in concentrated ammonia, so in it Br is present outside the coordination sphere.

(i) Thus, 'A' – $[Cr(NH_3)_4BrCl]Cl$

'B' – $[Cr(NH_3)_4Cl_2]Br$

(ii) Oxidation state of Cr in both the isomers 'A' and 'B' is 3 and thus, the configuration is $3d^3$. Therefore, the hybridisation of Cr is d^2sp^3.

For complex A and B: | 1 | 1 | 1 | | xx | xx | xx | xx | xx |

d^2sp^3

(iii) Both the isomers are paramagnetic due to presence of 3 unpaired electrons.

(iv) Magnetic moment is given by the formula

$$\mu = \sqrt{n(n+2)}$$

where, n = no. of unpaired electrons.

$\therefore$ Magnetic moment $(\mu) = \sqrt{3(3+2)}$ $[\because n = 3]$

$= \sqrt{15} = 3.87$ BM

(v) The strong field ligand EDTA forms stable complexes with Mg^{2+} and Ca^{2+} ions. Hence, these ions can be removed by adding EDTA to hard water.

Concept Enhancer The reactions involved in above questions are shown below for better understanding.

$[Cr(NH_3)_4ClBr]\,Cl + AgNO_3 \longrightarrow AgCl \downarrow$ (White ppt.) $+ [Cr(NH_3)_4ClBr]^+ + NO_3^-$

$[Cr(NH_3)_4Cl_2]\ Br + AgNO_3 \longrightarrow AgBr \downarrow$ (Pale yellow ppt.) $+ [Cr(NH_3)_4Cl_2]^+ + NO_3^-$

SPQ Code : **PB-05/15** Series ***i*-Succeed 05-25/15** Roll No. | | | | | | | |

Sample Question Paper 05

Chemistry 12th (Code 862)

General Instructions

1. This paper is divided into four sections-A, B, C and D. Answer all questions.
2. **Section A** consists of **one** question **having sub-parts** of **one** mark each. **Section B** consists of **ten** questions of **two** marks each. **Section C** consists of **seven** questions of **three** marks each and **Section D** consists of **three** questions of **five** marks each.
3. Internal choices have been provided in one question each in Section B, Section C and Section D.
4. All working, including rough work, should be done on the same sheet as, and adjacent to the rest of the answer.
5. The intended marks for questions or parts of questions are given in brackets [].
6. Balanced questions must be given, wherever possible and diagrams where they are helpful. When solving numerical problems, all essential working must be shown.
7. In working out problems, use the following data:
Gas constant (R) = 1.987 cal deg^{-1} mol^{-1} = 8.314 JK^{-1} mol^{-1} = 0.0821 dm^3 atm K^{-1} mol^{-1}
1L atm = 1 dm^3 atm =101.3 J, 1 Faraday =96500 Coulombs.
Avogadro's number (N_A) = 6.023 × 10^{23}.

Time : 3 Hrs.

Max. Marks : 70

Section A **[14 Marks]**

1. (A) Fill in the blanks by choosing the appropriate word(s) from those given below in the brackets.
(dihydric, monohydric, K_n, K_p, four times, unity, reactant, product, stepwise stability, overall stability, composition, azeotropic, trihydric.) [4 × 1]

(i) The rate constant of a reaction is equal to the rate of reaction when the concentration of each .... is .... • *Understanding*

(ii) Equilibrium constant for every step is known as .... constant of a complex and is denoted by .... • *Recall*

(iii) The solution of two completely miscible liquids which boils at a constant temperature like a pure liquid and distills over without a change in ...., is called .... mixture. • *Recall*

(iv) Glycol is an example of ...... alcohol and glycerol is an ...... alcohol. • *Understanding*

(B) Select and write the correct alternative from the choices given below. [7 × 1]

(i) IUPAC name of $CH_2{=}CH{-}CH_2{-}Br$ is • *Understanding*

(a) 1-bromo-2-propene (b) 3-bromopropene
(c) 3-bromopropane (d) 1-bromo-2-propane

(ii) Phenol on reacting with concentrated sulphuric acid followed by concentrated nitric acid, gives • *Analysis*

(a) 2,4,6-trinitrophenol (b) *o*-nitrophenol
(c) *p*-nitrophenol (d) nitrobenzene

(iii) Colourless complex ion in the following is • *Understanding*

(a) $[Cu(NH_3)_4]^{2+}$ (b) $[Zn(NH_3)_4]^{2+}$
(c) $[Fe(H_2O)_6]^{3+}$ (d) $[Fe(CN)_6]^{3-}$

(iv) The limiting molar conductivities Λ°_m for NaCl, KBr and KCl are 126, 152 and 150 $S\,cm^2\,mol^{-1}$ respectively. The Λ°_m for NaBr is • *Application*

(a) 128 $S\,cm^2\,mol^{-1}$ (b) 176 $S\,cm^2\,mol^{-1}$
(c) 278 $S\,cm^2\,mol^{-1}$ (d) 302 $S\,cm^2\,mol^{-1}$

(v) Which of the following statements are correct regarding potassium dichromate?

I. The structure of chromate ion is trigonal planar.
II. When potassium dichromate is strongly heated, it decomposes to give oxygen.
III. On acidifying the $K_2Cr_2O_4$ solution, the colour changes to yellow.
IV. $K_2Cr_2O_7$ is determined volumetrically using Fe^{2+} or I^- (iodometrically). • *Understanding*

(a) Only I and II (b) Only II and III
(c) Only II and IV (d) Only I and III

(vi) **Assertion** (A) Galvanised iron does not rust.

Reason (R) Zinc has a more negative electrode potential than iron. • *Analysis*

(a) Both Assertion and Reason are true and Reason is the correct explanation of Assertion.
(b) Both Assertion and Reason are true but Reason is not the correct explanation of Assertion.
(c) Assertion is true but Reason is false.
(d) Both Assertion and Reason are false.

(vii) **Assertion** (A) It is not always convenient to determine the instantaneous rate.

Reason (R) Instantaneous rate is measured by the determination of slope of the tangent at point 't' in concentration *versus* time plot.

• *Understanding and Analysis*

(a) Both Assertion and Reason are true and Reason is the correct explanation of Assertion.
(b) Both Assertion and Reason are true but Reason is not the correct explanation of Assertion.
(c) Assertion is true but Reason is false.
(d) Both Assertion and Reason are false.

(C) Read the passage given below carefully and answer the questions that follow. [3 × 1]

Alcohols and phenols consist of two parts, an alkyl/aryl group and a hydroxyl group. The properties of alcohols and phenols are chiefly due to the hydroxyl group.

Alcohol consumption, particularly heavier drinking is an important risk factor for many health problems and thus, is a major contributor to the global burden of disease. Alcohol or alcoholic bevarages contain ethanol, a psychoactive and toxic substance that can cause dependence. Worldwide, around 2.6 million deaths were caused by alcohol consumption in 2019. Infact, alcohol is a necessary underlying cause for more than 30 conditions and a contributing factor to many more.

The most common disease categories that are entirely or partly caused by alcohol consumption includes infectious diseases cancer, diabetes, neuropsychiatric diseases, cardiovascular disease, liver and pancreatic disease. Phenol is a historical disinfectant with continued use in industrial laboratories, and some health care settings.

Phenol is mildly acidic and requires careful handling due to its propensity to cause chemical burns. It is a protoplasmic poison that can result in multisystem organ failure in severe toxicity. This activity will describe the mechanism of toxicity of phenols, the expected clinical manifestations of phenol toxicity and the management of phenol poisoned patients.

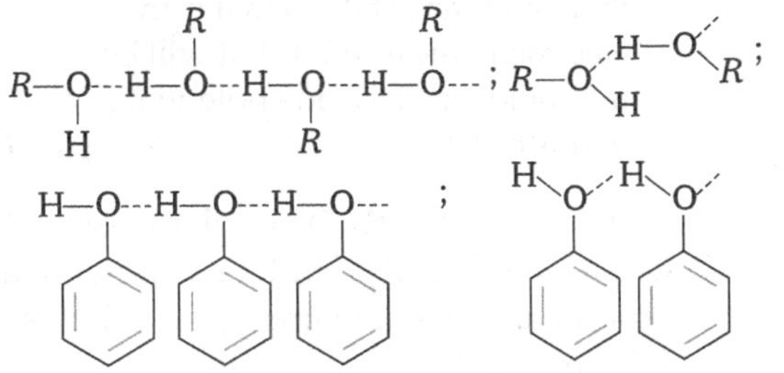

(i) Write the decreasing order of the boiling point of the following alcohols. • *Analysis*
(a) pentan-1-ol
(b) 2-methylbutan-2-ol
(c) 3-methylbutan-2-ol

(ii) Write the increasing order of the basicity of the following compounds.
$H_2O, OH^-, CH_3OH, CH_3O^-$ • *Analysis*

(iii) Which among the following, methanol, butanol-2-ol, butan-1-ol, 2-methyl-propan-2-ol, will have the highest boiling point? • *Understanding*

Section B **[20 Marks]**

2. Give reason for the following. • *Understanding* [2]
(i) Phenol is more acidic than methanol.
(ii) The C—O—H bond angle in alcohols is slightly less than the tetrahedral angle (109°28′).

3. Give reason for the following. • *Understanding* [2]
(i) Among lanthanoids, Ln (III) compounds are predominant. However, occasionally in solution or in solid compounds, +2 and +4 ions are also obtained.
(ii) Mn^{2+} is more stable than Fe^{2+} towards +3 oxidation state.

4. (i) A copper-silver cell is set-up. Given, $E^\circ_{Ag^+/Ag} = 0.80$ V, $E^\circ_{Cu^{2+}/Cu} = +0.34$ V.
Write the chemical reaction taking place [2]
(a) at the electrode that behaves as an anode. • *Recall*
(b) the electrode that behave as a cathode. • *Recall*

(ii) The standard reduction electrode potential of Cu^{2+}/Cu is +0.34 V and that of Cr^{3+}/Cr is −0.74 V. These two electrodes are connected in their standard state to make an electrochemical cell. What will be the standard electrode potential ($E°$) of this cell ? • *Application*

5. 18 g of glucose $C_6H_{12}O_6$ (molar mass = 180 g mol^{-1}) is dissolved in 1 kg of water in a saucepan. At what temperature will this solution boil? [2]
(K_b for water = 0.52 K kg mol^{-1} and boiling point of water = 373.15 K) • *Application*

6. How will the following be obtained? [Give chemical equations] • *Understanding* [2]
(i) Acetone from methyl chloride
(ii) Oxalic acid from formic acid

Or When liquid '*A*' is treated with a freshly prepared ammoniacal silver nitrate solution, it gives bright silver mirror. The liquid forms a white crystalline solid on treatment with sodium hydrogen sulphite. Liquid '*B*' also forms a white crystalline solid with sodium hydrogen sulphite but it does not give test with ammoniacal silver nitrate.
(a) Write the structures of *A* and *B*.
(b) Out of the liquids *A* and *B*, which one is aldehyde. Write the chemical equations of these reactions also. • *Understanding*

7. If the density of some lake water is 1.25 g mL^{-1} and it contains 92 g of Na^+ ions per kg of water. Calculate the molality of Na^+ ions in the lake. • *Evaluate and Application* [2]

8. Give the balanced equations for following reactions. • *Understanding* [2]
(i) How will you convert ethylamine to methylamine?
(ii) Aniline is treated with nitrous acid and HCl at low temperature.

9. During chemistry class, a teacher wrote $[Co(NH_3)_6]^{3+}$ as a coordination complex ion on the board. The students were asked to find out the magnetic behaviour and shape of the complex. Ali, a student, wrote the answer paramagnetic and tetrahedral

SP-05

whereas another student Rani wrote diamagnetic and octahedral.
Evaluate Ali's and Rani's responses. • *Evaluate*

10. Two compounds, (*R*)-2-bromobutane and (*S*)-2-bromobutane, are enantiomers of each other. [2]

Name one physical property that is

(i) same of (*R*)-2-bromobutane and (*S*)-2-bromobutane. • *Understanding*

(ii) different for (*R*)-2-bromobutane and (*S*)-2-bromobutane. • *Understanding*

11. (i) Give a reason to explain why Zn^{2+} salts are white but Cu^{2+} salts are blue in colour? • *Understanding* [2]

(ii) Copper atom has completely filled *d* orbitals ($3d^{10}$) in its ground state, yet it is regarded as a transition element. Why? • *Understanding*

Section C **[21 Marks]**

12. Consider the data given below for the reaction, $A + B \longrightarrow C + D$ [3]

	Initial concentration (mol/L)		Initial rate (mol/L/s)
	[*A*]	[*B*]	
(a)	1.0	1.0	2.0×10^{-3}
(b)	2.0	1.0	4.0×10^{-3}
(c)	1.0	2.0	2.0×10^{-3}

Answer the following questions.

(i) What is the order of reaction with respect to *A* and *B*. • *Application*

(ii) Determine the rate law expression for the reaction. • *Evaluate*

(iii) Calculate the rate constant. • *Application*

13. Arrange the following compounds. • *Analysis* [3]

$Cl—CH_2—COOH$, $F—CH_2—COOH$, $CH_3—COOH$

(i) In the increasing order of their acidic strength.

(ii) In the decreasing order of their pK_a value.

14. (i) What are the expected products of hydrolysis of lactose? • *Recall* [3]

(ii) What is meant by inversion of sugar? • *Recall*

(iii) Suresh visits a dentist as he was suffering from bleeding of gums. Which water-soluble vitamin should dentist prescribed to him? • *Understanding*

15. The freezing point of 0.02 m solution of hexacyanoferrate (III) is – 0.062°C. • *Application* [3]

(i) Calculate van't Hoff factor for this solution.

(ii) Calculate the percentage dissociation of it. (K_f for water = 1.86 K mol^{-1} kg).

16. Identify *A*, *B* and *C* in the following reactions. • *Understanding* [3]

(i)
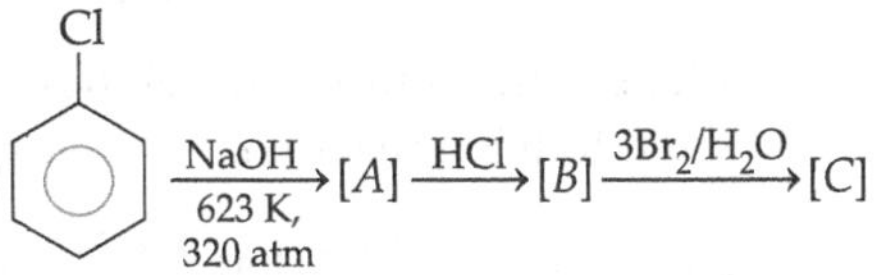

(ii)
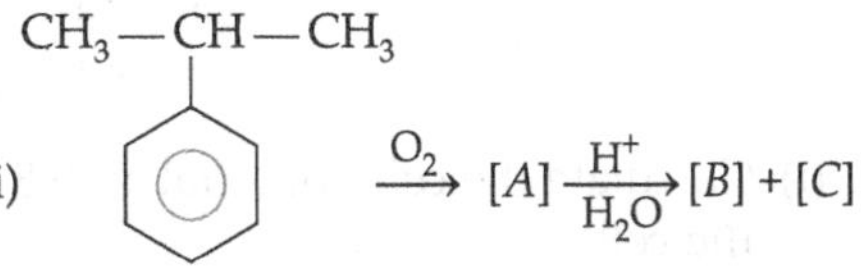

17. How will the following be converted? (Give chemical equations) • *Understanding* [3]

(i) Ethanoic acid into methanamine.

(ii) Hexane nitrile into 1-aminopentane.

(iii) Methanol into ethane nitrile.

Or

An aromatic compound '*A*' on treatment with aqueous ammonia and heating forms compound '*B*' which on heating with Br_2 and KOH forms a compound '*C*' of molecular formula C_6H_7N. Write the structure and IUPAC names of compound *A*, *B* and *C*. • *Understanding*

18. (i) The rate of most of the reactions become double when their temperature is raised from 298 K to 308 K. Calculate their activation energy. (Given, $R = 8.314$ J mol^{-1} K) • *Application* [3]

(ii) The rate constant for a zero order reaction in *A* is 0.0030 mol L^{-1}s^{-1}. How long will it take for the initial concentration of *A* to fall from 0.10 M to 0.075 M? • *Application*

Section D **[15 Marks]**

19. (i) An aliphatic unsaturated hydrocarbon (*A*) when treated with $HgSO_4 / H_2SO_4$ yields a compound (*B*) having molecular formula C_3H_6O. (*B*) on oxidation with concentrated HNO_3 gives two compounds (*C*) and (*D*). Compound (*C*) when treated with PCl_5 gives compound (*E*). (*E*) when reacts with ethanol gives a sweet smelling liquid (*F*). Compound (*F*) is also formed when (*C*) reacts with ethanol in the presence of concentrated H_2SO_4. Identify the compound *A, B, C, D, E* and *F*. • *Understanding* [5]

(ii) Identify the compounds *A, B* and *C* in the following reaction. • *Understanding*

$$CH_3—Br \xrightarrow{Mg / Ether} [A] \xrightarrow[(b)\ Water]{(a)\ CO_2} [B] \xrightarrow{CH_3OH/H^+} [C]$$

Or (i) The molar conductivity (λ_m) *vs* concentration $(\sqrt{C})$ curve is represented below.

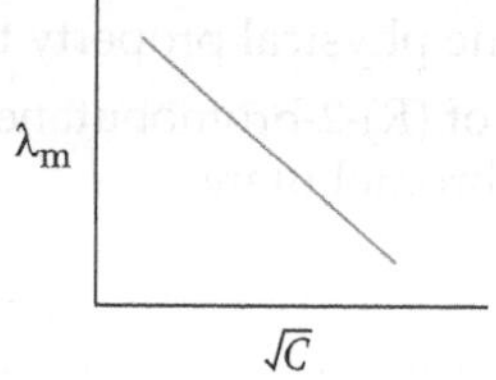

Identify the nature of electrolyte and also explain how molar conductivity vary with dilution? • *Recall*

(ii) The molar conductivity of a dilute solution of acetic acid is 42.8 S cm^2/mol. Calculate its degree of dissociation. Given : $\lambda^\circ_{(H^+)} = 349.6$ S cm^2/mol and $\lambda^\circ_{(CH_3COO^-)} = 56.7$ S cm^2/mol • *Application*

20. (i) Calculate the cell potential at 298 K for the cell, [5]

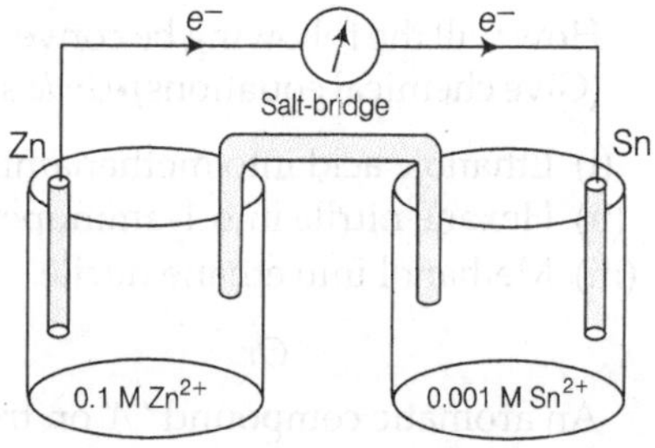

$Zn(s)|Zn^{2+}(0.1M)||Sn^{2+}(0.001M)|Sn(s)$

Given, $E^\circ_{Zn^{2+}/Zn} = -0.76$ V,

$E^\circ_{Sn^{2+}/Sn} = -0.14$ V • *Application*

(ii) Two electrolytic cells containing silver nitrate solution and dilute sulphuric acid solution were connected in series. A steady current of 2.5 A was passed through them till 1.078 g of silver was deposited (Ag = 107.8 g mol^{-1}, 1F = 96500 C mol^{-1}). What was the weight of the oxygen consumed? • *Application*

21. Isomerism is the phenomenon in which more than one compounds have the same chemical formula but different chemical structures. Chemical compounds that have identical chemical formulae but differ in properties and the arrangement of atoms in the molecule are called isomers. In chemistry, valence bond theory is one of the two basic theories that were developed to use the methods of quantum mechanics to explain chemical bonding.

(i) Name the type of isomerism shown by the following pairs of coordination compounds. • *Recall* [5]

(a) $[Co(NH_3)_5Cl]SO_4$ and $[Co(NH_3)_5SO_4]Cl$

(b) $[Co(NH_3)_2(NO_2)_2(py)_2]NO_3$ and $[Co(NH_3)_2(ONO)_2(py)_2]NO_3$

(c) $[Co(NH_3)_4Cl_2]^+$ and $[Co(NH_3)_4Cl_2]^+$

(ii) Using VBT, predict the hybridisation of the complex, $[Cr(NH_3)_6]^{3+}$. State whether it is a high spin or low spin complex. (Atomic number of Cr = 24) • *Understanding*

Solutions *in Topper's Style*

My Commitment *I affirm that I am reviewing these solutions only after I have solved the Sample Question Paper on my own. My purpose of looking the solutions is solely to verify whether my answers/solutions were correct or not and to identify my mistakes in case my solutions were wrong or I could not solve that.*

1. (A) (i) reactant, unity
(ii) stepwise stability, K_n
(iii) composition, azeotropic
(iv) dihydric, trihydric

(B) (i) (b) IUPAC name of $\overset{1}{C}H_2=\overset{2}{C}H—\overset{3}{C}H_2Br$ is 3-bromopropene. Here, the preference will be given to alkene group and —Br will be treated as substituent.

(ii) (a)

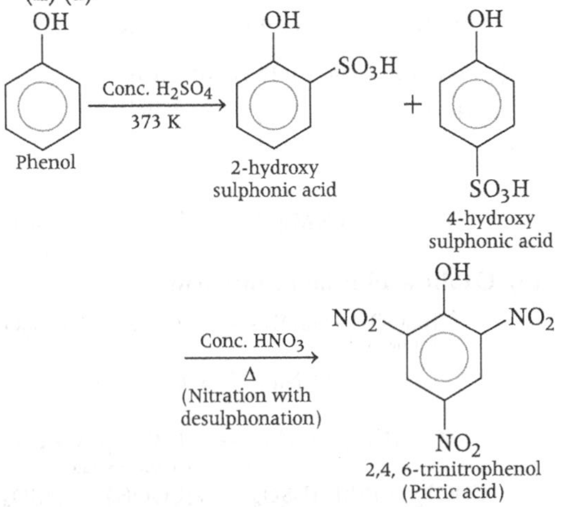

(iii) (b) $[Zn(NH_3)_4]^{2+}$ is colourless complex, as Zn^{2+} has no unpaired electrons.

$$Zn = [Ar]3d^{10}, 4s^2$$
$$Zn^{2+} = [Ar]3d^{10} = \underset{3d}{\boxed{\uparrow\downarrow|\uparrow\downarrow|\uparrow\downarrow|\uparrow\downarrow|\uparrow\downarrow}}$$

(iv) (a) Given, $\Lambda^\circ_{m(NaCl)} = 126\ S\ cm^2\ mol^{-1}$
$\Lambda^\circ_{m(KBr)} = 152\ S\ cm^2\ mol^{-1}$
$\Lambda^\circ_{m(KCl)} = 150\ S\ cm^2\ mol^{-1}$

According to Kohlrausch's law,
$$\Lambda^\circ_{NaBr} = \Lambda^\circ_{NaCl} + \Lambda^\circ_{KBr} - \Lambda^\circ_{KCl}$$
$$= 126 + 152 - 150 = 128\ S\ cm^2\ mol^{-1}$$

(v) (c) Statements II and IV are correct, while statements I and III are incorrect.

The correct form of statements I and III are as follows.

- The structure of chromate ion is tetrahedral.
- On acidifying the $K_2Cr_2O_4$ solution, the colour changes to orange-red due to the reformation of dichromate.

(vi) (a) Zinc metal has a more negative electrode potential than iron, so it will provide electrons in preference to iron and therefore corrodes first. Only when all the zinc has been oxidised, the iron starts to rust.

Thus, both (A) and (R) are true and (R) is the correct explanation of (A).

(vii) (a) It is not always convenient to determine the instantaneous rate, as it is measured by determining the slope of the tangent at point '*t*' in concentration *vs* time plot. This generally makes it difficult to determine the rate law and hence, the order of the reaction.

Thus, both (A) and (R) are true and (R) is the correct explanation of (A).

(C) (i) (a) $CH_3—CH_2—CH_2—CH_2—CH_2—OH$
Pentan -1 -ol

(b) $CH_3—CH_2—\overset{CH_3}{\underset{OH}{C}}—CH_3$
2 -methylbutan - 2 -ol

(c) $CH_3—\underset{CH_3}{CH}—\underset{OH}{CH}—CH_3$
3 -methylbutan - 2 -ol

The boiling point decreases with increase of branching in carbon chain. This is because of decrease in van der Waals' forces with decrease in surface area.

Therefore, order of decreasing boiling point is : (a) > (c) > (b).

(ii) Basicity can be described as the tendency to donate electrons by a chemical species. OH^- and CH_3O^- having a negative charge possess more tendency to donate electrons than H_2O and CH_3OH. $—CH_3$ shows + *I* effect, hence CH_3O^- is the most basic among the four groups and also CH_3OH is more basic than H_2O due to the same reason.

Hence, the correct order of increasing basicity is
$$H_2O < CH_3OH < OH^- < CH_3O^-.$$

(iii) The boiling point of alcohols increases with increase in number of carbon atoms and decreases with increase of branching in carbon chain. Therefore, butan-1-ol has the highest boiling point among the given options.

2. (i) The reaction of phenol with aqueous NaOH indicates that phenols are stronger acids than alcohols. It is because the phenoxide ion left after the release of a proton is stabilised by resonance but not the alkoxide ion.

$$R—\ddot{O}—H \rightleftharpoons R—\ddot{O}:^- + H^+$$

Alcohol — Alkoxide ion (not stabilised by resonance)

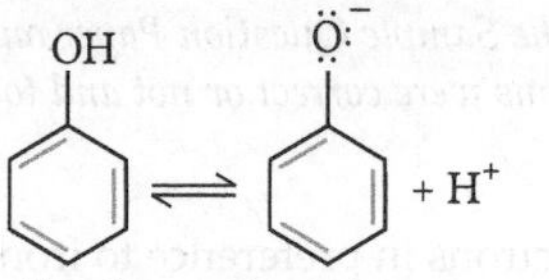

Phenol — Phenoxide ion

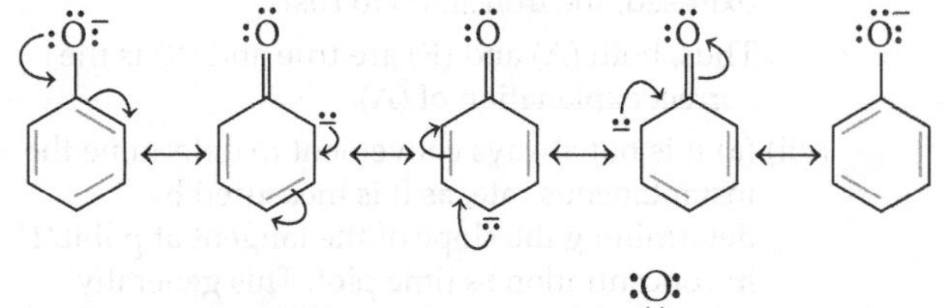

(ii) In alcohols, the bond angle of C–Ö–H is 108°9′. Due to the repulsion between the unshared electron pairs of oxygen, the bond angle in alcohols is lesser than the tetrahedral angle (109°28′).

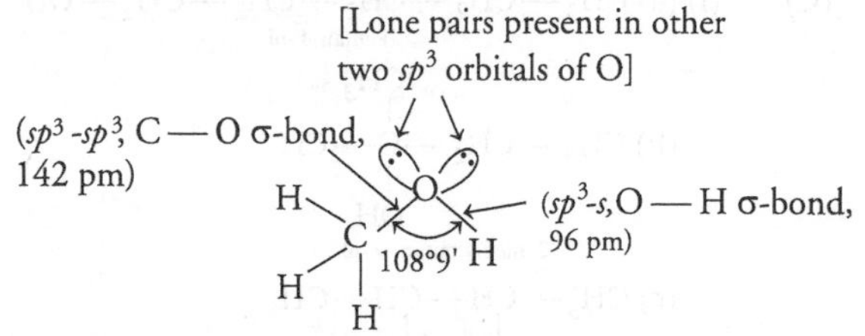

Structure of methanol

3. (i) Lanthanoid metals show +2 and +4 oxidation states in solution or in solid compounds to attain extra stable f^0, f^7 and f^{14} configurations.

For example, Eu and Yb exhibit +2 oxidation states due to extra stability of half-filled and completely filled 4f-subshell respectively.

Similarly, Ce and Tb exhibit +4 oxidation state due to the extra stability of empty and half-filled 4f-subshell respectively.

(ii) The electronic configuration of Mn^{2+} is $[Ar]3d^5$, which is considered stable due to its half-filled 3d-orbital.

Consequently, the third ionisation enthalpy is very high, making it difficult to remove the third electron.

However, Fe^{2+} can still lose electron easily to achieve a stable half-filled electronic configuration, $[Ar]3d^5$.

4. (i) Since, $E^\circ_{Ag^+/Ag} > E^\circ_{Cu^{2+}/Cu}$.
(0.80 V)

Therefore, following reaction takes place.

(a) At anode, $Cu(s) \longrightarrow Cu^{2+}(aq) + 2e^-$

(b) At cathode, $Ag^{2+}(aq) + 2e^- \longrightarrow Ag(s)$

(ii) At cathode, $Cu^{2+}(aq) + 2e^- \longrightarrow Cu(s)$, $E^\circ_{cell} = 0.34$ V

At anode, $Cr(s) \longrightarrow Cr^{3+}(aq) + 3e^-$, $E^\circ_{cell} = -0.74$ V

$$E^\circ_{cell} = E^\circ_{cathode} - E^\circ_{anode}$$
$$= 0.34 - (-0.74) = 1.08 \text{ V}$$

5. Given, weight of glucose, $w_2 = 18$ g

Molar mass of glucose, $M_2 = 180 \text{ g mol}^{-1}$

Weight of water, $W_1 = 1 \text{ kg} = 1000 \text{ g}$, $K_b = 0.52 \text{ K kg mol}^{-1}$

As we know that,

$$\text{Elevation in boiling point}, (\Delta T_b) = K_b \times \frac{w_2}{M_2} \times \frac{1000}{W_1}$$

$$(\Delta T_b) = 0.52 \times \frac{18}{180} \times \frac{1000}{1000} = 0.052 \text{ K}$$

$$\Delta T_b = T_b - T_b^\circ$$

(where, T_b is boiling point of solution)

$$\Rightarrow \quad 0.052\text{K} = T_b - 373.15\text{K}$$

$$T_b = 373.15 + 0.052\text{K} = 373.20\text{K}$$

$\therefore$ Boiling point of solution = 373.2 K

6. (i) **Acetone from methyl chloride**

$$\underset{\text{Methyl chloride}}{CH_3Cl} \xrightarrow{KCN} \underset{\text{Methyl cyanide}}{CH_3CN} \xrightarrow{CH_3MgCl}$$

$$CH_3—\overset{CH_3}{\overset{|}{C}}{=}NMgCl \xrightarrow{H_3O^+} \underset{\text{Acetone}}{CH_3—\overset{O}{\overset{||}{C}}—CH_3}$$

(ii) **Oxalic acid from formic acid**

$$\underset{\text{Formic acid}}{HCOOH} + NaOH \longrightarrow HCOO^-Na^+ + H_2O$$

$$2HCOO^-Na^+ \xrightarrow[-H_2]{633 \text{ K}} (COONa)_2$$

$$(COONa)_2 + CaCl_2 \longrightarrow \underset{\text{Calcium oxalate}}{(COO)_2Ca} + 2NaCl$$

$$(COO)_2Ca + \text{dil. } H_2SO_4 \longrightarrow \underset{\text{Oxalic acid}}{(COOH)_2} + CaSO_4\downarrow$$

Or Since, the liquid *A* reduces ammoniacal silver nitrate (Tollen's reagent), hence, *A* is an aldehyde and *B* does not give test with ammoniacal silver nitrate, thus, *B* is a ketone. Further, *B* forms a white crystalline solid on treatment with sodium hydrogen sulphite. This suggests that *B* is a methyl ketone.

(a) Thus, *A* is an aldehyde (*R*CHO) and *B* is a methyl ketone (*R*CO*R*)

(b) Following reactions takes place

$$\underset{\text{Aldehyde or ketone}}{>C{=}O} + \underset{\text{Sodium hydrogen sulphite}}{NaHSO_3} \rightleftharpoons >C\begin{matrix}OSO_2H \\ \overset{-\,+}{O}Na\end{matrix} \underset{\text{transfer}}{\overset{\text{Proton}}{\rightleftharpoons}} >C\begin{matrix}OSO_2Na \\ OH\end{matrix}$$

Bisulphite addition compound (White crystalline solid)

$$\underset{\text{Aldehyde}}{RCHO} + \underset{\text{Tollen's reagent}}{2[Ag(NH_3)_2]NO_3} + \underset{\text{Ammonium hydroxide}}{2NH_4OH} \longrightarrow$$

$$\underset{\text{Carboxylic acid}}{RCOOH} + \underset{\text{Silver mirror}}{2Ag\downarrow} + \underset{\text{Water}}{H_2O} + \underset{\text{Ammonia}}{4NH_3} + \underset{\text{Ammonium nitrate}}{2NH_4NO_3}$$

7. Number of moles in 92 g of Na^+ ions

$$=\frac{\text{Mass}}{\text{Molecular mass}}=\frac{92}{23}=4 \text{ moles}$$

$$\text{Molality of } Na^+ \text{ ions}=\frac{\text{Number of moles of solute}}{\text{Mass of solvent (kg)}}$$

$$=\frac{4 \text{ moles}}{1 \text{ kg}}=4 \text{ mol kg}^{-1}$$

8. (i) Ethylamine to methylamine

$$\underset{\text{Ethylamine}}{CH_3—CH_2—NH_2} + HNO_2 \xrightarrow{\text{Cold}} CH_3—CH_2—OH + N_2\uparrow + H_2O$$

$$CH_3—CH_2—OH \xrightarrow[\text{Dil. } H_2SO_4, \Delta]{K_2Cr_2O_7} CH_3COOH + H_2O$$

$$CH_3COOH \xrightarrow{SOCl_2} CH_3COCl \xrightarrow{NH_3} CH_3CONH_2$$

$$\xrightarrow{Br_2+NaOH} \underset{\text{Methylamine}}{CH_3NH_2}$$

(ii) When aniline is treated with nitrous acid and HCl at 0-5°C temperature, then benzene diazonium chloride is formed.

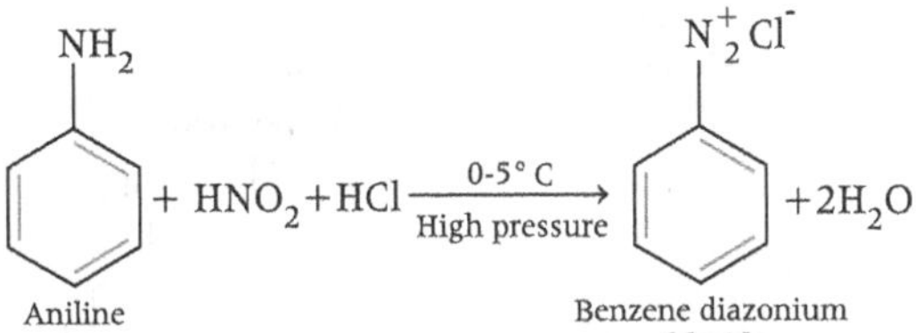

Aniline Benzene diazonium chloride

9. $[Co(NH_3)_6]^{3+}$

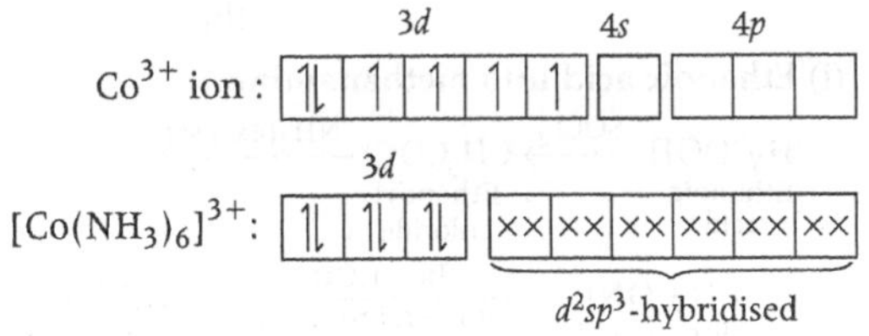

Six pair electrons from $6NH_3$ molecules.

Thus, $[Co(NH_3)_6]^{3+}$ is diamagnetic [absence of unpaired electron (s)] and octahedral.

Hence, Rani's response was correct.

10. (i) The boiling point is the same for (*R*)-2-bromobutane and (*S*)-2-bromobutane.

(ii) The specific rotation of plane-polarised light is different for (*R*)-2-bromobutane and (*S*)-2-bromobutane.

11. (i) The transition metal ions having completely filled *d*-orbitals or completely empty *d*-orbitals are colourless or white. Since, Zn^{2+} has completely filled *d*-orbitals with an electronic configuration of $1s^2, 2s^2\,2p^6, 3s^2\,3p^6, 3d^{10}$. Thus, its salts are white or colourless.

On the other hand, Cu^{2+} possesses an unpaired electron as its electronic configuration is $1s^2, 2s^2\,2p^6, 3s^2\,3p^6, 3d^9$.

Thus, it undergoes *d-d* transitions. Hence, Cu^{2+} salts are coloured.

(ii) Copper atom has incompletely filled *d*-orbitals in one of its oxidation states, i.e. Cu^{2+} ([Ar] $3d^9$).

Therefore, it is regarded as a transition element.

12. Rate of reaction $\propto$[concentration]^n, where n is the order of reaction.

Given reaction, $A+B \longrightarrow C+D$

Suppose the given reaction is of order p with respect to A and q with respect to B.

The rate law can also be written as

(a) $2.0\times10^{-3}=k[A]^p[B]^q=k(1)^p(1)^q$ ...(i)

(b) $4.0\times10^{-3}=k(2)^p(1)^q$ ...(ii)

(c) $2.0\times10^{-3}=k(1)^p(2)^q$ ...(iii)

From Eqs. (i) and (ii), we get

$$\frac{4.0\times10^{-3}}{2.0\times10^{-3}}=\frac{k(2)^p(1)^q}{k(1)^p(1)^q} \Rightarrow (2)^1=2^p$$

Hence, $p=1$

From Eqs. (i) and (iii), we get

$$\frac{2.0\times10^{-3}}{2.0\times10^{-3}}=\frac{k(1)^p(2)^q}{k(1)^p(1)^q}$$

$$\Rightarrow \quad 1=2^q \Rightarrow 2^0=2^q$$

Hence, $q=0$

(i) The order of reaction with respect to A is first order, i.e. $r\propto[A]^1$ and with respect to B is zero order, i.e. $r\propto[B]^0$.

(ii) Rate law equation is, $r=k[A]^1[B]^0$ where, k is rate constant.

(iii) Since, $r=k[A]^1$

Thus, rate constant, $k=\frac{r}{[A]}=\frac{2\times10^{-3}}{1.0}=2\times10^{-3}\text{s}^{-1}$

13. (i) The correct increasing order of their acidic strength is as follows

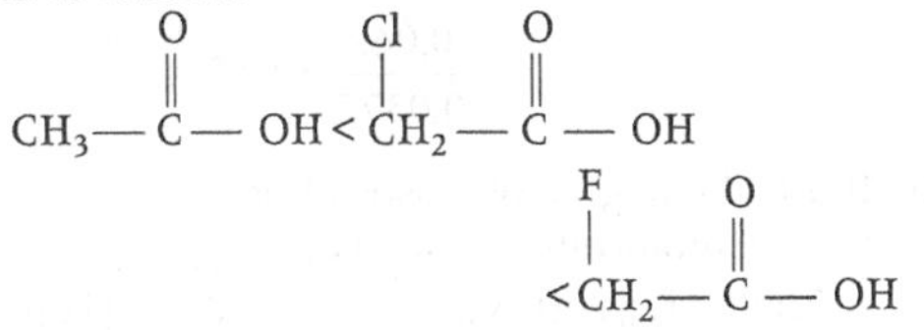

A more electronegative element such as fluorine produces a greater $-I$-effect than Cl-atom due to which F-atom withdraws electrons from the O—H bond, making it weaker and facilitating the release of H^+ ion from O—H bond.

Hence, FCH_2COOH is a stronger acid than $ClCH_2COOH$ and CH_3COOH. In case of CH_3COOH, the $+I$-effect of the methyl group increases the electron density in O—H bond. As a result, release of H^+ ions from CH_3COOH becomes more difficult.

(ii) $pK_a = -\log[K_a]$

i.e. $K_a \propto$ acidic nature of acid and $pK_a \propto \frac{1}{K_a}$

i.e. higher will be the pK_a value of a carboxylic acid, lower is its acidic strength and *vice-versa.*

So, the correct order is

$CH_3COOH > Cl—CH_2COOH > F—CH_2COOH.$

14. (i) Lactose on hydrolysis gives β-D-glucose and β-D-galactose.

$$\underset{\text{Lactose}}{C_{12}H_{22}O_{11}} + H_2O \xrightarrow{H^+} \underset{\beta\text{-D-glucose}}{C_6H_{12}O_6} + \underset{\beta\text{-D-galactose}}{C_6H_{12}O_6}$$

(ii) $$\underset{\substack{\text{Sucrose}\\(\text{dextrorotatory})\\+66.5^\circ}}{C_{12}H_{22}O_{11}} + \underset{\text{Water}}{H_2O} \xrightarrow{H^+} \underset{\substack{\text{Glucose}\\(\text{dextrorotatory})\\+52.5^\circ}}{C_6H_{12}O_6} + \underset{\substack{\text{Fructose}\\(\text{laevorotatory})\\-92.4^\circ}}{C_6H_{12}O_6}$$

Sucrose is dextrorotatory. On hydrolysis, it gives an equimolar mixture of glucose and fructose, which are dextrorotatory and laevorotatory respectively.

The mixture is laevorotatory because laevorotation of fructose (−92.4°) is more than dextrorotation of glucose (+52.5°). Therefore, hydrolysis of sucrose brings about a change in a sign of rotation and this process is known as inversion of sugar.

(iii) Vitamin C (water-soluble vitamin) should be prescribed to Suresh by dentist as its deficiency causes scurvy (bleeding of gums.)

15. (i) Given, T_f for hexacyanoferrate, $= -0.062\,°C$

$\therefore \Delta T_{(\text{observed})} = T_f{}^\circ - T_f = (273\,K - 272.939)\,K = 0.062\,K$

Molality of solution $= 0.02\,m$

We know that, $\Delta T = K_f \times \text{Molality}\,(m)$

$= 1.86 \times 0.02 = 0.0372\,K$

$\Delta T_{(\text{calculated})} = 0.0372\,K$

$$i = \frac{\text{Observed }(\Delta T)}{\text{Calculated }(\Delta T)} = \frac{0.062}{0.0372} = 1.67$$

(ii) If α is the degree of dissociation of hexacyanoferrate(III), $K_3[Fe(CN)_6]$.

Then, $K_3[Fe(CN)_6] \longrightarrow 3K^+ + [Fe(CN)_6]^{3-}$

	$K_3[Fe(CN)_6]$	$3K^+$	$[Fe(CN)_6]^{3-}$
Moles before dissociation	1	0	0
Moles after dissociation	$1-\alpha$	3α	α

$$i = \frac{(1-\alpha) + 3\alpha + \alpha}{1} = 1 + 3\alpha$$

$\therefore \quad 1 + 3\alpha = 1.67$

$\alpha = 0.223$ or 22.3%

Common Mistake Generally one can make mistake in dissociation of hexacyanoferrate (III).

16. (i)

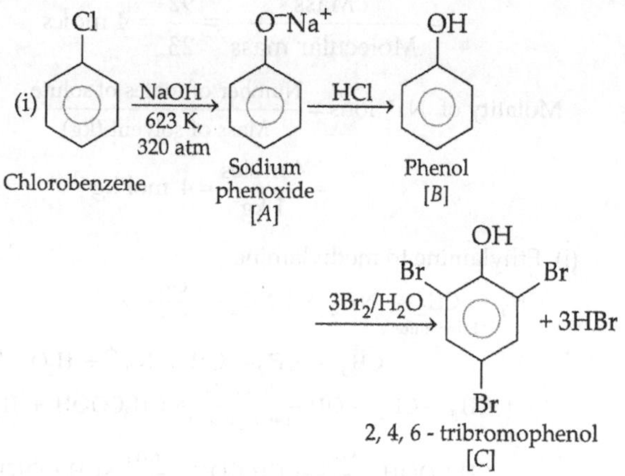

(ii)

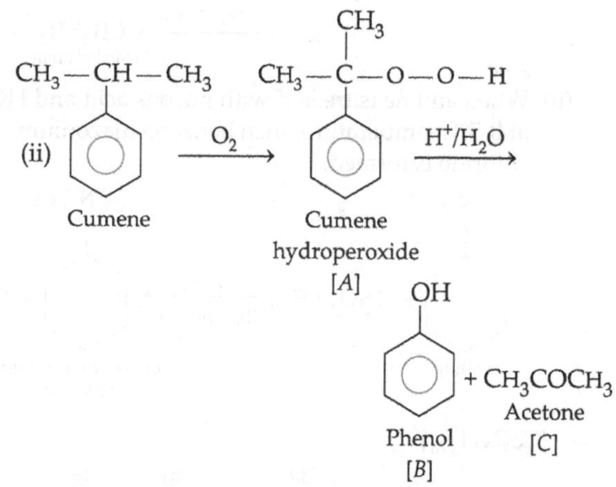

17. (i) **Ethanoic acid into methanamine**

$$\underset{\substack{\text{Ethanoic}\\\text{acid}}}{CH_3COOH} \xrightarrow{SOCl_2} \underset{\substack{\text{Ethanoyl}\\\text{chloride}}}{CH_3COCl} \xrightarrow{NH_3(\text{excess})}$$

$$\underset{\text{Ethanamide}}{CH_3CONH_2} \xrightarrow[\text{Hofmann bromamide reaction}]{Br_2/KOH} \underset{\text{Methanamine}}{CH_3NH_2}$$

(ii) **Hexane nitrile into 1-aminopentane**

$$\underset{\text{Hexane nitrile}}{CH_3(CH_2)_4CN} \xrightarrow[\text{Partial hydrolysis}]{H_3O^+} \underset{\text{Hexanamide}}{CH_3(CH_2)_4CONH_2}$$

$$\xrightarrow[\text{Hofmann bromamide reaction}]{Br_2/KOH} \underset{\text{1- aminopentane}}{CH_3(CH_2)_4NH_2}$$

(iii) **Methanol into ethane nitrile**

$$\underset{\text{Methanol}}{CH_3OH} \xrightarrow{PCl_5} \underset{\text{Chloromethane}}{CH_3Cl} \xrightarrow{KCN(\text{alc.})} \underset{\text{Ethane nitrile}}{CH_3CN}$$

Or

It is given that compound *C* having the molecular formula, C_6H_7N is formed by heating compound *B* with Br_2 and KOH. This is a Hofmann bromamide degradation reaction.

Therefore, compound *B* is amide and *C* is an amine.

The only amine having the molecular formula C_6H_7N is aniline.

Therefore, B must be benzamide ($C_6H_5CONH_2$), which is formed by heating compound A with aqueous ammonia. Therefore, compound A must be benzoic acid.

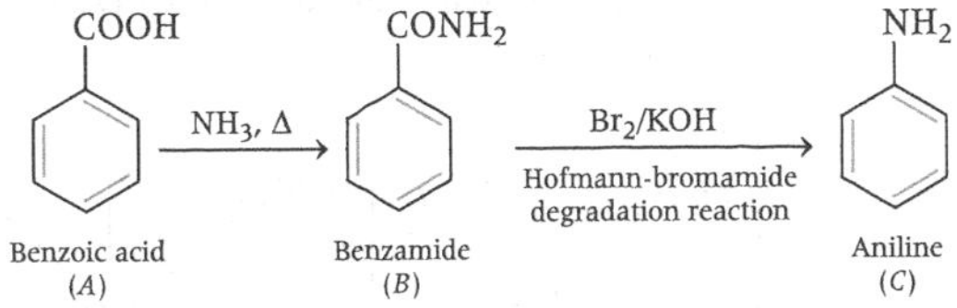

18. (i) According to Arrhenius equation,

$$\log\frac{k_2}{k_1}=\frac{E_a}{2.303R}\left[\frac{1}{T_1}-\frac{1}{T_2}\right] \quad \ldots(i)$$

Given, $\frac{k_2}{k_1}=2, T_1=298\text{K}, T_2=308\text{K}$,

$R=8.314\ \text{JK}^{-1}\ \text{mol}^{-1}$

On putting the values in Eq. (i), we get

$$\log 2=\frac{E_a}{2.303\times(8.314\,\text{JK}^{-1}\text{mol}^{-1})}\left[\frac{1}{298\text{K}}-\frac{1}{308\text{K}}\right]$$

$$\text{or } 0.3010=\frac{E_a}{2.303\times(8.314\,\text{J mol}^{-1})}\times\frac{10}{298\times308}$$

$$E_a=\frac{0.3010\times2.303\times8.314\times298\times308}{10}(\text{J mol}^{-1})$$

$$=52897.78\,\text{J mol}^{-1}$$

$$=52.90\,\text{kJ mol}^{-1}$$

$\therefore$ Activation energy for the reaction $=52.90\ \text{kJ mol}^{-1}$

(ii) For zero order reaction,

Rate constant, $k=\frac{[A]_0-[A]}{t}$

Given, $[A]_0=0.10$ M,

$[A]=0.075$ M and

$k=0.0030\ \text{mol L}^{-1}\ \text{s}^{-1}$

$\therefore \quad t=\frac{[A]_0-[A]}{k}$

$$t=\frac{0.10-0.075}{0.0030}=8.33\text{ s}$$

19. (i) The sequence of reactions take place as follows

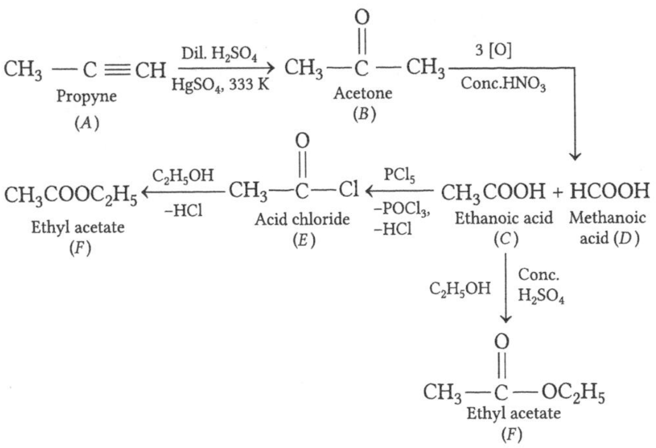

Thus, $[A]$ = Propyne ($CH_3C\equiv CH$),

$[B]$ = Acetone (CH_3COCH_3),

$[C]$ = Ethanoic acid (CH_3COOH),

$[D]$ = Methanoic acid ($HCOOH$)

$[E]$ = Acid chloride (CH_3COCl)

$[F]$ = Ethyl acetate ($CH_3COOC_2H_5$)

(ii) Complete chemical conversion can be done as

$$\underset{\text{Bromomethane}}{CH_3—Br}\xrightarrow{\text{Mg / Ether}}\underset{\substack{[A]\\ \text{Methyl magnesium}\\ \text{bromide}}}{CH_3MgBr}\xrightarrow[\text{(b) Water}]{\text{(a) }CO_2}$$

$$\underset{\substack{(B)\\ \text{Ethanoic acid}}}{CH_3COOH}\xrightarrow{CH_3OH/H^+}\underset{\substack{(C)\\ \text{Methyl ethanoate}}}{CH_3COOCH_3}$$

20. (i) The electrode reactions and the net cell reaction corresponding to the given cell are

At anode, $\quad Zn(s)\longrightarrow Zn^{2+}(aq\ 0.1\text{M})+2e^-$

At cathode, $\quad Sn^{2+}(aq.\ 0.001\text{M})+2e^-\longrightarrow Sn(s)$

Net cell reaction,

$Zn(s)+Sn^{2+}(aq\ 0.001\text{M})\longrightarrow Zn^{2+}(aq\ 0.1\text{M})+Sn(s)$

Here, number of electrons, $n=2$

Applying Nernst equation,

$$E_{\text{cell}}=E^\circ_{\text{cell}}-\frac{2.303RT}{nF}\log\frac{[Zn^{2+}(aq)]}{[Sn^{2+}(aq)]}$$

$$E^\circ_{\text{cell}}=E^\circ_{\text{cathode}}-E^\circ_{\text{anode}}=-[\,0.14-(-0.76)]\text{ V}=0.62\text{ V}$$

$$\therefore E_{\text{cell}}=0.62-\frac{2.303\times8.314\times298}{2\times96500}\log\frac{[0.1]}{[0.001]}$$

$$=0.62-0.0591=0.561\text{ V}$$

(ii) $Ag^+(aq)+e^-\longrightarrow Ag(s)$

107.8 g of Ag is deposited by 96500 C

$\therefore$ 1.078 g of Ag will be deposited by

$$\frac{96500}{107.8}\times1.078=965\text{ C}$$

If dilute sulphuric acid is used, then electrolysis of water takes place as SO_4^{2-}, ions do not dissociates.

$2H_2O\longrightarrow 4H^+ + O_2+4e^-$ (on each electrode)

4×96500 C of electricity liberates 32 g of O_2.

$$\therefore\ 965\text{ C liberates}=\frac{32\times965}{96500\times4}=0.08\text{ g of }O_2$$

$\therefore$ Total weight of O_2 liberated at both electrodes

$=2\times0.08=0.16$ g

Value Points

To get maximum marks in these type of questions following value point must be included in the answer.

- Do not skip the steps involved.
- Write the correct unit.

Or

(i) The linear plot corresponds to strong electrolyte. The molar conductance of strong electrolytes increases with dilution. This is because, as the volume increases, the mobility of ions and the conductance increases.

(ii) We are given, $\lambda^\circ_{(H^+)} = 349.6\ S\ cm^2/mol$

$\lambda^\circ_{(CH_3COO^-)} = 56.7\ S\ cm^2/mol$

According to Kohlrausch's law,

$$\Lambda^\circ_{(CH_3COOH)} = \lambda^\circ_{(H^+)} + \lambda^\circ_{(CH_3COO^-)}$$

$$= 349.6 + 56.7$$

$$= 406.3\ S\ cm^2/mol$$

$$\text{Degree of dissociation}\ (\alpha) = \frac{\Lambda^c_m}{\Lambda^\circ_m} = \frac{42.8}{406.3} = 0.1053$$

21. (i) (a) $[Co(NH_3)_5SO_4]Cl$ and $[Co(NH_3)_5Cl]SO_4$

These compounds will give different ions in solution, although they have same composition.
Hence, they represent ionisation isomerism.

(b) $[Co(NH_3)_2(NO_2)_2(py)_2]NO_3$ and $[Co(NH_3)_2(ONO)_2(py)_2]NO_3$. In these compounds, ambident ligand NO_2 is present. In $[Co(NH_3)_2(NO_2)_2(py)_2]NO_3$, NO_2 is coordinated through N and in $[Co(NH_3)_2(ONO)_2(py)_2]NO_3$, NO_2 is coordinated through O. Hence, they show linkage isomerism.

(c) Both the compounds have same molecular formula as well as structural formula but different arrangement in space, so they show geometrical isomerism or *cis-trans* isomerism.

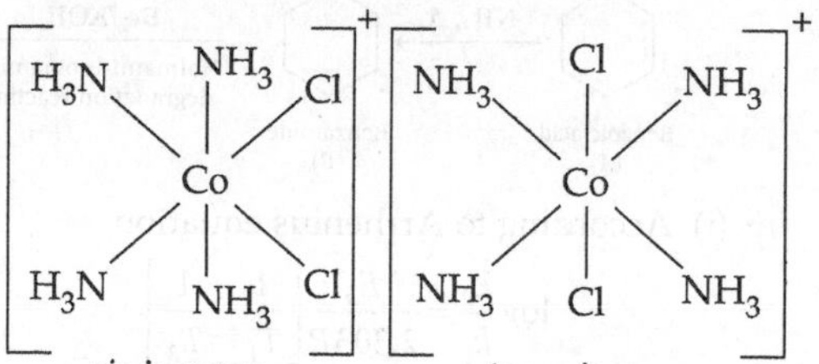

cis-isomer *trans*-isomer

(ii) Oxidation number of Cr in the complex $[Cr(NH_3)_6]^{3+}$ is

$$x + 6 \times 0 = +3$$

or $$x = +3$$

Electronic configuration of Cr is $[Ar]3d^5 4s^1$.

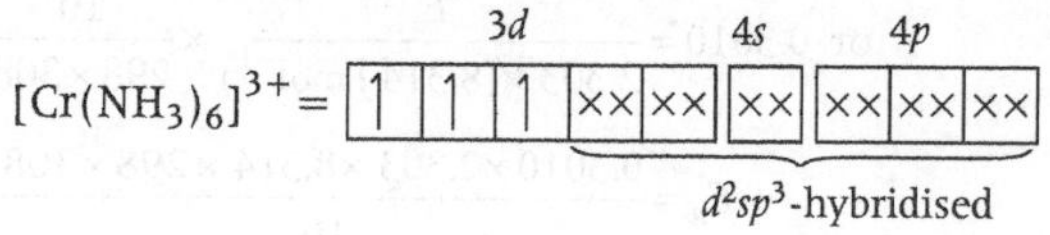

$[Cr(NH_3)_6]^{3+}$ is an inner orbital complex and it forms a high spin complex.

SPQ Code : **PB-06/15** Series ***i*-Succeed 06-25/15** Roll No. [ ]

Sample Question Paper 06

Chemistry 12th (Code 862)

General Instructions

1. This paper is divided into four sections-A, B, C and D. Answer all questions.
2. **Section A** consists of **one** question **having sub-parts** of **one** mark each. **Section B** consists of **ten** questions of **two** marks each. **Section C** consists of **seven** questions of **three** marks each and **Section D** consists of **three** questions of **five** marks each.
3. Internal choices have been provided in one question each in Section B, Section C and Section D.
4. All working, including rough work, should be done on the same sheet as, and adjacent to the rest of the answer.
5. The intended marks for questions or parts of questions are given in brackets [].
6. Balanced questions must be given, wherever possible and diagrams where they are helpful. When solving numerical problems, all essential working must be shown.
7. In working out problems, use the following data:
Gas constant (R) = 1.987 cal deg^{-1} mol^{-1} = 8.314 JK^{-1} mol^{-1} = 0.0821 dm^3 atm K^{-1} mol^{-1}
1L atm = 1 dm^3 atm =101.3 J, 1 Faraday =96500 Coulombs.
Avogadro's number (N_A) = 6.023×10^{23}.

Time : 3 Hrs.

Max. Marks : 70

Section A

[14 Marks]

1. (A) Fill in the blanks by choosing the appropriate word(s) from those given in the brackets. [4×1]
[ether, Pt, alcohol, Williamson synthesis, Etard reaction, 2, $5d^{10}6s^2$, 4, 3, $3d^{10}4s^1$, Hg, 0, 5, 1]
(i) Heating of alkyl halides and sodium alkoxide produces ...... and this reaction is known as .... • *Recall*
(ii) Among the transition elements, one which have lowest melting point is .... It has .... electronic configuration. • *Understanding*
(iii) In $[Fe(CN)_6]^{4-}$ and $[Fe(CN)_6]^{3-}$, the number of unpaired electrons respectively are .... and .... • *Understanding*
(iv) The values of van't Hoff factor for NaCl and K_2SO_4 respectively .... and ...... • *Application*

(B) Select and write the correct alternative from the choices given below. [7 × 1]
(i) Which of the following complex species is not expected to exhibit optical isomerism? • *Understanding*
(a) $[Co(en)_3]^{3+}$ (b) $[Co(en)_2Cl_2]^+$
(c) $[Co(NH_3)_3Cl_3]$ (d) $[Co(en)(NH_3)_2Cl_2]^+$
(ii) Equlibrium mixture of D-glucose contains • *Recall*
(a) 50% each of α-D-glucose and β-D-glucose.
(b) 64% of α-D-glucose and 36% of β-D-glucose.
(c) 36% of α-D-glucose and 64% of β-D-glucose.

(d) 33% of each α-D-glucose and β-D-glucose.

(iii) S_N1 reaction will be fastest in the case of • *Understanding*

(a) 1-chloro-2-methyl propane
(b) 1-iodo-2-methyl propane
(c) 1-chlorobutane
(d) 1-iodobutane

(iv) Which of the following reagent would not be a good choice for reducing an aryl nitro compound to an amine ? • *Understanding*

(a) H_2(excess)/Pt (b) $LiAlH_4$ in ether
(c) Fe and HCl (d) Sn and HCl

(v) Which of the following statements is correct regarding ethers?

I. Dimethyl ether and ethyl methyl ethers are gases at ordinary temperatures.
II. Lower ethers are insoluble in water.
III. Methoxy methane has lower boiling point than ethanol.
IV. The C—O—C bond angle in dimethyl ether is 120°.

• *Understanding*

(a) Only I and II (b) Only II and IV
(c) Only I and III (d) Only III and IV

(vi) **Assertion** (A) Formaldehyde is a planar molecule.

Reason (R) It contains sp^2-hybridised carbon atom. • *Analysis*

(a) Both Assertion and Reason are true and Reason is the correct explanation of the Assertion.
(b) Both Assertion and Reason are true but Reason is not the correct explanation of Assertion.
(c) Assertion is true but Reason is false.
(d) Both Assertion and Reason are false.

SP-06

(vii) **Assertion** (A) Cu is less reactive than hydrogen.

Reason (R) $E^\circ_{Cu^{2+}/Cu}$ is negative.

• *Analysis*

(a) Both Assertion and Reason are true and Reason is the correct explanation of the Assertion.
(b) Both Assertion and Reason are true but Reason is not the correct explanation of Assertion.
(c) Assertion is true but Reason is false.
(d) Both Assertion and Reason are false.

(C) Read the passage given below carefully and answer the questions that follow [3×1]

In the periodic table, the elements are classified into mainly four blocks, i.e. *s, p, d* and *f*. The *d*-block elements are called **transition elements**. The *d*-block contains the elements of the group 3-12 in the periodic table. They possess properties that are transitional between the s and *p*-block elements.

The two characteristics of transition elements are

(a) They show variable oxidation states.
(b) They generally form coloured compounds.

Zn, Cd and Hg do not exhibit characteristic properties of transition elements. All the elements belongs to this section are metals. Hence, they are lustrous and have good electrical and thermal conductivity.

There are four rows of the transition elements involving filling of 3*d*, 4*d*, 5*d* and 6*d* orbitals. They form useful alloys and are often employed as catalysts in elemental form or in compounds such as coordination complexes and oxides.

(i) Why does the transition element scandium not exhibit variable oxidation state? • *Understanding*

(ii) Why chromium is a typical hard metal while mercury is a liquid? • *Understanding*

(iii) What is the common oxidation state of Cu, Ag and Au? • *Understanding*

Section B **[20 Marks]**

2. How will be the following obtained? (Give chemical equations) [2]
   (i) 3-hydroxybutanal from ethanol
   (ii) 1-phenylethanol from bromobenzene
   • *Understanding*

   Or

   Give the simple chemical test to distinguish between
   (i) pentan-2-one and pentan-3-one
   (ii) ethanal and propanal • *Understanding*

3. Account for the following. [2]
   (i) Zn, Cd and Hg are quite soft and have low melting point.
   (ii) $La(OH)_3$ is more basic than $Lu(OH)_3$.
   • *Understanding*

4. A solution containing 0.5 g of KCl dissolves in 100 g of water and freezes at $-0.24°C$. Calculate the degree of dissociation of the salt. [2]
   (K_f for water $= 1.86°C\,mol\,kg^{-1}$).
   (Atomic weights of K = 39 u, Cl = 35.5 u).
   • *Application*

5. (i) Assume three samples of juices *A*, *B* and *C* have glucose as the only sugar present in them. The concentration of sample *A*, *B* and *C* are 0.1 M, 0.5 M and 0.2 M respectively. [2]
   (a) Which will have the highest freezing point? • *Analysis*
   (b) Which will have the highest boiling point? • *Analysis*
   (ii) Calculate the osmotic pressure of a solution containing 3.42 g of sucrose in 1 L of water at 400 K.
   (Molar mass $= 342\,g\,mol^{-1}$) • *Application*

6. Identify compounds [*A*] and [*B*] in the following reactions. [2]
   • *Understanding*

   (i) 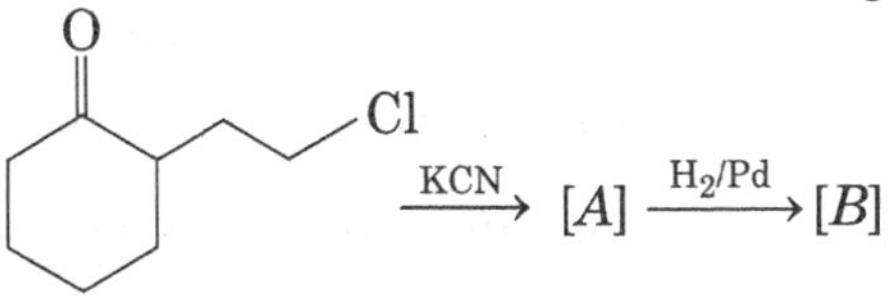

   (ii) $C_6H_5\overset{+}{N}_2Cl^- \xrightarrow{Cu/HCl} [A] \xrightarrow{Cl_2/FeCl_3} [B]$

7. Describe the oxidising action of potassium dichromate and write the ionic equations for its reactions with (i) iodide and (ii) H_2S.
   • *Recall* [2]

8. State reason for the following.
   • *Understanding* [2]
   (i) Aniline does not undergo Friedel-Crafts reaction.
   (ii) Acetylation of aniline reduces its activation effect. Explain.

9. (i) Given the standard electrode potentials,
   $K^+/K = -2.93$ V; $Ag^+/Ag = 0.80$ V;
   $Hg^{2+}/Hg = 0.79$ V; $Mg^+/Mg = -2.36$ V;
   $Cr^{3+}/Cr = -0.74$ V
   Arrange these metals in their increasing order of reducing power. • *Analysis*
   (ii) Calculate the potential of hydrogen electrode in contact with a solution whose pH is 10. [2]
   • *Application*

10. Devise a scheme for the synthesis of *n*-ethane using CH_3I as the only source of carbon. Is it possible to obtain butane in pure state by applying this scheme. Give a reason for your answer. • *Evaluate*

11. How will you convert the following?
    (i) Phenol to 2, 4, 6-tribromophenol [2]
    (ii) Phenol to benzoic acid • *Understanding*

Section C **[21 Marks]**

12. Vitamins are organic molecules that are essential to an organism in small quantities for proper metabolic function.
    (i) Classify the vitamins into fat soluble and water soluble. • *Recall*
    (ii) Why cannot vitamin C be stored in our body? • *Understanding*
    (iii) Harsh visits a doctor. He was suffering from muscular weakness in his body.

Which vitamin deficiency could be the reason told by the doctor? • *Understanding*

13. The experimental data for the decomposition of N_2O_5, [3]

$$[2N_2O_5 \longrightarrow 4NO_2 + O_2]$$

in gas phase of 318 K are given below :

t/s	$10^{-2} \times [N_2O_5]/\text{mol L}^{-1}$
0	1.63
400	1.36
800	1.14
1200	0.93
1600	0.78
2000	0.64
2400	0.53
2800	0.43
3200	0.35

Answer the following questions.

(i) What is the order of reaction? • *Application*

(ii) Deduce the rate expression. • *Evaluate*

(iii) Find out the rate constant of the reaction. • *Application*

14. Identify the compounds *A*, *B* and *C* in the following reactions. • *Understanding* [3]

(i) $\underset{\displaystyle OH}{CH_3-\underset{|}{CH}-CH_3} \xrightarrow{K_2Cr_2O_7/H_2SO_4} [A] \xrightarrow{CH_3MgBr} [B] \xrightarrow{H^+/H_2O} [C]$

(ii) $C_6H_5NH_2 \xrightarrow[0\text{-}5°C]{NaNO_2 + HCl} [A] \xrightarrow{H_2O,\ \text{warm}} [B] \xrightarrow{\text{Conc. } HNO_3} [C]$

15. At some temperature, the vapour pressure of pure C_6H_6 is 0.256 bar and that of pure $C_6H_5CH_3$ (toluene) is 0.0925 bar. If the mole fraction of toluene in solution is 0.6. Calculate, [3]

(i) the total pressure of the solution. • *Application*

(ii) mole fraction of toluene in vapour phase. • *Application*

16. Write the chemical equations to illustrate the following name reactions. • *Recall* [3]

(i) Wolff-Kishner reduction
(ii) Etard reaction
(iii) Fittig reaction

Or Explain the mechanism of acid catalysed dehydration of propanol to yield the corresponding alkene. • *Understanding*

17. A given mixture of alkyl halides is treated with water to convert them to alcohols through S_N1 reaction. Arrange them with respect to solvolytic reactivity. [3]

(i)
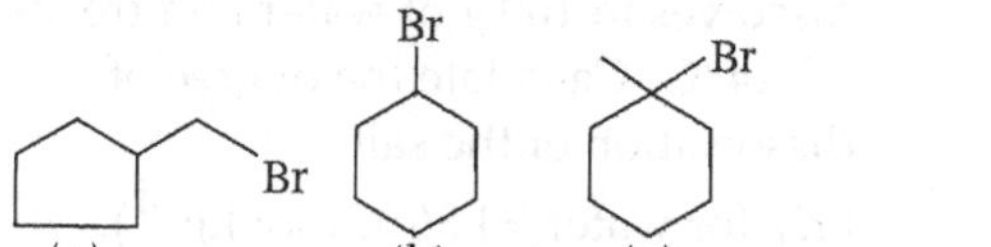

(a) (b) (c)

(ii)
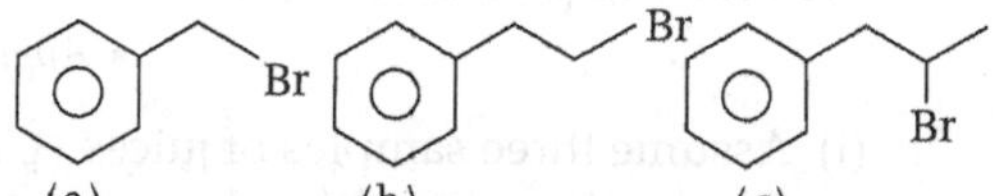

(a) (b) (c)

• *Analysis*

18. (i) Write the formulae for the following coordination compounds. [5] • *Understanding*

(a) Potassium tetracyanonickelate (II)
(b) Iron (II) hexacyanoferrate (II)

(ii) Consider the complex ion $[CoF_6]^{3-}$ and find the type of hybridisation of central metal atom, magnetic nature and geometry of the complex ion. • *Understanding*

SP-06

Section D **[15 Marks]**

19. (i) Give a reason for each of the following. • *Understanding*

(a) 2-propanone undergo nucleophilic addition reactions more readily than 2-propanal. [5]

(b) Trifluoroacetic acid is stronger acid than acetic acid.

(c) Carboxylic acids do not give characteristic reactions of carbonyl group.

(ii) An organic compound with molecular formula $C_5H_{10}O$ gets oxidised by Tollen's reagent. It does not respond to Fehling's test but undergoes Cannizzaro reaction. Identify the compound. Show how you used the above information to identify the compound. • *Understanding*

20. (i) For the given graph [5]

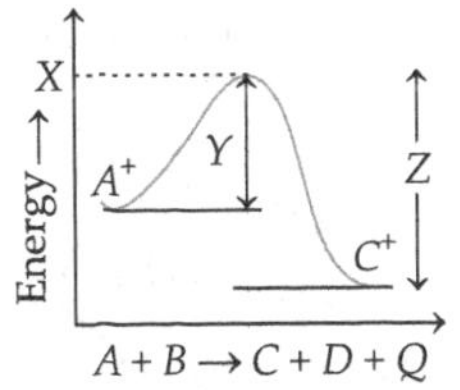

(a) Identify X, Y, Z and Q. • *Understanding*

(b) If the rate constant, the activation energy and Arrhenius parameter of a reaction at 25°C are $3 \times 10^{-4}\ s^{-1}$, $104.4\ kJ mol^{-1}$, and $6.0 \times 10^{14}\ s^{-1}$ respectively. What is the value of rate constant at $T \longrightarrow \infty$? • *Application*

(ii) Two reactions,

(a) $A \longrightarrow$ Products,

(b) $B \longrightarrow$ Products, follow first order kinetics.

The rate of reaction (a) is doubled when the temperature is raised from 300 K to 310 K. The half-life for this reaction at 310 K is 10 min. At the same temperature, B decomposes twice as fast as A. If the energy of activation for the reaction (b) is half that of reaction (a), calculate the rate constant of the reaction (b), at 300 K. • *Application*

21. A Daniell cell is a device that transforms chemical energy released by redox reactions into electrical energy. It has a 1.1 V electrical potential. Zinc (Zn) which serves as the anode in a Daniell cell and copper (Cu) which serves as the cathode are the two different metals in use as shown in the figure given below. Each of these electrodes continues to be immersed in ion-based chemical solutions.

In the Daniell cell, zinc dissolves in zinc sulphate. Cell electrodes are metal strips.

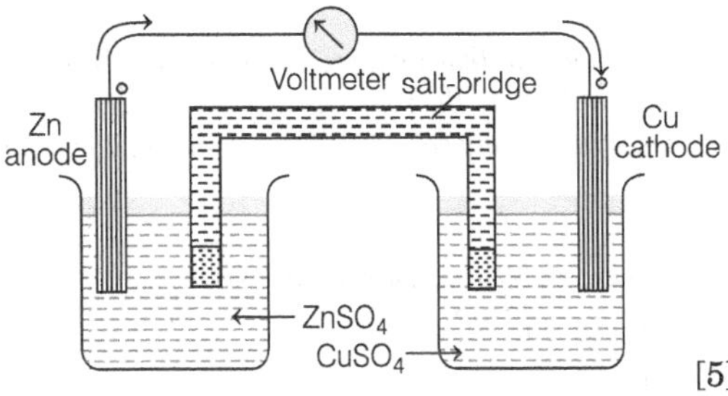

[5]

Answer the following questions.

(i) How salt bridge play an important role in working of Daniell cell? • *Recall*

(ii) Daniell cell is an example of which type of device? • *Recall*

(iii) If $E_{ext} < 1.1$ V, then what will be the direction of flow of current? • *Understanding*

(iv) What happens when external potential (E_{ext}) is equal to 1.1 V? • *Understanding*

(v) Calculate the maximum work that can be obtained from the Daniell cell,

$$Zn | Zn^{2+}(aq) || Cu^{2+}(aq) | Cu$$

[Given that, $E^\circ_{(Zn^{2+}/Zn)} = -0.76$ V

and $E^\circ_{(Cu^{2+}/Cu)} = 0.34$ V] • *Application*

Or (i) Conductivity of 0.00241 M acetic acid solution is $7.896 \times 10^{-5}\ S\ cm^{-1}$. If Λ°_m for acetic acid be $390.5\ S\ cm^2 mol^{-1}$.

Calculate its molar conductivity, degree of dissociation and dissociation constant. • *Application*

(ii) Calculating the thermodynamic equilibrium constant from the cell emf.

The standard emf for the following galvanic cell is 0.46 V.

$Cu(s) | Cu^{2+}(aq) || Ag^+(aq) | Ag(s)$

Determine the equilibrium constant, K_C for the reaction.

$Cu(s) + 2Ag^+(aq) \longrightarrow Cu^{2+}(aq) + 2Ag(s)$

• *Application*

Solutions in Topper's Style

My Commitment *I affirm that I am reviewing these solutions only after I have solved the Sample Question Paper on my own. My purpose of looking the solutions is solely to verify whether my answers/solutions were correct or not and to identify my mistakes in case my solutions were wrong or I could not solve that.*

1. (A) (i) ether, Williamson synthesis

(ii) Hg, $5d^{10}6s^2$

(iii) 0, 1

(iv) 2, 3

(B) (i) (c) Optical isomerism is exhibited by only those complexes which lacks element of symmetry.
$[Co(NH_3)_3Cl_3]$ shows *facial* as well as *meridional* isomerism. But both the forms contains plane of symmetry. Thus, the complex does not exhibit optical isomerism.

(ii) (c) D-glucose contains 36% of α-D-glucose and 64% of β-D-glucose.

(iii) (b) The order of reactivity of alkyl halides towards S_N1 reaction is as follows
Methyl halide < Primary halide < Secondary halide < Tertiary halide

Further for a given alkyl group, the reactivity of the halide R—X follows the order.

$$R—I > R—Br > R—Cl > R—F$$

Thus, S_N1 reaction will be fastest in case of 1-iodo-2-methyl propane.
This is because 1° carbocation formed in the reaction, rearranges itself to form 2° carbocation.

(iv) (b) Aryl nitro compound cannot be converted into amine using $LiAlH_4$ in ether.

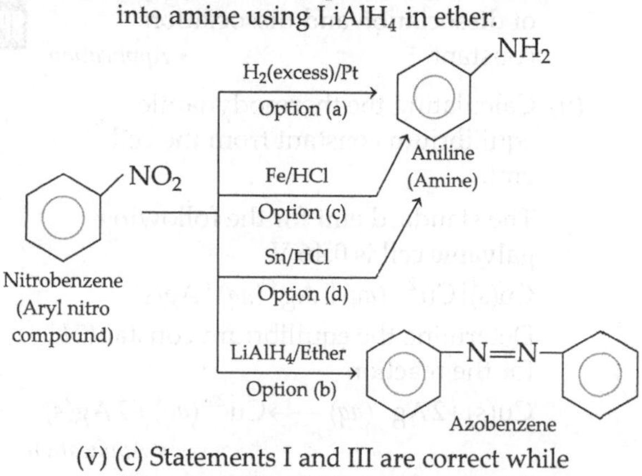

(v) (c) Statements I and III are correct while statements II and IV are incorrect. Their correct form are as follows

- Lower ethers (upto three carbon atoms) are soluble in water.
- The C—O—C bond angle in dimethyl ether is 111.7°.

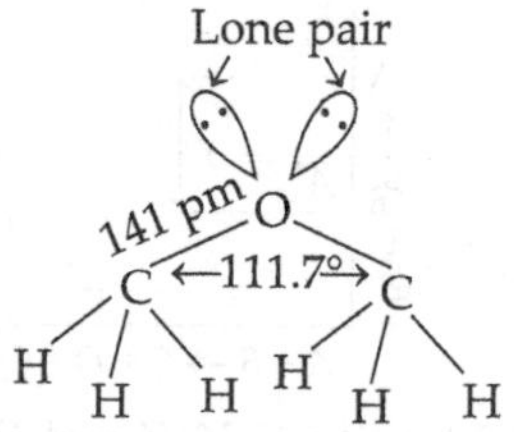

(vi) (a) Both Assertion and Reason are true and Reason is the correct explanation of Assertion.
Formaldehyde is a planar molecule due to presence of sp^2-hybridised carbon atom. Its structure is as follows

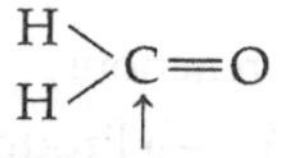

sp^2-hybridised carbon

(vii) (c) Electrode potential of Cu^{2+}/Cu is + 0.34 V and electrode potential of H^+/H_2 is 0V. Therefore, Cu is less reactive than hydrogen.
Thus, Assertion is true but Reason is false.

(C) (i) Outer electronic configuration of Sc is $[Ar]\,3d^1\,4s^2$.
Hence, it shows + 3 as the only oxidation state.

(ii) Cr have $3d^5\,4s^1$ electronic configuration. Hence, metallic bonds are very strong. In Hg ($[Xe]4f^{14}5d^{10}6s^2$), all the *d*-orbitals are fully-filled. Hence, the metallic bonds are very weak.

(iii) The common oxidation state of Cu, Ag and Au is +1.

2. (i) **3-hydroxybutanal from ethanol**

$$\underset{\text{Ethanol}}{CH_3CH_2OH} \xrightarrow[\text{(Oxidation)}]{K_2Cr_2O_7/H_2SO_4} \underset{\text{Ethanal}}{CH_3CHO} \xrightleftharpoons{\text{Dil. NaOH}}$$

$$\underset{\text{OH}}{CH_3\underset{|}{C}HCH_2CHO}$$

3-hydroxybutanal (Aldol)
(Formed from 2 molecules of ethanal)

(ii) **1-phenylethanol from bromobenzene**

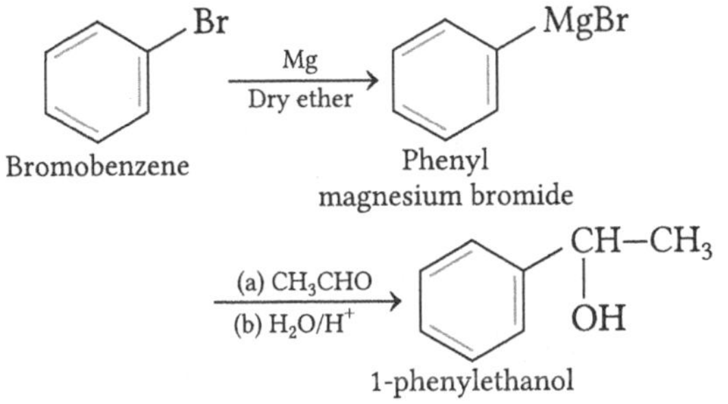

Or (i) **Distinguishing test between pentan-2-one and pentan-3-one** Pentan-2-one responds positively towards iodoform test, whereas pentan-3-one ($C_2H_5COC_2H_5$), due to the absence of

$$\underset{\|}{\overset{O}{}}\!\!-C-CH_3$$ group, do not give iodoform test.

$$\overset{1}{C}H_3-\overset{2}{C}O-\overset{3}{C}H_2-\overset{4}{C}H_2-\overset{5}{C}H_3 + 3NaOI$$
Pentan-2-one

$$\xrightarrow{\text{Heat}} \underset{\text{Yellow ppt.}}{CHI_3} + CH_3CH_2CH_2CO\bar{O}\overset{+}{N}a + 2NaOH$$

(ii) **Distinguishing test between ethanal and propanal** Ethanal, because of the presence of CH_3CO- skeleton gives iodoform test, whereas propanal due to the absence of such a skeleton does not.

$$\underset{\text{Ethanal or Acetaldehyde}}{CH_3CHO} + 4NaOH + 3I_2 \longrightarrow \underset{\substack{\text{Iodoform}\\ \text{(Yellow ppt.)}}}{CHI_3\downarrow}$$

$$+ \underset{\text{Sodium formate}}{HCO\bar{O}\overset{+}{N}a} + \underset{\text{Sodium iodide}}{3NaI} + 3H_2O$$

$$\underset{\text{Propanal}}{CH_3CH_2CHO} + 4NaOH + 3I_2 \longrightarrow \text{No reaction}$$

3. (i) Zn, Cd and Hg metals have completely filled d-orbitals (d^{10}). It means that d-electrons are not readily available for metallic bond formation. As a result, the metallic bonds which are present in them are weak.

Therefore, these metals are quite soft and have low melting point.

(ii) $Lu(OH)_3$ has greater covalent character than $La(OH)_3$ on account of lanthanoid contraction. Thus, the liberation of hydroxide ions from $La(OH)_3$ is easy and it is more basic than $Lu(OH)_3$.

4. Given,

Weight of KCl (solute) = 0.5 g

Weight of solvent (water) = 100 g

Depression in freezing point (ΔT_f)

$$= T_f^0 - T_f = 0 - (-0.24°C) = 0.24°C$$

$$K_f = 1.86°C \text{ mol kg}^{-1}$$

Molecular mass of KCl = 39 + 35.5 = 74.5 g mol^{-1}

From depression in freezing point, $\Delta T_f = i \times K_f \times m$

$$0.24°C = i \times 1.86°C \text{ mol kg}^{-1} \times \left(\frac{0.5}{74.5} \times \frac{1000}{100}\right) \text{mol kg}^{-1}$$

$$\Rightarrow i = 1.92$$

For KCl, $i = 1 + \alpha$

(where, α is the degree of dissociation)

$$\alpha = 1.92 - 1 = .92 \text{ or } 92\%$$

5. (i) (a) Juice A has highest freezing point as it has lowest concentration.

(b) Juice B has highest boiling point because more the concentration, more is the boiling point.

(ii) Given,

Mass of sucrose, $w = 3.42$ g

Molar mass of sucrose = 342 g mol^{-1}

$$\therefore \text{Osmotic pressure, } \pi = \frac{w \times R \times T}{M \times V}$$

$$= \frac{3.42 \text{ g} \times 0.0821 \text{ L atm K}^{-1}\text{mol}^{-1} \times 400 \text{K}}{1 \text{ g mol}^{-1} \times 342 \text{L}}$$

$$= 0.3284 \text{ atm}$$

6. (i)

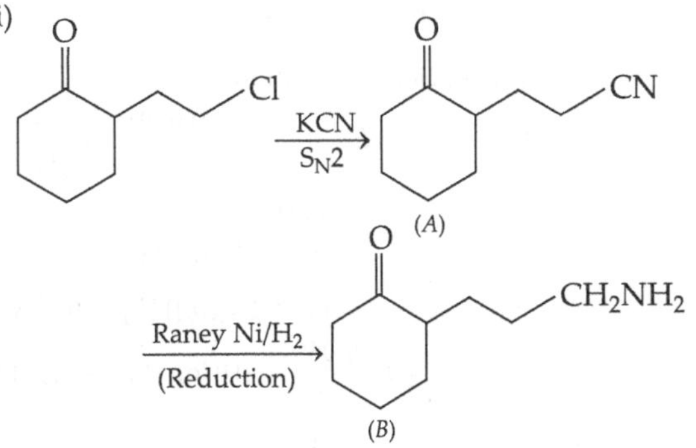

(ii)

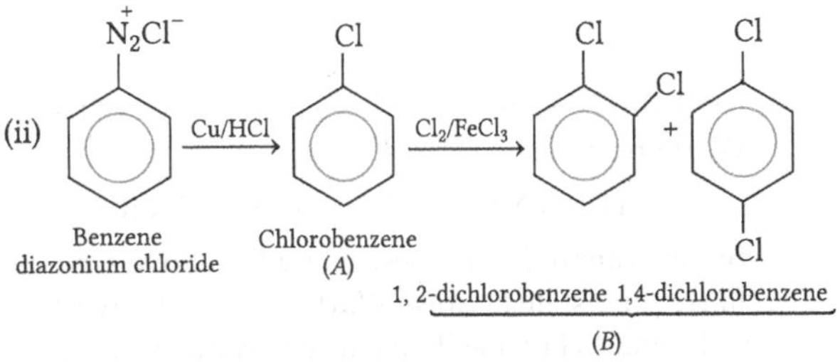

7. Potassium dichromate is a strong oxidising agent. In acidic solution, its oxidising action is represented as

$$Cr_2O_7^{2-} + 14H^+ + 6e^- \longrightarrow 2Cr^{3+} + 7H_2O$$

Ionic equations

(i) **Reaction of $K_2Cr_2O_7$ with I^-**

$$Cr_2O_7^{2-} + 14H^+ + 6I^- \longrightarrow 2Cr^{3+} + 3I_2 + 7H_2O$$

(ii) **Reaction of $K_2Cr_2O_7$ with H_2S**

$$Cr_2O_7^{2-} + 8H^+ + 3H_2S \longrightarrow 2Cr^{3+} + 3S + 7H_2O$$

8. (i) Aniline being a Lewis base, reacts with the Lewis acid $AlCl_3$ which is used in Friedel-Crafts reaction and produces complex salt.

The reaction involved is as follows

$$\underset{\text{Aniline}}{C_6H_5H_2} + AlCl_3 \longrightarrow \underset{\text{(Salt)}}{C_6H_5\overset{+}{N}H_2 \cdot AlCl_3^-}$$

As a result of this, nitrogen of aniline aquires positive charge and hence acts as a strong deactivating group. Therefore, it does not show Friedel-Crafts reaction.

(ii) In aniline, due to electron withdrawing effect of the acetyl group, the lone-pair of electrons present on N-atom is attracted by $-COCH_3$ group.

As a result, lone-pair of electrons on N-atom is not exclusively available for donation to the benzene ring and hence, activating effect of the $-NH_2$ group is reduced.

9. (i) We know that more negative is the reduction potential of the electrode, more is the reducing power.

Thus, the increasing order of reducing power is

$$Ag < Hg < Cr < Mg < K.$$

(ii) For hydrogen electrode,

$$H^+ + e^- \longrightarrow \frac{1}{2}H_2$$

Applying Nernst equation,

$$E_{(H^+/\frac{1}{2}H_2)} = E^\circ_{(H^+/\frac{1}{2}H_2)} - \frac{0.0591}{n}\log\frac{1}{[H^+]}$$

$$= 0 - \frac{0.0591}{1}\log\frac{1}{(10^{-10})}$$

$$(\because pH = 10, [H^+] = 10^{-10} M)$$

$$= 0 - \frac{0.0591}{1} \times (10 \log 10) = -0.591 \text{ V}$$

Thus, $E_{(H^+/\frac{1}{2}H_2)} = -0.591$ V

10. *n*-ethane can be obtained from CH_3I by carrying out Wurtz reaction.

$$CH_3I + 2Na + CH_3I \longrightarrow C_2H_6 + 2NaI$$

Butane cannot be synthesised by the above scheme in fairly pure state because Wurtz reaction between CH_3I and C_2H_5Cl will give three products i.e. ethane, butane and propane.

11. (i) **Phenol to 2, 4, 6-tribromophenol**

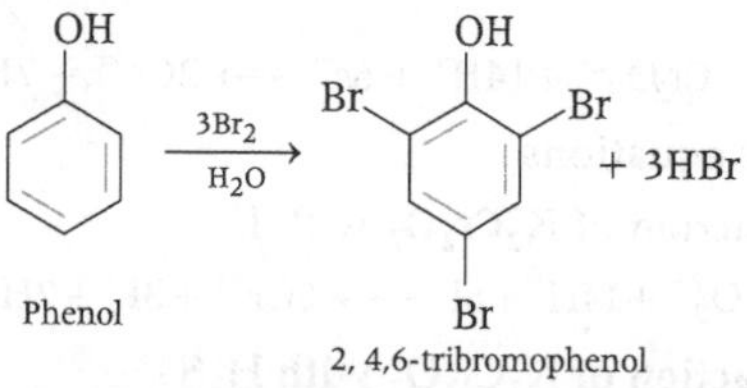

(ii) **Phenol to Benzoic Acid**

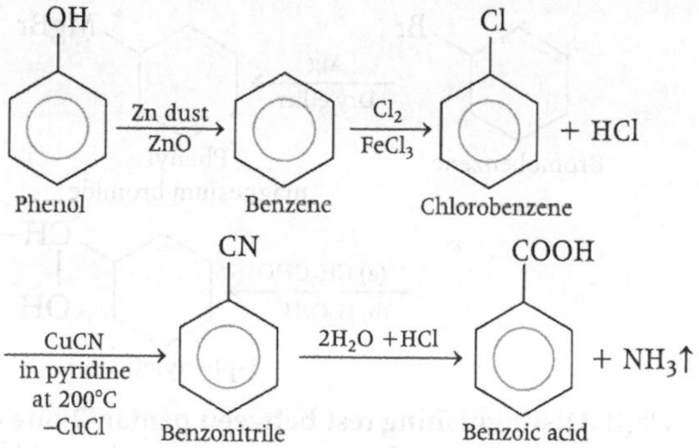

12. (i) Fat soluble vitamins are A, D, E and K whereas, water soluble vitamins are B and C.

(ii) Vitamin C cannot be stored in our body because it is soluble in water, excreted readily in urine Thus, vitamin C must be supplied regularly through diet.

(iii) Vitamin E deficiency causes muscular weakness and increased fragility of RBCs.

13. (i)

t/s	$10^{-2} \times [N_2O_5]$/mol L^{-1}	log $[N_2O_5]$
0	1.63	– 1.79
400	1.36	– 1.87
800	1.14	– 1.94
1200	0.93	– 2.03
1600	0.78	– 2.11
2000	0.64	– 2.19
2400	0.53	–2.28
2800	0.43	– 2.37
3200	0.35	– 2.46

The plot of log $[N_2O_5]$ and time can be represented as

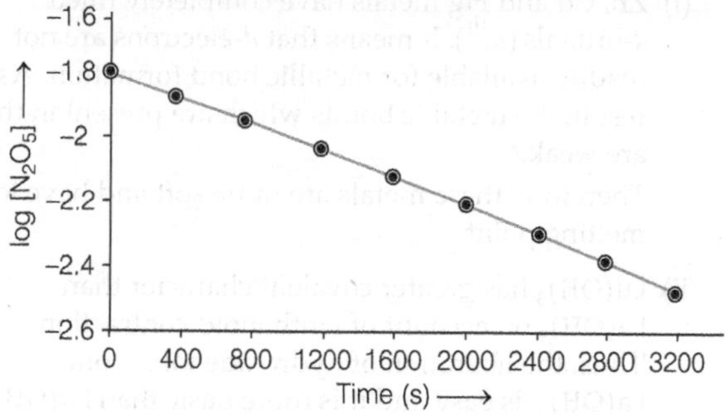

As the plot of log $[N_2O_5]$ *versus* time obtained is a straight line, hence it is a reaction of first order.

(ii) Rate expression for 1st order reaction is

$$\text{Rate} = k[N_2O_5]$$

(iii) For first order reaction, the slope of the line

$$= -\frac{k}{2.303} \quad \text{...(i)}$$

$\therefore$ Also, slope $= \dfrac{-2.46-(-1.79)}{3200-0} = \dfrac{-0.67}{3200}$ ...(ii)

Equating Eqs. (i) and (ii), we get

$$-\frac{k}{2.303} = \frac{-0.67}{3200}$$

or $$k = \frac{0.67 \times 2.303}{3200} = 4.82 \times 10^{-4}\ s^{-1}$$

14. (i)

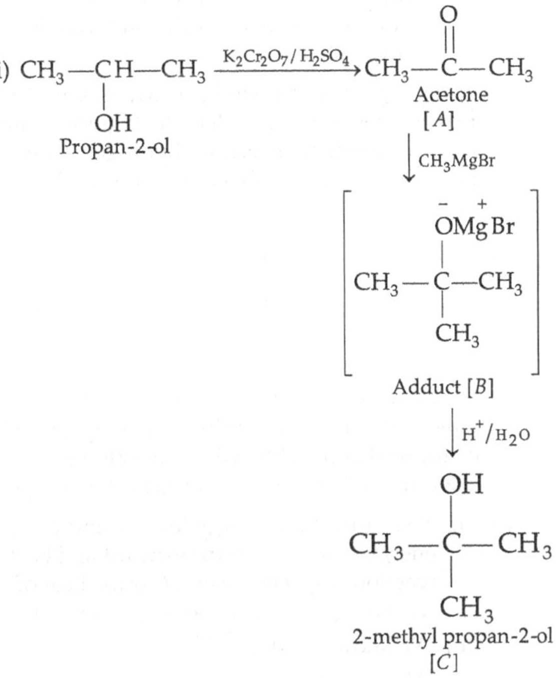

(ii)

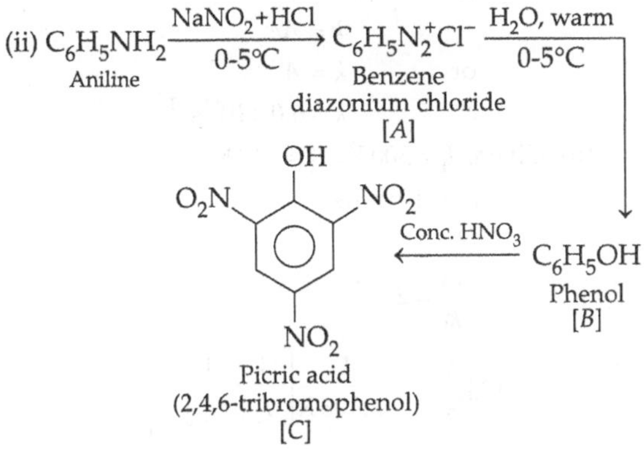

15. (i) According to Raoult's law,

For toluene, $p_1 = p_1^\circ \times \chi_1$

Since, $p_1^\circ = 0.0925$ bar and $\chi_1 = 0.6$

Therefore,, $p_1 = 0.0925 \times 0.6 = 0.0555$ bar

For benzene, $p_2 = p_2^\circ \times \chi_2$

Mole fraction of benzene,

$$\chi_2 = 1 - \chi_1 = 1 - 0.6 = 0.4$$

and $p_2^\circ = 0.256$ bar (Given)

Therefore, $p_2 = 0.256 \times 0.4 = 0.1024$ bar

Total vapour pressure of solution,

$$p_{total} = p_1 + p_2 = 0.0555 + 0.1024 = 0.158 \text{ bar}$$

(ii) Mole fraction of toluene in vapour phase,

$$y_1 = \frac{p_1}{p_{total}} = \frac{0.0555}{0.158} = 0.351$$

16. (i) **Wolff-Kishner reduction** Carbonyl group are easily reduced by hydrazine followed by heating with strong base like alkali to $>CH_2$.

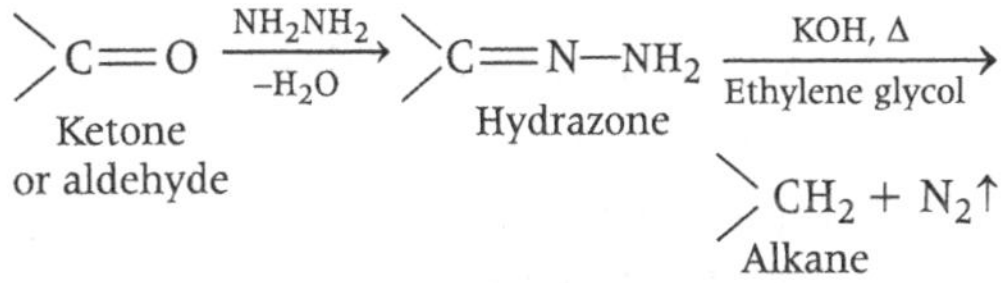

(ii) **Etard Reaction** Toluene on reaction with chromyl chloride in presence of CS_2 followed by hydrolysis produces benzaldehyde.

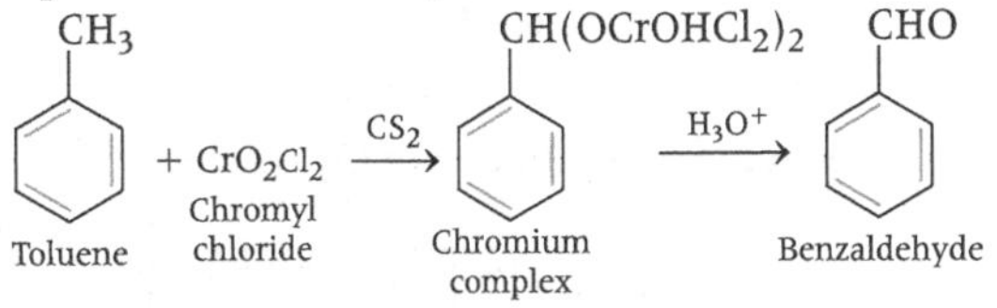

(iii) **Fittig reaction** Aryl halides give analogous compounds when treated with sodium in dry ether in which two aryl groups are joined together. It is called as Fittig reaction.

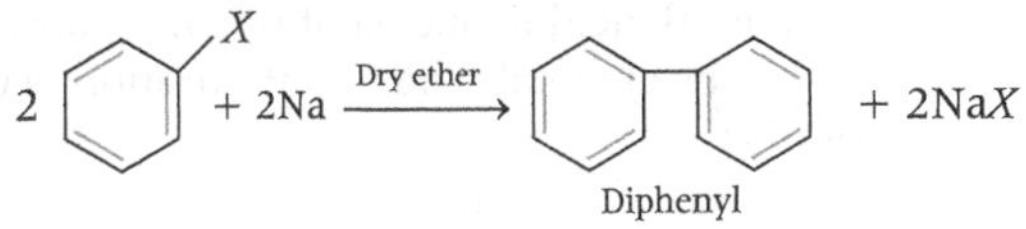

Or The mechanism for the acid catalysed dehydration of propanol is as follows:

$$2CH_3CH_2CH_2OH \xrightarrow[443\ K]{\text{Conc. } H_2SO_4} CH_3CH{=}CH_2 + H_2O$$

***Step* I** First step is the protonation of oxygen of —OH group.

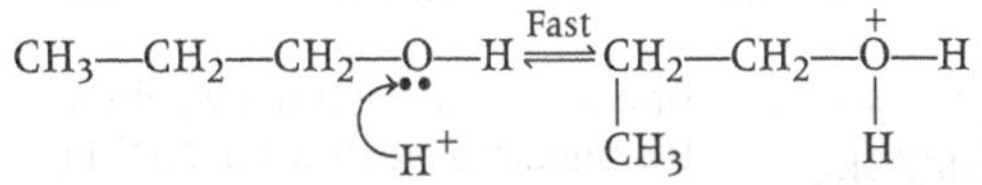

***Step* II** Second step is the loss of a molecule of water to form carbocation.

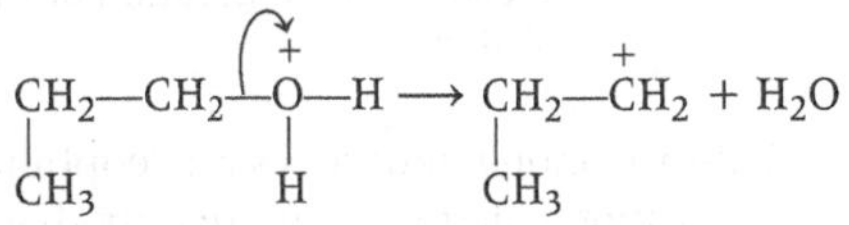

***Step* III** Last step is the deprotonation to form carbon-carbon double bond.

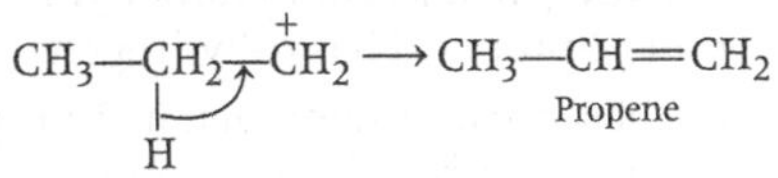

17. More stable is the carbocation, more is the solvolytic reactivity.

(i)

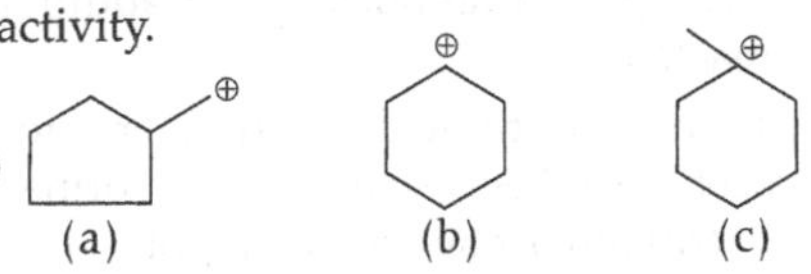

As, 3° > 2° > 1° (carbocation).

∴ (c) > (b) > (a)

(ii) 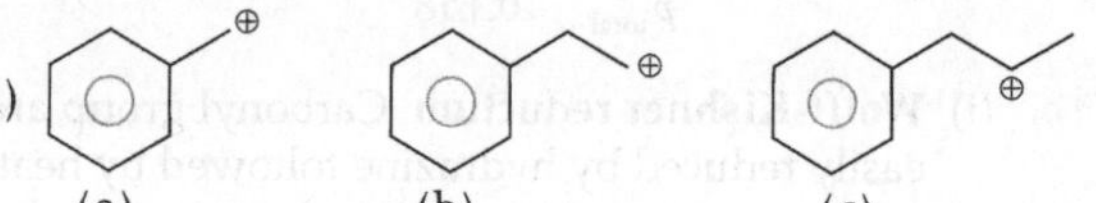

(a) (1°) (+*R*) (b) (1°) (c) (2°)

As, (a) is resonance stabilised.

∴ (a) > (c) > (b)

18. (i) (a) $K_2[Ni(CN)_4]$

(b) $Fe_4[Fe(CN)_6]_3$

(ii) Let the oxidation number of Co in the complex ion $[CoF_6]^{3-}$ be *x*, then

$$x + 6(-1) = -3$$

$$\Rightarrow \quad x = +3$$

Electronic configuration of Co $= [Ar]3d^7 4s^2$

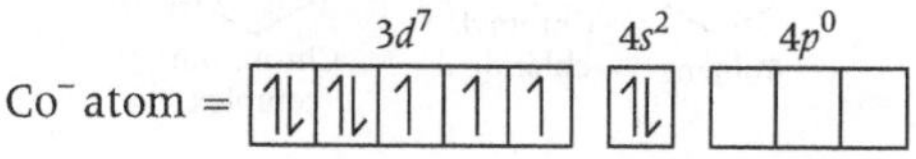

For $Co^{3+} = [Ar]\ 3d^6 4s^0$

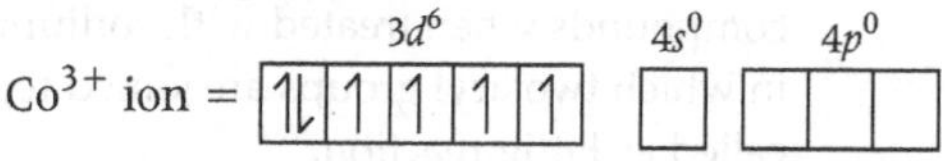

F^- is a weak field ligand, so it will not pair up the *d*-electrons of metal. Thus, configuration of Co^{3+} ion in $[CoF_6]^{3-}$ is

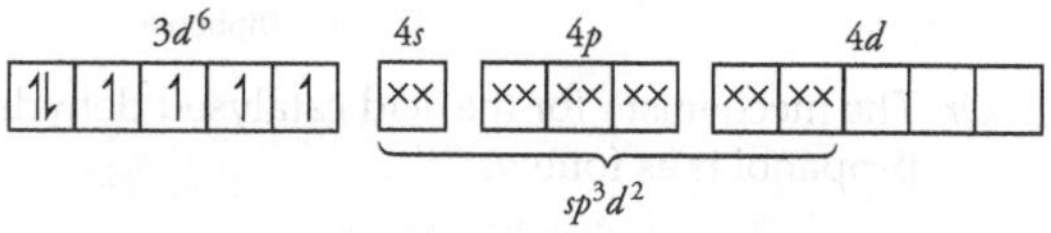

- The hybridisation of $[CoF_6]^{3-}$ complex is sp^3d^2.
- It contains four unpaired electrons. So, it is paramagnetic and geometry is octahedral.

Common Mistake One can make mistake by pairing the unpaired electrons of Co^{3+} in the presence of F^- ligand by assuming F^- as strong ligand while writing the electronic configuration of the complex $[CoF_6]^{3-}$.

19. (i) (a) 2-propanone undergoes nucleophilic addition reactions more readily than 2-propanal because 2-propanone lacks an α-hydrogen adjacent to carbonyl group, while 2-propanal has α-hydrogens.

The absence of α-hydrogen in 2-propanone makes the carbonyl carbon more electrophilic and more attractive to nucleophiles, leading to easier nucleophilic addition reaction.

(b) Trifluoroacetic acid is a stronger acid than acetic acid because the three fluorine atoms in trifluoroacetic acid are highly electronegative and withdraw electron density from the carboxylic acid group. This electron- withdrawing effect strengthens the acidic nature of trifluoroacetic acid, making it more acidic than acetic acid.

(c) Due to resonance, electrophilicity of carbonyl carbon is reduced.

Thus, carboxylic acids become less reactive and do not give characteristics reactions of carbonyl group.

(ii) Given organic compound gets oxidised by Tollen's reagent, hence it is an aldehyde. It gives Cannizzaro reaction, hence there is no α-hydrogen. Only possible structure with molecular formula, $C_5H_{10}O$ is

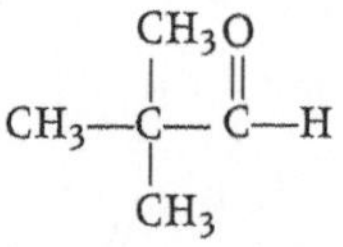

Cannizzaro reaction is disproportionation reaction which takes place in aldehydes having no α-H. It confirms that the aldehyde in question is 2, 2-dimethyl propanal as it has no α-hydrogen.

20. (i) (a) *X* is a threshold energy level; *Y* and *Z* are energy of activation for forward and backward reaction respectively and *Q* is the heat of reaction. (Here, reaction is exothermic).

(b) We know, $k = A \cdot e^{-E_a/RT}$

At $\quad T \longrightarrow \infty$

$$k = Ae^0$$

or $\quad k = A$

$$\therefore \quad k = 6.0 \times 10^{14} s^{-1}$$

(ii) Given, $T_1 = 300\,K$, $T_2 = 310\,K$

$$t_{\frac{1}{2}} = 10 \text{ mins}$$

$$\frac{k_2}{k_1} = 2$$

$$\because \quad \log \frac{k_2}{k_1} = -\frac{E_a}{2.303R}\left[\frac{1}{T_2} - \frac{1}{T_1}\right]$$

$$\therefore \quad \log 2 = -\frac{E_a}{2.303 \times 8.314}\left[\frac{1}{310} - \frac{1}{300}\right]$$

$$E_a = 53598.59\,J/mol$$

$$\Rightarrow \quad \log k_2 = \log A - \frac{E_a}{2.303RT}$$

$$\therefore \log 0.0693 = \log A - \frac{26799.3}{2.303 \times 8.314 \times 310}$$

$$\left[\because t_{1/2} = \frac{0.693}{k}\right]$$

$$\Rightarrow \quad \log A = 3.356$$

Now, $\log k_1 = \log 3.356 - \dfrac{53598.59}{2.303 \times 8.314 \times 300}$

$\Rightarrow \quad k_1 = 1.57 \times 10^{-9}\ \text{min}^{-1}$

21. (i) Salt-bridge completes the circuit and maintains the electrical neutrality of solutions in each of the respective half-cells.

(ii) Daniell cell is an example of galvanic or voltaic cell.

(iii) When $(E_{ext}) < 1.1$ V, then electrons flow from Zn rod to Cu rod. Hence, current flows from Cu to Zn.

(iv) When the external potential (E_{ext}) is equal to 1.1 V, then chemical reaction in the cell stop and there is no flow of electrons or current.

(v) The maximum work that can be obtained from a cell is equal to free energy change for the cell reaction.

$$Zn(s) + Cu^{2+}(aq) \longrightarrow Cu(s) + Zn^{2+}(aq)$$

$$E^\circ_{cell} = E^\circ_{cathode} - E^\circ_{anode}$$
$$= 0.34 - (-0.76) = 1.10\ \text{V}$$

Now, $\Delta G^\circ = -nFE^\circ_{cell}$

$$= -(2) \times 96500 \times 1.10\ [\text{as } n = 2]$$
$$= -212300\ \text{J/mol}$$
$$= -212.3\ \text{kJ/mol}$$

Or

(i) Given, $\kappa = 7.896 \times 10^{-5}\ \text{S cm}^{-1}$,

$\Lambda^\circ_{m\,(CH_3COOH)} = 390.5\ \text{S cm}^2\ \text{mol}^{-1}$

and molarity $(M) = 0.00241$ M

As we know that,

Molar conductivity,

$$\Lambda^C_m = \frac{\kappa \times 1000}{\text{Molarity}}$$
$$= \frac{7.896 \times 10^{-5}\text{S cm}^{-1} \times 1000}{0.00241\ \text{M (mol cm}^{-3})}$$
$$\Lambda^C_m = 32.76\ \text{S cm}^2\ \text{mol}^{-1}$$

Degree of dissociation,

$$\alpha = \frac{\Lambda^C_m}{\Lambda^\circ_m} = \frac{32.76}{390.5} = 8.4 \times 10^{-2}$$

For dissociation constant of acetic acid (CH_3COOH)

	CH_3COOH $\rightleftharpoons$	CH_3COO^- +	H^+
Initial conc.	C	0	0
After time t,	$C - C\alpha$	$C\alpha$	$C\alpha$

Dissociation constant,

$$K_a = \frac{[CH_3COO^-]\,[H^+]}{[CH_3COOH]} = \frac{C\alpha^2}{1-\alpha}$$
$$K_a = \frac{0.00241\ (8.4 \times 10^{-2})^2}{(1 - 0.084)}$$
$$= 1.86 \times 10^{-5}$$

(ii) As we know that, $E^\circ_{cell} = \dfrac{0.0591\text{V}}{n} \log K_{eq}$

and $\quad K_{eq} = K_C, n = 2$

$$0.46 = \frac{0.0591}{2} \log K_C \quad [\because E^\circ_{cell} = 0.46\ \text{V}]$$

or, $\quad \log K_C = 15.6$

and $\quad K_C = \text{antilog}\ (15.6) \approx 3.63 \times 10^{15}$

SPQ Code : **PB-07/15** Series ***i*-Succeed 07-25/15** Roll No.

Sample Question Paper 07

Chemistry 12th (Code 862)

General Instructions

1. This paper is divided into four sections-A, B, C and D. Answer all questions.
2. **Section A** consists of **one** question **having sub-parts** of **one** mark each. **Section B** consists of **ten** questions of **two** marks each. **Section C** consists of **seven** questions of **three** marks each and **Section D** consists of **three** questions of **five** marks each.
3. Internal choices have been provided in one question each in Section B, Section C and Section D.
4. All working, including rough work, should be done on the same sheet as, and adjacent to the rest of the answer.
5. The intended marks for questions or parts of questions are given in brackets [].
6. Balanced questions must be given, wherever possible and diagrams where they are helpful. When solving numerical problems, all essential working must be shown.
7. In working out problems, use the following data:
   Gas constant (R) = 1.987 cal deg^{-1} mol^{-1} = 8.314 JK^{-1} mol^{-1} = 0.0821 dm^3 atm K^{-1} mol^{-1}
   1L atm = 1 dm^3 atm =101.3 J, 1 Faraday =96500 Coulombs.
   Avogadro's number (N_A) = 6.023×10^{23}.

Time : 3 Hrs.

Max. Marks : 70

Section A

[14 Marks]

1. (A) Fill in the blanks by choosing the appropriate word(s) from those given in the brackets.
   [Trigonal coplanar, 108°.9, 120°, less, more, activation energy, catalyst, acidic, basic, poisons, greater, lesser]. [4 × 1]
   (i) At the same temperature, nitrogen gas is .... soluble in water than oxygen but ...... soluble than helium. • *Understanding*
   (ii) Greater the......strength of the ligand, ... is the stability of the complex. • *Understanding*
   (iii) The energy required to initiate a reaction is called ......, that can be lowered by the action of .... • *Recall*
   (iv) The carbonyl carbon possesses a ...... structure with bond angles of .... • *Recall*

   (B) Select and write the correct alternative from the choices given below. [7 × 1]
   (i) The correct order of the decreasing density of haloalkanes is • *Anaslysis*
   (a) $CH_3I > C_2H_5I > C_3H_7I$
   (b) $CH_3I > C_3H_7I > C_2H_5I$
   (c) $C_3H_7I > C_2H_5I > CH_3I$
   (d) $C_2H_5I > C_3H_7I > CH_3I$
   (ii) Which of the following cell is used in low current devices like watches and hearing acids? • *Recall*
   (a) Mercury cell (b) Dry cell
   (c) Daniell cell (d) Fuel cell

(iii) The emf of the cell in which the reaction,
$2Ag^+(aq) + H_2(g) \longrightarrow 2Ag(s) + 2H^+(aq)$
occurs is 0.57 V. The standard reduction potential of Ag electrode is • *Application*

(a) 0.57 V (b) – 0.57 V
(c) 0.40 V (d) 1.14 V

(iv) The product formed when aniline is warmed with chloroform and caustic potash is • *Understanding*

(a) methyl isocyanide
(b) phenyl isocyanide
(c) phenyl chloride
(d) nitrophenol

(v) Which of the following statements are correct?

I. Primary amines show intermolecular hydrogen bonding.
II. Secondary amines do not show intermolecular hydrogen bonding.
III. Tertiary amines show intermolecular hydrogen bonding.
IV. Amines have lower boiling point as compared to those of alcohols and carboxylic acids of comparable molar masses. • *Understanding*

(a) Only I and III (b) Only II and IV
(c) Only I and IV (d) Only III and IV

(vi) **Assertion** (A) Separation of Zr and Hf is difficult.

Reason (R) Zr and Hf lies in the same group of the periodic table. • *Analysis*

(a) Both Assertion and Reason are true and Reason is the correct explanation of Assertion.
(b) Both Assertion and Reason are true but Reason is not the correct explanation of Assertion.
(c) Assertion is true but Reason is false.
(d) Both Assertion and Reason are false.

(vii) **Assertion** (A) Low concentration of oxygen in the blood and tissues of people living at high altitude.

Reason (R) Low atmospheric pressure at high altitude. • *Analysis*

(a) Both Assertion and Reason are true and Reason is the correct explanation of Assertion.
(b) Both Assertion and Reason are true but Reason is not the correct explanation of Assertion.
(c) Assertion is true but Reason is false.
(d) Both Assertion and Reason are false.

(C) Read the passage given below carefully and answer the questions that follow [3 × 1]

Nucleophilic substitution reaction of haloalkane can be conducted according to both S_N1 and S_N2 mechanisms. S_N1 is a two step reaction while S_N2 is a single step reaction. For any haloalkane which mechanism is followed depends on factors such as structure of haloalkane, properties of leaving group, nucleophilic reagent and solvent.

Influences of solvent polarity In S_N1 reaction, the polarity of the system increases from the reactant to the transition state, because a polar solvent has a greater effect on the transition state than the reactant, thereby reducing activation energy and accelerating the reaction. In S_N2 reaction, the polarity of the system generally does not change from the reactant to the transition state and only charge dispersion occurs.

At this time, polar solvent has a great stabilising effect on Nu than the transition state, thereby increasing activation energy and slow down the reaction rate. For example, the decomposition rate (S_N1) of tertiary chlorobutane at 25°C in water (dielectric constant 79) is 300000 times faster than in ethanol (dielectric constant 24).

The reaction rate (S_N2) of 2-bromopropane and NaOH in ethanol containing 40% water is twice slower than in absolute ethanol. Hence, the level of solvent polarity has influence on both S_N1 and S_N2 reaction, but with different results.

Generally, weak polar solvent is favourable for S_N1.

The substitution reaction of tertiary haloalkane is based on S_N1 mechanism in solvents with a strong polarity (for example ethanol containing water).

(i) Why racemisation occurs in S_N1 reactions? • *Understanding*

(ii) Why is ethanol less polar than water? • *Understanding*

(iii) Which one of the following in each pair is more reactive towards S_N2 reaction? • *Understanding*

(a) $CH_3—CH_2—I$ or $CH_3—CH_2—Cl$

(b) 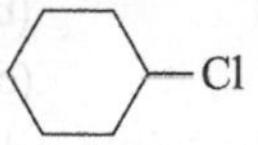 or 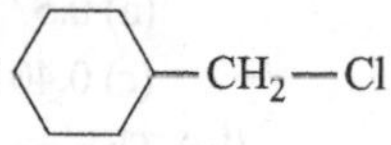

Section B **[20 Marks]**

2. Consider the following reaction, [2]

$$Cu(s) + 2Ag^+(aq) \longrightarrow 2\,Ag(s) + Cu^{2+}(aq)$$

(i) Depict the galvanic cell in which the given reaction takes place. • *Analysis*

(ii) Write the half-cell reactions taking place at cathode and anode. • *Understanding*

3. During chemistry class, a teacher wrote Mn as a transition element on the board. The students were asked to find out oxoanion of Mn in which it shows the oxidation state equal to its group number and the type (acidic, basic and neutral) of this oxoanion. Raja, a student, wrote the answer $KMnO_4$ and neutral whereas another student Vijay wrote MnO_2 and acidic.

Evaluate Raja's and Vijay's responses. • *[Evaluate]*

4. (i) Arrange the following compounds in decreasing order of their basic strength. *p*-methyl aniline, aniline, *p*-nitroaniline. • *Analysis* [2]

(ii) The diazonium salts of aromatic amines are more stable than aliphatic amines. Justify the statement. • *Understanding*

5. Give one chemical test to distinguish between the following pair of compounds. [2]

(i) Primary amine and secondary amine

(ii) Ethylamine and acetamide • *Understanding*

Or

A compound [*A*] on treatment with excess NH_3 and in the presence of $ZnCl_2$ at 300°C gives [*B*]. [*B*] on treatment with $CHCl_3$ and KOH gives phenyl isocyanide. The diazonium salt formed from [*B*] gives [*C*] with ethanol. Identify [*A*], [*B*] and [*C*]. • *Understanding*

6. A 2 molal solution of sodium chloride in water causes an elevation in the boiling point of water by 1.88 K. ($K_b = 0.52\ \text{K kg mol}^{-1}$) [2]

(i) What is the value of van't Hoff factor? • *Application*

(ii) What does it signify? • *Understanding*

7. What amount of water is required to make 10% ethanol in water solution using 10 mL of pure ethanol? • *Application* [2]

8. How will the following be obtained? (Give chemical equations) [2]

(i) Methyl salicylate from phenol

(ii) Benzoic acid from phenol

• *Understanding*

9. Complete and balance the following chemical equations. • *Recall* [2]

(i) $KMnO_4 + H_2S + H_2SO_4 \longrightarrow$

(ii) $Cr_2O_7^{2-} + H^+ + NO_2^- \longrightarrow$

10. Give reasons to support the answer. • *Understanding* [2]

(i) Presence of α-hydrogen in aldehydes and ketones is essential for aldol condensation.

(ii) 3-hydroxypentan -2- one shows positive Tollen's test.

11. (i) Explain the following. • *Understanding* [2]

(a) Scandium forms white coloured ions, yet it is regarded as a transition element.

(b) Transition elements have many irregularities in electronic configurations.

(ii) Calculate the number of moles of $K_2Cr_2O_7$ reduced by one mole of Sn^{2+} ion. • *Application*

Section C

[21 Marks]

12. (i) Show that the time required for the completion of 75% of a reaction of first order is twice the time required for the completion of 50% of the reaction. • *Application* [3]

(ii) At 500 K, half-life period of a gaseous reaction at an initial pressure of 80 kPa is 350s. When pressure is 40 kPa, the half-life period is 175 s. What is the order of reaction? • *Application*

13. Arrange the following esters in the decreasing order of alkaline hydrolysis. • *Analysis* [3]

(i) $HCOOCH_3$, CH_3COOCH_3, $(CH_3)_3C—COOCH_3$, $(CH_3)_2CHCOOCH_3$

(ii) CH_3COOCH_3, $CH_3COOC_2H_5$, $CH_3COOCH(CH_3)_2$, $CH_3COOC(CH_3)_3$

14. The following results have been obtained during the kinetic studies of the reaction, [3]

$$2A + B \longrightarrow C + D.$$

Exp.	$[A]$ / mol L^{-1}	$[B]$ / mol L^{-1}	Initial rate of formation of $[D]$ / mol L^{-1} min^{-1}
1.	0.1	0.1	6.0×10^{-3}
2.	0.3	0.2	7.2×10^{-2}
3.	0.3	0.4	2.88×10^{-1}
4.	0.4	0.1	2.40×10^{-2}

Answer the following questions.

(i) What is the order of reaction with respect to A and B? • *Application*

(ii) Calculate the rate constant. • *Application*

(iii) Determine the reaction rate when the concentration of A and B are 0.3 mol L^{-1} min^{-1} and 0.45 mol L^{-1} respectively. • *Evaluate*

15. Identify the compounds A, B and C in the following reactions. [3]

(i) 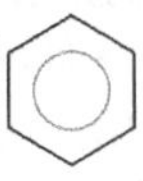 $\xrightarrow[\text{Anhy. } AlCl_3]{CH_3Cl} [A] \xrightarrow[(CH_3CO)_2O]{CrO_3} [B] \xrightarrow{\bar{O}H/H_2O} [C]$

(ii) $CH_3CH_2COOH \xrightarrow[\text{(in ether)}]{LiAlH_4} [A] \xrightarrow{PBr_3} [B] \xrightarrow[\Delta]{\text{Alc.KCN}} [C]$

• *Understanding*

16. Draw the structure and name the product formed, if the following alcohols are oxidised. Assuming that an excess of oxidising agent is used.

(i) $CH_3CH_2CH_2CH_2OH$

(ii) Butan-2-ol

(iii) 2-methylpropan-1-ol • *Understanding*

Or Compound A having molecular formula $C_4H_{10}O$ is found to be soluble in concentrated sulphuric acid. It does not react with sodium metal or potassium permanganate.

On heating with excess of HI, it gives a single alkyl halide. Deduce the structure of compound A and explain all the reactions. • *Understanding*

17. (i) What mass of ethylene glycol (Molar mass 62 g mol^{-1}) must be added to 5.50 kg of water to lower the freezing point of water from 0°C to −10°C? (K_f for water =1.86 K kg mol^{-1}) • *Application* [3]

(ii) If density of methanol is 0.793 g/mL, what is its volume needed for making 2.5 L of its 0.25 M solution? • *Application*

18. (i) Write the product when D-glucose reacts with conc. HNO_3. • *Recall*

(ii) Saurav while studying about vitamins; found out that not all the vitamins can be stored in our body. What do you think can be the possible reason?

Name the vitamins which must be supplied regularly in our diet. • *Recall*

(iii) Write one difference between α-helix and β-pleated structures of proteins. • *Recall*

Section D

[15 Marks]

19. (i) Starting with ethanol, how will the following compounds be synthesised? [5]

(a) But-1-yne

(b) Propane nitrile

(c) Propanol • *Understanding*

(ii) Sulphuric acid is not used during the reaction of alcohols in the conversion of an alcohol to the alkyl iodide. Explain. • *Understanding*

20. (i) Name the type of isomerism shown by the following pairs of coordination compounds. [5]

(a) $[Cu(NH_3)_4][PtCl_4]$ and $[Pt(NH_3)_4][CuCl_4]$

(b) $[Cr(SCN)(H_2O)_5]^{2+}$ and $[Cr(NCS)(H_2O)_5]^{2+}$

(c) $[Cr(H_2O)_6]Cl_3$ and $[CrCl(H_2O)_5]Cl_2 \cdot H_2O$ • *Understanding*

(ii) Explain the following cases giving appropriate reasons.

(a) Nickel does not form low spin octahedral complexes.

(b) Co^{2+} is easily oxidised to Co^{3+} in the presence of a strong ligand. • *Understanding*

Or To explain bonding in coordination compounds various theories were proposed. One of the important theory was valence bond theory. According to that, the central metal ion in the complex makes available a number of empty orbitals for the formation of coordination bonds with suitable ligands. The appropriate atomic orbitals of the metal hybridise to give a set of equivalent orbitals of definite geometry.

The various complex ion are $[Fe(H_2O)_6]^{2+}$ and $[Mn(CN)_6]^{3-}$.

Answer the following questions

(i) Write the type of hybridisation in $[Fe(H_2O)_6]^{2+}$ and $[Mn(CN)_6]^{3-}$ respectively. • *Understanding*

(ii) Write the magnetic nature of $[Fe(H_2O)_6]^{2+}$. • *Understanding*

(iii) Calculate the magnetic moment value of $[Mn(CN)_6]^{3-}$. • *Application*

(iv) What type of complex is $[Mn(CN)_6]^{3-}$ (inner, outer orbital complex)? • *Understanding*

(v) Write the limitations of VBT. • *Recall*

21. (i) (a) The representation of lead storage battery is given below.

$Pb(s)|PbSO_4(s)|H_2SO_4(aq)|PbSO_4(s)|PbO_2(s)|Pb(s)$

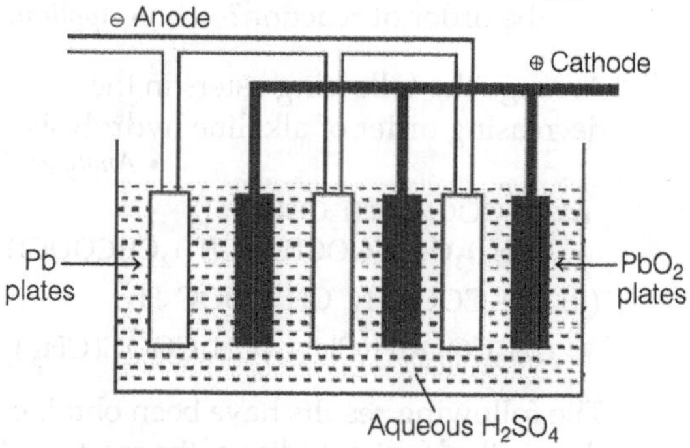

Calculate the E°_{cell} value that can be obtained under standard conditions at 25°C and write the reactions of anode and cathode.

Given, E°_{red} at anode $= -0.356$ V

E°_{red} at cathode $= 1.685$ V • *Application*

(b) How much electricity in terms of Faraday is required to produce 20 g of Ca from molten $CaCl_2$? • *Application*

(ii) (a) The given plot represents the variation of molar conductance against $\sqrt{C}$ (where, C = molar concentration of the electrolyte).

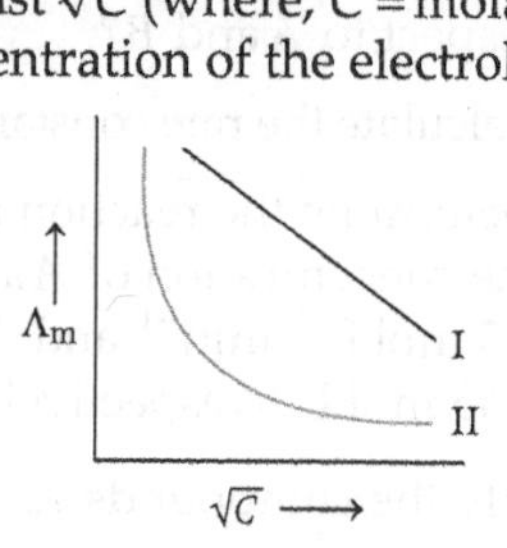

Identify the curve I and II. Justify your answer. • *Understanding*

(b) The resistance of a conductivity cell containing 0.001 M KCl solution at 298 K is 1500 Ω. What is the value of cell constant, if conductivity of 0.001 M KCl solution at 298 K is 0.146×10^{-3} S cm^{-1}? • *Application*

Solutions *in Topper's Style*

My Commitment *I affirm that I am reviewing these solutions only after I have solved the Sample Question Paper on my own. My purpose of looking the solutions is solely to verify whether my answers/solutions were correct or not and to identify my mistakes in case my solutions were wrong or I could not solve that.*

1. (A) (i) less, more
   (ii) basic, greater
   (iii) activation energy, catalyst
   (iv) trigonal coplanar, 120°

(B) (i) (c) Haloalkanes are more dense than alkene, from which they are derived and usually more dense than water. Moreover, density increases as the number of carbon and halogen atom increases.

(ii) (a) Mercury cell is suitable for low current devices like watches, hearing aids etc.

(iii) (a) The cell formed will be

$$H_2(g)\,|\,H^+(aq)\,||\,Ag^+(aq)\,|\,Ag(s)$$

$$E^\circ_{cell} = E^\circ_{cathode} - E^\circ_{anode}$$

$$0.57 = E^\circ_{cathode} - 0.00\text{ V}$$

$$E^\circ_{cathode} = 0.57\text{ V}$$

∴ Standard reduction potential of Ag = 0.57 V

(iv) (b) The product formed is phenyl isocyanide.

$$\underset{\text{Aniline}}{PhNH_2} + 3KOH + CHCl_3 \xrightarrow{\Delta} \underset{\substack{\text{Phenyl}\\ \text{isocyanide}}}{PhNC} + 3KCl + 3H_2O$$

(v) (c) Only I and IV are correct statements while II and III are incorrect as 2° amines shows intermolecular H-bonding while 3° amines do not show intermolecular H-bonding.

(vi) (b) Assertion and Reason are true but Reason is not the correct explanation of Assertion. The correct explanation is,

Separation of Zr and Hf is difficult. This is due to lanthanoid contraction which causes almost similar radii to both of them.

(vii) (a) At high altitudes, the partial pressure of oxygen is less than that at the ground level. This leads to low concentration of oxygen in the blood and tissues of people living at high altitudes.

Thus, both Assertion and Reason are correct and Reason is the correct explanation of Assertion.

(C) (i) In S_N1 reactions, racemisation occurs because in this case when reaction takes place, a reacting group can attacks from both sides, i.e. from back and front.

(ii) Water has two hydrogen atoms bonded to an oxygen while ethanol has a hydrogen and a methyl group bonded to an oxygen. And the electronegativity difference between carbon and oxygen is smaller than that between oxygen and hydrogen in water.

Correspondingly, the polarity of ethanol is lower than that of water.

(iii)(a) CH_3CH_2I and CH_3CH_2Cl both are primary halogen compounds. The reactivity will depend upon the size of halogen atom. Iodine is a better leaving group because of larger size, therefore, CH_3CH_2I will have more reactivity will than CH_3CH_2Cl.

(b)

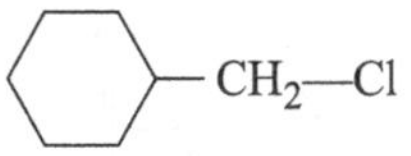

will react faster towards S_N2 reaction because it is a primary alkyl halide whereas

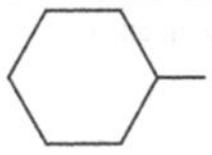

Cl is a secondary halide.

2. (i) $Cu\,|\,Cu^{2+}(aq\ 1M)\,||\,Ag^+(aq.\ 1M)\,|\,Ag$

(ii) At anode, $Cu(s) \longrightarrow Cu^{2+}(aq) + 2e^-$

At cathode, $2Ag^+(aq) + 2e^- \longrightarrow 2Ag(s)$

Net reaction,

$$Cu(s) + 2Ag^+(aq) \longrightarrow Cu^{2+}(aq) + 2Ag(s)$$

3. Permanganate ion, i.e. MnO_4^- with oxidation number +7. Potassium permanganate ($KMnO_4$) is a salt made from strong acid and strong base. So, it is a neutral salt.

Thus, Raja's response was correct.

4. (i) The decreasing order of basic strength is,

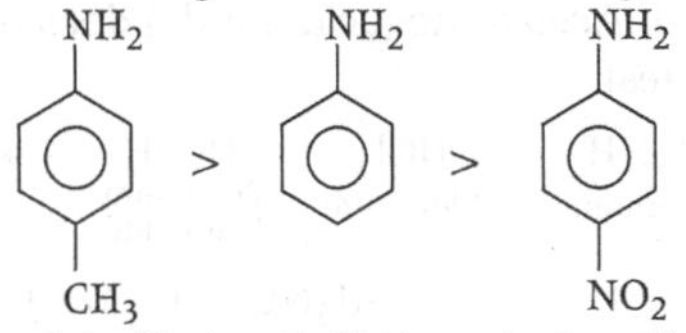

(*p*-methyl aniline) (Aniline) (*p*-nitroaniline)

The electron donating group (+ *I* effect) increases the basic strength. Whereas, electron withdrawing group (– *I* effect) decreases the electron density on the nitrogen atom, hence, the basic strength decreases.

(ii) The arene diazonium ion in diazonium salts of aromatic amines is stabilised by resonance.

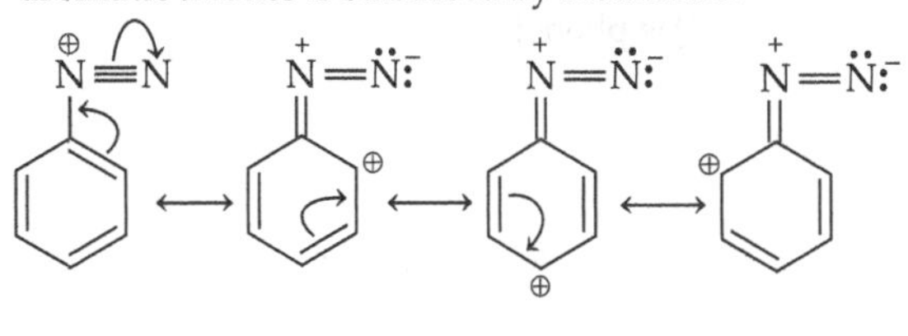

But, no such resonance stabilisation is possible in diazonium salts of aliphatic amines.

5. (i) With Hinsberg's reagent (benzene sulphonyl chloride), primary amine gives N-alkyl benzene sulphonamide. Hydrogen attached to nitrogen is strongly acidic due to presence of strong electron withdrawing sulphonyl group. Hence, it is soluble in alkali.

On the other hand, secondary amine on reaction with benzene sulphonyl chloride yields N, N-dialkylbenzene sulphonamide. It does not have any H-atom attached to N-atom. It is not acidic and hence, insoluble in alkali.

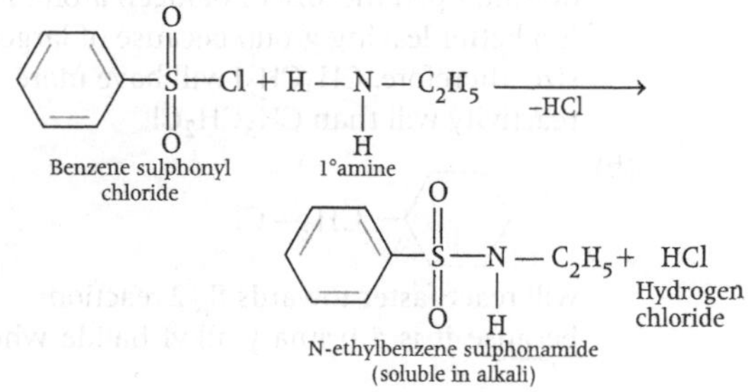

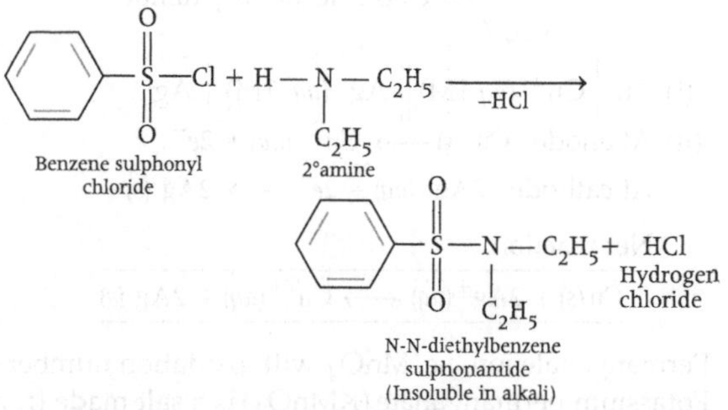

(ii) Ethylamine (1° amine) when heated with chloroform and alcoholic KOH, it forms ethyl carbylamine which has peculiar offensive smell. Acetamide (acid amide) does not give this test.

$$\underset{\text{Ethylamine}}{C_2H_5NH_2} + \underset{\text{Chloroform}}{CHCl_3} + \underset{\text{Potassium hydroxide}}{3KOH} \longrightarrow \underset{\substack{\text{Ethyl isocyanide}\\ \text{(Offensive smell)}}}{C_2H_5NC} + \underset{\text{Potassium chloride}}{3KCl} + \underset{\text{Water}}{3H_2O}$$

Or

$[B]$ on treatment with $CHCl_3$ and KOH gives phenyl isocyanide thus, $[B]$ is aniline. Further, $[A]$ on treatment with excess of NH_3 in presence of $ZnCl_2$ of 300°C gives aniline. Thus, $[A]$ is phenol.

The reaction takes place as follow

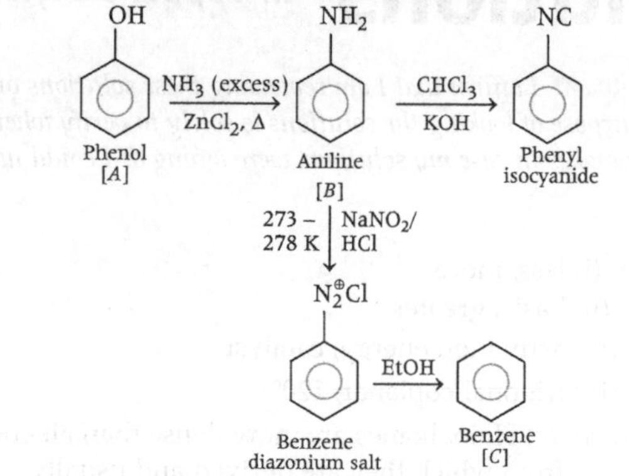

Thus, $[A]$ = phenol, $[B]$ = aniline, $[C]$ = benzene.

6. (i) Given,

Molality $(m) = 2$ molal

Elevation in boiling point, $\Delta T_b = 1.88$ K,

van't Hoff factor, $i = ?$

$$K_b = 0.52 \text{ K kg mol}^{-1}$$

We know that, $\Delta T_b = i\ K_b m$

van't Hoff factor,

$$(i) = \Delta T_b / K_b \times m = \frac{1.88}{0.52 \times 2} = 1.808$$

(ii) Since, value of van't Hoff factor is greater than one, it signifies that solute undergoes dissociation.

7. Given, volume of pure ethanol = 10 mL

Volume % of ethanol = 10%

Total amount of solution = ?

$$\text{Volume \% of ethanol} = \frac{\text{Volume of ethanol}}{\text{Total volume of solution}} \times 100$$

or $$10 = \frac{10}{\text{Total volume of solution}} \times 100$$

$\Rightarrow$ Total volume of solution = 100 mL

Thus, the amount of water used

= 100 − amount of ethanol

= (100 − 10) mL = 90 mL

8. (i) **Methyl salicylate from phenol**

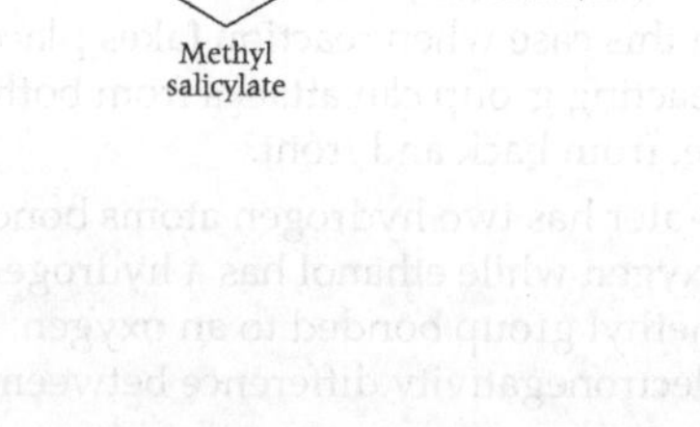

(ii) **Benzoic acid from phenol**

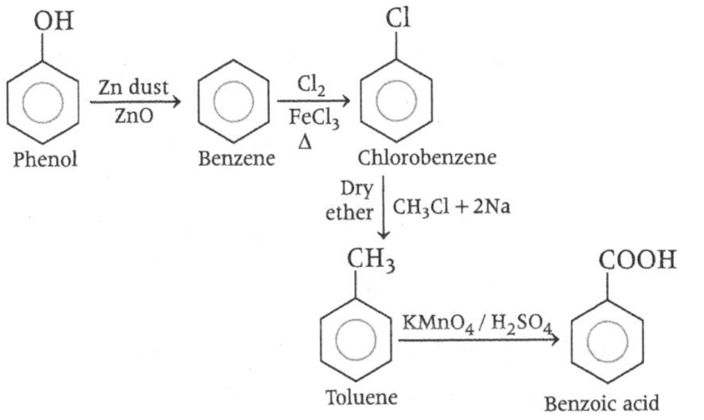

9. (i) $2KMnO_4 + 3H_2SO_4 + 5H_2S \longrightarrow K_2SO_4 + 2MnSO_4 + 8H_2O + 5S$

(ii) $Cr_2O_7^{2-} + 8H^+ + 3NO_2^- \longrightarrow 2Cr^{3+} + 3NO_3^- + 4H_2O$

Common Mistake One can make mistake in balancing the chemical reaction.

10. (i) The presence of α-hydrogen in aldehydes and ketones is essential for aldol condensation because they are acidic in nature (due to the presence of electron withdrawing carbonyl group).
As a result, the electron density at alpha C—H bond decreases and hence, H-atom becomes weakly held which can be easily abstracted by strong bases forming enolate ion, which are stabilised by resonance.

(ii) The structure of 3-hydroxypentan-2-one is

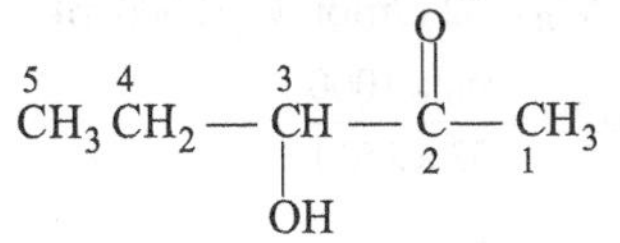

All α-hydroxy ketones give Tollen's test. Since, α-hydroxy ketones have the ability to tautomerise to aldehydes which gives Tollen's test.
The given compound is also a α-hydroxy ketone. Thus, it gives this test.

11. (i) (a) Scandium in ground state has one *d*-electron. Hence, it is regarded as transition element.

(b) In transition elements, the $(n-1)d$ subshell and *ns* subshell have very small difference in energy. The incoming electron may enter into either *ns* or $(n-1)d$ subshell.
Thus, they show irregularities in their electronic configuration.

(ii) $Cr_2O_7^{2-} + 14H^+ + 6e^- \longrightarrow 2Cr^{3+} + 7H_2O$

$(Sn^{2+} \longrightarrow Sn^{4+} + 2e^-) \times 3$

$Cr_2O_7^{2-} + 14H^+ + 3Sn^{2+} \longrightarrow 2Cr^{3+} + 3Sn^{4+} + 7H_2O$

Thus, from the equation, it is clear that 3 moles of Sn^{2+} reduce one mole of $Cr_2O_7^{2-}$ ion. Hence, 1 mole of Sn^{2+} will reduce 1/3 mole of $Cr_2O_7^{2-}$ ion.

12. (i) For a first order reaction, rate constant

$$k = \frac{2.303}{t} \log \frac{[A]_0}{[A]}$$

where, *t* is time, $[A]_0$ is initial concentration and $[A]$ is concentration left after time *t*.

For 75% completion, suppose $[A]_0 = 100$ M, then $[A] = 100 - 75 = 25$ M

$$k = \frac{2.303}{t} \log \frac{100}{25} = \frac{1.386}{t}$$

[As $\log 4 = 2 \log 2 = 2 \times 0.3010$]

For 50% completion, $k = \frac{0.693}{t_{1/2}}$

But, for a given reaction, *k* is constant.

$$\therefore \quad \frac{1.386}{t} = \frac{0.693}{t_{1/2}} \Rightarrow \frac{t}{t_{1/2}} = \frac{1.386}{0.693} = 2$$

or $t = 2t_{1/2}$

So, time (t) required for completion of 75% of a reaction is twice the time required for completion of 50% (half-life) of the reaction.

(ii) $$\frac{(t_{1/2})_1}{(t_{1/2})_2} = \left(\frac{p_2}{p_1}\right)^{n-1}$$

$$\frac{350}{175} = \left(\frac{40}{80}\right)^{n-1} \quad \text{or} \quad (2)^1 = \left(\frac{1}{2}\right)^{n-1}$$

$\therefore$ $n = 0$ (zero-order reaction)

13. The greater is the steric hindrance either on alcoholic portion or on the acidic portion, the more difficult will be the hydrolysis.
Therefore, the order of given compounds towards hydrolysis is

(i) $HCOOCH_3 > CH_3COOCH_3 > (CH_3)_2CHCOOCH_3 > (CH_3)_3C—COOCH_3$

(ii) $CH_3COOCH_3 > CH_3COOC_2H_5 > CH_3COOCH(CH_3)_2 > CH_3COOC(CH_3)_3$

14. (i) Rate law may be expressed as,

Rate $= k[A]^x[B]^y$

$(\text{Rate})_1 = 6.0 \times 10^{-3} = k\,(0.1)^x(0.1)^y$ ...(i)

$(\text{Rate})_2 = 7.2 \times 10^{-2} = k\,(0.3)^x(0.2)^y$ ...(ii)

$(\text{Rate})_3 = 2.88 \times 10^{-1} = k(0.3)^x(0.4)^y$ ...(iii)

$(\text{Rate})_4 = 2.40 \times 10^{-2} = k(0.4)^x(0.1)^y$ ...(iv)

By dividing Eqs. (i) with (ii) we get,

$$\frac{(\text{Rate})_1}{(\text{Rate})_4} = \frac{6.0 \times 10^{-3}}{2.40 \times 10^{-2}} = \frac{k\,(0.1)^x\,(0.1)^y}{k\,(0.4)^x(0.1)^y}$$

or $$\frac{1}{4} = \frac{(0.1)^x}{(0.4)^x} = \left(\frac{1}{4}\right)^x$$

$\therefore$ $x = 1$

By dividing Eqs. (ii) with (iii) we get,

$$\frac{(\text{Rate})_2}{(\text{Rate})_3} = \frac{7.2 \times 10^{-2}}{2.88 \times 10^{-1}} = \frac{k(0.3)^x\,(0.2)^y}{k(0.3)^x(0.4)^y}$$

or $$\frac{1}{4} = \frac{(0.2)^y}{(0.4)^y} = \left(\frac{1}{2}\right)^y$$

$\therefore \quad y = 2$

Thus, rate law expression is given by

$$\text{Rate} = k[A][B]^2$$

(ii) Rate $= k[A][B]^2$

$$k = \frac{\text{Rate}}{[A][B]^2} = \frac{6\times10^{-3}}{[0.1][0.1]^2}$$

$$= \frac{6\times10^{-3}}{0.1\times0.1\times0.1} = 6\times10^{-6}\,\text{mol}^{-2}\,\text{L}^2\,\text{min}^{-1}$$

(iii) Rate $= 6\times10^{-6}\times[0.3][0.45]^2$

$$= 0.3645\times10^{-6}\ \text{mol L}^{-1}\ \text{min}^{-1}$$

15. (i)

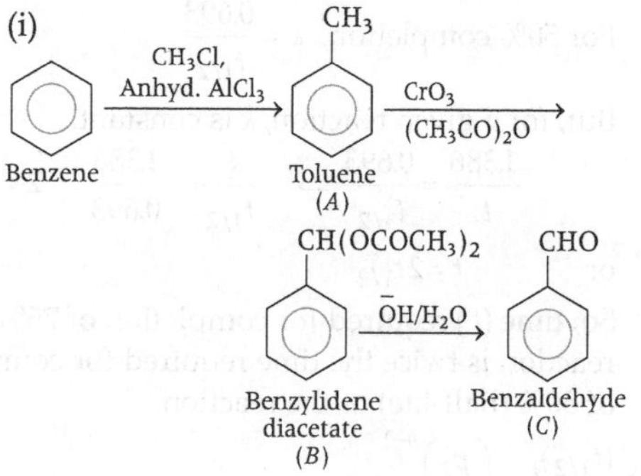

(ii) $CH_3CH_2—COOH \xrightarrow[\text{(in ether)}]{LiAlH_4}$
Propanoic acid

$CH_3CH_2CH_2—OH \xrightarrow{PBr_3} CH_3CH_2CH_2—Br$
n-propyl alcohol (*A*) → *n*-propylbromide (*B*)

$\xrightarrow[\Delta]{\text{Alc. KCN}} CH_3CH_2CH_2—CN$
n-butylnitrile (*C*)

16. (i) $CH_3CH_2CH_2CH_2OH \xrightarrow[\text{Oxidation}]{[O]} CH_3CH_2CH_2COOH$
n-Butanol → Butanoic acid

(ii) $CH_3CH(OH)—CH_2CH_3 \xrightarrow[\text{Oxidation}]{[O]} CH_3—C(=O)—CH_2CH_3$
Butan-2-ol → Butan-2-one

(iii) $CH_3—CH(CH_3)—CH_2OH \xrightarrow[\text{Oxidation}]{[O]} CH_3—CH(CH_3)—COOH$
2-methyl propan-1-ol → 2-methyl propanoic acid

Or (i) As compound *A* does not react with sodium metal or potassium permanganate, it cannot be an alcohol.

(ii) As compound *A* dissolves in conc. H_2SO_4, it may be an ether.

(iii) As compound *A* on heating with excess of HI, gives a single alkyl halide, therefore compound *A* must be a symmetrical ether.

(iv) The only symmetrical ether having molecular formula $C_4H_{10}O$ is diethyl ether. Thus, compound *A* is diethyl ether.

$CH_3—CH_2—O—CH_2—CH_3$.

$CH_3CH_2—O—CH_2CH_3 \xrightarrow{\text{Conc. } H_2SO_4} \left[CH_3—CH_2—\overset{+}{O}(H)—CH_2—CH_3\right]HSO_4^-$
Soluble oxonium salt

$CH_3CH_2OCH_2CH_3 \xrightarrow[\Delta]{HI} 2\,CH_3CH_2—I$
(*A*) Diethyl ether → Ethyl iodide

17. (i) Given, *M* (ethylene glycol) $= 62\ \text{g mol}^{-1}$,

W_1 (water) $= 5.50\ \text{kg} = 5500\ \text{g}$

$\Delta T_f = 0°\text{C} - (-10°\text{C}) = 10°\text{C} = 10\ \text{K}$

w_2 (ethylene glycol) =?

$K_f = 1.86\ \text{K kg mol}^{-1}$

$$\because \quad \Delta T_f = \frac{K_f \times w_2 \times 1000}{M \times W_1}$$

$$\therefore \quad w_2 = \frac{\Delta T_f \times M \times W_1}{K_f \times 1000} = \frac{10\times62\times5500}{1.86\times1000}$$

$$= 1833.33\ \text{g} = 1.833\ \text{kg}$$

(ii) As we know that molarity,

$$M = \frac{w_B \times 1000}{M_B \times V}$$

Given, Molarity $= 0.25\ \text{M}$,

$M_B = 32\ \text{g/mol}$, $V = 2500\ \text{mL}$

$$\therefore \quad 0.25 = \frac{w_B \times 1000}{32\times2500}$$

$$\Rightarrow \quad w_B = 20\ \text{g}$$

As, mass = volume × density

$\therefore \quad 20\ \text{g} = \text{volume} \times 0.793\ \text{g/mL}$

[$\because$ Given, $\rho = 0.793$ g/mL]

Volume $= 25.22$ mL

18. (i) It is saccharic acid which is formed as per the reaction given below.

$CHO—(CHOH)_4—CH_2OH \xrightarrow[HNO_3]{\text{Oxidation}} COOH—(CHOH)_4—COOH$
D-Glucose → Saccharic acid

(ii) Water soluble vitamins like vitamin B and vitamin C (except vitamin B_{12}) are readily excreted in urine and thus, cannot be stored in our body.
Therefore, they must be regularly supplied in our diets.

(iii) Difference between α-helix and β-pleated structures

α-helix structure	β-pleated structure
If the size of *R*-group is large, intramolecular H-bonds are formed between C=O of molecule and NH of amino acid in polypeptide chain that gives right handed α-helix structure, i.e. it is formed by the folding of a single polypeptide chain due to hydrogen bonding.	If size of *R*-group is small, intermolecular H-bonds forms between C=O of polypeptide chain with N—H of other giving β-pleated sheet structure, i.e. it is formed by the folding in more than one polypeptide chain due to hydrogen bonding.

19. (i) (a) $\underset{\text{Ethanol}}{CH_3—CH_2—OH} \xrightarrow{SOCl_2} CH_3—CH_2—Cl \xrightarrow{CH\equiv CMgBr} \underset{\text{But-1-yne}}{CH_3—CH_2—C\equiv CH}$

(b) $\underset{\text{Ethanol}}{CH_3—CH_2—OH} \xrightarrow{\text{Red P}/Br_2} \underset{\text{Ethyl bromide}}{CH_3CH_2Br} \xrightarrow{\text{KCN, } aq. \text{ ethanol}} \underset{\text{Propane nitrile}}{CH_3CH_2—CN}$

(c) $\underset{\text{Ethanol}}{CH_3CH_2OH} \underset{-H_2O}{\xrightarrow{HI}} CH_3CH_2I \xrightarrow{\text{Alc. KCN}} \underset{\text{Ethyl cyanide}}{CH_3CH_2CN} \underset{Na/C_2H_5OH}{\xrightarrow{4[H]}} \underset{\text{Propanamine}}{CH_3CH_2CH_2NH_2} \underset{HNO_2}{\xrightarrow{NaNO_2/HCl}} \underset{\text{Propanol}}{CH_3CH_2CH_2OH}$

(ii) If sulphuric acid is used, then HI gets used up to produce I_2 gas because H_2SO_4 is an oxidising agent. As a result, the action of alcohol on acid to produce alkyl iodide cannot occur.

$$KI + H_2SO_4 \xrightarrow{\text{Heat}} KHSO_4 + HI$$

$$2HI + H_2SO_4 \longrightarrow I_2 + SO_2 + 2H_2O$$

20. (i) (a) In both the given compounds, interchange of ligands (NH_3 and Cl) between cationic and anionic entities of different metal ion (Cu and Pt) takes place. Hence, they show **coordination isomerism.**

(b) In both the given compounds, ambidentate ligand SCN is present. In $[Cr[(SCN)(H_2O)_5]^{2+}$ complex, SCN is attached through S with Cr while in $[Cr(NCS)(H_2O)_5]^{2+}$ complex, NCS is attached through N with Cr. Hence, they show **linkage isomerism.**

(c) In both the given compounds, number of solvent ligand molecules and counter ions differ in the crystal lattice. So, they show **hydrate isomerism.**

(ii) (a) In case of Ni, electronic configuration of Ni = $3d^8\,4s^2$ and when it forms Ni^{2+} ion its electronic configuration becomes $3d^8 4s^0$.

Ni^{2+} = 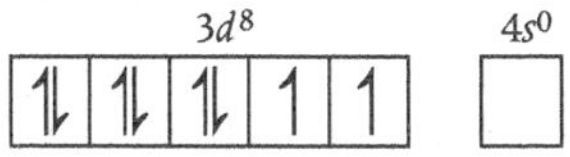

For low spin complexes, electrons gets pair up. Thus, will produce only one empty *d*-orbital.

Hence, d^2sp^3-hybridisation is not possible in Ni to form octahedral complexes.

(b) The electronic configuration of Co^{3+} is $3d^6\,4s^0$. So, pairing occurs in the presence of a strong ligand.

Thus, there are no unpaired electrons and it is highly stable.

$Co^{3+} = 3d^6$, 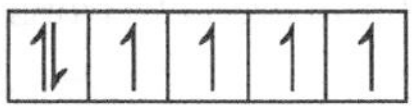

In the presence of a strong ligand,

However, in Co^{2+}, electronic configuration is $3d^7$, there is one unpaired electron even after pairing occurs in the presence of a strong ligand.

$Co^{2+} = 3d^7$, 

In the presence of a strong ligand

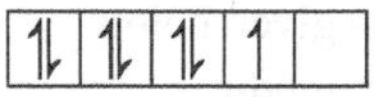

This unpaired electron can be easily lost and shows an oxidation state of +3.

Hence, Co^{2+} is oxidised to more stable Co^{3+}.

Or

(i) (a) Let oxidation number of Fe in the complex ion $[Fe(H_2O)_6]^{2+}$ is *x*, then

$$x + 6 \times 0 = +2$$
$$x = +2$$

Electronic configuration of Fe is $[Ar]3d^6 4s^2$.

Fe-atom = $[Ar]\ 3d^6 4s^2$ = 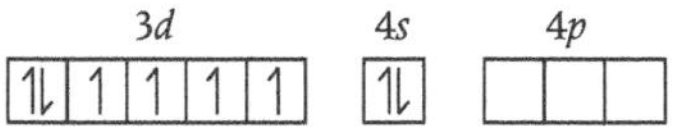

Fe^{2+} atom = $[Ar]3d^6$ = 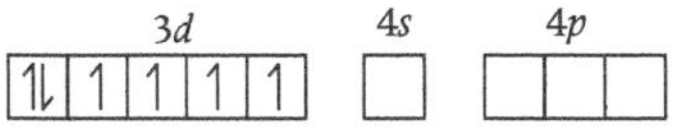

H_2O is a weak field ligand, so it will not pair up $3d^6$ electrons. Thus,

$[Fe(H_2O)_6]^{2+}$ 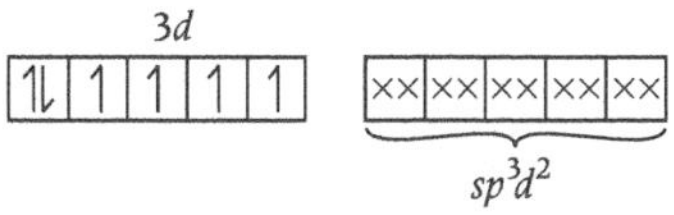

Coordination number of complex is 6.

Hence, hybridisation is sp^3d^2.

(b) In$[Mn(CN)_6]^{3-}$, Mn is in +3 oxidation state.

Mn= [Ar] $3d^5 4s^2$ = 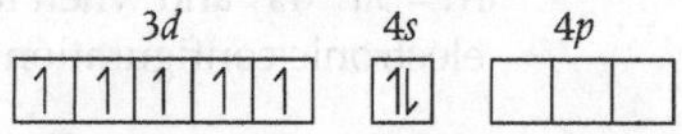

Mn^{3+}= [Ar] $3d^4$ = 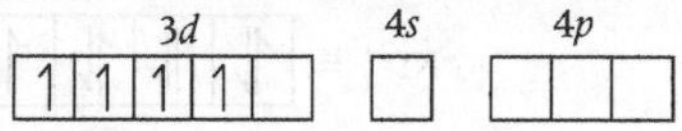

As CN^- is a strong field ligand, So, pairing of electrons will take place

$[Mn(CN)_6]^{3-}$ = 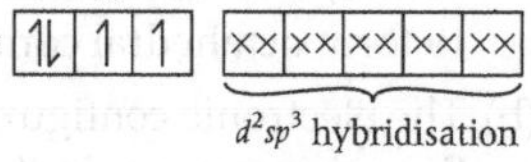

(ii) It contains four unpaired electrons. So, it is paramagnetic.

(iii) Magnetic moment $= \sqrt{n(n+2)} = \sqrt{2(2+2)}$

(as 2 unpaired electrons are present)

$= \sqrt{8} = 2.83$ BM

where, n = no. of unpaired electrons

(iv) Type of complex – Inner orbital

(v) Valence Bond Theory (VBT) suffers from the following shortcomings.

(a) It involves number of assumptions.

(b) It does not give quantitative interpretation of magnetic data.

(c) It does not explain the colour exhibited by coordination compounds. (Any one)

21. (i) (a) The cell reaction when the battery is in use are given below.

At anode,

$Pb(s) + SO_4^{2-}(aq) + H_2O \longrightarrow PbSO_4(s) + 2e^-$;

$E^\circ_{red} = -0.356$ V

At cathode,

$PbO_2(s) + SO_4^{2-}(aq) + 4H^+(aq) + 2e^- \longrightarrow PbSO_4(s) + 2H_2O$; $E^\circ_{red} = 1.685$ V

Overall reaction,

$Pb(s) + 2H_2SO_4(aq) + PbO_2(s) \longrightarrow 2PbSO_4(s) + 2H_2O(l)$

$E^\circ_{cell} = E^\circ_{cathode} - E^\circ_{anode}$

$= 1.685 - (-0.356)$

$E^\circ_{cell} = 2.041$ V

(b) Electrode reaction :

$$\underset{2F}{Ca^{2+}(aq) + 2e^-} \longrightarrow \underset{40g}{Ca(s)}$$

To produce 40g of Ca from molten $CaCl_2$, 2F electricity is required.

∴ To produce 20g of Ca from molten $CaCl_2$, 1F of electricity is required.

(ii) (a)

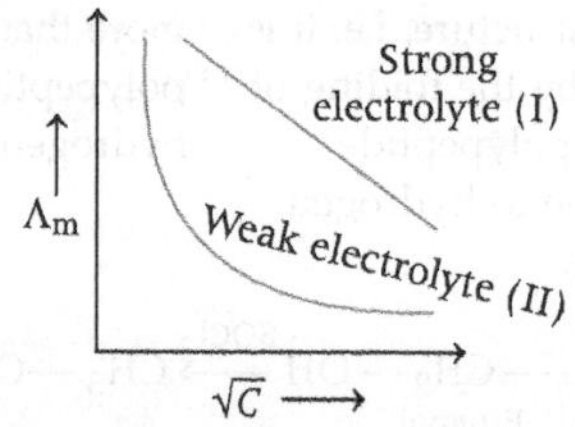

The linear plot (I) corresponds to strong electrolyte. This is because in case of strong electrolyte, it has already dissociated completely and thus, on dilution, the rise in conductivity is not very much. However, the exponential curve (II) represents weak electrolyte as on dilution, complete dissociation of weak electrolyte occurs and therefore, their is a steep increase in molar conductivity.

(b) Given, $\kappa = 0.146 \times 10^{-3}$ S cm^{-1}, $R = 1500\Omega$

∵ Conductivity (κ)

$$= \frac{1}{\text{Resistance } (R)} \times \text{Cell constant}$$

$$\therefore 0.146 \times 10^{-3} \text{ S cm}^{-1} = \frac{1}{1500\Omega} \times \text{Cell constant}$$

$\Rightarrow$ Cell constant $= 0.146 \times 10^{-3}$ S cm^{-1} $\times 1500\Omega$

$= 219 \times 10^{-3}$ cm^{-1}

$= 0.219$ cm^{-1}

SPQ Code : **PB-08/15** Series ***i*-Succeed 08-25/15** Roll No.

Sample Question Paper 08

Chemistry 12th (Code 862)

General Instructions

1. This paper is divided into four sections-A, B, C and D. Answer all questions.
2. **Section A** consists of **one** question **having sub-parts** of **one** mark each. **Section B** consists of **ten** questions of **two** marks each. **Section C** consists of **seven** questions of **three** marks each and **Section D** consists of **three** questions of **five** marks each.
3. Internal choices have been provided in one question each in Section B, Section C and Section D.
4. All working, including rough work, should be done on the same sheet as, and adjacent to the rest of the answer.
5. The intended marks for questions or parts of questions are given in brackets [].
6. Balanced questions must be given, wherever possible and diagrams where they are helpful. When solving numerical problems, all essential working must be shown.
7. In working out problems, use the following data:
   Gas constant (R) = 1.987 cal deg^{-1} mol^{-1} = 8.314 JK^{-1} mol^{-1} = 0.0821 dm^3 atm K^{-1} mol^{-1}
   1L atm = 1 dm^3 atm =101.3 J, 1 Faraday =96500 Coulombs.
   Avogadro's number (N_A) = 6.023×10^{23}.

Time : 3 Hrs.

Max. Marks : 70

Section A

[14 Marks]

1. (A) Fill in the blanks by choosing the appropriate word(s) from those given in the brackets. [4×1]

[CrO_4^{2-}, CrO_4^{-}, dry acetone, Fe^{3+}, $A_0/2k$, initial concentration, Fe^{2+}, Finkelstein reaction, final concentration, A_0/k, alkaline oxygen, carbon dioxide]

(i) Alkyl iodides are often prepared by the reaction of alkyl chloride/bromides with NaI in ...... This reaction is known as ....
• *Recall*

(ii) Haemoglobin, the .... carrier in blood, is a coordination compound of .... with porphyrin ring. • *Recall*

(iii) For zero order reaction, $A \longrightarrow$ products, with rate constant k, the half-life period is given by $t_{1/2}$ = ...
Thus, half-life period of a zero order is directly proportional to ....
• *Understanding*

(iv) In .... medium, dichromate ion exist as .... ion. • *Understanding*

(B) Select and write the correct alternative from the choices given below. [7 ×1]

(i) The correct order of the increasing magnitude of Δ_o for the octahedral complexes of Co (atomic number = 27) is
• *Analysis*

(a) $[Co(CN)_6]^{3-} < [Co(C_2O_4)_3]^{3-} < [Co(H_2O)_6]^{3+} < [Co(NH_3)_6]^{3+}$

(b) $[Co(C_2O_4)_3]^{3-} < [Co(H_2O)_6]^{3+} < [Co(NH_3)_6]^{3+} < [Co(CN)_6]^{3-}$

(c) $[Co(H_2O)_6]^{3+} < [Co(NH_3)_6]^{3+} < [Co(CN)_6]^{3-} < [Co(C_2O_4)_3]^{3-}$

(d) $[Co(NH_3)_6]^{3+} < [Co(H_2O)_6]^{3+}$ $[Co(C_2O_4)_3]^{3-} < [Co(CN)_6]^{3-}$

(ii) The compound that reacts fastest with Lucas reagent at room temperature is • *Understanding*

(a) butan -1-ol

(b) butan -2-ol

(c) 2- methyl propan-1-ol

(d) 2- methyl propan-2- ol

(iii) If α is the degree of dissociation of Na_2SO_4, then the van't Hoff factor (i) used for calculating the molecular mass is • *Application*

(a) $1-2\alpha$ (b) $1+2\alpha$

(c) $1-\alpha$ (d) $1+\alpha$

(iv) An electrochemical cell can behave like an electrolytic cell when • *Understanding*

(a) $E_{cell} = 0$ (b) $E_{cell} > E_{ext}$

(c) $E_{ext} > E_{cell}$ (d) $E_{cell} = E_{ext}$

(v) Which of the following are true about diazonium salts?

I. Diazonium salts are colourless crystalline solids, but become coloured on exposure to air.

II. Diazonium salts of aromatic amines are comparatively less stable in solution than corresponding salts of aliphatic amine.

III. Diazonium salts are highly reactive and thus undergo substitution or coupling reactions.

IV. They are covalent in nature and thus soluble in water.

• *Understanding*

(a) I and II only (b) I and III only

(c) II and IV only (d) III and IV only

(vi) **Assertion** (A) *Iso*-propyl bromide on Wurtz reaction gives 2, 3-dimethyl butane.

Reason (R) When same alkyl halides react with sodium in dry ether to give hydrocarbon which contains double the number of carbon atoms present in the alkyl halide, it is called Wurtz reaction. • *Analysis*

(a) Both Assertion and Reason are true and Reason is the correct explanation of Assertion.

(b) Both Assertion and Reason are true but Reason is not the correct explanation of Assertion.

(c) Assertion is true but Reason is false.

(d) Both Assertion and Reason are false.

(vii) **Assertion** (A) Zn metal is formed when a Cu plate is dipped in $ZnSO_4$ solution.

Reason (R) Zn is placed below Cu in electrochemical series. • *Analysis*

(a) Both Assertion and Reason are true and Reason is the correct explanation of Assertion.

(b) Both Assertion and Reason are true but Reason is not the correct explanation of Assertion.

(c) Assertion is true but Reason is false.

(d) Both Assertion and Reason are false.

(C) Read the passage given below carefully and answer the questions that follows [3×1]

The characteristic chemical properties of carboxylic acids are the properties of the carboxyl group (—COOH). This group is made up of carbonyl group ($>$C=O) and a hydroxyl group. Thus, the properties of the carboxylic acids should be due to these groups. The properties of the COOH group get modified due to the presence of the carbonyl group. The carboxylic acids do not give the properties of the C=O group of the aldehydes and ketones due to resonance.

Most of the reactions of the carboxylic acids can be divided into four principal types which are reactions due to cleavage of O—H bond, OH part of —COOH, —COOH group and alkyl group and benzene ring.

(i) What happens when benzoic acid undergoes electrophilic substitution in presence of conc. HNO_3 and conc. H_2SO_4? • *Understanding*

(ii) Carbonyl group in carboxylic acid does not give its usual nucleophilic addition reactions, why? • *Understanding*

(iii) Write a simple chemical test to distinguish between benzaldehyde and benzoic acid. • *Understanding*

Section B

[20 Marks]

2. What will be the osmotic pressure of a 0.1 M monobasic acid, if its pH is 2.0 at 25°C ? • *Application* [2]

3. (i) The cell in which the following reaction occurs
$$2Fe^{3+}(aq) + 2I^-(aq) \longrightarrow 2Fe^{2+}(aq) + I_2(s)$$
has $E^\circ_{cell} = 0.236$ V at 298 K.
Calculate the standard Gibbs energy of the cell reaction. • *Application*
(Given: 1 F = 96500 C mol^{-1})
(ii) How many electrons flow through a metallic wire if a current of 0.5 A is passed for 2 h? • *Application*
(Given: 1 F = 96500 C mol^{-1}) [2]

4. Which compound in each of the following pairs will react faster towards S_N2 reaction with $-OH$? Why? • *Understanding*
(i) CH_3Br or CH_3I
(ii) $(CH_3)_3CCl$ or CH_3Cl [2]

Or A compound is formed by the substitution of two chlorine atoms for two hydrogen atoms in propane. Write the structures of the isomers possible. Give the IUPAC name of the isomer which can exhibit enantiomerism. • *Understanding*

5. When a coordination compound $CoCl_3 \cdot 6NH_3$ is mixed with $AgNO_3$, 3 moles of AgCl are precipitated per mole of the compound. Write. • *Understanding* [2]
(i) Structural formula of the complex.
(ii) IUPAC name of the complex.

6. During chemistry class, a teacher wrote $[Ni(CO)_4]$ as a coordination complex ion on the board. The students were asked to find out the magnetic behaviour and shape of the complex. Ajay, a student, wrote the answer paramagnetic and tetrahedral whereas another student Neelam wrote diamagnetic and tetrahedral. Evaluate Ajay's and Neelam's responses. • *Evaluate* [2]

7. Account for the following. • *Understanding* [2]
(i) The boiling points of alcohols decreases with increase in branching of the alkyl chain.
(ii) Phenol does not give protonation reaction readily.

8. Give reason of the following. • *Understanding* [2]
(i) Cr^{2+} is a stronger reducing agent than Fe^{2+} in an aqueous solution ?
(ii) HCl is not used to make the medium acidic in oxidation reactions of $KMnO_4$.

9. (i) The elevation of boiling point produced by dilute equimolal solutions of three substances is in the order, $A >$ glucose $> B$. Suggest a reason for this observation. • *Understanding* [2]
(ii) People living at high altitudes feel weak both physically and mentally. Explain. • *Understanding*

10. An optically active compound 'X' has molecular formula $C_4H_8O_3$. It evolves CO_2 gas with *aq*. $NaHCO_3$. 'X' reacts with $LiAlH_4$ to give an achiral compound 'Y'. [2]
(i) Write the optically active compound 'X' (marking the chiral centre). • *Understanding*
(ii) Write the optically inactive compound 'Y'. • *Understanding*

11. Complete and balance the following reactions. • *Recall* [2]
(i) $FeCr_2O_4 + Na_2CO_3 + \ldots\ldots \longrightarrow \ldots\ldots + \ldots\ldots + \ldots\ldots$
(ii) $KMnO_4 + H_2SO_4 + KI \longrightarrow \ldots\ldots\ldots + \ldots\ldots\ldots + \ldots\ldots\ldots + \ldots\ldots\ldots$

SP-08

Section C **[21 Marks]**

12. A complex is represented as $CoCl_3 \cdot xNH_3$. Its 0.1 m solution in aqueous medium shows [3]

$\Delta T_f = 0.558°C$ and $K_f(H_2O) = 1.86$ K kg/mol.

(i) Calculate the van't Hoff factor. • *Application*

(ii) Assuming 100% ionisation and coordination number of Co(III) is six. What is the formula of the complex? • *Application*

13. How will the following be converted? (Give chemical equations) • *Understanding* [3]

(i) Benzamide to aniline

(ii) Aliphatic primary amine to alcohol

(iii) Aromatic amine to benzene diazonium chloride

Or Give one chemical test each to distinguish between the compounds in the following pairs. • *Understanding*

(i) Methylamine and dimethylamine

(ii) Aniline and benzylamine

(iii) Ethylamine and aniline

14. (i) If first order reaction takes 32 minutes for 75% completion, then what is the time required for 50% completion? • *Application* [3]

(ii) How much faster would a reaction proceed at 25°C than 0°C if the activation energy is 65 kJ? • *Application*

15. (i) Which of the following biomolecules is insoluble in water? Justify. • *Analysis* [3]

Insulin, Haemoglobin, Keratin

(ii) Draw the Haworth structure of α-D-glucopyranose. • *Recall*

(iii) Write chemical reaction to show that glucose contains aldehyde as carbonyl group. • *Recall*

16. Identify the compounds *A, B* and *C* in the following reactions • *Understanding* [3]

(i) $CH_3—COOH \xrightarrow{NH_3/\Delta} [A] \xrightarrow{Br_2/KOH(aq)} [B] \xrightarrow{CHCl_3 + alc.KOH} [C]$

(ii) $C_6H_5N_2^+BF_4^- \xrightarrow[\Delta]{NaNO_2/Cu} [A] \xrightarrow{Fe/HCl} [B] \xrightarrow{CH_3COCl/pyridine} [C]$

17. The reaction between *A* and *B* is of first order with respect to *A* and zero order with respect to *B*. [3]

Exp. No.	$[A]$/ mol L^{-1}	$[B]$/ mol L^{-1}	Initial rate/ mol L^{-1} min^{-1}
1.	0.1	0.1	2.0×10^{-2}
2.	—	0.2	4.0×10^{-2}
3.	0.4	0.4	—
4.	—	0.2	2.0×10^{-2}

Answer the following questions.

(i) Calculate the rate constant of reaction. • *Application* [1]

(ii) Show how the above data can be used to find concentration of (*A*) in experiment number 2 and 4. • *Evaluate*

(iii) Find the initial rate in experiment 3. • *Application*

18. Complete the following • *Understanding* [3]

(i) 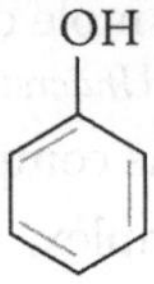 + (Dil.)$HNO_3 \longrightarrow$

(ii) 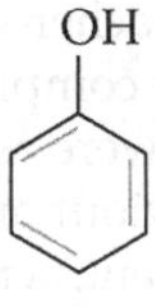 + $CHCl_3$ + NaOH $\xrightarrow{343\ K}$

(iii) 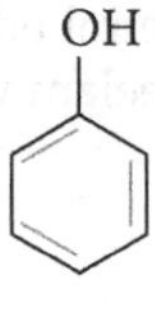 + $CH_3COCl \xrightarrow{Base}$

Section D

[15 Marks]

19. The accurate measurement of an unknown resistance can be performed on a Wheatstone bridge. However, for measuring the resistance of an ionic solution we face two problems. Firstly, passing direct current (DC) changes the composition of the solution. Secondly, a solution cannot be connected to the bridge like a metallic wire or other solid conductor.

The first difficulty is resolved by using an (alternating current) AC source of power. The second problem is solved by using conductivity cell.

The resistance of a conductivity cell when filled with 0.05 M solution of an electrolyte x is 100 Ω at 40°C.

The same conductivity cell filled with 0.01 M solution of electrolyte y has a resistance of 50 Ω.
The conductivity of 0.05 M solution electrolyte x is 1.0×10^{-4} S cm^{-1}.

Answer the following questions. [5]

(a) How conductivity cell is made? • *Recall*

(b) How cell constant is determined. • *Recall*

(c) Calculate cell constant of 0.01 M, y solution. • *Application*

(d) Determine molar conductivity of 0.01 M, y solution. • *Application*

(e) Draw a plot showing molar conductivity *versus* $C^{1/2}$ for weak and strong electrolyte in aqueous solutions. • *Understanding*

20. (i) Acetone on reaction with HCN gives one compound whereas acetaldehyde gives two compounds that are difficult to separate. Explain why?
• *Understanding* [5]

(ii) Why is it necessary to control the pH during the reaction of aldehydes and ketones with ammonia derivatives?
• *Understanding*

21. (i) Starting with butan-1-ol, how will but-2-ene be synthesised?
• *Understanding* [5]

(ii) Show how would you synthesise the following alcohols from alkenes ?

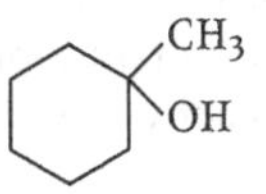

and

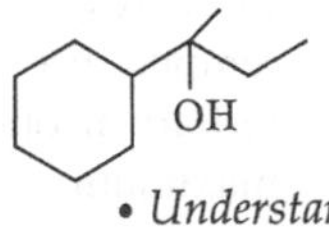

• *Understanding*

Or (i) Discuss how Lucas reagent is used to distinguish 1°, 2° and 3° alcohols.
• *Understanding*

(ii) Illustrate with examples, the limitations of the Williamson's synthesis for the preparation of certain types of ethers. • *Recall*

Solutions *in Topper's Style*

My Commitment *I affirm that I am reviewing these solutions only after I have solved the Sample Question Paper on my own. My purpose of looking the solutions is solely to verify whether my answers/solutions were correct or not and to identify my mistakes in case my solutions were wrong or I could not solve that.*

1. (A) (i) dry acetone, Finkelstein reaction

(ii) oxygen, Fe^{2+}

(iii) $\frac{A_0}{2k}$, initial concentration

(iv) alkaline, CrO_4^{2-}

(B) (i) (b) CFSE (Δ_o) for octahedral complex depends on the strength of the ligands. The order of strength of the ligands is

$$C_2O_4^{2-} < H_2O < NH_3 < CN^-$$

Thus, the increasing order of magnitude of Δ_o for octahedral complexes is

$$[Co(C_2O_4)_3]^{3-} < [Co(H_2O)_6]^{3+} < [Co(NH_3)_6]^{3+} < [Co(CN)_6]^{3-}$$

(ii) (d) The compound that reacts fastest with Lucas reagent (HCl + anhyd. $ZnCl_2$) at room temperature is 2-methyl propan-2-ol as it is a tertiary alcohol, so it's reactivity will be maximum.

(iii) (b) $Na_2SO_4 \rightleftharpoons 2Na^+ + SO_4^{2-}$

van't Hoff factor, $i = [1 + (y-1)\alpha]$

where, y is the number of ions obtained from one mole solute (in this case, $y = 3$) and α is the degree of dissociation.

$\therefore \quad i = 1 + 2\alpha$

(iv) (c) An electrochemical cell can behave like an electrolytic cell when its $E_{ext} > E_{cell}$. At this stage, the reaction proceeds in the opposite direction.

(v) (b) (I) and (III) are the only correct statements whereas, statements (II) and (IV) are incorrect. Their correct form are as follows:

- Diazonium salts of aromatic amines are more stable due to resonance stabilisation, whereas, no such resonance is possible in diazonium salts of aliphatic amines.
- They are ionic in nature and hence, water soluble.

(vi) (a) Both Assertion and Reason are true and Reason is the correct explanation of Assertion.

(vii) (d) The formation of Zn is not possible by placing Cu plate in $ZnSO_4$ solution because Zn is placed above Cu in electrochemical series. Thus, both Assertion and Reason are false.

(C) (i) In the presence of conc. H_2SO_4, and conc. HNO_3, benzoic acid gives *m*-nitrobenzoic acid.

(ii) It is stabilised by resonance, therefore, electrophilicity of carbonyl carbon is reduced and hence, carbonyl group in carboxylic acid is different from normal carbonyl group.

(iii) **Benzaldehyde and benzoic acid** Add $NaHCO_3$ solution to both the compounds, benzoic acid will give effervescence and liberate CO_2, while benzaldehyde will not.

2.

	HA	$\rightleftharpoons$	H^+	+	A^-
Initial conc.	C		0		0
At equilibrium conc.	$(C - C\alpha)$		$C\alpha$		$C\alpha$

i.e. $\quad [H^+] = C\alpha$

But $\quad [H^+] = 10^{-2}$ M $\quad [\because pH = 2.0]$

$\therefore \quad C\alpha = 10^{-2}$

or $\quad \alpha = \frac{10^{-2}}{C} = \frac{10^{-2}}{0.1} = 0.1 \quad [\because C = 0.1 \text{ M (given)}]$

Now, total number of particles after dissociation

$$= C - C\alpha + C\alpha + C\alpha = C(1+\alpha)$$

van't Hoff factor (i) $= \frac{C(1+\alpha)}{C} = 1 + \alpha = 1 + 0.1 = 1.1$

Osmotic pressure (π) $= iCRT$

$$= 1.1 \times 0.1 \times 0.0821 \times 298 \text{ atm}$$
$$= 2.69 \text{ atm}$$

3. (i) Standard Gibbs free energy is given by

$$\Delta G° = -nFE°_{cell} \quad \ldots(i)$$

where, n = number of moles of electrons transferred, F = Faraday's constant $= 96500 \text{ C mol}^{-1}$

$E°_{cell}$ = cell potential

Two half-reactions for the given redox reaction can be written as

$$2Fe^{3+}(aq) + 2e^- \longrightarrow 2Fe^{2+}(aq)$$
$$2I^-(aq) \longrightarrow I_2(s) + 2e^-$$

2 moles of electrons are involved in the reaction, hence $n = 2$. Therefore, by substituting all the values in Eq. (i) we get

$$\Delta_r G° = -(2 \text{ mol}) \times (96500 \text{ C mol}^{-1}) \times (0.236 \text{ V})$$
$$= -45548 \text{ J}$$
$$\Delta_r G° = -45.55 \text{ kJ}$$

(ii) Given, current (i) = 0.5 A, time (t) = 2 h

Quantity of charge (Q) passed = Current (i) × time (t) = (0.5 A) × (2 × 60 × 60 s) = 3600 C

Again, $Q = ne^-$

where, n = number of electrons

e^- = charge on electron

$$\therefore \quad n = \frac{Q}{e^-} = \frac{3600\text{C}}{1.6 \times 10^{-19}\text{C}}$$

$$= 2250 \times 10^{19}$$

Thus, number of electrons $= 2.250 \times 10^{22}$

4. **KEY IDEA**

(i) Lesser the bond dissociation energy, faster is the reaction. So, find the molecule in which bond dissociation enthalpy is less.

(ii) If both halide groups are same, steric hindrance will be considered in case of S_N2 reaction. More the steric hindrance, lesser the reactivity towards S_N2 reaction.

(i) CH_3I will react faster as compared to CH_3Br because CH_3I has lower bond dissociation energy and I^- is a better leaving group than Br^-. Thus, in the presence of nucleophile, iodide ion will be released at a faster rate.

(ii) In S_N2 reactions, reactivity depends upon the steric hindrance. CH_3Cl being a 1° halide will react faster as compared to $(CH_3)_3CCl$ which is a 3° halide because 1° halides undergo S_N2 mechanism faster than 3° halides.

Or

Propane on substitution of two chlorine atoms for hydrogen atoms forms respective isomers as shown below.

$$CH_3—CH_2—CH_3 + Cl_2 \xrightarrow{h\nu} CH_3—CH(Cl)—CH_2(Cl) + CH_2(Cl)—CH_2—CH_2(Cl)$$

$$+ CH_3—CH_2—CHCl_2 + CH_3—C(Cl)_2—CH_3$$

Out of these, $CH_3—CH(Cl)—CH_2—Cl$ having **IUPAC name** 1,2-dichloropropane, will exhibit enantiomerism.

5. (i) When one mole of $CoCl_3 \cdot 6NH_3$ is mixed with $AgNO_3$, three moles of AgCl are precipitated which indicates that three ionisable chloride ions in the complex are present. Hence, its structural formula is $[Co(NH_3)_6]Cl_3$.

(ii) IUPAC name of the complex, $[Co(NH_3)_6]Cl_3$ is hexaamminecobalt (III) chloride.

6. Electronic configuration of $Ni_{28} = [Ar]3d^8 4s^2$

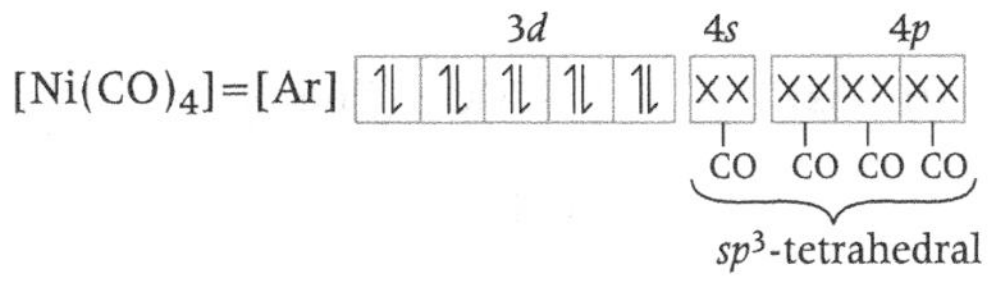

Since, no unpaired electrons are present thus, diamagnetic.

Hence, Neelam's response was correct.

7. (i) Since, branched chain alcohols have minimum surface area, therefore, minimum force of attraction occur between them, hence boiling point decreases with increase in branching of alkyl chain.

(ii) In phenols, the lone pair of electrons on the oxygen atoms are delocalised over the benzene ring due to resonance and hence, are not easily available for protonation.

8. (i) Cr^{2+} is a stronger reducing agent than Fe^{2+} in aqueous solution. This is because when Cr^{2+} loses one electron, it forms Cr^{3+} with electronic configuration d^3, while Fe^{2+} changes to Fe^{3+} with electronic configuration d^5 which is highly stable.

Thus, Cr^{2+} can lose more than one electron, but Fe^{2+} can lose only one electron.

Moreover, the values of reduction potentials of Cr^{2+} and Fe^{2+} are = 0.90 and = 8.44 V respectively. More the reduction potential, greater will be its reducing power.

(ii) HCl is not used to make the medium acidic in oxidation reactions of $KMnO_4$. The reason is that if HCl is used, then their is a formation of Cl_2 gas which itself acts as an oxidising agent and partially oxidises the reducing agent.

9. (i) This observation suggests that substance A dissociates, while substance B associates in the solution. It is because elevation in boiling point depends upon the number of particles of the solute present in the solution and not on the molal concentration.

(ii) At high altitudes, the partial pressure of oxygen is less than that at the ground level. This leads to low concentration of oxygen in the blood and tissues of people living at high altitudes or climbers. Consequently, they feel weak both physically and mentally.

10. • Since, the compound (X) is optically active thus, chiral carbon (C^*) is present.

• As, it evolves CO_2 with $NaHCO_3$, thus —COOH is present.

• $LiAlH_4$ converts —COOH into —CH_2OH.

$$CH_3\overset{*}{C}H(CH_2OH)COOH \xrightarrow{LiAlH_4} CH_3CH(CH_2OH)CH_2OH$$

(X) (Chiral) (Y) (Achiral)

(i) X is $CH_3—\overset{*}{C}H—COOH$ (Chiral)
$\qquad\qquad\quad|$
$\qquad\qquad CH_2OH$

(ii) Y is $CH_3—CH—CH_2OH$ (Achiral)
$\qquad\qquad\quad|$
$\qquad\qquad CH_2OH$

11. (i) $4FeCr_2O_4 + 8Na_2CO_3 + 7O_2 \longrightarrow 2Fe_2O_3 + 8Na_2CrO_4 + 8CO_2$

(ii) $2KMnO_4 + 8H_2SO_4 + 10KI \longrightarrow 6K_2SO_4 + 2MnSO_4 + 8H_2O + 5I_2$

12. Given,

Molality of solution $(m) = 0.1$ m

Depression in freezing point $= \Delta T_f = 0.558°C$

$K_f(H_2O) = 1.86$ K kg/mol

(i) As we know, $\Delta T_f = i\, K_f m$ (i = van't Hoff's factor)

$$0.558 = 1.86 \times 0.1 \times i$$

$$i = \frac{0.558}{0.186} = 3$$

$\Rightarrow$ $i = 3$ indicates that complex dissociate to form three ions.

(ii) $CoCl_3 \cdot xNH_3 \longrightarrow [Co(NH_3)_xCl_{6-x}]Cl_{3-(6-x)}$

After complete ionisation number of molecule, $\alpha = 1$

$$i = 1 + (n-1)\alpha$$
$$3 = 1 + n - 1$$
$$n = 3$$

Since, coordination number is 6 and hence, $x = 5$

So, the complex is $[Co(NH_3)_5Cl]Cl_2$.

13. (i) Benzamide forms aniline with solution of KOH and Br_2.

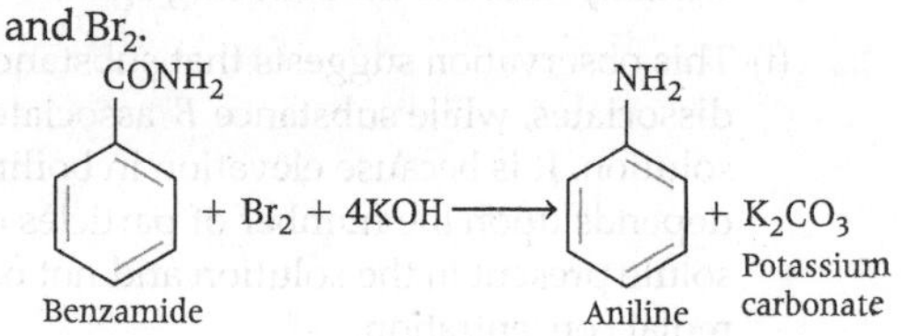

$+ 2KBr + 2H_2O$
Potassium bromide Water

(ii) Aliphatic primary amine forms alcohol with nitrous acid at 273-278 K.

$$\underset{\text{Aliphatic primary amine}}{R—NH_2} + \underset{\text{Nitrous acid}}{HONO} \xrightarrow{273\text{-}278\,K} \underset{\text{Alcohol}}{R—OH} + \underset{\text{Nitrogen}}{N_2\uparrow} + \underset{\text{Hydrogen chloride}}{HCl}$$

(iii) Aromatic amine on reaction with nitrous acid at 273-278 K forms benzene diazonium chloride.

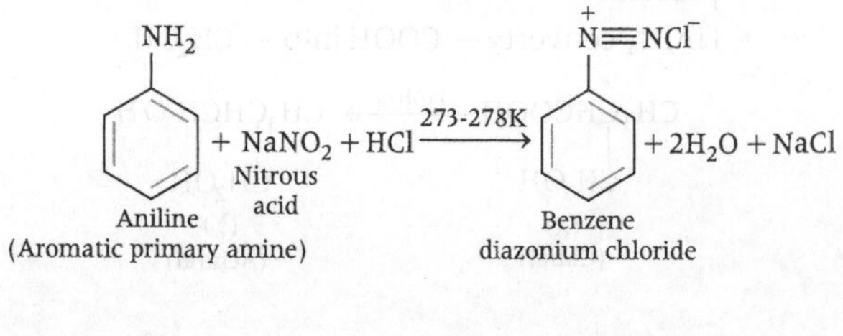

Or (i) Methylamine being a primary amine gives carbylamine test, i.e. on treatment with alc. KOH and chloroform, followed by heating, it gives offensive odour of methyl isocyanide. Dimethylamine being a secondary amine does not give this test.

(ii) Aniline and benzylamine can be distinguished by azo dye test. Aniline reacts with HNO_2 at 273-278 K to form stable benzene diazonium chloride which on treatment with an alkaline solution of β-naphthol gives an orange dye. While benzylamine does not give this test.

(iii) Ethylamine is a primary aliphatic amine, while aniline is a primary aromatic amine. Both can be distinguished by azo dye test.

$$\underset{\text{Ethylamine}}{C_2H_5NH_2} + HONO \xrightarrow{273\text{-}278K} \underset{\text{Ethanol}}{C_2H_5OH} + N_2\uparrow + H_2O$$

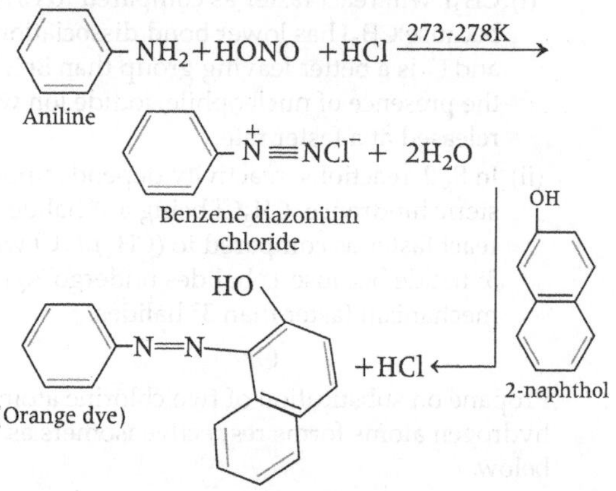

14. (i) We know, for first order reaction,

$$k = \frac{2.303}{t}\log\left(\frac{a}{a-x}\right)$$

When, $a = 100$, $x = 75$, $t = 32$

$$k = \frac{2.303}{32}\log\left(\frac{100}{25}\right) = 0.0433\ \text{min}^{-1}$$

Time for 50% completion $(t_{1/2}) = \dfrac{0.693}{k} = \dfrac{0.693}{0.0433}$

$$t_{1/2} = 16\ \text{mins}$$

(ii) We know,

$$2.303\log\frac{k_2}{k_1} = \frac{E_a}{R}\left[\frac{T_2 - T_1}{T_1T_2}\right]$$

Given : $E_a = 65 \times 10^3$ J

$T_1 = 0°C = 273$ K

and $T_2 = 25°C = 298$ K

$$\therefore\ 2.303\log\frac{k_2}{k_1} = \frac{65 \times 10^3}{8.314}\left[\frac{25}{298 \times 273}\right]$$

$$\frac{k_2}{k_1} = 11.05$$

15. (i) Keratin being a fibrous protein is insoluble in water.

(ii)

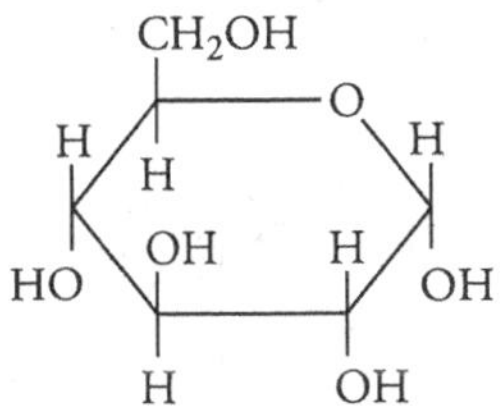

α-D-(+)-glucopyranose

(iii) Glucose reduces Tollen's reagent to metallic silver.

$$\underset{\text{D-(+)-Glucose}}{\begin{matrix}CHO\\|\\(CH-OH)_4\\|\\CH_2OH\end{matrix}} + \underset{\text{Tollen's reagent}}{2[Ag(NH_3)_2]^+} + 3\bar{O}H \longrightarrow \underset{\text{Gluconic acid}}{\begin{matrix}COO^-\\|\\(CHOH)_4\\|\\CH_2-OH\end{matrix}} + \underset{\text{Silver mirror}}{4Ag\downarrow} + 2H_2O$$

16. (i) $\underset{\text{Acetic acid}}{CH_3COOH} \xrightarrow[-H_2O]{NH_3/\Delta} \underset{\text{Acetamide }(A)}{CH_3CONH_2} \xrightarrow{Br_2/KOH\,(aq)}$

$\underset{\underset{(B)}{\text{Methylamine}}}{CH_3NH_2} \xrightarrow{CHCl_3 + \text{Alc. KOH}} \underset{\underset{(C)}{\text{Methyl isocyanide}}}{CH_3NC}$

(ii) $C_6H_5N_2^+BF_4^- \xrightarrow[-N_2,\,-NaBF_4]{NaNO_2/Cu,\,\Delta} \underset{\underset{(A)}{\text{Nitrobenzene}}}{C_6H_5NO_2}$

$\xrightarrow[\text{Reduction}]{Fe/HCl} \underset{\underset{(B)}{\text{Aniline}}}{C_6H_5NH_2} \xrightarrow[-HCl]{CH_3COCl/\text{pyridine}} \underset{\underset{(C)}{\text{Acetanilide}}}{C_6H_5NHCOCH_3}$

17. (i) The rate expression, Rate $= k[A]^1[B]^0 = k[A]$

For experiment 1, $[A] = 0.1\ \text{mol L}^{-1}$

So, Rate $= 2.0 \times 10^{-2} = k\ [0.1\ \text{mol L}^{-1}]$

$\therefore \quad k = \dfrac{2.0\times 10^{-2}\ \text{mol L}^{-1}\text{min}^{-1}}{0.1\ \text{mol L}^{-1}} = 0.2\ \text{min}^{-1}$

(ii) **For experiment 2,** rate $= k[A]$

$4.0 \times 10^{-2}\ \text{mol L}^{-1}\text{min}^{-1} = 0.2\ \text{min}^{-1}[A]$

$[A] = \dfrac{4.0\times 10^{-2}\text{mol L}^{-1}\text{min}^{-1}}{0.2\ \text{min}^{-1}}$

$= 0.2\ \text{mol L}^{-1}$

$\therefore \quad [A] = 0.2\ \text{mol L}^{-1}$

For experiment 4, rate $= k[A]$

$\Rightarrow \quad [A] = \dfrac{\text{Rate}}{k}$

$\Rightarrow \quad [A] = \dfrac{2.0\times 10^{-2}\ \text{mol L}^{-1}\ \text{min}^{-1}}{0.2\ \text{min}^{-1}}$

$= 0.1\ \text{mol L}^{-1}$

(iii) **For experiment 3,** rate $= 0.2\,\text{min}^{-1} \times 0.4\ \text{mol L}^{-1}$

$= 0.08\ \text{mol L}^{-1}\ \text{min}^{-1}$

18. (i)

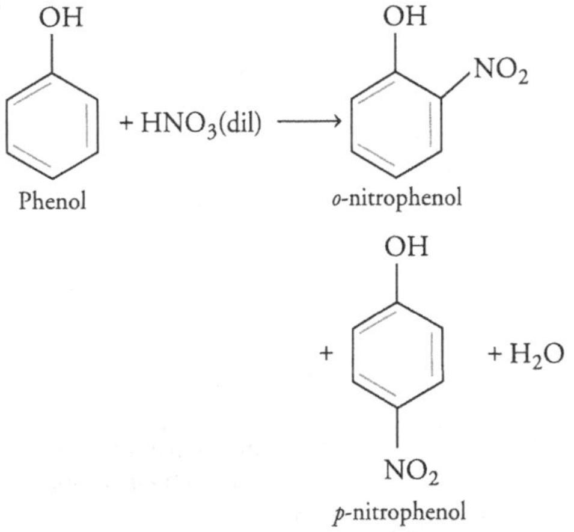

(ii)

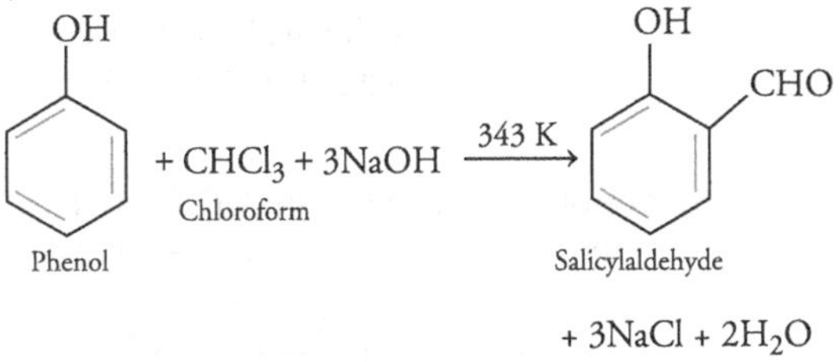

(iii)

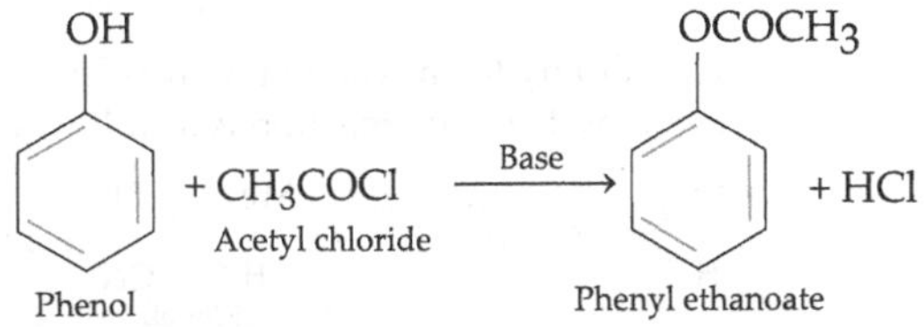

19. (a) The conductivity cell consists of two different types of conductivity cell consisting of two platinum electrodes coated with platinum black.

(b) The cell constant can be determined by measuring the resistance of the cell containing a solution, whose conductivity is already known.

(c) Given, for electrolyte x, molarity = 0.05 M

Resistance = 100 Ω and

Conductivity $= 1.0 \times 10^{-4}\ \text{S cm}^{-1}$

For electrolyte y, molarity = 0.01 M,

Resistance = 50 Ω and Conductivity = ?

⇒ Cell constant,

$G^* =$ Resistance $(R) \times$ Conductivity (κ)

$= 100 \times 1.0 \times 10^{-4} = 10^{-2}\ \text{cm}^{-1}$

(d) Conductivity of solution y is given as

$\kappa = \dfrac{\text{Cell constant}}{\text{Resistance}} = \dfrac{10^{-2}\ \text{cm}^{-1}}{50\Omega}$

$= 2 \times 10^{-4}\ \text{S cm}^2\ \text{mol}^{-1}$

Conductivity,

$\Lambda_m = \dfrac{\kappa \times 1000}{\text{Molarity}} = \dfrac{2\times 10^{-4} \times 1000}{0.01}$

$= 2 \times 10^{-4}\ \text{Scm}^2\text{mol}^{-1} = 20\ \text{S cm}^2\ \text{mol}^{-1}$

(e)

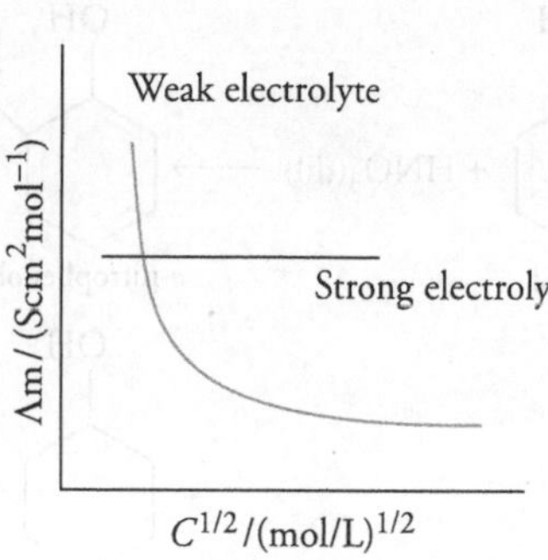

Value Points

For getting maximum marks, following points should be included in the answer.

- SI units of the numerical answers.
- Write the formula used in the solution of the question.

20. (i) Acetone on reaction with HCN gives cyanohydrin. The reaction is as follows

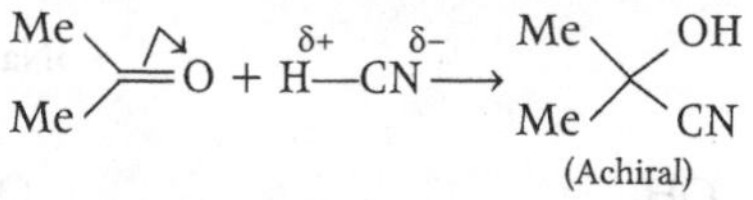

Acetaldehyde on reaction with HCN gives chiral cyanohydrin. The reaction is as follows

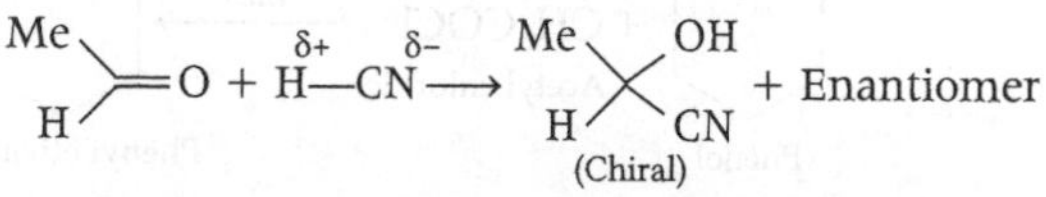

So, acetaldehyde gives enantiomer (optical isomers) due to the chiral centre. They are difficult to separate as the chemical and physical properties of enantiomers are same.

(ii) The reaction of ammonia derivatives with aldehyde and ketone is catalysed by acids. In acidic medium, the carbonyl oxygen gets protonated and ammonia act as nucleophile and attacks on it.

But if the medium is highly acidic then the NH_2OH being basic in nature form their respective salt and cannot act as nucleophile and consequently no reaction will occur.

21. (i) $\underset{\text{Butan-1-ol}}{CH_3CH_2CH_2CH_2—OH} \xrightarrow{H^+} \underset{\text{Protonated alcohol}}{C_4H_9—\overset{\oplus}{O}H_2} \xrightarrow{-H_2O}$

$\underset{\text{1°carbocation}}{CH_3CH_2—\underset{\displaystyle H}{\underset{|}{C}H}—\overset{\oplus}{C}H_2} \xrightarrow{\text{1,2-H shift}}$

$\underset{\text{2°carbocation}}{CH_3—CH_2—\overset{\oplus}{C}H—CH_3} \xrightarrow{-H^+} \underset{\text{But-2-ene}}{CH_3CH=CH—CH_3}$

(ii) On adding H_2O to 1-methylcyclohexene in the presence of an acid, we get 1-methylcyclohexan-1-ol.

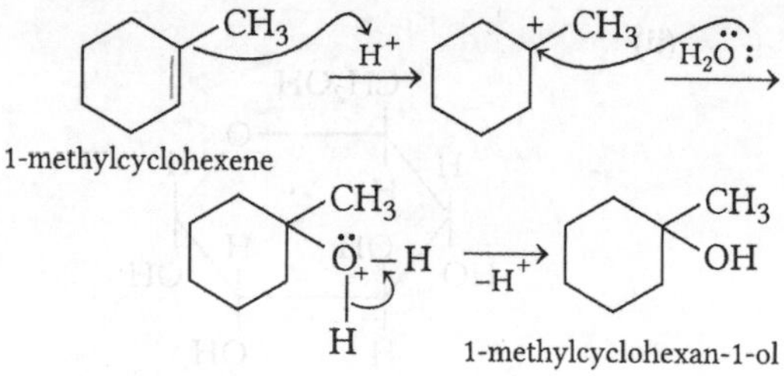

When we add H_2O to 2-cyclohexylbut-2-ene or 2-cyclohexylidenebutane, in the presence of an acid, the product obtained is same, in both the cases, i.e. 2-cyclohexylbutan-2-ol.

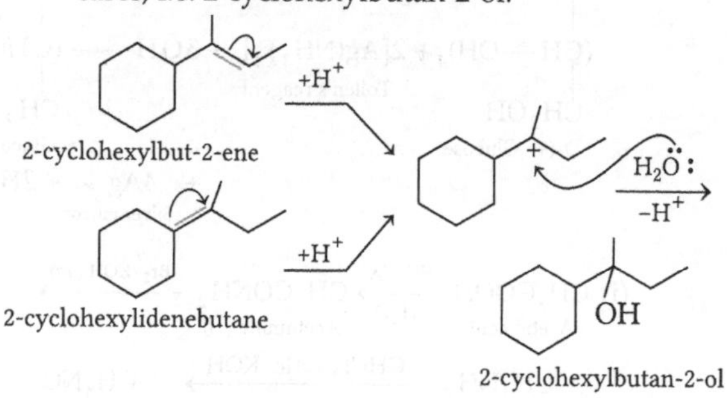

Or

(i) **Lucas test** is based on the difference in reactivity of 1°, 2° and 3° alcohols with anhydrous $ZnCl_2$ and conc. HCl, i.e. Lucas reagent.

When primary alcohol is treated with the reagent no turbidity is observed at room temperature while secondary alcohols give turbidity after five minutes and tertiary alcohols give turbidity immediately.

Turbidity is observed due to the formation of insoluble alkyl chlorides.

(ii) **Limitations**

(a) Williamson's synthesis is not applicable for tertiary alkyl halides as they yield alkenes instead of ethers. The reaction of CH_3ONa with $(CH_3)_3C—Br$ gives exclusively 2-methylpropene.

$$\underset{\textit{tert}\text{-butyl bromide}}{CH_3—\underset{CH_3}{\overset{CH_3}{C}}—Br} + Na—\ddot{\underset{\cdot\cdot}{O}}—CH_3 \longrightarrow \underset{\text{2-methyl propene}}{CH_3—\underset{CH_3}{C}=CH_2} + NaBr$$

(b) Aryl and vinyl halides cannot be used as substrates because of their low reactivity in nucleophilic substitution.

SPQ Code : **PB-09/15** Series ***i*-Succeed 09-25/15** Roll No. [ ]

Sample Question Paper 09

Chemistry 12th (Code 862)

General Instructions

1. This paper is divided into four sections-A, B, C and D. Answer all questions.
2. **Section A** consists of **one** question **having sub-parts** of **one** mark each. **Section B** consists of **ten** questions of **two** marks each. **Section C** consists of **seven** questions of **three** marks each and **Section D** consists of **three** questions of **five** marks each.
3. Internal choices have been provided in one question each in Section B, Section C and Section D.
4. All working, including rough work, should be done on the same sheet as, and adjacent to the rest of the answer.
5. The intended marks for questions or parts of questions are given in brackets [].
6. Balanced questions must be given, wherever possible and diagrams where they are helpful. When solving numerical problems, all essential working must be shown.
7. In working out problems, use the following data:
Gas constant (R) = 1.987 cal deg^{-1} mol^{-1} = 8.314 JK^{-1} mol^{-1} = 0.0821 dm^3 atm K^{-1} mol^{-1}
1L atm = 1 dm^3 atm =101.3 J, 1 Faraday =96500 Coulombs.
Avogadro's number (N_A) = 6.023 × 10^{23}.

Time : 3 Hrs.

Max. Marks : 70

Section A **[14 Marks]**

1. (A) Fill in the blanks by choosing the appropriate word(s) from those given in the brackets. [4 × 1]
[cane sugar, first order, [Xe]$4f^{14}$, [Xe]$4f^{13}$ solvent, solute, less, more, vapour, pseudo first order, reductant, oxidant, antioxidant]
(i) The .... pressure of an aqueous solution of 0.1M cane sugar is .... than that of pure water. • *Understanding*
(ii) Ytterbium (Yb) in +2 oxidation state has ...... configuration and it acts as a .... • *Understanding*
(iii) Inversion of .... is an example of a .... reaction. • *Recall*
(iv) Methanol is used as a .... in paints, varnishes and as an ...... in formaldehyde formation. • *Recall*

(B) Select and write the correct alternative from the choices given below. [7 × 1]
(i) The reaction,
$$Ar\overset{+}{N}_2Cl^- \xrightarrow{Cu/HCl} ArCl + N_2 + CuCl$$
is named as • *Recall*
(a) Sandmeyer reaction
(b) Gattermann reaction
(c) Claisen reduction
(d) Carbylamine reaction

(ii) The standard reduction potential for the half-cell reaction, $Cl_2 + 2e^- \longrightarrow 2Cl^-$ will be
($Pt^{2+} + 2Cl^- \longrightarrow Pt + Cl_2, E^\circ_{cell} = -0.15$ V;
$Pt^{2+} + 2e^- \longrightarrow Pt, E^\circ_{cell} = 1.20$ V) • *Application*
(a) 1.05 V (b) 1.35 V
(c) 2.1 V (d) 0.9 V

(iii) Transition metal shows variable oxidation states. Which of the following metal does NOT show variable oxidation state ? • *Analysis*

(a) Zn (b) Cr
(c) Fe (d) Cu

(iv) In the equation,

$$C_2H_5OH \xrightarrow[\Delta]{H_2SO_4} A + \text{byproduct},$$

the compound A is • *Understanding*

(a) CH_3CHO
(b) C_2H_4
(c) C_2H_2
(d) CH_3COOH

(v) Which of the following statements are correct?

I. In octahedral complexes, d_{z^2}, $d_{x^2-y^2}$ orbitals have higher energy than d_{xy}, d_{yz} and d_{zx} orbitals.

II. In tetrahedral complexes, d_{xy}, d_{yz}, d_{zx} orbitals have higher energy than d_{z^2} and $d_{x^2-y^2}$ orbitals.

III. The colours of complexes are due to electronic transitions from one set of p-orbitals to another set of orbitals.

IV $\Delta_{(\text{tetrahedral})} = \frac{9}{4}\Delta_{(\text{octahedral})}$

• *Understanding*

(a) I and II only (b) III and IV only
(c) II and III only (d) II and IV only

SP-09

(vi) **Assertion** (A) Hydrolysis of (−)-2-bromooctane proceeds with inversion of configuration.

Reason (R) This reaction proceeds through the formation of a carbocation. • *Analysis*

(a) Both Assertion and Reason are true and Reason is the correct explanation of Assertion.
(b) Both Assertion and Reason are true but Reason is not the correct explanation of Assertion.
(c) Assertion is true but Reason is false.
(d) Both Assertion and Reason are false.

(vii) **Assertion** (A) All naturally occurring α-amino acids except glycine are optically active.

Reason (R) Most naturally occurring amino acids have L-configuration.

• *Analysis*

(a) Both Assertion and Reason are true and Reason is the correct explanation of Assertion.
(b) Both Assertion and Reason are true but Reason is not the correct explanation of Assertion.
(c) Assertion is true but Reason is false.
(d) Both Assertion and Reacton are false.

(C) Read the passage given below carefully and answer the questions that follow [3 × 1]

Carbohydrates are optically active polyhydroxy aldehydes and ketones. They are also called saccharides. All those carbohydrates which reduce Fehlings solution and Tollen's reagent are referred to as reducing sugars. Those carbohydrates which cannot reduce either Fehling solution and Tollen's reagent are referred to as non-reducing sugars. Carbohydrates are mainly synthesised by plants during photosynthesis. Glucose, the most important source of energy for mammals, is obtained by the hydrolysis of starch. Glucose contains one aldehydic group, one 1° alcoholic group and four 2° alcoholic group in its open chain structure.

Vitamins are accessory food factors required in structural and dynamic functions in the organisms. They have diverse biochemical functions. Deficiency of vitamins leads to many diseases.

(i) The penta-acetate of glucose does not react with hydroxylamine. What does it indicate? • *Understanding*

(ii) Why cannot vitamin C be stored in our body? • *Understanding*

(iii) Define the following as related to carbohydrates. • *Recall*

(a) Anomers (b) Glycosidic linkage

Section B **[20 Marks]**

2. 6.02×10^{20} molecules of urea are present in 100 mL of its solution. What is the concentration of solution? • *Application* [2]

3. Give reason for the following. [2]
   (i) Of the d^4 species, Cr^{2+} is strongly reducing agent while manganese (III) is strongly oxidising agent.
   (ii) The paramagnetic character in 3*d*-transition series elements increases upto Mn and then decreases.
   • *Understanding* [2]

4. (i) What should be the signs (positive/negative) for E°_{cell} and ΔG° for a spontaneous redox reaction occurring under standard conditions? [2] • *Recall*
   (ii) State Faraday's first law of electrolysis. • *Recall*

5. How would you account for the following? [2] • *Understanding*
   (i) Actinoid contraction is greater than lanthanoid contraction.
   (ii) Cd^{2+} salts are white.

6. An organic compound (*A*) having molecular formula ($C_8H_{16}O_2$) was hydrolysed with dilute sulphuric acid to give a carboxylic acid (*B*) and alcohol (*C*). Oxidation of (*C*) with chromic acid produced (*B*). (*C*) on dehydration gives but-1-ene. Identify the compounds [*A*], [*B*] and [*C*]. • *Understanding* [2]

7. Account for the following.
   (i) pK_b of aniline is more than that of methylamine.
   (ii) Ethylamine is soluble in water, whereas aniline is not. • *Understanding* [2]

8. Devise a scheme for the synthesis of hexane-2, 3-diol using propane as the only source of carbon. Is it you may use any other required organic or inorganic reagents. • *Evaluate* [2]

Or Arun was sitting in the chemistry laboratory. He was studying about the nature of phenol and propanol. He was in favour of the statement that phenol is more acidic than propanol. What can be the possible reason for his statement? • *Analysis* [2]

9. (i) In order to know about the extent of association or dissociation of solutes in solution van't Hoff introduced a factor (*i*). [2]
   (a) Write the formula for relation of van't Hoff factor and degree of association. • *Recall*
   (b) Write the formula for relation of van't Hoff factor and degree of dissociation. • *Recall*
   (ii) Find the cryoscopic constant if the freezing point of benzene is 278.4 K. Given, 0.4 molal solution of acetic acid in benzene and molar heat of fusion $= 10.42 \text{ kJ mol}^{-1}$. • *Application*

10. Write the main products in each of the following reactions. • *Understanding* [2]

(i)

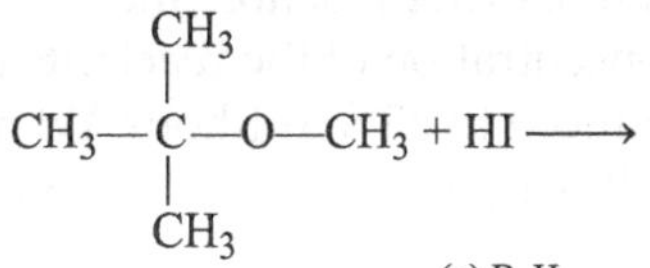

(ii) $CH_3—CH=CH_2 \xrightarrow[\text{(b) } 3H_2O_2/OH^-]{\text{(a) } B_2H_6}$

11. (i) Magnetic moment of $[MnCl_4]^{2-}$ is 5.92 BM. Give reason. [2] • *Understanding*
    (ii) $[Co(NH_3)_6]^{3+}$ has d^2sp^3-hybridisation and octahedral geometry. Justify. • *Understanding*

Section C **[21 Marks]**

12. How are the following conversions carried out? [3]
• *Understanding*
   (i) Benzyl chloride $\rightarrow$ Benzyl alcohol
   (ii) Ethyl magnesium chloride $\rightarrow$ Propan-1-ol
   (iii) Methyl magnesium bromide $\rightarrow$ 2-methyl propan-2-ol.

13. When liquid '*A*' is treated with a freshly prepared ammoniacal silver nitrate solution, it gives bright silver mirror. [3]
The liquid forms a white crystalline solid on treatment with sodium hydrogen sulphite. Liquid '*B*' also forms a white crystalline solid with sodium hydrogen sulphite but it does not give test with ammoniacal silver nitrate. Which of the two liquids is aldehyde? Write the chemical equations of these reactions also.
• *Analysis*

14. (i) Two reactions of the same order have equal exponential factors but their activation energies differ by 24.9 kJ/mol. Calculate the ratio between the rate constants of their reactions at 27° C. $(R = 8.314 \text{JK}^{-1}\text{mol}^{-1})$ • *Application* [3]
   (ii) In first order reaction, the concentration of the reactants is reduced to 25% in 1 hour. What is the half-life period? • *Application*

SP-09

15. Colligative properties include the lowering of vapour pressure, elevation of boiling point, depression of freezing point and osmotic pressure. [3]
   (i) Calculate the mass of compound (molar mass = 256 g mol^{-1}) to be dissolved in 75 g of benzene to lower its freezing point by 0.48 K. $(K_f = 5.12 \text{ K kg mol}^{-1})$ • *Application*
   (ii) If elevation in boiling point of sucrose solution is 0.1°C, then what will be the boiling point of NaCl solution for the same molal concentration? • *Application*

16. How will the following be converted? (Give chemical equations) [3]
   (i) Benzene diazonium chloride to fluorobenzene.
   (ii) Nitrobenzene to phenol.
   (iii) Chloromethane to ethylamine.
• *Understanding*

Or

Write chemical equations to illustrate the following name reactions,
   (i) Hofmann bromamide degradation reaction
   (ii) Gabriel phthalimide synthesis
   (iii) Sandmeyer reaction • *Recall*

17. Suppose a reaction between *A* and *B*, the initial rate of reaction (r_0) was measured for different initial concentrations of *A* and *B* as given below. [3]

$A/\text{ mol L}^{-1}$	0.20	0.20	0.40
$B/\text{mol L}^{-1}$	0.30	0.10	0.05
$r_0/\text{ mol L}^{-1}\text{s}^{-1}$	4.08×10^{-5}	4.08×10^{-5}	2.34×10^{-4}

Answer the following questions.
   (i) Find the order of reaction with respect to *A* and *B*. • *Application*
   (ii) Determine the rate law expression for the reaction. • *Evaluate*
   (iii) Calculate the rate constant. • *Application*

18. Identify the compounds *A*, *B* and *C* in the following reactions. [3]
   (i) $CH_3{-}CH{=}CH_2 \xrightarrow[\text{Peroxide}]{\text{HBr}} [A] \xrightarrow[\text{Acetone}]{\text{NaI}} [B] \xrightarrow{\text{KCN}} [C]$
   (ii) $CH_3Cl \xrightarrow{\text{KCN}} [A] \xrightarrow{CH_3MgCl} [B] \xrightarrow{H_3O^+} [C]$
• *Understanding*

Section D [15 Marks]

19. (i) The standard electrode potential ($E°$) for Daniell cell is +1.1 V. Calculate the $\Delta G°$ for the reaction.

$$Zn(s) + Cu^{2+}(aq) \longrightarrow Zn^{2+}(aq) + Cu(s),$$
$$(1\ F = 96500\ C\ mol^{-1})$$

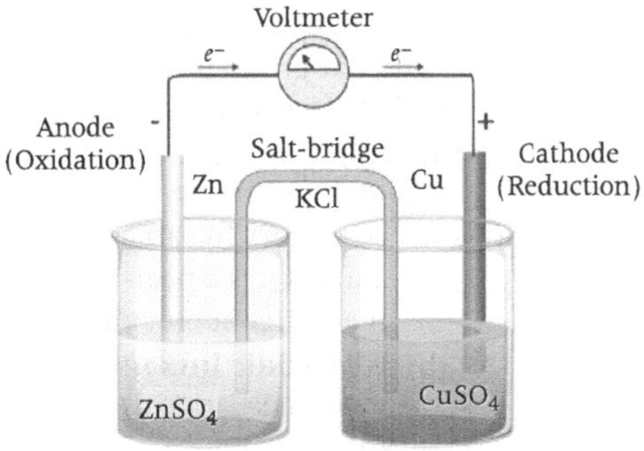

$Zn(s)|ZnSo_4(aq)||CuSO_4(aq)|Cu(s)$

• *Application*

(ii) A steady current of 1.8 amperes was passed through three electrolytic cells *A*, *B* and *C* (connected in a series) containing $CuSO_4$, $ZnSO_4$ and $AgNO_3$ solutions respectively till 2.16g of silver was deposited at the cathode.

(a) Calculate the time for which the current was passed.

(b) Calculate the weight of copper and zinc deposited. • *Application* [5]

20. (i) Using VBT, predict the geometry, hybridisation and magnetic behaviour of $[Fe(CN)_6]^{3-}$. [5]

• *Understanding*

(ii) For the coordination complex ion, $[Co(NH_3)_6]^{3+}$.

Write the IUPAC name and oxidation number of cobalt in the complex ion.

• *Understanding*

Or

Crystal field theory considers the metal-ligand bond to be ionic arising from electrostatic interaction between the metal ion and the ligands. In coordination compounds, the interaction between the ligand and the metal ion causes the five *d*-orbitals to split-up. This is called crystal field splitting and the energy difference between the two sets of energy level is called crystal field splitting energy. The crystal field splitting energy (Δ_o) depends upon the nature of the ligand.

Answer the following questions.

(i) $[Ni(H_2O)_6]^{2+}(aq)$ is green in colour whereas $[Ni(H_2O)_4(en)]^{2+}(aq)$ is blue in colour, give reason in support of your answer. • *Understanding*

(ii) In a coordination entity, the electronic configuration of the central metal ion is $t_{2g}^3\, e_g^1$.
Predict whether it is high spin or low spin complex. • *Understanding*

(iii) Draw the crystal field splitting diagram for the splitting of *d*-orbitals in an octahedral field. • *Recall*

(iv) Write any one limitation of crystal field theory. • *Recall*

(v) How is the crystal field splitting energy in tetrahedral complex and octahedral complex related to each other. • *Recall*

21. (i) Starting with cyclohexane carbaldehyde, how will cyclohexyl phenyl carbinol, cyclohexane carbaldehyde diethyl acetal and 1-methylcyclohexane compounds be synthesised? [5]

• *Understanding*

(ii) Acetone reacts with hydroxylamine to form only one product which has no geometrical isomer, but acetaldehyde reacts with hydroxylamine to form a product which has two geometrical isomers. Explain. • *Understanding*

Solutions in Topper's Style

My Commitment *I affirm that I am reviewing these solutions only after I have solved the Sample Question Paper on my own. My purpose of looking the solutions is solely to verify whether my answers/solutions were correct or not and to identify my mistakes in case my solutions were wrong or I could not solve that.*

1. (A) (i) vapour, less

(ii) $[Xe]4f^{14}$, reductant

(iii) cane sugar, pseudo first order

(iv) solvent, antioxidant

(B) (i) (b) The given reaction is known as Gattermann reaction.

In this reaction, aryl chloride is formed from aryl diazonium chloride by reacting it with copper in presence of HCl.

(ii) (*b*) Since, $E^{\circ}_{cell} = E^{\circ}_{reduction} - E^{\circ}_{oxidation}$

$\therefore \quad E^{\circ}_{cell} = 1.20\text{ V} - (-0.15\text{V}) = 1.35\text{ V}$

(iii) (a) Zn shows only +2 oxidation state as in this state, it attains stable noble gas configuration.

(iv) (b)The given equation represents the dehydration of the C_2H_5OH which takes place as follows

$$\underset{\text{Ethanol}}{C_2H_5OH} \xrightarrow[\Delta]{H_2SO_4} \underset{\text{Ethene }(A)}{H_2C = CH_2} + H_2O$$

Thus, compound '*A*' is ethene.

(v) (a) I and II are the correct statements whereas, statements III and IV are incorrect. Their correct form are as follows:

- The colours of complexes are due to electronic transitions from one set of *d*-orbitals to another set of orbitals.
- $\Delta_{(octahedral)} = \frac{9}{4}\Delta_{(tetrahedral)}$

(vi) (c) Assertion is true but Reason is false. The correct form of reason is as follows:

This reaction proceeds through S_N2 mechanism, in which OH^- ion attacks at 180° to the halogen atom of 2-bromooctane which leads to the inversion of configuration.

(vii) (b) Both Assertion and Reason are true, but Reason is not the correct explanation of Assertion.

The correct explanation is as follows

Glycine is optically inactive because it does not have four different substituents as shown below.

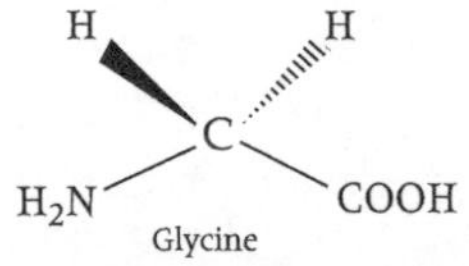

Glycine

(C) (i) The pentaacetate of glucose does not react with hydroxylamine. It indicates that the carbonyl group of glucose is not free and is present in cyclic form.

(ii) Vitamin C is water soluble and that's why it cannot be stored in our body.

(iii) (a) **Anomers** In carbohydrates, a pair of anomers, is a near-identical stereoisomers that differ at only the anomeric carbon.

(b) **Glycosidic linkage** The two monosaccharide units are joined together through amide linkage, known as glycosidic linkage.

2. Given number of molecules of urea = 6.02×10^{20}

[Number of moles = No. of molecules of urea/Avogadro's number]

$\therefore$ Number of moles = $\frac{6.02 \times 10^{20}}{6.02 \times 10^{23}} = 1 \times 10^{-3}$ moles

Volume of the solution = 100 mL = $\frac{100}{1000}$ L = 0.1 L

Concentration of urea solution (in mol L^{-1})

$$= \frac{1 \times 10^{-3}}{0.1} = 1 \times 10^{-2} \text{ mol L}^{-1}$$

$$= 0.01 \text{ mol/L or } 0.01 \text{ M}$$

3. (i) The electronic configuration of Cr^{2+} is $3d^4 4s^0$. After loosing one electron, it changes to Cr^{3+} whose configuration is $3d^3$, which is a more stable configuration and hence, it can act as a reducing agent. While Mn^{3+} after gaining one electron becomes Mn^{2+} whose electronic configuration is $3d^5 4s^0$, which is highly stable configuration. Thus, it acts as an oxidising agent.

(ii) Paramagnetic character increases with the increase in the number of unpaired electrons. The larger is the number of unpaired electron in central atom or ion, greater is the paramagnetic character.

From Sc to Mn, number of unpaired electron increases and then decreases from Fe to Zn. Hence, paramagnetic character also increases from Sc to Mn and then decreases from Fe to Zn.

4. (i) ΔG° gives the maximum work.

$$\Delta G^{\circ} = -nFE^{\circ}_{cell}$$

If E°_{cell} is + ve.

ΔG° = negative, cell will work.

(ii) Faraday's first law of electrolysis states that "the amount of chemical reaction occurring at any electrode by passing current is directly proportional to the quantity of electricity passed through the electrolyte (in solution or molten state)".

5. (i) In actinoids, 5 *f*-orbitals are filled which have more poor shielding effect than 4 *f*-orbitals in lanthanoids. Thus, the effective nuclear charge experienced by electrons in valence shells in case of actinoids is much more than that experienced by lanthanoids. Hence, the size contraction in actinoids is greater as compared to that of lanthanoids.

(ii) Cd^{2+} ion has completely filled *d*-orbitals ($4d^{10}$). Thus, there is no *d-d* transition possible in this case. Hence, in the absence of *d-d* transition, it is white in colour.

6. (i) The reaction involved is as follows

$$\underset{\text{Butyl butanoate [A]}}{CH_3CH_2CH_2-\overset{O}{\overset{\|}{C}}-OCH_2CH_2CH_2CH_3} \xrightarrow[\text{Hydrolysis}]{\text{Dil. } H_2SO_4} \underset{\text{Butanoic acid [B]}}{CH_3CH_2CH_2-\overset{O}{\overset{\|}{C}}-OH} + \underset{\text{Butan-1-ol [C]}}{CH_3CH_2CH_2CH_2OH}$$

$$\underset{\text{Butan-1-ol [C]}}{CH_3CH_2CH_2CH_2OH} \xrightarrow[H_2CrO_4 \text{ (Oxidation)}]{[O]} \underset{\text{Butanoic acid [B]}}{CH_3CH_2CH_2COOH}$$

$$\text{[C]} \xrightarrow[\text{Dehydration } (-H_2O)]{\text{Conc. } H_2SO_4} \underset{\text{But-l-ene}}{CH_3CH_2CH=CH_2}$$

7. (i) In aniline, the electron pair on nitrogen atom is involved in conjugation with ring and is less available for protonation than that in methylamine.
Therefore, pK_b value of aniline is more than that of methylamine and thus aniline is less basic (as higher the pK_b value, weaker is the base).

(ii) Ethylamine is soluble in water due to hydrogen bonding.

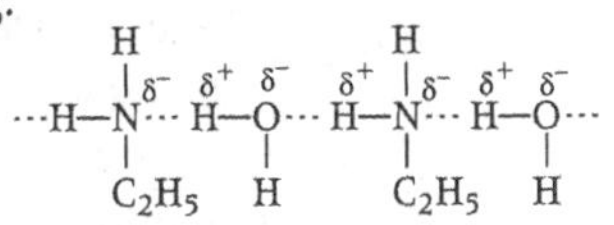

In aniline, due to bulky hydrocarbon part, the extent of hydrogen bonding is less and hence, it is not soluble in water.

Common Mistake One can make mistakes in the representation of the partial charges on the elements while showing hydrogen bonding.

8. (i)

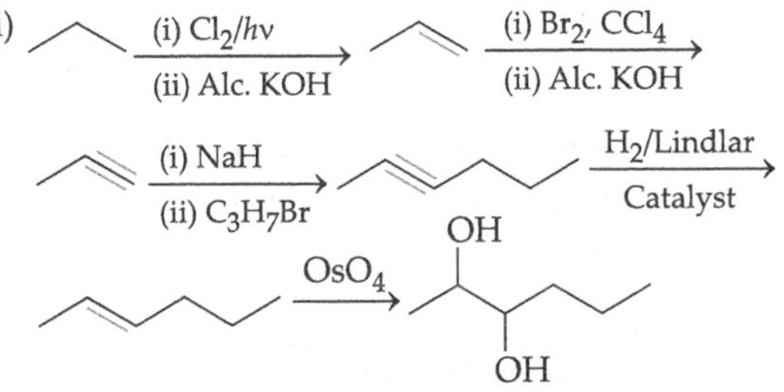

Or

Acidic nature of phenol can be checked by reaction with aqueous NaOH. Phenol can react with aqueous NaOH to form sodium phenoxide which shows that phenol is more acidic than propanol. This is because phenoxide ion left after the release of a proton is stabilised by resonance but not the alkoxide ion.

9. (i) (a) Degree of association, $\alpha = \dfrac{(1-i)}{\left(1-\dfrac{1}{n}\right)}$

(b) Degree of dissociation, $\alpha = \dfrac{i-1}{n-1}$

(ii) Given, molality = 0.4 molal
Freezing point of benzene, $T_f = 278.4$ K
Molar heat of fusion, $\Delta H_{fus} = 10.42 \text{ kJ mol}^{-1}$

$$\because \; K_f = \frac{RT_f^2 M}{1000 \times \Delta H_{fus}}$$
$$= \frac{8.314 \times 10^{-3} \times (278.4)^2 \times 78}{1000 \times 10.42}$$
$$= 4.82 \text{ K kg mol}^{-1}$$

10. (i)
$$\underset{\text{2-methoxy-2-methyl propane}}{CH_3-\overset{CH_3}{\overset{|}{\underset{CH_3}{\underset{|}{C}}}}-O-CH_3} + HI \longrightarrow \underset{tert\text{-butyliodide}}{CH_3-\overset{CH_3}{\overset{|}{\underset{CH_3}{\underset{|}{C}}}}-I} + \underset{\text{Methanol}}{CH_3OH}$$

(ii)
$$\underset{\text{Propene}}{CH_3-CH=CH_2} \xrightarrow[\text{(b) } 3H_2O_2/OH^-]{\text{(a) } B_2H_6} \underset{\text{(Propanol)}}{3CH_3CH_2CH_2OH}$$

11. (i) The magnetic moment of 5.92 BM corresponds to the presence of five unpaired electrons in the *d*-orbital of Mn^{2+} ion. Thus, the hybridisation involved is sp^3 rather than dsp^2.
Hence, the tetrahedral structure of $[MnCl_4]^{2-}$ complex will show 5.92 BM magnetic moment value.

(ii) The oxidation state of cobalt in the complex is +3. The electronic configuration of Co^{3+} ion is

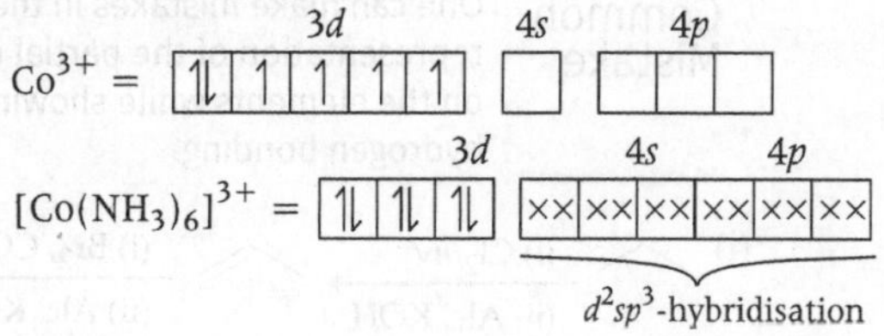

Hence, geometry is octahedral.

12. (i) **Benzyl chloride ⟶ Benzyl alcohol**

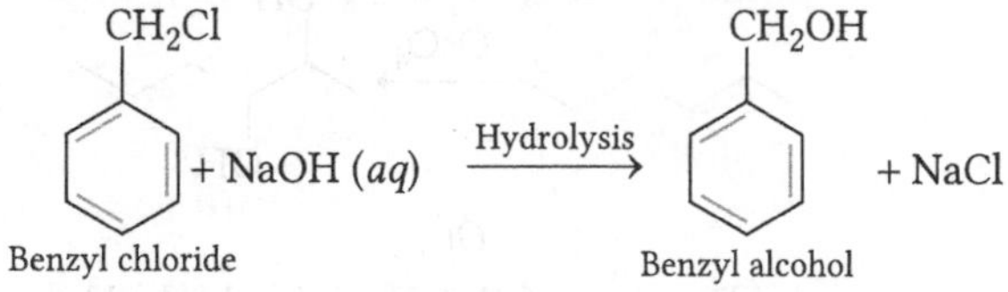

(ii) **Ethyl magnesium chloride ⟶ Propan-1-ol**

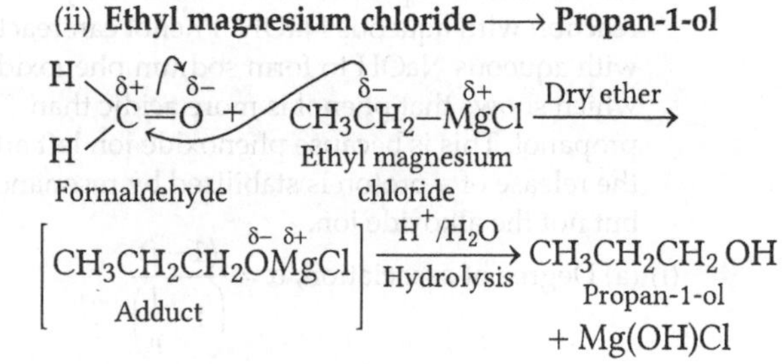

(iii) **Methyl magnesium bromide ⟶ 2-methylpropan-2-ol**

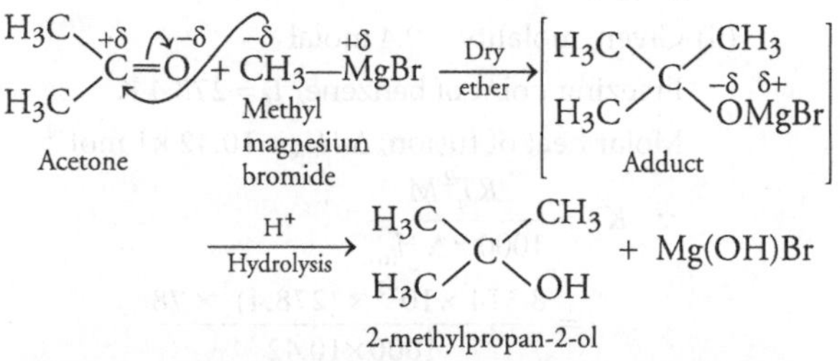

13. Since, the liquid *A* reduces ammoniacal silver nitrate (Tollen's reagent), hence *A* is aldehyde and *B* does not give test with ammoniacal silver nitrate, thus, *B* is a ketone.

Further, *B* forms a white crystalline solid on treatment with sodium hydrogen sulphite. This suggests that *B* is a methyl ketone.

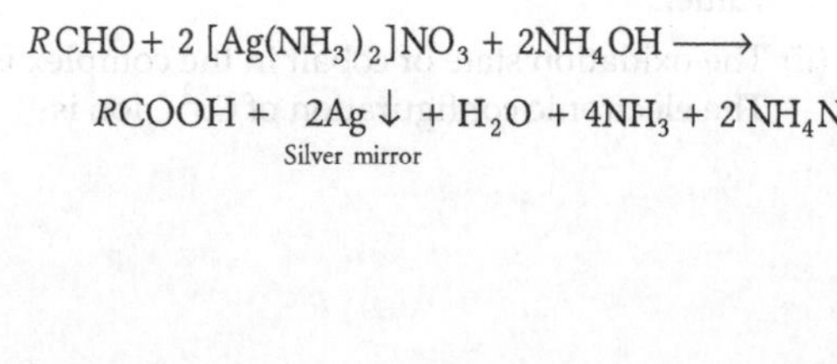

$$RCHO + 2[Ag(NH_3)_2]NO_3 + 2NH_4OH \longrightarrow RCOOH + 2Ag\downarrow + H_2O + 4NH_3 + 2NH_4NO_3$$

Silver mirror

Note Aldehyde and ketone both gives white crystalline solid with sodium hydrogen sulphite but only aldehyde gives Tollen's test and Fehling's test.

14. (i) Given, $E_1 - E_2 = 24.9$ kJ/mol

$T = 27°C = 300$ K

$R = 8.314$ J/mol/K

According to Arrhenius equation,

$$\log_{10} k = \log_{10} A - \frac{E}{2.303RT}$$

so, $$\log_{10} k_1 = \log_{10} A - \frac{E_1}{2.303RT} \quad \ldots(i)$$

and $$\log_{10} k_2 = \log_{10} A - \frac{E_2}{2.303RT} \quad \ldots(ii)$$

From Eqs. (i) and (ii) we get,

$$\log_{10}\left(\frac{k_2}{k_1}\right) = \frac{(E_1 - E_2)}{2.303RT}$$

$$\log_{10}\left(\frac{k_2}{k_1}\right) = \frac{24.9 \times 1000}{2.303 \times 8.314 \times 300}$$

$$\log_{10}\left(\frac{k_2}{k_1}\right) = 4.33$$

$$\Rightarrow \quad \frac{k_2}{k_1} = 2.138 \times 10^4$$

(ii) Given, $t = 1$ hour $a_0 - x = 0.25\,a$

For 1st order reaction,

$$k = \frac{2.303}{t} \log \frac{a_0}{a_0 - x}$$

$$k = \frac{2.303}{1} \log \frac{a}{0.25a}$$

$$= \frac{2.303}{1} \log 4 = 2.303 \times 2 \times 0.3010$$

$$= 1.386 \text{ hr}^{-1}$$

$$t_{1/2} = \frac{0.693}{k} = \frac{0.693}{1.386} = 0.5 \text{ hours}$$

15. (i) Given that, $K_f = 5.12$ K kg mol^{-1}

Mass of benzene, $W_1 = 75$ g

Depression in freezing point,

$\Delta T_f = 0.48$ K, $M_2 = 256$ g mol^{-1}

If w_2 is the mass of compound,

Then, $$\Delta T_f = \frac{K_f \times w_2 \times 1000}{W_1 \times M_2}$$

(where, M_2 is molar mass of compound)

or $$0.48 = \frac{5.12 \times w_2 \times 1000}{75 \times 256}$$

$$\therefore \quad w_2 = \frac{0.489 \times 75 \times 256}{5.12 \times 1000} = 1.8 \text{ g}$$

(ii) Elevation in boiling point is a colligative property as it depends upon the number of particles.

$$\Delta T_b \propto n$$

For sucrose, $n = 1$, $\Delta T_b = 0.1°C$

Therefore, for NaCl, $n = 2$ $\Delta T_b = 0.2°C$ (i.e. double of sucrose).

16. (i) **Benzene diazonium chloride to fluorobenzene**

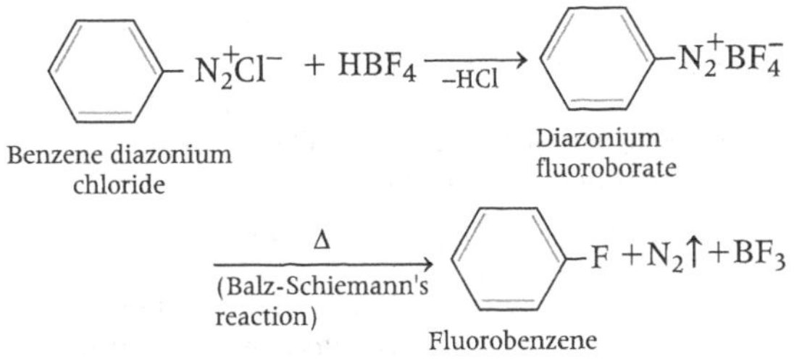

(ii) **Nitrobenzene to phenol**

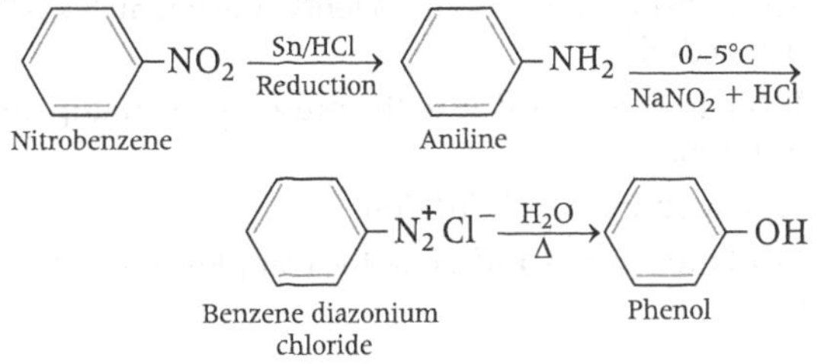

(iii) **Chloromethane to Ethylamine**

$$\underset{\text{Chloromethane}}{CH_3Cl} \xrightarrow{KCN} \underset{\text{Methylcyanide}}{CH_3CN} \xrightarrow{LiAlH_4} \underset{\text{Ethanamine}}{CH_3CH_2NH_2}$$

Or

(i) **Hofmann bromamide degradation reaction** This reaction is used for preparing primary amine containing one carbon less than the starting amide.

$$R{-}\overset{O}{\overset{\|}{C}}{-}NH_2 + Br_2 + 4NaOH \longrightarrow R{-}NH_2 + Na_2CO_3 + 2NaBr + 2H_2O$$

(ii) **Gabriel phthalimide synthesis** In this reaction, phthalimide is treated with ethanolic KOH, it forms potassium salt of phthalimide which on heating with alkyl halide followed by alkaline hydrolysis forms corresponding primary amines.

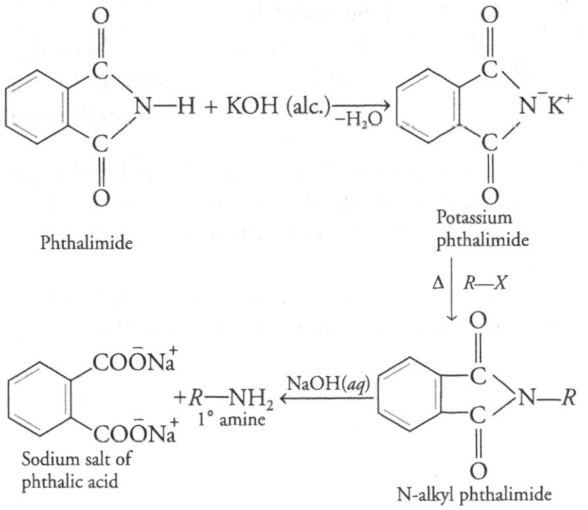

(iii) **Sandmeyer reaction** The Cl^-, Br^- and CN^- nucleophiles can easily be introduced in the benzene ring in the presence of Cu (I) ion. This reaction is called Sandmeyer reaction.

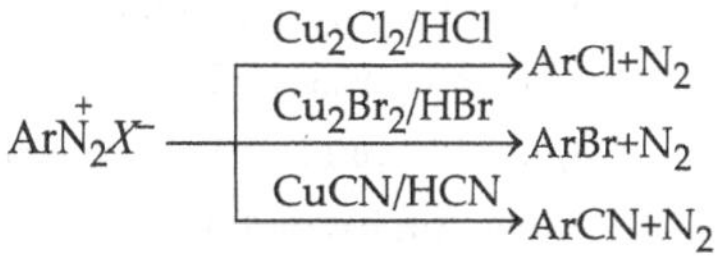

17. According to rate law $= k[A]^x[B]^y$

$(\text{Rate})_1 = k[0.20]^x[0.30]^y = 4.08 \times 10^{-5}$ ...(i)

$(\text{Rate})_2 = k[0.20]^x[0.10]^y = 4.08 \times 10^{-5}$ ...(ii)

$(\text{Rate})_3 = k[0.40]^x[0.05]^y = 2.34 \times 10^{-4}$ ...(iii)

On dividing Eq. (i) by Eq. (ii), we get

$$\frac{(\text{Rate})_1}{(\text{Rate})_2} = \frac{k(0.20)^x(0.30)^y}{k(0.20)^x(0.10)^y} = \frac{4.08 \times 10^{-5}}{4.08 \times 10^{-5}} = 1$$

$$[3]^y = [3]^0$$

$$y = 0$$

On dividing Eq. (iii) by Eq. (ii), we get

$$\frac{(\text{Rate})_3}{(\text{Rate})_2} = \frac{k\,(0.40)^x(0.05)^y}{k\,(0.20)^x(0.10)^y} = \frac{2.34 \times 10^{-4}}{4.08 \times 10^{-5}}$$

$$5.7352 = 2^x$$

$$\log 5.7352 = x \log 2$$

$$x = \frac{0.7585}{0.3010} = 2.5$$

(i) Thus, order of reaction with respect to A is 2.5. and order of the reaction with respect to B is 0.

(ii) Rate law equation is, $r = k[A]^{2.5}[B]^0$

(iii) Since, $r = k[A]^{2.5}$

Thus, rate constant,

$$k = \frac{r}{[A]^{2.5}} = \frac{4.08 \times 10^{-5}\,\text{mol/L/s}}{[0.20\,\text{mol/L}]^{2.5}}$$

$$= 2.28 \times 10^{-3}\,\text{mol}^{-1.5}\text{L}^{1.5}\text{s}^{-1}$$

18. (i) $\underset{\text{Propene}}{CH_3{-}CH{=}CH_2} \xrightarrow[\text{Peroxide}]{HBr} \underset{\text{1-bromopropane (A)}}{CH_3CH_2CH_2{-}Br}$

$$\xrightarrow[\text{(Finkelstein reaction)}]{\text{NaI acetone}} \underset{\text{1-iodopropane (B)}}{CH_3CH_2CH_2{-}I} \xrightarrow{KCN} \underset{\text{Butanenitrile (C)}}{CH_3CH_2CH_2CN}$$

(ii) $CH_3Cl \xrightarrow{KCN} \underset{\text{Methyl cyanide (A)}}{CH_3CN} \xrightarrow{CH_3MgCl}$

$$\underset{(B)}{CH_3{-}\overset{CH_3}{\overset{|}{C}}{=}NMgCl} \xrightarrow{H_3O^+} \underset{\text{Acetone (C)}}{CH_3{-}\overset{O}{\overset{\|}{C}}{-}CH_3}$$

19. (i) For the reaction,

$$Zn(s) + Cu^{2+}(aq) \longrightarrow Zn^{2+}(aq) + Cu(s)$$

$$E° = +1.1\,V, \Delta G° = ?$$

$$1F = 96500\,C\,mol^{-1}, n = 2$$

As we know that, $\Delta G^\circ = -nFE^\circ$

$\therefore \quad \Delta G^\circ = -2 \times 96500 \times 1.1$

$= -212300 \text{ J mol}^{-1}$

(ii) (a) Weight of Ag deposited = 2.16 g

Current passed = 1.8 amperes,

Quantity of electricity passed, Q = ?

Reaction involved is

$$\underset{1\text{ mol}}{Ag^+} + \underset{1\text{ mol}}{e^-} \longrightarrow \underset{1\text{ mol} = 108\text{ g}}{Ag}$$

[$\because$ Atomic weight of Ag = 108 g]

108 g Ag is deposited by charge = 96500 C

2.16 g of Ag is deposited by charge

$= \dfrac{96500}{108} \times 2.16$

= 1930 Coulombs

We know, Q = current in amperes × time in sec

$$t = \frac{Q}{i} = \frac{1930 \text{ Coulombs}}{1.8 \text{ Amperes}} = 1072 \text{ s}$$

(b) Equivalent weight of Cu = $\dfrac{\text{At. wt.}}{\text{Valency}}$

$\dfrac{63.5}{2} = 31.75$ g

$\because$ Equivalent weight of Ag

$= \dfrac{\text{Atomic weight of Ag}}{\text{Valency}} = \dfrac{108}{1}$

Let weight of Cu deposited = x g

But,

$$\frac{\text{weight of Cu}}{\text{weight of Ag}} = \frac{\text{Equivalent weight of Cu}}{\text{Equivalent weight of Ag}}$$

$\Rightarrow \quad \dfrac{x}{2.16} = \dfrac{31.75}{108}$

$\Rightarrow \quad x = 0.635$ g

Now, Equivalent weight of Zn

$= \dfrac{\text{Atomic weight}}{\text{valency}}$

$= \dfrac{65}{2} = 32.5$

Let weight of Zn = y g

But,

$$\frac{\text{weight of Zn}}{\text{weight of Ag}} = \frac{\text{Equivalent weight of Zn}}{\text{Equivalent weight of Ag}}$$

$\dfrac{y}{2.16} = \dfrac{32.5}{108}$

$\Rightarrow \quad y = 0.65$ g

20. (i) Let the oxidation number of Fe in the complex ion $[Fe(CN)_6]^{3-}$ be x.

Then, $x + 6(-1) = -3 \Rightarrow x = +3$

Electronic configuration of Fe = $[Ar]3d^6 4s^2$

For Fe^{3+} = [Ar] $3d^5$: [1][1][1][1][1] $4s^0$: [ ] $4p^0$: [ ][ ][ ]

CN^- being strong field ligand, will pair up the d-electrons of the metal. Thus,

$[Fe(CN)_6]^{3-}$ = $3d$: [⥮][⥮][1] [XX][XX][XX][XX][XX][XX] (d^2sp^3-hybridisation; Six pairs of electrons from six CN^- ions)

The hybridisation is d^2sp^3. Hence, the geometry is octahedral.

It is paramagnetic due to the presence of an unpaired electron.

(ii) Hexaammine cobalt (III) ion

Oxidation number of Co in the complex $[Co(NH_3)_6]^{3+}$ is

$$x \times 6 \times (0) = +3 \Rightarrow x = +3$$

Or

(i) Ligands play an important role in exhibiting the colour to the complex. H_2O is a weak field ligand, which causes small d-d splitting and correspondingly complex gives green colour, whereas, ethane-1, 2- diamine (en) is a strong field ligand due to which d-d splitting is increased and correspondingly complex gives blue colour.

(ii) In $t_{2g}^3 e_g^1$ configuration, as the fourth electron enters in one of the e_g-orbitals, thus it is a high spin complex.

(iii) **Crystal field splitting diagram in octahedral crystal field**

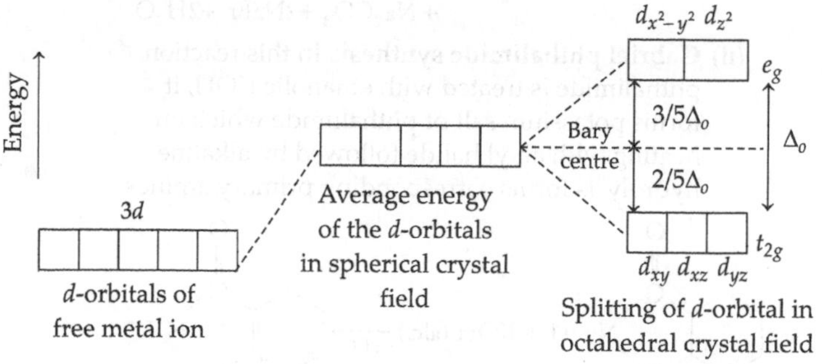

Splitting of d-orbital in octahedral crystal field

(iv) Crystal field theory treats the metal-ligand bond as purely ionic and it does not take into account the covalent character of bonding between the ligand and the central atom.

(v) The crystal field splitting energy of octahedral and tetrahedral complexes are related to each other as

$$\Delta t = \left(\frac{4}{9}\right)\Delta_o$$

21. (i) •

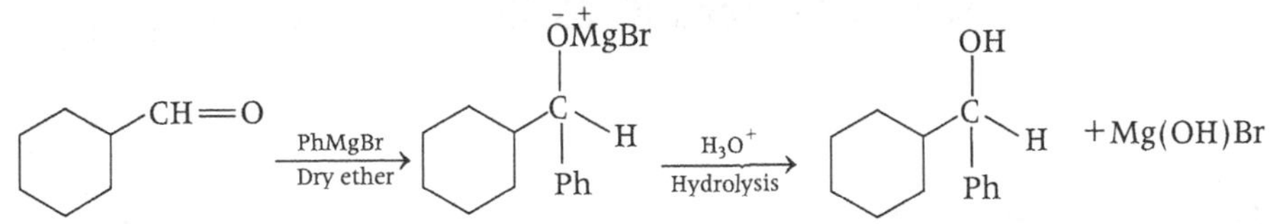

Cyclohexane carbaldehyde → Cyclohexyl phenyl carbinol

Also,

•

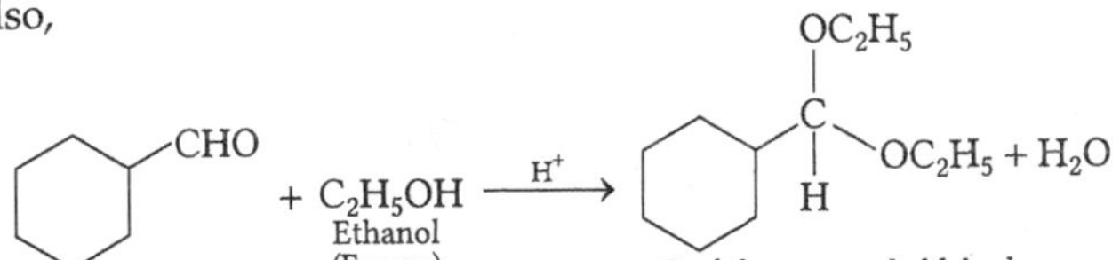

Cyclohexane carbaldehyde diethyl acetal

•

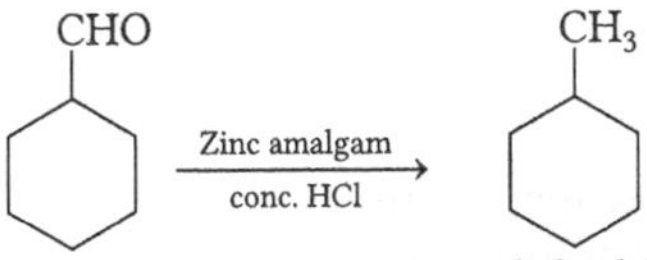

1-methylcyclohexane

(ii) When acetone reacts with —NH_2OH, the acetoxime formed has two identical —CH_3 groups attached to carbon with which N forms a double bond. This does not fulfill conditions for geometrical isomerism. But when acetaldehyde reacts with NH_2OH, acetaldoxime is formed which has two different groups attached to C forming double bond with nitrogen. Therefore, it exhibits geometrical isomerism.

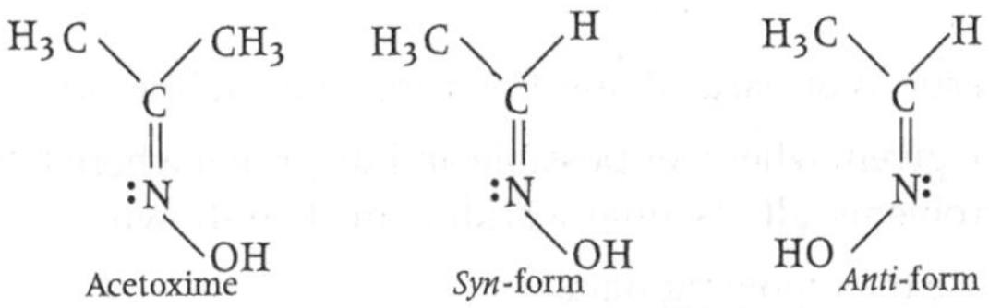

Acetoxime *Syn*-form *Anti*-form

(Acetaldoxime)

SQP Code : **PB-10/15** Series ***i*-Succeed 10-25/15** Roll No. [ ]

Sample Question Paper 10

Chemistry 12th (Code 862)

General Instructions

1. This paper is divided into four sections-A, B, C and D. Answer all questions.
2. **Section A** consists of **one** question **having sub-parts** of **one** mark each. **Section B** consists of **ten** questions of **two** marks each. **Section C** consists of **seven** questions of **three** marks each and **Section D** consists of **three** questions of **five** marks each.
3. Internal choices have been provided in one question each in Section B, Section C and Section D.
4. All working, including rough work, should be done on the same sheet as, and adjacent to the rest of the answer.
5. The intended marks for questions or parts of questions are given in brackets [].
6. Balanced questions must be given, wherever possible and diagrams where they are helpful. When solving numerical problems, all essential working must be shown.
7. In working out problems, use the following data:
Gas constant (R) = 1.987 cal deg^{-1} mol^{-1} = 8.314 JK^{-1} mol^{-1} = 0.0821 dm^3 atm K^{-1} mol^{-1}
1L atm = 1 dm^3 atm =101.3 J, 1 Faraday =96500 Coulombs.
Avogadro's number (N_A) = 6.023×10^{23}.

Time : 3 Hrs.

Max. Marks : 70

Section A

[14 Marks]

1. (A) Fill in the blanks by choosing the appropriate word(s) from those given in the brackets. [4 ×1]

[ideal, +ve, –ve, positive, zero, acidic, basic, first, mesomeric, negative, inductive (+*I*), rate constant, concentration].

(i) The slope of the curve for the variation in the concentration (R) *versus* time (t) plot for a .... order reaction is equal to the negative of .... for the reaction.

• *Understanding*

(ii) For a non-spontaneous reaction, ΔG° and E°_{cell} are .... and .... respectively.

• *Recall*

(iii) Methylamine is more .... than ammonia because of .... effect.

• *Understanding*

(iv) Maximum boiling azeotropes show ...... deviation from .... behaviour.

• *Recall*

(B) Select and write the correct alternative from the choices given below. [7 ×1]

(i) The reaction of CH_2OCH_2 with $RMgX$ gives

• *Understanding*

(a) $RCHOHCH_3$ (b) $RCHOHR$
(c) R_2CHCH_2OH (d) RCH_2CH_2OH

(ii) The standard electrode potentials of four elements P, Q, R, S are –3.05 V, –1.66 V, –0.40 V and –0.80 V respectively. Correct order of increasing chemical reactivity of the elements is

• *Analysis*

(a) $S < R < Q < P$ (b) $Q < P < R < S$
(c) $R < S < P < Q$ (d) $S < Q < R < P$

(iii) Which set of ions exhibit specific colours? (Atomic number of Sc = 21, Ti = 22, V = 23, Mn = 25, Fe = 26, Ni = 28, Cu = 29 and Zn = 30) • *Understanding*

(a) Sc^{3+}, Ti^{4+}, Mn^{3+}
(b) Sc^{3+}, Zn^{2+}, Ni^{2+}
(c) V^{3+}, V^{2+}, Fe^{3+}
(d) Ti^{3+}, Ti^{4+}, Ni^{2+}

(iv) The half-life of a first order reaction is 69.35 seconds. The value of rate constant of the reaction is • *Application*

(a) $1.0\ s^{-1}$ (b) $0.1\ s^{-1}$
(c) $0.01\ s^{-1}$ (d) $0.001\ s^{-1}$

(v) Consider the following statements regarding $[MnO_4]^-$ complex ion.

I. It is pink in solution.
II. The oxidation state of Mn is +7.
III. It is diamagnetic in nature.
IV. MnO_4^- possess planar structure.

The incorrect statement(s) is/are • *Understanding*

(a) I and II (b) II and III
(c) I and IV (d) II and IV

(vi) **Assertion** (A) Linkage isomerism arises in coordination compounds containing ambidentate ligand. [2 ×1]

Reason (R) Ambidentate ligand has two different donor atoms. • *Analysis*

(a) Both Assertion and Reason are true and Reason is the correct explanation of Assertion.
(b) Both Assertion and Reason are true but Reason is not the correct explanation of Assertion.
(c) Assertion is true but Reason is false.
(d) Both Assertion and Reason are false.

(vii) **Assertion** (A) Nitration of aniline can be conveniently done by protecting the amino group by acetylation.

Reason (R) Acetylation increases the electron-density in the benzene ring. • *Analysis*

(a) Both Assertion and Reason are true and Reason is the correct explanation of Assertion.
(b) Both Assertion and Reason are true but Reason is not the correct explanation of Assertion.
(c) Assertion is true but Reason is false.
(d) Both Assertion and Reason are false.

(C) Read the passage given below carefully and answer the questions that follows [3 ×1]

Haloalkanes and haloarenes are the hydrocarbons in which one or more hydrogen atoms have been replaced with halogen atoms.

Haloarenes undergo the usual electrophilic substitution reactions of the benzene ring such as halogenation, nitration, sulphonation and Friedel-Crafts reaction.

In electrophilic substitution reactions, the formation of an intermediate carbocation is the slow rate determining step and the factors which stabilise the intermediate carbocation, favour the electrophilic substitution. Halogens attached directly to a benzene ring exhibit dual nature.

The lone pair of electrons present on halogens participitates in delocalisation with π-electrons of the benzene ring, through +*R*-effect, stabilises the carbocation formed by *ortho* and *para* attack.

(i) What happens when chlorobenzene is treated with Cl_2 and anhydrous $FeCl_3$? • *Understanding*

(ii) What happens when 2, 4-dinitrochlorobenzene is treated with aqueous NaOH? • *Understanding*

(iii) In the presence of light, toluene reacts with Br_2 to give benzyl bromide, while in presence of $FeBr_3$, the product is *p*-bromotoluene. Why? • *Understanding*

Section B **[20 Marks]**

2. Give reason for the following. [2] • *Understanding*

(i) The lowest oxide of a transition metal is basic, the highest one is amphoteric or acidic.

(ii) Acidified $KMnO_4$ solution is treated with KI and forms I_2.

3. Write the equation for the following reactions. [2] • *Understanding*

(i) Conversion of propan-2-ol to 2-methyl propan-2-ol

(ii) Phenol is treated with $Na_2Cr_2O_7$ in the presence of sulphuric acid.

4. Identify compounds [*A*] and [*B*] in the following reactions. [2] • *Understanding*

(i) $$CH_3-\underset{\displaystyle CH_3}{\underset{|}{CH}}-Br + Mg \xrightarrow{\text{Dry ether}} [A] \xrightarrow{D_2O} [B]$$

(ii) $$CH_3-\underset{\displaystyle CH_3}{\underset{|}{CH}}-CH_2-Br \xrightarrow{\text{KOH(alc.)}} [A] \xrightarrow{\text{HBr}} [B]$$

5. (i) How does a change of temperature influence the value of molarity and molality of a solution ? [2] • *Recall*

(ii) Why does aquatic animals feel more comfortable in cold water rather in warm water? • *Understanding*

6. 0.05 M NaOH solution offered a resistance of 31.6 Ω in a conductivity cell at 298 K. If the cell constant of the cell is 0.367 cm^{-1}, calculate the molar conductivity of the NaOH solution. [2] • *Application*

7. Write the chemical equation for the following named organic reactions. [2]

(i) Coupling reaction

(ii) Carbylamine reaction • *Recall*

8. During chemistry class, a teacher wrote $[Fe(H_2O)_6]^{3+}$ as coordination complex ion on the board. The students were asked to find out the magnetic behaviour and shape of the complex. Pooja, a student wrote the answer paramagnetic and octahedral whereas another student Anjali wrote diamagnetic and square planar. [2]

Evaluate Pooja's and Anjali's responses. • *Evaluate*

9. (i) Ethyl benzene is generally prepared by acetylation of benzene followed by the reduction and not by direct alkylation. Think of a possible reason. • *Analysis*

(ii) Can Gattermann-Koch reaction be considered similar to Friedel-Crafts acylation? Discuss. • *Recall* [2]

Or

(i) Which of the following pair is a stronger acid ? • *Understanding*

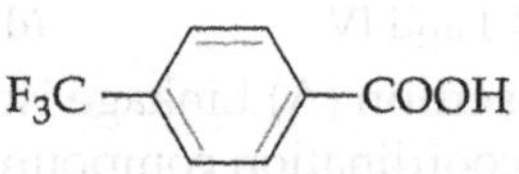

or

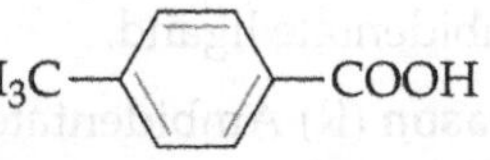

(ii) Why are α-hydrogen atoms of aldehydes and ketones acidic in nature? • *Understanding*

10. Give reason for the following questions. [2] • *Understanding*

(i) The $E^\circ_{M^{2+}/M}$ value of copper is positive (+0.34 V).

(ii) The enthalpy of atomisation of zinc is lowest.

11. H_2S, a toxic gas with rotten egg like smell, is used for qualitative analysis. If the solubility of H_2S in water at STP is 0.195 m. Calculate, [2] • *Application*

(i) mole fraction of H_2S in water.

(ii) Henry's law constant.

SP-10

Section C

[21 Marks]

12. The order of reaction can be defined as the power dependence of rate on the concentration of all reactants.

A reaction is first order in *A* and second order in *B*. [3]

(i) Write the differential rate equation. • *Application*

(ii) How is the rate affected on increasing the concentration of *B* three times? • *Application*

(iii) How is the rate affected when the concentration of both *A* and *B* are doubled? • *Application*

13. Arrange the following compounds in order of the feature given. [3] • *Analysis*

(i) *o*-cresol, phenol, *o*-nitrophenol (Acidic character).

(ii) Phenol, benzene, chlorobenzene (Reactivity towards electrophilic substitution).

14. (i) Write one main function of carbohydrate in plants. • *Recall* [3]

(ii) Shivansh found out that their is coagulation of an egg while on boiling. What can be the possible reason behind it ? • *Understanding*

(iii) Write the products of hydrolysis of maltose. • *Recall*

15. A hydrocarbon (*A*) with molecular formula C_5H_{10} on ozonolysis gives two products (*B*) and (*C*). Both (*B*) and (*C*) gives a yellow precipitate when heated with iodine in presence of NaOH while only (*B*) gives a silver mirror on reaction with Tollen's reagent. • *Understanding* [3]

(i) Identify (*A*), (*B*) and (*C*).

(ii) Write the reaction of *B* with Tollen's reagent.

(iii) Write the equation for iodoform test of *C*.

Or

Compare the reactivity of benzaldehyde and ethanal towards nucleophilic addition reactions. Write the Cross-aldol condensation product between benzaldehyde and ethanal. • *Understanding*

16. Vapour pressure of pure water at 298 K is 23.8 mm of Hg. 50 g of urea (NH_2CONH_2) is dissolved in 850 g of water. Calculate, • *Application* [3]

(i) the vapour pressure of water for this solution.

(ii) its relative lowering.

17. Identify the compounds *A*, *B* and *C* in the following reactions. [3] • *Understanding*

(i) $CH_3COCH_3 \xrightarrow[2[H]]{LiAlH_4} [A] \xrightarrow[Heat]{H_2SO_4(conc.)} [B] \xrightarrow[Peroxide]{HBr} [C]$

(ii) 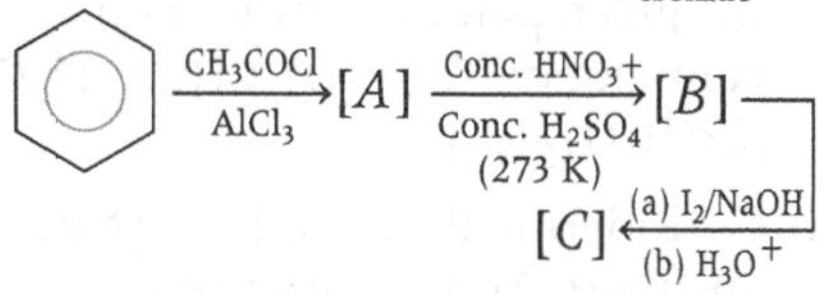

18. Suppose for the first order decomposition of azo *iso*-propane to hexane and nitrogen at 543 K, the following data is obtained. [3]

t (s)	*p* (mm of Hg)
0	35.0
360	54.0
720	63.0

Answer the following questions

(i) What is the rate constant after 360 s. • *Application*

(ii) What is the rate constant after 720. • *Application*

(iii) Determine average rate constant. • *Evaluate*

Section D **[15 Marks]**

19. (i) A ketone $A(C_4H_8O)$ which undergoes a haloform reaction gives compound *B* on reduction. *B* on heating with sulphuric acid gives a compound *C* which forms mono-ozonide *D*. *D* on hydrolysis with zinc dust gives only acetaldehyde *E*. Identify *A*, *B*, *C*, and *D*. Write an explanation for your answer. • *Understanding* [3]

(ii) (a) Write the reaction when propan-2-one is reduced with zinc amalgam. • *Understanding*

(b) Write the name of this reaction. The IUPAC name of the product formed in above reaction. • *Recall* [5]

20. (i) Explain linkage isomerism. Give an example of complexes which exhibit this type of isomerism.

Also, find out the type of isomerism in the given pair of coordination compounds $[Cr(H_2O)_5Cl]Cl_2 \cdot H_2O$ and $[Cr(H_2O)_6]Cl_3$. • *Recall*

(ii) Considering the complexes $[Ni(CN)_4]^{2-}$ and $[Ni(CO)_4]$. Explain the differences in their geometry and hybridisation. • *Understanding*

21. Faradays laws of electrolysis in chemistry are quantitative laws being used to express magnitude of eletrolytic effects.

The First law states that the amount of chemical change being produced by a current at an electrode-electrolyte interface is proportional to the quantity of electricity used.

The second one tells that the amounts of chemical changes produced by the same quantity of electricity in different substances are proportional to their equivalent weights.

(i) A current of 1.70 A is passed through 300.0 mL of 0.160 M solution of $ZnSO_4$ for 230 s with a current efficiency of 90 percent.

Find out the molarity of Zn^{2+} after the deposition of zinc. • *Application*

Assume the volume of the solution to remain constant during electrolysis. [5]

(ii) A current of 10 A is passed for 80 min and 27 s through a cell containing dilute sulphuric acid. How many moles of oxygen gas will be liberated at the anode? • *Application*

Or (i) How long a current of 3A has to be passed through a solution of silver nitrate to coat a metal surface of 80 cm^2 with a 0.005 mm thick layer ? [Density of Ag = 10.5 g cm^{-3} and atomic weight of Ag = 108.0 u] • *Application*

(ii) From the graph given below, which will be the weakest electrolyte and which will be the strongest and why? • *Understanding*

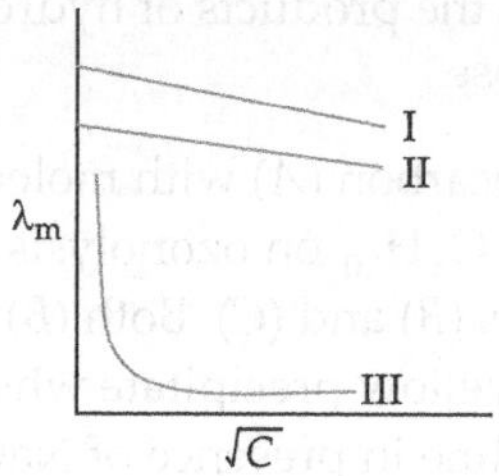

SP-10

Solutions in Topper's Style

My Commitment *I affirm that I am reviewing these solutions only after I have solved the Sample Question Paper on my own. My purpose of looking the solutions is solely to verify whether my answers/solutions were correct or not and to identify my mistakes in case my solutions were wrong or I could not solve that.*

1. (A) (i) Zero, rate constant
   (ii) +ve, –ve,
   (iii) basic, inductive (+*I*)
   (iv) negative, ideal

(B) (i) (d)

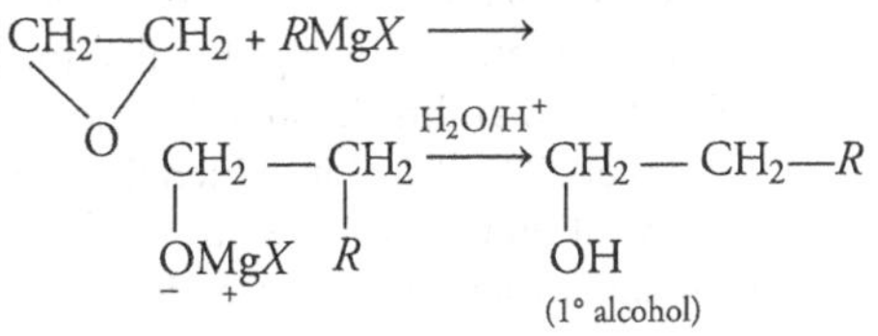

(ii) (a) Lower the standard electrode (reduction) potential of an element, higher is their chemical reactivity.

Thus, the correct increasing order of chemical reactivity is S < R < Q < P.

(iii) (c) V^{3+}, V^{2+} and Fe^{3+} exhibit colours due to *d-d* transition.

Transition metal ion having d^0 and d^{10}-configuration are colourless as *d- d* transition is not possible.

$V^{3+}(3d^2) \longrightarrow$ Green
$V^{2+}(3d^3) \longrightarrow$ Violet
$Fe^{3+}(3d^6) \longrightarrow$ Green

(iv) (c) For first order, $t_{1/2} = \dfrac{0.693}{k}$

$$\Rightarrow \quad k = \frac{0.693}{t_{1/2}} = \frac{0.693}{69.35} = 0.01\,s^{-1}$$

(v) (c) Statements II and III are correct while statements I and IV are incorrect. Their correct form are as follows:

- Solution of MnO_4^- is not pink in colour. It is deep purple.
- MnO_4^- possess tetrahedral structure.

(vi) (a) Linkage isomerism arises in coordination compounds containing ambidentate ligands because ambidentate ligands has two different donor atoms, e.g. SCN, NO_2 etc.

Thus, both Assertion and Reason are true and Reason is the correct explanation of Assertion.

(vii) (c) Assertion is true but Reason is false.

The correct form of reason is,

Acetylation decreases the electron-density in the benzene ring thereby preventing oxidation.

(C) (i) When chlorobenzene is treated with Cl_2 and anhydrous $FeCl_3$, two types of products are formed as

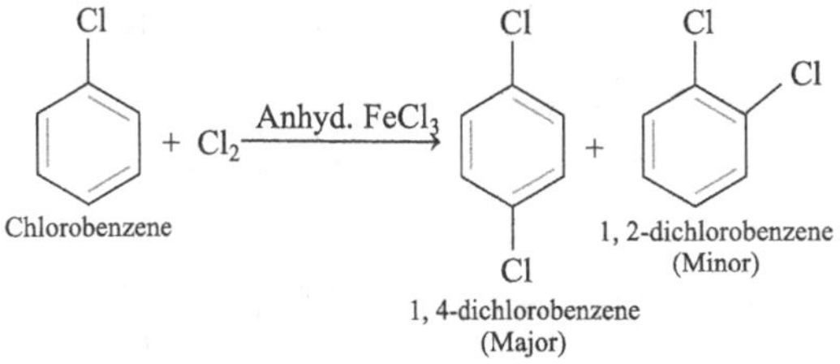

(ii) 2, 4-dinitrochlorobenzene reacts with NaOH(*aq*) to yield 2, 4-dinitrophenol.

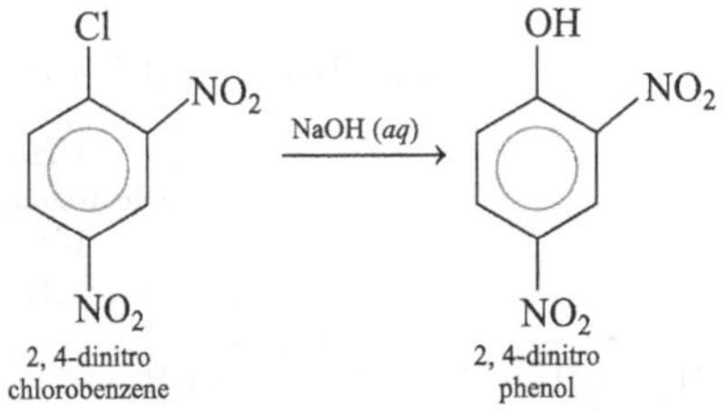

(iii) In the presence of light, side chain is brominated by free radical mechanism, while in presence of $FeBr_3$, electrophilic substitution occurs in the ring.

2. (i) In the lowest oxidation state of the transition metal, some of the valence electrons are not involved in bonding. Therefore, they can donate electrons and behave as a base.

While in higher oxidation state, the valence electrons are involved in bonding and hence are not available.

Therefore, transition metals in higher oxidation states behave as an acid.

(ii) An acidified $KMnO_4$ solution oxidises potassium iodide to iodine.

$$2KMnO_4 + 8H_2SO_4 + 10KI \longrightarrow 6K_2SO_4 + 2MnSO_4 + 8H_2O + 5I_2$$

3. (i) **Propan-2-ol to 2-methylpropan-2-ol**

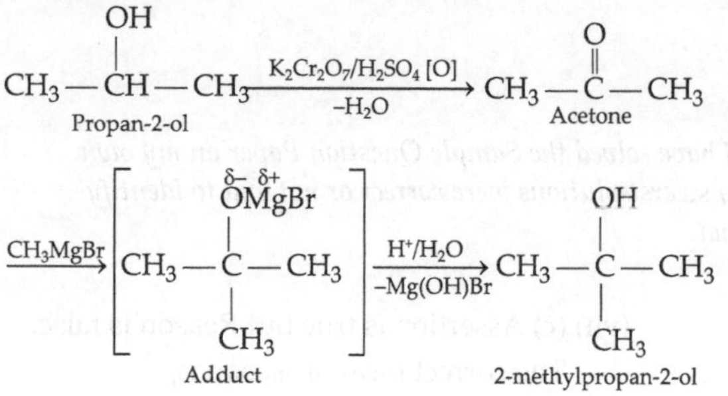

(ii) Oxidation of phenol is done with $Na_2Cr_2O_7$ in the presence of sulphuric acid and benzoquinone is formed alongwith water.

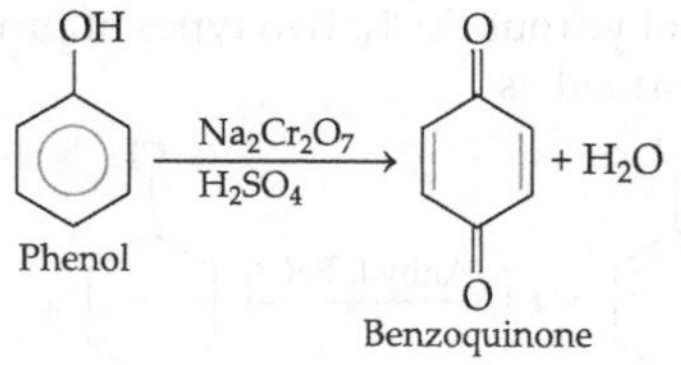

4. (i)

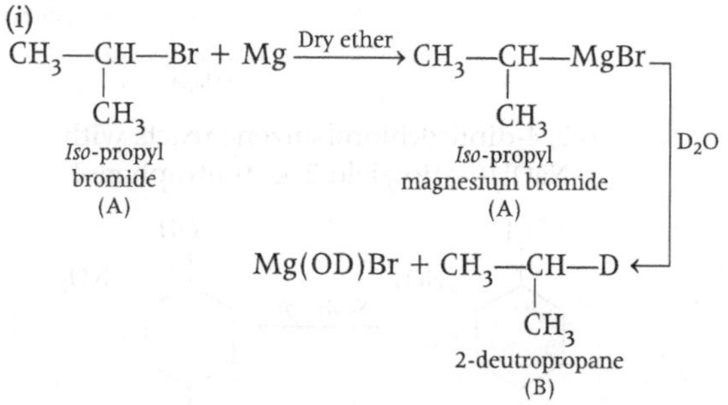

(ii)

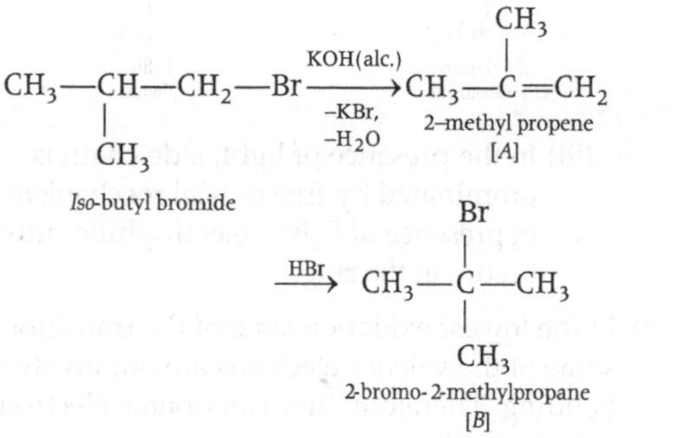

5. (i) Molality does not change with change in temperature while molarity decreases with rise in temperature.

(ii) K_H values for both N_2 and O_2 increases with increase of temperature indicating that the solubility of gas in liquid decreases with increase of temperature.

This is the reason that aquatic species are more comfortable in cold water rather than in warm water.

6. Molar conductivity, $\Lambda_m = \frac{1000}{C} \times \kappa$

where, κ = specific conductivity

$$\kappa = \frac{l}{RA} = \frac{\text{cell constant } (G^*)}{R}$$

Given, concentration, $C = 0.05$ M,

Resistance $(R) = 31.6\,\Omega$

Cell constant $(G^*) = 0.367\ \text{cm}^{-1}$

$$\because \quad \Lambda_m = \frac{1000}{C} \times \kappa = \frac{1000}{C} \times \frac{G^*}{R}$$

$$\therefore \quad \Lambda_m = \frac{1000}{0.05} \times \frac{0.367}{31.6} = 232.278\ \Omega^{-1}\ \text{cm}^2\ \text{mol}^{-1}$$

7. (i) **Coupling reaction** Benzene diazonium chloride reacts with phenol in slightly alkaline medium [pH = 9 – 10] and aniline in slightly acidic medium (pH = 4 – 5) at 273 – 278 K in which the molecule at its *para*-position is coupled with the diazonium salt to form azo products. This reaction is called coupling reaction.

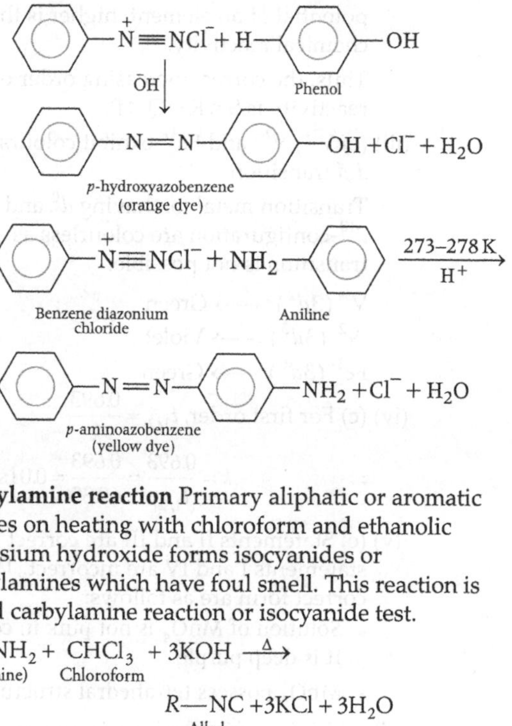

(ii) **Carbylamine reaction** Primary aliphatic or aromatic amines on heating with chloroform and ethanolic potassium hydroxide forms isocyanides or carbylamines which have foul smell. This reaction is called carbylamine reaction or isocyanide test.

$$\underset{(1^\circ \text{ amine})}{R—NH_2} + \underset{\text{Chloroform}}{CHCl_3} + 3KOH \xrightarrow{\Delta} \underset{\substack{\text{Alkyl or} \\ \text{aryl isocyanide}}}{R—NC} + 3KCl + 3H_2O$$

8.

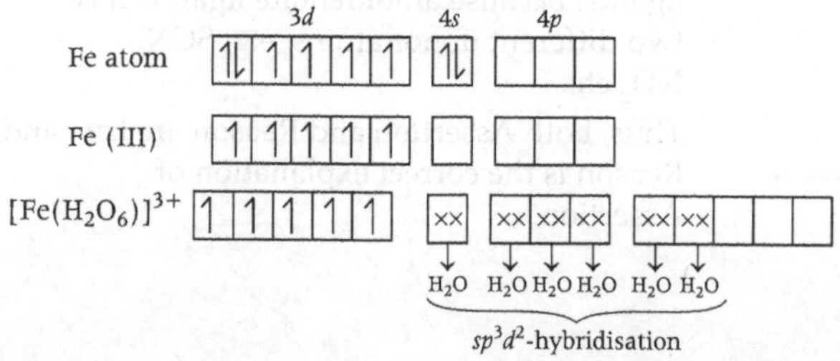

Thus, the complex is octahedral and paramagnetic due to presence of unpaired electrons.

Hence, Pooja's response was correct.

9. (i) Acetylation of benzene yields acetophenone which on reduction gives ethyl benzene. The complete reactions can be shown as:

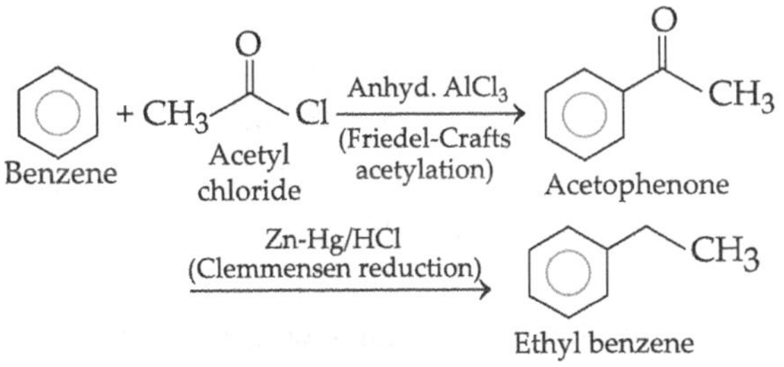

The direct alkylation cannot be performed because polysubstitution product is formed.

Due to disadvantage of polysubstitution, the Friedel-Crafts alkylation reaction is not used for the preparation of alkyl benzene. Instead of that, Friedel-Crafts acetylation is used.

(ii) In Gattermann-Koch reaction, benzene or its derivative is treated with CO and HCl in the presence of anhydrous aluminium chloride to produce benzaldehyde. In this reaction, CO and HCl combine to form HCOCl, i.e. formyl chloride which gets substituted on benzene by the replacement of H-atom.

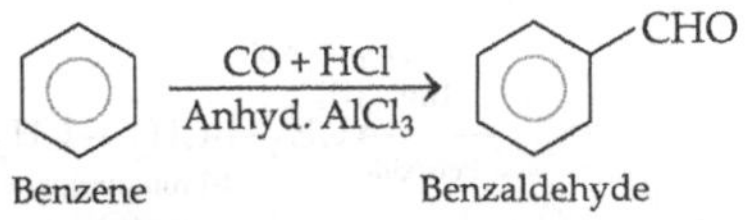

While in Friedel-Crafts acylation, acyl group is also transferred to carbon of benzene and acyl benzene is obtained as a result.This can be done by reaction of benzene with acyl chloride in the presence of anhydrous $AlCl_3$.

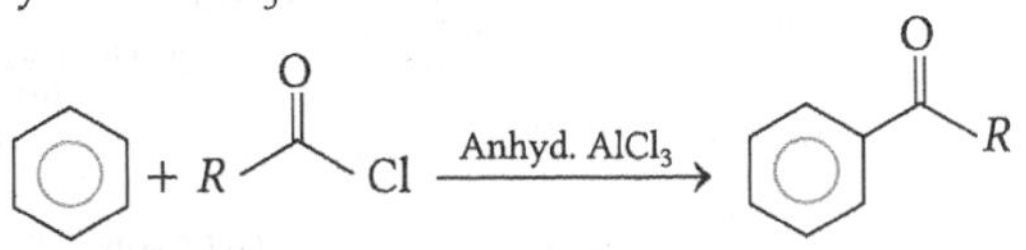

As, formyl chloride is unstable in nature. So, it can be prepared *in situ* by treating CO and HCl in the presence of anhy. $AlCl_3$ by only Gattermann-Koch reaction, not by Friedel-Crafts reaction.

Or

(i) 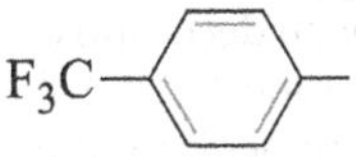

is stronger acid as compared to 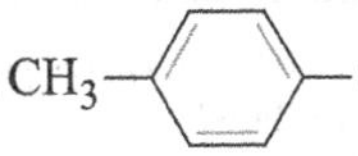

due to CF_3 group. CF_3 group is an electron withdrawing group which will stabilise the anion formed after loss of proton while CH_3 is an electron donating group which destabilise the anion.

(ii) The α-hydrogen of aldehydes and ketones are acidic due to the strong electron withdrawing nature of carbonyl group and resonance stabilisation of the anion (base) formed after loss of proton.

10. (i) $E^\circ_{M^{2+}/M}$ value of copper is positive as the value of hydration enthalpy is less than the sum of values of ionisation enthalpy and enthalpy of atomisation.

(ii) Zinc has stable ground state configuration due to its completely filled *d*-orbitals. It is therefore, has least tendency to form metallic bonds in the series. Thus, it requires least enthalpy of atomisation.

11. (i) Solubility of H_2S gas = 0.195 m, i.e. 0.195 moles in 1 kg of the solvent (water).

∵ Number of moles of H_2O in 1 kg of the solvent

$$\text{(water)} = \frac{1000\,\text{g}}{18\,\text{g mol}^{-1}} = 55.55\ \text{mol}$$

∴ Mole fraction of H_2S gas in the solution (χ)

$$= \frac{0.195}{0.195 + 55.55}$$

$$= \frac{0.195}{55.745} = 0.0035$$

(ii) Pressure at STP = 1 bar

According to Henry's law,

$$p_{H_2S} = K_H \times \chi_{H_2S}$$

$$\text{or} \quad K_H = \frac{p_{H_2S}}{\chi_{H_2S}} = \frac{1\ \text{bar}}{0.0035} = 285.7\ \text{bar}$$

12. A reaction is first order in *A* and second order in *B*

(i) Differential rate equation = (Rate),

$$= \frac{-d[R]}{dt} = k[A][B]^2$$

(ii) When the concentration of *B* is increased to three times (3*B*), the rate would be

$$(\text{Rate})_2 = k\,[A]\,[3B]^2$$

$$(\text{Rate})_2 = 9k\,[A]\,[B]^2 = 9 \times (\text{Rate})_1$$

∴ Rate is increased by 9 times.

(iii) $(\text{Rate})_3 = k\,[2A]\,[2B]^2$

$(\text{Rate})_3 = 2 \times 2 \times 2 \times k\,[A]\,[B]^2 = 8 \times (\text{Rate})_1$

∴ Rate is increased by 8 times.

13. (i) Acidity order of the given organic compounds will be

o-nitrophenol > phenol > *o*-cresol.

o-nitrophenol has electron withdrawing NO_2 group to stabilise the phenoxide ion. Hence, it is more acidic than phenol.

Whereas, *o*-cresol has CH_3 group attached at *ortho*-position to OH. It is a $+I$ inducing group and hence, it reduces the stability of phenoxide ion. Therefore, it is less acidic than phenol.

(ii) Electrophilic substitution reaction rate increases if benzene is attached to the electron donating group but rate decreases if the benzene is attached to the electron withdrawing group. So, the correct order is phenol > benzene > chlorobenzene.

14. (i) Carbohydrates are used as storage materials as starch in plants.

(ii) Coagulation of an egg white on boiling occurs due to denaturation of protein. When a native protein is subjected to change in temperature, the hydrogen bonds are disturbed. As a result, globules unfold and helix get uncoiled and protein loses its biological activity.

(iii) On hydrolysis, maltose gives two molecules of α-D-glucose.

$$\underset{\text{Maltose}}{C_{12}H_{22}O_{11}}\ (aq) + H_2O(l) \longrightarrow \underset{\alpha\text{-D-Glucose}}{2C_6H_{12}O_6}\ (aq) \qquad (1)$$

15. (i) $A \rightarrow$ An alkene

$B \rightarrow$ An aldehyde with $-CH_3$ group, i.e.(CH_3CHO)

$C \rightarrow$ Methylketone (CH_3COCH_3)

(ii) $$\underset{\substack{\text{Acetaldehyde}\\(B)}}{CH_3CHO} + \underset{\substack{\text{Tollen's}\\\text{reagent}}}{[Ag(NH_3)_2]^+} + OH^- \longrightarrow$$

$$CH_3COO^- + Ag + NH_3 + H_2O$$

(iii) $$\underset{\text{Acetone}}{CH_3COCH_3} + NaOH + I_2 \longrightarrow \underset{\text{Iodoform}}{CHI_3} + CH_3COONa$$

$A: CH(CH_3){=}C(CH_3)_2 \quad B: CH_3CHO$

$C: O{=}C(CH_3)_2$

Or

Comparison of reactivity of benzaldehyde and ethanal towards nucleophilic addition reaction.

The reactivity of benzaldehyde is less than the ethanal. Because electron donating resonance effect (+ *R*-effect) of benzene ring in benzaldehyde increases the electron density on the carbonyl carbon. This makes the carbonyl carbon less electrophilic than the carbon atom of carbonyl group present in ethanal.

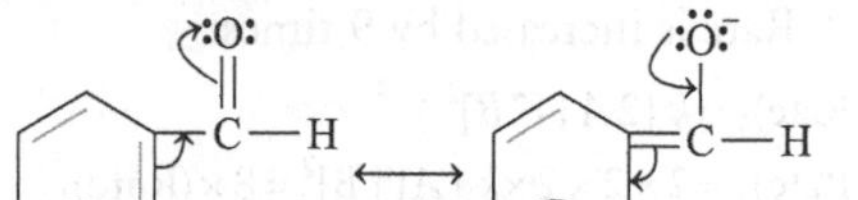

The cross-aldol condensation product between benzaldehyde and ethanal is given as,

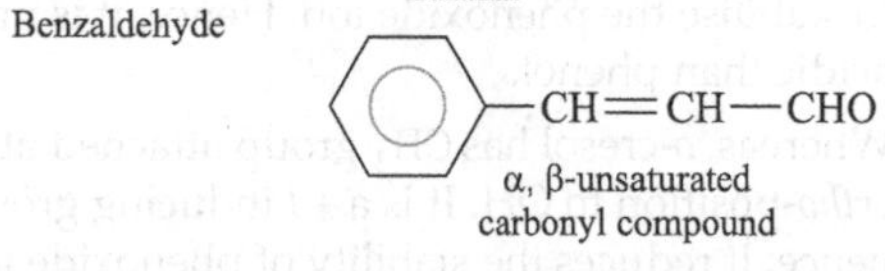

16. Here, $p^\circ = 23.8$ mm of Hg, $w_2 = 50$ g, $W_1 = 850$ g

For solute, urea (NH_2CONH_2), $M_2 = 60\ g\ mol^{-1}$

For solvent (H_2O), $M_1 = 18\ g\ mol^{-1}$

(i) According to relative lowering in vapour pressure,

$$\frac{p_1^\circ - p_1}{p_1^\circ} = \frac{n_2}{n_1 + n_2}$$

or $$\frac{p_1^\circ - p_1}{p_1^\circ} = \frac{n_2}{n_1} = \frac{w_2 / M_2}{W_1 / M_1}$$

(for dilute solution, $n_1 + n_2 \simeq n_1$)

or $$1 - \frac{p_1}{p_1^\circ} = \frac{w_2 \times M_1}{W_1 \times M_2}$$

Substituting the values, we get

$$1 - \frac{p_1}{23.8} = \frac{50}{60} \times \frac{18}{850} = \frac{3}{170}$$

$$\frac{p_1}{23.8} = 1 - \frac{3}{170} = \frac{167}{170}$$

$$p_1 = \frac{167 \times 23.8}{170} = \frac{3974.6}{170} = 23.38 \text{ mm of Hg}$$

(ii) Relative lowering of vapour pressure

$$= \frac{p_1^\circ - p_1}{p_1^\circ} = \frac{23.80 - 23.38}{23.80} = \frac{0.42}{23.80} = 0.018$$

17. (i) $$\underset{\text{Propanone}}{CH_3COCH_3} \xrightarrow[2[H]]{LiAlH_4} \underset{\substack{|\\ OH \\ \text{Propan-2-ol}\\ [A]}}{CH_3CHCH_3} \xrightarrow[\text{Heat}]{H_2SO_4\,(\text{conc.})} \underset{\substack{\text{Propene}\\(B)}}{CH_3CH{=}CH_2}$$

$$\xrightarrow[\text{Peroxide}]{HBr} \underset{\substack{\text{1-bromopropane}\\(C)}}{CH_3{-}CH_2{-}CH_2{-}Br}$$

(ii)

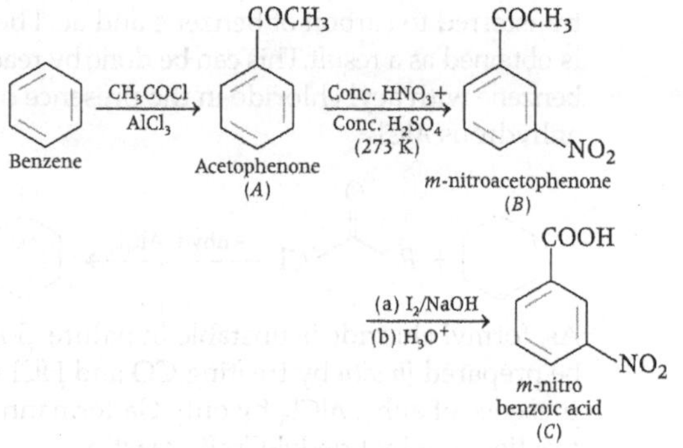

18. Let the pressure of azoisopropane decreases by x atm. As 1 mole of azoisopropane decomposes to give 1 mole of N_2 and 1 mole of hexane (C_6H_{14}), the pressure of N_2 and hexane increases by x atm.

$$\underset{\text{Azoisopropane}}{(CH_3)_2CHN{=}NCH(CH_3)_2(g)} \longrightarrow N_2(g) + C_6H_{14}(g)$$

At $t = 0$	35.0 atm	0 atm	0 atm
At time, t	$(35.0 - x)$ atm	x atm	x atm

$$p_t = p_{\text{azoisopropane}} + p_{N_2} + p_{C_6H_{14}}$$
$$p_t = 35.0 - x + x + x$$
$$p_t = 35 + x \quad \Rightarrow x = p_t - 35$$
$$\therefore \; p_{\text{azoisopropane}} = 35.0 - (p_t - 35) = 70 - p_t$$

(i) Rate constant after 360 s $= k_1$

At $t = 360$ s, $p_i = 35$ atm, $p_t = 54$ atm

$\therefore \; p_{\text{azoisopropane}} = (70 - 54)$ atm $= 16$ atm

$\therefore$ Rate constant, k_1

$$= \frac{2.303}{360}\log\frac{35}{16} = \frac{2.303}{360}\log 2.188$$
$$= \frac{2.303 \times 0.3400}{360} = 2.18 \times 10^{-3}\ \text{s}^{-1}$$

(ii) Rate constant after 720 s, k_2

$p_i = 35$ atm, $p_t = 63.0$ atm

$\therefore \; p_{\text{azoisopropane}} = (70 - 63)$ atm $= 7$ atm

$\therefore$ Rate constant,

$$k_2 = \frac{2.303}{720}\log\frac{35}{7} = \frac{2.303}{720}\log 5$$
$$= \frac{2.303 \times 0.6990}{720} = 2.24 \times 10^{-3}\ \text{s}^{-1}$$

(iii) Average rate constant, $k = \frac{(2.18 + 2.24)}{2} \times 10^{-3}$

$$= 2.21 \times 10^{-3}\ \text{s}^{-1}$$

19. (i) Since, *A* gives haloform test, it must contain $-COCH_3$ group.

Thus, its possible formula is $C_2H_5COCH_3$. On reduction, it gives butan-2-ol, i.e. compound *B* which on dehydration with sulphuric acid gives but-2-ene (*C*). Ozonolysis of butan-2-ene gives only acetaldehyde (*E*). (1)

The reactions involved are

A gives iodoform reaction as

$$\underset{(A)}{CH_3COCH_2CH_3} + 3I_2 + 4\,NaOH \longrightarrow CHI_3 \downarrow$$
$$+ C_2H_5COONa + 3NaI + 3H_2O.$$

$$\underset{\substack{\text{Butan-2-one}\\(A)}}{CH_3COCH_2CH_3} \xrightarrow[LiAlH_4]{[H]} \underset{\substack{\text{Butan-2-ol}\\(B)}}{CH_3-\underset{OH}{\underset{|}{CH}}-CH_2CH_3}$$

$$\xrightarrow[-H_2O]{\text{Conc. } H_2SO_4,\ \Delta} \underset{\substack{\text{But-2-ene}\\(C)}}{CH_3-CH{=}CH-CH_3} \xrightarrow[\text{Ozonolysis}]{O_3}$$

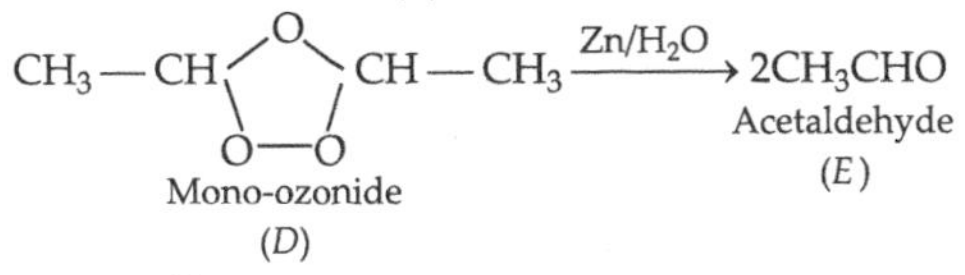

(ii)

(a) $$\underset{\text{Propan-2-one}}{CH_3-\overset{O}{\overset{\|}{C}}-CH_3} + 4[H] \xrightarrow[\text{Conc. HCl}]{\text{Zn-Hg}} CH_3-CH_2-CH_3 + H_2O$$

(b) The above reaction is called as Clemmensen reduction reaction. The IUPAC name of the product formed in above reaction is propane.

20. (i) **Linkage isomerism** It is shown by the compounds when both have same ligand but differs in the atom through which the ligand binds to the metal. For this, the ligand should be an ambidentate ligand having two donor sites.

e.g. $[Co(NH_3)_5(NO_2)]Cl_2$ and $[Co(NH_3)_5(ONO)]Cl_2$

In the pair $[Cr(H_2O)_5Cl]Cl_2 \cdot H_2O$ and $[Cr(H_2O)_6]Cl_3$ the complexes differ in number of water molecule as ligands.

In first, there are 5 H_2O ligands in coordination sphere but in the second, there are 6 H_2O ligands in coordination sphere. The extra water molecule is transferred from outside the sphere to the inside. So, it shows hydrate isomerism.

(ii) $[\mathbf{Ni(CN)_4}]^{2-}$

Here, Ni is in +2 oxidation state.

CN^- is a strong field ligand.

Orbital electronic configuration of

Ni^{2+} = [⥮ | ⥮ | ⥮ | ⥮ | ××] [××] [×× | ×× |] (3*d*, 4*s*, 4*p*)

Due to CN^- (strong field ligand) pairing of electrons takes place in 3*d*-orbital. The incoming ligand bonds with the dsp^2 hybridised orbitals. Its geometry is square planar.

In $Ni(CO)_4$, Ni is in 0 oxidation state.

The electronic configuration will be

Ni(O) = [⥮ | ⥮ | ⥮ | ↿ | ↿] [⥮] [| |] (3*d*, 4*s*, 4*p*)

In presence of CO, a strong field ligand, pairing will occur.

[⥮ | ⥮ | ⥮ | ⥮ | ⥮] [××] [×× | ×× | ××] (3*d*, 4*s*, 4*p*)

Inner orbital is not available. Hence, $Ni(CO)_4$ is sp^3-hybridised and its geometry is tetrahedral.

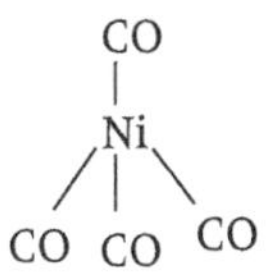

21. (i) Quantity of electricity passed $= i \times t$

$$= 1.70 \times 230 = 391\,\text{C}$$

As current efficiency $= 90\%$

$$\text{Effective charge} = \frac{90}{100} \times 391\,\text{C}$$
$$= 351.9\,\text{C}$$

$$Zn^{2+} + 2e^- \longrightarrow Zn$$

2×96500 C deposit $Zn^{2+} = 1$ mol

$\therefore$ 351.9C will deposit $= \dfrac{1}{2 \times 96500} \times 351.9$ moles

$= 0.0018$ moles

Zn^{2+} ions present originally in 300 mL of 0.160 M

$ZnSO_4 = \dfrac{0.160}{1000} \times 300 = 0.048$ moles

$\therefore$ Amount of Zn^{2+} in 300 mL of solution after deposition of Zn $= 0.048 - 0.0018 = 0.0462$ mol

$\therefore$ Molarity (M) of Zn^{2+} after deposition of Zn

$= \dfrac{0.0462}{300} \times 1000$

$= 0.154$M

(ii) According to Faraday's first law of electrolysis,

$$W = Zit = \frac{Eit}{96500}$$

Given, current $i = 10$ A, $t = 80$ mins and 27 s

$= (80 \times 60 + 27)$ s $= 4827$ s

Equivalent weight, E for oxygen $= 8$

Weight of O_2 liberated $= \dfrac{8 \times 10 \times 4827}{96500} = 4$ g

Moles of oxygen $= \dfrac{\text{Weight}}{\text{Molecular weight}} = \dfrac{4}{32}$

$= 0.125$ moles

Or (i) $Ag^+ (aq) + e^- \longrightarrow Ag(s)$

We know that, volume = area × thickness

Given : Density = 10.5 g cm^{-3}

Area = 80 cm^2

Thickness = 0.005 mm $= \dfrac{0.005}{10}$ cm

$\therefore$ Volume, $V = 80 \times \dfrac{0.005}{10} = 0.04\ cm^3$

Mass (w) of Ag = volume × density

$= 0.04 \times 10.5 = 0.42$ g

From the Faraday's first law, $m = Zit$

where, i = current, t = time,

$$Z = \frac{\text{Equivalent weight}}{96500}$$

Equivalent weight of Ag

$= \dfrac{\text{Atomic weight}}{\text{Valency}} = \dfrac{108}{1} = 108$

$\therefore \quad w = \dfrac{108}{96500} \times 3 \times t$ or $0.42 = \dfrac{108 \times 3 \times t}{96500}$

$\therefore \quad t = \dfrac{0.42 \times 96500}{3 \times 108} = 125.09$ s

(ii) Graph I is the strongest electrolyte, as its molar conductivity is proportional to concentration and increases on dilution linearly.

Graph III is the weakest as it's molar conductivity is the lowest but on extreme dilution, it increases as its molar conductivity increases exponentially.

SPQ Code : **PB-11/15** Series ***i*-Succeed 11-25/15** Roll No.

Sample Question Paper 11

Chemistry 12th (Code 862)

General Instructions

1. This paper is divided into four sections-A, B, C and D. Answer all questions.
2. **Section A** consists of **one** question **having sub-parts** of **one** mark each. **Section B** consists of **ten** questions of **two** marks each. **Section C** consists of **seven** questions of **three** marks each and **Section D** consists of **three** questions of **five** marks each.
3. Internal choices have been provided in one question each in Section B, Section C and Section D.
4. All working, including rough work, should be done on the same sheet as, and adjacent to the rest of the answer.
5. The intended marks for questions or parts of questions are given in brackets [].
6. Balanced questions must be given, wherever possible and diagrams where they are helpful. When solving numerical problems, all essential working must be shown.
7. In working out problems, use the following data:
Gas constant (R) = 1.987 cal deg^{-1} mol^{-1} = 8.314 JK^{-1} mol^{-1} = 0.0821 dm^3 atm K^{-1} mol^{-1}
1L atm = 1 dm^3 atm =101.3 J, 1 Faraday =96500 Coulombs.
Avogadro's number (N_A) = 6.023×10^{23}

Time : 3 Hrs.

Max. Marks : 70

Section A

[14 Marks]

1. (A) Fill in the blanks by choosing the appropriate word(s) from those given in the brackets.
[sp^2, more, fluorine, oxygen, less, ethanol, carbon, concentrated, methanol, propanoic acid, osmosis, dilute, sp^3] [4 × 1]
(i) In phenol, the —OH group is attached to .... hybridised carbon. The C—O bond length in phenol is slightly .... than in methanol. • *Understanding*
(ii) Transition metals show their highest oxidation states with .... and .... elements. • *Recall*
(iii) Hydrolysis of methyl propanoate gives .... and .... • *Recall*
(iv) A raw mango placed in .... salt solution loses water *via* .... and shrivel into pickle. • *Understanding*
(B) Select and write the correct alternative from the choices given below. [7 ×1]
(i) Al_2O_3 may be electrolysed at 1000°C to furnish Al metal (atomic mass =27 amu, 1F =96500 C). The cathode reaction is
$$Al^{3+} + 3e^- \longrightarrow Al.$$
To prepare 5.12 kg of Al metal by this method, it would require • *Application*
(a) 5.49×10^{10} C of electricity
(b) 1.83×10^7 C of electricity
(c) 5.49×10^4 C of electricity
(d) 5.49×10^7 C of electricity

(ii) The incorrect statement among the following.

I. Order of reaction is the sum of powers of concentration of the reactants in the rate law expression.

II. Elementary reactions are only one step reactions.

III. Rate of elementary reactions depends upon the slowest step, i.e. rate determining step of reaction.

IV. Order of reaction is always a whole number. • *Understanding*

(a) I and II (b) III and IV
(c) II and IV (d) I and III

(iii) The correct order of decreasing acid strength of the following is • *Analysis*

(a) 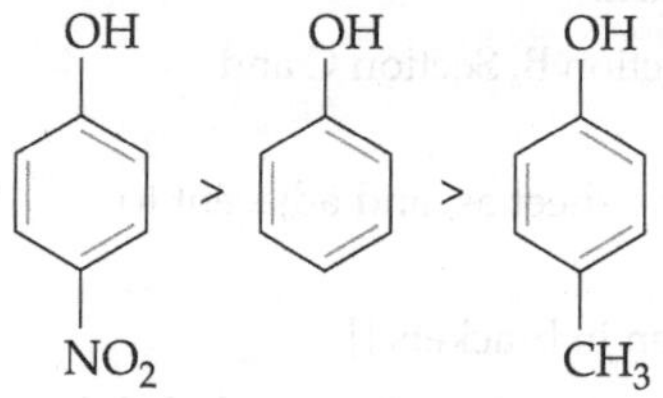

(b) 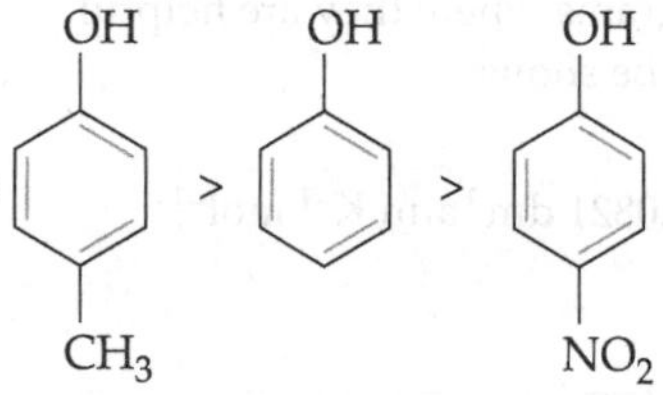

(c) 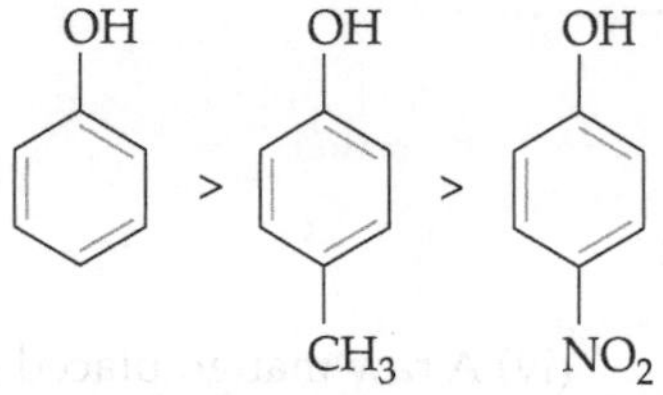

(d) 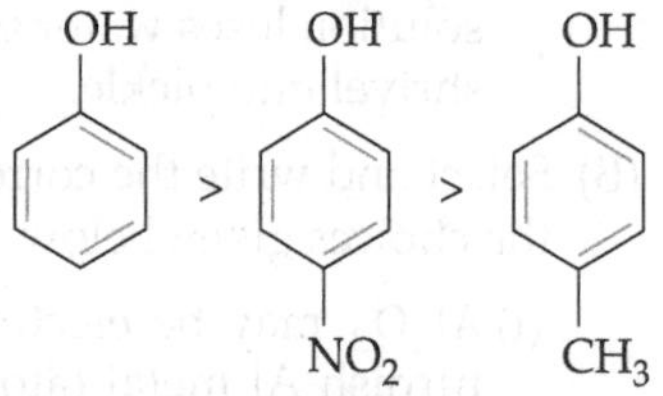

(iv) —NH_2 group in the aniline is an activating group and it proceeds reaction at • *Understanding*

(a) only *para*-position
(b) only *ortho*-position
(c) only *meta*-position
(d) Both *ortho* and *para*-position

(v) The major product of the acid catalysed reaction of 3, 3-dimethylbutene is • *Understanding*

(a) 2-methylbutanol
(b) 2, 3-dimethylbutan-2-ol
(c) 3, 3-dimethylbutan-2-ol
(d) 2, 2-dimethylbutanol

(vi) **Assertion** (A) Valine is an essential amino acid.

Reason (R) The lack of essential amino acids in the diet causes Kwashiorkor. • *Analysis*

(a) Both Assertion and Reason are true and Reason is the correct explanation of Assertion.
(b) Both Assertion and Reason are true but Reason is not the correct explanation of Assertion.
(c) Assertion is true but Reason is false.
(d) Both Assertion and Reason are false.

(vii) **Assertion** (A) During charging of lead storage battery, cathode is converted into Pb and PbO_2 respectively.

Reason (R) Lead storage battery consists of a lead anode and a grid of lead packed with lead dioxide as cathode. • *Analysis*

(a) Both Assertion and Reason are true and Reason is the correct explanation of Assertion.
(b) Both Assertion and Reason are true but Reason is not the correct explanation of Assertion.
(c) Assertion is true but Reason is false.
(d) Both Assertion and Reason are false.

(C) Read the passage given below carefully and answer the questions that follow. [3×1]

Arrhenius equation for first order reactions are useful for modeling the timing and temperature of petroleum generation from organic rich shales and **kerogens** at laboratory scales (e.g. per minute), based on pyrolysis 52 peak data is measured at multiple heating rates, and for burial histories occurring over geological time scales (e.g. per millions of years).

First order reactions are accompanied by second order reactions and physical changes impacting the kerogens as they thermally mature, so simple Arrhenius equation first order reaction modeling can only provide an approximation of the complete petroleum generation process. Thermally immature shale and/or kerogen samples yield less complex pyrolysis S2-peaks than thermally mature sample and provide more credible kinetic distributions when modeled at multiple heating rates with the Arrhenius equation.

More credible kinetic fits to the S2-peak pyrolysis data are derived by allowing the activation energy (E) and the frequency factor (A) to vary for each reaction to derive good-fit kinetic distributions than by applying the commonly used assumption that the A value remain constant for the set of parallel reactions included in the distribution.

(i) The plot of ln k *versus* $\frac{1}{T}$ gives a straight line.
What is the value of slope and intercept in this graph ? • *Understanding*

(ii) If the activation energy for a reaction is zero and rate constant is $1.72 \times 10^5 s^{-1}$ at 300 K. Calculate the rate constant at 310 K. • *Application*

(iii) Give the relation between rate constant and activation energy. • *Recall*

Section B **[20 Marks]**

2. (i) Solution A contains 7 g/L $MgCl_2$ and solution B contains 7 g/L of NaCl. At room temperature, which solution has greater osmotic pressure? • *Understanding*

(ii) What are isotonic solutions? • *Recall* [2]

3. Give reasons for the following. • *Understanding* [2]

(i) Cu^+ is diamagnetic but Cu^{2+} is paramagnetic ($Z = 29$).

(ii) The transition metals and many of their compounds act as good catalyst.

4. How will the following be obtained? (Give chemical equations) • *Understanding* [2]

(i) Ethylbenzene from acetophenone

(ii) 3-hydroxy butanal from acetaldehyde

Or Devise a scheme for the synthesis of propanone using CH_3MgBr. Is it possible to prepare secondary product by applying this scheme. Give reason for your answer. • *Evaluate*

5. Give reasons of the following observations. • *Understanding*

(i) Gabriel phthalimide synthesis is not preferred for synthesising aromatic primary amines. [2]

(ii) *Tert*-butylamine cannot be prepared by the action of NH_3 on *tert*-butyl bromide.

6. The cell in which the following reaction occurs, • *Application* [2]

$$2Fe^{3+}(aq) + 2I^-(aq) \longrightarrow 2Fe^{2+}(aq) + I_2(s)$$

has $E^\circ_{cell} = 0.236$ V at 298 K, calculate

(i) standard Gibbs energy.

(ii) equilibrium constant of the cell reaction.

7. (i) Why is chemistry of actinoids complicated as compared to lanthanoids? • *Understanding* [2]

(ii) The given graph shows the trends in melting points of transition metals.

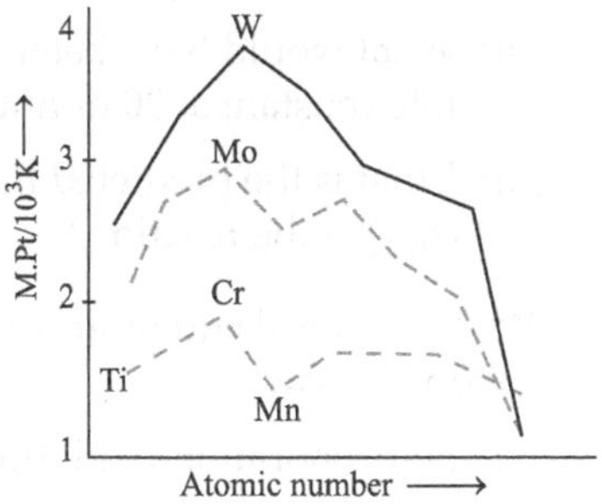

Explain the reason why chromium (Cr) has highest melting point and manganese (Mn) has lower melting point? • *Understanding*

8. Which compound in each of the following pairs will react faster in S_N2 reaction with OH^- and why? • *Understanding* [2]

(i) CH_3Br or CH_3I

(ii) $(CH_3)_3CCl$ or CH_3Cl

9. (i) What happens to the vapour pressure of water when a table spoon of sugar is added to it? • *Understanding* [2]

(ii) How is van't Hoff factor related to degree of dissociation and association of an electrolyte? • *Recall*

10. Give one chemical test for each to distinguish between the following pairs of compounds. • *Understanding* [2]

(i) Phenol and cyclohexanol

(ii) Butan-2-ol and 2-methylpropan-2-ol

11. An organic compound *A* which has characteristic odour, on treatment with NaOH forms two compounds *B* and *C*. [3]

Compound *B* has molecular formula C_7H_8O which on oxidation gives back *A*. The compound *C* is a sodium salt of an acid. When *C* is treated with soda lime, it yields an aromatic hydrocarbon *D*.

(i) Write the sequence of reactions involved. • *Understanding*

(ii) Deduce the structures of *A*, *B*, *C* and *D*. • *Understanding*

Section C **[21 Marks]**

12. Richa performed an experiment to check the chemical kinetics of bacteria. This experiment at 35°C gave the following results.

Time (in min)	0	15	30	45	60
Number of bacteria	100	200	400	800	1600

Answer the following questions on the basis of above data. [3]

(i) Which order of the reaction was followed in the multiplication of bacteria? Justify your answer. • *Analysis*

(ii) What would have been the value of rate constant at 30 minutes? • *Application*

(iii) What is the predicted half-life period ($t_{1/2}$) of the reaction? • *Application*

13. Write chemical equations to illustrate the following reactions: • *Recall*

(i) Hydroboration-oxidation reaction [3]

(ii) Friedel-Crafts alkylation of anisole

(iii) Reimer-Tiemann reaction

Or

Write the equations for the following reaction. • *Understanding*

(i) Phenol is treated with zinc dust and then with conc. HNO_3 and H_2SO_4. [3]

(ii) Ethanol is treated with PCC.

(iii) Chloroethane is treated with *aq*. NaOH and then followed by $KMnO_4$.

14. (i) Write the structural difference between starch and cellulose. • *Recall* [3]

(ii) What type of linkage is present in nucleic acid? • *Recall*

(iii) Give one example each for fibrous protein and globular protein. • *Recall*

15. (i) A 0.1539 molal aqueous solution of cane sugar (molar mass = 342 g mol^{-1}) has a freezing point of 271 K, while the freezing point of pure water is 273.15 K. What will be the freezing point of an aqueous solution containing 5 g of glucose per 100 g of solution (Molar mass = 180 g mol^{-1})? • *Application* [3]

(ii) How does Henry's constant (K_H) of a gas in a particular solvent vary with temperature? • *Understanding*

16. How will the following be converted? (Give chemical equations) • *Understanding* [3]

(i) Acetamide to ethylamine

(ii) Ethylamine to methylamine

(iii) Benzene to acetanilide

17. Identify the compounds *A*, *B* and *C* in the following reactions. • *Understanding* [3]

(i) $C_6H_5NH_2 \xrightarrow[0-5°C]{NaNO_2+HCl} [A] \xrightarrow[\Delta]{H_2O,\ warm} [B] \xrightarrow{Zn} [C]$

(ii) $\xrightarrow{Oleum} [A] \xrightarrow{NaOH} [B] \xrightarrow{H^+/H_2O} [C]$

SP-11

18. The magnetic moments of few transition metal ions are given below. [3]

Metal ion	Magnetic moment (BM)
Sc^{3+}	0.00
Cr^{2+}	4.90
Ni^{2+}	2.84
Ti^{3+}	1.73

(Atomic no. of Sc = 21, Ti =22, Cr = 24, Ni = 28)

(i) Which of the given metal ions has the maximum number of unpaired electrons and forms colourless aqueous solution respectively? • *Application*

(ii) On the basis of crystal field theory, write the electronic configuration of d^5 ion if • *Recall*

(a) $\Delta_o > P$

(b) $\Delta_o < P$

Section D **[15 Marks]**

19. (i) An unknown aldehyde '*A*' on reacting with alkali gives a β-hydroxy aldehyde, which loses water to form an unsaturated aldehyde, but-2-enal. Another aldehyde '*B*' undergoes disproportionation reaction in the presence of conc. alkali to form products *C* and *D*. *C* is an aryl alcohol with the formula C_7H_8O. Identify *A* and *B*. Write the sequence of reactions involved. • *Understanding* [5]

(ii) Give reason for the following. • *Understanding*

(a) Carboxylic acids are stronger acids than phenol.

(b) Sodium bisulphite is used for the purification of aldehydes.

20. (i) (a) What kind of isomerism exists between $[Cr(H_2O)_6]Cl_3$ (violet) and $[Cr(H_2O)_5Cl]Cl_2 \cdot H_2O$ (greyish-green)? • *Recall* [5]

(b) Write the formula of diammine chloridonitrito-N-platinum(II). • *Recall*

(c) Different colours are observed in octahedral and tetrahedral complexes for the same metal and same ligands. Explain. • *Understanding*

(ii) The formula $[Pt(en)_2Cl_2]^{2+}$ represent a coordination compound. Write IUPAC name and structures of possible isomers. • *Recall*

21. (i) The specific conductance of a 0.01 M solution of acetic acid at 298 K is $1.65 \times 10^{-4}\ \Omega^{-1}\ cm^{-1}$. The molar conductance at infinite dilution for H^+ ion and CH_3COO^- ion are $349.1\ \Omega^{-1}\ cm^2\ mol^{-1}$ and $409\ \Omega^{-1}\ cm^2\ mol^{-1}$ respectively. Calculate the molar conductance of the solution and degree of dissociation of CH_3COOH • *Application* [5]

(ii) Calculate the emf of the following cell reaction at 298 K.

$$Mg(s) + Cu^{2+}(0.0001\ M) \longrightarrow Mg^{2+}(0.001\ M) + Cu(s)$$

The standard potential ($E°$) of cell is 2.71V. • *Application*

Or Standard electrode potentials are used for various processes.

- It is used to measure relative strengths of various oxidants and reductants.
- It is used to calculate standard cell potential.
- It is used to predict possible reactions.

For the cell,

$Cu | Cu^{2+} (0.13\ M) || Ag^+ (0.01\ M) | Ag$

the standard reduction potential for copper and silver electrodes are 0.34 V and 0.80 V respectively.

(a) Write the net cell reaction. • *Recall*

(b) Calculate the standard emf of the cell. • *Application*

(c) Predict the cell reaction is spontaneous or not. • *Understanding*

(d) Will nickel displace copper from a 1 M solution of copper sulphate? Justify your answer.

($E^\circ_{Ni^{2+}/Ni} = -0.25$ V) • *Understanding*

(e) Write the limitation of standard electrode potentials. • *Recall*

Solutions *in Topper's Style*

My Commitment *I affirm that I am reviewing these solutions only after I have solved the Sample Question Paper on my own. My purpose of looking the solutions is solely to verify whether my answers/solutions were correct or not and to identify my mistakes in case my solutions were wrong or I could not solve that.*

1. (A)(i) sp^2, less

(ii) fluorine, oxygen

(iii) methanol, propanoic acid

(iv) concentrated, osmosis

(B) (i) (d) From Faraday's first law,

$$w = Z \times Q$$

where, w = weight

Z = electrochemical equivalent

Q = quantity of electricity

Also, $E = Z \times F$

Where, E = equivalent weight

F = Faraday's constant

$$\therefore \quad w = \frac{E}{F} \times Q \text{ or } Q = \frac{w \times F}{E}$$

$$\text{or} \quad Q = \frac{w \times F}{\dfrac{\text{Atomic wt. }(A)}{\text{Valency of ion }(n)}} \Rightarrow \frac{n \times w \times F}{A}$$

$$\therefore \quad Q = \frac{3 \times 5.12 \times 10^3 \times 96500}{27}$$

$$= 5.49 \times 10^7 \text{C of electricity}$$

(ii) (b) Statements I and II are correct while statements III and IV are incorrect.

The correct form of statements III and IV are as follows

- Rate of complex reactions depends upon the slowest step, i.e. rate determining step of reaction.
- Order of reaction may be zero, whole number or fractional number.

(iii) (a) Acidity increases with $-I$ effect and decreases with $+I$ effect. Since, $—NO_2$ is an electron withdrawing group, thus it increases acidity and $—CH_3$ is an electron donating group, it decreases acidity. Thus, the correct order is

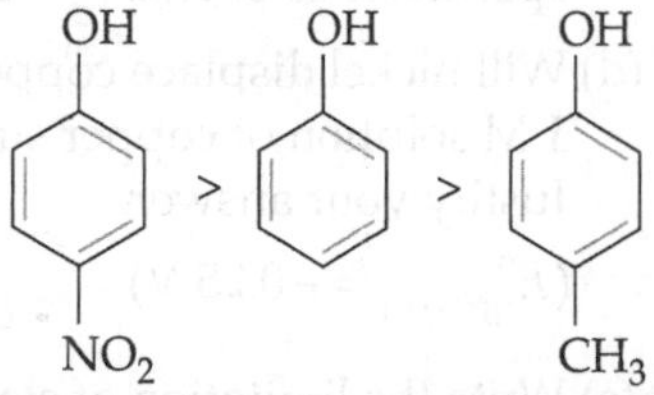

(iv) (d) *Ortho* and *para*-positions to the $—NH_2$ group have high electron density. Thus, $—NH_2$ group is *ortho* and *para*-directing and a powerful activating group.

(v) (b)

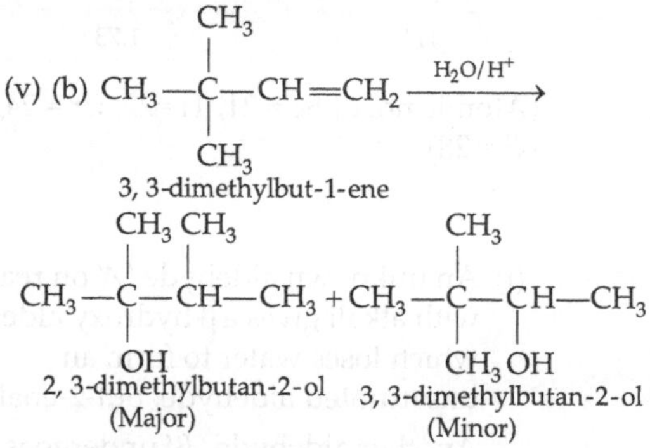

(vi) (b) Both Assertion and Reason are true but Reason is not the correct explanation of Assertion. The amino acids which the body can not synthesise are called essential amino acid.

(vii) (b) Both Assertion and Reason are true but Reason is not the correct explanation of Assertion. The correct explanation is as follows During charging of lead storage battery, current is passed through the terminals from external source and the reactions are reversed. Thus, $PbSO_4(s)$ is liberated at anode and cathode is converted into Pb and PbO_2 respectively.

(C) (i) The plot of ln k *versus* $1/T$ is given as

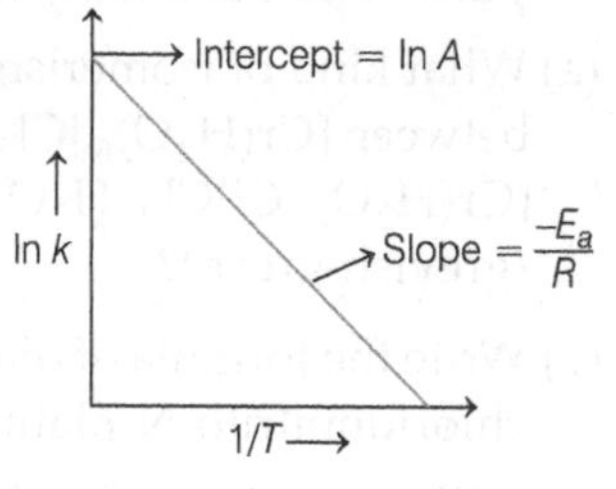

(ii) Given, $E_a = 0$

$$\Rightarrow \log\frac{k_2}{k_1} = 0 \Rightarrow \frac{k_2}{k_1} = 1$$

Therefore, $k_2 = k_1 = 1.72 \times 10^5 \text{ s}^{-1}$

(iii) The relationship between rate constant and activation energy is as follows

$$\log k = \log A - \frac{E_a}{2.303\,RT}$$

2. (i) Solution A (7 g/L $MgCl_2$) has greater osmotic pressure than solution B (7g/L NaCl). This is because osmotic pressure is directly proportional to van't Hoff factor (i).

$$MgCl_2 \rightleftharpoons Mg^{2+} + 2Cl^-$$

$$NaCl \rightleftharpoons Na^+ + Cl^-$$

For $MgCl_2$, $i = 3$, for NaCl, $i = 2$

(ii) Solutions having the same value of osmotic pressure are called **isotonic solutions**.
e.g. 0.1 M solution of glucose is isotonic with 0.1 M fructose solution.

3. (i) The electronic configuration of

$$Cu^+ = 1s^2, 2s^2, 2p^6, 3s^2, 3p^6, 4s^0, 3d^{10}$$

$$\text{and } Cu^{2+} = 1s^2, 2s^2, 2p^6, 3s^2, 3p^6, 4s^0, 3d^9$$

In Cu^+ ion, all electrons are paired. Hence, Cu^+ is diamagnetic in nature. Whereas, Cu^{2+} has one unpaired electron and thus, shows paramagnetic character.

(ii) The catalytic activity of the transition elements can be explained by two basic facts. Firstly, transition metals because of their variable oxidation state form unstable intermediate compounds and provide a new path by lowering the activation energy, for the reaction. Secondly, transition metals also provide a suitable surface for the reactions to occur.

4. (i) **Ethylbenzene from acetophenone**

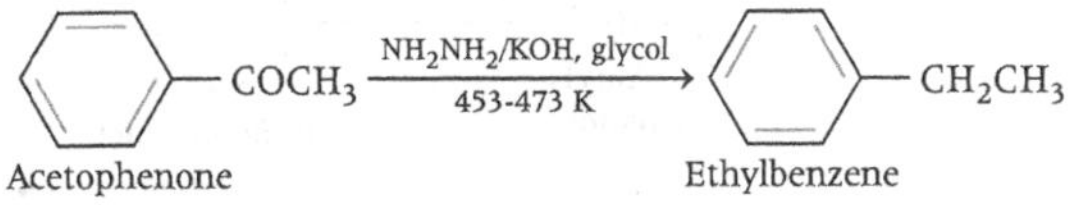

(ii) **3-hydroxy butanal from acetaldehyde**

$$\underset{\text{Acetaldehyde or Ethanal}}{2CH_3CHO} \xrightarrow{\text{Dil. NaOH}} \underset{\text{3-hydroxy butanal (Aldol)}}{CH_3-\underset{|}{C}H(OH)-CH_2CHO}$$

Or

When propanone reacts with Grignard reagent, CH_3MgBr in presence of dry ether then additional product is obtained which on acidic hydrolysis gives *tert*-butyl alcohol.

The reaction is as follows

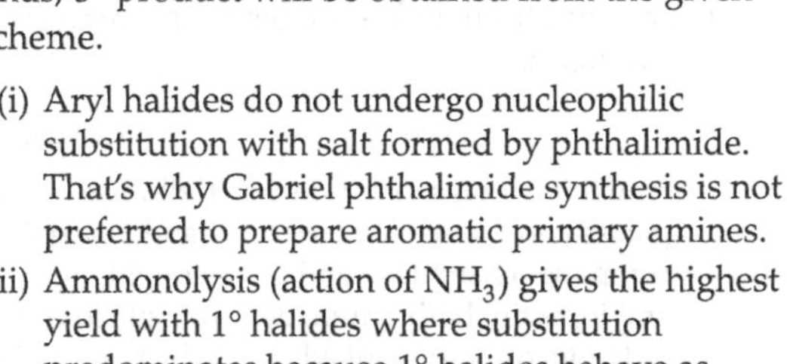

Thus, 3° product will be obtained from the given scheme.

5. (i) Aryl halides do not undergo nucleophilic substitution with salt formed by phthalimide. That's why Gabriel phthalimide synthesis is not preferred to prepare aromatic primary amines.

(ii) Ammonolysis (action of NH_3) gives the highest yield with 1° halides where substitution predominates because 1° halides behave as nucleophile. While in case of 3° halides, elimination predominates where 3° halides acts as base.

Therefore, *tert*-butylamine cannot be prepared by the action of NH_3 on *tert*-butyl bromide.

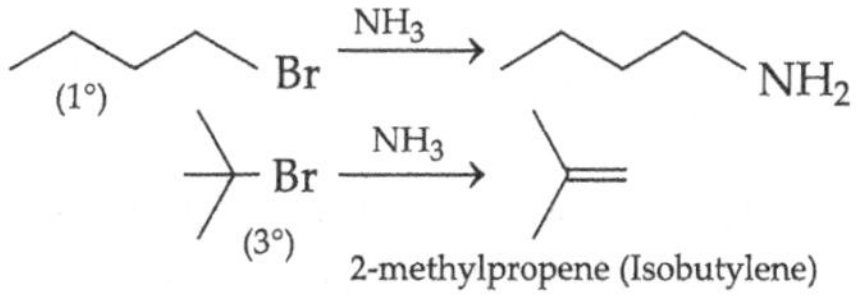

6. (i) Two half-reactions for the given redox reaction may be written as

$$2\,Fe^{3+}(aq) + 2e^- \longrightarrow 2Fe^{2+}(aq)$$

$$2I^-(aq) \longrightarrow I_2(s) + 2e^-$$

2 moles of electrons are involved in the reaction, so $n = 2$

$$\Delta_r G^\circ = -nFE^\circ_{cell}$$

$$= -(2\text{ mol}) \times (96500\text{ C mol}^{-1}) \times (0.236\text{ V})$$

$$= -45548\text{ C V} = -45548\text{ J}$$

$$\Delta_r G^\circ = -45.55\text{ kJ}$$

(ii) $\log K_C = -\dfrac{\Delta G^\circ}{2.303\,RT}$

$$= -\frac{(-45.55\text{ kJ})}{2.303 \times (8.314 \times 10^{-3}\text{ kJ K}^{-1}) \times (298\text{ K})} = 7.983$$

$$K_C = \text{antilog}\,(7.983) = 9.616 \times 10^7$$

7. (i) Chemistry of the actinoids is more complicated in the view of their ability to exist in different oxidation states. Further, many of the actinoid elements are radioactive which makes study of these elements rather difficult.

(ii) Manganese has a half-filled *d*-orbital configuration with all the electrons, spinning in the same direction. This makes it stable and less likely to form bonds with other atoms. Hence, Mn has a lower melting point. On the other hand, the highest melting point of Cr is attributed to the involvement of greater number of unpaired electrons from 3*d*-orbitals.

8. (i) CH_3Br and CH_3I both are primary halogen compounds. The reactivity will depend upon the size of the halogen atom. Iodine is a better leaving group because of larger size, therefore, CH_3I will react faster than CH_3Br.

(ii) Out of $(CH_3)_3CCl$ and CH_3Cl, the molecule being a primary halide, i.e. CH_3Cl, will react faster with OH^- because in S_N2 reaction, 1° halide reacts faster than 3° halide.

9. (i) The vapour pressure of water gets lowered due to the addition of sugar in it. This is because the surface has both solvent and solute molecules, on adding sugar, the fraction covered by water molecule gets reduced.
Hence, the number of water molecules escaping from the surface is reduced, resulting in the lowering of vapour pressure.

(ii) Degree of dissociation or association (α) is related to van't Hoff factor by the following relations.

Degree of association, $\alpha = \dfrac{(i-1)}{\left(\dfrac{1}{n}-1\right)}$

Degree of dissociation, $\alpha = \dfrac{(i-1)}{(m-1)}$

Here, n = number of solute particles associated to make bigger molecular species.

m = number of particles formed from molecule of the electrolyte.

10. (i) **Phenol and cyclohexanol** Phenol gives violet colouration with $FeCl_3$ solution, while cyclohexanol does not.

$$\underset{\text{Phenol}}{6C_6H_5OH} + FeCl_3 \longrightarrow \underset{\text{Violet colouration}}{[Fe(OC_6H_5)_6]^{3-}} + 3H^+ + 3HCl$$

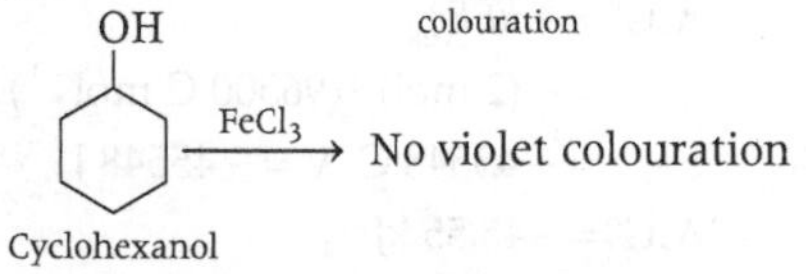

(ii) **Butan 2-ol and 2-methylpropan-2-ol** Butan-2-ol when warmed with NaOI (I_2/NaOH) gives yellow precipitate of iodoform, while 2-methylpropan-2-ol does not give this test.

$$\underset{\text{Butan-2-ol}}{CH_3CH_2\overset{OH}{\overset{|}{C}}HCH_3} + 4I_2 + 6NaOH \xrightarrow{\Delta} \underset{\text{Iodoform}}{CHI_3} \downarrow + CH_3CH_2COO^-Na^+ + 5NaI + 5H_2O$$

$$\underset{\text{2-methylpropan-2-ol}}{(CH_3)_3COH} + I_2 + NaOH \longrightarrow \text{No yellow ppt. of iodoform}$$

11. Since, compound '*A*' having a characteristic odour on treatment with NaOH forms two compounds '*B*' and '*C*' and '*C*' is a sodium salt of an acid.

Therefore, *A* must be an aldehyde. Since, '*B*' having molecular formula C_7H_8O gives back '*A*' on oxidation. Therefore, '*B*' must be alcohol.

(i) The reactions involve are as follows

$$\underset{\substack{\text{Benzaldehyde}\\(A)}}{2C_6H_5CHO} \xrightarrow[\text{solution}]{NaOH} \underset{\substack{\text{Benzyl alcohol}\\(B)}}{C_6H_5CH_2OH} + \underset{\substack{\text{Sodium}\\ \text{benzoate}\\(C)}}{C_6H_5CO\overset{-}{O}\overset{+}{N}a}$$

$$\underset{\substack{\text{Benzyl alcohol}\\(B)}}{C_6H_5CH_2OH} \xrightarrow{[O]} \underset{\substack{\text{Benzaldehyde}\\(A)}}{C_6H_5CHO}$$

$$\underset{\substack{\text{Sodium benzoate}\\(C)}}{C_6H_5CO\overset{-}{O}\overset{+}{N}a} \xrightarrow{\text{Sodalime}} \underset{\substack{\text{Benzene}\\(D)}}{C_6H_6}$$

(ii) $A = C_6H_5CHO$, $B = C_6H_5CH_2OH$, $C = C_6H_5CO\overset{-}{O}\overset{+}{N}a$, $D = C_6H_6$.

12. (i) As the rate of the reaction increases with increase in concentration, the order of reaction is the first order. Rate $\propto$ [No. of bacteria]

(ii) For first order reaction,

$$\text{Rate constant, } k = \frac{-2.303}{t}\log\frac{[A]_0}{[A]}$$

$$k = \frac{-2.303}{30}\log\frac{100}{400} = -0.076[\log 1 - \log 4]$$

$$k = -0.076[-0.602] = 0.046\ \text{min}^{-1}$$

(iii) Half-life period ($t_{1/2}$) for first order reaction is

$$t_{1/2} = \frac{0.693}{k}$$

For $k = 0.046$, $t_{1/2} = \dfrac{0.693}{0.046} = 15.065$ mins.

13. (i) Hydroboration-oxidation reaction is the addition of borane followed by oxidation.

$$\underset{\text{Propene}}{3CH_3{-}CH{=}CH_2} + (BH_3)_2 \text{ or } B_2H_6 \longrightarrow (CH_3CH_2CH_2)_3B \xrightarrow{H_2O_2/OH} H_3BO_3 + 3CH_3CH_2CH_2OH$$

(ii) Anisole reacts with alkyl halide in presence of anhydrous $AlCl_3$ to give the desired products as shown below.

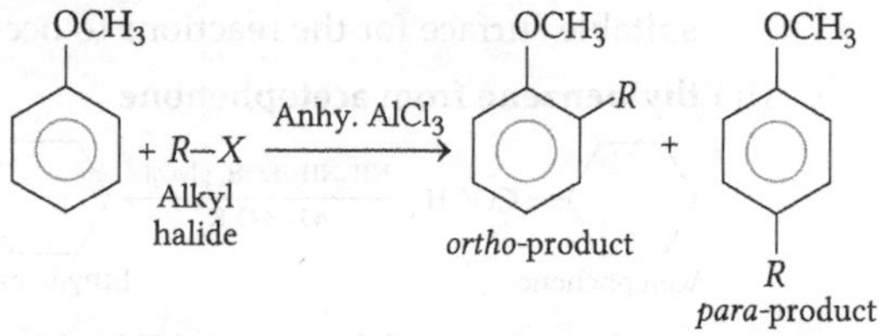

(iii) A chemical reaction in which phenol is converted into *ortho*-hydroxy benzaldehyde using chloroform, a base and an acidic hydrolysis is known as Reimer-Tiemann reaction.

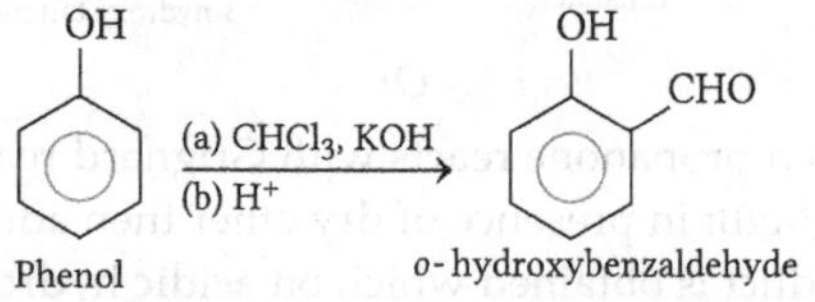

Or (i)

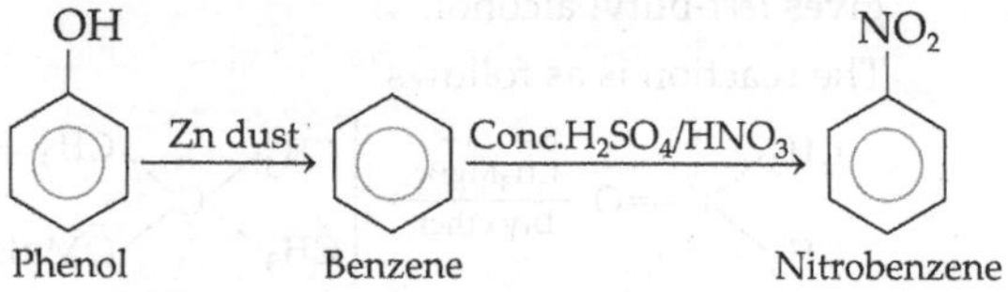

(ii) $$\underset{\text{Ethanol}}{CH_3CH_2OH} \xrightarrow{PCC} \underset{\text{Ethanal}}{CH_3CHO}$$

(iii) $$\underset{\text{Chloroethane}}{CH_3CH_2Cl} \xrightarrow{Aq.\ NaOH} \underset{\text{Ethanol}}{CH_3CH_2OH} \xrightarrow{KMnO_4} \underset{\text{Ethanoic acid}}{CH_3COOH}$$

14. (i) The structural difference between starch and cellulose is

Starch	Cellulose
Starch is a polysaccharide of plants and consists of two components amylose and amylopectin, both are made of D-glucose units linked through α-glycosidic linkage. Amylose is water soluble while amylopectin is not.	Cellulose on the other hand is a polymer of straight chain β-D-glucose units which are linked together by β-glycosidic linkage.

(ii) Nucleotides in nucleic acids are joined together by phosphodiester linkage between 5′ and 3′ carbon atoms of the pentose sugar.

(iii) Fibrous protein ⟶ Keratin (found in skin, hair, nails, wool, silk)
Globular protein ⟶ Insulin

15. (i) Given,
The molality of the cane sugar solution = 0.1539 m
and the depression in the freezing point
$(\Delta T_f) = 273.15 - 271 = 2.15\,K$ [$\because \Delta T_f = T_f^\circ - T_f$]
Since, $\Delta T_f = K_f\, m$
or $K_f = \dfrac{\Delta T_f}{m} = 2.15\,K/0.1539\,m$
$= 13.97\,K\,kg\,mol^{-1}$

Now, weight of glucose, $w_2 = 5\,g$
Also, molecular mass of glucose,
$M_2 = 180\,g\,mol^{-1}$

Then, $\Delta T_f = K_f \times m$
$$\Delta T_f = \frac{K_f \times w_2 \times 1000}{M_2 \times W_1} = \frac{13.97 \times 5 \times 1000}{180 \times 100} = 3.88\,K$$
Thus, $T_f = 273.15 - 3.88 = 269.27\,K$

(ii) The Henry's constant of a gas in a particular solvent increases with increase in temperature. This indicates that the solubility of a gas in liquid decreases with increase in temperature.

16. (i) **Acetamide to ethylamine**

$$\underset{\text{Acetamide}}{CH_3-\overset{\overset{O}{\|}}{C}-NH_2} \xrightarrow[P_2O_5]{\Delta} \underset{\text{Methyl cyanide}}{CH_3C\equiv N} \xrightarrow[LiAlH_4]{+4\,[H]} \underset{\text{Ethylamine}}{CH_3CH_2NH_2}$$

(ii) **Ethylamine to methylamine**

$$\underset{\text{Ethylamine}}{CH_3CH_2NH_2} \xrightarrow[-NH_2,\,-H_2O]{+HNO_2} \underset{\text{Ethanol}}{CH_3CH_2OH} \xrightarrow[\Delta]{Cu/573K}$$
$$\underset{\text{Acetaldehyde}}{CH_3CHO} \xrightarrow[KMnO_4]{\text{Alkaline}} \underset{\text{Acetic acid}}{CH_3COOH} \xrightarrow{SOCl_2}$$
$$\underset{\text{Acetyl chloride}}{CH_3COCl} \xrightarrow[-H_2O]{NH_3/\Delta} \underset{\text{Acetamide}}{CH_3CONH_2} \xrightarrow[\Delta\ \text{(Hofmann bromamide reaction)}]{Br_2+NaOH}$$
$$\underset{\text{Methylamine}}{CH_3NH_2} + \underset{\text{Sodium bromide}}{2NaBr} + \underset{\text{Sodium carbonate}}{Na_2CO_3} + \underset{\text{Water}}{2H_2O}$$

(iii) **Benzene to acetanilide**

$$\underset{\text{Benzene}}{C_6H_6} \xrightarrow[-H_2O]{HNO_3/H_2SO_4} \underset{\text{Nitrobenzene}}{C_6N_5NO_2} \xrightarrow[(Sn+HCl),\,-2H_2O]{4[H]}$$
$$\underset{\text{Aniline}}{C_6H_5NH_2} \xrightarrow[-HCl]{CH_3COCl} \underset{\text{Acetanilide}}{C_6H_5NHCOCH_3}$$

17. (i)

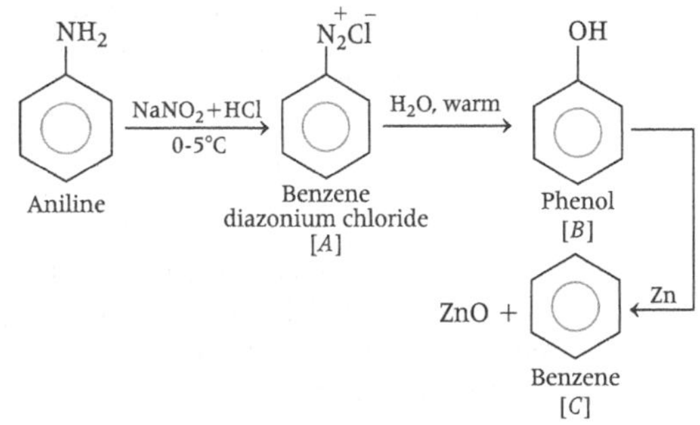

(ii)

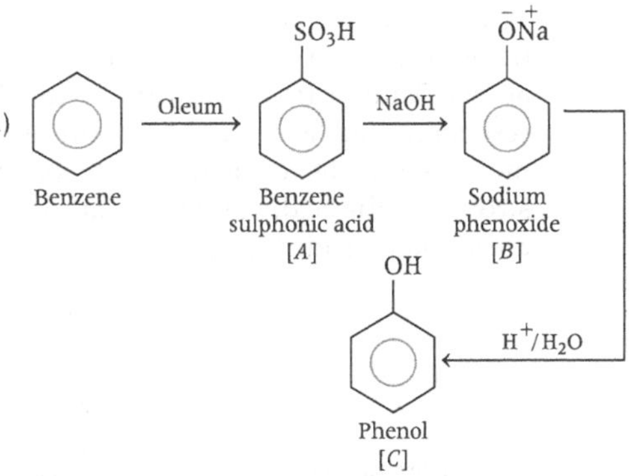

18. (i) Magnetic moment $(\mu) = \sqrt{n(n+2)}$ BM
where, n = number of unpaired electrons.

Metal ion	Electronic configuration	Magnetic moment (BM)	Unpaired electrons
Sc^{3+}	$3d^0$	0.00	0
Cr^{2+}	$3d^4$	4.90	4
Ni^{2+}	$3d^8$	2.84	2
Ti^{3+}	$3d^1$	1.73	1

$\therefore Cr^{2+}$ has the maximum number of unpaired electrons.

The metal ion which does not contain unpaired electrons form colourless aqueous solution.

$\because$ $Sc^{3+} \longrightarrow 3d^0$

$\therefore$ Sc^{3+} forms colourless aqueous solution.

(ii) (a) $\Delta_o > P$, low spin, strong field, $t_{2g}^5 e_g^0$.
(b) $\Delta_o < P$, high spin, weak field, $t_{2g}^3 e_g^2$.

> **Value Point** For getting maximum marks, one should include the brief explanation of the answers instead of writing answer in one word.

19. (i) A is CH_3CHO (ethanal).
B is C_6H_5CHO (benzaldehyde).

$$\underset{\substack{\text{Ethanal}\\(A)}}{2CH_3CHO} \overset{NaOH}{\rightleftharpoons} \underset{\beta\text{-hydroxyaldehyde}}{CH_3\overset{\overset{OH}{|}}{CH}CH_2CHO} \xrightarrow{-H_2O} \underset{\text{But-2-enal}}{CH_3CH{=}CH{-}CHO}$$

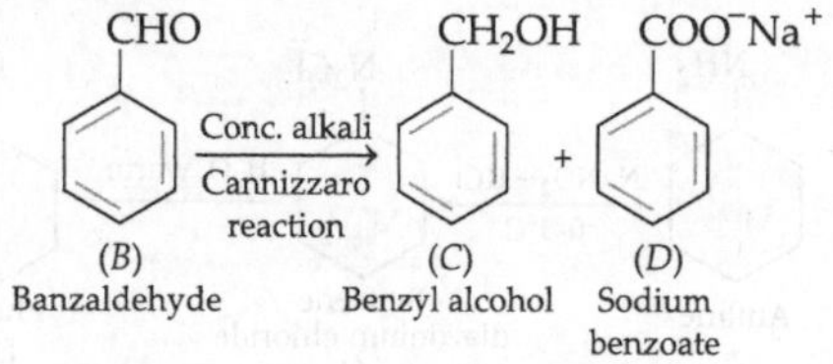

(ii) (a) Phenoxide ion has non-equivalent resonance structures in which the negative charge is less effectively delocalised over less electronegative carbon atom and one oxygen atom.

While in carboxylate ion, the negative charge is delocalised over two electronegative oxygen atoms. Thus, carboxylate ion is much more resonance stabilised than phenoxide ion. Since, more stable the conjugate base of an acid, stronger is the acid. Therefore, carboxylic acids are stronger acids than phenol.

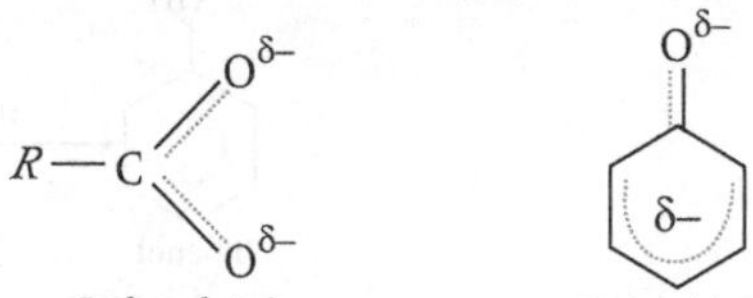

Carboxylate ion Phenoxide ion

(b) The bisulphite addition compound is water soluble whereas impurities do not. So, on hydrolysis we get pure aldehydes.

Therefore, sodium bisulphite can be used for purification of aldehydes.

20. (i) (a) Coordination compound $[Cr(H_2O)_6]Cl_3$ and $[Cr(H_2O)_5Cl]Cl_2 \cdot H_2O$ are solvate isomers, because water is exchanged by chloride ion. This is why both of them show different colour on exposure to sunlight.

(b) The formula is $[Pt(NH_3)_2Cl(NO_2)]$.

(c) Crystal field splitting energy (CFSE) in the octahedral and tetrahedral field are closely related as $\Delta_t = \left(\frac{4}{9}\right)\Delta_o$.

The colour of complexes is due to *d-d* transition. Higher the CFSE, higher will be the energy radiated in *d-d* transition.

(ii) $\mathbf{[Pt(en)_2Cl_2]^{2+}}$

IUPAC name Dichlorido*bis*-(ethylenediamine) platinum(II) ion.

Geometrical isomers of $[Pt(en)_2Cl_2]^{2+}$ are

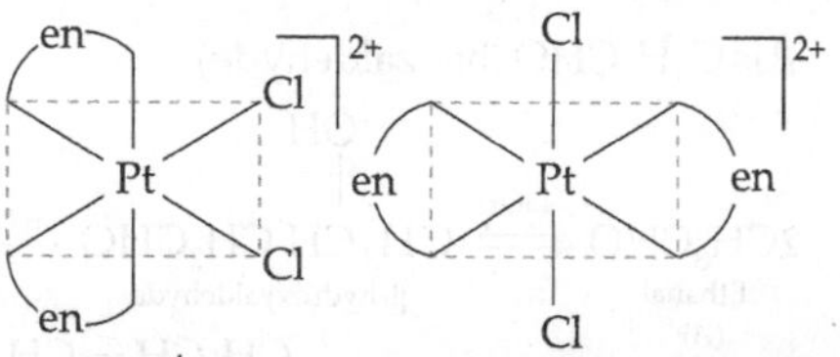

cis *trans*

21. (i) Specific conductance (κ) $= 1.65 \times 10^{-4}\,\Omega^{-1}\,cm^{-1}$

Concentration $= 0.01\,M$

$$\Lambda_m = \frac{\kappa \times 1000}{C} = \frac{1.65 \times 10^{-4}\,\Omega^{-1}cm^{-1} \times 1000}{0.01}$$

$$= 16.5\,\Omega^{-1}cm^2\,mol^{-1}$$

Degree of dissociation,

$$\alpha = \frac{\text{Molar conductance of substance}}{\text{Molar conductance at infinite dilution}} = \frac{\Lambda_m}{\Lambda_m^\infty}$$

According to Kohlrausch's law,

$$\Lambda^\infty_{m\,(CH_3COOH)} = \Lambda^\infty_{CH_3COO^-} + \Lambda^\infty_{H^+}$$

$$= (349.1 + 40.9)\,\Omega^{-1}cm^2\,mol^{-1}$$

$$= 390\,\Omega^{-1}\,cm^2\,mol^{-1}$$

∴ Degree of dissociation of CH_3COOH,

$$\alpha = \frac{16.5}{390} = 0.042$$

(ii) (a) $Mg(s) + Cu^{2+}\,(0.0001\,M) \longrightarrow Mg^{2+}\,(0.001\,M) + Cu(s)$

Standard electrode potential, $E^\circ_{cell} = 2.71\,V$

Applying Nernst equation,

$$E_{cell} = E^\circ_{cell} - \frac{0.0591}{n}\log\frac{[Mg^{2+}]}{[Cu^{2+}]}$$

$$= 2.71 - \frac{0.0591}{2}\log\frac{0.001}{0.0001}$$

$$= 2.71 - \frac{0.0591}{2}\log 10 = 2.71 - 0.02955$$

$$\therefore E_{cell} = 2.68\,V$$

Or

(a) Cell reaction,

At cathode, $2Ag^+(aq) + 2e^- \longrightarrow 2Ag(s)$

At anode, $Cu(s) \longrightarrow Cu^{2+}(aq) + 2e^-$

Net reaction, $Cu(s) + 2Ag^+(aq) \longrightarrow Cu^{2+}(aq) + 2Ag(s)$

(b) $E^\circ_{cell} = E^\circ_{cathode} - E^\circ_{anode} = E^\circ_{Ag^+/Ag} - E^\circ_{Cu^+/Cu}$

$$E^\circ_{cell} = 0.80 - 0.34 = +\,0.46\,V$$

$$E^\circ_{cell} = E^\circ_{cell} - \frac{0.0591}{n}\log\frac{[Cu^{2+}]}{[Ag^+]^2}$$

$$= 0.46\,V - \frac{0.0591}{2}\log\frac{0.13}{(0.01)^2}$$

$$= 0.46\,V - \frac{0.0591}{2}\log(13 \times 10^2)$$

$$= 0.46 - 0.092 = 0.368\,V$$

(c) For a reaction to be spontaneous, ΔG should be negative. For this cell, E_{cell} is positive and $\Delta G = -nFE^\circ$. Hence, this cell reaction is spontaneous.

(d) Since, $E^\circ_{Ni^{2+}/Ni}\,(-0.25\,V) < E^\circ_{Cu^{2+}/Cu}\,(0.34\,V)$

Therefore, Ni possesses a greater reducing power. Hence, Ni can displace Cu from $CuSO_4$ solution.

(e) Standard electrode potentials can be applied to aqueous equilibrium only. We cannot predict reaction possibilities, but we cannot predict the rate of reaction by using standard electrode potentials.

SPQ Code : **PB-12/15** Series ***i*-Succeed 12-25/15** Roll No.

Sample Question Paper 12

Chemistry 12th (Code 862)

General Instructions

1. This paper is divided into four sections-A, B, C and D. Answer all questions.
2. **Section A** consists of **one** question **having sub-parts** of **one** mark each. **Section B** consists of **ten** questions of **two** marks each. **Section C** consists of **seven** questions of **three** marks each and **Section D** consists of **three** questions of **five** marks each.
3. Internal choices have been provided in one question each in Section B, Section C and Section D.
4. All working, including rough work, should be done on the same sheet as, and adjacent to the rest of the answer.
5. The intended marks for questions or parts of questions are given in brackets [].
6. Balanced questions must be given, wherever possible and diagrams where they are helpful. When solving numerical problems, all essential working must be shown.
7. In working out problems, use the following data:
Gas constant (R) = 1.987 cal deg^{-1} mol^{-1} = 8.314 JK^{-1} mol^{-1} = 0.0821 dm^3 atm K^{-1} mol^{-1}
1L atm = 1 dm^3 atm =101.3 J, 1 Faraday =96500 Coulombs.
Avogadro's number (N_A) = 6.023×10^{23}.

Time : 3 Hrs.
Max. Marks : 70

Section A

[14 Marks]

1. (A) Fill in the blanks by choosing the appropriate word(s) from those given in the brackets.
[molecularity, fractional, integer, silver mirror, CH_3CH_2OH, 2, 1, potassium trioxalato chromate(III), order, alkaline, CH_3OCH_3, acidic, neutral] [4 × 1]

(i) The functional group isomers having formula C_2H_6O are ...... and .... • *Understanding*

(ii) The IUPAC name of the complex $K_3[Cr(C_2O_4)_3]$ is .... The denticity of $C_2O_4^{2-}$ in the given complex is .... • *Application*

(iii) .... of reaction may have zero, whole number or .... values. • *Recall*

(iv) When an aldehyde is heated with freshly prepared Tollen's reagent, a bright ...... is produced. The reaction occurs in .... medium. • *Understanding*

(B) Select and write the correct alternative from the choices given below. [7×1]

(i) During depression of freezing point in a solution, the following are in equilibrium. • *Recall*

(a) Liquid solvent, solid solvent
(b) Liquid solvent, solid solute
(c) Solid solvent, solid solute
(d) Liquid solute, solid solvent

(ii) Transition metals exhibit a range of oxidation states in different compounds.

Which of the following is the reason for zinc not exhibiting variable oxidation state? • *Analysis*

(a) Inert pair effect
(b) Completely filled 3*d*-subshell
(c) Completely filled 4*s*-subshell
(d) Common ion effect

(iii) Among the following, the strongest base in aqueous medium is .... • *Understanding*

(a) CH_3NH_2 (b) $NCCH_2NH_2$
(c) $(CH_3)_2NH$ (d) $C_6H_5NHCH_3$

(iv) For a cell reaction involving two electrons change, the standard emf of the cell is found to be 0.295 V at 25°C. The equilibrium constant for the reaction at 25°C will be • *Application*

(a) 2.95×10^2 (b) 10
(c) 1×10^{10} (d) 1×10^{-10}

(v) Which of the following statements is/are incorrect?

I. Law of mass action and rate law expression are the same for single step reactions.
II. Both order of reaction and molecularity have normally a maximum value of 3.
III. Order and molecularity for elementary reactions are different.
IV. Molecularity of a complex reaction, $A + 2B \longrightarrow C$ is 3.

• *Recall*

(a) Only I and II (b) Only II and III
(c) Only III and IV (d) Only I and IV

(vi) **Assertion** (A) Molarity of a solution in liquid state changes with temperature.

Reason (R) The volume of a solution changes with change in temperature. • *Analysis*

(a) Both Assertion and Reason are true and Reason is the correct explanation of Assertion.
(b) Both Assertion and Reason are true but Reason is not the correct explanation of Assertion.
(c) Assertion is true but Reason is false.
(d) Both Assertion and Reason are false.

(vii) **Assertion** (A) Chlorobenzene is resistant to nucleophilic substitution reaction at room temperature.

Reason (R) C—Cl bond gets weaker due to resonance. • *Analysis*

(a) Both Assertion and Reason are true and Reason is the correct explanation of Assertion.
(b) Both Assertion and Reason are true but Reason is not the correct explanation of Assertion.
(c) Assertion is true but Reason is false.
(d) Both Assertion and Reason are false.

(C) Read the passage given below carefully and answer the questions that follow [3×1]

The chemical properties of aldehydes and ketones are due to the properties of carbonyl group ($>C=O$) in them. In carbonyl group, the more electronegative oxygen atom pulls the π-electron cloud towards itself. It acquires the partial negative charge, while the less electronegative carbon atom acquires the partial positive charge ($>\overset{\delta+}{C}=\overset{\delta-}{O}$). Carbonyl group is flat due to sp^2-hybridisation of its C-atom. Thus, it can be attacked easily from above or below. As the carbonyl carbon is electron deficient (acidic), therefore, it can be attacked easily by nucleophiles (bases).

Thus, the typical reactions of aldehydes and ketones are nucleophilic addition reactions. The many reactions involving aldehydes and ketones are sufficient for different synthesis reactions.

A general mechanism for such reactions is given below.

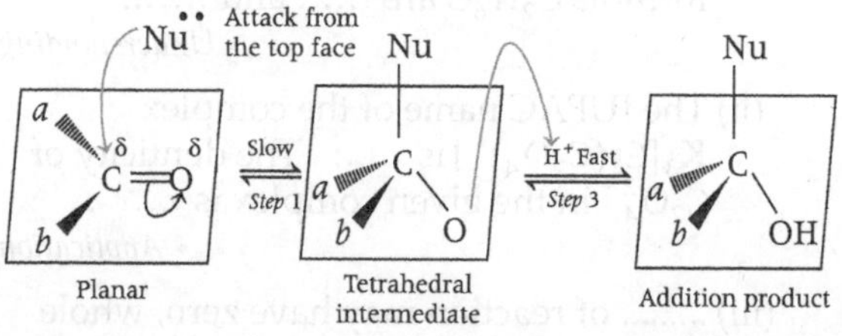

These reactions are considered very important in organic chemistry since they enable the conversion of carbonyl groups into a variety of functional groups.

(i) What type of aldehyde undergo Cannizzaro reaction? • *Understanding*

(ii) Write down the name of the product which is formed by the reaction of formaldehyde and ammonia. • *Understanding*

(iii) Why ethanol undergoes aldol condensation but trichloroethanol does not? • *Understanding*

Section B

[20 Marks]

2. A solution of glucose in water is labelled as 10% w/w. • *Application* [2]

   (i) What would be the molality and mole fraction of each component in the solution ?

   (ii) If the density of the solution is 1.2 g mL^{-1}, then what shall be the molarity of the solution?

3. (i) Write the product formed when benzaldehyde reacts with CH_3CHO in presence of dilute NaOH • *Understanding*

   (ii) Distinguish between following. [2]

   $CH_3—CH{=}CH—CO—CH_3$ and $CH_3—CH_2—CO—CH{=}CH_2$ • *Understanding*

4. Depict the galvanic cell in which the reaction [2]

   $Zn(s) + 2Ag^+(aq) \longrightarrow Zn^{2+}(aq) + 2Ag(s)$

   takes place.

   Further show which of the above electrode is • *Recall*

   (i) negatively charged?

   (ii) positively charged?

5. When a chromite ore (A) is fused with an aqueous solution of sodium carbonate in free excess of air, a yellow solution of compound (B) is obtained. [2]

   This solution is filtered and acidified with sulphuric acid to form compound (C). Compound (C) on treatment with solution of KCl gives orange crystals of compound (D). Identify the compounds [A], [B], [C] and [D]. • *Understanding*

6. Predict the products of the following reactions. • *Understanding*

   (i) 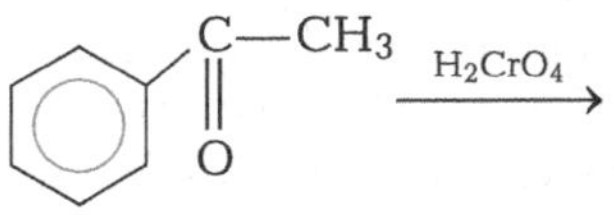

   (ii) 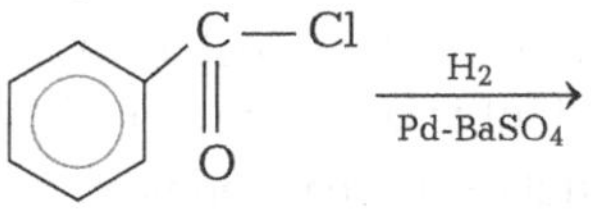

   [2]

7. During chemistry class, a teacher wrote MnO_4^{2-} as one of the compound of transition metals on board. The students were asked to find out the magnetic behaviour and shape of the compound. Umar, a student, wrote the answer paramagnetic and tetrahedral whereas another student Sunny wrote diamagnetic and square planar. Evaluate Umar's and Sunny's responses. • *Evaluate* [2]

8. How will you carry out the following conversions? • *Analysis*

   (i) 2-bromopropane to 1-bromopropane [2]

   (ii) Benzene to *p*-nitrochlorobenzene

   Or

   A hydrocarbon, C_5H_{10} does not react with chlorine in dark but gives a single monochloro compound, C_5H_9Cl in bright sunlight. Identify the hydrocarbon. • *Analysis*

9. Account for the following. • *Understanding* [2]

   (i) Diazonium salts of aromatic amines are more stable than those of aliphatic amines.

   (ii) Amines are more basic than alcohols of comparable molecular masses.

10. (i) Arrange the following compounds in the increasing order of their acidic strength : • *Analysis* [2]

    p-cresol, *p*-nitrophenol, phenol

(ii) Write the mechanism (using curved arrow notation) of the following reaction. • *Understanding*

$$CH_2{=}CH_2 \xrightarrow{H_3O^+} CH_3-\overset{+}{C}H_2 + H_2O$$

11. What happens when • *Understanding*

(i) H_2S reacts with acidified $K_2Cr_2O_7$ solution?

(ii) ethanol is oxidised with acidified $K_2Cr_2O_7$ solution? [2]

Section C **[21 Marks]**

12. A first order reaction is a chemical reaction in which the rate of the reaction is directly proportional to the concentration of the reactants. Half life ($t_{1/2}$) is the time required for a quantity to reduce to half its initial value. Consider the two cases given below and answer the questions that follow. [3]

(A) In a first order reaction 10% of the reactant is consumed in 25 mins.

(B) A first order reaction is 50% complete in 30 mins at 27°C.

Answer the following questions.

(i) Calculate the rate constant in both the cases. • *Application*

(ii) Calculate the time required for completing 17% of the reaction in case (A). • *Application*

(iii) Calculate the half life of the reaction in case (A). • *Application*

13. Rank the transition states of dehydration of alcohols that occur during the following reactions in • *Analysis* [3]

(a) $CH_3-\overset{+}{O}H_2 \longrightarrow CH_3^+ + H_2O$

(b) $(CH_3)_3C-\overset{+}{O}H_2 \longrightarrow (CH_3)_3C^+ + H_2O$

(c) $(CH_3)_2CH-\overset{+}{O}H_2 \longrightarrow (CH_3)_2CH^+ + H_2O$

(i) In the increasing order of stability of carbocation.

(ii) In the increasing order for rate of nucleophilic substitution reaction.

14. (i) Name an amino acid, which is not optically active and also give reason. • *Recall* [3]

(ii) Show that how three moles of phenyl hydrazine are consumed in reaction with glucose. • *Understanding*

(iii) Sohan while studying about the reactions of glucose found out that glucose on reaction with HI gives *n*-hexane. What does it suggests about the structure of glucose? • *Understanding*

15. When 10 g of $CH_3CH_2CHClCOOH$ is added to 250 g of water. Calculate • *Application* [3]

[Degree of dissociation, $\alpha = 0.065$, $K_f = 1.86 \text{ K kg mol}^{-1}$]

(i) the molality.

(ii) the van't Hoff factor (i).

(iii) the depression in the freezing point of water.

16. Give reasons for the following. [3]

(i) When 2g of benzoic acid is dissolved in 25 g of benzene, the experimentally determined molar mass is always greater than the true value. • *Application*

(ii) Mixture of ethanol and acetone shows positive deviation from Raoult's law. • *Understanding*

(iii) The preservation of fruits by adding concentrated sugar solution protects them against bacterial action. • *Understanding*

Or The air is a mixture of a number of gases. The major components are oxygen and nitrogen with approximate proportion of 20% and 79% by volume at 298 K, respectively. The water is in equilibrium with air at a pressure of 10 atm. At 298 K, if the Henry's law constant for oxygen and nitrogen are 3.30×10^7 mm and 6.51×10^7 mm respectively, calculate the composition of these gases in water. • *Application*

17. Identify the compounds *A*, *B* and *C* in the following reactions. • *Understanding* [3]

(i) 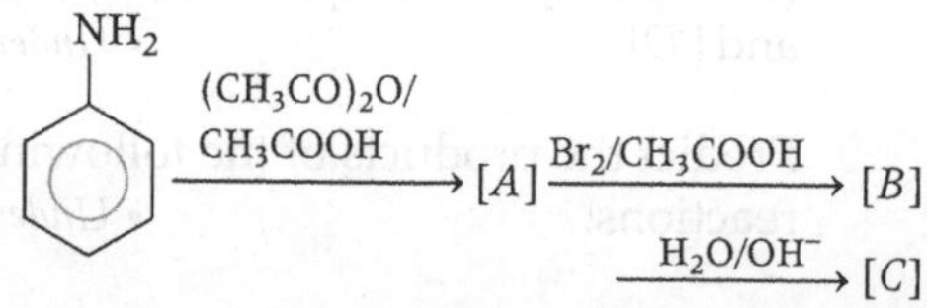

(ii) 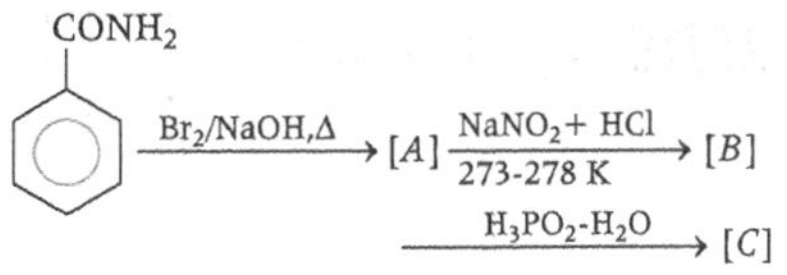

18. Data given below is for the reaction.

$$2SO_3(g) \longrightarrow 2SO_2(g) + O_2(g)$$

S.No.	$[SO_3]$ (mol L^{-1})	Rate of disappearance of $[SO_3]$ (mol L^{-1} min^{-1})
1.	1.13×10^{-2}	34×10^{-5}
2.	0.84×10^{-2}	25×10^{-5}
3.	0.62×10^{-2}	18×10^{-5}

(i) What is the order of reaction? • *Application*

(ii) Determine the rate law expression for the reaction. • *Evaluate*

(iii) Calculate the rate constant of the reaction. • *Application*

Section D **[15 Marks]**

19. (i) (a) Define term molar conductance. • *Recall*

(b) How Nernst equation can be applied in the calculation of equilibrium constant of any cell reaction? • *Understanding*

(ii) Calculate the emf of the cell. [5]

$Cr|Cr^{3+}(0.1\ M)||Fe^{2+}(0.01\ M)|Fe$

Given : $E^\circ_{Cr^{3+}/Cr} = -0.75$ V,

$E^\circ_{Fe^{2+}/Fe} = -0.45$ V • *Application*

20. For understanding the structure and bonding in transition metal complexes, the magnetic properties are very helpful. Low spin complexes are generally diamagnetic because of pairing of electrons, whereas high spin complexes are usually paramagnetic because of unpaired electrons. Iron forms many complexes such as $[Fe(CN)_6]^{3-}$ (*A*), $[Fe(CN)_6]^{4-}$ (*B*), $[Fe(en)_2Cl_2]Cl$ (*C*) etc. They exhibit different magnetic properties and undergo different hybridisation of iron.

Answer the following questions.

(i) State the reason, why $[Fe(CN)_6]^{3-}$ is weakly paramagnetic while $[Fe(CN)_6]^{4-}$ is diamagnetic? • *Understanding* [5]

(ii) Consider the complex ion $[Fe(en)_2Cl_2]Cl$. Find the type of hybridisation of central metal atom. • *Understanding*

(iii) Write the IUPAC name of $[Fe(en)_2Cl_2]Cl$. • *Recall*

(v) Find the geometry of the complex ion $[Fe(en)_2Cl_2]Cl$. Using VBT theory. • *Understanding*

(v) Magnetic moment of $[Fe(CN)_6]^{3-}$ is 1.73 B.M. Give reason • *Understandng*

Or (i) Write the IUPAC name of $[Cu(NH_3)_4]SO_4$ and $K_2[Zn(OH)_4]$. [5]

Also, draw the total number of possible isomers of $[Cu(NH_3)_4][PtCl_4]$ • *Understanding*

(ii) $[Co(NH_3)_6]^{3+}$ and $[CoF_6]^{3-}$ both are complexes of Co(III), but $[Co(NH_3)_6]^{3+}$ is diamagnetic while $[CoF_6]^{3-}$ is paramagnetic with magnetic moment 4.90 B.M. Explain. • *Understanding*

21. (i) How is phenol obtained from ? [5]

(a) Chlorobenzene (b) Aniline

(c) Cumene • *Understanding*

(ii) Explain the following.

$(CH_3)_3C—O—CH_3$ on reaction with HI gives $(CH_3)_3C—I$ and $CH_3—OH$ as the main products and not $(CH_3)_3C—OH$ and $CH_3—I$. • *Understanding*

SP-12

Answer Key

1. (B) (i) (a) (ii) (b) (iii) (c) (iv) (c) (v) (c) (vi) (a) (vii) (c)

Scan this QR code from your mobile phone to get the explanations of this Sample paper.

SPQ Code : **PB-13/15** Series ***i*-Succeed 13-25/15** Roll No.

Sample Question Paper 13

Chemistry 12th (Code 862)

General Instructions

1. This paper is divided into four sections-A, B, C and D. Answer all questions.
2. **Section A** consists of **one** question **having sub-parts** of **one** mark each. **Section B** consists of **ten** questions of **two** marks each. **Section C** consists of **seven** questions of **three** marks each and **Section D** consists of **three** questions of **five** marks each.
3. Internal choices have been provided in one question each in Section B, Section C and Section D.
4. All working, including rough work, should be done on the same sheet as, and adjacent to the rest of the answer.
5. The intended marks for questions or parts of questions are given in brackets [].
6. Balanced questions must be given, wherever possible and diagrams where they are helpful. When solving numerical problems, all essential working must be shown.
7. In working out problems, use the following data:
   Gas constant (R) = 1.987 cal deg^{-1} mol^{-1} = 8.314 JK^{-1} mol^{-1} = 0.0821 dm^3 atm K^{-1} mol^{-1}
   1L atm = 1 dm^3 atm =101.3 J, 1 Faraday =96500 Coulombs.
   Avogadro's number (N_A) = 6.023×10^{23}.

Time : 3 Hrs.

Max. Marks : 70

Section A

[14 Marks]

1. (A) Fill in the blanks by choosing the appropriate word(s) from those given in the brackets. [4×1]

[straight line, delocalisation, stronger, weaker, mole fraction, solute, solvent, number of moles, $-k/2.303$, sodium chloride, *o*-chlorotoluene, toluene, $\frac{2.303}{K}$]

(i) Chlorobenzene on reaction with chloromethane in presence of dry ether forms ...... and .... • *Understanding*

(ii) Benzoic acid is ...... acid than acrylic acid. This is because .... destroys the aromatic character of the benzene ring. • *Understanding*

(iii) The relative lowering vapour pressure of a solvent at a given temperature due to dissolution of a non-volatile solute is equal to .... of ...... in the solution. • *Recall*

(iv) A variation of $\log_{10}[A]$ *versus* t is a ...... with a slope equal to .... • *Recall*

(B) Select and write the correct alternative from the choices given below. [7×1]

(i) The number of Faraday's which will be required to reduce 4g equivalents of Cu^{2+} to Cu metal is • *Application*

(a) 1 (b) 2
(c) 3 (d) 4

(ii) The correct order of the increasing magnetic moment of the given complexes is • *Analysis*

(a) $[CoCl_6]^{4-} < [Cu(NH_3)_4]^{2+} < [Ni(CN)_4]^{2-}$

(b) $[Cu(NH_3)_4]^{2+} < [CoCl_6]^{4-} < [Ni(CN)_4]^{2-}$

(c) $[Ni(CN)_4]^{2-} < [CoCl_6]^{4-} < [Cu(NH_3)_4]^{2+}$

(d) $[Ni(CN)_4]^{2-} < [Cu(NH_3)_4]^{2+} < [CoCl_6]^{4-}$

(iii) When 1 mole of $CrCl_3{\cdot}6H_2O$ is treated with excess of $AgNO_3$, 3 moles of AgCl are obtained. The formula of the complex is • *Understanding*

(a) $[CrCl_3(H_2O)_3]{.}\,3H_2O$

(b) $[CrCl_2(H_2O)_4]Cl.2H_2O$

(c) $[CrCl(H_2O)_5]Cl_2.H_2O$

(d) $[Cr(H_2O)_6]Cl_3$

(iv) IUPAC name of the compound,

$CH_3—\underset{\displaystyle CH_3}{\underset{|}{CH}}—OCH_3$ is • *Recall*

(a) 1-methoxy-1-methylethane

(b) 2-methoxy-2-methylethane

(c) 2-methoxypropane

(d) *iso*-propylmethyl ether

(v) Consider the following statements regarding vitamins.

I. Vitamins are the organic compounds required in small amounts in the diet but their deficiency causes specific disease.

II. Vitamins cannot be synthesised by plant but our body can synthesise them.

III. Vitamins are necessary to perform the specific biological functions for the normal maintenance of optimum growth and health of the organism.

IV. Vitamin B_{12} being water soluble, cannot stored in body.

Select the incorrect statements about the vitamins and choose the correct option. • *Understanding*

(a) Only I

(b) Only II and IV

(c) Only I and II

(d) Only II and III

(vi) **Assertion** (A) As a lead storage battery gets discharged, density of electrolyte present in it decreases.

Reason (R) Lead and lead dioxide both react with sulphuric acid to form lead sulphate. • *Analysis*

(a) Both Assertion and Reason are true and Reason is the correct explanation of Assertion.

(b) Both Assertion and Reason are true but Reason is not the correct explanation of Assertion.

(c) Assertion is true but Reason is false.

(d) Both Assertion and Reason are false.

(vii) **Assertion** (A) Glucose give α, 2, 4-DNP test.

Reason (R) Glucose does not have an aldehyde group. • *Analysis*

(a) Both Assertion and Reason are true and Reason is the correct explanation of Assertion.

(b) Both Assertion and Reason are true but Reason is not the correct explanation of Assertion.

(c) Assertion is true but Reason is false.

(d) Both Assertion and Reason are false.

(C) Read the passage given below carefully and answer the questions that follow. [3 × 1]

Amines constitute one of the most important class of organic compounds. Amines are alkyl or aryl derivatives of ammonia formed by replacement of one or more hydrogen atoms. Alkyl derivatives are called aliphatic amines and aryl derivatives are known as aromatic amines. Both aliphatic and aromatic primary amines can be prepared by the reduction of nitro compounds catalytically with H_2 in the presence of active metal in acidic medium.

The presence of aromatic amines can be identified by performing dye test. Aniline is the simplest example of aromatic amine. It undergoes electrophilic substitution reactions in which $—NH_2$ group strongly activates the aromatic ring through delocalisation of lone pair of electrons of N-atom.

Aniline undergoes electrophilic substitution reactions.
Ortho and *para*-positions to the $—NH_2$ group become centres of high electron density.
Thus, $—NH_2$ group is *ortho* and *para*-directing powerful activating group.

(i) Propylamine reacts with which reagent to form an alkali soluble product? • *Recall*

(ii) Which compound is produced by oxidation of aniline with $K_2Cr_2O_7$ / H_2SO_4? • *Understanding*

(iii) Why amines are reactive?• *Understanding*

Section B **[20 Marks]**

2. (i) Give reason to explain why the C— O bond is much shorter in phenol than in ethanol. • *Understanding*

(ii) Alcohols are more soluble in water than the hydrocarbons of comparable molecular masses. • *Understanding* [2]

3. Account for the following. • *Understanding*

(i) Transition metals form alloys.

(ii) Transition elements acts as catalyst. [2]

4. 15.0 g of unknown molecular material is dissolved in 450 g of water, resulting solution freezes at −0.34°C. What is the molar mass of the material?
(K_f of water = 1.86 K kg mol^{-1})
• *Application* [2]

5. Following compounds are given to you: [2]
2-bromopentane, 2-bromo-2-methylbutane, 1-bromopentane. • *Analysis*

(i) Write the compound which is most reactive towards S_N2 reaction.

(ii) Write the compound which is optically active.

6. (i) During working of a mercury cell, write the reaction taking place at
(a) anode (b) cathode • *Recall*

(ii) Given that the standard reduction potential for $Cr^{3+}/Cr = -0.72$ V and $Fe^{2+}/Fe = -0.42$ V. What will be the standard potential of the cell?
• *Application* [2]

7. A violet compound of manganese, [*W*] decomposes on heating to liberate oxygen and compounds [*X*] and [*Y*] of manganese are also formed. Compound [*Y*] reacts with KOH in the presence of oxygen to give compound [*X*].
On reacting compound [*W*] with H_2SO_4, a compound [*Z*] of manganese alongwith other products is formed. Identify the compounds [*W*], [*X*], [*Y*] and [*Z*].
• *Understanding* [2]

Or

What happens when $KMnO_4$ is treated with (write chemical reactions only).

(i) KI in alkaline medium ?

(ii) Ferrous sulphate in acidic medium ?
• *Understanding*

8. (i) Among the following dihalobenzenes, which one will exhibit high melting point? • *Analysis* [2]

m-dichlorobenzene, *p*-dichlorobenzene, *o*-dichlorobenzene.

(ii) The dipole moment of chlorobenzene is lower than that of cyclohexyl chloride. Justify the statement. • *Analysis*

9. Devise a scheme for the synthesis of phenol using chlorobenzene and ethanol from diethyl ether. • *Evaluate* [2]

10. A reactant has a half-life of 10 min.
• *Application* [2]

(i) Calculate the rate constant for the first order reaction.

(ii) What fraction of the reactant will be left after an hour of the reaction has occurred?

11. The first few members of the lanthanoid series are quite reactive. They usually form oxides and hydroxides. Complete the following reactions of lanthanoids. • *Analysis* [2]

(i) $Ln \xrightarrow{\text{Heated with N}}$ (ii) $Ln \xrightarrow{\text{Heated with } X}$

(iii) $Ln \xrightarrow{\text{Heated with S}}$ (iv) $Ln \xrightarrow[\text{2773K}]{\text{With C}}$

Section C **[21 Marks]**

12. An aqueous solution of a non-volatile solute freezes at 272.4 K, while pure water freezes at 273.0 K. Determine the following :

(Given, $K_f = 1.86$ K kg mol^{-1}, $K_b = 0.512$ K kg mol^{-1} and vapour pressure of water at 298 K = 23.756 mm of Hg) • *Application* [3]

(i) The molality of solution.

(ii) Boiling point of solution.

13. Arrange the following compounds in the increasing order of their property as indicated.

$CH_3CH_2CH(Br)COOH$, $CH_2CH(Br)CH_2COOH$, $(CH_3)_2CHCOOH$, $CH_3CH_2CH_2COOH$ • *Analysis* [3]

(i) In the increasing order of their acidic strength.

(ii) In the increasing order of their pK_a values.

14. (i) Account for the following. • *Understanding*

(a) A solution containing non-volatile solute have higher boiling point than the pure solvent.

(b) Elevation of boiling point is a colligative property.

(ii) What happens when blood cells are placed in water? • *Understanding* [3]

15. Write the reaction and IUPAC name of the product formed.

(i) When ethanal is treated with ethyl magnesium bromide followed by hydrolysis.

(ii) Phenol is treated with conc. H_2SO_4 and conc. HNO_3. • *Understanding* [3]

16. Write the equation for the reaction of hydrogen iodide with • *Understanding* [3]

(i) 1-propoxy propane

(ii) methoxy benzene

(iii) benzyl ethyl ether

Or

How may be the following transformation carried out (in not more than six steps)?

Ethyl alcohol to vinyl acetate. • *Evaluate*

17. Identify the compounds *A*, *B* and *C* in the following reactions. • *Understanding* [3]

(i)  $\xrightarrow[\text{and conc. } H_2SO_4]{\text{Conc. } HNO_3} [A] \xrightarrow{\text{Sn/HCl}} [B] \xrightarrow{\text{HCl}} [C]$

(ii) $C_6H_5NO_2 \xrightarrow{\text{Fe/HCl}} [A] \xrightarrow[(273\text{-}298\text{ K})]{HNO_2} [B] \xrightarrow{C_6H_5OH} [C]$

18. For the reaction: • *Application* [3]

$2H_2 + 2NO \rightleftharpoons 2H_2O + N_2$, the following rate data was obtained:

S.No.	[NO], mol L^{-1}	[H_2], mol L^{-1}	Rate, mol L^{-1} s^{-1}
1.	0.40	0.40	4.6×10^{-3}
2.	0.80	0.40	18.4×10^{-3}
3.	0.40	0.80	9.2×10^{-3}

Using the data given above.

(i) Find the overall order of the reaction. • *Application*

(ii) Determine the rate law expression for the reaction. • *Application*

(iii) Calculate the value of rate constant • *Evaluate*

SP-13

Section D

[15 Marks]

19. (i) An organic compound $A(C_3H_8O)$ on treatment with copper at 573 K gives *B*. *B* does not reduce Fehling's solution but gives a yellow ppt. of compound *C* with I_2 / NaOH. Deduce the structures of *A*, *B*, and *C*. • *Understanding* [5]

(ii) (a) Explain why cyclohexanone forms cyanohydrin in good yield but 2,2,6-trimethyl cyclohexanone does not. • *Understanding*

(b) How will you obtain tertiary butyl alcohol from acetone?• *Understanding*

20. (i) Conductivity of 2.5×10^{-4} M methanoic acid is 5.25×10^{-5} S cm^{-1}. Given, $\Lambda^{\circ}_{(H^+)} = 349.5$ S cm^2 mol^{-1} and $\Lambda^{\circ}_{(HCOO^-)} = 50.5$ S cm^2 mol^{-1}. Calculate its molar conductivity and degree of dissociation. • *Application* [5]

(ii) Calculate the emf of the cell in which the following reaction takes place :

$$Ni(s) + 2Ag^+(0.002\ M) \longrightarrow Ni^{2+}(0.160\ M) + 2Ag\ (s)$$

• *Application*

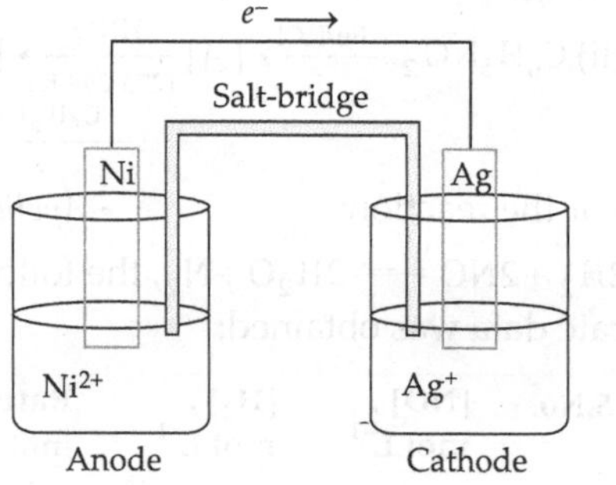

Given that, $E^{\circ}_{cell} = 1.05$ V

Or (i) The resistance of 0.5 N solution of an electrolyte in a conductivity cell was found to be 25 Ω. Calculate the conductance and equivalent conductivity of the solution if the electrodes in the cell are 1.6 cm apart and have an area of 3.2 cm^2. • *Application*

(ii) A current of 5 A is flowing through a wire for 193s. Calculate the number of electrons flowing through the cross-section of wire for 193s. • *Application*

21. The Crystal Field Theory (CFT) is an electrostatic model which considers the metal-ligand bond to be ionic arising purely from electrostatic interactions between the metal ion and the ligand. The splitting of the *d*-orbitals provides different electronic arrangements in strong and weak crystal fields. The treatment provides quantitative estimations of orbital separation energies, magnetic moments and spectral and stability parameters.

Answer the following questions.

(a) Predict the number of unpaired electrons in $[Fe(CN)_6]^{4-}$ complex. • *Understanding* [5]

(b) Calculate the number of unpaired electrons in $[Fe(H_2O)_6]^{2+}$ complex. • *Understanding*

(c) Calculate the spin magnetic moment of cobalt in the compound $Hg[Co(SCN)_4]$. • *Application*

(d) Why Co(III) forms paramagnetic octahedral complex with weak field ligands whereas it forms diamagnetic octahedral complex with strong field ligands? • *Understanding*

(e) State the factor that affect stability of complexes. • *Recall*

Answer Key

1. (B) (i) (d) (ii) (d) (iii) (d) (iv) (c) (v) (b) (vi) (a) (vii) (d)

Scan this QR code from your mobile phone to get the explanations of this Sample paper.

SP-13

SPQ Code : **PB-14/15** Series *i*-**Succeed 14-25/15** Roll No.

Sample Question Paper 14

Chemistry 12th (Code 862)

General Instructions

1. This paper is divided into four sections-A, B, C and D. Answer all questions.
2. **Section A** consists of **one** question **having sub-parts** of **one** mark each. **Section B** consists of **ten** questions of **two** marks each. **Section C** consists of **seven** questions of **three** marks each and **Section D** consists of **three** questions of **five** marks each.
3. Internal choices have been provided in one question each in Section B, Section C and Section D.
4. All working, including rough work, should be done on the same sheet as, and adjacent to the rest of the answer.
5. The intended marks for questions or parts of questions are given in brackets [].
6. Balanced questions must be given, wherever possible and diagrams where they are helpful. When solving numerical problems, all essential working must be shown.
7. In working out problems, use the following data:
   Gas constant (R) = 1.987 cal deg^{-1} mol^{-1} = 8.314 JK^{-1} mol^{-1} = 0.0821 dm^3 atm K^{-1} mol^{-1}
   1L atm = 1 dm^3 atm =101.3 J, 1 Faraday =96500 Coulombs.
   Avogadro's number (N_A) = 6.023 × 10^{23}.

Time : 3 Hrs.

Max. Marks : 70

Section A **[14 Marks]**

1. A. Fill in the blanks by choosing the appropriate word(s) from those given in the brackets. [4 × 1]

[first, second, half-life, trihalides, valence bond, crystal field, anaesthetics, plasticisers, L. Pauling, Alfred Werner, antioxidants, dihalides, transition state]

(i) Ethers plays an important role for the use of .... They are also used as .... • *Recall*

(ii) Presence of two and three halogen atoms respectively of same type in the structure of haloalkanes are called ...... and .... • *Recall*

(iii) .... theory for coordinate compounds was put forward by .... • *Recall*

(iv) For a .... order reaction, ... is independent of the initial concentration of the reactant. • *Understanding*

(B) Select and write the correct alternative from the choices given below. [7 × 1]

(i) When acetic acid reacts with calcium hydroxide and the product is dry distilled the compound formed is • *Understanding*

(a) calcium acetate
(b) acetone
(c) acetaldehyde
(d) acetic anhydride

(ii) Conductivity of an electrolyte solution is a measure of its ability to conduct electricity. Which of the following about conductivity is not correct? • *Analysis*

(a) It is the inverse of resistivity.
(b) Its SI unit is Sm^{-1}.
(c) It is equal to conductance when $\frac{l}{A} = 1 m^{-1}$.
(d) Gold defines conductivity

(iii) The mass of urea required for making 3.5 kg of 0.35 molal aqueous solution will be • *Application*

(a) 167 g (b) 72 g
(c) 75 g (d) 139 g

(iv) In which of the following solvents, the $C_4H_8NH_3^+X^-$ is soluble? • *Understanding*

(a) Ether (b) Acetone
(c) Water (d) Bromine water

(v) Which of the following statements are correct? • *Understanding*

I. Benedict's solution and Fehling's solution are used for the test of sugar in blood sample.
II. Glucose and fructose gives false test with Fehling's solution.
III. Fructose give positive test with Fehling's solution due to absence of hydroxyl group.
IV. Glucose and fructose gives positive test with Fehling's solution.

(a) Only I and II
(b) Only I and IV
(c) Only II and III
(d) Only III and IV

(vi) **Assertion** (A) Transition metals are good catalysts.

Reason (R) V_2O_5 is used in the preparation of H_2SO_4 by contact process. • *Analysis*

(a) Both Assertion and Reason are true and Reason is the correct explanation of Assertion.
(b) Both Assertion and Reason are true but Reason is not the correct explanation of Assertion.
(c) Assertion is true but Reason is false.
(d) Both Assertion and Reason are false.

(vii) **Assertion** (A) Alkyl halide are insoluble in water. • *Analysis*

Reason (R) Alkyl halides have halogen attached to sp^3 hybrid carbon.

(a) Both Assertion and Reason are true and Reason is the correct explanation of Assertion.
(b) Both Assertion and Reason are true but Reason is not the correct explanation of Assertion.
(c) Assertion is true but Reason is false.
(d) Both Assertion and Reason are false.

(C) Read the passage given below carefully and answer the questions that follow. [3×1]

Werner, a Swiss chemist in 1892 prepared and characterised a large number of coordination compounds and studied their physical and chemical behaviour. He proposed that in coordination compounds, metals possess two types of valencies, i.e. primary valencies which are normally ionisable and secondary valencies which are non-ionisable.

In a series of compounds of cobalt (III) chloride with ammonia, it was found that some of the chloride ions could be precipitated as AgCl on adding excess of $AgNO_3$ solution, but some remained in solution. The number of ions furnished by a complex in a solution can be determined by precipitation reactions.

The measurement of molar conductance of solutions of coordination compounds helps to estimate the number of ions formed by the compound in solution.

(i) Assign the secondary valency for the compound $NiCl_2 \cdot 6H_2O$ which precipitate 2 moles of AgCl with excess of $AgNO_3$. • *Analysis*

(ii) The compound $CoCl_3 \cdot 4NH_3$ contains only one Cl^- ion that is precipitated immediately on the addition of Ag^+ ions. Write the structural formula of the compound. • *Understanding*

(iii) A coordination compound $CrCl_3 \cdot 4H_2O$ precipitates silver chloride when treated with silver nitrate. The molar conductance of its solution corresponds to a total of two ions. Write the structural formula of the compound. • *Understanding*

Section B

[20 Marks]

2. For a certain chemical reaction variation in concentration $[A]$ *vs* time (s) plot is given below:

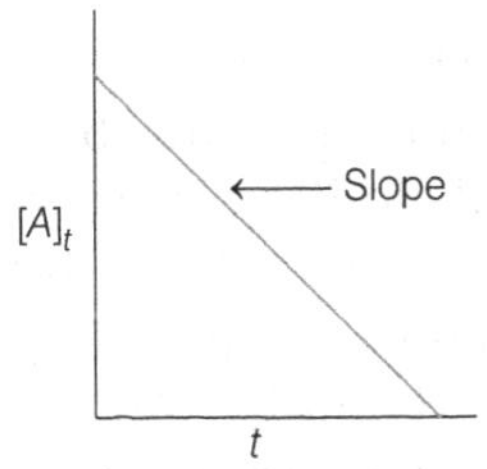

(i) Predict the order of the given reaction. • *Understanding*

(ii) What does the slope of the line and intercept indicate ? • *Understanding*

3. (i) Arrange the following in the increasing order of their basic character in an aqueous solution.

$C_2H_5NH_2$, $(C_2H_5)_2NH$, $(C_2H_5)_3N$ • *Analysis*

(ii) Boiling points of amines are lesser than alcohols and acids of comparable molar weight. Justify. • *Understanding* [2]

4. How will the following be obtained? (Give chemical equations)• *Understanding* [2]

(i) Benzamide to benzene

(ii) Aniline to toluene

Or

When aniline reacts with nitrous acid and HCl, it forms $[A]$, which on reaction with β-naphthol in presence of dil. NaOH forms $[B]$. Identify $[A]$ and $[B]$. • *Understanding* [2]

5. Draw the structures of the compounds whose IUPAC names are as follows

(i) 1-ethoxypropane

(ii) 2-ethoxy-3-methyl pentane • *Recall* [2]

6. (i) In the button cells, widely used in watches and other devices, the following reaction takes place • *Understanding* [2]

$$Zn(s) + Ag_2O(s) + H_2O(l) \longrightarrow Zn^{2+}(aq) + 2Ag(s) + 2OH^-(aq)$$

(a) Write the anode reaction.

(b) Write the cathode reaction.

(ii) Determine $E°$ for the reaction. • *Application*

(Given, $E^\circ_{Ag^+/Ag} = +0.80$ V, $E^\circ_{Zn^{2+}/Zn} = -0.76$ V)

7. The molecular masses of polymers are determined by osmotic pressure method and not by measuring other colligative properties. Give two reasons. • *Understanding* [2]

8. Give reasons for the following. • *Understanding* [2]

(i) La^{3+} (Z = 57) and Lu^{3+} (Z = 71) do not show any colour in solutions.

(ii) From element to element, the actinoid contraction is greater than the lanthanoid contraction.

9. Avinash while studying about non ideal solutions found out that on mixing liquid *X* and liquid *Y*, volume of the resulting solution decreases. [2]

(i) What type of deviation from Raoult's law is shown by the resulting solution? • *Analysis*

(ii) What change in temperature would you observe after mixing liquids *X* and *Y*? • *Analysis*

10. During chemistry class, a teacher wrote $[Fe(CN)_6]^{3-}$ as a coordination complex ion on the board. The students were asked to find out the magnetic behaviour and hybridisation of the complex. Isha, a student, wrote the answer paramagnetic and d^2sp^3 whereas another student Sameer wrote diamagnetic and sp^3d^2. Evaluate Isha's and Sameer's responses. • *Evaluate*

11. Write chemical equation when • *Understanding* [2]

(i) ethyl chloride is treated with *aq.*KOH.

(ii) propene is treated with B_2H_6 followed by H_2O_2/OH^-.

SP-14

Section C **[21 Marks]**

12. (i) Give a chemical test to distinguish between N-methylethanamine and N,N-dimethyl ethanamine. • *Understanding*

(ii) Write the reaction for catalytic reduction of nitrobenzene followed by reaction of product so formed with bromine water. • *Understanding*

(iii) Out of butan-1-ol and butan-1-amine, which will be more soluble in water and why? • *Understanding* [3]

13. Arrange the following in the increasing order of their property indicated. • *Analysis*

(i) CH_3CHO, CH_3COCH_3, $C_6H_5COCH_3$ (Reactivity towards nucleophilic addition)

(ii) $CH_3CH_2CH_3$, CH_3CHO, CH_3OCH_3, CH_3CH_2OH (Boiling point) [3]

14. The three solutions of fructose, sucrose and glucose are prepared in 10% water at 20°C. The optical rotation values are measured by the student using a polarimeter and are given in the following table.

Solution	Student Result $[\alpha]_{592}$	Teacher $[\alpha]_{592}$
(A) D-(–)-fructose	–94.8° ± 3.3	– 93.5°
(B) D(+)-sucrose	+ 66.5° ± 2.5	+ 66.8°
(C) D-(+)-glucose	+ 52.9° ± 2.2	+ 54.5°

SP-14

(i) What does the positive and negative optical rotation in the above results indicate? • *Understanding*

(ii) There can be a change in the sign of rotation from *dextro* to *laevo* in a reaction. Justify your answer with example. • *Understanding* [3]

(iii) If glucose reacts with acetic anhydride, then compound *A* is obtained. Identify the compound *A*. • *Analysis*

15. All the properties which depend on the number of solute particles irrespective of their nature relative to the total number of particles present in the solution is called colligative properties. Consider the two cases given below and answer the questions that follow.

(A) A non-volatile solute 'X' (molar mass $= 50\ g\ mol^{-1}$) when dissolved in 78 g of benzene reduced its vapour pressure to 90%.

(B) A solution prepared by adding 10g of $MgCl_2$ to 200 g of water assuming $MgCl_2$ is completely dissociated. [3]

(K_b for water $= 0.512\ Kkg\ mol^{-1}$, molar mass of $MgCl_2 = 95\ g\,mol^{-1}$).

(i) Calculate the mass of X dissolved in the solution. • *Application*

(ii) Calculate the boiling point elevation in case (*B*). • *Application*

(iii) Why is boiling of 1 M NaCl solution more than that of 1M glucose solution ? • *Understanding*

16. How will the following be converted? (Give chemical equations) • *Understanding* [3]

(i) Benzoic acid to *p*-nitrotoluene

(ii) Ethanol to 3-hydroxy butanal

(iii) Propanoic acid to acetic acid

Or

An organic compound contains 69.77% carbon, 11.63% hydrogen and rest oxygen. The molecular mass of the compound is 86. It does not reduce Tollen's reagent but forms an addition compound with sodium hydrogen sulphite and gives positive iodoform test. On vigorous oxidation, it gives ethanoic acid and propanoic acid. Write the possible structure of the compound. • *Understanding* [3]

17. Identify the compounds *A*, *B* and *C* in the following reactions. • *Understanding* [3]

(i) $$CH_3CH_2OH \xrightarrow{K_2Cr_2O_7/H_2SO_4} [A] \xrightarrow{CaCO_3} [B] \xrightarrow{\text{Dry distillation}} [C]$$

(ii) $$CH_3{-}\overset{\overset{\displaystyle O}{\|}}{C}{-}CH_3 \xrightarrow[\text{(b) } H_2O]{\text{(a) } CH_3MgBr} [A] \xrightarrow[\text{Ether}]{\text{Na metal}} [B] \xrightarrow{CH_3-Br} [C]$$

18. The decomposition of *A* into product has values of *k* as $4.5 \times 10^3\ s^{-1}$ at 10°C and energy of activation 60 kJ mol^{-1}. At what temperature would *k* be $1.5 \times 10^4\ s^{-1}$? • *Application* [3]

Section D [15 Marks]

19. (i) Chromium metal is electroplated using an acidic solution containing CrO_3 according to the following equation.

$CrO_3(aq) + 6H^+ + 6e^- \longrightarrow Cr(s) + 3H_2O$

Calculate how many grams of chromium will be electroplated by 24000 coulombs. How long will it take to electroplate 1.5 g chromium using 12.5 A current?

[Atomic mass of Cr = 52 g mol^{-1}, 1 F = 96500 C mol^{-1}] • *Application* [5]

(ii) Write applications of Kohlrausch's law. • *Recall*

Or (i) The molar conductivity of A is 46.1 S cm/mol and that of B is 0.025 S cm/mol. at 0.02 M. Which of the two is most likely to be methanoic acid? • *Application*

(ii) How many moles of mercury will be produced by electrolysing 10 M $Hg(NO_3)_2$ solution with a current of 2.00 A for three hours? • *Application*

[$Hg(NO_3)_2$ = 200.6 g mol^{-1}]

(iii) Following reactions occur at cathode during the electrolysis of aqueous silver chloride solution.

$Ag^+(aq) + e^- \longrightarrow Ag(s); \quad E° = 0.80\,V$

$H^+(aq) + e^- \longrightarrow \frac{1}{2}H_2(g); \quad E° = 0.00\,V$

On the basis of their standard reduction electrode potential ($E°$) values, which reaction is feasible at the cathode and why? • *Understanding*

20. The *d*-block of the periodic table contains the elements of the group 3-12 in which the *d*-orbitals are progressively filled in each of the four long periods. The *f*-block consists of elements in which $4f$ and $5f$ orbitals are progressively filled. They are placed in a separate panel at the bottom of the periodic table.

Answer the following questions. [5]

(i) Why orange colour of $Cr_2O_7^{2-}$ ion changes to yellow when treated with an alkali? • *Understanding*

(ii) Explain the observation, $E^\circ_{M^{2+}/M}$ values are not regular for first row transition metals of 3*d*-series. • *Understanding*

(iii) What are the similarities between the chemistry of lanthanoids and that of actinoids? • *Recall*

(iv) Ni^{2+} is more stable than Pt^{2+} but the trend is reverse where Pt^{4+} is more stable than Ni^{4+}. Explain. • *Understanding*

(v) Name a compound of transition metal which is used in Haber's process for the manufacture of ammonia. • *Recall*

21. (i) Write the names of reagents and equations for the preparation of the following ethers by Williamson's synthesis. • *Understanding* [5]

(a) 1-propoxypropane

(b) Ethoxybenzene

(c) 2-methoxy-2-methylpropane

(ii) Explain the fact that in aryl alkyl ether, the alkoxy group activates the benzene ring towards electrophilic substitution reactions. • *Understanding*

SP-14

Answer Key

1. (B) (i) (b) (ii) (d) (iii) (b) (iv) (c) (v) (b) (vi) (b) (vii) (b)

Scan this QR code from your mobile phone to get the explanations of this Sample paper.

SPQ Code : **PB-15/15** Series *i*-**Succeed 15-25/15** Roll No.

Sample Question Paper 15

Chemistry 12th (Code 862)

General Instructions

1. This paper is divided into four sections-A, B, C and D. Answer all questions.
2. **Section A** consists of **one** question **having sub-parts** of **one** mark each. **Section B** consists of **ten** questions of **two** marks each. **Section C** consists of **seven** questions of **three** marks each and **Section D** consists of **three** questions of **five** marks each.
3. Internal choices have been provided in one question each in Section B, Section C and Section D.
4. All working, including rough work, should be done on the same sheet as, and adjacent to the rest of the answer.
5. The intended marks for questions or parts of questions are given in brackets [].
6. Balanced questions must be given, wherever possible and diagrams where they are helpful. When solving numerical problems, all essential working must be shown.
7. In working out problems, use the following data:
Gas constant (R) = 1.987 cal deg^{-1} mol^{-1} = 8.314 JK^{-1} mol^{-1} = 0.0821 dm^3 atm K^{-1} mol^{-1}
1L atm = 1 dm^3 atm =101.3 J, 1 Faraday =96500 Coulombs.
Avogadro's number (N_A) = 6.023×10^{23}.

Time : 3 Hrs.

Max. Marks : 70

Section A

[14 Marks]

1. (A) Fill in the blanks by choosing appropriate word(s) from those given in the bracket.
[Strong, amino, alcoholic, carboxylic, coloured, paired, unpaired, colourless, lower, higher, weak, dehydration, decreases, alkene] [4×1]

(i) Liquids having …… intermolecular forces possess …… vapour pressure at a given temperature. • *Understanding*

(ii) Amino acids may be acidic, basic or neutral depending upon the relative number of active …….. and …….. group present in their molecule. • *Recall*

(iii) Tertiary alcohols when passed over heated copper at 573 K undergo ……to give ……. • *Understanding*

(iv) Paramagnetic compounds are generally …… and contain …… electrons. • *Recall*

(B) Select and write the correct alternative from the choices given below. [7×1]

(i) The reduction potential for the following half-cell reaction at 298 K will be
(Given : $[Ag^+] = 0.1$ M and $E^\circ_{cell} = +0.80$ V) • *Application*

(a) 0.859 V (b) 0.741 V
(c) 0.80 V (d) 0.771 V

(ii) Which of the following compounds is used as the starting material for the preparation of potassium dichromate? • *Recall*

(a) $K_2SO_4 \cdot Cr_2(SO_4)_3 \cdot 24H_2O$ (Chrome alum)
(b) $PbCrO_4$ (Chromite yellow)
(c) $FeCr_2O_4$ (Chromite)
(d) $PbCrO_4 \cdot PbO$ (Chrome red)

(iii) The correct IUPAC name for $CH_2=CHCH_2NHCH_3$ is • *Understanding*

(a) 2-aminopent-4-ene
(b) 4-aminopent-1-ene
(c) allyl methylamine
(d) N-methylprop-2-en-1 amine

(iv) In a first order reaction, reactant concentration 'C' varies with time 't' as • *Recall*

(a) C decreases with $\frac{1}{t}$
(b) $\log C$ decreases with $\frac{1}{t}$
(c) $\frac{1}{C}$ increases linearly with t
(d) $\log C$ decreases linearly with t

(v) Consider the following statements.

I. If $\Delta_o < P$, low spin state is more stable.
II. CO is a very weak ligand.
III. Tetrahedral complexes exhibit nearly 50% CFSE value than octahedral complexes.
IV. The colour of a complex depends on the nature of ligands.

The incorrect statements are • *Understanding*

(a) III and IV (b) I and IV
(c) I and II (d) II and IV

(vi) **Assertion** (A) Benzaldehydes and formaldehydes which do not contain α-hydrogen, undergo Cannizzaro reaction.

Reason (R) Benzaldehydes are almost as reactive as formaldehyde. • *Analysis*

(a) Both Assertion and Reason are true and Reason is the correct explanation of Assertion.
(b) Both Assertion and Reason are true but Reason is not the correct explanation of Assertion.
(c) Assertion is true but Reason is false.
(d) Both Assertion and Reason are false.

(vii) **Assertion** (A) Mercury cell does not give steady potential.

Reason (R) In the cell reaction, ions are involved in solution. • *Analysis*

(a) Both Assertion and Reason are true and Reason is the correct explanation of Assertion.
(b) Both Assertion and Reason are true but Reason is not the correct explanation of Assertion.
(c) Assertion is true but Reason is false.
(d) Both Assertion and Reason are false.

(C) Read the passage given below carefully and answer the questions that follows [3 × 1]

When the solutions of certain organic compounds are placed in the path of plane polarised light, they rotate the path of the light either to left or right. Such substances are called optically active substances.

A substance which rotates the plane polarised light to the right is called dextrorotatory or *d*-form. The substance which rotates the plane polarised light towards the left is called laevorotatory or *l*-form. Such *d*-and *l*-forms of compound are called optical isomers.

The four valencies of carbon atom are directed towards the corners of regular tetrahedron. If all the atoms or groups attached to a carbon atom are different, such carbon atom is called asymmetric carbon atom or stereocentre.

The resulting molecule would lack symmetry and the molecule is called asymmetric molecule. The asymmetry of the molecule is responsible for the optical activity in such organic compounds. An object or molecule which is not superimposable on its mirror image is called chiral and this property is called chirality, e.g. human hand. Chiral molecules are optically active.

The objects which are superimposable on their mirror images are called achiral and are optically inactive. The optical isomers which are non-superimposable mirror images of each other are called enantiomers and the phenomenon is called enantiomerism.

If one of the enantiomer is dextrorotatory then other will be laevorotatory. A mixture containing two enantiomers in equal proportions will have zero optical rotation, as the rotation due to one isomer will be cancelled by the rotation due to the other isomer. Such a mixture is called racemic mixture. It is represented as *dl* or ± forms and will be optically inactive.

The process of converting *d*- or *l*-form of an optically active compound into racemic form (*d*, *l*) is called racemisation.

(i) An alcohol having molecular formula, $C_4H_{10}O$ is optically active. What is its structure? • *Understanding*

(ii) What are enantiomers? Draw the structures of the possible enantiomers of butan-2-ol. • *Recall*

(iii) Identify the chiral molecule in the following pair

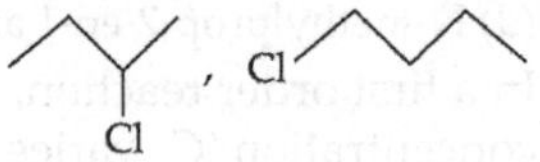

• *Analysis*

Section B **[20 Marks]**

2. Complete and balance the following chemical equations. [2]

(i) $MnO_4^{2-} + H^+ \longrightarrow$

(ii) $Mn^{2+} + S_2O_8^{2-} + H_2O \longrightarrow$ • *Recall*

3. Give reason for the following. [2]

(i) Metal-metal bonding is more extensive in the 4*d* and 5*d*-series of transition elements than the 3*d*-series.

(ii) Mn(III) undergoes disproportionation reaction easily. • *Understanding*

4. Write the reaction for the formation of each of the following. [2]

(i) Dichloromethane

(ii) Phosgene • *Recall*

5. Account for the following.

(i) N-ethylbenzene sulphonyl amide is soluble in alkali.

(ii) Reduction of nitrobenzene using Fe and HCl is preferred over Sn and HCl. [2] • *Understanding*

6. Consider the following cell reaction at 298 K. [2]

$$2Ag^+ + Cd \longrightarrow 2Ag + Cd^{2+}$$

The standard reduction potential ($E°$) for Ag^+/Ag and Cd^{2+}/Cd are +0.80 V and −0.40V respectively.

(i) Give the cell representation. • *Recall*

(ii) Calculate the standard cell emf, E°_{cell}. • *Application*

7. A decimolar solution of sodium chloride exerts an osmotic pressure of 4.82 atmosphere at 27°C, calculate the degree of dissociation of sodium chloride. [2] • *Application*

8. Devise a scheme for the synthesis of the following. [2]

(i) *p*-methoxy acetophenone from anisole.

(ii) *iso*-propyl alcohol from acetaldehyde. • *Evaluate*

Or

(i) Write hydroboration-oxidation reaction with an example. • *Recall*

(ii) Write the products of the following reaction.

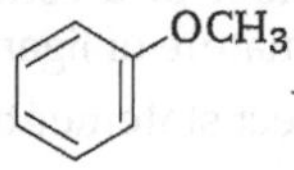

+ HBr ⟶

• *Understanding*

9. (i) Distinguish the structure of chromate ion from that of dichromate ion. • *Recall*

(ii) Give two equations that explains the nature of $K_2Cr_2O_7$ as oxidising agent. [2] • *Recall*

10. Write the products of the following reactions: • *Understanding* [2]

(i) 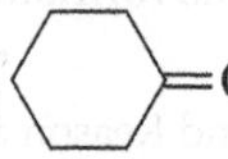 $=O + NH_2—NH—\overset{\overset{O}{\|}}{C}—NH_2 \xrightarrow{H^+}$

(ii) $CH_3CH_2COOH + Br_2 \xrightarrow{\text{Red Phosphorus}}$

11. Answer the following questions. [2]

(i) What type of deviation is shown by a mixture of ethanol and acetone? • *Recall*

(ii) What will be the value of van't Hoff factor for a dilute solution of K_2SO_4 in water? • *Application*

Section C [21 Marks]

12. The rate constant for the decomposition of N_2O_5 at various temperatures is given below.

$T/°C$	0	20	40	60	80
$10^5 \times K/s^{-1}$	0.0787	1.70	25.7	178	2140

(i) Draw a graph between $\ln k$ and $1/T$. • *Application*

(ii) Evaluate the value of slope. • *Evaluate*

(iii) Calculate the value of E_a. • *Application* [3]

13. When 3-methylbutan-2-ol is treated with HBr, the following reaction takes place:

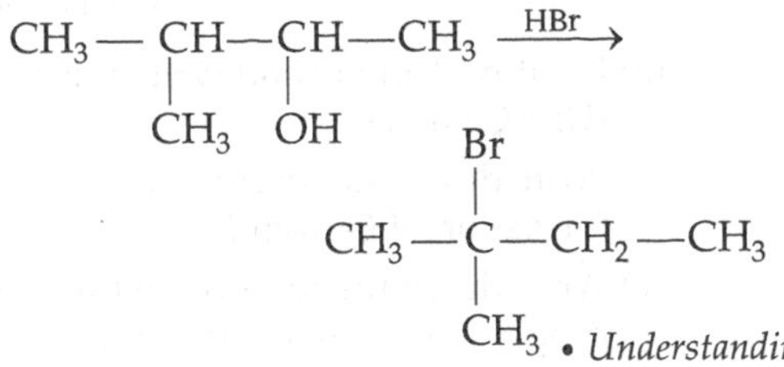

• *Understanding*

Give a mechanism for this reaction. [3]

14. Define the following terms.

(i) Denaturation (ii) Peptide linkage
(iii) Polysaccharides • *Recall* [3]

15. The boiling point of a liquid is that temperature at which its vapour pressure becomes equal to the atmospheric pressure. The difference in the boiling points of the solution and pure solvent is called as elevation in boiling point. It depends on the number of solute molecules.

Consider the case given below and the questions that follows

Prerna dissolves 4g of $MgSO_4$ (M=120 g mol^{-1}) in 100 g of water assuming $MgSO_4$ undergoes complete ionisation. (K_b for water =0.52 K kg mol^{-1}) [3]

(i) Calculate elevation in boiling point of solution. • *Application*

(ii) Calculate the boiling point of solution. • *Application*

(iii) Arrange the following aqueous solution in the order of their increasing boiling points. 10^{-3}M NaCl, 10^{-3} M $MgCl_2$, 10^{-3} M urea. • *Analysis*

16. Write the equations for the following reaction.

(i) Benzyl chloride is treated with aqueous KOH followed by hydrolysis.

(ii) Cumene hydroperoxide undergoes acid hydrolysis.

(iii) Benzene diazonium chloride is treated with water. • *Understanding* [3]

17. Write the structures of *A*, *B* and *C* in the following reactions.

(i) $C_6H_5—CONH_2 \xrightarrow{Br_2/Aq.\ KOH} A \xrightarrow{NaNO_2,HCl} B \xrightarrow{KI} C$

(ii) $CH_3Cl \xrightarrow{KCN} A \xrightarrow{LiAlH_4} B \xrightarrow{CHCl_3 + Alc.\ KOH} C$ [3]

• *Understanding*

Or

Write chemical equations to illustrate the following name reactions.

(i) Etard reaction (ii) Stephen reaction
(iii) Rosenmund's reduction • *Recall*

18. An aqueous solution of copper sulphate, $CuSO_4$ was electrolysed between platinum electrodes using a current of 0.1287 A for 50 min.

[Given : Atomic mass of Cu = 63.5 g mol^{-1}]

(i) Write the cathodic reaction. • *Recall*

(ii) Calculate

(a) electric charge passed during electrolysis.

(b) mass of copper deposited at the cathode. • *Application*

[Given, 1F =96500 C mol^{-1}] [3]

SP-15

Section D [15 Marks]

19. The half-life of a reaction is the time required for the concentration of reactant to decrease by half, i.e. $[A]_t = \frac{1}{2}[A]$

For first order reaction, $t_{1/2} = \frac{0.693}{k}$

This means $t_{1/2}$ is independent of initial concentration.

The decomposition of phosphine, PH_3 proceeds according to the following equation:

$$4PH_3(g) \longrightarrow P_4(g) + 6H_2(g)$$

It is found that the reaction follows the following rate equation.

$$\text{Rate} = k[PH_3]$$

Secondly, the C-14 content of an ancient piece of wood was found to have three-tenths of that in living trees.

Answer the following questions.

(i) How much time is required for 3/4th of PH_3 to decompose, if the half-life of PH_3 is 37.9s at 120°C? • *Application*

(ii) Why does radioactive disintegration follows first order kinetics? • *Understanding*

(iii) What fraction of the original sample of PH_3 remains behind after 1 min? • *Application*

(iv) What does the slope of the graph represent? • *Understanding*

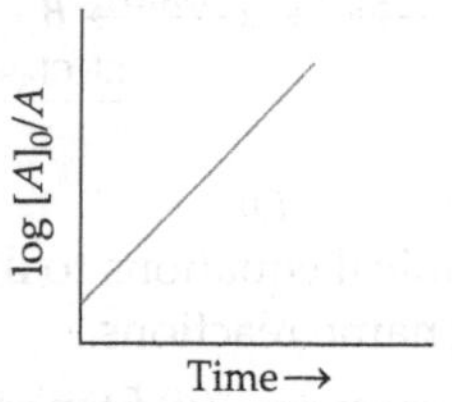

(v) How old is that piece of wood ? ($\log 3 = 0.4771$, $\log 7 = 0.8540$, half-life of C-14 = 5730 years) • *Application* [5]

20. (i) (a) Give an example of linkage isomerism. • *Recall* [5]

(b) The complex ion $[CuCl_4]^{2-}$ is formed in solution when chloride ions are added to the solution containing Cu^{2+} ions.

$$Cu^{2+}(aq) + 4Cl^-(aq) \longrightarrow [CuCl_4]^{2-}$$

However, the solution does not give the test for Cl^- ions. Why? • *Understanding*

(c) What is the denticity of coordination compound used for the treatment of lead poisoning? • *Recall*

(ii) Consider the complex ion $[Mn(CN)_6]^{3-}$ and find out the type of hybridisation of central metal atom and magnetic nature. (Atomic number of Mn = 25) • *Understanding*

21. A hydrocarbon, *P*, with the formula C_6H_{12} readily decolourises bromine.

(i) On reaction with hot, concentrated, acidified potassium manganate (VII) solution a single organic product, *Q*, is obtained. *Q* gives an orange precipitate when reacted with 2, 4-DNP reagent, but has no reaction with Tollen's reagent. • *Understanding*

(a) Identify *P* and *Q* and write their IUPAC names.

(b) Write down the reaction for the formation of *Q* from *P*.

(c) Write down the reaction to prepare propan-2-ol from compound *Q*.

(ii) Arrange the following compounds in the increasing order of their property as indicated. • *Analysis*

(a) Acetaldehyde, acetone, di-*tert*-butyl ketone, methyl *tert*-butyl ketone (reactivity towards HCN).

(b) Benzoic acid, 4-nitrobenzoic acid, 3, 4-dinitrobenzoic acid, 4 methoxy benzoic acid (acid strength). [5]

Or

(i) An organic compound with molecular formula $C_5H_{10}O$ does not reduce Tollen's reagent but forms an addition compound with sodium hydrogen sulphite and gives a positive iodoform test. On vigorous oxidation, it gives ethanoic acid and propanoic acid.

Identify the compound and write all chemical equations for the reactions. • *Understanding*

(ii) Name the electrophile produced in the reaction of benzene with benzoyl chloride in the presence of anhydrous $AlCl_3$. Name the reaction also. • *Recall*

Answer Key

1. (B) (i) (b) (ii) (c) (iii) (d) (iv) (d) (v) (c) (vi) (c) (vii) (d)

Scan this QR code from your mobile phone to get the explanations of this Sample paper.

Knowledge Booster Zone

Welcome to the Knowledge Booster Zone !

This section is dedicated to enhancing your understanding of key concepts. Here, you will find chapter-wise revision notes designed to solidify your **foundational knowledge**. Use these notes to review and reinforce what you've learned, ensuring you're well-prepared for each topic.

Progress Tracker Tick the papers as you complete them.

- [ ] Solutions
- [ ] Chemical Kinetics
- [ ] Coordination Compounds
- [ ] Alcohols, Phenols and Ethers
- [ ] Organic Compounds Containing Nitrogen
- [ ] Electrochemistry
- [ ] *d* and *f*-block Elements
- [ ] Haloalkanes and haloarenes
- [ ] Aldehydes, Ketones and Carboxylic Acids
- [ ] Biomolecules

Chapter 1 Solutions

*Solutions are homogeneous mixtures of two or more than two components. The solutions containing two components are called **binary solutions**, e.g. salt solution.*

*In solution, a **solute** is a substance which is dissolved in another substance known as **solvent**. Solvent is present in a larger quantity than the solute.*

1. Expressing Concentrations of Solutions

The ways by which we can describe the concentration of the solution are given in the tabular form below.

S. No.	Concentration term with symbol	Formula	Definition
1.	Mass percentage $\%\left(\frac{W}{W}\right)$	$\frac{\text{Mass of solute}}{\text{Total mass of solution}} \times 100$	Amount of solute in grams present in 100 g of solution.
2.	Mass by volume percentage $\%\left(\frac{W}{V}\right)$	$\frac{\text{Mass of solute}}{\text{Total volume of solution (in mL)}} \times 100$	Amount of solute in grams dissolved in 100 mL of the solution
3.	Volume percentage $\%\left(\frac{V}{V}\right)$	$\frac{\text{Volume of solute}}{\text{Total volume of solution}} \times 100$	Volume of solute in mL dissolved in 100mL of the solution
4.	Strength (g/L) or (g/dm^3)	$\frac{\text{Mass of solute in grams}}{\text{Volume of solution (in L or } dm^3)}$	Amount of solute in grams present in one litre (or one dm^3) of solution
5.	Parts per million (ppm)	$\frac{\text{No. of parts of solute}}{\text{Total no. of parts of all components of solution}} \times 10^6$	Number of parts of solute present in million (10^6) parts of solution.
6.	Mole fraction (χ)	$\chi_A = \frac{n_A}{n_A + n_B}$	Ratio of number of moles of one component to the total number of moles of all the components
7.	Molarity (M)	$\frac{\text{Moles of solute}}{\text{Volume of solution (in L or } dm^3)}$	Number of moles of solute dissolved in one litre (or one dm^3) of solution.
8.	Molality (m)	$\frac{\text{Moles of solute}}{\text{Mass of solvent (in kg)}}$	Number of moles of solute per kilogram of the solvent.

2. Solubility of Gas in Liquid

The maximum amount of a solute that can be dissolved in a given amount of solvent at a given temperature is termed as **solubility** at that temperature.

(i) **Henry's law** Henry stated that, "the partial pressure of the gas in vapour phase (p) is proportional to the mole fraction (χ) of the gas in the solution". This is known as Henry's law. It is expressed as

$$p \propto \chi \quad \text{or} \quad p = K_H \chi$$

where, K_H is called Henry's constant.

(ii) Higher the value of K_H at a particular temperature, lower is the solubility of the gas in the liquid. K_H increases with increase of temperature implying that solubility decreases with increase of temperature.

3. Vapour Pressure of Solution

The pressure exerted by the vapours above the liquid surface in equilibrium with the liquid at a given temperature is called vapour pressure.

4. Raoult's Law

For solutions containing volatile solutes This law states that, for a solution of volatile solutes, the partial vapour pressure of each component in the solution is directly proportional to its mole fraction.

For component 1, $p_1 \propto \chi_1$ or $p_1 = p_1^\circ \chi_1$

Similarly, for component 2, $p_2 = p_2^\circ \chi_2$

$$p_{total} = p_1 + p_2 = p_1^\circ \chi_1 + p_2^\circ \chi_2$$

(where, p_1 and p_2 are partial vapour pressures, χ_1 and χ_2 are mole fractions and p_1° and p_2° are the *vapour pressures in the pure state of components 1 and 2, respectively).*

If y_1 and y_2 are the mole fractions of the components 1 and 2 respectively, in vapour phase, then $p_1 = y_1 \times p_{total}$

Similarly, $p_2 = y_2 \times p_{total}$

Raoult's law as a special case of Henry's law. *In the solution of a gas in a liquid, Raoult's law becomes a special case of Henry's law in which K_H becomes equal to pure component, p^0.*

5. Ideal Solutions

They obey Raoult's law over entire range of concentrations and temperatures. For these solutions, $\Delta H_{mix} = 0$ and $\Delta V_{mix} = 0$. In ideal solutions, A—B intermolecular interactions are nearly equal to A—A or B—B molecular interactions.

Solution of n-hexane and n-heptane, bromoethane and chloroethane, benzene and toluene etc., are nearly ideal in behaviour.

6. Non-ideal Solutions

They do not obey Raoult's law over entire range of concentrations and temperatures.

For such solutions, $\Delta H_{mix} \neq 0$ and $\Delta V_{mix} \neq 0$.

The vapour pressure of these solutions are either higher (solution exhibits positive deviation) or lower (solution exhibits negative deviation) than that predicted by Raoults' law.

Azeotropic mixtures

*The solutions of completely miscible liquids, which boils at constant temperature and can distilled over without any change in composition are called **azeotropes** or azeotropic mixtures.*

*The solutions which shows large negative deviation from Raoult's law, form **maximum boiling azeotropes** and the solutions which shows large positive deviation from Raoult's law, form **minimum boiling azeotropes**.*

7. Colligative Properties and Relative Molecular Mass of Non-volatile Solute

(i) ***Relative lowering of vapour pressure*** *of an ideal solution containing the non-volatile solute is equal to the mole fraction of the solute at a given temperature.*

Relative lowering of vapour pressure (Raoult's law for non-volatile solutes) is given by,

$$\frac{p^\circ - p}{p^\circ} = \chi_{solute} = \frac{n}{n + N}$$

where, p° = *vapour pressure of pure solvent*
p = *vapour pressure of solution*
χ = *mole fraction of solute*
n = *number of moles of solute*
N = *number of moles of solvent*

Its relation with molecular mass of solute (M′) is given as

$$M' = \frac{wM}{W\left(\frac{p^\circ - p}{p^\circ}\right)}$$

where, w = *given mass of the solute*
W = *given mass of the solvent*
M = *molecular mass of the solvent*

(ii) ***Depression in freezing point*** *When a non-volatile solute is added to a solvent, the freezing point of the solution is always lower than that of pure solvent as the vapour pressure of the solvent decreases in the presence of non-volatile solute. This difference in freezing point is known as depression in freezing point (ΔT_f).*

$$\Delta T_f = K_f m$$

where, K_f = *molal depression constant or cryoscopic constant*
m = *molality*

Its relation with molecular mass of solute (M′) is given as

$$M' = \frac{K_f \times w \times 1000}{\Delta T_f \times W \text{ (in gram)}}$$

where, all notations have their usual meaning.

(iii) ***Elevation in boiling point*** *The boiling point of a liquid is the temperature at which its vapour pressure becomes equal to the atmospheric pressure.*

When a non-volatile solute is added to a solvent, the boiling point of the solution is always higher than that of pure solvent as the vapour pressure of the solvent decreases in the presence of non-volatile solute and to make it boil, we have to increase the vapour pressure to atmospheric pressure by raising the temperature. This difference in boiling point is known as elevation in boiling point (ΔT_b).

$$\Delta T_b = K_b m$$

where, K_b = *molal elevation constant or ebullioscopic constant*
m = *molality*

Its relation with molecular mass of solute (M′) is given as

$$M' = \frac{K_b \times w \times 1000}{\Delta T_b \times W \text{ (in gram)}}$$

where, all the notations have their usual meaning.

(iv) ***Osmosis and osmotic pressure*** *The process of flow of solvent molecules through semipermeable membrane from the solution of lower concentration to solution of higher concentration is known as* ***osmosis****. The* ***osmotic pressure*** *of the solution is the pressure which just prevents the flow of solvent molecules.*

In other words, the pressure that must be applied to the solution in order to prevent the passage of solvent molecules into the solution through a semipermeable membrane separating the two is called ***osmotic pressure****.*

Vegetable membranes and animal membranes are natural membranes while copper ferrocyanide, silicates of iron, cobalt and nickel are chemical semipermeable membranes. When the pressure applied on the solution is greater than the osmotic pressure of the solution, the solvent molecules starts flowing from solution into the solvent, through the semipermeable membrane. This phenomenon is known as ***reverse osmosis****.*

$$\pi = CRT = \frac{n}{V}RT$$

where, C = concentration of solution,
R = gas constant, T = temperature,
n = number of moles of solute
V = volume

Its relation with molecular mass of solute (M′) is given as

$$M' = \frac{wRT}{\pi V}$$

where, all the notations have their usual meaning.

8. Abnormal Molecular Mass

For the substances undergoing association, dissociation, etc., in the solution, experimentally observed molecular mass determined from colligative properties is different from the normal value as expected from its chemical formula. This observed molecular mass is known as ***abnormal molecular mass****.*

(i) ***Association*** *Certain solutes undergoes molecular association in solution to form their aggregates. e.g. 2 molecules of solute after association forms a dimer.*

$$\underset{\text{Benzoic acid}}{2C_6H_5COOH} \rightleftharpoons \underset{\text{Dimer of benzoic acid}}{(C_6H_5COOH)_2}$$

Thus, the number of solute particles present in solution is less than the number of particles expected to be present, due to association.

(ii) ***Dissociation*** *Certain electrolytic solutes undergoes dissociation when dissolved in a solvent.*

(a) ***In case of strong electrolytic solutes*** *The number of particles of the solute in the solution is an exact multiple of the number of ions present in one mole of the solute.*

e.g. $$\underset{1.0\ mol}{KCl\ (aq)} \longrightarrow \underset{1.0\ mol}{K^+(aq)} + \underset{1.0\ mol}{Cl^-(aq)}$$

(b) ***In case of weak electrolytic solutes*** *The number of particles of the solute in the solution is not an exact multiple of the number of ions present in one mole of the solute but a part of it and depends on the degree of dissociation.*

e.g. $$CH_3COOH(aq) + H_2O(l) \rightleftharpoons H_3O^+(aq) + CH_3COO^-(aq)$$

$$NH_3(aq) + H_2O(l) \rightleftharpoons NH_4^+(aq) + \bar{O}H(aq)$$

9. van't Hoff Factor

It is the ratio of the experimental (observed) value of the colligative property to the calculated (normal) value of the same colligative property. It is used to find out the extent of dissociation or association.

$$\text{van't Hoff factor, } i = \frac{\text{Normal molar mass}}{\text{Abnormal molar mass}}$$

$$= \frac{\text{Total number of moles of particles after association or dissociation}}{\text{Number of moles of particles before association or dissociation}}$$

$$= \frac{\text{Observed colligative property}}{\text{Calculated colligative property}}$$

If $i > 1$*, solute undergoes dissociation and if* $i < 1$*, solute undergoes association.*

10. Calculation of Degree of Association or Dissociation

- *For association, when molecules of solute form dimer, n = 2.*

$$\text{Degree of association, } \alpha = \frac{i-1}{\left(\frac{1}{n}-1\right)}$$

where, n = number of solute molecules associating to make bigger molecular species.

- *For dissociation, of the solute AB type, m = 2 and of the solute* AB_2 *or* A_2B *type (*$CaCl_2$*,* Na_2SO_4*), m = 3.*

Degree of dissociation, $\alpha = \frac{i-1}{m-1}$.

where, m = number of particles formed per molecule of the electrolyte.

Inclusion of van't Hoff factor modifies the equations for colligative properties are as follows

(i) Relative lowering in vapour pressure of solvent.

$$\frac{p^\circ - p}{p^\circ} = i\frac{n}{N}$$

(ii) Elevation in boiling point, $\Delta T_b = iK_b m$

(iii) Depression in freezing point, $\Delta T_f = iK_f m$

(iv) Osmotic pressure of solution,

$$\pi = i\,(n/V)\,RT.$$

Chapter 2 Electrochemistry

1. Electrical Conductors and Electrical Insulators

The substances which allow the passage of current through them are called **electrical conductors.** The substances which do not allow the passage of electric current through them are called **electrical insulators.**

Classification of electrical conductors These are classified into two categories

(i) **Metallic conduction** The phenomenon of conduction of current by metals is called metallic conduction. It decreases with increase in temperature.

(ii) **Electrolytic conduction** The phenomenon of the flow of current due to the movement of ions is called electrolytic conduction. It increases with increase in temperature.

2. Electrolytes

The substances which conduct electric current either in aqueous state or fused state, on account of the movement of ions and undergo a chemical change (decomposition) during the passage of electric current through them are called electrolytes, e.g. ionic compounds like NaCl, KCl, NaOH, HCl, NH_4OH etc.

3. Voltaic or Galvanic or Electrochemical Cell

A device which can generate electricity by means of a chemical reaction is called an **electrochemical cell.** It converts chemical energy into electrical energy.

A **galvanic cell** generates electric current, on account of a redox reaction occurring in it.

4. Representation of Galvanic Cell

While representing a galvanic cell, the oxidation electrode (anode) is always written at the left and the reduction electrode (cathode) always at the right. Direct contact of the two solutions (i.e. through a porous diaphragm) is shown by a single vertical line (|) while the contact of the two solutions through a salt bridge is shown by two parallel vertical lines (||).

$$\underset{\text{Anode}}{Zn(s)\,|\,Zn^{2+}(aq, C_1)}\,||\,\underset{\text{Cathode}}{Cu^{2+}(aq, C_2)\,|\,Cu(s)}$$

$$\underset{\substack{\text{Oxidation electrode} \\ \text{(Oxidation half-cell)}}}{\text{Negative electrode } (-)} \xrightarrow{\text{Flow of electrons}} \underset{\substack{\text{Reduction electrode} \\ \text{(Reduction half-cell)}}}{\text{Positive electrode } (+)}$$

5. Electrode Potential

The potential difference developed between a metal and a solution containing its own ions (in equilibrium) is called electrode potential of that metal or electrode. It is the tendency of an electrode to lose or gain electrons, when it is in contact with its own ions in a solution.

Factors affecting electrode potential are

(i) nature of metal or electrode

(ii) concentration of metal ions in solution

(iii) temperature.

6. Electrochemical Series

The arrangement of various standard half-cells in order of their decreasing values of standard reduction potentials is called electrochemical series.

7. Standard Electrode Potential (E°)

The potential difference between the standard hydrogen half-cell and the half-cell placed in contact with Standard Hydrogen Electrode (SHE) is called standard electrode potential, provided all dissolved species at unit molarity, all gases at one atmospheric pressure, all solids in their most stable form and temperature is maintained at 25°C.

8. EMF of an Electrochemical Cell

The difference between the electrode potentials of two half-cells is known as cell potential or cell voltage. If no current is drawn from the cell, it is called electromotive force (emf) of the cell.

$$E_{cell} = E_{cathode} - E_{anode} = E_{right} - E_{left}$$

9. Nernst Equation

For an electrode involving the process of reduction, Nernst equation can be written as follows

$$M^{n+}(aq) + ne^- \longrightarrow M(s)$$

or $$E_{cell} = E^{\circ}_{cell} - \frac{2.303RT}{nF} \log \frac{[M(s)]}{[M^{n+}(aq)]}$$

For emf of cell under standard conditions,

$$E_{cell} = E^{\circ}_{cell} - \frac{0.0591}{n}$$

$$\log \frac{(\text{Concentration of products})}{(\text{Concentration of reactants})}$$

10. Relationship between Equilibrium constant and Standard potential of the cell.

$$E_{cell} = E^{\circ}_{cell} - \frac{2.303RT}{nF} \log K_c$$

[where, K_C is equilibrium constant]

or, $$E^{\circ}_{cell} = \frac{2.30RT}{nF} \log(K_c)$$

[$\because E_{cell} = 0$ at equilibrium]

$$= \frac{0.059}{n} \log K_C$$

11. Gibbs Free Energy and EMF of a Cell

The relation between emf of a cell in the standard state and the standard free energy change is

$$\Delta G^{\circ} = -nFE^{\circ}_{cell} = W_{max}$$

where, W_{max} = maximum work, n = number of moles of electrons transferred, F = Faraday constant ⇒ 96500C.

12. Electrolytic Conductance

The ease of flow of current through an electrolytic solution is called electrolytic conductance.

13. Conductance of Electrolytic solutions

Terms related to conductance of electrolytic solutions are given in the tabular form below.

S. No.	Terms with Symbol	Formula	Unit	Definition
1.	Conductance (G)	$G = \frac{1}{R} = \rho \frac{A}{l}$ where, ρ = Resistivity or specific resistance	S or Ohm^{-1}	It is the reciprocal of resistance (R)
2.	Resistance (R)	$R = \frac{\rho l}{A}$ where, $G^* = \frac{l}{A}$ = cell constant	Ohm	It is directly proportional to length and inversely proportional to area of cross-section
3.	Specific conductance or conductivity (k)	$K = \frac{1}{\rho} = \frac{l}{R \cdot A}$	$Ohm^{-1}cm^{-1}$ or Scm^{-1}	It is the conductance of a solution of 1 m length with area of cross section of 1 m^2
4.	Molar conductivity or Molar conductance	$\Lambda_m = \frac{K \times 1000}{M}$ where, M = Molarity of solution	$Scm^2 mol^{-1}$ or $Ohm^{-1}cm^2 mol^{-1}$	Conductance of a solution whose volume contains one mole of solute placed between parallel electrodes separated by 1 cm and having area to hold whole of the solution.
5.	Equivalent conductance or Equivalent conductivity (Λ_{eq})	$(\Lambda_{eq}) = \frac{k \times 1000}{N}$ where, N = normality of Solution	$Scm^2 eq^{-1}$ or $Ohm^{-1}cm^2 eq^{-1}$	It is the conductance of a solution containing 1g equivalent of the electrolyte

14. Variation of Conductivity and Molar Conductivity with Concentration

Conductivity always decreases with decrease in concentration of both strong and weak electrolytes. This is due to the fact that the number of ions that carry current in a unit volume of solution always decreases with decrease in concentration. On the other hand, molar conductivity increases with decrease in concentration.This is because the total volume V of solution containing one mole of electrolyte also increase.

In case of weak electrolytes, the Λ^{∞}_m values increases steeply with dilution, especially in the low concentration region.

15. Kohlrausch's Law

Molar conductance of an electrolyte at infinite dilution is equal to the sum of the individual molar conductances of cations and anions with each *conductance term multiplied by the number of respective ions present in the formula unit of the electrolyte.*

$$\Lambda_m^\infty = \Lambda_+^\infty + \Lambda_-^\infty \quad \text{or} \quad \nu_+\Lambda_+^\infty + \nu_-\Lambda_-^\infty$$

(where, Λ_+^∞ and Λ_-^∞ are the molar conductivities of cations and anions respectively and ν_+ and ν_- are the number of cations and anions per formula unit of the electrolyte, respectively.

16. Degree of Dissociation

The ratio of molar conductivity (Λ_m) at a specific concentration, C to the molar conductivity at infinite dilution, i.e. limiting molar conductivity, Λ_m^∞ is known as degree of dissociation.

At any concentration C, if α is the degree of dissociation, then for a weak electrolyte, $\alpha = \frac{\Lambda_m}{\Lambda_m^\infty}$.

17. Electrolysis

It is the process of decomposition of an electrolyte by passing electricity through its aqueous solution or molten state.

18. Faraday's Laws of Electrolysis

Michael Faraday studied the phenomenon of electrolysis and formulated two important quantitative laws governing electrolysis. These are

(i) ***Faraday's first law of electrolysis*** *It states the amount of substance deposited at a particular electrode as a result of electrolysis is directly proportional to the quantity of electricity passed*

$$w = Z \times Q \text{ or } w = Z \times i \times t$$

(ii) ***Faraday's second law of electrolysis*** *When the same quantity of electricity is passed through the solutions of different electrolytes connected in series, the masses of the substances produced at the electrodes are directly proportional to their equivalent weights.*

$$\frac{\text{Weight of A}}{\text{Weight of B}} = \frac{\text{Equivalent weight of A}}{\text{Equivalent weight of B}}$$

Products of Electrolysis

Electrolyte	Products		Reactions involved	
	At Cathode	At anode	At Cathode	At anode
Molten NaCl	Na metal	Cl_2 gas	$Na^+(aq) + e^- \longrightarrow Na(s)$	$Cl^-(l) \longrightarrow \frac{1}{2}Cl_2(g) + e^-$
Aqueous NaCl	H_2 gas	Cl_2 gas	$H_2O(l) + e^- \longrightarrow \frac{1}{2}H_2(aq) + OH^-(aq)$	$Cl^-(aq) \longrightarrow \frac{1}{2}Cl_2(g) + e^-$
Dil. H_2SO_4	H_2 gas	O_2 gas	$H^-(aq) + e^- \longrightarrow \frac{1}{2}H_2(g)$	$2H_2O(l) \longrightarrow O_2(g) + 4H^+(aq) + 4e^-$
Conc. H_2SO_4	H_2 gas	$S_2O_8^{2-}$	$H^+(aq) + e^- \longrightarrow \frac{1}{2}H_2(g)$	$2SO_4^{2-}(aq) \longrightarrow S_2O_8^{2-}(aq) + 2e^-$

19. Battery

It is the arrangement of two or more galvanic cells connected, together in series.

Commercial cells *(Batteries)*

These are of two types

(i) ***Primary cell*** *In this cell, redox reaction occurs once and, hence it becomes dead after sometime, e.g. dry cell and mercury cell.*

(ii) ***Secondary cell*** *It can be recharged by passing a direct current in it. It is also called rechargeable cell, e.g. lead storage battery and nickel cadmium storage cell.*

20. Fuel Cells

It converts chemical energy of fuel directly into electrical energy, e.g. H_2-O_2 fuel cell. The electrode reactions of H_2-O_2 fuel cell are

Cathode $O_2(g) + 2H_2O(l) + 4e^- \longrightarrow 4OH^-(aq)$

Anode $2H_2(g) + 4OH^-(aq) \longrightarrow 4H_2O(l) + 4e^-$

21. Corrosion

The process of slow conversion of metals into their undesirable compounds by the action of moisture and other gases present in the atmosphere is called corrosion, e.g. rusting of iron involves the following reaction:

$$2Fe(s) + O_2(g) + 4H^+(aq) \longrightarrow 2Fe^{2+}(aq) + 2H_2O(l), \; E^\circ_{cell} = 1.67 \text{ V}$$

Methods of prevention of corrosion *are barrier protection sacrificial protection and antirusto solutions.*

Chapter 3 Chemical Kinetics

1. Scope and Importance of Kinetics of Reaction

In kinetics, we study the rate of chemical reaction along with the course of all physical and chemical processes induced during the reaction. This helps in finding the conditions to maximise the yield of products.

2. Classification of Reactions on the Basis of Rate of Reaction

(i) **Very fast reactions** The reactions (involving ions), which proceed, so rapidly that they may be practically considered instantaneous, are called very fast reactions, e.g. neutralisation of a strong acid by a strong base.

(ii) **Very slow reactions** The reactions, which proceed very slowly and may take even several months for their completion are called very slow reactions, e.g. rusting of iron.

(iii) **Slow or moderate reactions** The reactions that are neither very fast nor very slow and whose rates can be measured conveniently are called slow reactions, e.g. hydrolysis of esters.

3. Reaction Rate and Factors Affecting Rate of Reaction

The rate of a chemical reaction may be defined as the change in concentration of any of the reactants or products per unit time.

Units of rate of reaction is mol $L^{-1}s^{-1}$ or atm s^{-1} (when reactants and products are in gaseous state).

Average Rate of a Reaction

The change in concentration of any of the reactants or products per unit time over a specified interval of time is called the rate of the given reaction.

For a reaction like,

$$A + 2B \longrightarrow 3C$$

$$\text{Rate} = -\frac{\Delta[A]}{\Delta t} = \frac{-1\Delta[B]}{2\Delta t} = \frac{1\ \Delta[C]}{3\ \Delta t}$$

Instantaneous Rate of Reaction

The rate of change of concentration of any of the reactants or products at a particular instant of time for a given temperature is called instantaneous rate of a given reaction at that instant of time.

It is expressed as $r_{inst} = \frac{-d[R]}{dt} = \frac{d[P]}{dt}$

Factors Affecting the Rate of Reaction

(i) **Nature of reactants** The reactions involving polar and ionic substances are quite fast, whereas the reactions involving covalent compounds are much slower.

(ii) **Concentration of reactants** Rate of reaction increases on increasing the concentration of reactants due to increase in molecular collisions.

(iii) **Temperature** Usually, rate increases with increase in temperature.

For most of the homogeneous reactions, the rate becomes doubled for every 10° rise in temperature.

Temperature coefficient

$$= \frac{\text{Rate constant } k \text{ at } T + 10°K}{\text{Rate constant at } T°C}$$

(iv) **Presence of catalyst** The presence of catalyst in a reaction, also affects the rate of many reactions. If a catalyst increases the rate of a reaction, it is called **positive catalyst** and if it slows down the reaction, it is called **negative catalyst**.

(v) **Surface area** The rate of a reaction increases with an increase in surface area of the reactant.

4. Law of Mass Action

At constant temperature, the rate of a chemical reaction is directly proportional to the product of active masses of reacting species, with each active mass term raised to the power equal to the stoichiometric coefficient of that species in the chemical reaction.

e.g. For a general reaction, $aA + bB \longrightarrow$ Products, rate of reaction $\propto [A]^a\ [B]^b$, where $[A]$ and $[B]$ are active masses of reactants A and B, respectively.

5. Rate Law

It is the expression in which the reaction rate is given in terms of molar concentration of reactants with each term raised to some power, which may or may not be same as the stoichiometric coefficient of the reacting species in a balanced chemical equation.

Rate law for a chemical reaction cannot be decided from the balanced chemical equation, i.e. theoretically. It has to be determined experimentally.

6. General Rate Equation

For equation, $aA + bB \longrightarrow$ Products, if rate of reaction depends upon the pth power of concentration of A and qth power of concentration of B, we have

$$Rate = k[A]^p[B]^q \quad ...(i)$$

$\therefore$ General rate of equation is,

$$Rate = k \text{ (concentration of the reactant)}^n$$

where, n is the order of the reaction (discussed below).

For equation (i), $p + q = n$

7. Rate Constant (Specific Reaction Rate)

For reaction, $aA + bB \longrightarrow$ Products, rate law is given by, $rate \propto [A]^a\,[B]^b$

$$Rate = k\,[A]^a\,[B]^b$$

If $[A] = [B] = 1 \text{ mol L}^{-1}$

$\therefore \quad Rate = k$

Thus, the rate constant of a reaction is equal to the rate of reaction, when the concentration of each of the reactants is unity.

Units of Rate Constant

The general unit of rate constant is $(\text{mol L}^{-1})^{1-n}$ s^{-1} where, n represents the overall sum of the powers appearing in the rate law.

For a gaseous reaction, unit of rate constant is $atm^{1-n}\ s^{-1}$.

Characteristics of Rate Constant

(i) Higher the value of k, greater is the rate of the reaction.
(ii) A particular reaction has a definite value of k at a particular temperature.
(iii) The value of rate constant for a particular reaction increases with an increase in temperature.
(iv) The rate constant does not depend upon the initial concentration of reactants.
(v) Its units depend upon the overall order of the reaction (the sum of powers to which the concentration terms have been raised in the rate law).

8. Order of a Reaction

The power to which concentration term of a particular reactant in the rate law is raised, is called the order of reaction with respect to that reactant.

The sum of all the powers to which all the concentration terms in the rate law are raised to express the observed rate of reaction is called the **overall order of reaction.**

e.g. For the general reaction,

$$aA + bB + cC \longrightarrow \text{Products},$$

$$Rate = k[A]^p[B]^q[C]^r$$

where, p represents the order of reaction with respect to A. Similarly, q and r represent the order of reaction with respect to B and C, respectively.

Hence, overall order of reaction, $n = p + q + r$.

Order of reaction usually differ from the stoichiometric coefficients (a, b, c) of the reactant.

9. Molecularity

It is the number of reacting species taking part in an elementary reaction, which must collide simultaneously in order to bring about a chemical reaction. It is a theoretical concept and can never be zero or fractional.

10. Mechanism of a Reaction

A sequence of intermediate steps or all elementary processes proper to account for the overall stoichiometry of a reaction is called the mechanism of the reaction.

The simple chemical reactions, which occur only in one step are called elementary reactions, whereas the reactions which occur in two or more steps are called complex reactions.

The overall rate of a complex reaction is governed by the rate of slowest elementary step, which is known as **rate determining step.**

11. Different Order Reactions

(i) **Zero Order Reaction** It means the rate of the reaction is directly proportional to zeroth power of the concentration of reactant A, i.e. rate does not depend upon the concentration of reactants.

$$Rate = k[A]^0$$

or $$k = \frac{[A]_0 - [A]}{t}$$

where, $[A]_0$ is the initial concentration of reactant and $[A]$ is the concentration of reactant at time t.

A plot of concentration [A] with time, t is a straight line with slope = – K

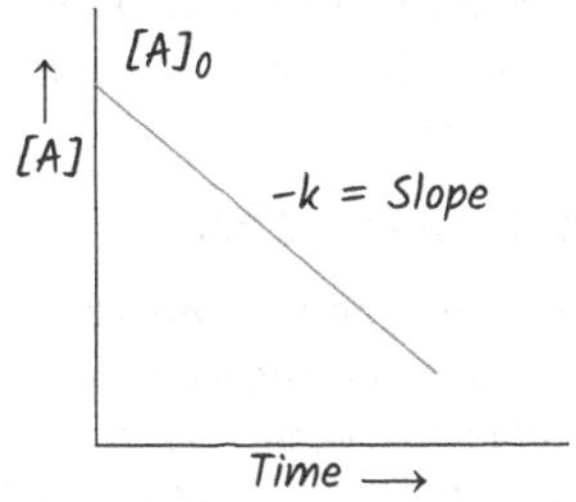

Variation in the concentration vs time plot for zero order reaction

The photochemical reactions follow zero order reaction.

(ii) **First Order Reaction** It means that rate of reaction is directly proportional to the concentration of the reactant A.

i.e. Rate = $k[A]$

or $$k = \frac{2.303}{t}\log\frac{[A]_0}{[A]}$$

A plot of $\log\frac{[A]_0}{[A]}$ with time, t for a Ist order reaction is a straight line with slope $= \frac{k}{2.303}$

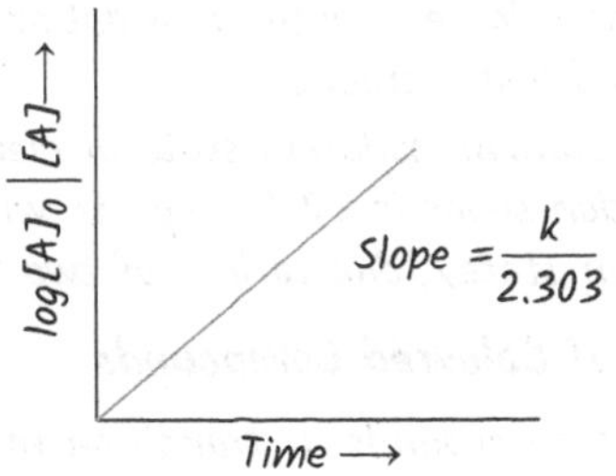

variation of $\log\frac{[A]_0}{[A]}$ vs time plot for Ist order reaction.

Radioactive disintegration follows first order kinetics.

(iii) **Pseudo First Order Reaction** The reactions which apparently seem to be of higher order but behave as first order reaction under certain conditions, are known as pseudo first order reactions, e.g. hydrolysis of ethyl acetate in the presence of acid and inversion of cane sugar.

12. Half-life ($t_{1/2}$)

The time taken for half of the reactant to react or the time taken for half of the reaction to get completed or the time in which the concentration of a reactant is reduced to half of its original value is called half-life of the reaction.

For a zero order reaction, $k = \frac{[A]_0 - [A]}{t}$

At, $t = t_{1/2}$, $[A] = \frac{1}{2}[A]_0$

$$\therefore \quad k = \frac{[A]_0 - \frac{1}{2}[A]_0}{t_{1/2}}$$

$$\Rightarrow \quad t_{1/2} = \frac{[A]_0}{2k}$$

For a first order reaction,

$$k = \frac{2.303}{t}\log\frac{[A]_0}{[A]}$$

At, $t = t_{1/2}$, $$k = \frac{2.303}{t_{1/2}}\log\frac{[A]_0}{[A]_0/2}$$

$$\therefore \quad t_{1/2} = \frac{0.693}{k}$$

Amount of reactant left after n half-lives $= \frac{[A]_0}{2^n}$

where, $[A]_0$ is the initial concentration of reactant.

13. Types of Reactions on the Basis of Concept of Energy

(i) **Endothermic reaction** A reaction in which energy is supplied to the reactants from the surroundings for the reaction is called endothermic reaction.

(ii) **Exothermic reaction** A reaction in which energy is evolved alongwith the products is called exothermic reaction.

14. Arrhenius Equation

It can be expressed as $k = Ae^{-E_a/RT}$ where, A is a constant (pre-exponential factor) known as frequency factor.

It denotes the frequency of binary collisions of reactant molecules per second per unit volume. E_a is activation energy, R is gas constant, T represents temperature (in K) and k is the rate constant of the reaction.

On taking log on both side of the above reaction.

or $$\log_{10} k = \frac{-E_a}{2.303\,RT} + \log_{10} A$$

If k_1 and k_2 are the rate constants measured at two temperatures T_1 and T_2 respectively, then

$$\log_{10}\frac{k_2}{k_1} = \frac{E_a}{2.303\,R}\left[\frac{1}{T_1} - \frac{1}{T_2}\right]$$

15. Activation Energy

It is the minimum amount of energy that the reactant molecules must acquire in order to cross the energy barrier and to change into the products.

Thus, Activation energy = Threshold energy – Average energy possessed by the reactant molecules.

16. Effect of Catalyst on Activation Energy

The formation of activated complex provides an alternative path of lower activation energy as compared to uncatalysed reaction. This allows a large number of reactant molecules to cross over the energy barrier in order to transform into products.

17. Collision Theory

It is based on kinetic theory of gases. It produces greater insight into the energetic and mechanastic aspects of reactions.

Conditions for a Chemical Change

(i) A reaction occurs only when the reactant molecules encounter together, i.e. undergo effective collisions with one another.

(ii) Only those collisions are effective which acquire a definite amount of energy. The minimum amount of energy required by the reacting molecules to produce effective collisions is called ***threshold energy****. As the temperature increases, the number of effective collisions increases. Hence, the rate of a reaction increases appreciably with small rise in temperature.*

Chapter 4 d and f-block Elements

1. d-Block Elements

The elements in which outermost electron lies into the d-subshell of penultimate shell are called d-block elements. The elements of d-block of the periodic table are known as transition elements.

They have the general electronic configuration, $(n-1)\,d^{1-10}ns^{1-2}$.

Exception in electronic configuration

Cr : $3d^5 4s^1$ instead of $3d^4 4s^2$

Cu : $3d^{10} 4s^1$ instead of $3d^9 4s^2$

General Characteristics of d-Block Elements

Some important compounds of transition elements are as follows

1. Atomic Radii and Ionic Radii

Atomic radii of 3d series decreases till the middle with an increase in atomic number.

However, there is a slight increase in the atomic radii near the end of series. The atomic radii of corresponding elements of second (4d) and third (5d) transition series are nearly same due to ***lanthanoid contraction****.*

2. Metallic Character

Almost all transition elements exhibit typical metallic properties, like metallic lustre, malleability, ductility, high tensile strength, etc.

3. Ionisation Enthalpy

The ionisation enthalpies of transition elements are quite high and lies between those of s-block and p-block elements.

The first ionisation enthalpy increases with increase in atomic number across a given transition series, although the increase is not very regular.

4. Oxidation State

They exhibit a large variety of oxidation state except the first and last element.

The most common oxidation state of elements of first transition series is +2 (except Sc which has only +3 oxidation state), due to loss of two 4s electrons.

5. Formation of Coloured Compounds

Most of the compounds of transition metals are coloured both in solid state and in aqueous solution, due to d-d transitions and charge transfer.

6. Magnetic Properties

Due to presence of unpaired electrons in d-orbital, many compounds of transition elements are paramagnetic in nature. As the number of unpaired electron increases, paramagnetic character increases.

7. Complex Compounds

The tendency to form complex ions/compounds is due to (i) small size, (ii) high charge on the transition metal ions, (iii) availability of vacant d-orbitals of suitable energy to accommodate lone pair of electrons donated by the ligand atoms, e.g. $[Fe(CN)_6]^{3-}$, $[Fe(CN)_6]^{4-}$, etc.

8. Catalytic Property

Most of the transition metals and their compounds act as a catalyst because of the variable oxidation states and the presence of vacant d-orbitals due to which they can form a variety of unstable intermediates.

9. Alloy Formation

A large number of alloys are formed due to their similar atomic size. Alloys, so formed are very hard with high melting points. Some examples are brass (Cu-Zn), bronze (Cu-Sn).

10. Applications of Transition metals

(i) TiO_2 is used in pigment industry.

(ii) V_2O_5 is used as a catalyst in the manufacturing of sulphuric acid.

(iii) Light sensitive properties of AgBr are used in photographic industries.

Potassium Dichromate ($K_2Cr_2O_7$)

Preparation from chromite ore

($FeO \cdot Cr_2O_3$ or $FeCr_2O_4$) Potassium dichromate is generally manufactured from chromite ore, $FeO \cdot Cr_2O_3$ or $FeCr_2O_4$.

$$4FeO.Cr_2O_3 + 8Na_2CO_3 + 7O_2 \longrightarrow \underset{\text{Sodium chromate}}{8Na_2CrO_4} + 2Fe_2O_3 + 8CO_2$$

$$2Na_2CrO_4 + H_2SO_4 \longrightarrow \underset{\text{Sodium dichromate}}{Na_2Cr_2O_7} + Na_2SO_4 + H_2O$$

$$Na_2Cr_2O_7 + 2KCl \longrightarrow \underset{\text{Potassium dichromate}}{K_2Cr_2O_7} + 2NaCl$$

Structure of chromate and dichromate ion

The structure of chromate ion is tetrahedral and dichromate ion consists of two tetrahedra sharing one corner with Cr— O— Cr bond angle of 126°.

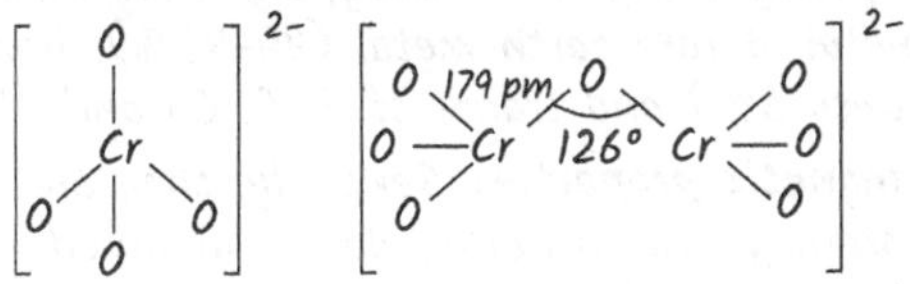

Chemical Properties

(i) **Oxidising properties in acidic medium**

$K_2Cr_2O_7$ acts as a good oxidising agent in acidic medium.

$$K_2Cr_2O_7 + 4H_2SO_4 \longrightarrow K_2SO_4 + Cr_2(SO_4)_3 + 4H_2O + 3[O]$$

Or

$$\underset{\text{Orange}}{Cr_2O_7^{2-}} + 14H^+ + 6e^- \longrightarrow \underset{\text{Green}}{2Cr^{3+}} + 7H_2O$$

It oxidises iodides, sulphides, nitrites, etc.

$$6I^- \longrightarrow 3I_2 + 6e^-,$$

$$3H_2S \longrightarrow 6H^+ + 3S + 6e^-$$

$$6Fe^{2+} \longrightarrow 6Fe^{3+} + 6e^-$$

(ii) **Oxidising properties in basic medium** In alkaline solution (pH >7), orange colour of $Cr_2O_7^{2-}$ (dichromate ion) changes to yellow colour due to the formation of CrO_4^{2-} (chromate ion).

$$\underset{\text{Orange red}}{K_2Cr_2O_7} + 2KOH \longrightarrow \underset{\text{Yellow}}{2K_2CrO_4} + H_2O$$

(iii) **Interconversion of K_2CrO_4 and $K_2Cr_2O_7$**

On acidifying the K_2CrO_4 solution, the colour changes to orange-red due to the reformation of dichromate.

$$2K_2CrO_4 + H_2SO_4 \longrightarrow K_2Cr_2O_7 + K_2SO_4 + H_2O$$

or $2CrO_4^{2-} + 2H^+ \longrightarrow Cr_2O_7^{2-} + H_2O$

Reason for inter conversion In dichromate solution, the orange-red $Cr_2O_7^{2-}$ ions are invariably in equilibrium with yellow CrO_4^{2-} ions.

$$\underset{\text{Orange-red}}{Cr_2O_7^{2-}} + H_2O \rightleftharpoons \underset{\text{Yellow}}{2CrO_4^{2-}} + 2H^+$$

Uses

(i) Oxidising agent in organic chemistry.

(ii) In volumetric analysis, for tanning of leather and in chromyl chloride test.

Potassium Permanganate ($KMnO_4$)

Preparation

(i) **From pyrolusite ore**

$$2MnO_2 + 4KOH + O_2 \xrightarrow[\text{KNO}_3 \text{ (Oxidising agent)}]{\text{Heat}} \underset{\text{Potassium manganate (Dark green)}}{2K_2MnO_4} + 2H_2O$$

(ii) Commercially, it is prepared by alkaline oxidative fusion of MnO_2 followed by electrolytic oxidation of manganate VI.

$$MnO_2 \xrightarrow[\text{Oxidised with air}]{\text{Fused with KOH}} \underset{\text{Managanate ion}}{MnO_4^{2-}}$$

$$MnO_4^{2-} \xrightarrow[\text{In alkaline solution}]{\text{Electrolytic oxidation}} \underset{\text{Permanganate ion}}{MnO_4^{-}}$$

Structure of Manganate and Permanganate ion

The manganate ($M_nO_4^{2-}$) and permanganate (MnO_4^-) ions are tetrahedral.

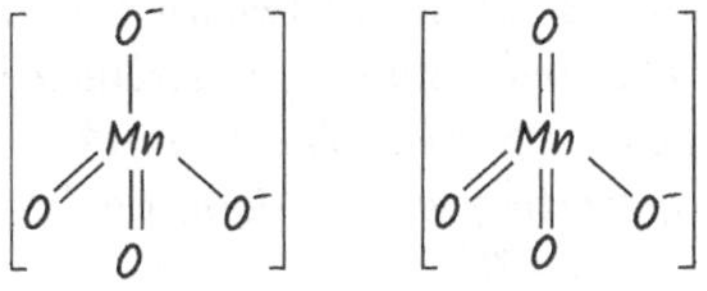

(Paramagnetic) (Diamagnetic)

Properties of Redox Reaction

$KMnO_4$ shows oxidising nature in acidic medium, basic medium and neutral medium. These are as follows

(i) **Acidic medium**

(a) **Ferrous salts to ferric salts**

$$2KMnO_4 + 3H_2SO_4 \longrightarrow K_2SO_4 + 2MnSO_4 + 3H_2O + 5O$$

$$[2FeSO_4 + H_2SO_4 + [O] \longrightarrow Fe_2(SO_4)_3 + H_2O] \times 5$$

$$\underset{\text{Ferrous sulphate}}{2KMnO_4 + 8H_2SO_4 + 10FeSO_4} \longrightarrow K_2SO_4 + 2MnSO_4 + \underset{\text{Ferric sulphate}}{5Fe_2(SO_4)_3} + 8H_2O$$

(b) **Iodide to iodine**

$$[MnO_4^- + 8H^+ + 5e^- \longrightarrow Mn^{2+} + 4H_2O] \times 2$$

$$[2I^- \longrightarrow I_2 + 2e^-] \times 5$$

$$2MnO_4^- + 10I^- + 16H^+ \longrightarrow 2Mn^{2+} + 5I_2 + 8H_2O$$

(c) **Oxalate to carbon dioxide**

$$[MnO_4^- + 8H^+ + 5e^- \longrightarrow Mn^{2+} + 4H_2O] \times 2$$

$$[C_2O_4^{2-} \longrightarrow 2CO_2 + 2e^{2-}] \times 5$$

$$2MnO_4^- + 5C_2O_4^{2-} + 16H^+ \longrightarrow 2Mn^{2+} + 10CO_2 + 8H_2O$$

(ii) **Basic medium and neutral medium**

Oxidises potassium iodide to potassium iodate

$$2KMnO_4 + H_2O \longrightarrow 2MnO_2 + 2KOH + 3O$$

$$KI + 3[O] \longrightarrow KIO_3$$

$$2KMnO_4 + KI + H_2O \longrightarrow 2MnO_2 + 2KOH + KIO_3$$

Uses

(i) Widely used in laboratory and industry as an oxidising agent in redox reaction.

(ii) Germicide, sterilising wells of drinking water, washing wounds.

II. f-Block Elements

The elements in which the differentiating electrons enter into (n – 2) f-subshell, are called f-block elements or **inner-transition elements**. f-block elements consist of two series called lanthanoid series and actinoid series.

I. Lanthanoids or Lanthanoid Series

These elements follow lanthanum (La) in the periodic table and resemble, it strongly in physical and chemical properties. There are 14 elements in this series, starting with cerium, Ce (Z=58) to lutetium, Lu (Z=71).

Lanthanoid Contraction and its Consequences

On moving from La to Lu in lanthanoid series, the size of atoms and ions decreases regularly.

The 4f-orbitals containing electrons are too diffused to screen the nucleus as effectively as the more localised inner shell.

Hence, the attraction of the nucleus for the outermost electrons increases steadily with increase in atomic number.

Thus, due to imperfect shielding of 4f-electrons, a contraction in the electron cloud of 4f-subshell increases.

Due to lanthanoid contraction, the basic character of oxides and hydroxides decreases from La $(OH)_3$ to Lu $(OH)_3$. Zr/Hf; Nb/Ta and Mo/W are almost identical in size.

General Characteristics of Lanthanoids

(i) **General electronic configuration** In general, the electronic configuration of f-block elements is $[Xe]4f^{1-14}5d^{0-1}6s^2$. Only Ce, Gd and Lu have electrons in 5d orbitals as well.

(ii) **Oxidation state** The most common oxidation state of lanthanoids is + 3. Oxidation states +2 and +4 also exist but they relapse to +3.

(iii) **Formation of coloured compounds** Several trivalent lanthanide ions are coloured in solid state as well as in aqueous solution.

Colour of compounds of members of this series arises due to f-f electronic transition.

(iv) **Complex formation** Lanthanide ions have very less tendency to form complexes, because of their low density due to large size and high charge.

(v) **Alloy formation** With other metals especially Fe, they easily forms alloy, e.g. alloy misch metal of rare earth metal (94-95%), iron (upto 5%) and traces of S, C, Ca and Al.

(vi) **Magnetic properties** Generally, they are paramagnetic in nature due to unpaired electrons in f-orbital.

(vii) **Chemical reactivity** Lanthanoids react with oxygen, hydrogen, halogens, sulphur, nitrogen, carbon and water. The reactions are given below

(a) $4Ln + 3O_2 \longrightarrow 2Ln_2O_3$

(b) $2Ln + 3H_2 \longrightarrow 2LnH_3$

(c) $2Ln + 3X_2 \longrightarrow 2LnX_3$

(d) $Ln + 2C \xrightarrow{2773\text{ K}} LnC_2$

(e) $2Ln + 3S \longrightarrow Ln_2S_3$

(f) $2Ln + N_2 \longrightarrow 2LnN$

2. Actinoids or Actinoid Series

These elements from actinium (Ac) to lawrencium (Lr) closely resemble in physical and chemical properties.

General electronic configuration Actinoids follow the general electronic configuration of $[Rn]5f^{1-14}6d^{0-1}7s^2$.

Comparison with lanthanoides

(i) The decrease in atomic (or ionic) radii in actinoid elements (actinoid contraction) is greater than lanthanoid contraction because 5 f-electrons have poor shielding effect as compared to 4 f-electrons.

Therefore, the effect of increased nuclear charge leading to contraction in size is more in case of actinoid elements.

(ii) Actinoids exhibit more number of oxidation states than lanthanoids. This is due to the fact that 5f, 6d and 7s levels are of comparable energies.

(iii) Actinoids have stronger tendency towards complex formation as compare to lanthanoids.

Uses of Lanthanoids and Actinoids

(i) U and Pu are used as fuels in atomic reactors.

(ii) Uranium salts are used in medicine, in the treatment of cancer.

(iii) Lanthanoids are useful in the form of their alloys and compounds, e.g. an alloy containing Mg and about 3% misch metal is used in jet engine parts.

(iv) Mixed oxides of lanthanoids are used as catalysts in petroleum cracking.

Chapter 5 Coordination Compounds

1. Double Salts

These are the addition compounds that lose their identity in solution. They exist only in solid state and have properties same as those of constituent compounds.

2. Coordination Compounds

These are those addition compounds which retain their identity in solid as well as in aqueous solution. Their properties are different from their constituents.

3. Some Important Terms Used in Coordination Compounds

(i) **Central metal atoms or ions** In a coordination entity, the metal atoms or ions with which a definite number of ligands are attached in a definite geometry are called central metal atoms or ions.

e.g. Fe^{2+}, Cu^{2+}, Ni^{2+}, Pt^{2+} are central metal ions which are also known as **Lewis acids**.

(ii) **Ligand** It is a charged ion or neutral molecule which is capable of donating a pair of electrons to the central atom or ion for the formation of a coordinate bond. It is also as known **Lewis base**.

Ligands can be classified as :

(a) **Monodentate ligands** These have only one donor atom which is bound to central metal ion, e.g. Cl^-, NH_3, CO, H_2O, etc.

(b) **Bidentate ligands** These ligands can bind through two donor atoms, e.g. 1, 2-ethanediamine (en).

(c) **Polydentate ligands** These have more than two donor atoms in the molecule. e.g. Ethylenediamine tetraacetate (EDTA) is a hexadentate ligand.

(d) **Chelating ligands** The ligands coordinating through two or more donor groups leading to formation of a ring with metal ion are called chelating ligands and such complexes are chelate complexes, e.g. $[Pt(en)_2]Cl_2]^+$.

(e) **Ambidentate ligands** When a ligand containing two different donor atoms attach to the central metal atom through any of its donor atoms, is called ambidentate ligand.

e.g. NO_2, SCN^-, ONO^- etc.

(iii) **Coordination entity** (Complex ion) Coordination entity constitutes a central metal atom or ion attached to a fixed number of ions or molecules which may be positive, negative or neutral.

(iv) **Coordination sphere** The central atom/ion and the ligands present in the square brackets are collectively known as coordination sphere.

(v) **Coordination number** The total number of ligands to which the metal is directly attached is called coordination number (C.N) e.g. $[Co(NH_3)_6]^{3+}$, C.N = 6.

(vi) **Ionisation sphere** The part of the coordination compound which is present outside the square brackets of coordination sphere is known as ionisation sphere.

(vii) **Oxidation state** It is defined as the charge it would carry if all the ligands are removed along with the electrons pairs that are shared with central atom. It is represented by roman numeral in parantheses.

4. Nomenclature of Coordination Compounds

The formula and names adopted for coordination entities are based on the recommendations of the IUPAC.

Formulae of Mononuclear Coordination Entities

Following rules are applied while writing the formulae

(i) The central atom is listed first.

(ii) The ligands are then listed in alphabetical order. The placement of a ligand, in the list does not depend on its charge.

(iii) Polydentate ligands are also listed alphabetically. In case of abbreviated ligand, the first letter of the abbreviation is used to determine the position of the ligand in the alphabetical order.

(iv) The formula for the entire coordination entity, whether charged or not, is enclosed in square brackets.
When ligands are polyatomic, their formulae are enclosed in parentheses. Ligand abbreviations are also enclosed in parentheses.

(v) There should be no space between the ligands and the metal within a coordination sphere.

(vi) When the formula of a charged coordination entity is to be written without that of the counter ion, the charge is indicated outside the square brackets as a right superscript with the number before the sign.

(vii) The charge of the cation(s) is balanced by the charge of the anion(s).

IUPAC Rules for Naming Complex Compounds

(i) If the counter ions are positively charged (cations), they are named first and if they are negatively charged (anions) they are named at the end.

(ii) In complex ions, ligands are named first. The number of a particular type of ligand is written as di for 2, tri for 3, tetra for 4, penta for 5, hexa for 6 and so on.
If the name of ligand involves numerical prefix such as di, tri, tetra etc. the number of such ligands are : bis for 2, tris for 3, tetrakis for 4.
If there are more than one type of ligands, their names are written in alphabetical order.
The negative and positive ligands are named by putting suffix –o and –ium, respectively.

(iii) The oxidation state of central metal ion can be indicated by roman numerals I, II, III and IV etc., in bracket at the end of the name of the complex.

(iv) For cationic and neutral complex, the name is written as it is but for anionic complex, the name of the central atom ends with 'ate'.

(v) When a ligand coordinates through more than one atom, the point of attachment of the ligand is indicated by putting the symbol of the atom through which coordination occurs after the name of ligand.

(vi) For bridging ligand, μ followed by hyphen is used before the name of ligand.

(vii) Geometrical isomers are differentiated by cis and trans and optical isomers by (+) and (–) or d-and l-form.

e.g. $[Cr(NH_3)_3(H_2O)_3]Cl_3$
Triamminetriaquachromium (III) chloride,
$[Co(H_2NCH_2CH_2NH_2)_3]SO_4$
tris(ethane-1, 2-diammine)cobalt (II) sulphate.
$[Ag(NH_3)_2][Ag(CN)_2]$
Diamminesilver (I) dicyanoargentate.

5. Isomerism in Coordination Compounds

Compounds having same molecular formula but different structures are called **isomers** and this phenomenon is called **isomerism**. Coordination compounds show two major types of isomerism, structural isomerism and stereoisomerism.

(i) **Structural Isomerism** The coordination compounds having same chemical formula and chemical bonds but are different due to different structural arrangement.
These are of four types

(a) **Ionisation isomerism** It is shown by those compounds which have same composition but give different ions in solution,
e.g. $[Co(NH_3)_5Br]SO_4$ and
$[Co(NH_3)_5(SO_4)]Br$.

(b) ***Hydrate isomerism*** *It is shown by the compounds having difference in number of water molecules present as ligand and as molecules of hydration, e.g.* $[Cr(H_2O)_5Cl]Cl_2 \cdot H_2O$ *and* $[Cr(H_2O)_6]Cl_3$.

(c) ***Linkage isomerism*** *It is shown by the compounds having ambidentate ligand, e.g.* $[Co(NH_3)_5(NO_2)]Cl_2$ *and* $[Co(NH_3)_5ONO]Cl_2$.

(d) ***Coordination isomerism*** *It is shown by the compounds when both positive and negative ions of the compound are complex ions and the two isomers differ in the distribution of ligands in the cation and the anion, e.g.* $[Co(CN)_6][Cr(NH_3)_6]$ *and* $[Cr(CN)_6][Co(NH_3)_6]$.

(ii) ***Stereoisomerism*** *Coordination compounds having same molecular as well as structural formulae but different arrangement in three dimensional space around the central atom in the polyhedral are called stereoisomers. It is of two types.*

(a) ***Geometrical or cis-trans isomerism*** *When two identical ligands occupy adjacent position, we have cis-isomer and when they are arranged opposite to each other, we have trans-isomer.*

This phenomenon is called geometrical isomerism, e.g. $[Co(en)_2Cl_2]^+$ *have two geometrical isomers as shown below:*

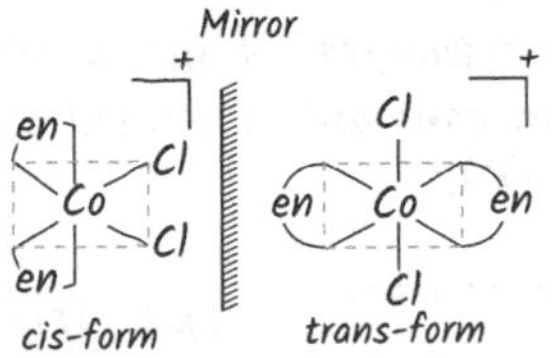

cis-form *trans-form*

Ma_3B_3 *shows facial and meridonial isomer*

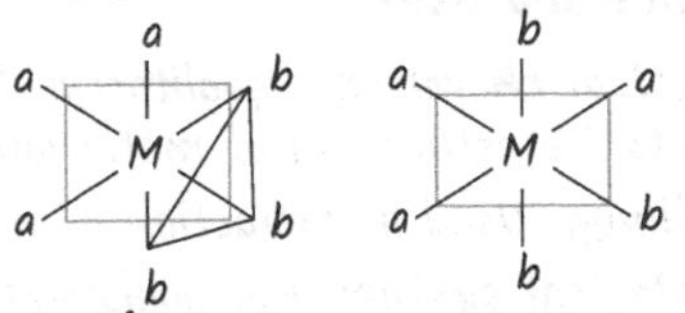

fac- *mer-*

(b) ***Optical isomerism*** *The compounds which do not have a plane of symmetry show optical isomerism.*

The isomer which rotates the plane of polarised light to the right is called dextro (d) ***rotatory****, whereas the isomer which rotates the plane of polarised light to the left is called laevo (l)* ***rotatory****.*

$[Co(en)_3]^{3+}$ *has two optical isomers as shown below*

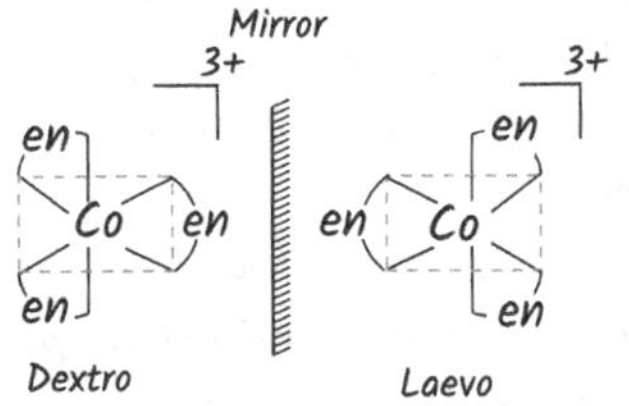

Dextro *Laevo*

6. Werner's Theory

According to Werner' theory, primary valency is ionisable (i.e. oxidation number) whereas secondary valencies are not. (i.e. the coordination number)

7. Valence Bond Theory (VBT)

It was developed by ***Linus Pauling****. It's various postulates are also follows*

(i) *Central atom/ion makes available required number of empty orbitals.*

(ii) *These orbitals undergo hybridisation to give same number of hybrid orbitals of equal energy. These hybridised orbitals are allowed to overlap with ligand orbitals that can donate electron pairs for bonding, and form strong ligand-metal coordinate covalent bonds.*

(iii) *Ligands must have one sigma orbital containing lone pair of electrons.*

(iv) *During complex formation, the Hund's rule of maximum multiplicity is followed while, in case of strong ligands, unpaired electrons get paired.*

(v) *A complex is paramagnetic if it contains unpaired electrons. If all the electrons are paired, the complex is diamagnetic in nature.*

(vi) *The outer orbital (high spin) or inner orbital (low spin) complexes are formed depending whether outer d-orbitals or inner d-orbitals are used.*

e. g. Using VBT, formation of inner orbital complex $[Fe(CN)_6]^{3-}$ *can be represented as*

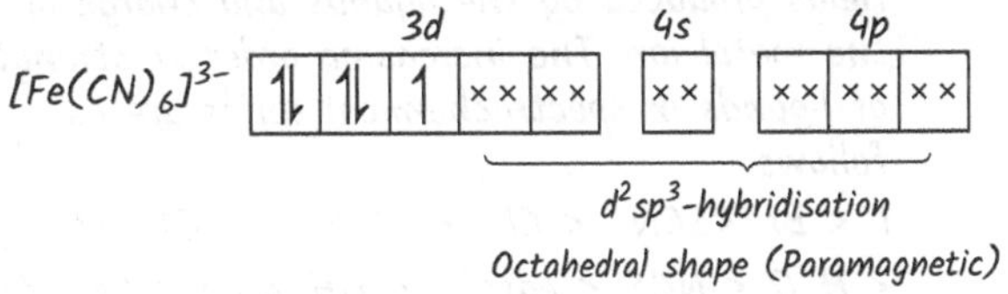

Using VBT, formation of outer orbital complex $[COF_6]^{3-}$ *can be represented as*

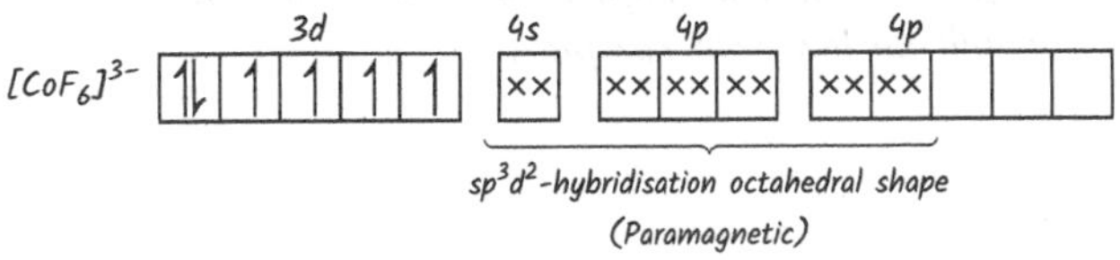

8. Crystal Field Theory

It is an electrostatic model which considers the metal-ligand bond to be ionic arising purely from electrostatic interactions between the metal ion and the ligand.

The main characteristics of CFT are as follows

(i) The metal ion and ligand act as point charges and the interaction is purely electrostatic.

(ii) When ligand approaches free metal ion, all five degenerate (having similar energy) d-orbitals get split into two groups t_{2g} (d_{xy}, d_{yz}, d_{zx}) and e_g ($d_{x^2-y^2}, d_{z^2}$).

This type of splitting is called **crystal field splitting.**

(iii) Due to different orientation, orbitals experience different interaction from ligand. Orbitals lying in the direction of ligand will have energy more than in the relative energy in the spherical crystal field.

Whereas orbitals lying in between the ligands will have lower energy.

On the approach of ligands, two sets of d-orbitals having different energies are obtained.

This difference in energies is called crystal field splitting energy (Δ_o or 10 Dq).

CFSE in Octahedral Field

CFSE = no. of e^-s in $t_{2g} \times -0.4\Delta_o$ + no. of e^-s in $e_g \times 0.6\ \Delta_o$

CFSE in tetrahedral field = no. of electrons in $e \times -0.6\Delta_t$ + no. of electrons in $t_2 \times 0.4\Delta_t$.

(iv) Due to electrical field of ligand, the accommodation of electron in splitted d-orbitals is in accordance to Hund's rule.

(v) The crystal field splitting Δ_o depends upon the fields produced by the ligands and charge on the metal ion. The increasing order of strength of ligands in spectrochemical series are as follows

$I^- < Br^- < SCN^- < Cl^- < S^{2-} < F^- < OH^- < C_2O_4^{2-} < H_2O < NCS^- < edta^{4-} < NH_3 < en < CN^- < CO$

9. High Spin and Low Spin Complex

If $\Delta < P$ it will be high spin complex and if $\Delta > P$ it will be low spin complex.

where, Δ = crystal field splitting energy, P = energy required for electron pairing in an orbital. Weak field ligands form high spin complexes while strong field ligands form low spin complexes.

10. Colour of Coordination Compounds

According to the crystal field theory, colour of complexes is due to d-d transitions of electrons. For example, the complex $[Ti(H_2O)_6]^{3+}$ appears violet in colour due to the transition of electron from t_{2g} level to the e_g level ($t^1_{2g}e^0_g \rightarrow t^0_{2g}e^1_g$).

In the absence of ligands, crystal field splitting does not occur and hence the substance is colourless. The compounds can also be colourless in case of paired electrons or no electrons in d-orbitals.

11. Magnetic Property of Coordination Compounds

Coordination compounds containing unpaired electrons are paramagnetic while coordination compounds containing all electrons paired are diamagnetic in nature.

Diamagnetic compounds are weakly repelled by magnetic field and paramagnetic compounds are attracted to applied magnetic field.

12. Stability of Complex Ion

It depends on the charge present on central atom, nature of metal ion, basic nature of ligand, presence of chelate ring and effect of multidentate cyclic ligand.

For the reaction, $M^{a+} + nL^{x-} \rightleftharpoons [ML_n]^{b+}$ the equilibrium constant is termed as stability constant (K).

It is expressed as, $K = \dfrac{[ML_n]^{b+}}{[M^{a+}][L^{x-}]^n}$

13. Importance and Uses

(i) **Analytical chemistry**, qualitative detection and quantitative estimation of metal ions.

(ii) **Metallurgy**, Used in extraction of metal.

(iii) **In biological system**, Haemoglobin (complex of iron with porphyrin ring), chlorophyll (complex of magnesium with prophyrin ring).

(iv) **In industry**, As catalyst, in electroplating.

(v) **In medicine**, cis-platin (cis-$[PtCl_2(NH_3)_2]$) is used in the treatment of cancer.

Chapter 6 Haloalkanes and Haloarenes

I. Haloalkanes

Haloalkanes are obtained by the replacement of a hydrogen atom of an alkane by a halogen atom (F, Cl, Br, I).

(i) Nomenclature

In common system, monohalogen derivatives of alkanes (alkyl halides) are named by adding the word 'halide' to the name of the corresponding alkyl group.

Here, the prefixes n-, iso-, sec-, tert- etc., are used.

In IUPAC system, alkyl halides are named as halo substituted hydrocarbons, i.e. haloalkanes. The names are written by prefixing the word 'halo' to the name of alkane corresponding to the longest continuous straight carbon chain having the halogen atom.

e.g.

	$CH_3CH_2CH_2Br$,	$H_3C—CH(Cl)—CH_3$,
Common name	n-propyl bromide	iso-propyl chloride
IUPAC name	1-bromopropane	2-chloropropane

$H_3C—CH(CH_3)—CH_2Cl$

iso-butyl chloride

1-chloro-2-methylpropane

(ii) Nature of C—X Bond

Due to the greater electronegativity of halogen atom, the halogen atom in C—X bond acquires partial negative charge, whereas C-atom acquires partial positive charge.

(iii) Preparation

(a) **From alkane and halogen** Chloroalkane and bromoalkane can be prepared by the reaction of alkane with chlorine or bromine in the presence of sunlight or heat. For higher alkanes, a mixture of 1°, 2° and 3° alkyl halide is obtained.

(b) **From alkene and hydrohalide** Halogen acid when treated with alkene undergoes addition reaction to yield haloalkane.

Unsymmetrical alkene follows Markownikoff's rule.

$$\underset{\text{Propene}}{CH_3—CH=CH_2} + HBr \longrightarrow \underset{\text{2-bromopropane}}{CH_3—CH(Br)—CH_3}$$

(c) **From alcohols** Most common method for preparation of haloalkanes is the replacement of —OH group of an alcohol by required halogen atom.

With phosphorus halides Chloroalkanes can be prepared by the reaction of PCl_5 or PCl_3.

$$ROH + PCl_5 \longrightarrow \underset{\text{Chloroalkane}}{RCl} + POCl_3 + HCl$$

$$3\,ROH + PCl_3 \longrightarrow 3\,RCl + H_3PO_3$$

With thionyl chloride In the presence of pyridine.

$$ROH + SOCl_2 \xrightarrow{\text{Pyridine}} RCl + SO_2\uparrow + HCl\uparrow$$

(d) **Preparation by halogen exchange method**

Finkelstein reaction Alkyl iodides are often prepared by the reaction of alkyl chlorides/bromides with NaI in dry acetone. This is called Finkelstein reaction.

$$R—X + NaI \xrightarrow[\Delta]{\text{Acetone}} R—I + NaX (X=Cl, Br)$$

Swart's reaction Fluoroalkanes are best prepared by treating alkyl chloride/bromide in the presence of a metallic fluoride such as AgF, Hg_2F_2. This is known as Swart's reaction.

$$\underset{\text{Bromomethane}}{CH_3Br} + AgF \longrightarrow \underset{\text{Fluoromethane}}{CH_3F} + AgBr$$

(e) **Borodine-Hunsdiecker reaction** Bromoalkanes are prepared by refluxing silver salts of acids with bromine in CCl_4.

$$CH_3COO^-Ag^+ + Br_2 \xrightarrow[\text{Re flux}]{CCl_4,\ 350K} CH_3Br + CO_2 + AgBr$$

(iv) Physical Properties

(a) Alkyl halides are highly combustible.

(b) For the same alkyl group, the boiling point decreases in the order $RI > RBr > RCl > RF$.

As the size of alkyl group decreases, boiling points decreases, for the same halogen,

$$CH_3CH_2CH_2X > CH_3CH_2X > CH_3X$$

(c) Alkyl halides are slightly solube in water because they do not form H-bonds with water.

(v) Chemical Properties

(a) **Nucleophilic Substitution Reactions (S_N)**
Nucleophile attacks at electron deficient sites. S_N reactions are of two types- S_N1 and S_N2. In S_N1 reaction, rate is proportional to the concentration of alkyl halide and it is unimolecular.
While, in S_N2. reaction, rate is proportional to the concentration of both alkyl halide and nucleophile and it is bimolecular.

The order of reactivity of alkyl halides for: S_N1 is 3° > 2° > 1° and S_N2 is 1° > 2° > 3°.

(b) **Elimination reaction** Haloalkanes having β – hydrogen atom undergoes β – elimination when heated with alcoholic solution of KOH. Due to involvement of elimination of β – hydrogen atom, the process is often called β – elimination reaction.

Some chemical reactions of alkyl halides are shown below in the form of flowchart.

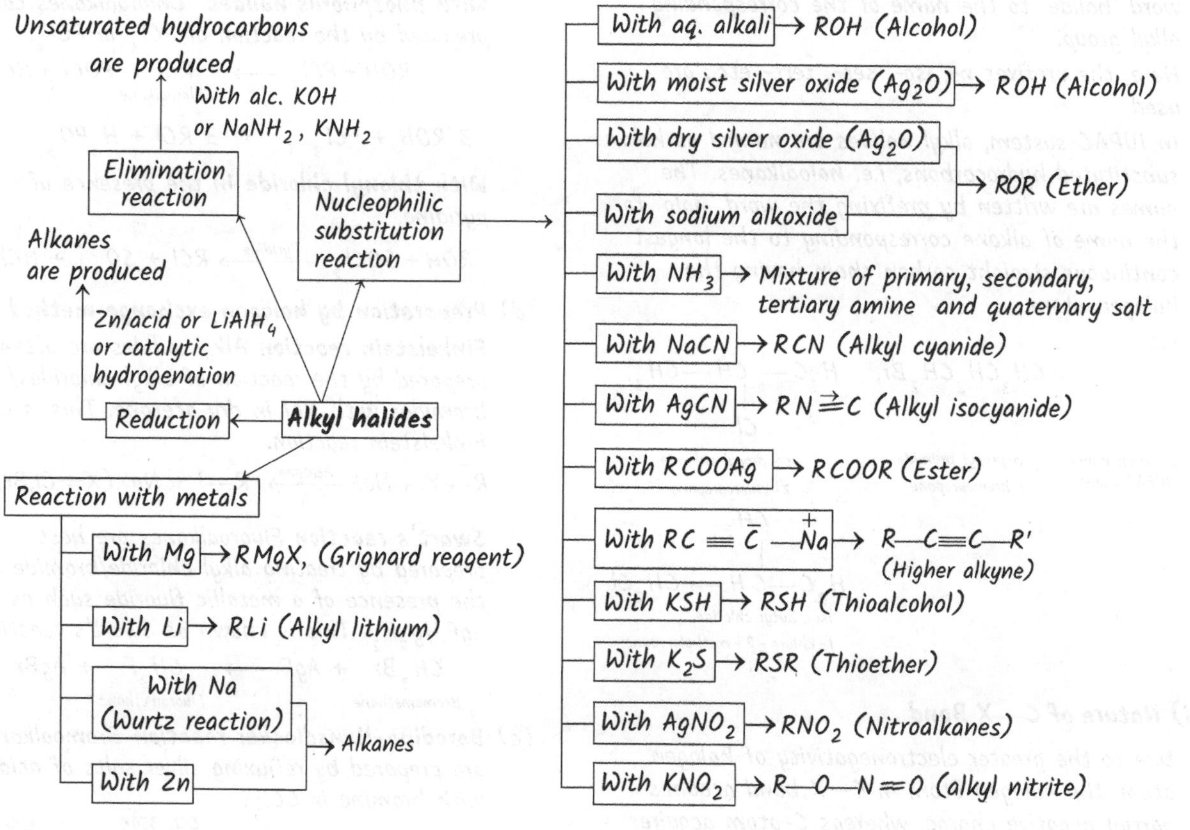

(vi) Uses

- Synthesis of large variety of organic compounds.
- Ethyl chloride is used as a local anaesthetic and as refrigerant.
- Ethyl bromide is used for the preparation of barbiturate drugs.

2. Haloarenes

Haloarenes are obtained by the replacement of a hydrogen atom of an aromatic hydrocarbon by a halogen atom (F, Cl, Br, I).

(i) Nomenclature

They are named by prefixing 'halo' before the name of the aromatic hydrocarbon. Haloarenes are the common name as well as IUPAC names of aryl halides. For dihalogen derivatives, the prefixes, o-, m-, p- are used in common system but in IUPAC system, the numerals 1,2; 1,3 and 1,4 are used.

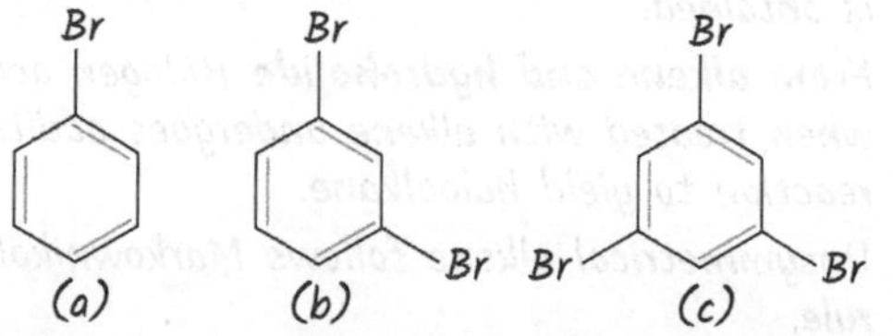

Common and IUPAC names of above figures are given below

	Common name	IUPAC name
(a)	Bromobenzene	Bromobenzene
(b)	m -dibromobenzene	1,3-dibromobenzene
(c)	sym -tribromobenzene	1,3,5-tribromobenzene

(ii) Nature of C—X Bond

In haloarenes, sp^2-hybridised carbon of benzene is bonded to halogen and C—X bond is also polar as in haloalkanes.

Also, as lone pairs of electrons of halogen atom are involved in resonance with benzene ring. So, this C—X bond acquires partial double bond character.

(iii) Preparation

- **By halogenation of aromatic hydrocarbons** Haloarenes can be prepared by the halogenation of aromatic hydrocarbons in dark or at ordinary temperature in presence of $FeCl_3$ as given below

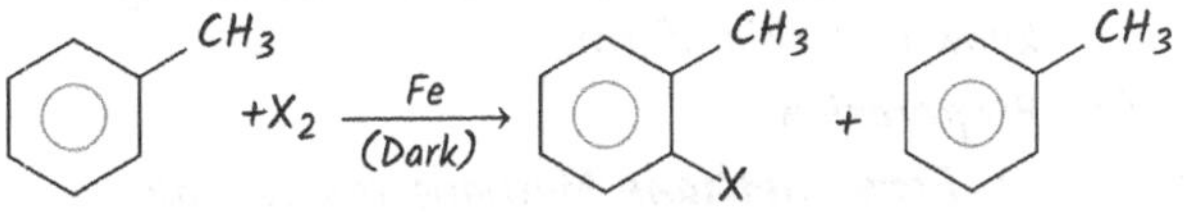

o-haloarenes p-halotoluene

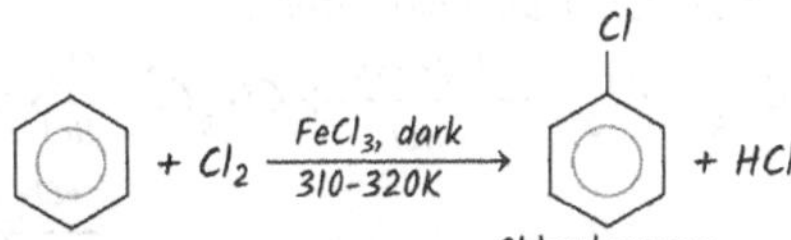

Chlorobenzene

- **From benzene diazonium salts**

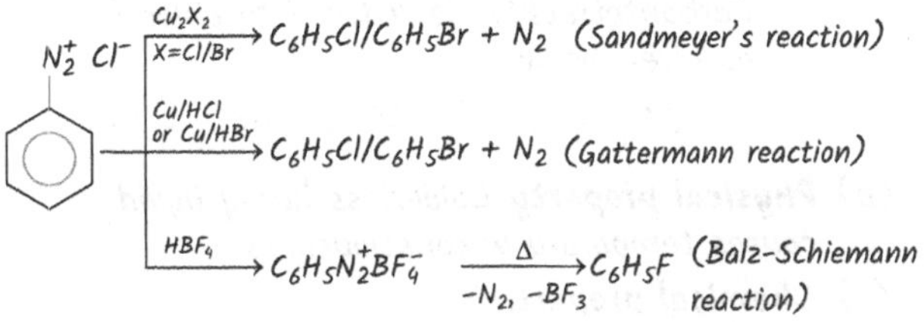

(iv) Physical Properties

(a) These are colourless with pleasant smell, insoluble in water.

(b) Isomeric haloarenes have similar boiling points. However, p-isomers have higher melting point than other two, i.e. meta and ortho because of the symmetry in p-isomer which occupies crystal structure better than ortho and meta-isomers.

(v) Chemical Properties

- Haloarenes are less reactive than haloalkanes towards nucleophilic substitution reactions, due to resonance effect, sp^2-hybridisation of a carbon bearing halogen atom and instability of phenyl cation.
- **Nucleophilic Substitution Reactions Under** drastic condition, haloarenes undergo nucleophilic substitution reactions as given below.

  Some nucleophilic substitution reactions are.
- **Substitution by hydroxyl group** Chlorobenzene when heated in aq. NaOH solution at 623 K and 300 atm, phenol is formed. This is known as **Dow's process.**

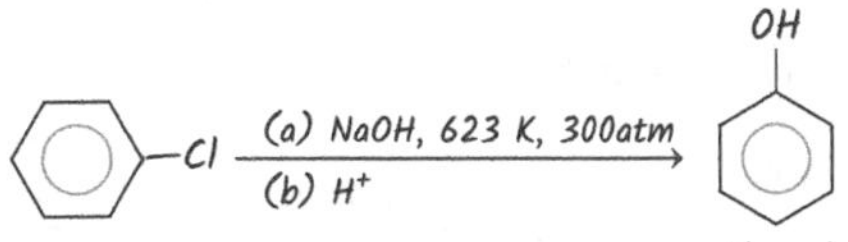

Phenol

The presence of electron withdrawing group ($—NO_2$) at ortho and para positions increases the reactivity of haloarenes.

- **Substitution by $—NH_2$ group**

  Chlorobenzene in presence of strong base such as $NaNH_2$ undergoes nucleophilic substitution reaction.

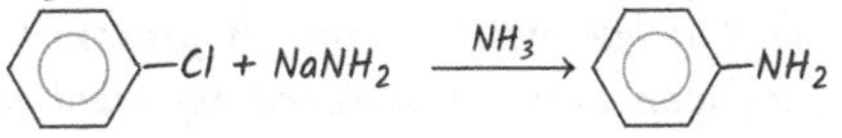

Aniline

Electrophilic Substitution Reactions

Electrophilic substitution reactions of haloarenes yield ortho (minor) and para products (major).

The common electrophilic substitution reactions of haloarenes are depicted as below:

- **Halogenation**

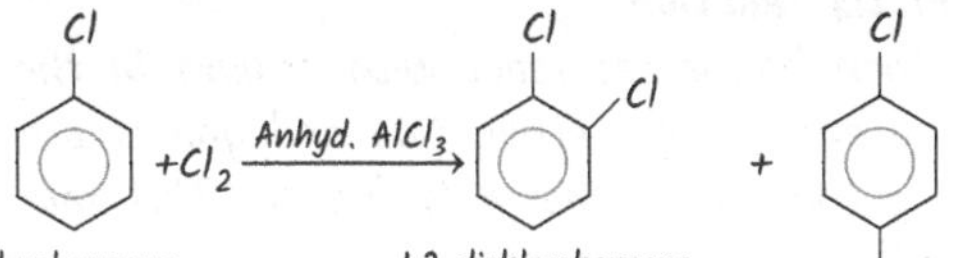

Chlorobenzene 1,2-dichlorobenzene (Minor) 1,4-dichlorobenzene (Major)

- **Nitration**

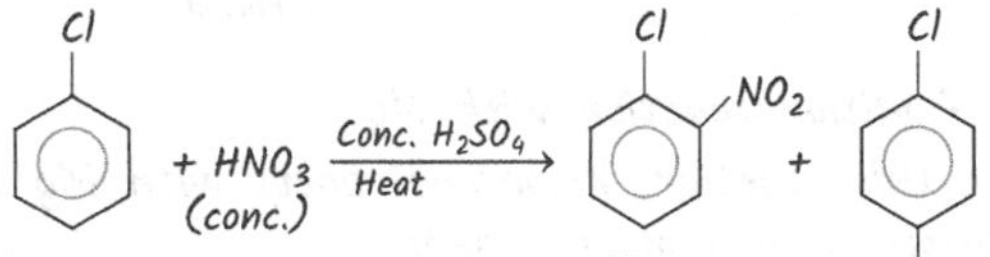

Chlorobenzene 1-chloro-2-nitrobenzene 1-chloro-4-nitrobenzene

- **Sulphonation**

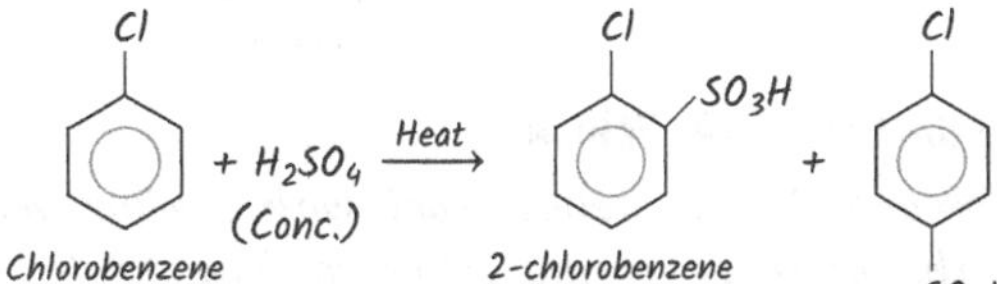

Chlorobenzene 2-chlorobenzene sulphonic acid 4-chlorobenzene sulphonic acid

- ***Friedel-Craft alkylation***

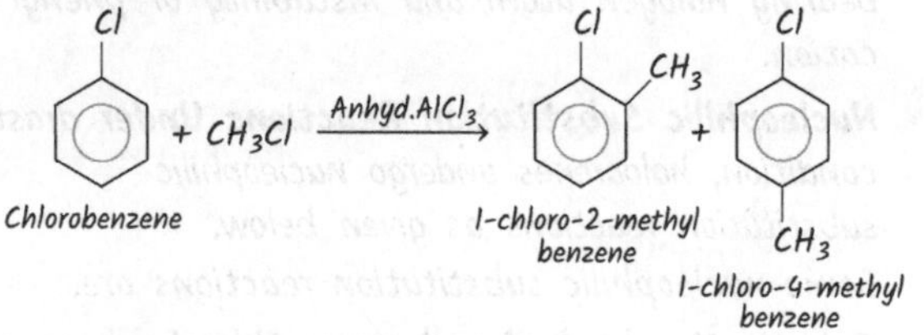

- ***Friedel-Craft acylation***

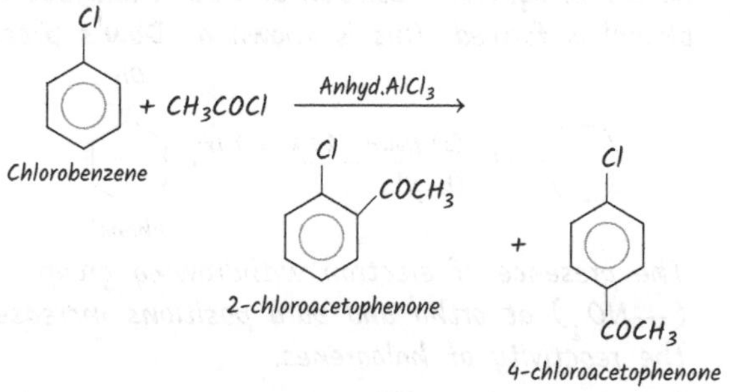

Reaction with metals

- ***Wurtz-Fittig reaction*** *When aryl halide is heated with alkyl halide with sodium in presence of dry ether, halogen atom is replaced by alkyl group and alkylarene is formed.*

  The reaction is called Wurtz-Fittig reaction.

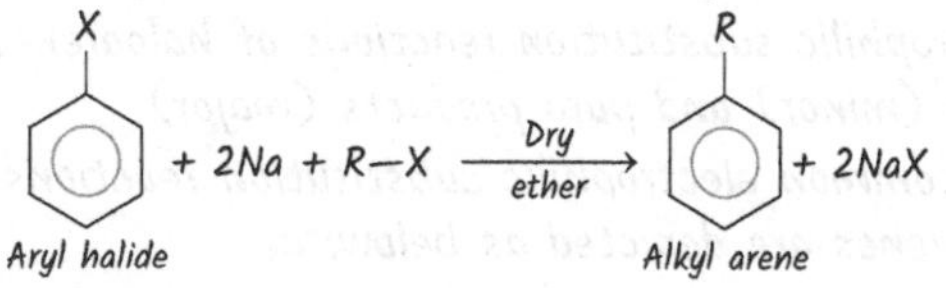

- ***Fittig reaction***
  When haloarenes react with sodium in the presence of dry ether, two aryl groups are joined together and diphenyl is formed. This reaction is called Fittig reaction.

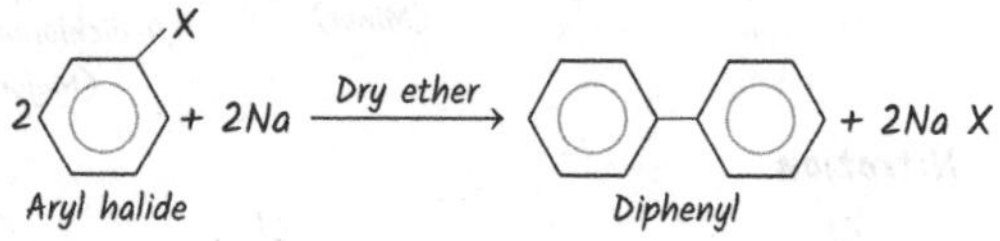

- ***Addition reaction with Mg***
  In this reaction, haloarene reacts with Mg then Grignard reagent is formed.

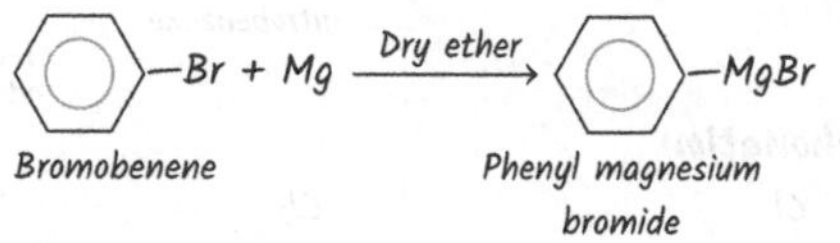

- ***Addition with lithium***
  Bromo and iodo arenes react with lithium metal in the presence of dry ether to form their corresponding organometallic compounds.

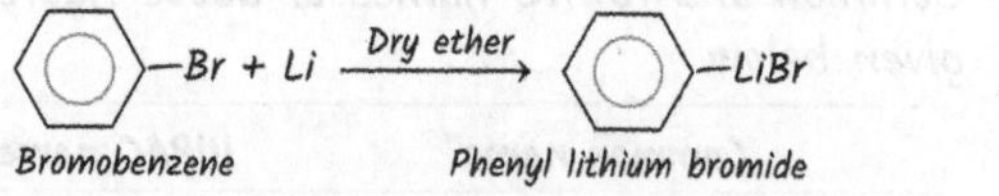

- ***Reaction with copper powder*** *(Ullmann reaction)*
  In this reaction, iodobenzene is heated with copper powder in a sealed tube and biphenyl is formed.

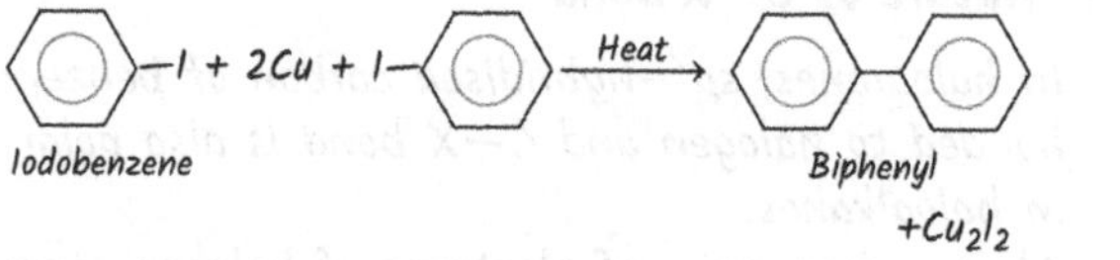

(vi) Reduction *On reduction of haloarenes, hydrocarbons are formed.*

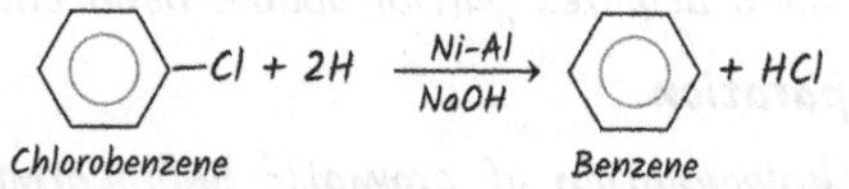

3. Polyhalogen Compounds

(i) Chloroform *($CHCl_3$) Trichloromethane is the trichloro derivative of methane commonly known as chloroform.*

(a) Preparation

I. **From methane** *Methane reacts with chlorine in the presence of light to form chloroform as given below*

$$CH_4 + Cl_2 \xrightarrow[-HCl]{Light/675K} CH_3Cl \xrightarrow[-HCl]{+Cl_2} CH_2Cl_2 \xrightarrow[-HCl]{+Cl_2} \underset{Chloroform}{CHCl_3}$$

II. **Partial reduction of carbon tetrachloride** *Carbontetrachloride reduced to chloroform as given below*

$$CCl_4 + 2H \xrightarrow{Fe + steam} CHCl_3 + HCl$$

(b) Physical property *Colourless heavy liquid causes temporary unconsciousness.*

(c) Chemical properties

I. **Oxidation** *When exposed to air and sunlight form highly poisonous gas,carbonyl chloride or phosgene.*

II. **Reduction** *With zinc and hydrochloric acid, it reduces to methylene chloride.*

III. **Hydrolysis** *When boiled with aqueous or alcoholic potassium hydroxide, it gets hydrolysed to give formic acid, which combines with KOH to give potassium formate.*

IV. **Nitration** *It may be nitrated by concentrated nitric acid to form chloropicrin.*

(d) **Uses** *It is used as anaesthetic, solvent for oils, fats, medicines.*

(e) **Harmful effects** *It affects the CNS. Inhaling at, 900 ppm for a short time cause dizziness, fatigue and headache. Skin develops sore if immersed directly into the chloroform.*

(ii) Iodoform (CHI_3)

(a) **Preparation** (Haloform reaction)

I. **From ethanol** Iodoform is prepared by ethanol by the following manner

$$\underset{\text{Ethanol}}{CH_3CH_2OH} + 4I_2 + 6NaOH \xrightarrow{\text{Heat}} \underset{\text{Iodoform}}{CHI_3} + \underset{\text{Sodium formate}}{HCOONa} + 5NaI + 5H_2O$$

II. **From acetone** Acetone reacts with I_2 and NaOH to form iodoform as given below :

$$\underset{\text{Acetone}}{CH_3-\overset{\overset{\large O}{\|}}{C}-CH_3} + 3I_2 + 4NaOH \xrightarrow{\text{Heat}} \underset{\substack{\text{Iodoform}\\\text{(Yellow ppt.)}}}{CHI_3} + 3NaI + \underset{\text{Sodium acetate}}{CH_3-\overset{\overset{\large O}{\|}}{C}-ONa} + 3H_2O$$

(b) **Physical properties**

I. It is a pale yellow crystalline solid and insoluble in water.

II. On heating, it decomposes to give iodine vapour.

(c) **Chemical properties**

I. **Reduction** When reduced with red phosphorus and hydroiodic acid, it gives methylene iodide.

II. **Hydrolysis** Hydrolysis of iodoform can be done as follows

$$\underset{\text{(alc.)}}{CHI_3 + 3KOH} \xrightarrow{-3KI} \underset{\text{(Unstable)}}{[H-C(OH)_3]} \xrightarrow[-H_2O]{} \underset{\text{Formic acid}}{H-\overset{\overset{\large O}{\|}}{C}-OH} \xrightarrow[-H_2O]{KOH} \underset{\text{Potassium formate}}{H-\overset{\overset{\large O}{\|}}{C}-OK}$$

III. **Dehalogenation** Iodoform undergoes dehalogenation to form ethyne as given below:

$$CHI_3 + 6Ag + CHI_3 \xrightarrow{\text{Heat}} \underset{\text{Ethyne}}{HC \equiv CH} + 6AgI$$

IV. **Reaction with silver nitrate** CHI_3 reacts with silver nitrate (alc.) to form yellow ppt. of AgI.

$$\text{Iodoform} + \underset{\text{(alc.)}}{\text{silver nitrate}} \xrightarrow{\text{Heat}} \text{Yellow ppt. of AgI}$$

(d) **Uses** It is used as an antiseptic due to liberation of iodine.

(iii) Tetrachloromethane (CCl_4)

It is colourless oily liquid with sticky smell.

(a) **Uses**

- It is used in large quantities in the manufacture of refrigerants and propellants for aerosol cans.
- It is used as fire extinguisher.

(b) **Harmful Effects**

- Exposure to CCl_4 causes liver cancer in humans.
- The most common effects are dizziness, headache, nausea and vomiting.

(iv) Freons

Chlorofluorocarbons compounds of methane and ethane are collectively known as freons. Freon-12 is one of the most common freons in industrial use.

(a) It is manufactured as,

$$3CCl_4 + 2SbF_3 \xrightarrow{SbCl_5} 2SbCl_3 + \underset{\text{Freon-12}}{3CCl_2F_2}$$

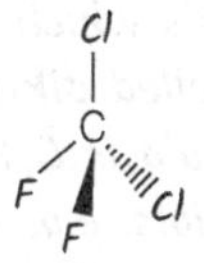

Structure of freons (tetrahedral)

(b) **Uses** These are used as refrigerants in refrigerators and air conditioning. These are used as propellants for aerosols and foams to spray out deodrants, hair creams and insecticides.

(c) **Harmful effects** Most freons make its way into the atmosphere where it undergoes photochemical decomposition and initiate radical chain reactions for depletion of the ozone layer.

Therefore, the use of freons as propellants and refrigerants has been drastically discouraged.

(v) DDT [1,1,1-trichloro-2,2-bis (p-chlorophenyl) ethane or (p,p'- dichlorodiphenyltrichloroethane)

(a) **Preparation** It can be prepared by reacting chloral with chlorobenzene as given below

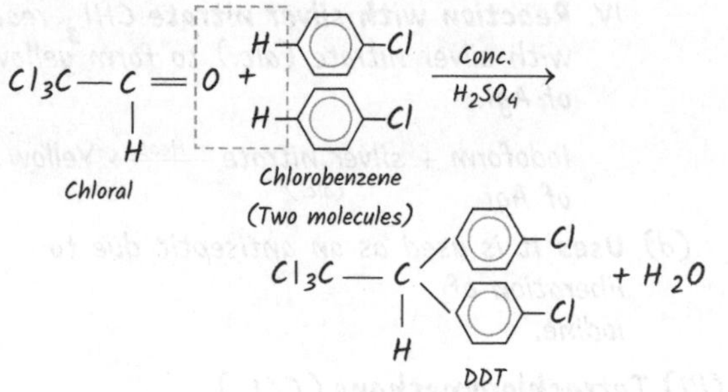

(b) Uses

This white powder is used as insecticide. It is popularly very effective against anopheles mosquitoes and lices which carry typhus.

(c) Harmful effects

Its use has been restricted as it is toxic, non-biodegradable and highly stable once entered a food chain.

Chapter 7 Alcohols, Phenols and Ethers

I. Alcohols

Hydroxy derivatives of aliphatic hydrocarbons are called alcohols. They possess the general formula R—OH, where R is an alkyl or substituted alkyl group. These are named by replacing 'e' of parent alkane with suffix 'ol'. The general formula of alcohols is $C_nH_{2n+1}OH$.

(i) Classification of Alcohols

(a) On the basis of no. of —OH groups present in the molecules

I. Those alcohols which contain one —OH group are called **monohydric alcohols**. e.g. CH_3OH, C_2H_5OH etc.

II. Those alcohols which contain two —OH groups are called **dihydric alcohols**. Their general formula is $C_nH_{2n}(OH)_2$ They are also called diols. e.g. 1, 2-ethanediol.

III. Those alcohols which contain three hydroxyl groups are called **trihydric alcohols**. They are also called triols. e.g. 1, 2, 3-propanetriol.

(b) On the basis of position of —OH group in the carbon chain

I. The alcohol in which —OH group is attached to 1° carbon atom is called **primary alcohol**. e.g. CH_3OH, C_2H_5OH, etc.

II. The alcohol in which —OH group is attached to 2° carbon atom is called **secondary alcohol**, e.g. propan-2-ol

III. The alcohol in which —OH group is attached to 3° carbon atom is called **tertiary alcohol**. e.g. 2-methylbutan-2-ol.

(ii) Structure

The structure of an alcohol resembles the structure of water with an alkyl group replacing one of hydrogen atoms of water.

Both have sp^3-hybridised oxygen atoms, but the C—O—H bond angle in methanol is considerably larger than H—O—H bond angle in water due to the large size of methyl group in alcohol.

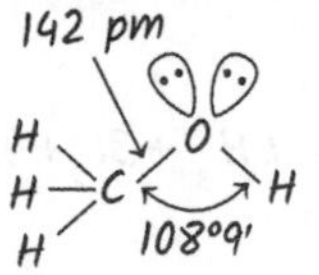

(iii) Methods of Preparation

(a) **Hydrolysis of alkyl halide** Haloalkanes when treated with aqueous solution of an alkali (NaOH/KOH) give corresponding alcohols.

$$\underset{\text{Haloalkane}}{R—X} + KOH(aq) \longrightarrow \underset{\text{Alcohol}}{R—OH} + KX$$

(b) **From Grignard reagent** Aldehydes and ketones react with Grignard reagent to form alcohol.

I. HCHO gives primary alcohols.

II. Aldehyde other than formaldehyde give secondary alcohols.

III. RCOR' gives tertiary alcohols.

(c) **From alkenes**

- **Direct hydration of alkenes** Alkenes react with water in the presence of acid as catalyst to form alcohols.

$$\underset{\text{Propene}}{H_3C—CH{=}CH_2} + H_2O \overset{H^+}{\rightleftharpoons} \underset{\text{Propan-2-ol}}{H_3C—\underset{|}{\overset{}{C}}H(OH)—CH_3}$$

- **Indirect hydration of alkenes** In this method, sulphuric acid and alkene react at elevated temperature ad under pressure to form sulphate esters which upon hydrolysis give alcohol.

$$RCH{=}CH_2 + H_2SO_4 \longrightarrow RCH(SO_2OH)CH_3$$

$$+ (R—\overset{CH_3}{\overset{|}{C}}HO)_2SO_2 \xrightarrow[H_2SO_4]{H_2O} R\underset{OH}{\underset{|}{C}}H—CH_3$$

- ***Hydroboration-oxidation process*** *Diborane reacts with alkenes to give trialkyl boranes as an addition product which upon subsequent oxidation by H_2O_2 in presence of aq. NaOH give alcohols.*

$$\underset{\text{Propane}}{3CH_3—CH{=}CH_2} \xrightarrow[\text{Ether}]{H—BH_2 \text{ or } (B_2H_6)} (CH_3—CH_2—CH_3)_3B$$

$$\xrightarrow{OH^-/H_2O_2} \underset{\text{Propan-1-ol}}{3\,CH_3CH_2CH_2OH} + H_3BO_3$$

(d) *By the reduction of carbonyl and carboxyl compounds*

- ***Aldehydes and Ketones*** *are reduced to the primary and secondary alcohols respectively.*

$$R—CHO + H_2 \xrightarrow{Ni/Pd} \underset{1^\circ \text{ alcohol}}{R—CH_2OH}$$

$$\begin{matrix}R\\H/R'\end{matrix}\!\!>C{=}O \xrightarrow[LiAlH_4 \text{ or } Ni/Pd]{NaBH_4/} \underset{2^\circ\text{alcohol}}{\begin{matrix}R\\H/R'\end{matrix}\!\!>CH—OH}$$

- ***Carboxylic acids*** *are reduced to primary alcohols by $LiAlH_4$.*

$$R—COOH \xrightarrow[(ii)\ H_3O^+]{(i)\ LiAlH_4} RCH_2OH$$

(e) ***From primary amines*** *Aliphatic primary amines react with nitrous acid to give primary alcohols.*

$$NaNO_2 + HCl \xrightarrow{0-5^\circ C} HNO_2 + HCl$$

$$R—NH_2 + HNO_2 \xrightarrow{0-5^\circ C} R—OH + N_2\uparrow + H_2O$$

(iv) Physical Properties of Alcohols

(a) *These are colourless volatile liquids having characteristic alcoholic odour and burning taste.*

(b) *Alcohols are polar in nature and capable of forming intermolecular hydrogen bonding due to which alcohols are soluble in water.*

(c) *The solubility of alcohols in water decreases with increase in molecular mass.*

(d) *The boiling points of alcohols are considerably higher than those of corresponding hydrocarbons, haloalkanes, ethers etc. due to H-bonding.*

(v) Chemical Properties of Alcohols

Alcohols R—OH

- $\xrightarrow{Na} R\overset{-}{O}\overset{+}{Na} + H_2\uparrow$
- $\xrightarrow[\text{(Esterification)}]{R'COOH} R—OCOR' + H_2O$
- $\xrightarrow[\text{(Esterification)}]{(R'CO)_2O} R—OCOR' + R'COOH$
- $\xrightarrow[\text{Acetylation}]{R'COCl,\ \text{Pyridine}} R—OCOR' + HCl$
- $\xrightarrow{HX} R—X + H_2O$
- $\xrightarrow{PCl_5} R—Cl + POCl_3 + HCl$
- $\xrightarrow[P/Br_2]{PBr_3} 3R—Br + H_3PO_3$
- $\xrightarrow{SOCl_2} RCl + SO_2\uparrow + HCl\uparrow$
- with conc. $H_2SO_4 \xrightarrow{\text{At } 443\ K}$ Alkene is formed due to dehydration.
- Oxidation →
  - 1° alcohol ⟶ Aldehyde ⟶ Carboxylic acid
  - 2° alcohol ⟶ Ketones
- Dehydrogenation with Cu at 573 K →
  - 1° alcohol ⟶ Aldehydes
  - 2° alcohol ⟶ Ketones
  - 3° alcohol ⟶ Alkenes

(vi) Some Commercially Important Alcohols

(a) **Methanol** (CH_3OH)

It is also known as 'wood spirit', as it was produced by the destructive distillation of wood.

Preparation (Bosch Process)

Now-a-days, methanol is produced by the catalytic hydrogenation of carbon monoxide at high pressure and temperature in the presence of $ZnO\text{-}Cr_2O_3$ catalyst.

$$CO + 2H_2 \xrightarrow[\substack{200-300\ atm\\575-673\ K}]{ZnO-Cr_2O_3} \underset{\text{Methyl alcohol or methanol}}{CH_3—OH}$$

Uses

It is used as a solvent in paints, varnishes and in formaldehyde formation as antioxidant.

(b) **Ethanol** (C_2H_5OH)

Preparation

It is obtained commercially by the fermentation of sugar present in molasses, sugarcane or fruits like grapes.

$$\underset{\text{Sucrose}}{C_{12}H_{22}O_{11}} + H_2O \xrightarrow{\text{Invertase}} \underset{\text{Glucose}}{C_6H_{12}O_6} + \underset{\text{Fructose}}{C_6H_{12}O_6}$$

$$\underset{\text{Glucose or Fructose}}{C_6H_{12}O_6} \xrightarrow{\text{Zymase}} \underset{\text{Ethanol}}{2C_2H_5OH} + 2CO_2\uparrow$$

Fermentation takes place in anaerobic conditions, i.e. in the absence of air.

Carbon dioxide is released during fermentation. If air gets into fermentation mixture, the oxygen of air oxidises ethanol to ethanoic acid which destroys the taste of alcoholic drinks.

Uses

It is used as a sovlent in paint industry and in wine making 100% ethanol is called absolute alcohol.

(vii) Distinction between Primary, Secondary and Tertiary Alcohols

(a) **Lucas Test** *A small quantity of unknown alcohol is added to Lucas reagent (anhy. $ZnCl_2$ + conc. HCl) at room temperature and the mixture is shaken.*

A tertiary alcohol forms turbidity immediately, secondary alcohol forms turbidity within five minutes and primary alcohol shows no turbidity at room temperature.

(ii) Iodoform Test

All alcohols containing the group $CH_3CH(OH)$ linked to carbon or hydrogen atom can be distinguished from other alcohols by the iodoform test.

$$\underset{\text{Ethyl alcohol}}{CH_3CH_2OH} + 4I_2 + 6NaOH \xrightarrow{\Delta} \underset{\text{Iodoform}}{CHI_3} + HCO\overset{-}{O}\overset{+}{Na} + 5NaI$$

$$\underset{\text{(Methyl alcohol)}}{CH_3OH} + I_2 + NaOH \xrightarrow{\Delta} \text{No reaction}$$

Phenols and alcohols can also be distinguished using this test.

(viii) Conversion of One Alcohol into Another.

(a) Conversion of a Lower Alcohol into a Higher Alcohol

$$\underset{\text{Lower alcohol}}{R-OH} \xrightarrow[-H_2O]{HI} RI \xrightarrow[-KI]{KCN} RCN$$

$$\xrightarrow[\text{Reduction}]{4[H]} RCH_2NH_2 \xrightarrow{HNO_2} \underset{\text{Higher alcohol}}{RCH_2OH}$$

(b) Conversion of Higher Alcohol into a Lower Alcohol

$$\underset{\text{Higher alcohol}}{RCH_2OH} \xrightarrow[K_2Cr_2O_7]{[O]} RCHO \xrightarrow{[O]} RCOOH$$

$$\xrightarrow{NaOH} RCO\overset{-}{O}\overset{+}{Na} \xrightarrow[\text{Heat}]{NaOH + CaO} Na_2CO_3 + RH$$

$$\xrightarrow{Cl_2} R-Cl \xrightarrow{Aq.\ KOH} \underset{\text{Lower alcohol}}{R-OH} + Na_2CO_3$$

(c) Conversion of Primary Alcohol to a Secondary Alcohol

$$\underset{1^\circ\ \text{alcohol}}{RCH_2-CH_2-OH} \xrightarrow{SOCl_2} RCH_2CH_2Cl \xrightarrow{KOH\ (alc.)}$$

$$RCH{=}CH_2 \xrightarrow{HBr} R-CH(Br)-CH_3 \xrightarrow{aq.\ KOH} \underset{2^\circ\ \text{alcohol}}{R-CH(OH)-CH_3}$$

(d) Conversion of Secondary Alcohol to a Tertiary Alcohol

$$\underset{2^\circ\ \text{alcohol}}{R^1-CH(R^2)-OH} \xrightarrow[K_2Cr_2O_7]{[O]} R^1-C(R^2){=}O \xrightarrow{R_3MgBr}$$

$$R^1-C(R^3)(R_2)-\overset{-}{O}\overset{+}{Mg}Br \xrightarrow[-\ MgBr(OH)]{H_2O} \underset{3^\circ\ \text{alcohol}}{R^1-C(R^3)(R^2)-OH}$$

(e) Conversion of Primary Alcohol to a Tertiary Alcohol

$$\underset{1^\circ\ \text{alcohol}}{R-CH_2-CH_2OH} \xrightarrow[433\ K]{Conc.\ H_2SO_4} R-CH{=}CH_2$$

$$\xrightarrow{HBr} R-CH(Br)-CH_3 \xrightarrow[-KBr]{Aq.KOH} \underset{2^\circ\ \text{alcohol}}{R-CH(OH)-CH_3}$$

$$\xrightarrow{K_2Cr_2O_7} R-C(=O)-CH_3 \xrightarrow{R'MgBr} R-C(\overset{-}{O}\overset{+}{Mg}Br)(R')-CH_3$$

$$\xrightarrow[-MgBr(OH)]{H_2O} \underset{3^\circ\ \text{alcohol}}{R-C(OH)(R')-CH_3}$$

2. Phenols

Phenols are the hydroxy derivatives of arenes in which one or more —OH groups are directly attached to the carbon atoms of an aromatic ring.

(i) Preparation of Phenols

(a) **Dow's process** In this process, phenol is prepared by heating chlorobenzene with 10% NaOH solution at 623 K under 300 atm followed by hydrolysis.

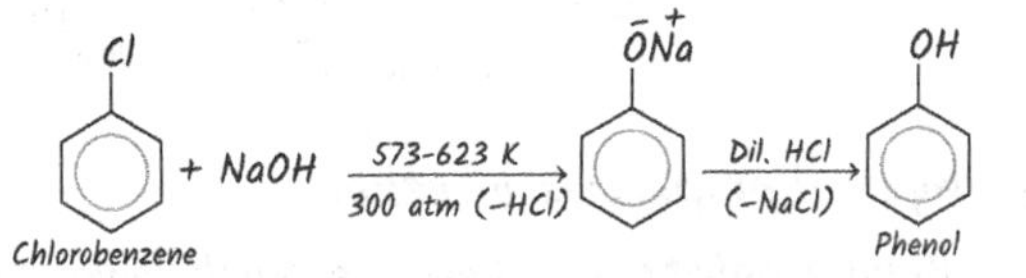

(b) **From benzene sulphonic acids** When benzene is sulphonated with oleum then benzene sulphonic acid is formed which gets further converted to sodium phenoxide on heating with molten sodium hydroxide followed by acidification phenols are obtained.

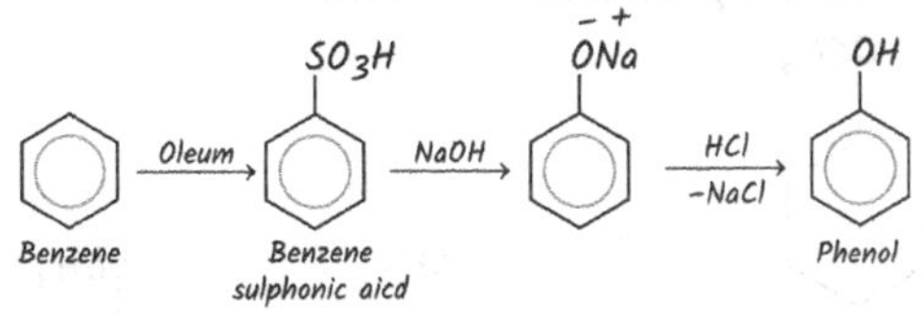

(c) **From diazonium salts** Diazonium salts are hydrolysed in the presence of dil. H_2SO_4 or warm water to give phenols.

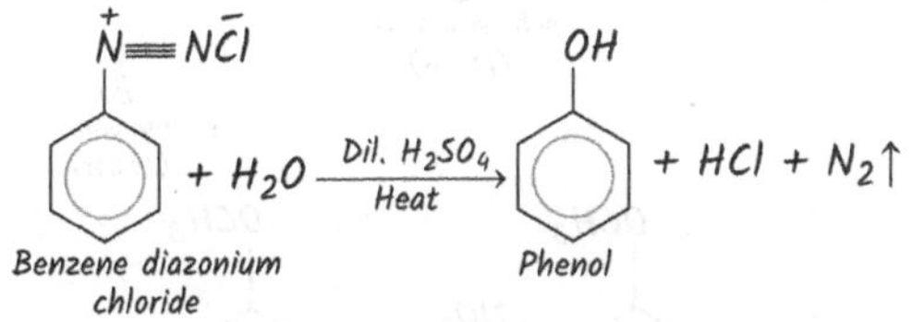

(d) **From cumene** This method is used for the commercial preparation of phenol. This reaction proceed at 150°C in the presence of HBr as a catalyst. The reaction is also called auto oxidation.

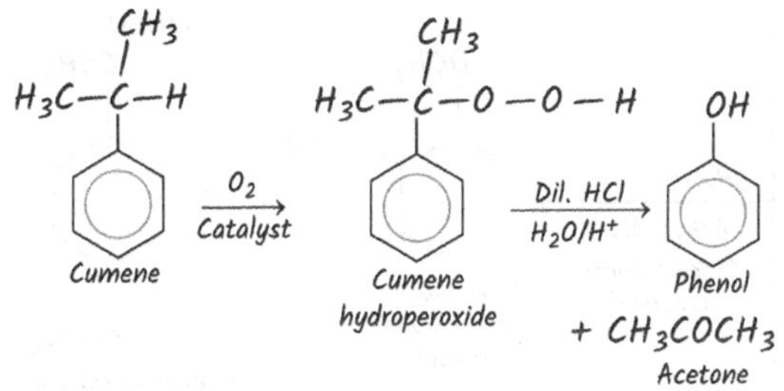

(ii) Physical Properties

(a) Phenols are either colourless liquids or colourless crystalline solids with low melting points.

(b) Phenols are slightly soluble in water.

(c) Phenols possess higher boiling points as compared to those of the corresponding aromatic hydrocarbons and haloarenes.

(iii) Chemical Properties

Phenols show various chemical reaction. Some of them are discussed below

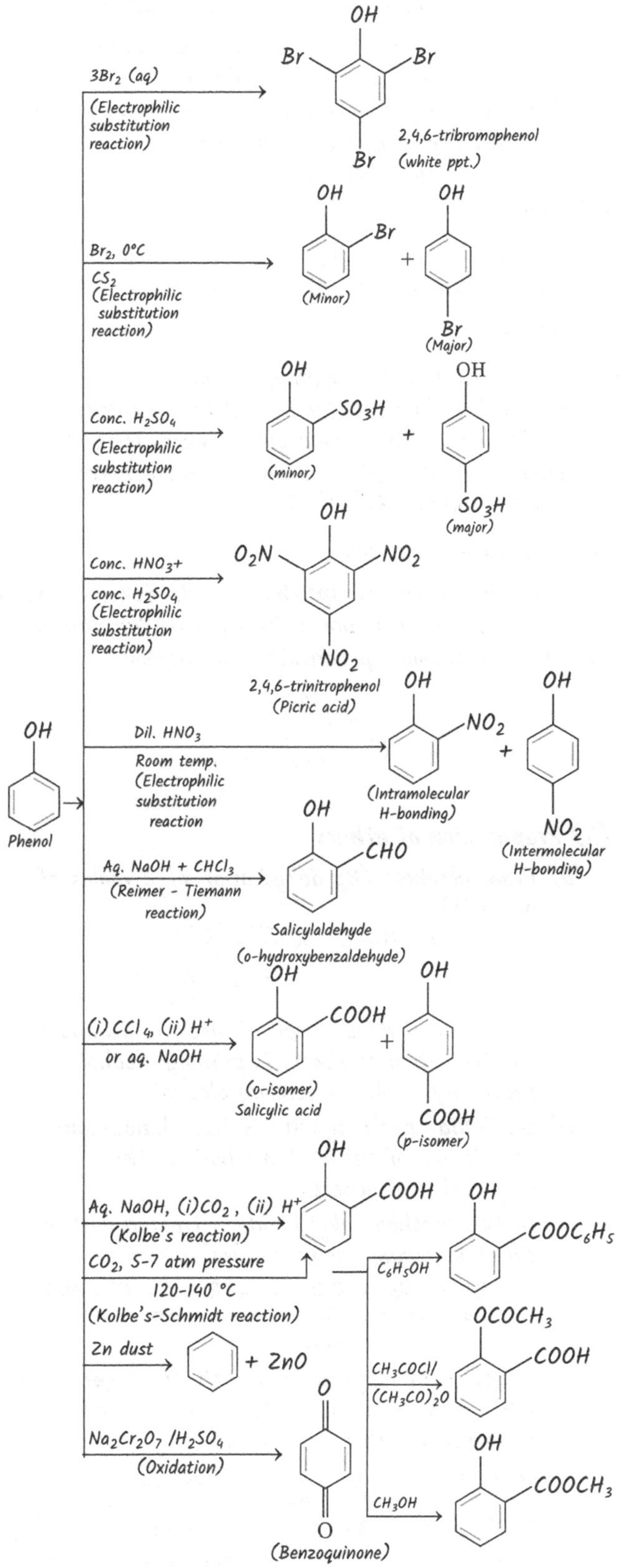

(iv) Test for Phenols

(a) **Reaction with ferric chloride** Unlike alcohols, phenols react with neutral $FeCl_3$ and give violet coloured water soluble complex$[Fe(OC_6H_5)_3]^{3-}$. Thus, this reaction is used to distinguish phenol and known as **FerriC chloride test.**

(b) **Coupling reaction** (Azo dye test) Phenol reacts with diazonium salt to form azo dye but alcohol does not form azo dye.

(v) Uses

It is used in perfumery. It is widely used in the manufacture of dyes, plastics etc.

3. Ethers

The substitution of a hydrogen atom in a hydrocarbon (aliphatic/aromatic) by an alkoxy (OR)/aryloxy (OAr) group yield ethers. These have general formula $C_nH_{2n+2}O$ and are represented by general structure R—O—R′.

(i) Structure of ethers

O-atom in ethers is sp^3-hybridised. Ethers have a bent or angular structure. Ethers are dialkyl derivatives of water or monoalkyl derivatives of alcohols.

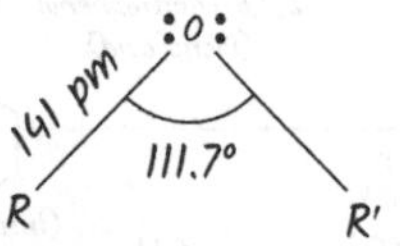

(ii) Preparation of ethers

(a) **From alcohols** (By dehydration of 2 moles of alcohols)

$$R—O—H + H—O—R' \xrightarrow[413\ K]{Conc.\ H_2SO_4} \underset{Ether}{R—O—R'} + H_2O$$

The order of dehydration of alcohols leading to the formation of ethers is primary alcohol > secondary alcohol > tertiary alcohol

(b) **By Williamson's synthesis from haloalkanes** This is one of the best method for the preparation of ethers.

In this method, alkyl halide is treated with a suitable sodium (or potassium) alkoxide.

$$\underset{Sodium\ alkoxide}{R—O^-Na^+} + \underset{Alkyl\ halide}{R'X} \longrightarrow \underset{Ether}{R—O—R'} + NaX$$

(c) **Reaction of alkyl halides with dry silver oxide** When alkyl halide is heated with silver oxide, symmetrical ether is formed.

$$\underset{Ethyl\ bromide}{\begin{matrix} CH_3CH_2—Br \\ + \\ CH_3CH_2—Br \end{matrix}} + \underset{Dry\ silver\ oxide}{\begin{matrix} Ag \\ \ \ \ \ \rangle O \\ Ag \end{matrix}} \longrightarrow \underset{Diethyl\ ether}{\begin{matrix} CH_3CH_2 \\ \ \ \ \ \rangle O \\ CH_3CH_2 \end{matrix}} + \underset{Silver\ bromide}{2AgBr}$$

(d) **From Grignard's reagent** Higher ethers can be prepared by treating α-haloethers with suitable Grignard's reagent.

$$\underset{Chloromethoxy\ methane}{CH_3—O—CH_2Cl} + CH_3MgI \xrightarrow[Ether]{Dry} \underset{Ethyl\ methyl\ ether}{CH_3—O—CH_2CH_3} + \underset{Chloromagnesium\ iodide}{Mg(Cl)I}$$

(iii) Physical properties of ethers

(a) **Boiling points** of ethers are much lower than those of alcohols.

(b) **Solubility** Lower ethers (upto three carbon atoms) are soluble in water and their miscibility with water resembles those of alcohols of the same molecular masses.

(iv) Chemical properties of ethers

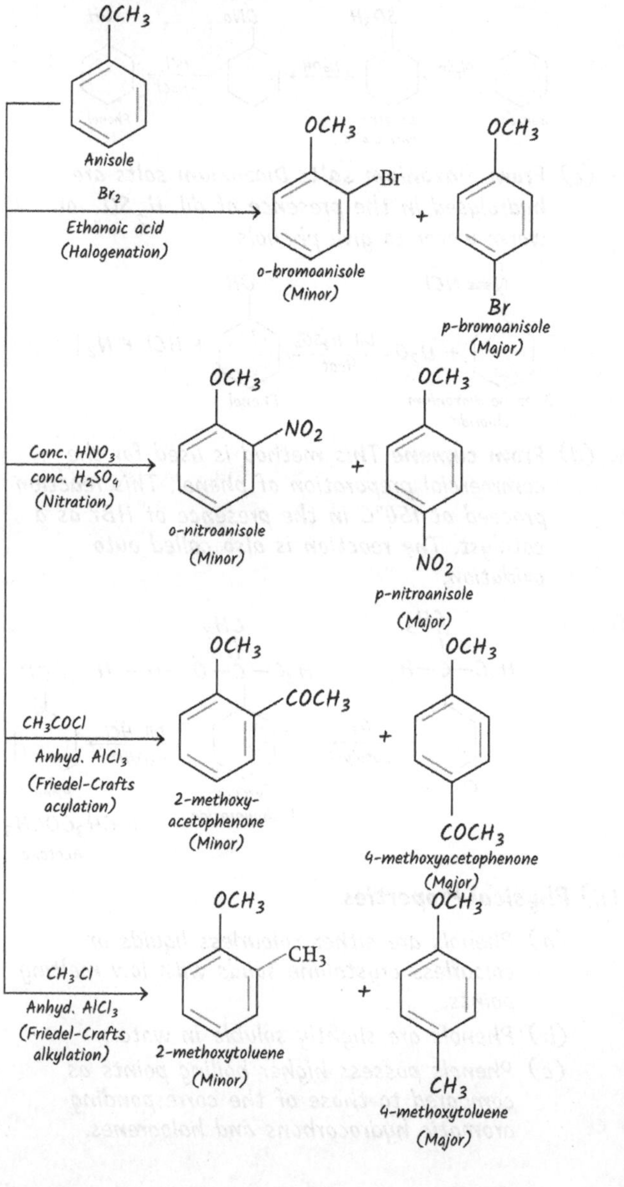

(vi) Uses of ethers

(a) Dimethyl ether is used as a refrigerant and as a solvent at low temperatures.

(b) Used as an industrial solutions for oils, resins, gums, etc.

(c) As an extracting solvent in laboratory and industry because of their almost inert nature and good dissolving power.

Chapter 8 Aldehydes, Ketones and Carboxylic Acids

I. Carbonyl Compounds or Aldehydes and Ketones

The >C = O group is known as the **carbonyl group** and the compounds containing >C = O group are known as **carbonyl compounds**.

In aldehydes, the carbonyl group is bonded to carbon and hydrogen while in ketones, it is bonded to two carbon atoms.

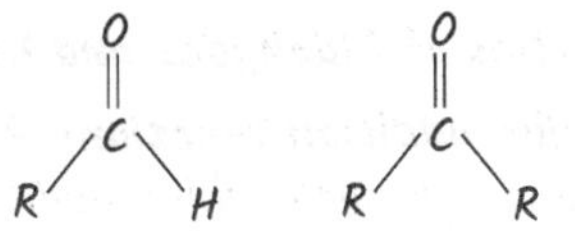

Aldehyde Ketone

Aldehydes and ketones have molecular formula, $C_nH_{2n}O$ and are functional isomers of each other.

Structure of carbonyl compounds

It possesses a trigonal coplanar structure with bond angle of 120°. The carbon-oxygen double bond is polarised due to higher electronegativity of oxygen relative to carbon.

Methods of Preparation

Aliphatic Aldehydes and Ketones

(i) From alcohols

(a) By oxidation of alcohols with $K_2Cr_2O_7$/ H_2SO_4 or $KMnO_4$ / KOH.

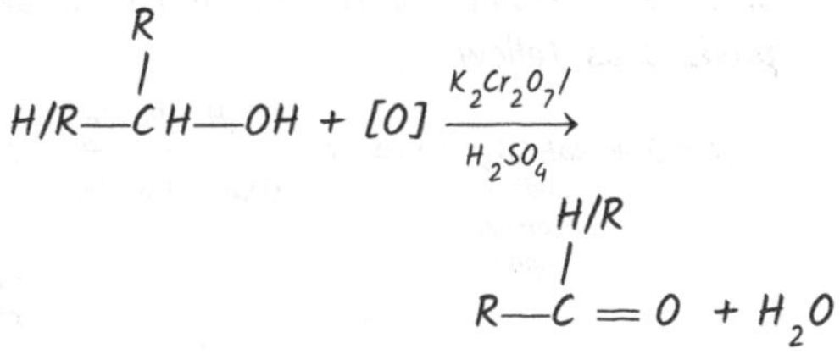

(b) By catalytic dehydrogenation of alcohols with Cu at 573K.

$$R{-}CH_2OH \xrightarrow{Cu/573\ K} R{-}CHO + H_2$$

1° alcohol Aldehyde

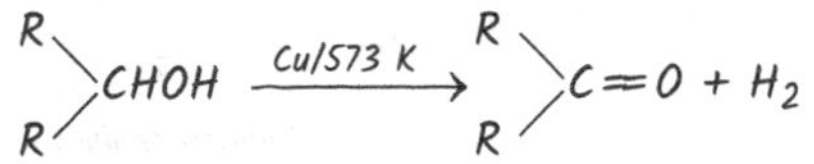

2° alcohol Ketone

(ii) From alkenes (Ozonolysis) By reductive ozonolysis of alkenes, carbonyl compounds are formed.

(iii) From alkynes Ethyne on hydration in presence of dil. H_2SO_4 and $HgSO_4$ gives acetaldehyde (by terminal alkynes) whereas all other alkynes give ketones.

(iv) From calcium salts of carboxylic acids

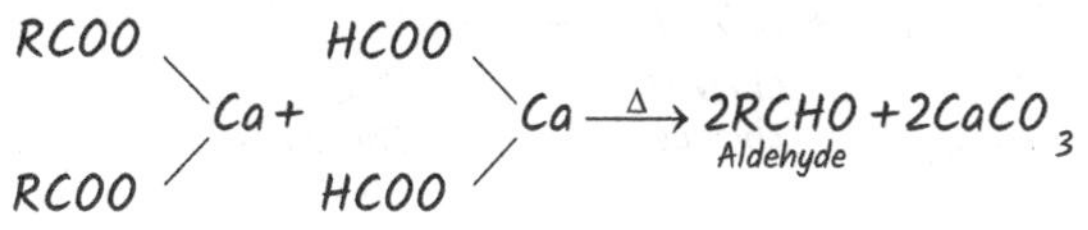

Calcium salt of carboxylic acid Calcium formate

(v) From acid chloride (Rosenmund's reaction) Aldehydes can be obtained from acid chlorides by the catalytic hydrogenation known as **Rosenmund's reduction**.

$$\underset{\text{Acid chloride}}{R{-}\overset{O}{\overset{\|}{C}}{-}Cl} + H_2 \xrightarrow[\text{Boiling xylene}]{Pd/BaSO_4,\ S} \underset{\text{Aldehyde}}{RCHO} + HCl$$

Ketones cannot be prepared by this method. They are prepared by treating acid chlorides with dimethyl cadmium in the presence of dry ether.

(vi) From nitriles

- Nitriles are also reduced to corresponding imine with stannous chloride in the presence of hydrochloric acid which on hydrolysis give corresponding aldehydes.

$$\underset{\text{Nitrile}}{RCN} + SnCl_2 + HCl \longrightarrow \underset{\text{amine}}{RCH{=}NH} \xrightarrow{H_3O^+} \underset{\text{Aldehyde}}{RCHO}$$

This reaction is known as **Stephen reaction.**

- When nitriles reacts with Grignard reagent followed by hydrolysis yields a ketone.

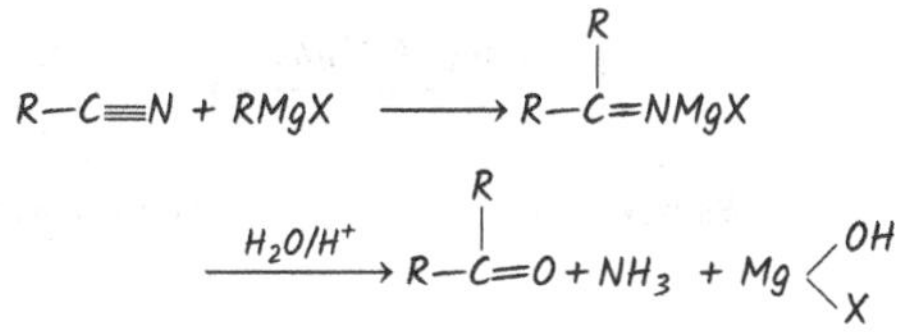

(vii) **From esters** Esters can also be reduced to aldehydes with DIBAL-H.

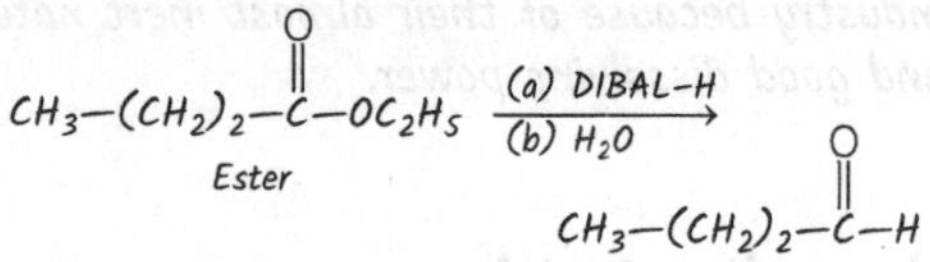

(viii) Aromatic aldehydes (benzaldehydes and its derivatives) are prepared from aromatic hydrocarbons by the following methods.

(a) **By Etard reaction** (From toluene)

Toluene on oxidation with chromyl chloride oxidises methyl group to a chromium complex which on hydrolysis gives corresponding benzaldehyde.

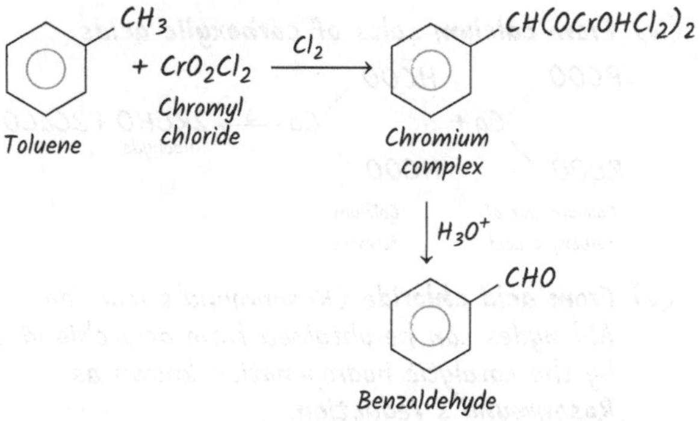

(b) **By side chain chlorination followed by hydrolysis**

Toluene on chlorination gives benzal chloride which on hydrolysis gives benzaldehyde.

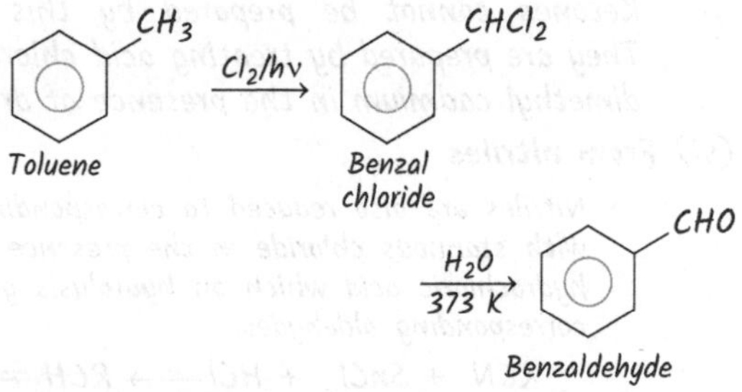

(c) **By Gattermann-Koch reaction**

When benzaldehyde or its derivative is treated with carbon monoxide and hydrogen chloride in the presence of anhydrous $AlCl_3$ or CuCl, it gives benzaldehyde or substituted benzaldehyde.

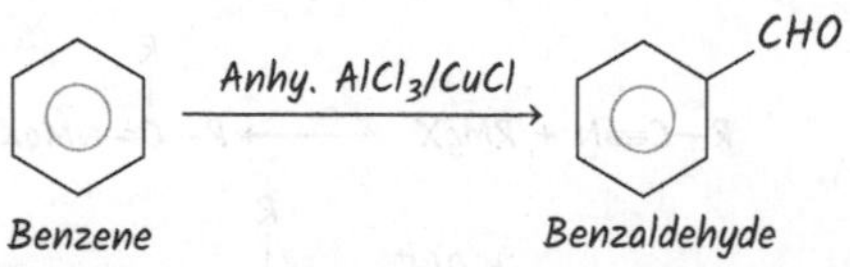

Aromatic Ketones can be prepared by Friedel-crafts acylation reaction.

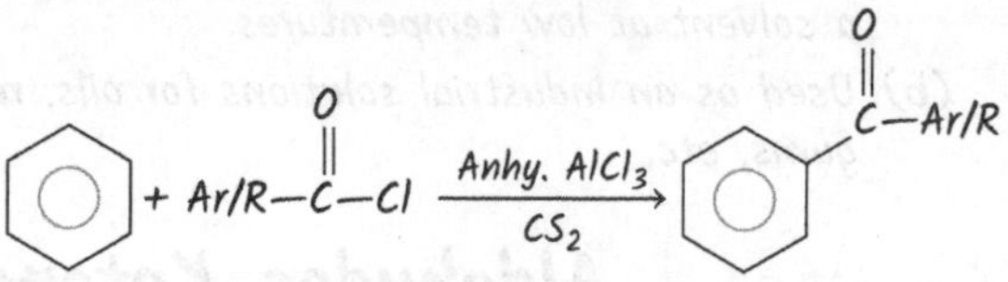

Physical Properties of Aldehydes and Ketones

(i) Methanal is a gas while ethanal is a volatile liquid at room temperature.

(ii) Boiling points of aldehydes and ketones are higher than hydrocarbons and ethers of comparable molecular masses.

(iii) All aldehydes and ketones are fairly soluble in organic solvents like benzene, ether, methanol, chloroform, etc.

Chemical Properties of Aldehydes and Ketones

(a) **Nucleophilic addition reactions** Aldehydes and ketones undergo nucleophilic addition reactions. These reactions are catalysed by both acids and bases.

Some Important Nucleophilic Addition Reactions are

- Aldehydes and ketones on reaction with HCN give cyanohydrins. This reaction is slow, so it is catalysed by a base.

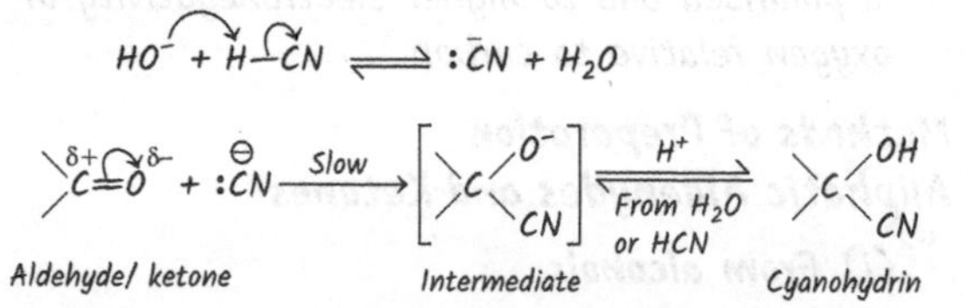

- Addition of sodium hydrogen sulphite to aldehydes or ketones results in the formation of an addition product as follow

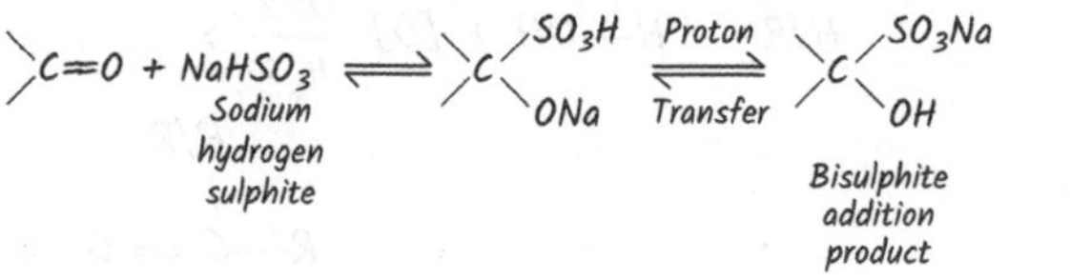

- Aldehydes and ketones on reaction with Grignard reagent give addition products which upon hydrolysis with water/dil. mineral acids gives alcohol.

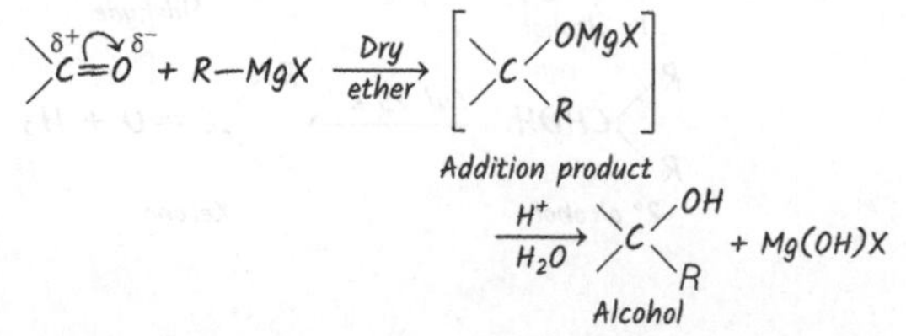

- Aldehyde react with one equivalent of monohydric alcohols in the presence of dry HCl gas to give hemiacetals which on further reaction with 1 more molecule of alcohols give acetals. The reaction is given as

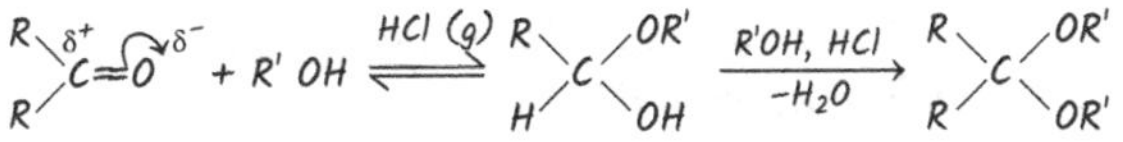

Hemiacetal Acetal

Ketones react with dihydric alcohols to give cyclic ketals.

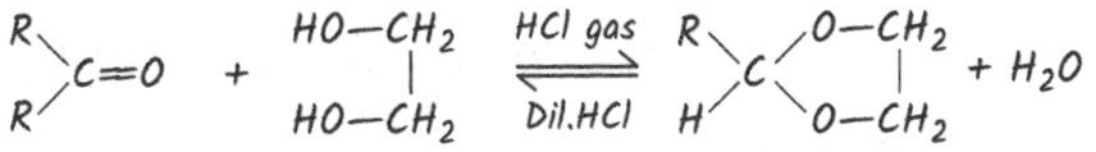

Ethylene glycol Cyclic ketal

- Nucleophiles such as ammonia and its derivative, $H_2N—Z$ add to the carbonyl group of aldehyde and ketones in presence of weakly acidic medium.

The reaction is given as below

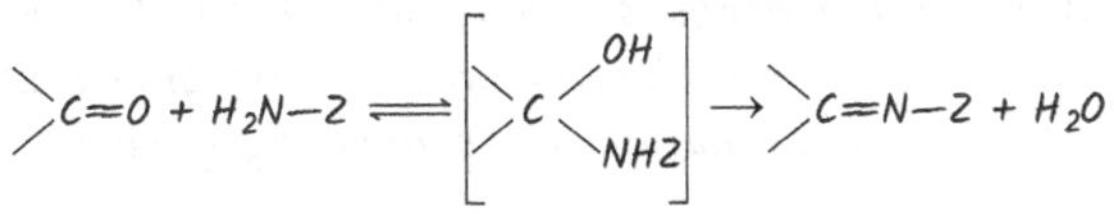

[Z = H, alkyl, aryl, —OH, $—NH_2$, $—C_6H_5NH$,

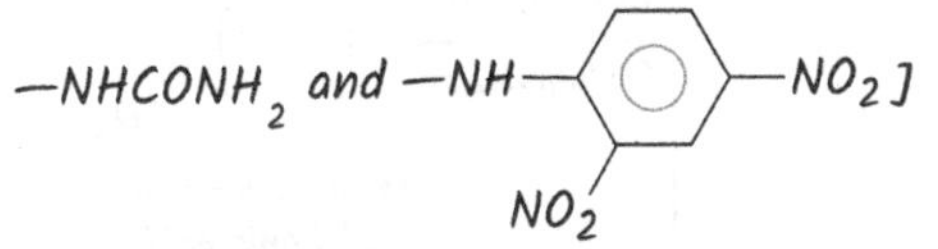

(b) Base catalysed reactions

- **Aldol condensation** Aldehydes and ketones containing α -H atoms undergo aldol condensation in presence of dilute alkali as catalyst to form β-hydroxy aldehyde (aldol) or β-hydroxy ketones (ketol).

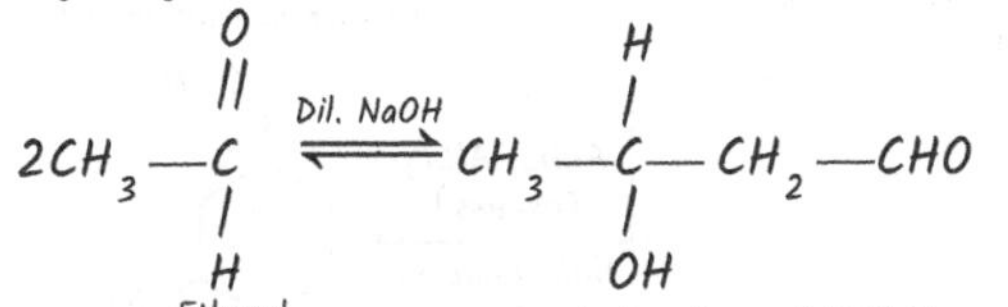

Ethanal 3 - hydroxybutanol (Aldol)

But - 2 - enal

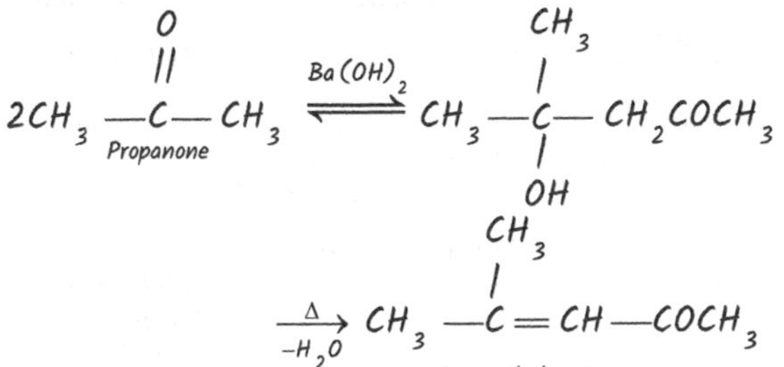

Propanone

4 - methylpent 3 - en - 2 - one

- **Cross-aldol condensation** When two different aldehydes or different ketones or one aldehyde and one ketone each containing α-H atoms, undergo cross aldol condensation.

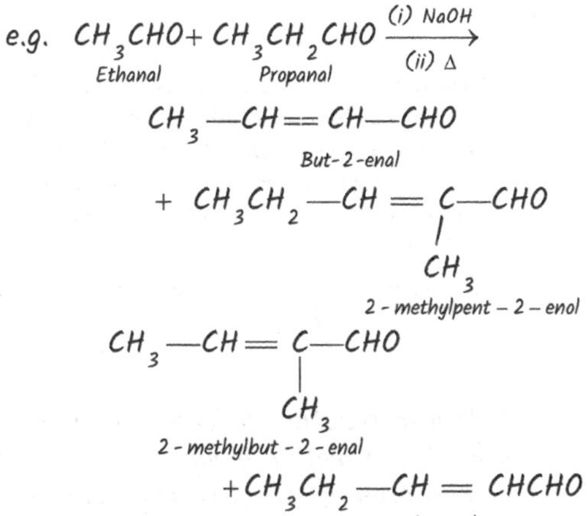

Ethanal Propanal

But-2-enal

2 - methylpent – 2 – enol

2 - methylbut - 2 - enal

pent - 2 - enal

(c) Cannizzaro's reaction

Cannizzaro's reaction Aldehydes which do not have α-H atoms undergo self oxidation and reduction on treatment with conc. alkali.

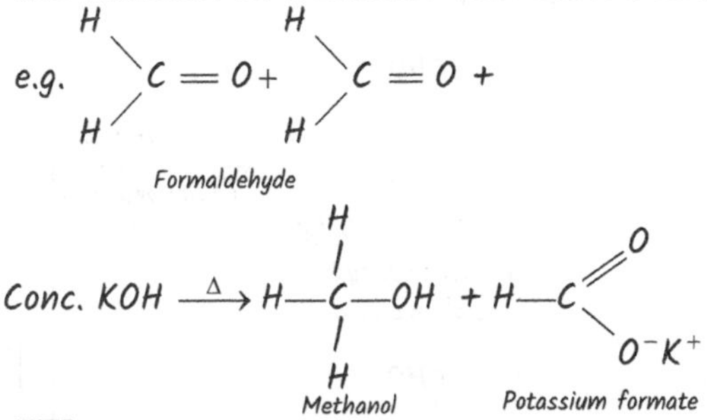

Formaldehyde

Methanol Potassium formate

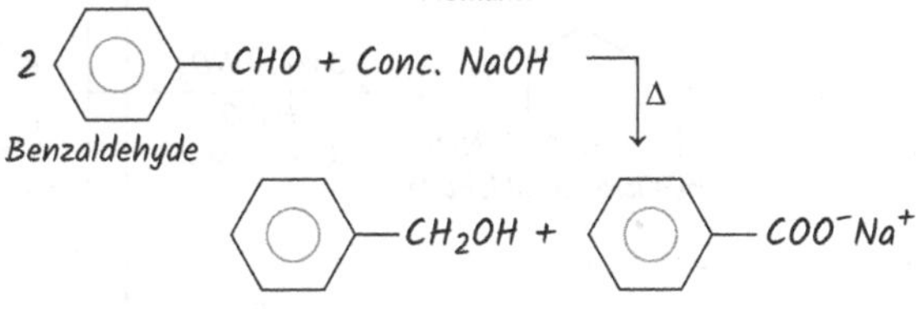

Benzaldehyde

Benzyl alcohol Sodium benzoate

(d) Reaction with Grignard reagent

Reaction with Grignard reagent Aldehydes and ketones on reaction with Grignard reagent give addition products which upon hydrolysis give alcohols.

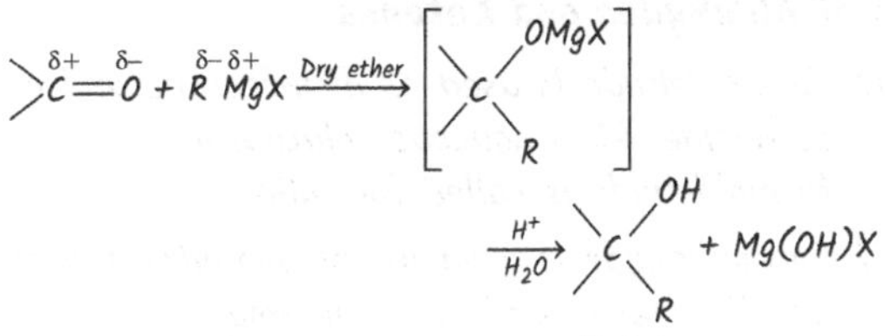

Alcohol

(e) Oxidation

- **Oxidation of aldehydes to carboxylic acids** Aldehydes differ from ketones in their oxidation reactions. Aldehydes are easily oxidised to *carboxylic acids containing the same number of carbon atom, because aldehydes contain H-atom attached to carbonyl group, which can be converted into —OH group without involving cleavage of any other bond.*

$$RCHO \xrightarrow{[O]} R—COOH$$

- ***Oxidation of ketones*** *Unlike aldehydes, ketones do not contain H-atom attached to C=O group and hence they cannot be oxidised by weak oxidising agents. They are oxidised by strong oxidising agents, like $KMnO_4$, acidified $K_2Cr_2O_4$at high temperature.*

$$R—CH_2—\underset{\underset{O}{||}}{C}—CH_2—R' \xrightarrow{[O]} R—COOH + RCH_2COOH + R'COOH$$

(f) ***Iodoform reaction*** *Aldehyde and ketones having atleast one methyl group linked to carbonyl carbon atom (methyl ketone) are oxidised by sodium hypohalite to sodium salts of corresponding carboxylic acids having one carbon atom less than that of carbonyl compound.*

$$R—\overset{\overset{O}{||}}{C}—CH_3 \xrightarrow{NaOI} R—\underset{\underset{O}{||}}{C}—O^-Na^+ + CHI_3$$

(g) ***Reduction*** *Aldehydes and ketones can be reduced to a variety of compounds under different conditions.*

$$>C=O \xrightarrow[\text{Conc. HCl}]{\text{Zn-Hg}} >CH_2 + H_2O$$

(Clemmensen reduction)

$$>C=O \xrightarrow[-H_2O]{NH_2NH_2} >C=NNH_2 \xrightarrow[\text{glycol, heat}]{\text{KOH / ethylene}} >CH_2 + N_2$$

(Wolff-kishner reduction)

Electrophilic Substitution Reactions

In aromatic aldehydes and ketones, both aldehydic and ketonic group are electron withdrawing groups so they act as deactivating and meta-directing groups.

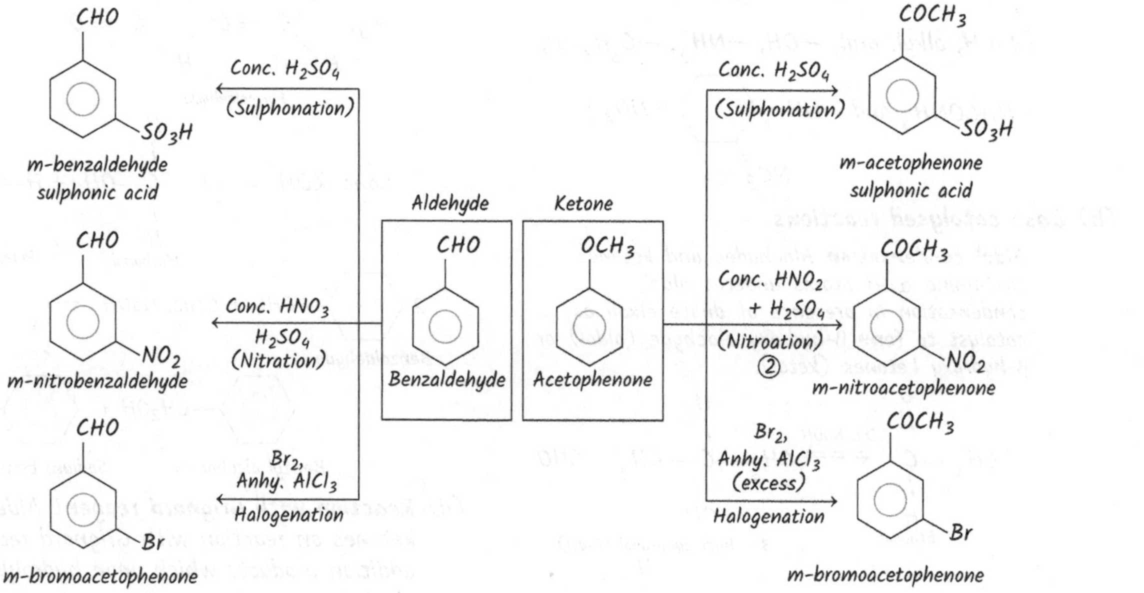

Uses of Aldehydes and Ketones

(i) *Formaldehyde is used as disinfectant and as a germicide, 40% aqueous solution of formaldehyde is called formalin.*

(ii) *Formaldehyde is used in the manufacture of bakelite, resin, and other polymers.*

(iii) *Formaldehyde is used in making urotropine, a medicine for urine infections.*

(iv) *Paraldehyde is used in medicine as a hypnotic.*

(v) *Acetone is used as a constituent of liquid nail polish.*

Test to Distinguish between Aldehydes and Ketones

Test	Aldehydes	Ketones
Tollen's reagent test	Give silver mirror	No response
Fehling's solution test	Give red precipitate (Aromatic aldehydes do not give this test)	No response
Schiff's reagent test	Give pink colour	No response, (acetone restore the pink colour but very slowly)
Reaction with $LiAlH_4$	Form primary alcohols	Form secondary alcohols

2. Aromatic Aldehyde or Benzaldehyde (C_6H_5CHO)

It is commercially known as oil of bitter almonds.

Preparation

From toluene Toluene on oxidation with chromyl chloride, oxidises methyl group to a chromium complex which on hydrolysis gives corresponding benzaldehyde.

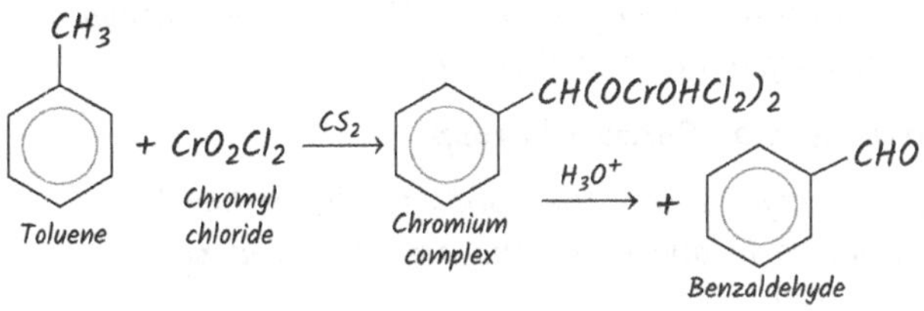

This reaction is known as **Etard reaction.**

Physical Properties

(i) It is highly refractive liquid.

(ii) It has boiling point of 452 K.

Chemical Properties

(i) **Oxidation** It gets oxidised to benzoic acid in the presence of dil. HNO_3 or alkaline $KMnO_4$.

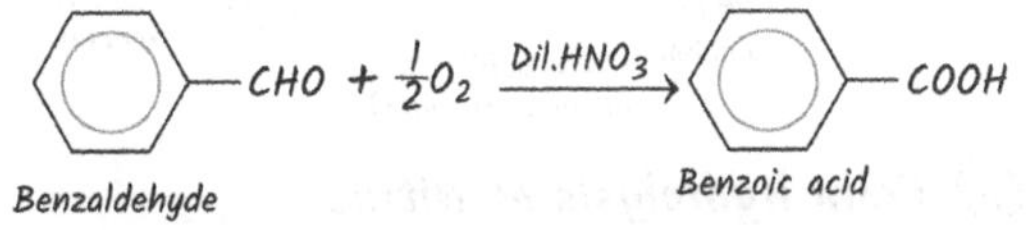

(ii) **Reduction** It is reduced to benzyl alcohol.

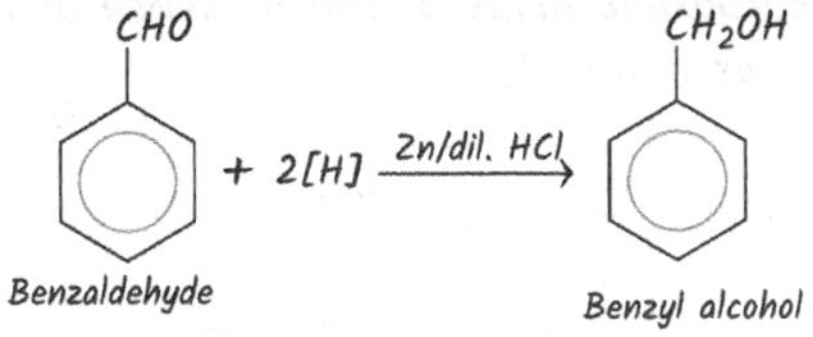

(iii) **Nucleophilic addition reaction**

(a) **With HCN**

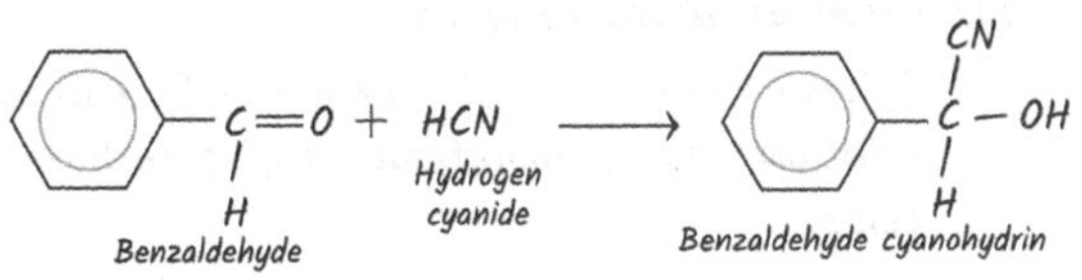

(b) **With $NaHSO_3$**

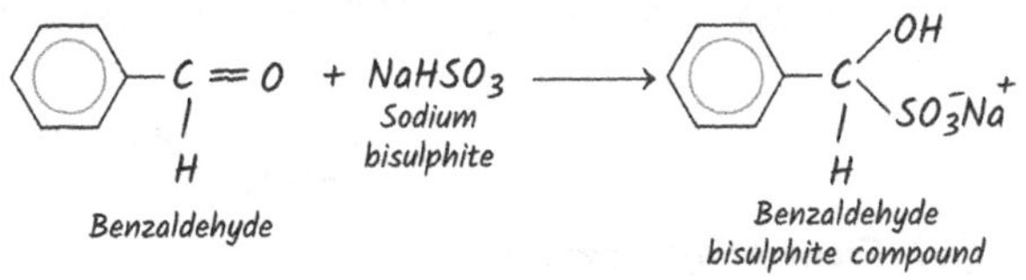

(iv) **Addition of Ammonia and its Derivatives**

(a) **With ammonia** It reacts with NH_3 to form complex product called **hydrobenzamide.**

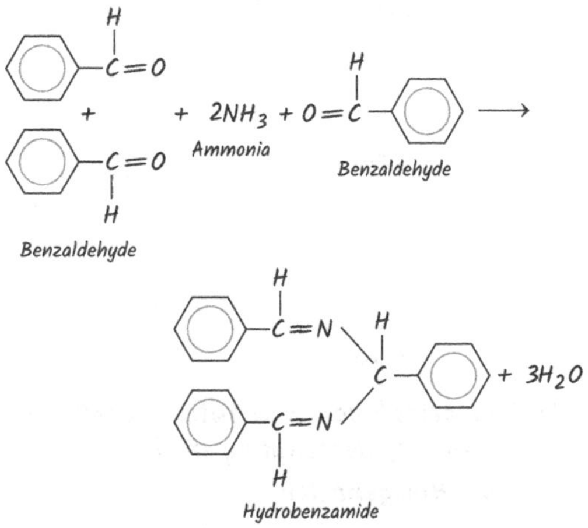

(b) **With ammonia derivatives**

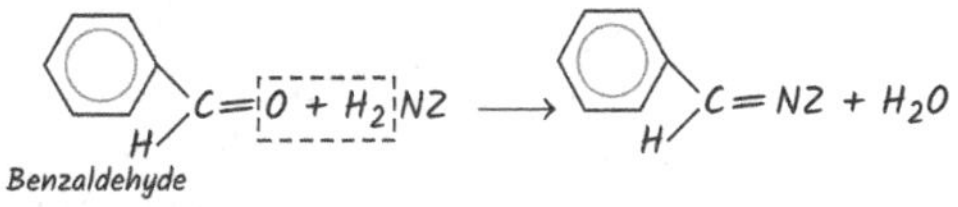

[Z = OH, NH_2, C_6H_5NH, 2,4-DNP, etc.]

(v) **Reaction with PCl_5** Benzal chloride is formed when benzaldehyde reacts with PCl_5.

$$\underset{\text{Benzaldehyde}}{C_6H_5CHO} + PCl_5 \longrightarrow \underset{\text{Benzal chloride}}{C_6H_5CHCl_2} + POCl_3$$

(vi) **Cannizzaro's reaction** When benzaldehyde is heated with strong alkali solution, it undergoes simultaneous oxidation and reduction forming salt of benzoic acid and benzyl alcohol.

$$\underset{\text{Benzaldehyde}}{2C_6H_5CHO} + \underset{\text{conc.}}{NaOH} \longrightarrow \underset{\text{Benzyl alcohol}}{C_6H_5CH_2OH} + \underset{\text{Sodium benzoate}}{C_6H_5COONa}$$

(vii) **Benzoin condensation** When two molecules of benzaldehyde are heated with an alcoholic solution of KCN, they undergo self condensation to form benzoin.

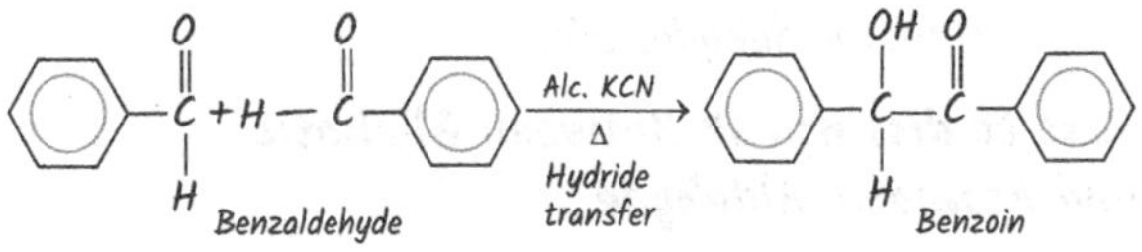

(viii) **Perkin's reaction** When benzaldehyde is heated with aliphatic acid anhydride in presence of sodium salt of the acid corresponding to the anhydride, they form α, β-unsaturated acid on hydrolysis.

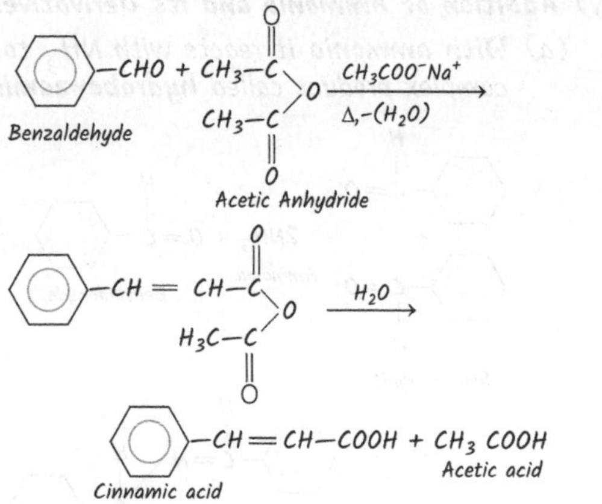

(ix) **Electrophilic substitution reactions** —CHO group is deactivating m-directing group.

(a) **Halogenation**

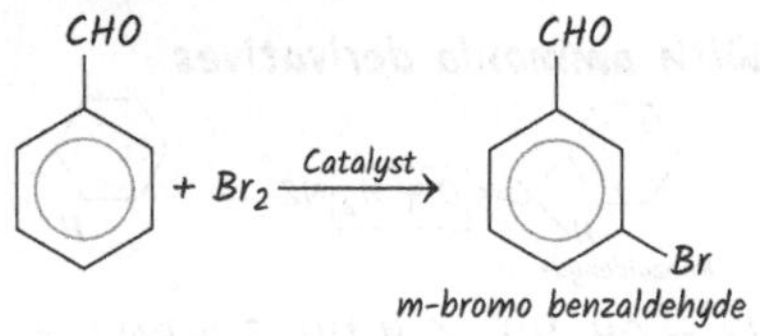

(b) **Nitration**

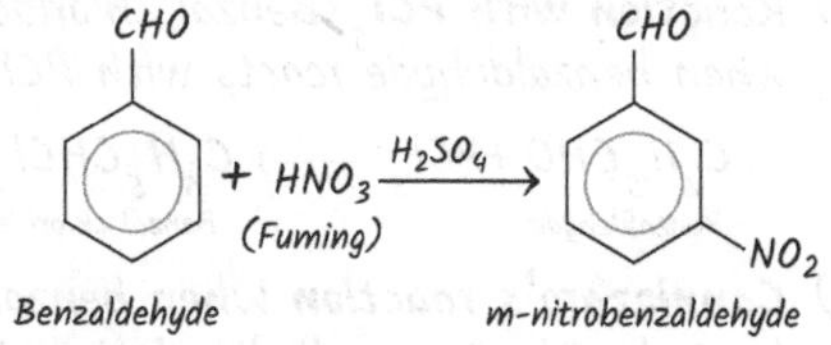

(c) **Sulphonation**

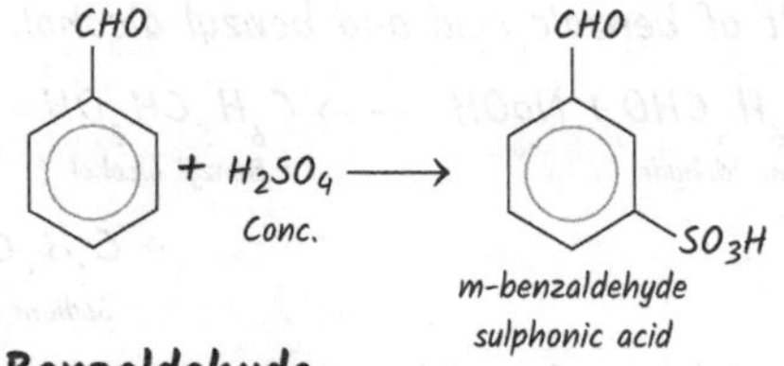

Uses of Benzaldehyde

(i) As a flavouring essence in perfumery.

(ii) In the manufacture of dyes.

(iii) In the synthesis of cinnamic acid, cinnamaldehyde, etc.

Test to distinguish Between Aliphatic and Aromatic Aldehyde

They can be distinguished by iodoform test. Acetaldehyde gives a yellow precipitate of iodoform, when heated with iodine in the presence of alkali.

$$\underset{\text{Acetaldehyde}}{CH_3CHO} + 4NaOH + 3I_2 \xrightarrow{\Delta} \underset{\substack{\text{Iodoform}\\\text{(yellow ppt.)}}}{CHI_3} + H\overset{-}{COO}\overset{+}{Na} + 3NaI + 3H_2O$$

Benzaldehyde does not give iodoform test.

3. Carboxylic Acids

The organic compounds which contain the carboxyl group

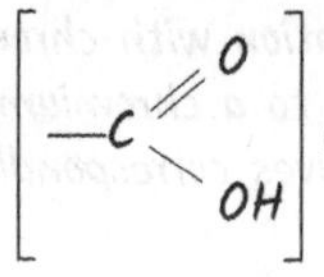

as the functional group are known as carboxylic acids. The general formula of carboxylic acids is $C_nH_{2n}O_2$.

Structure of Carboxyl Group

In carboxylic acids, the bonds to the carboxyl carbon lie in one plane and are separated by about 120°.

Preparation of Carboxylic Acids

(i) **From Oxidation of Primary Alcohols and Aldehydes**

Alcohols on oxidation with strong oxidising agent gives aldehyde which on further oxidation gives carboxylic acids.

$$\underset{\substack{\text{Primary}\\\text{alcohol}}}{RCH_2OH} \xrightarrow[\substack{KMnO_4 \text{ or}\\K_2Cr_2O_7\\\text{(in acidic or}\\\text{alkaline medium)}}]{[O]} \underset{\text{Aldehyde}}{RCHO} \xrightarrow[\substack{\text{Tollen's}\\\text{reagent}}]{[O]} \underset{\substack{\text{Carboxylic}\\\text{acid}}}{RCOOH}$$

(ii) **From Hydrolysis of Nitriles**

Nitriles are first hydrolysed to amides and then to carboxylic acids in the presence of H^+ or OH^- as catalyst.

$$\underset{\text{Nitrile}}{RC \equiv N} + 2H_2O \xrightarrow[\Delta]{H^+ \text{ or } OH^-} \underset{\text{Amide}}{R-\overset{\overset{\displaystyle O}{\|}}{C}-NH_2} \xrightarrow[H_2O]{H^+ \text{ or } OH^-} \underset{\substack{\text{Carboxylic}\\\text{acid}}}{RCOOH} + NH_3$$

(iii) **From Grignard reagent**

Grignard reagent with dry ice (CO_2) in etheral solution and on acidification give carboxylic acids.

$$RMgX + O{=}C{=}O \xrightarrow{\text{Dry ether}} R-\overset{\overset{\displaystyle O}{\|}}{C}-\overset{-}{O}\overset{+}{Mg}X \xrightarrow[H^+/H_2O]{-Mg(OH)X} R-COOH$$

(iv) **From Alkyl benzene**

Aromatic acids are obtained by vigorous oxidation of alkyl benzene with chromic acids or acidic or alkaline $KMnO_4$.

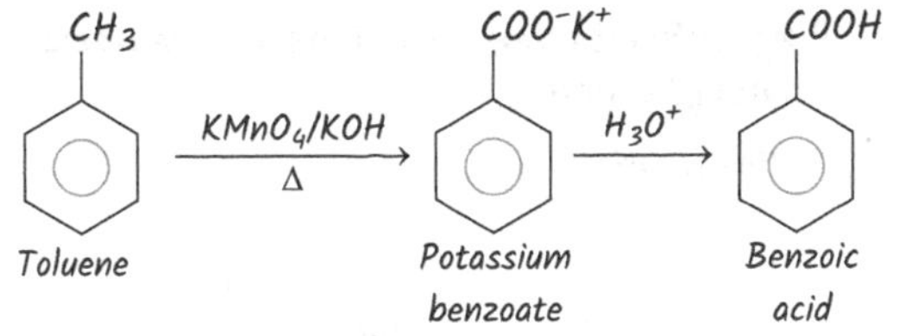

(v) **From Acyl Halides and Anhydrides**

$$RCOCl \begin{cases} \xrightarrow{H_2O} RCOOH + Cl^- \\ \xrightarrow{OH^-/H_2O} RCOO^- + Cl^- \xrightarrow{H_3O^+} RCOOH \end{cases}$$

$$\underset{\text{Benzoic anhydride}}{(C_6H_5CO)_2} \xrightarrow{H_2O} \underset{\text{Benzoic acid}}{2C_6H_5COOH}$$

(vi) **From Esters**

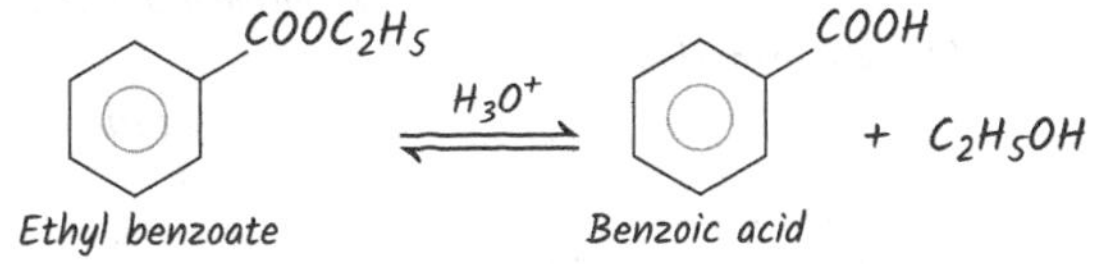

$$CH_3CH_2CH_2COOC_2H_5 \underset{}{\overset{NaOH}{\rightleftharpoons}} CH_3CH_2CH_2COO^-Na^+ + C_2H_5OH$$

Physical Properties of Carboxylic Acids

The physical properties of carboxylic acids are described below

(i) **Solubility** Simple aliphatic carboxylic acids having upto four carbon atoms are miscible in water because of hydrogen bond formation with water.

(ii) **Boiling point** As compared to hydrocarbons, aldehydes and ketones, carboxylic acids have higher boiling points because they have high extent of hydrogen bonding with water due to which they exists as associated molecules.

(iii) **Melting point** The melting points of aliphatic carboxylic acids do not show a regular pattern rather they show oscillation or alteration effect, i.e. melting point of an acid containing even number of carbon atoms is higher than the next member containing odd number of carbon atoms.

Chemical Properties of Carboxylic Acids

(i) **Acidic nature of carboxylic acids**

$$R\text{—}\overset{\overset{O}{||}}{C}\text{—}OH + H_2O \rightleftharpoons R\text{—}\overset{\overset{O}{||}}{C}\text{—}O^- + H_3O^+$$

Greater the extent of ionisation, greater is the strength of the acid.

Presence of an electron donating substituent (+I-effect) decreases the acidic strength of the carboxylic acid.

Presence of an electron withdrawing substituent (–I effect) increases the acidic strength of the carboxylic acid.

Reactions showing acidic character of carboxylic acids

(a) **Reaction with metals**

$$2RCOOH + 2Na \longrightarrow \underset{\text{Sodium carboxylate}}{2RCO\overset{-}{O}\overset{+}{Na}} + H_2\uparrow$$

(b) **Reaction with alkalies,**

$$RCOOH + NaOH \longrightarrow RCO\overset{-}{O}\overset{+}{Na} + H_2O$$

(c) **Reaction with carbonates and bicarbonates**

$$2RCOOH + \underset{\text{Sodium carbonate}}{Na_2CO_3} \longrightarrow 2RCO\overset{-}{O}\overset{+}{Na} + CO_2\uparrow + H_2O$$

$$R\text{—}COOH + NaHCO_3 \longrightarrow R\text{—}CO\overset{-}{O}\overset{+}{Na} + H_2O + CO_2\uparrow$$

18. Reaction involving cleavage of C—OH bond

(a) **Formation of acid chlorides** Carboxylic acids can be converted into corresponding and chlorides by treating with PCl_5, PCl_3 or $SOCl_2$

$$R\text{—}\underset{\underset{O}{||}}{C}\text{—}OH + \underset{\text{Thionyl chloride}}{SOCl_2} \longrightarrow \underset{\text{Acid chloride}}{R\text{—}\underset{\underset{O}{||}}{C}\text{—}Cl} + SO_2\uparrow + HCl\uparrow$$

(b) **Formation of esters** When carboxylic acids reacts with alcohols in presence of Conc. H_2SO_4, esters are formed.

$$\underset{\text{Acid}}{R\text{—}\underset{\underset{O}{||}}{C}\text{—}OH} + \underset{\text{Alcohol}}{R'OH} \overset{\text{Conc. } H_2SO_4}{\rightleftharpoons} \underset{\text{Ester}}{R\text{—}\underset{\underset{O}{||}}{C}\text{—}OR'} + H_2O$$

(c) **Formation of amides** They react with ammonia to form ammonium salts which upon heating form acid amides.

$$R\text{—}\underset{\underset{O}{||}}{C}\text{—}OH + NH_3 \longrightarrow \underset{\text{Ammonium carboxylate}}{R\text{—}\underset{\underset{O}{||}}{C}O^-\ NH_4^+} \xrightarrow{\Delta} \underset{\text{Acid amides}}{R\text{—}\underset{\underset{O}{||}}{C}\text{—}NH_2} + H_2O$$

Ammonium carboxylate

(d) **Formation of acid anhydride** Carboxylic acids in presence of strong dehydrating agents such as P_2O_5 or H_2SO_4 give acid anhydrides.

$$2\,R-\overset{\overset{O}{\|}}{C}-OH \xrightarrow[\Delta]{P_2O_5 \text{ or } H_2SO_4} \begin{matrix} R-\overset{\overset{O}{\|}}{C} \\ \quad\;\rangle O \\ R-\underset{\underset{O}{\|}}{C} \end{matrix} + H_2O$$

(ii) ***Decarboxylation of carboxylic acid*** *By electrolysis of aqueous solution of sodium or potassium salt.*

$$\underset{\text{Sodium salt of carboxylic acid}}{R-\overset{\overset{O}{\|}}{C}-O^- Na^+} + NaOH \xrightarrow[CaO]{\Delta} \underset{\text{Alkane}}{R-H} + Na_2CO_3$$

Electrolytic decarboxylation

(Kolbe electrolysis)

Alkali metal salts of carboxylic acids also undergo decarboxylation on electrolysis of their aqueous solutions and form hydrocarbons having twice the number of carbon atoms present in the alkyl group of acid. This reaction is known as ***Kolbe electrolysis.***

e.g. $2CH_3CO\overset{-}{O}\overset{+}{Na} + 2H_2O \xrightarrow{\text{Electrolysis}} CH_3-CH_3 + 2CO_2 + H_2 + 2NaOH$

The reaction follows the following path

(i) $2CH_3COONa \longrightarrow 2CH_3CO\bar{O} + 2N\dot{a}$

(ii) **At anode,** $2CH_3CO\bar{O} \xrightarrow{-2e^-} \underset{\text{(Unstable)}}{2CH_3COO} \longrightarrow \underset{\text{Alkane}}{2C\dot{H}_3} + 2CO_2\uparrow$

(iii) $\dot{C}H_3 + \dot{C}H_3 \rightarrow CH_3-CH_3\uparrow$

(iv) **At cathode,** $H_2O^\bullet + e^- \longrightarrow OH^- + \dot{H}$

$$2\dot{H} \longrightarrow H_2\uparrow$$

(v) ***Halogenation***

Carboxylic acids (except formic acid) react with chlorine or bromine in presence of small amount of red phosphorus gives α- halogenated carboxylic acids.

$$\underset{\text{Acetic Acid}}{CH_3COOH} \xrightarrow[(-HCl)]{Cl_2,\text{ Red P}} \underset{\text{Monochloro Acetic acid}}{CH_2ClCOOH}$$

$$\xrightarrow[(-HCl)]{Cl_2,\text{ Red P}} \underset{\text{Dichloro acetic acid}}{CHCl_2COOH} \xrightarrow[(-HCl)]{Cl_2,\text{ Red P}} \underset{\text{Trichloro acetic acid}}{CCl_3COOH}$$

This reaction is called ***Hell-Volhard-Zelinsky*** *(HVZ) reaction.*

(vi) ***Ring substitution reactions in aromatic carboxylic acids***

(a) **Halogenation**

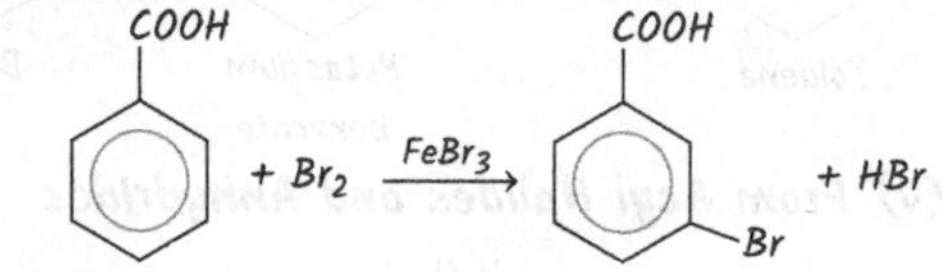

Benzoic acid → m-bromobenzoic acid

(b) **Nitration**

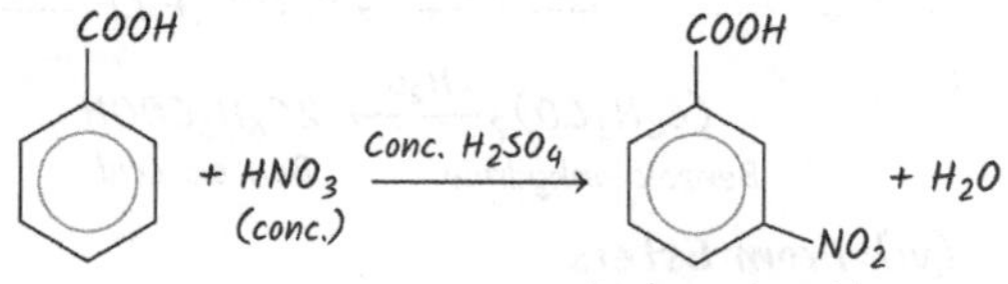

m-nitrobenzoic acid

(c) **Sulphonation**

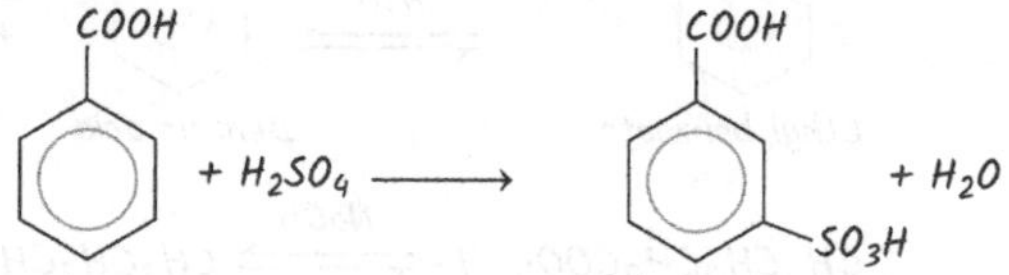

m-sulphobenzoic acid

Test For

(i) **Formic acid**

(a) *It gives silver mirror or black precipitate with Tollen's reagent.*

(b) *It gives red precpitate with Fehling's solution.*

(c) *It gives decolourises pink colour of acidified* $KMnO_4$.

(ii) **Acetic acid**

(a) *It liberates carbon dioxide gas with bicarbonates and carbonates. With ferric chloride, it produces wine red colour.*

(b) *When warmed with ethyl alcohol and conc.* H_2SO_4, *a pleasant fruity odour of ethyl acetate is formed.*

(iii) **Benzoic acid**

(a) *It dissolves in water on boiling but separate out in the form of white precipitate on cooling.*

(b) *It gives buff coloured ppt with* $FeCl_3$.

Uses

(i) **Formic acid**

(a) *As an antiseptic.*

(b) *For dye baths in textiles.*

(c) *As a coagulating agent in rubber industry.*

(ii) **Acetic acid**

(a) As a solvent for resins, cellulose etc.
(b) In the production of dyes, perfumes, esters, acetone etc.
(c) For the manufacture of cellulose which is used for making packaging materials, varnishes, rayon etc.

(iii) **Benzoic acid**

(a) As a food preservative either in the pure form or mostly in the form of sodium benzoate.
(b) As urinary antiseptic in medicine.
(c) In the manufacture of antiseptics and dyes.

Chapter 9 Organic Compounds Containing Nitrogen

I. Amines

Amines can be considered as derivatives of ammonia obtained by the replacement of hydrogen atoms by alkyl or aryl groups.
In the IUPAC system, they are named as alkanamines, derived by the replacement of 'e' of alkane by the word amines.

Classification

They are classified as primary (RNH_2) secondary (R_2NH) and tertiary (R_3N) amines according to the number of alkyl groups attached directly with N-atom.

Structure

In aliphatic amines, N-atom is always sp^3-hybridised.
Each of the three sp^3-hybridised orbitals overlap with overlap of hydrogen or carbon.
Due to presence of unshared pair of electrons, the angle C—N—E (E is C or H) is less than 109.5°.

(i) General Methods of Preparation of Amines

(a) **From haloalkanes** A mixture of primary, secondary and tertiary amines alongwith quaternary salt, is obtained by the cleavage of C—X bond by ammonia. This process is known as ammonolysis.

$$\underset{\text{Haloalkane}}{RX} + NH_3 \xrightarrow[-HX]{373\text{ K}} \underset{\text{Primary amine}}{RNH_2} \xrightarrow[-HX]{RX}$$

$$\underset{\text{sec - amine}}{R_2NH} \xrightarrow[-HX]{RX} \underset{\text{tert - amine}}{R_3N} \xrightarrow[-HX]{RX} \underset{\text{quartenery - amine}}{R_4N^+X^-}$$

(b) **By the reduction of nitro compounds** Reduction of nitro compounds to primary amines can occur by using Sn/HCl or Fe/HCl or $LiAlH_4$ or H_2/Ni.

$$R—NO_2 + 6[H] \xrightarrow[\text{or } LiAlH_4 \text{ (or } H_2/Ni)]{Sn/HCl \text{ or } Fe/HCl} RNH_2 + 2H_2O$$

(c) **By the reduction of cyanides and isocyanides** Alkyl nitriles and isocyanide on reduction gives primary and secondary amines respectively. Reduction of nitriles to primary amines by using Na and alcohol is called Mendius reaction.

$$R—C \equiv N + 4[H] \xrightarrow[\text{(or } H_2 Ni)]{LiAlH_4 \text{ or Na/alc.}} \underset{1°\text{ amine}}{RCH_2NH_2}$$

$$R—N \Rightarrow C + 4[H] \xrightarrow[\text{(or } H_2/Ni)]{LiAlH_4} \underset{2°\text{amine}}{RNHCH_3}$$

(d) **From alcohols** When vapour of a mixture of alcohol and ammonia are passed over heated alumina at 620 K, a mixture of amines is obtained.

$$CH_3OH + NH_3 \xrightarrow[347°C]{Al_2O_3} CH_3NH_2 + H_2O$$

$$\downarrow CH_3OH$$

$$(CH_3)_3N + H_2O \xleftarrow{CH_3OH} (CH_3)_2NH + H_2O$$

(e) **From amides** Amides on reaction with Br_2 in an aqueous or ethanolic solution of NaOH give 1° amine with one C atom less than that present in the amide.

$$R—\overset{O}{\overset{\|}{C}}—NH_2 + Br_2 + 4NaOH \longrightarrow RNH_2 + Na_2CO_3 + 2NaBr + 2H_2O$$

This reaction is known as **Hofmann bromamide degradation reaction**. Also, amides on reduction with $LiAlH_4$ yield amines.

$$R—\overset{O}{\overset{\|}{C}}—NH_2 \xrightarrow[(ii)\ H_2O]{(i)\ LiAlH_4} R—CH_2NH_2$$

(f) **Gabriel's phthalimide synthesis** In this reaction, phthalimide on treatment with ethanolic KOH forms potassium salt of phthalimide which on heating with RX followed by either alkaline hydrolysis produces 1° amines.

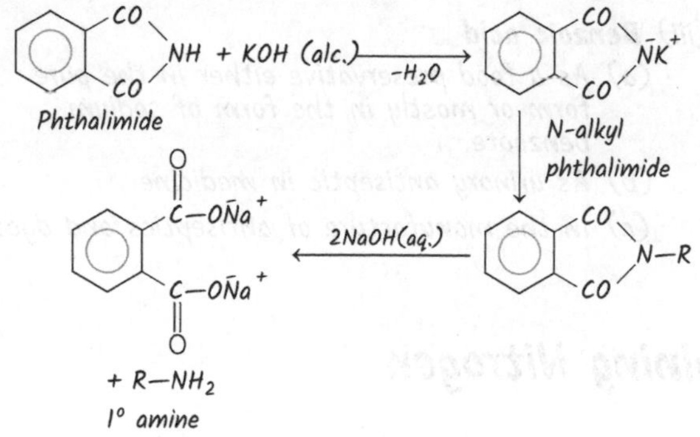

(ii) Physical Properties of Amines

(a) Amines exhibit hydrogen bonding which influence their physical properties. Aliphatic amines (1° and 2°) forms H-bonds with water and hence, are soluble in water while 3° amines are insoluble in water. Aromatic amines however, insoluble in water due to large hydrocarbon part.

(b) Boiling points of 1° amine is higher than that of 3° amine due to the presence of two H-atoms attached directly with N, which results in H-bonding in 1° amines.

$$1^\circ \text{ amine} > 2^\circ \text{ amine} > 3^\circ \text{ amine}$$

(iii) Chemical Properties of Amines

(a) **Basic character of amines**

- Aliphatic amines are stronger bases than ammonia due to +I-effect (electron donating power) of alkyl groups, due to which electron density on nitrogen atom increases and hence they can easily donate their electrons as compared to ammonia. Aromatic amines are weaker bases than ammonia due to presence of configuration of unshared pair of electrons in N-atom with benzene ring.
- Larger the value of K_b or smaller the value of pK_b, stronger is the base.
- Order of basicity of amines in **gaseous phase** follows the expected order:
  Tertiary amine > Secondary amine > Primary amine > Ammonia
- Combined effect of +I-group, steric effect and solvation effect decides the basic character of amines in aqueous phase. If the alkyl group is small, i.e. CH_3, then there is no steric hindrance to H-bonding and hence H-bonding predominates over +I-effect. Since, all these effect are favourables for 2° amine, therefore order of basicity is 2° amine > 1° amine > 3° amine (in aqueous phase).
- If the alkyl group is bigger than CH_3 group, there is steric hindrance to H-bonding and hence +I-effect predominates over H-bonding. Therefore, the order is 2° amine > 3° amine > 1° amine (in aqueous phase).
- In case of aniline, presence of electron withdrawing group decreases the basicity whereas presence of electron donating group increases the basicity.
- In aniline or any other arylamines, unshared electron pair present on nitrogen atom is in conjugation with the benzene ring and making, it is less available for protonation.
- Electron donating groups such as $—CH_3$, $—OCH_3$, $—NH_2$ increase the basicity while electron withdrawing groups such as $— NO_2$, — CN, —(halogens) decrease the basicity of amines. The effect of these substituents is more pronounced at p- than at m-positions.

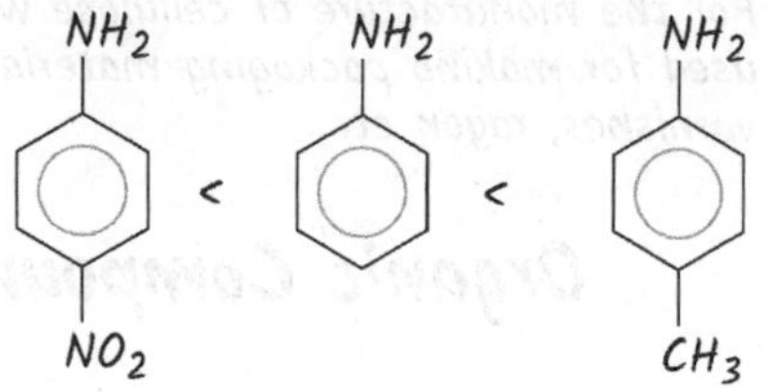

- o-substituted anilines are weaker bases than aniline regardless of the nature of the substituent whether electron-donating or electron-withdrawing. This is called ortho-effect and is due to steric hindrance.

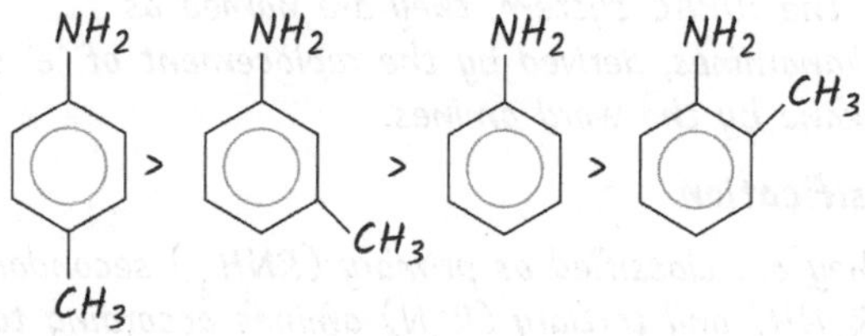

Note Aliphatic amines are more basic than aromatic amines. As in aromatic amines, lone pair of electrons present on nitrogen takes part in resonance, hence not available for donation whereas in aliphatic amines, it is available.

(b) **Alkylation** H-atoms of amine get replaced one by one by alkyl group of alkyl halide.

$$\underset{1^\circ \text{ amine}}{RNH_2} \xrightarrow[-HX]{RX} \underset{2^\circ \text{ amine}}{R_2NH} \xrightarrow[-HX]{RX} \underset{3^\circ \text{ amine}}{R_3N} \xrightarrow[-HX]{RX} \underset{\text{Quaternary salt}}{[R_4N]^+ X^-}$$

(c) **Acylation** 1° amines gives N-substituted amide while 2° amine give N, N-disubstituted amides.

$$R— NH_2 + R'COCl \longrightarrow R—NH—COR' + HCl$$

In aromatic amines, acylation occurs in the presence of base such as pyridine as catalyst.

Benzoylation of amines in the presence of NaOH is known as Schotten-Baumann reaction.

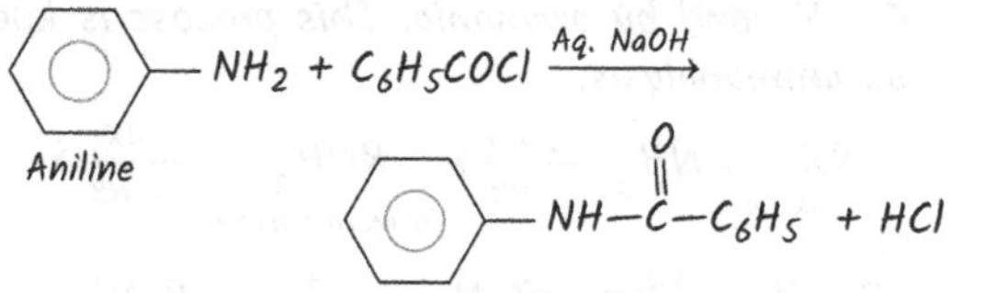

N-phenyl benzamide

(d) **Formation of Schiff's bases** Primary amines react with aldehydes and ketones in the presence of a trace of an acid as a catalyst to form azomethines called anils or Schiff's bases.

(iv) Tests to Distinguish 1°, 2° and 3° Amines

(a) **Carbylamine test** This test is used to distinguish primary amines from secondary and tertiary amines. Both aliphatic and aromatic primary amines on heating with chloroform and alcoholic KOH from isocyanides or carbylamines which is foul smelling compound.

$$R{-}NH_2 + CHCl_3 + 3KOH(alc.) \xrightarrow{\Delta} R{-}NC + 3KCl + 3H_2O$$

1° a min e ; Isocyanide

Secondary and tertiary amines do not show this reaction.

(b) **Nitrous acid test** Aliphatic amines react with nitrous acid to form aliphatic diazonium salts which further liberate nitrogen gas and alcohols.

$$R{-}NH_2 + HNO_2 \xrightarrow{NaNO_2 + HCl} [R{-}\overset{+}{N}_2\overset{-}{C}l] \xrightarrow{H_2O} ROH + N_2\uparrow + HCl$$

Aromatic primary amines also react with nitrous acid but at low temperature giving only diazonium salt.

$$C_6H_5{-}NH_2 \xrightarrow[273\text{-}278\ K]{NaNO_2 + 2HCl} C_6H_5{-}N_2^+\overset{-}{C}l + NaCl + 2H_2O$$

Secondary and tertiary amines also react with nitrous acid in different manner.

(c) **Hinsberg's test**

- Primary amine when reacts with Hinsberg's reagent (benzene sulphonyl chloride), it yields derivative of mono-alkyl sulphonamide which is soluble in KOH.

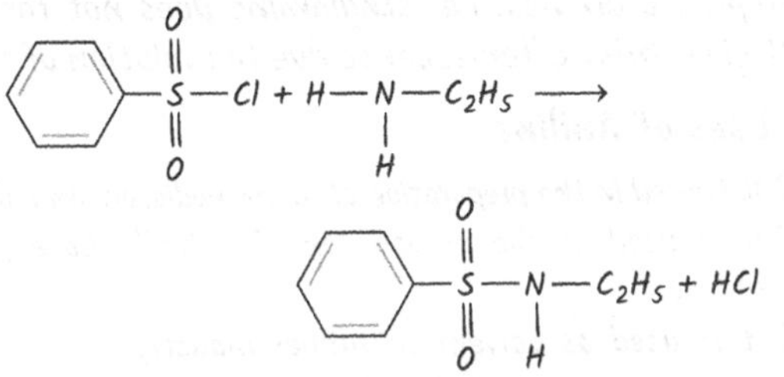

N-ethyl benzene sulphonamide
(soluble in alkali)

- Secondary amines forms dialkyl sulphonamide derivative with Hinsberg's reagent which is insoluble in KOH.

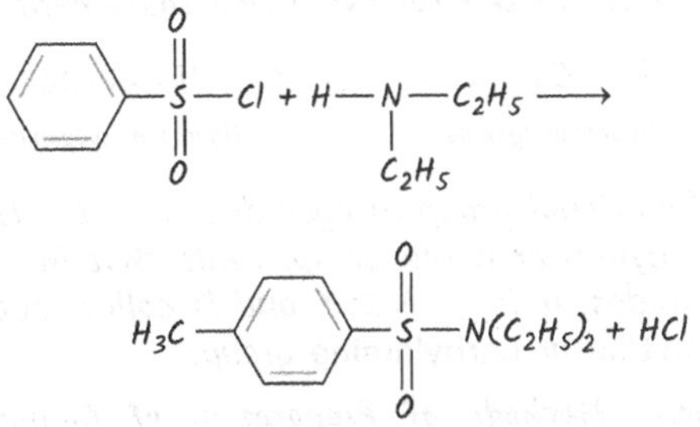

N-diethyl benzene sulphonamide
(soluble in alkali)

- Tertiary amines do not reacts with Hinsberg's reagent.

(v) Uses of Amines

(a) Aliphatic amines are used as solvents and intermediates in the manufacturing of drugs.

(b) They are used as reagents in organic synthesis.

(c) Aromatic amines are used in the formation of polymers, dyes and drugs.

2. Aniline ($C_6H_5NH_2$)

(i) Preparation of Aniline

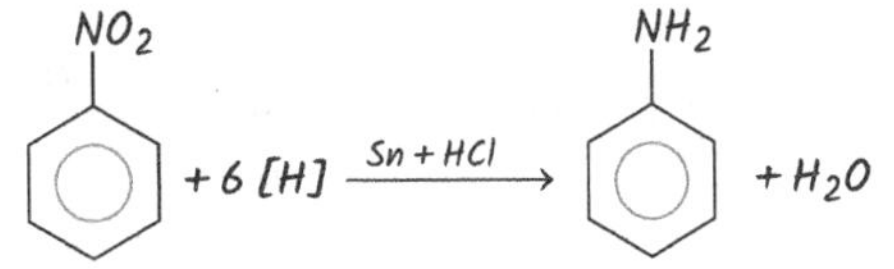

Nitrobenzene — Aniline

(ii) Physical Properties of Aniline

- It is steam volatile and toxic in nature.
- Aniline is slightly soluble in water and sometimes freely soluble in chemicals such as alcohol and ether.

(iii) Chemical Properties of Aniline

(a) **Reaction with HCl and H_2SO_4** (Basic nature)

$$C_6H_5NH_2 + HCl \longrightarrow C_6H_5NH_2 \cdot HCl$$

Benza min e — Anilinium chloride

$$2C_6H_5NH_2 + H_2SO_4 \longrightarrow (C_6H_5NH_2)_2 \cdot H_2SO_4$$

Benza min e — Anilinium sulphate

(b) **Alkylation**

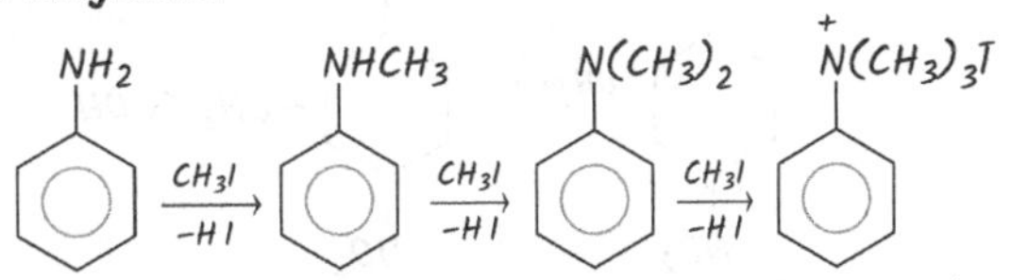

1° amine — 2° amine — 3° amine — Quaternary salt

(c) **Acetylation**

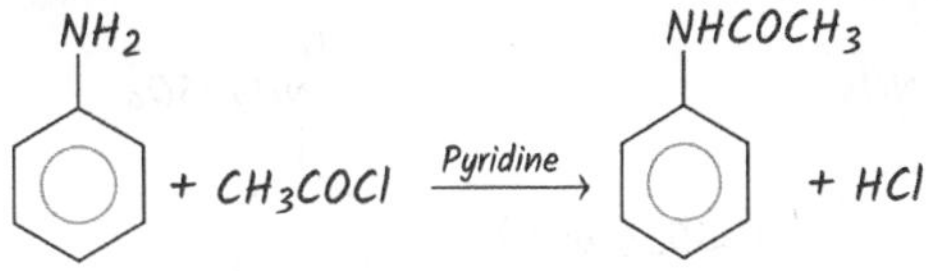

N-phenylacetamide

(d) **Carbylamine reaction**

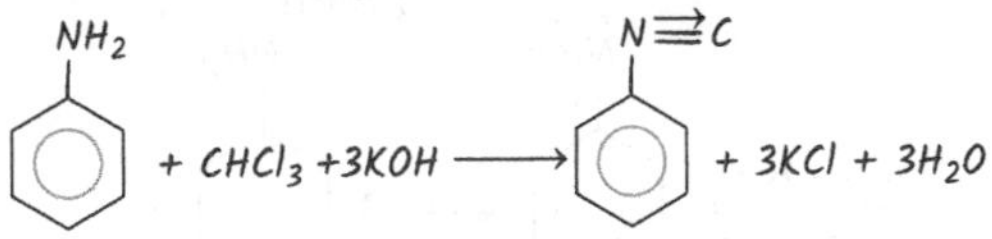

Phenyl cyanide

(e) **Electrophilic substitution reaction** In aniline, electron density at ortho and para-positions (due to $-NH_2$) is high. Therefore, $-NH_2$ group is ortho or para directing and powerful activating.

To control its activity, aniline is subjected to acetylation before subjecting to electrophilic substitution reactions to get mono-substituted product.

Halogenation

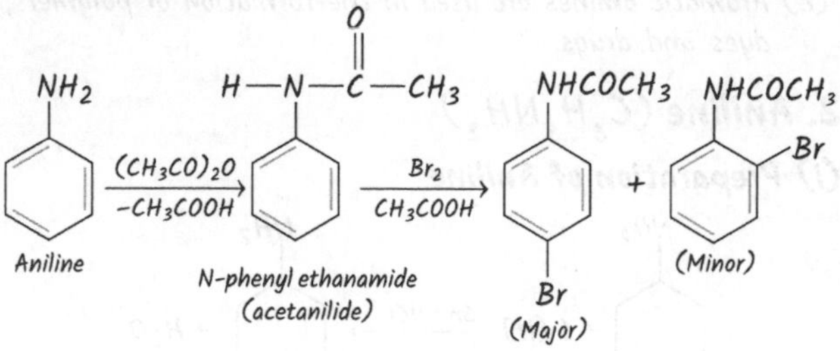

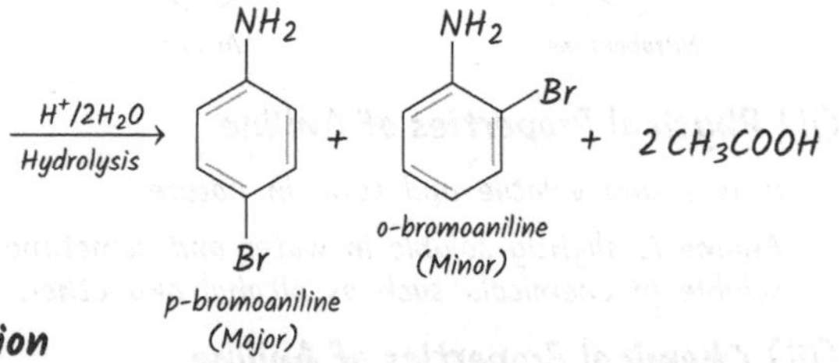

Nitration

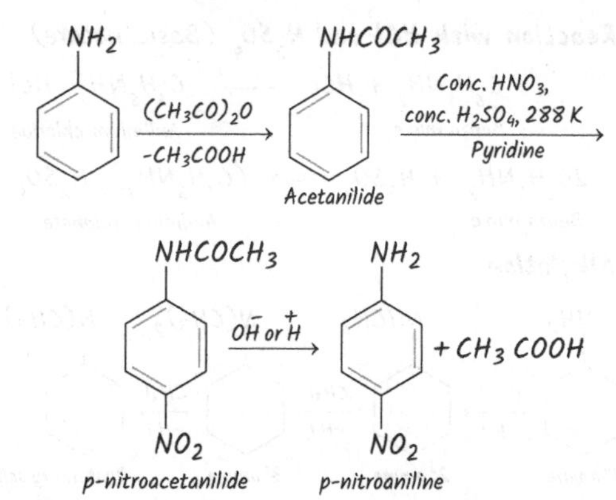

Sulphonation

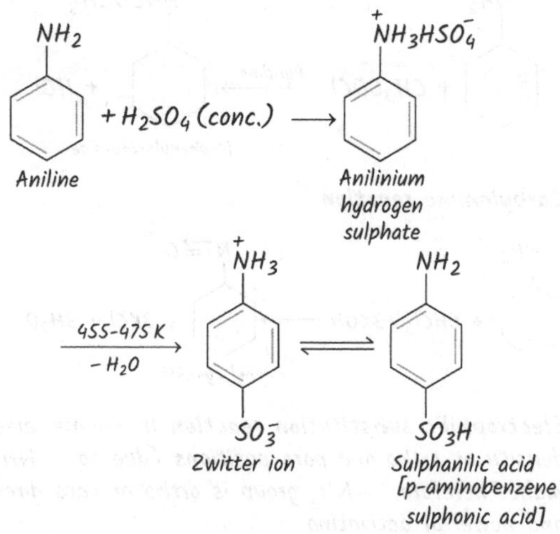

Test for Aniline

Aniline gives following test :

Azo Dye Test *This test is used to distinguish aromatic primary (1°) amines from aliphatic 1° amines.*

Aniline on treatment with (HNO_2 + dilute.HCl) followed by the treatment with alkaline solution of β-naphthol forms an orange or red dye.

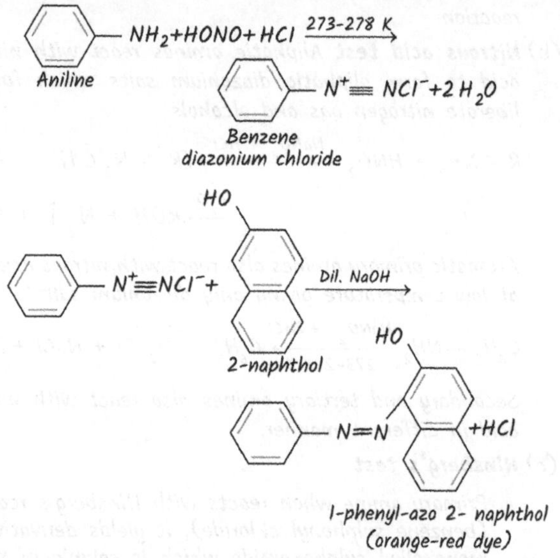

Aliphatic amines, i.e. ethylamine does not form dye. It gives brisk effervescence due to evolution of N_2.

(v) Uses of Aniline

(a) It is used in the preparation of benzenediazonium chloride.

(b) It is used in the preparation of Schiff's bases, sulpha drugs.

(c) It is used as solvent in rubber industry.

3. Cyanides and Isocyanides

The cyanide group is an ambident group and can attach itself to H through both C as well as N-atom.

HCN exists in the following two tautomeric forms :

$$\underset{\text{Hydrogen cyanide}}{H—C \equiv N} \rightleftharpoons \underset{\text{Hydrogen isocyanide}}{H—N \overset{\rightarrow}{=} C}$$

The functional group in cyanides is —C≡N and is called cyano *or* nitrile *group, while that in isocyanides, it is —N⇉C and is called* isocyano *or* isonitrile *or* carbylamine *group.*

(i) General Methods of Preparation of Cyanides and Isocyanides

(a) Cyanides

- *From alkyl halides When an alkyl halide is heated with an alcoholic solution of sodium or potassium cyanide, alkyl cyanides are obtained.*

$$RX + K^+CN^-(alc.) \xrightarrow{\Delta} R—C \equiv N + K^+X^-$$

- *From acid amides When an acid amide is heated with P_2O_5 or $SOCl_2$, the amide undergoes dehydration to give corresponding cyanide.*

$$R-\overset{\overset{O}{||}}{C}-NH_2 \xrightarrow[\Delta]{P_2O_5 \text{ or } SOCl_2} R-C \equiv N + H_2O$$

(b) ***Isocyanides***

From alkyl halides *When an alkyl halide is treated with an alcoholic solution of silver cyanide, alkyl isocyanide is formed.*

$$RX + AgCN(alc.) \longrightarrow R-N \overrightarrow{\leftarrow} C + AgX$$

(ii) ***Physical Properties of Cyanides and Isocyanides***

Cyanides and isocyanides both are polar but isocyanides possess lesser dipole moments than the cyanides.

(iii) ***Chemical Properties of Cyanides and Isocyanides***

(a) ***Hydrolysis***

I. ***Cyanides*** *can be hydrolysed by mineral acids or alkali to form the corresponding carboxylic acids and ammonia, through the formation of an amide as an intermediate.*

$$\underset{\text{Cyanide}}{RCN} \xrightarrow{H_2O,\ H^+} \underset{\text{Acid amide}}{RCONH_2} \xrightarrow{H_2O,\ H^+} \underset{\text{Carboxylic acid}}{RCOOH} + NH_3$$

II. ***Isocyanides*** *are hydrolysed only by dilute acids and not by alkalis to form primary amine and formic acid.*

$$\underset{\text{Isocyanide}}{R-N \overrightarrow{\leftarrow} C} + H_2O \xrightarrow{H^+} \underset{\text{N - alkyl amide form}}{[R-NH-\overset{\overset{O}{||}}{C}-H]}$$

$$\xrightarrow{H^+,\ H_2O} \underset{\text{Primary amine}}{RNH_2} + \underset{\text{Formic acid}}{HCOOH}$$

4. Diazonium Salts

Diazonium salts have the general formula $Ar\overset{+}{N}_2 X^-$

where X^- *ion may be* Cl^-, Br^-, HSO_4^-, NO_3^-, *etc.*

(i) Preparation of Diazonium Salts

$$C_6H_5NH_2 + NaNO_2 + 2HCl \xrightarrow{273\text{-}278\ K} \underset{\text{Diazonium salt}}{C_6H_5\overset{+}{N}_2}\ Cl^- + NaCl + 2H_2O$$

This process of conversion of a primary aromatic amine into their diazonium salts is called ***diazotisation.***

(ii) Physical Properties of Diazonium Salts

(a) They are highly soluble in water.

(b) These are unstable and explode in dry state, hence used in solution state.

(c) Their aqueous solutions are neutral to litmus and conduct electricity due to the presence of ions.

(iii) Chemical Properties of Diazonium Salts

The reactions of diazonium salts can be divided into two following categories

(a) ***Reactions involving displacement of nitrogen***

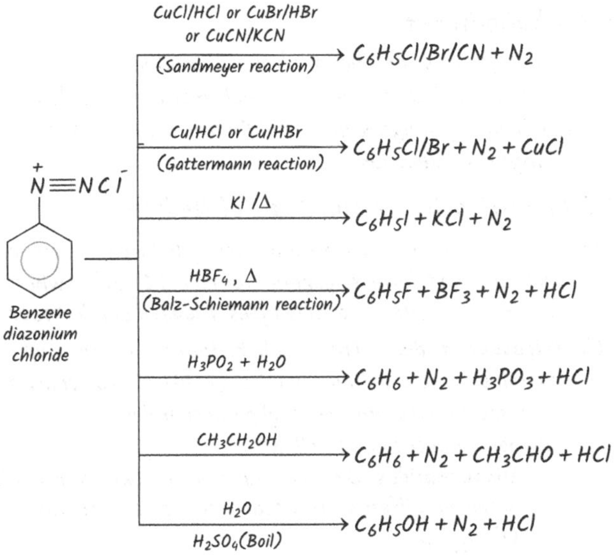

(b) ***Coupling reaction*** *Benzene diazonium chloride coupled with phenol molecule having —OH group at para-position to give p-hydroxyazobenzene, hence, the reaction is known as* coupling reaction. *The azo products obtained, are coloured and used as dyes.*

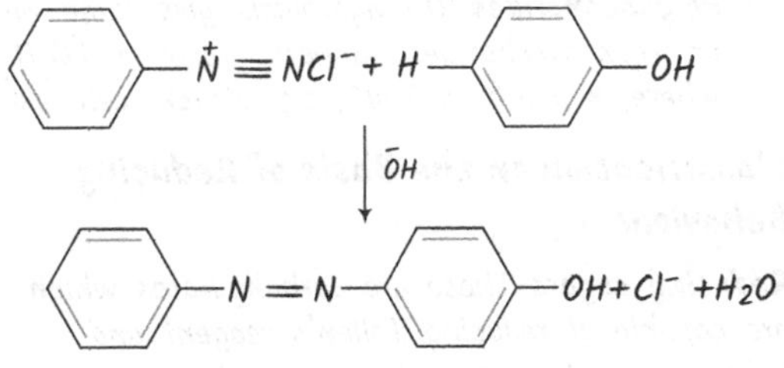

p-hydroxyazobenzene
(Orange dye)

Also, diazonium salt react with amine to yield p-aminoazobenzene.

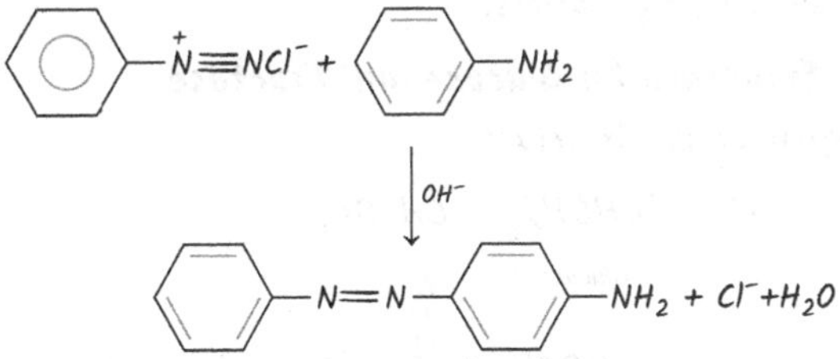

p- aminoazobenzene
(yellow dye)

(iv) Uses of Diazonium Salt

(a) It is a standard reagent in synthesis of organic compounds especially aryl derivatives.

(b) It's major applications remain in the dye and pigment industry.

Chapter 10 Biomolecules

I. Carbohydrates

Carbohydrates are polyhydroxy aldehydes or polyhydroxy ketones or large polymeric molecules which on hydrolysis yield polyhydroxy aldehydes or polyhydroxy ketones.

(i) Classification on the Basis of Hydrolysis

(a) **Monosaccharides** These cannot be hydrolysed to simpler molecule and have a general formula $(CH_2O)_n$, where, $n = 3$ to 7. These are of two types. **Aldoses** and **ketoses**.

(b) **Oligosaccharides** The carbohydrates which upon hydrolysis give a definite number (2-10) of molecules of monosaccharides are called oligosaccharides.
Further categorised as follows :

I. **Disaccharides** On hydrolysis give two units of same or different monosaccharides, e.g. sucrose $(C_{12}H_{22}O_{11})$.

II. **Trisaccharides** On hydrolysis give three units of same or different monosaccharides. e.g. raffinose $(C_{18}H_{32}O_{16})$.

III. **Tetrasaccharides** On hydrolysis give four units of same or different monosaccharides. e.g. stachyrose $(C_{24}H_{42}O_{21})$.

IV. **Polysaccharides** On hydrolysis give large number of monosaccharides. General formula $(C_6H_{10}O_5)_n$ where, $n = 100$ to 3000, e.g. starch, cellulose.

(ii) Classification on the Basis of Reducing Behaviour

(a) **Reducing sugars** These are carbohydrates which are capable of reducing Tollen's reagent and Fehling's solution, e.g. all monosaccharides and the disaccharides except sucrose.

(b) **Non-reducing sugars** These are carbohydrates which are unable to reduce Tollen's reagent and Fehling's solution, e.g. sucrose.

(iii) Structure for Glucose and Fructose

- **Open Chain Structure**

$$OHC—(CHOH)_4—CH_2OH;$$

Glucose

$$HOCH_2—\overset{\overset{\Large O}{||}}{C}—(CHOH)_3—CH_2OH$$

Fructose

- **Cyclic Structure** (Haworth structure)
All the pentoses and hexoses exist in cyclic hemiacetal or hemiketal structures.
In the free state, they have generally six-membered cyclic structures called **pyranose form**. However, in the combined state, some of these such as ribose, 2-deoxyribose, fructose, etc. have five-membered cyclic structure called the **furanose form**.

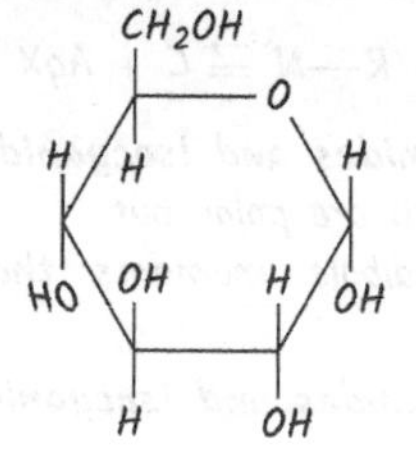

α-D(+)-gluco pyranose

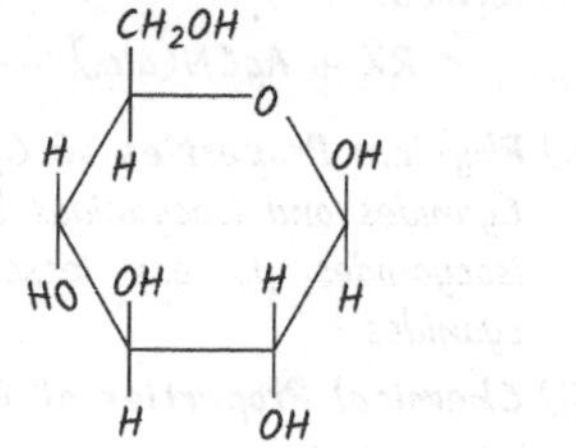

β-D(+)-glucopyranose

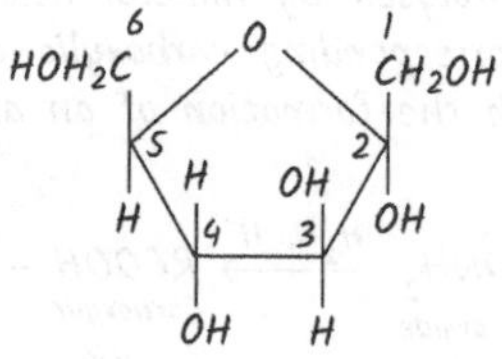

α-D-(–)-fructofuranose

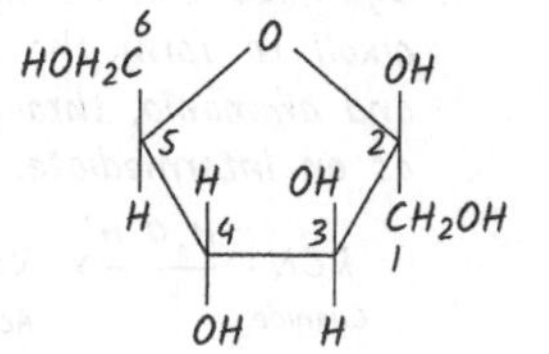

β-D-(–)-fructofuranose

Sucrose on hydrolysis with acids or enzymes gives equimolar mixture of D – (+) – glucose and D – (–) – fructose.

$$\underset{\text{Sucrose}}{C_{12}H_{22}O_{11}} + H_2O \xrightarrow{HCl} \underset{D-(+)-\text{glucose}}{C_6H_{12}O_6} + \underset{D-(-)-\text{fructose}}{C_6H_{12}O_6}$$

Hydrolysis of sucrose brings about a change in the sign of rotation from dextro (+) to leavo (–) and the product is named as invert sugar.

(b) Properties of Glucose and Fructose

I. Glucose and fructose are functional isomers.
Glucose has aldehyde group (—CHO), whereas fructose has ketone ($\rangle C = O$) group at second carbon atom.

II. Glucose condenses with hydroxylamine to form oxime called **D-glucose oxime**.

$$\underset{D-\text{glucose}}{\begin{matrix} CHO \\ | \\ (CHOH)_4 \\ | \\ CH_2OH \end{matrix}} + \underset{\text{Hydroxyl a min e}}{NH_2OH} \longrightarrow \underset{D-\text{glucose amine}}{\begin{matrix} H—C = NOH \\ | \\ (CHOH)_4 \\ | \\ CH_2OH \end{matrix}} + H_2O$$

III. When heated with HI for a long time, it forms n-hexane which shows that all six carbon atoms are linked in a straight chain.

$$\underset{\text{Glucose}}{\begin{matrix} CHO \\ | \\ (CHOH)_4 \\ | \\ CH_2OH \end{matrix}} \xrightarrow{HI,\ \Delta} \underset{n-\text{hexane}}{CH_3CH_2CH_2CH_2CH_2CH_3}$$

IV. *Acetylation of glucose with* ***acetic anhydride*** *gives glucose pentaacetate which confirms the presence of five —OH groups.*

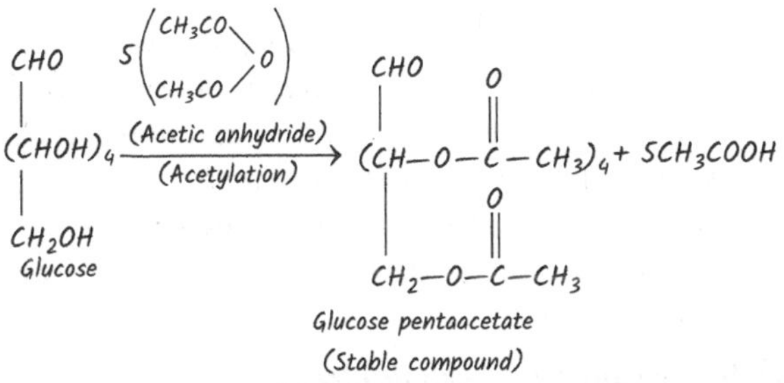

V. Bromine Water Test

When glucose is treated with bromine water, red colour of bromine water disappears as —CHO group changes to —COOH group, whereas fructose does not decolourise the red colour of bromine water. This confirms the presence of aldehyde group.

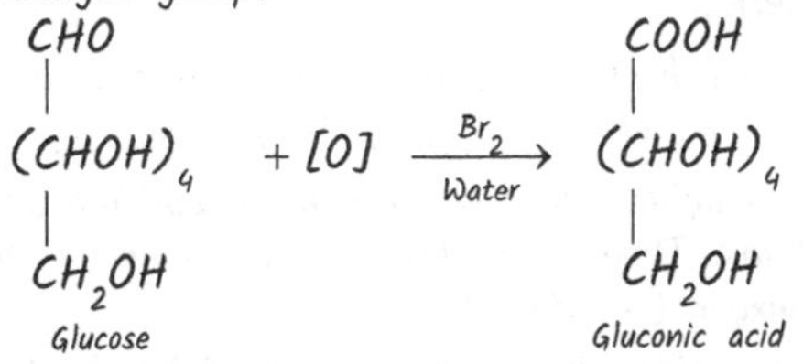

VI. *Both glucose and fructose react with phenylhydrazine to form osazone.*

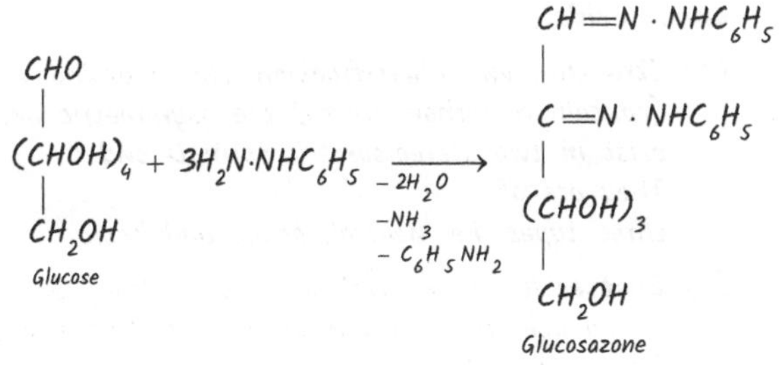

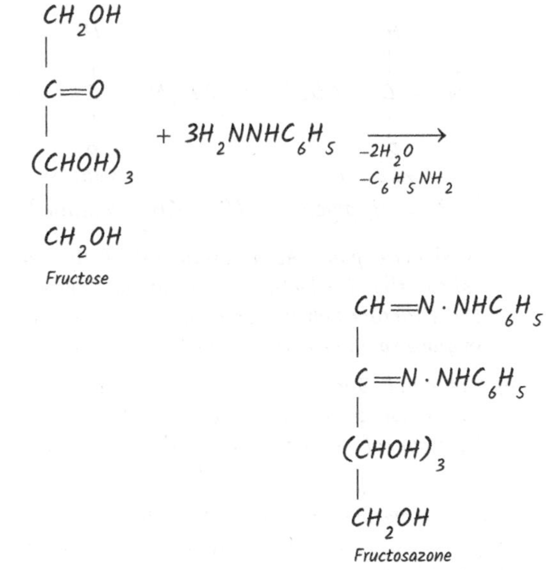

VII. *On oxidation with nitric acid, glucose forms saccharic acid. This indicates the presence of one (—OH) group.*

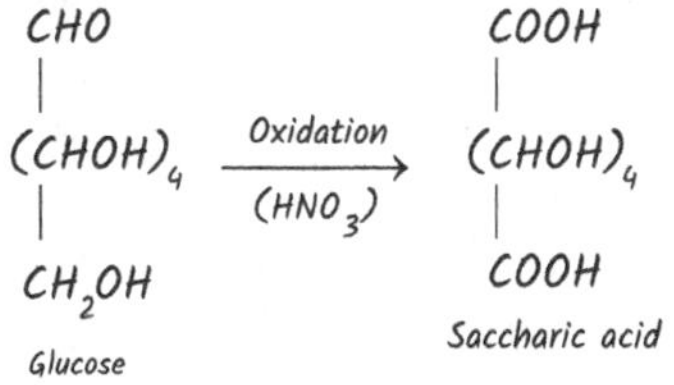

Fructose, when oxidised with nitric acid, it get converted into a mixture of trihydroxy glutaric, glycolic and tartaric acids.

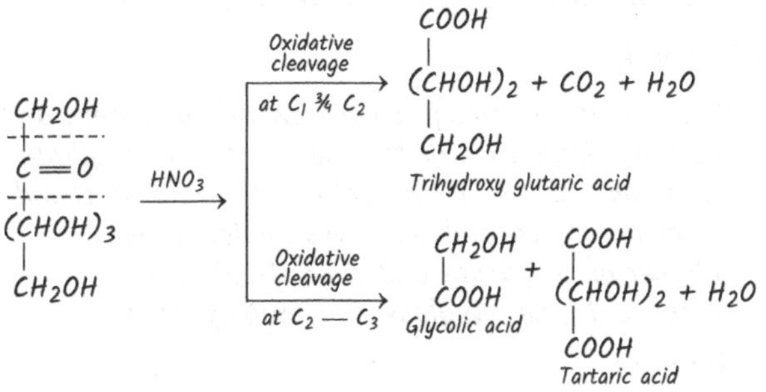

(iv) Disaccharides

The linkage between two monosaccharide units through an oxygen atom is called ***glycosidic linkage****.*

Some important disaccharides are

(a) Sucrose

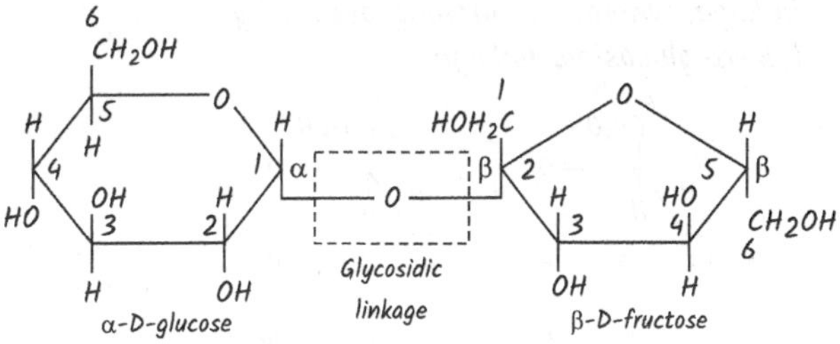

Haworth structure of sucrose

(b) Maltose

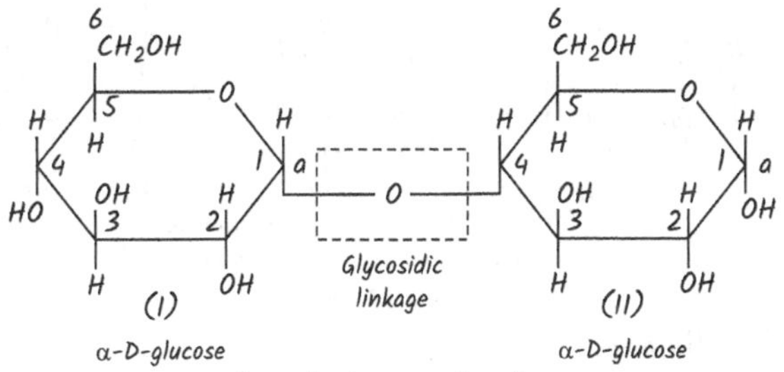

Haworth structure of maltose

(c) Lactose

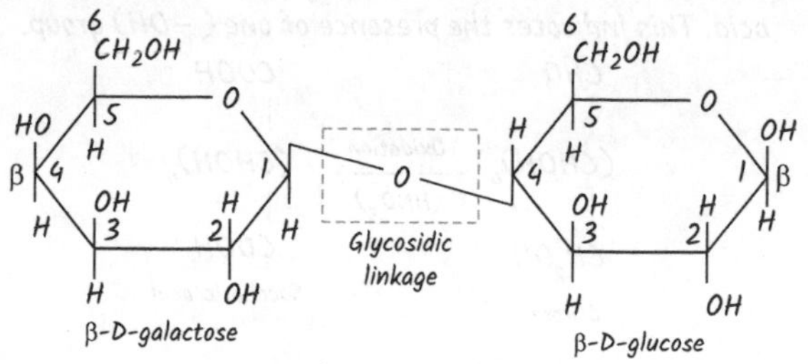

Haworth structure of lactose

(v) Polysaccharides

Some important polysaccharides are as follows

(a) Starch

It is important storage polysaccharide of plants and the most important dietary source of carbohydrate for human beings. High content of starch is found in cereals, roots, and some vegetables. It is a polymer of α-glucose and consists of two components, i.e. **amylose** and **amylopectin.**

Amylose

It is a long unbranched chain with $200-1000\ \alpha-\mathrm{D}-(+)-$ glucose units held by $1,4\ \alpha-$ glycosidic linkage. It is non-reducing in water.

Amylopectin

It is a branched chain polymer of α-D-glucose units. In this, chain is formed by 1, 4-α-glcosidic linkage, whereas branching occurs by 1, 6-α-glucosidic linkage.

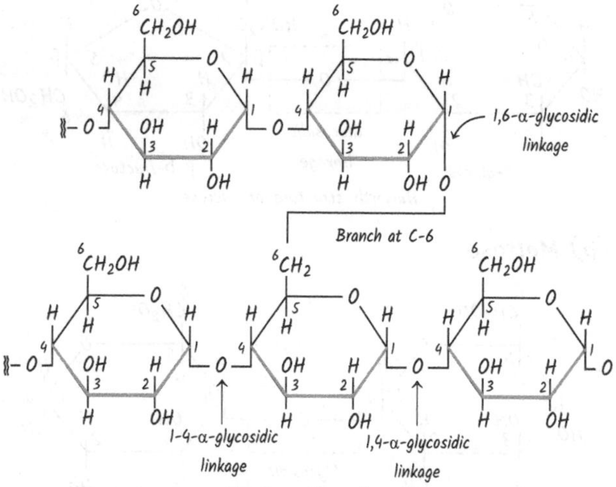

Structure of amylopectin

(b) Cellulose

It occurs exclusively in plants and it is the most abundant organic substance in plant kingdom. It is the main constituent of cell wall of plant cells. It is a straight chain polysaccharide composed only of β-D-glucose units that are linked together by glycosidic linkage between C-1 of one glucose unit and C-4 of the next glucose unit.

(c) Glycogen

It is known to be the storage material of animals. Its structure is similar to amylopectin and is highly branched that is why also known as animal starch. It is found in liver, muscles and brain.

When body requires energy, it breaks down to glucose by the action of enzymes. It is also found in yeast and fungi.

(vi) Importance of Carbohydrates

(a) It acts as the major source of energy for human beings and animals.

(b) It acts as food reserve in animals and plants.

(c) They are the structural materials for the cell walls.

2. Proteins

These are highly complex nitrogenous organic compounds of very high molecular masses.

(i) **Amino acids** These are the basic building units of proteins. Their molecules contain amino $(-NH_2)$ and carboxylic (—COOH) group.

Amino acids which are synthesised by the body are called **non-essential amino acids** and which cannot be synthesised in body are called **essential amino acids.**

(a) **Structure and classification** The α-amino acids (contain α-carbon atoms) are asymmetric and exist in two stereoisomeric form D and L.
They are of
three types, i.e. neutral, acidic and basic.

(b) **Zwitter ion** In neutral aqueous solution, the amino acid forms a dipolar ion structure called Zwitter ion structure.

$$\underset{\text{Amino acid}}{H_2\ddot{N}-\underset{\substack{|\\R}}{\overset{\substack{H\\|}}{C}}-COOH} \rightleftharpoons \underset{\text{Zwitter ion}}{H_3\overset{+}{N}-\underset{\substack{|\\R}}{\overset{\substack{H\\|}}{C}}-COO^-}$$

(If R = H, glycine) $(R = CH_3$, alanine)

(c) **Isoelectric point** At a certain pH of the medium, called the isoelectric point of an amino acid, the structure behaves as a dipolar ion and does not migrate to any electrode on passing current.

(ii) **Peptide bond** When two α-amino acids combine, —COOH group of one amino acid condense with $-NH_2$ group of second amino acid with elimination of water molecule, forming $-\overset{\overset{O}{\|}}{C}-NH-$ or peptide linkage. These form proteins which are condensed polymer of amino acids.

(iii) **Classification of proteins** On the basis of molecular structure.

(a) **Fibrous proteins** Linear thread like molecules tend to lie side by side to form fibres. The polypeptide chains are held at many points by H— bonds, e.g. keratin found in skin and hair.

(b) **Globular proteins** Polypeptide chains are folded into compact units to give a spheroidal shape.

(iv) **Structure of proteins**

(a) **Primary structure** The sequence in which various amino acids are linked to one another by peptide linkage.

(b) **Secondary structure** Refers to the arrangement of polypeptide chains that arises as a result of H-bonding.

They are of two types:

(i) α-helix

(ii) β- pleated sheet

(c) **Tertiary Structure** The further folding of the secondary structure of proteins is known as **tertiary structure.** It gives rise to two major molecular shapes, fibrous and globular.

The main forces that, stabilise 2° and 3° structures of protein are hydrogen bonds, disulphide bonds, van der Waals' forces and electrostatic forces of attraction.

(d) **Quaternary Structure** Although many proteins exist as a single polypeptide chain, but some of the proteins are composed of two or more polypeptide chains called **subunits.**

The spatial arrangement of these subunits with respect to each other is known as **quaternary structure.**

(v) **Denaturation of proteins** A change in physical and biological properties of a protein without affecting its chemical composition, is called denaturation of protein. It may be affected by the action of heat, alcohol, acid, radiation, etc.

During denaturation, 2° and 3° structures are destroyed but 1° structure remains intact.

3. Enzymes

These are essential biological catalysts which are needed to catalyse biochemical reactions. Almost all the enzymes are globular proteins. Enzymes have specificity, i.e. specific for a particular substrate and reaction.

4. Hormones

These are the chemical substances produced by the endocrine glands in the body and are release directly in blood stream. On the basis of constitution, they are of two types (steroid and non-steroid).

5. Vitamins

These are the organic compounds required in small amounts in our diet but their deficiency causes specific diseases. Most of the vitamins cannot be synthesised in our body but plants can synthesize almost all of them.

Vitamins are designated by alphabets A,B,C,D, etc.

Some of them are further named as sub-groups, e.g. B_1, B_2, B_6, B_{12} etc.

Classification of Vitamins

These are classified into two groups depending upon their solubility in water or fat:

(i) **Fat soluble vitamins** These are vitamins A,D,E and K that are stored in liver and adipose (fat storing) tissues.

(ii) **Water soluble vitamins** B group vitamins and vitamin C are soluble in water. Water soluble vitamins must be supplied regularly in diet because they are readily excreted in urine and cannot be stored (except vitamin B_{12}) in our body.

Some Important Vitamins, their Sources and their Deficiency Diseases

Name of vitamins	Sources	Deficiency diseases
Vitamin A	Fish, cod liver oil, carrots, butter and milk	Xerophthalmia (hardening of cornea of eye), night blindness
Vitamin B_1 (Thiamine)	Yeast, milk, green vegetables and cereals	Beri-beri (loss of appetite, retarded growth)
Vitamin B_2 (Riboflavin)	Milk, egg yolk, liver, kidney	Cheilosis (fissuring at corners of mouth and lips), digestive disorders and burning sensation of the skin.
Vitamin B_6 (Pyridoxine)	Yeast, milk, egg yolk, cereals and rice bran	Convulsions, anaemia
Vitamin B_{12}	Meat, fish, egg and curd	Pernicious anaemia (RBC deficient in haemoglobin)
Vitamin C (Ascorbic acid)	Citrus fruits, amla and green leafy vegetables	Scurvy (bleeding of gums)
Vitamin D	Exposure to sunlight, fish and egg yolk	Rickets (bone deformities in children) and osteomalacia (soft bones and joint pain in adults)
Vitamin E	Vegetable oils, wheat, milk, sunflower oil etc.	Increased fragility of RBCs and muscular weakness
Vitamin K	Green leafy vegetables	Increased blood clotting time, haemorrhage

6. Nucleic Acids

Nucleic acids are biomolecules found in the nuclei of all living cells in the form of nucleoproteins (long chain polymers). These are the chemical carrier's of a cell's genetic information. These are of two types:

- *DNA (deoxyribose nucleic acid) RNA (ribo-nucleic acid)*

(i) Chemical composition of nucleic acids

(a) **Nucleoside** *A nucleoside consists of two basic components of nucleic acids; a pentose sugar and nitrogenous base. In this unit, base is attached at 1' position of sugar and sugar carbons are numbered as 1', 2', 3', etc., in order to distinguish these from the bases.*

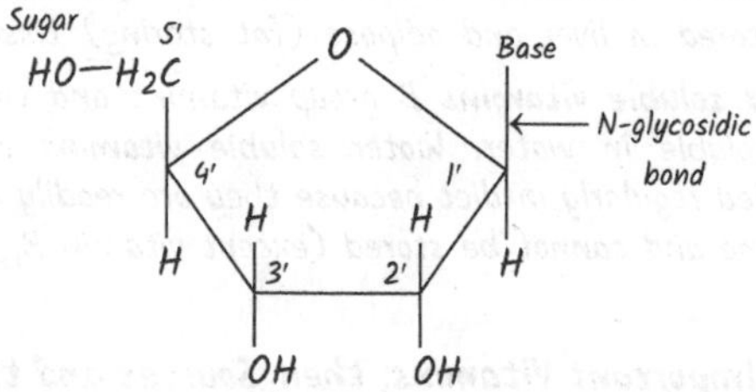

(b) **Nucleotides** *The monomeric units of nucleic acids are called nucleotides.*

Each nucleotide consists of three components:

- *A pentose sugar is D(–) ribose or 2-deoxy – D(–) ribose.*
- *A heterocyclic base – These are of two types:*
  I. ***Purines*** *Adenine (A) and guanine (G).*
  II. ***Pyrimidines*** *Uracil (U), thymine (T) and cytosine (C).*
- **Phosphoric acid** *Nucleic acids are of two types:* ***Deoxyribosenucleic acid (DNA)*** *and* ***ribonucleic acid (RNA).***
  DNA consists adenine (A) and guanine (G) as purine bases and cytosine (C) and thymine (T) as pyrimidine bases, while in RNA, purine bases are adenine (A) and guanine (G) and pyrimidine bases are cytosine (C) and uracil (U).
  In this unit, phosphoric acid is linked at 5'-position of a sugar moiety.

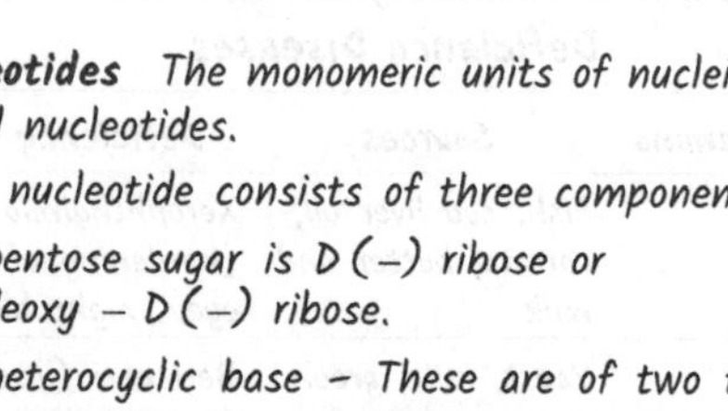

Nucleotides are linked together, between 5' and 3' carbon atoms of the pentose sugar by phosphodiester linkages.

(ii) Structure of DNA

James Watson *and* ***Francis Crick*** *proposed a double helical structure of DNA. According to this model, DNA consists of two separate polynucleotide strands leading in opposite directions (3' or 5').*
The polynucleotide chains of the double helix are held together at definite intervals through hydrogen bonds.
The two strands are complementary, i.e. adenine of one strand is hydrogen bonded to thymine of the other (through two hydrogen bonds), whereas cytosine of one strand is hydrogen bonded with guanine of the other (through three hydrogen bonds). i.e.

$A{=}T$ (↓ 2 hydrogen bonds) and $C{\equiv}G$ (↓ 3 hydrogen bonds)

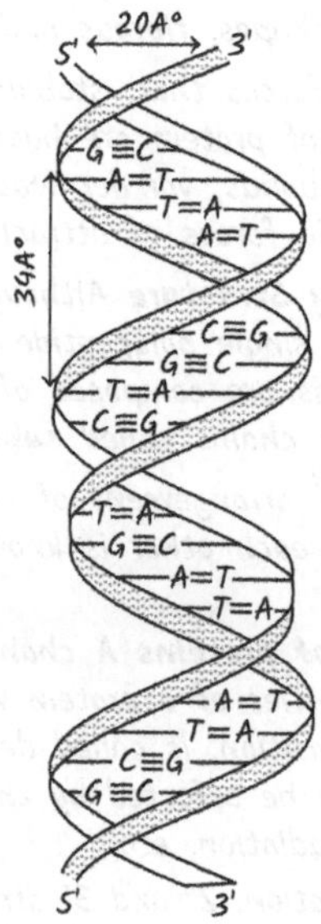

(iii) Structure of RNA

Secondary structure of RNA consists of a single strand but sometimes they fold back on themselves to form a double helix structure. RNA molecules are of three types namely, ***messenger RNA*** *(m-RNA),* ***ribosomal RNA*** *(r-RNA) and* ***transfer RNA*** *(t-RNA), they perform different functions.*